REA: THE LEADER IN TEACHER CERTIFICATION PREP

FTCE SOCIAL SCIENCE 6–12

Cynthia Metcalf, Ph.D.
Visiting Assistant Professor
Manhattanville College
Purchase, New York

Revised and Edited by
Rhonda Atkinson, Ph.D.
Professor of Education
Valencia College
Orlando, Florida

Research & Education Association
www.rea.com

Research & Education Association
1325 Franklin Ave., Suite 250
Garden City, NY 11530
Email: info@rea.com

Florida FTCE Social Science 6–12 Test with Online Practice Tests, 3rd Edition

Published 2023
Copyright © 2017 by Research & Education Association.
Prior editions copyright © 2011, 2009 by Research & Education Association. All rights reserved. No part of this book may be reproduced in any form without permission of the publisher.

Printed in the United States of America

Library of Congress Control Number 2017932505

ISBN-13: 978-0-7386-1215-7
ISBN-10: 0-7386-1215-4

The competencies presented in this book were created and implemented by the Florida Department of Education. All trademarks cited in this publication are the property of their respective owners.

LIMIT OF LIABILITY/DISCLAIMER OF WARRANTY: Publication of this work is for the purpose of test preparation and related use and subjects as set forth herein. While every effort has been made to achieve a work of high quality, neither Research & Education Association nor the authors and other contributors of this work guarantee the accuracy or completeness of or assume any liability in connection with the information and opinions contained herein and in REA's software and/or online materials. REA and the authors and other contributors shall in no event be liable for any personal injury, property or other damages of any nature whatsoever, whether special, indirect, consequential or compensatory, directly or indirectly resulting from the publication, use or reliance upon this work. Links to external sites in this publication or companion online materials are provided as a convenience to readers and for informational purposes only. Though every reasonable effort has been made to publish current links, URLs may change over time. No endorsement of any external link is made or implied, and neither the publisher nor the author(s) are responsible for the accuracy, legality, or content of any external site or for that of subsequent links.

Cover image: © iStockphoto.com/monkeybusinessimages

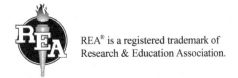

REA® is a registered trademark of Research & Education Association.

CONTENTS

5.9. Evaluate the impact of immigration on social, cultural, political, and economic development in the late 19th and early 20th centuries 240

5.10. Identify the causes, significant individuals, and effects of the events associated with the World War I era 242

5.11. Identify social, cultural, political, and economic developments between World War I and World War II 247

5.12. Identify the causes, significant individuals, and effects of the events associated with the World War II era 262

5.13. Identify the causes, significant individuals, and effects of the events associated with domestic and foreign affairs during the Cold War era 268

5.14. Identify the causes, significant individuals, and effects of the events associated with movements for equality, civil rights, and civil liberties in the 19th and 20th centuries 277

5.15. Identify the causes, significant individuals, and effects of the events associated with contemporary domestic and foreign affairs 294

5.16. Identify key individuals, events, and issues related to Florida history 296

Chapter 6. Social Science and Its Methodology 307
6.1. Identify social science disciplines 307
6.2. Identify social science concepts 309
6.3. Analyze the interrelationships between social science disciplines 314
6.4. Interpret tabular and graphic representations of information related to the social sciences 314
6.5. Identify appropriate strategies, methods, tools, and technologies for the teaching of social science 316
6.6. Evaluate examples of primary and secondary sources 321

FTCE: Social Science 6–12 Practice Tests
Also available online at www.rea.com/studycenter

Practice Test 1 323
Answer Sheet 325
Practice Test 1 326
Answer Key 352
Self-Assessment Guide 357
Detailed Explanations 358

Practice Test 2 379
Answer Sheet 381
Practice Test 2 382
Answer Key 410
Self-Assessment Guide 415
Detailed Explanations 416

Index 439

About Our Author

Dr. Cynthia Metcalf earned her Ph.D. in history from the University of Virginia. She received several major fellowships to conduct her research from the Social Science Research Council, American Research Center in Egypt, American Institute of Maghrebi Studies, and the United States Information Agency Documentation of Cultural Properties Program.

Dr. Metcalf is a Visiting Assistant Professor in the History Department at Manhattanville College in Purchase, N.Y., where she teaches both graduate and undergraduate courses in Middle Eastern history, South Asian history, and World History. She also serves as a senior thesis advisor for history majors and as a freshman advisor and freshman seminar instructor for incoming students. Dr. Metcalf also teaches online as an Adjunct Instructor in History for Baker College Online. Currently, Dr. Metcalf is revising her dissertation manuscript and contributing entries to the *Dictionary of African Bibliography*.

About Our Editor

Rhonda Atkinson, Ph.D., has an extensive background in reading and psychology, and a deep understanding of how people learn. She has applied this knowledge to a variety of content areas and learner needs, and is an expert in instructional design.

After earning her doctorate in curriculum and instruction from Louisiana State University, Dr. Atkinson went on to become a faculty member and administrator in post-secondary education programs in Louisiana, Missouri, and Florida. Along the way, she has created courses and workshops to meet different content and learner needs in online, face-to-face, and hybrid formats.

She has also developed educational materials for Northrop Grumman, the Institute for Healthcare Advancement, Novartis, the Public Broadcasting System, the Louisiana Office of Elder Affairs, the Louisiana Office of Nutrition Education, and the Louisiana Department of Education.

Dr. Atkinson is the co-author of seven college textbooks—many of them in multiple editions—in reading and learning strategies. She is currently a Professor of Education at Valencia College, Orlando, Florida, where she teaches undergraduate education courses in student success and technology as well as post-graduate certification courses in education.

About REA

Founded in 1959, Research & Education Association (REA) is dedicated to publishing the finest and most effective educational materials—including study guides and test preps—for students of all ages.

Today, REA's wide-ranging catalog is a leading resource for students, teachers, and other professionals. Visit *www.rea.com* to see a complete listing of all our titles.

Acknowledgments

We would like to thank Pam Weston, Publisher, for setting the quality standards for production integrity and managing the publication to completion; John Cording, Technology Director, for coordinating the design and development of the REA Study Center; Larry B. Kling, Editorial Director, for his overall direction; Diane Goldschmidt, Managing Editor, for coordinating development of this edition; and Jennifer Calhoun, Graphic Designer, for page design and file preparation.

In addition, we would like to thank Transcend Creative Services for typesetting this edition; Karen Lamoreux for copyediting; and Ellen Gong for proofreading.

INTRODUCTION

Passing the FTCE Social Science 6–12 Test

Congratulations! By taking the Florida Teacher Certification Examinations (FTCE) Social Science 6–12 test, you're on your way to a rewarding teaching career. Our book, and the online tools that come with it, focus on what you need to succeed on this important exam, bringing you one step closer to being certified to teach social studies in grades 6–12 in Florida.

This FTCE Social Science 6–12 Book + Online test prep package includes:

- **Complete overview** of the FTCE Social Science 6–12 test
- **Focused content review** for all six subjects tested on the FTCE Social Science 6–12 test
- An **online diagnostic test** to pinpoint your strengths and weaknesses and focus your study
- **Two full-length practice tests** (both in the book and online) that come with powerful diagnostic tools to help you personalize your prep

There are many different ways to prepare for your FTCE Social Science test. What's best for you depends on how much time you have to study and how comfortable you are with the subject matter. Our book and online tests give you the tools you need to customize your prep so you can make the most of your study time.

HOW TO USE THIS BOOK + ONLINE PREP

About Our Review

The review chapters are designed to help you sharpen your command of all the skills you'll need to pass the FTCE Social Science test. The test assesses six competencies. Each of the skills required is discussed at length in this book to optimize your understanding of what the test covers.

Keep in mind that your schooling has taught you most of what you need to know to answer the questions on the test. Our review will reinforce what you have learned and show you how to relate that information to the specific competencies on the test. Studying your class notes and textbooks together with our review will give you an excellent foundation for passing the test.

About the REA Study Center

We know your time is valuable and you want an efficient study experience. At the online REA Study Center (*www.rea.com/studycenter*), you will get feedback right from the start on what you know and what you don't to help make the most of your study time.

Here is what you will find at the REA Study Center:

- **Diagnostic Test**—Before you review with the book, take our online diagnostic test. Your score report will pinpoint topics for which you need the most review to help focus your study.

- **2 Full-Length Practice Tests**—These practice tests give you the most complete picture of your strengths and weaknesses. After you've studied with the book, test what you've learned by taking the first of two online practice exams. Review your score reports, then go back and study any topics you missed. Take the second practice test to ensure you've mastered the material.

Our online exams simulate the computer-based format of the actual FTCE test and come with these features:

- **Automatic Scoring**—Find out how you did on your test, instantly.

- **Diagnostic Score Reports**—Get a specific score tied to each competency, so you can focus on the areas where you need the most help.

- **Detailed Answer Explanations**—Learn not just why a response option is correct, but also why the other answer choices are incorrect.

- **Timed testing**—Manage your time as you practice, so you'll feel confident on test day.

Introduction

AN OVERVIEW OF THE TEST

Who Takes the FTCE Social Science 6–12 Test and What Is it Used for?

The FTCE Social Science 6–12 test is a criterion-referenced examination constructed to measure the knowledge and skills that an entry-level social science educator must have to teach in public schools in Florida. The test is a requirement for candidates seeking to teach grades 6–12 social science, and is used to determine if teacher candidates have the necessary knowledge to effectively teach the subject matter.

What is the Format of the FTCE Social Science Test?

The test has approximately 100 multiple-choice questions and you will have 2.5 hours to complete it. Each question has four answer choices. You will select the best option by choosing A, B, C, or D.

The FTCE Social Science test is a computer-administered test and is available throughout the year at numerous locations across the state and at select locations nationally. To find a test center near you, visit *www.fldoe.org*.

What is Assessed on the FTCE Social Science 6–12 Test?

Below are the competencies used as the basis for the FTCE Social Science 6–12 examination, as well as the approximate percentage of the total test that each competency accounts for. These competencies represent the knowledge that teams of teachers, subject area specialists, and district-level educators have determined to be important for beginning teachers.

Competencies	Approx. Percentage
1. Knowledge of Geography	10%
2. Knowledge of Economics	15%
3. Knowledge of Political Science	15%
4. Knowledge of World History	25%
5. Knowledge of U.S. History	25%
6. Knowledge of Social Science and its Methodology	10%

When Should the FTCE Test Be Taken?

Florida law requires that teacher candidates demonstrate mastery of basic skills, professional knowledge, and the content area in which they choose to specialize. If you've graduated from a

Florida state-approved teacher preparation program and made the decision to teach Social Science 6–12, you need to begin the process by applying for a Florida Temporary Certificate in that subject. The Bureau of Educator Certification will evaluate your eligibility only in the subject(s) you request on your application form. The Temporary Certificate is valid for three school years, which allows you time to complete the certification tests while teaching full-time.

For high school graduates and out-of-state educators, the Bureau of Educator Certification will provide you with official information about which test(s) to take to complete requirements for the professional certificate. The FTCE Social Science exam is administered by appointment, year round in several locations throughout Florida. Special accommodations also can be made for applicants who are visually impaired, hearing impaired, physically disabled, or specific learning disabled.

To receive information on upcoming administrations of the FTCE, you should consult the FTCE Registration Bulletin, which can be obtained by contacting:

> Florida Department of Education
> Educator Certification
> Room 201, Turlington Building
> 325 West Gaines Street
> Tallahassee, FL 32399-0400
> U.S. Toll-Free: 800-445-6739
> Website: *www.fldoe.org* or *www.fl.nesinc.com*
> Bureau of Educator Certification: *www.fldoe.org/edcert*

The FTCE Registration Bulletin also includes information regarding test retakes and score reports. You must pay a registration fee to take the FTCE Social Science test. Utilize the contact information above for any questions.

What's the Passing Score?

A scaled score of at least 200 is required to pass the exam. The Florida Department of Education estimates that, as of spring 2022, in order to pass, test-takers need to get 74% of the questions correct. Thus, to achieve a minimum passing score you'll need to get approximately 74 questions correct. For the latest information on scale scoring, see the "Scores" tab at *www.fl.nesinc.com*.

When Will I Receive My Score Report?

Because the FTCE Social Science 6–12 test has only multiple-choice questions, you will receive an *unofficial* pass/non-pass status at your test site immediately after your exam. Official reports will be released within 4 weeks of the test date.

Introduction

Can I Retake the Test?

A score on the FTCE that does not match your expectations does not mean that you should change your plans about teaching. If you do not achieve a passing grade on the FTCE, don't panic. The test can be taken again after 31 calendar days, so you can seriously work on improving your score in preparation for your next FTCE. To retake the Social Science test, you must reregister and pay a retake fee.

What Else Do I Need to Know About Test Day?

The day before your test, check for any updates in your testing account. This is where you'll learn of any changes to your reporting schedule or if there's a change in the test site.

On the day of the test, be sure to make time for a good breakfast and dress in layers that can be removed or added as the conditions in the test center require.

Your admission ticket lists your appointment time, but you should arrive at the test center 30 minutes beforehand. Administrative preparations must take place before the actual test begins. As an added incentive to make sure that you arrive early, keep in mind that no one will be admitted into the test center after the test has begun.

Before you leave for the testing site, carefully review your registration materials. Make sure you bring your admission ticket and two unexpired forms of identification. Primary forms of identification must be government-issued and include a photo and your signature. Such forms of ID include:

- Passport
- Government-issued driver's license
- State-issued ID card
- Military ID card

You may need to produce a supplemental identification document if any questions arise with your primary ID or if your primary ID is otherwise valid but lacks your full name, photo, and signature. Secondary forms of identification must have a photo or a signature; examples include a Social Security card, work ID, or student ID. Remember, without proper identification you will not be admitted to the test center.

Strict rules limit what you can bring into the test center. We recommend that you consult the "Test Site Rules" found at *www.fl.nesinc.com/policies* for a complete rundown. You may not bring watches of any kind, cellphones, smartphones, any other electronic communication devices or weapons of any kind. Scrap paper, written notes, books, and any printed material is prohibited. In addition, no smoking, eating, or drinking is allowed in the testing room. Personal items must be placed in the secure storage area provided at the testing center.

Consider bringing a small snack and a bottle of water to partake of beforehand to keep you sharp during the test.

STUDYING FOR THE TEST

It is never too early to start studying for the Florida Social Science 6–12 test. The earlier you begin, the more time you will have to sharpen your skills. Do not procrastinate. Cramming is not an effective way to study, since it does not allow you the time needed to learn the test material.

When you take REA's practice tests, simulate the conditions of the actual test as closely as possible. Turn your television and radio off. Mute your social media alerts, and go to a quiet place free from distraction. Read each question carefully, consider all answer choices, and pace yourself.

As you complete each test, review your score reports, study the diagnostic feedback, and review the explanations to the questions you answered incorrectly. But don't overdo it. Take one problem area at a time; review it until you are confident that you understand the material. Give extra attention to the areas giving you the most difficulty, as this will help raise your score. After further review, you may want to retake the practice tests online.

Keep track of your scores. By doing so, you will be able to gauge your progress and discover your strengths and weaknesses. Take notes or create flashcards for the material you will want to go over again. Using notecards gives you essential information at a glance, keeps you organized, and helps you build your confidence.

STUDY SCHEDULE

Week	Activity
1	Take the online Diagnostic Test at the REA Study Center (*www.rea.com/studycenter*). Your detailed score report will identify the topics where you need the most review.
2–3	Study the review chapters. Use your score report from the Diagnostic Test to focus your study. Useful study techniques include highlighting key terms and information and taking notes as you read the review. Learn all the competencies by making flashcards and targeting questions you missed on the diagnostic test.
4	Take Practice Test 1 either in the book or online at the REA Study Center. Review your score report and identify topics where you need more review.
5	Reread all your notes, refresh your understanding of the test's competencies and skills, review your college textbooks, and read class notes you've taken. This is also the time to consider any other supplementary materials that your advisor or the Florida Department of Education suggests. Review the agency's website at *http://www.fl.nesinc.com*
6	Take Practice Test 2 online at the REA Study Center. Review your score report and restudy the appropriate review section(s) until you are confident you understand the material.

Introduction

TEST-TAKING TIPS TO BOOST YOUR SCORE

Even though you have probably taken standardized tests like the FTCE Social Science test before, you may still be anxious about the exam. This is perfectly normal, and there are several ways to help alleviate test-day nervousness. Here are some tips to help you raise your score and build your comfort level with the test.

1. Guess Away!

One of the most frequently asked questions about the FTCE Social Science test is: Can I guess? The answer: absolutely! There is no penalty for guessing on the test. That means if you refrain from guessing, you may lose points. To guess smartly, use the process of elimination (see Strategy No. 2). Your score is based strictly on the number of correct answers. So answer all questions and take your best guess when you don't know the answer.

2. Process of Elimination

Process of elimination is one of the most important test-taking strategies at your disposal. Process of elimination means looking at the choices and eliminating the ones you know are wrong, including answers that are partially wrong. Your odds of getting the right answer increase from the moment you're able to get rid of a wrong choice.

3. All in

Review all the response options. Just because you believe you've found the correct answer, look at each choice so you don't mistakenly jump to any conclusions. If you are asked to choose the *best* answer, be sure your first answer is really the best one.

4. Choice of the Day

What if you are truly stumped and can't use the process of elimination? It's time to pick a fallback answer. On the day of the test, choose the position of the answer (e.g., the third of the four choices) that you will pick for any question you cannot smartly guess. According to the laws of probability, you have a higher chance of getting an answer right if you stick to one chosen position for the answer choice when you have to guess an answer instead of randomly picking one.

5. Use Choices to Confirm Your Answer

The great thing about multiple-choice questions is that the answer has to be staring back at you. Have an answer in mind and use the choices to *confirm* it.

6. Watch the Clock

Among the most vital point-saving skills is active time management. Keep an eye on the timer on your computer screen. Make sure you stay on top of how much time you have left and never spend too much time on any one question. Remember: Most multiple-choice questions are worth one raw point. Treat each one as if it's the one that will put you over the top. You never know, it just might.

7. Read, Read, Read

It's important to read through all the multiple-choice options. Even if you believe answer choice A is correct, you can misread a question or response option if you're rushing to get through the test. While it is important not to linger on a question, it is also crucial to avoid giving a question short shrift. Slow down, calm down, read all the choices. Verify that your choice is the best one, and click on it.

8. Take Notes

The test center will provide you with a pen and erasable notepad. Make sure you get this notepad and use it just like scratch paper to make notes as you work your way toward the answer(s).

9. Isolate Limiters

Pay attention to any limiters in a multiple-choice question stem. These are words such as *initial*, *best*, *most* (as in *most appropriate* or *most likely*), *not*, *least*, *except*, *required*, or *necessary*. Especially watch for negative words, such as "Choose the answer that is *not* true." When you select your answer, double-check yourself by asking how the response fits the limitations established by the stem. Think of the stem as a puzzle piece that perfectly fits only the response option(s) that contain the correct answer. Let it guide you.

10. It's Not a Race

Ignore other test-takers. Don't compare yourself to anyone else in the room. Focus on the items in front of you and the time you have left. If someone finishes the test 30 minutes early, it does not necessarily mean that person answered more questions correctly than you did. Stay calm and focus on *your* test. It's the only one that matters.

11. Confirm Your Click

In the digital age, many of us are used to rapid-clicking, be it in the course of emailing or gaming. Look at the screen to be sure to see that your mouse-click is acknowledged. If your answer doesn't register, you won't get credit. However, if you want to mark it for review so you can return

Introduction

later, that's your call. Before you click "Submit," use the test's review screen to see whether you inadvertently skipped any questions.

12. Creature of Habit? No Worries.

We are all creatures of habit. It's therefore best to follow a familiar pattern of study. Do what's comfortable for you. Set a time and place each day to study for this test. Whether it is 30 minutes at the library or an hour in a secluded corner of your local coffee shop, commit yourself as best you can to this schedule every day. Find quiet places where it is less crowded, as constant background noise can distract you. Don't study one subject for too long. Take an occasional breather and treat yourself to a healthy snack or some exercise. After your short break—5 or 10 minutes can do the trick—return to what you were studying or start a new section.

13. Knowledge is Power

Purchasing this book gives you an edge on passing the FTCE Social Science 6–12 test. Make the most of this edge: Review the sections on how the test is structured, what types of questions will be asked, and so on. Take our practice tests to familiarize yourself with what the test looks and feels like.

Most test anxiety occurs because people feel unprepared when they are taking the test, and they psych themselves out. You can whittle away at anxiety by learning the format of the test and by knowing what to expect. Fully simulating the test even once will boost your chances of getting the score you need.

Meanwhile, the knowledge you've gained will also save you the valuable time that would have been eaten up puzzling through what the directions are asking. As an added benefit, previewing the test will free up your brain's resources so you can focus on racking up as many points as you can.

14. B-r-e-a-t-h-e

What's the worst that can happen when you take a test? You may have an off day, and despite your best efforts, you may not pass. Well, the good news is that a test can be retaken. In fact, you may already be doing this—this book is every bit for you as it is for first-timers. Fortunately, the FTCE Social Science 6–12 test is something you can study and prepare for, and in some ways to a greater extent than other tests you may have taken.

Good luck on the Florida Social Science 6–12 test!

CHAPTER 1

Geography

Geography is the study of the Earth's surface, including such aspects as its climate, topography, vegetation, and population.

Geography is much more than just memorizing names and places and studying the physical features of the Earth. While geography requires an understanding of the Earth's surface, it also is concerned with the distribution of living things and Earth's features around the Earth. Geography focuses on three questions: *Where? Why there? What are the consequences of it being there?* Geographers look at the Earth's physical space and investigate patterns. For example, a geographer might look at the space of your bedroom and ask several questions: How are things distributed? Why are they where they are? What processes operate in that space? How does this space relate to other nearby spaces? Geographers call this way of identifying, explaining, and predicting human and physical patterns in space and the interconnectedness of various spaces the **spatial perspective**. Geography views the Earth through a lens of location and space and seeks to find patterns of place or interactions between places and people. Thus, geography is the science of space and place.

Branches of Geography

Generally, geography can be divided into four main branches:

Human Geography focuses on humans and the cultures they create relative to their space. It encompasses population geography, economics, and political geography and looks at how people's activities relate to the environment politically, culturally, historically, and socially.

Physical Geography addresses Earth's physical environment: water (**hydrosphere**), air (**atmosphere**), plants and animals (**biosphere**), and land (**lithosphere**). Physical geographers study land formation, water, weather, and **climate** (weather patterns, specifically precipitation and temperature, over time), as well as more specific topics such as geomorphology, biogeography, and environmental geography.

Regional Geography organizes areas of Earth that have some degree of similarity and divides the world into different **realms**.

Topical/Systemic Geography is the orderly and methodical study of climate, landforms, economics, and culture.

The main focus of geographers, no matter the subfield, is the spatial perspective. For example, **population geography** deals with the relationships between geography and population patterns, including birth and death rates. **Political geography** concerns the effect of geography on politics, especially on national boundaries and relations between states. **Economic geography** focuses on the interaction between Earth's landscape and the economic activity of the human population.

COMPETENCY 1.1

Apply the six essential elements of geography.

Geographic Education: 18 Standards, 6 Elements

The National Geography Standards *(http://nationalgeographic.org/standards/national-geography-standards/)* were published in 1994 to guide the teaching and learning of geography in the United States. The 18 standards are organized under six essential elements. These elements indicate what a geographically informed person should know and understand in terms of factual knowledge of geographic concepts and information, mental maps and tools, and thinking in geographic terms.

Element 1: The World in Spatial Terms

Geography connects the relationships between people, places, and environments by structuring the knowledge of them into real and mental maps and then conducting a spatial analysis of that information. So, maps become a primary tool that geographers use in order to present, acquire, process, and decipher information in spatial terms. Standards that address this element are:

Competency 1: Geography

1. how to use maps and other geographic representations, tools, and technologies to acquire, process, and report information;

2. how to use mental maps (a person's internalized picture of a part of Earth's surface) to organize information about people, places, and environments;

3. how to analyze the spatial organization of people, places, and environments on Earth's surface.

One of the first things geographers do is identify a location in spatial terms: absolute and relative location.

Absolute location is the physical whereabouts of a place as shown on a map or geographic representation. Every point on Earth has a specific location that is determined by an imaginary grid of lines denoting **latitude** and **longitude**. Parallels of latitude measure distances north and south of the line called the **equator**. **Meridians** of longitude measure distances east and west of another imaginary line called the **prime meridian**. Geographers use latitude and longitude to pinpoint a place's absolute, or exact, location. Addresses (e.g., 200 Main Street, Orlando, Florida) also denote absolute locations.

Relative location is the type of location most commonly used: a description of a place in terms of other places. Relative locations reflect a person's mental map (internalized picture of a part of Earth's surface) to organize information about people, places, and environments. Relative location is usually described by landmarks, time, direction, or distances from one thing to another. So while the absolute address might be described as 200 Main Street, Orlando, Florida, the relative location might be "the three story-building on Main Street across from the public parking lot and next to Joe's Pizzeria." While the absolute location (200 Main Street) may remain the same, the relative location could change if Joe's Pizzeria becomes a grocery store or if the public parking lot becomes a dog park.

Element 2: Places and Regions

The basic units of geography are **place** and **region**. Geographers use these units to explore the physical and human characteristics of areas to understand how the areas work. Places and regions also involve people's perceptions of areas, the mental regions that people create from their own view of the world, and people's methods of organizing these perceptions or biases. Standards within the element of places and regions are:

1. the physical and human characteristics of places;

2. that people create regions to interpret Earth's complexity;

3. how culture and experience influence people's perceptions of places and regions.

Place addresses the question: *What's it like there?* Place is a unique combination of physical and cultural attributes that give each location on the Earth its individual "stamp" and help us understand its nature. A place's **physical characteristics** comprise its natural environment and emanate from geological, hydrological, atmospheric, and biological processes present in that location. Physical characteristics of a place include mountains, rivers, beaches, topography, flora (plant life), fauna (animal life), resources (trees, oil, petroleum, and diamonds), landforms (rivers, plateaus, plains), bodies of water, climate, soils, and natural vegetation. The **human characteristics** of a place are derived from the changes to an environment as a result of human ideas and actions. Such characteristics include architecture, religion, food, and transportation and communication networks. Looking at the physical and human characteristics of a place helps answer two major questions that geographers ask: "Where is it?" and "Why is it there?"

Geographers divide the world into more manageable units called **regions**. Regions have unifying characteristics that may be physical, cultural, or human-based. They may occur over large spaces and can be found across great distances. Physical characteristics of a region include landforms such as a mountain range, climate, soil, and natural vegetation. Regions may also be distinguished by human characteristics, including language, economic, social, political, and cultural similarities.

There are three basic types of regions:

- **Formal regions** (sometimes referred to as uniform regions) are areas that have common (or uniform) cultural or physical features. They are often defined by governmental or administrative boundaries (i.e., United States, Jacksonville, Brazil). However, formal regions can show other characteristics. For example, a climate region is a formal region because it links places that share a climate. The places on a map that shows where a specific language is spoken make up a formal region because they share the feature of a common language.

- **Functional regions** (sometimes referred to as **nodal regions**) are linked together by some function's influence on them. However, if the function ceases to exist, the region no longer exists. Functional regions are created through the movement of some phenomenon, like a disease; or a perceived interaction among places, like pizza delivery routes. For example, a functional region might appear on a map of Delta Airlines' flights from Atlanta, Georgia. A mapmaker would plot all the places to which Delta travels from its hub in Atlanta, the node. Then the mapmaker would draw a boundary enclosing all of those places into one functional region. The area affected by the spread of a flu epidemic is another example of a functional region. Functional regions are defined by the places affected by the movement of some phenomenon from its source, or from the node of other places.

- **Vernacular regions** are those loosely defined by people's perception (e.g., the South, the Middle East). The boundaries of a perceptual region are determined by people's beliefs, not a scientifically measurable process. For example, the space in which the "cool kids" sit at lunch would be a perceptual region because its boundaries are totally determined by the region maker's perception of who is cool and who is not—something that could be debated by any other person in the room. Another example of a perceptual region is the American South. People differ in their perceptions of which places are considered part of the South.

Element 3: Physical Systems

Physical processes shape Earth's surface and interact with plant and animal life to create, sustain, and modify ecosystems. This element of geography looks at environmental phenomena and their interaction through ecosystems, renewable resources, and the water cycle. Standards involving physical systems include:

1. the physical processes that shape the patterns of Earth's surface;
2. the characteristics and distribution of ecosystems on Earth's surface.

A place's **physical characteristics** comprise its natural environment and emanate from geological, hydrological, atmospheric, and biological processes present in that location. Some physical characteristics of a place include mountains, rivers, beaches, topography, flora (plant life), fauna (animal life), resources (trees, oil, petroleum, diamonds), landforms (rivers, plateaus, plains), bodies of water, climate, soils, and natural vegetation.

Element 4: Human Systems

People are central to geography in that human activities help shape Earth's surface. Human settlements and structures are part of Earth's surface, and humans compete for control of Earth's surface. This element looks at characteristics, distribution, and migration of human populations. It also tries to find patterns—in culture, economic interdependence, human settlement, conflict and cooperation—and how these patterns influence people's relationships with each other and the Earth. This element consists of the following standards:

1. the characteristics, distribution, and migration of human populations;
2. the characteristics, distribution, and complexity of Earth's cultural mosaics;
3. the patterns and networks of economic interdependence;
4. the processes, patterns, and functions of human settlement;
5. how forces of cooperation and conflict among people influence the division and control of Earth's surface.

Movement is a key factor in human systems. Movement involves transportation (imports and exports), flow of people (immigration and migration), and spread of ideas and information (communications, Internet usage). For example, **cultural diffusion** is an aspect of movement that focuses on how ideas, innovation, and ideology spread from one area to another. **Spatial interaction** describes how places interact through movement. Although everything is theoretically linked to everything else, nearer things are usually related more to each other than to faraway things. Thus, the extent of spatial interaction often depends on distance.

In evaluating movement and spatial interaction, geographers often evaluate the **friction of distance**, the degree to which distance interferes with an interaction. For example, the friction of distance for a working-class Ohio man wanting to visit a dentist in Ethiopia is quite high, meaning that the distance gets in the way of this interaction occurring. However, the friction of distance has been reduced in many aspects of life with improved transportation and communication infrastructures. Thus, the friction of distance is not as much of a problem for a business in Florida to sell something to a business in Taiwan. Businesses can now communicate over the Internet, buying and selling their goods in transactions that would have taken months to complete just 30 years ago. This increasing sense of accessibility and connectivity seems to bring humans in distant places closer together, a phenomenon known as **space-time compression**. Note that space-time compression is reducing perceived distance, which is the friction of distance thought by humans, not the actual distance on the land.

Related to space-time compression is the effect of **distance decay**, in which the interaction between two places declines as the distance between the two places increases. Imagine putting a magnet on your desk and putting an iron nail on it. The farther you pull the iron nail away from the magnet, the less of a pull effect the magnet has on the nail. It is the same with distance decay; as the distance between two entities increases, the effect of their interaction decreases. However, improved transportation and communication technologies have reduced the effect of distance decay on most human interactions. On any given day in 1850, a person living in Atlanta probably never interacted with someone from 30 miles outside the city. Now a person in Atlanta can interact with people from all over the world via the Internet and improved transportation.

Element 5: Environment and Society

Humans modify the Earth's environment through their actions. Such actions happen largely as a consequence of the way people value or devalue the Earth's resources. This element consists of the following standards:

1. how human actions modify the physical environment;

2. how physical systems affect human systems;

3. the changes that occur in the meaning, use, distribution, and importance of resources.

Geographers look at both the positive and negative effects that result from human interaction with the environment: how humans rely on the environment, alter it, and adapt to it—and how the environment may limit what people are able to do. Much of the way that people relate to the environment reflects their economic and political circumstances, as well as their culture and their

Competency 1: Geography

technological capabilities. One significant issue is that the interaction between humans and the environment can change quickly, and such change might be temporary. For instance, building a dam changes the environment, but then floods, earthquakes, drought, or mudslides could destroy the dam and change the environment again.

Element 6: The Uses of Geography

Geography informs people about the relationships they have between place and environment over time. This element explores how humans modify the physical environment, how physical systems affect human systems, and how the changes occur in the meaning, use, distribution, and importance of resources both in the past and potentially in the future. This element addresses the following standards:

1. how to apply geography to interpret the past;

2. how to apply geography to interpret the present and plan for the future.

COMPETENCY 1.2

Identify the ways natural processes and human–environment interactions shape the Earth's physical systems and features.

The Earth's physical systems and features are shaped and reshaped by natural processes and human interactions with it. Physical processes are nature's way of producing, maintaining, or altering the physical systems of the Earth. Physical processes can be categorized into four areas:

- Air—referred to as **atmospheric** and includes examinations of climate and meteorology.

- Land—referred to as **lithospheric** and includes examinations of plate tectonics, erosion, and soil formation.

- Water—referred to as **hydrospheric** and examines things like the circulation of the oceans and the hydrologic cycle.

- Animals—referred to as **biospheric** and examines plant and animal communities and ecosystems.

There are seven main categories of natural processes that have shaped Earth's landforms and physical systems and features:

- weathering

- transportation

- erosion

- freezing and thawing
- gravity
- deposition
- plate tectonics

Much of Earth's **landforms** were the byproducts of interactions among these natural processes that produced sediments, which were then deposited together to form sand dunes, deltas, and glacial moraines. Some of the natural processes, like earthquakes and volcanic eruptions, produce dramatic alterations of the Earth's surface. Others, like weathering and erosion, take longer to happen.

Studying the interactions within and between these categories of physical processes and the parts that the natural cycles of water, rocks, and atmospheric gasses play reveals how the Earth functions. Earth's natural processes shape the land and environment by reworking, conserving, and renewing its materials. For instance, the interaction between the hydrosphere and the atmosphere might produce floods, hurricanes, and cyclones that in turn reshape the Earth where they land. Plants alter the Earth's atmosphere in multiple ways: first, they remove the carbon dioxide, then they transform the carbon into sugar, and then they release the oxygen.

Weathering is the physical and chemical breakdown of rocks at or near the Earth's surface. As rocks fragment, crack, and crumble, due to physical, chemical, or biological interactions, they become soil. As that soil and rock debris loosen and get transported, **erosion** happens. Without it, rock debris would just stay where it was formed. Erosion can happen for a variety of reasons and through a variety of natural agents, each producing distinctive changes both in the material that it transports and creating distinctive characteristics in the surface and landscape. There are various agents of erosion:

- **Streams** (running water): Sediments get transported by streams and shape the Earth as a result.
- **Glaciers** (moving ice): Glacial erosion can cause the formation of glacial **moraines** (material transported by a glacier and then deposited somewhere else), **drumlins** (streamlined long hills composed of sediment from glacial drift), and **finger lakes** (caused by glaciers advancing and retreating and dragging sediment along with them). For example, the **Ice Age** was an age where a significant amount of glacier formation and erosion happened during its waning and waxing.
- **Wave Action**: Erosion and deposition by waves cause changes in shoreline features, including beaches, sandbars, and barrier islands. Wave action is the most potent erosive force on Earth as it is powered by the force of gravity, and the world's rivers alone move about 20 billion tons of rock and sediment to the oceans each year.
- **Wind**: Wind can aid the erosion of sediments and create dunes and sandblasted bedrock.
- **Mass Movement**: This can cause Earth materials to move downslope under the influence of gravity.

Competency 1: Geography

Plate tectonics is the theory that Earth's lithosphere is broken down into a dozen plates that float. It focuses on the movement in the Earth and the forces that produce movement. When forces deep in the Earth make pieces of the Earth's crust separate, collide, and slide past each other, we get a variety of new forms—like mountains, islands, trenches, and valleys. Earthquakes occur along the boundaries between colliding tectonic plates; sometimes the molten rock below creates so much pressure that it gets released by volcanoes and then these help to construct mountains. Under the ocean, volcanic activity along the ocean floor may form undersea mountains that can thrust above the Earth's surface and become islands.

COMPETENCY 1.3

Identify the ways natural processes and human–environment interactions shape cultural features (e.g., communities, language, technology, political and economic institutions).

Geographers also look at the impact of humans on the physical environment. **Culture** is the way of life (e.g., language, technology, political and economic institutions, religion, work ethics, values, education, art, music) that characterizes a group of people. The study of culture and Earth interactions is called **cultural ecology**. **Political ecology** is a multi-disciplinary study of how social and environmental change occurs in the context of power relations, social structures, economic issues, and human–environment interactions.

Humans depend on the environment to provide them with their basic needs: food, shelter, and clothing. Humans also modify that same environment in order to meet their needs. For instance, people build dams to change the way water flows, plow and irrigate fields to grow food, clear forests to build houses, and dig mines for minerals and natural resources that help sustain life. Humans adapt to their environment if they cannot change it. For instance, people put on warm coats and use heaters when they live in cold climates. How people adapt to their environment depends to a large extent on their ability to do so—and it reflects their economic and political circumstances and their technological abilities.

Human–environment interaction has also shaped Earth's physical systems and features. For example, building on oceanfronts may increase erosion and alter the landscape. Clearing forests to make room for agriculture or cities changes the appearance of the landscape. Building dams and canals changes the way water flows.

Geographers approach the study of human–environment interaction in a variety of ways:

Environmental determinism: This is the view that the environment can overpower people and determine their culture and the direction and extent of their development. This is widely considered a "not politically correct" belief in geography. The main train of thought in environmental determinism is that an area's physical characteristics, like climate, impact how people develop over time. For instance, a widely held idea was that "the higher the civilization, the higher the latitude," as it was believed that people in hot climates had to rest a lot in order to keep their body temperature cool—so, over time, they became lazy and did not work very hard.

Human–cultural determinism: This is the view that culture overpowers and shapes the environment. This informs the view of many environmentalists that people are destroying the environment. The problem with this way of thinking is that it is an inadequate way to consider the relationship between humans and the environment because environment does much to shape our cultural activities.

Human–environment interaction: This is the idea that there is a cycle of interaction between humans and the environment that is complex and tautological—the environment shapes people and people shape the environment. We can look at this interaction through a variety of lenses:

- **Impact of climate on the interaction:** Climate influences humans and cultures, as people avoid places that are too hot, cold, wet, or dry. It also influences what kind of agriculture can be produced. But, on the other hand, people have learned to adapt to the environment—they developed air conditioning and heating and have used trade to get the goods they need if they cannot be produced where they live.

- **Impact of vegetation on the interaction:** The quality of soil and vegetation and access to irrigation can affect how people interact with the environment. For example, they can leave an area, develop it and find another use for it, use technology to provide an area for water, etc.

- **Impact of landforms on the interaction:** Landforms can shape human and cultural activities, like hunting. But humans and cultures can also adapt and change landforms to meet their needs, like building highways through mountains to make communication and transportation easier.

COMPETENCY 1.4

Analyze geographic information from maps, charts, and graphs.

During the FTCE Social Science 6–12 test, you will have to use maps, charts, and graphs. Familiarize yourself with the information provided before reading the questions. Typically, a map, chart, or graph will be displayed with a set of questions following it. Be sure you understand what the data reveals before proceeding to the questions.

Competency 1: Geography

Maps

What is a map? A map shows a view of an area. Maps are made for a variety of reasons: to represent an area that we cannot see, to show a phenomenon or process, to present information concisely, or to show spatial relationships. Maps are one of the basic tools of geography because they depict spatial information on paper so that the geographer can read and use information effectively.

A **map** is a two-dimensional model of the Earth or a portion of its surface. The process of mapmaking is called **cartography**. All maps include a somewhat simplified view of the Earth's surface. Simplification is what a cartographer does to get rid of unnecessary details and focuses on the information needed to be displayed on the map. For example, when designing a map of Europe for high school students to use to help them learn the names of countries and capitals, a mapmaker would present a simplified map of Europe's political states and boundaries, eliminating details such as vegetation or climate. Another example of simplification involves a cartographer designing a map of London's Underground subway for tourists. Such a cartographer might eliminate unnecessary details such as unrelated buildings and streets from their maps because tourists do not need these details to understand London's subway tracks. Tourists are simply interested in getting on and off at the correct subway stops.

Maps are categorized based on the kind of information they include: **General reference maps** show a variety of information—geological, geographical, political—about a location. **Political maps** show political boundaries, states, cities, capitals, countries. **Physical maps** show landforms and bodies of water found in an area. **Thematic,** or **special purpose maps,** focus on a specific aspect of geography such as climate, vegetation, population density, historical trends, etc. For example, a **contour** map depicts elevation. The closer the **contour lines** are together, the steeper the elevation. An **atlas** is a collection of maps.

Map Properties

Every map has four main map properties: shape, size (area), distance, and direction.

- **Shape** refers to the geometric shapes of the objects on the map.
- **Size (area)** refers to the relative amount of space taken up on the map by the landforms or objects on the map.
- **Distance** refers to the represented distance between objects on the map.
- **Direction** refers to the degree of accuracy representing the cardinal directions—north, south, east, and west—and their intermediate directions—northwest, northeast, southwest, and southeast. Less accurate are the relative directions that people commonly use to describe a location, such as right, left, up, and down, among many others.

All four properties cannot be accurately represented, so a cartographer must choose which of the properties to distort. Cartographers make this decision by considering the map's purpose.

When designing a map for navigational purposes, the cartographer would keep direction and distance accurate; size (area) and shape are not as important. It is impossible to take the Earth's round surface and put it onto a flat surface without some form of distortion, or error, resulting from the "flattening" process. Think of distortion as being caused by a process similar to trying to flatten an orange peel. Every map is, in some way, wrong as a result. The globe is the most accurate representation of the Earth.

Maps have several parts.

- **Title** reveals the subject of a map and identifies what the map conveys.

- **Compass** (or a **compass rose**) helps you orient a map. Look carefully on the maps in the test to make sure you can identify north—sometimes it just has an N with an arrow.

- **Scale** tells you how much smaller the distance is on a map compared to the actual distance. The smaller the scale, the more detailed the map.

- **Grid** of a map consists of **longitude** and **latitude** lines that show coordinates of locations. Latitudes are parallel and measure distances north and south of the line called the **equator**. **Meridians** of longitude measure distances east and west of another imaginary line called the **prime meridian**. Meridians meet at the poles.

- **Labels** are words or phrases that explain features on a map.

- **Key** (**legend**) explains or shows what the symbols or colors on a map mean.

Graphs and Charts

Graphs and **charts** are graphical representations that summarize data and show relationships between the parts of data. Graphs and charts have the capability of strengthening the implications about data through the use of visual images, colors, and other tools. Graphs and charts usually have the following parts.

Features of Graphs and Charts

- **Title:** The title usually appears above the main graphic and provides a description of the information contained in the chart or graph.

- **Diagram:** A diagram represents the visualization of the underlying data.

- **Dimensions:** Dimensions in the data are expressed along **axes**. All charts, with the exception of pie charts (circle graphs), have one or more axis—usually an *x*-**axis** (horizontal) and a *y*-**axis** (vertical).

- **Scale:** Each chart or graph has a scale marked by periodic gradations and accompanied by numerical or categorical indications.

Competency 1: Geography

- **Labels:** Each axis will have a label displayed outside or beside it that describes what sort of dimensions it represents.

- **Data:** All charts and graphs represent data of some sort.

- **Legend:** When the chart or graph represents multiple variables, a legend is usually included that lists the variables in the chart and an example of their appearance.

Types of Charts and Graphs

- **Area Chart:** An area chart (**area graph**) is used to show how something changes with respect to time. It shows the contribution, over time, of each type of data in a series, in the form of a whole picture.

- **Bar Chart:** A bar chart (also referred to as **a bar graph**) uses horizontal or vertical blocks or bars to compare the amounts or frequency of distinct items or shows single items at distinct intervals. Bar charts are useful for comparing groups of data that are in competition with one another. Usually, a bar chart is laid out with categories along the vertical axis and values along the horizontal axis.

- **Column Chart:** Column charts are similar to bar charts because they compare items at distinct intervals. However, they differ from bar charts in that they arrange the categories along the horizontal axis and place the values along the vertical axis. As a result, the bars are vertical on the chart. Column charts are often used to show how values can change over a certain period of time.

- **Line Chart:** A line chart (also referred to as **a line graph**) compares two or more sets of information. A line chart plots the value of data in a **data point** and then "connects the dots" in order to illustrate the relationship of consecutive points. Line charts are usually used to show how something changes over time. Unlike bar and column charts, which show change over a small amount of time, line charts imply continuous change.

- **Pie Chart:** A pie chart (also referred to as **a circle graph**) is used to represent a part-to-whole relationship between data groups. In these charts, the circle represents the whole and the pie is split into parts called **sectors** that represent a part of the whole. Each sector typically is in proportion in size to the amount each sector represents. **Sector labels** indicate the category of information the sector relates to and may also give numeric data, like percentages. While pie charts show the relationship between component values, they only reflect a snapshot of *one* moment in time.

- **Scatter Plot:** A scatter plot (also referred to as a **scattergraph**) is the simplest type of graph. The data are displayed as a collection of points that simply plots the data points against their values, without making any connecting lines, columns, or bars. It usually shows one variable on the horizontal axis and another value on the vertical axis.

CHAPTER 2

Economics

Adam Smith (1723–1790) is widely considered to be the founder of the field of economics. Smith was a Scottish economist whose writings can be said to have inaugurated the modern era of economic analysis. His *Wealth of Nations,* published in 1776, can be read as an analysis of a market economy. It was Smith's belief that a market economy was a superior form of organization from the standpoint of both economic progress and human liberty. Smith acknowledged that self-interest was a dominant motivating force in a market economy, yet this self-interest was ultimately consistent with the public interest. In Smith's view, market participants were guided by an invisible hand to act in ways that promoted the public interest. Firms may only be concerned with profits, he said, but profits were only earned by firms that satisfied consumer demand and kept costs down. Since his work was published, many others have furthered the study of economics, though they certainly have not always agreed with Smith. Four general—and differing—viewpoints have evolved regarding the workings of markets: **Classical** (based on Smith's theory that markets function best with minimal government interference); **Keynesian** (suggests that in the short run, and especially during recessions, economic output is strongly total spending in the economy); **Monetary** (an analysis of money in its functions as a medium of exchange, store of value, and unit of account); and **Neoclassical** (a focus on the determination of goods, outputs, and income distributions in markets through supply and demand).

Most contemporary definitions of economics involve the notions of choice and scarcity and their relationship to one another. Perhaps the earliest of these is by Lionel Robbins in 1935: "Economics is a science which studies human behavior as a relationship between ends and scarce means which have alternative uses." Virtually all textbooks have definitions that are derived from this definition, though the exact wording differs from author to author.

The standard definition of economics is something like this: "**Economics** is the social science that examines how people choose to use limited or scarce resources to obtain maximum satisfaction of unlimited wants."

Macroeconomics is the study of the economy as a whole and includes topics such as inflation, unemployment, and economic growth. **Microeconomics** is the study of the individual parts (e.g., households, business firms, and government agencies) that make up the economy. It particularly emphasizes both how these units make decisions and the consequences of these decisions.

COMPETENCY 2.1

Analyze how scarcity and opportunity cost influence choices about how to allocate resources.

Economists believe that human wants are unlimited while the resources to satisfy those needs are limited. Consequently, society is never able to produce enough goods and services to satisfy everybody, or almost anyone, completely. Alternatively, resources are scarce relative to human needs and desires. When resources are limited, the limitation affects prices (the amount of money needed to buy goods, services, or resources). **Scarcity** means that choices have to be made when either purchasing or producing goods. Theoretically, a society that does not have scarcity is a lucky society that has no problems and, thus, never has to make any decisions. In the real world, all societies must make three crucial decisions:

1. which and how many goods and services it should produce;

2. how it should produce these goods and services;

3. how the goods and services should then be distributed among the people.

If a society chooses to produce more of some goods, then there are fewer resources available to produce other goods. These seemingly local decisions may affect other people and even other nations.

There are two important components of the idea of scarcity: a good has to be limited AND people have to want it. If no one wants a good, no matter how limited it is, it is not scarce.

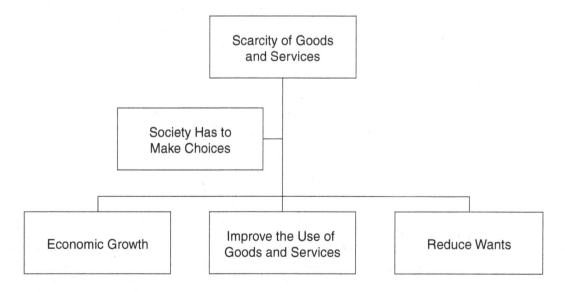

Competency 2: Economics

Economic Growth: One way to deal with scarcity is to grow the economy to produce more of the goods and services that people want so that whatever is wanted is in abundant supply. In order to accomplish this, you would need more resources, better resources, and better technology to get those resources.

Improve the Use of Goods and Services: If society uses its resources wisely, then scarcity is less likely to be an issue.

Reduce Wants: Another way to deal with scarcity is to get a society to not want so much of an item. If people did not want so much, then an item would not be scarce. In the long term, however, this is difficult to do.

There are four ways that society can use its existing resources to reduce scarcity and obtain the maximum satisfaction possible. These universal economic goals are sometimes referred to as the 4 E's:

- Allocative **E**fficiency
- Production **E**fficiency
- **E**quity
- Full **E**mployment

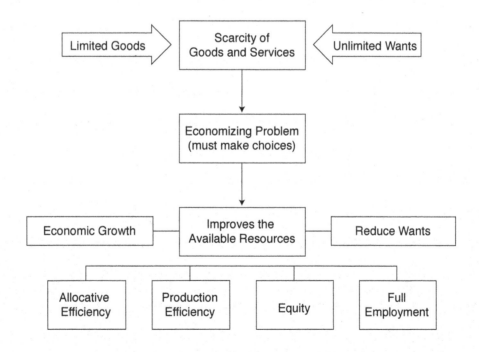

Universal Economic Goals

Allocative Efficiency (Economic Efficiency)—A society achieves allocative efficiency if it produces the types and quantities of goods and services that most satisfy its people. Allocative efficiency is using our limited resources to produce the right mix of goods, so that society makes more of what people want, and less of what people do not want. Failure to do so wastes resources by producing a lot of things people do not want and few things that people want.

Production Efficiency (Technical Efficiency)—A society achieves production/technical efficiency when it is producing the greatest quantity of goods and services possible from its resources at a minimum cost, thus using fewer resources and increasing production quantities. In turn, scarcity is reduced. Failure to do so is also a waste of resources. There are three methods that can be used to achieve production efficiency:

- not using more resources than necessary;
- using resources where they are best suited;
- using technology that minimizes costs.

Equity—A society wants the distribution of goods and services to conform with its notions of "fairness." Equity is not necessarily synonymous with equality. There is no objective standard of equity, and all societies have different notions of what constitutes equity. Three widely held **Standards of Equity** are as follows:

- **Contributory standard**—Under a contributory standard, people are entitled to a share of goods and services based on what they contribute to society. Those making larger contributions receive correspondingly larger shares. The measurement of contribution and what to do about those who contribute very little or are unable to contribute (i.e., individuals with chronic illnesses or other debilitating conditions) are continuing issues.

- **Needs standard**—Under a needs standard, a person's contribution to society is irrelevant. Goods and services are distributed based on the needs of different households. Measuring need and inducing people to contribute to society when goods and services are guaranteed are continuing issues.

- **Equality standard**—Under an equality standard, every person is entitled to an equal share of goods and services, simply because he or she is a human being. Some of the ongoing issues with this theory are how to allow for needs and how to induce individuals to maximize their productivity when the reward is the same for everyone. Economists remain divided over whether the goals of equity and efficiency (allocative and technical) are complementary or in conflict.

Full Employment—Full employment means using all available resources, not just labor. If an economy has full employment, it produces more; if all resources are not employed, it produces less.

Trade-Offs and Opportunity Cost

Another basic axiom of economics is that the economic choices that are made result in trade-offs that can be measured. As those trade-offs are measured, various combinations of goods and services can be produced. However, when more of one good is produced, there is a cost in the form of lost production of an alternative good or service. The **Production Possibilities Frontier Curve**, the **Law of Diminishing Marginal Returns**, and the **Law of Increasing Opportunity Cost** help explain this axiom. Together, these realities govern the behavior of the supplier in the free market system.

Production Possibilities Frontier Curve

The **Production Possibilities Frontier Curve** is a model of the economy used to illustrate the problems associated with scarcity. It shows the maximum feasible combinations of two goods or services that society can produce, assuming all resources are used in their most productive manner.

Assumptions of the Model

- Society is capable of producing only two goods (guns and butter).
- At a given point in time, society has a fixed quantity of resources.
- All resources are used in their most productive manner.

Table 2.1 shows selected combinations of the two goods that can be produced given the assumptions.

Table 2.1
Selected Combinations of Guns and Butter

Point	Guns	Butter
A	0	16
B	4	14
C	7	12
D	9	9
E	10	5
F	11	0

Figure 2.1, below, shows the Production Possibilities Curve (curve FA).

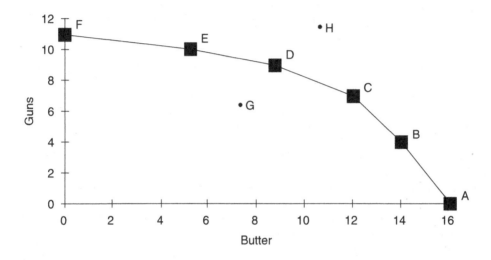

**Figure 2.1
Production Probabilities Curve (Opportunity Costs as Variant)**

Technical Efficiency—All points on the curve are points of technical efficiency. By definition, **technical efficiency** is achieved when more of one good cannot be produced without producing less of the other good. Find point D on the curve. Any move to a point with more guns (such as point E) will necessitate a reduction in butter production. Any move to a point with more butter (such as point C) will necessitate a reduction in gun production. Any point inside the curve (such as point G) represents technical inefficiency. Either inefficient production methods are being used or resources are not fully employed. A movement from G to the curve will allow more of one or both goods to be produced without any reduction in the quantity of the other good. Points outside the curve (such as H) are technically infeasible given society's current stock of resources and technological knowledge.

Opportunity Cost—This is the loss of potential gain from other options when one option is chosen. For example, consider a move from D to E. Society gets one more unit of guns but must sacrifice four units of butter. The four units of butter is the opportunity cost of the gun. One gun costs four butters at that point in time.

Law of Increasing Costs—Starting from point A and moving up along the curve, note that the opportunity cost of guns increases. From point A to point B, two butter are sacrificed to get four guns (one gun costs one-half butter); from B to C, two butters are sacrificed to get three guns (one gun costs two-thirds butter); from C to D, three butters are sacrificed for two guns (one gun costs one and one-half butter); from D to E, one gun costs four butters; and from E to F, one gun cost five butters. The law of increasing costs says that as more of a good or service is produced, its opportunity cost will rise. It is a consequence of resources being specialized in particular uses. Some resources are particularly good in gun production and not so good for butter production, and vice versa.

At the commencement of gun production, the resources shifted out of butter will be those least productive in butter (and most productive in guns). Consequently, gun production will rise with little cost in terms of butter. As more resources are diverted, those more productive in butter will be affected, and the opportunity cost will rise. This is what gives the production possibilities curve its characteristic convex shape. If resources are not specialized in particular uses, opportunity costs will remain constant and the Production Possibilities Curve will be a straight line (see Figure 2.2 below).

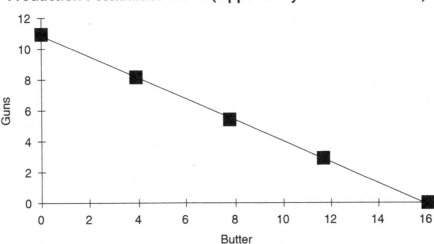

**Figure 2.2
Production Possibilities Curve (Opportunity Costs as Constant)**

- **Allocative Efficiency**—Allocative efficiency will be presented by the point on the curve that best satisfies society's needs and wants. It cannot be located without additional knowledge of society's likes and dislikes. A complicating factor is that the allocative efficiency point is not independent of society's distribution of income and wealth.

- **Economic Growth**—Society's production of goods and services is limited by its resources. Economic growth, then, requires that society increase the amount of resources it has or make those resources more productive through the application of technology. Graphically, economic growth is represented by an outward shift of the curve to IJ (see Figure 2.3). Economic growth will make more combinations of goods and services feasible but will not end the problem of scarcity.

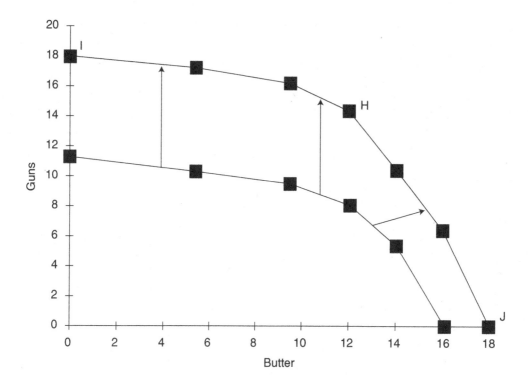

Figure 2.3
Production Possibilities Curve (Economic Growth)

COMPETENCY 2.2

Identify how economic systems (e.g., market, command, traditional) answer the three basic economic questions.

An economic system of a country manages goods and services. All economic systems must answer the same basic economic questions: *What to produce? How to produce it? For whom to produce?* Different economic systems answer these questions in different ways.

Traditional Economies—Traditional systems usually rely on custom/tradition to determine production and distribution questions. While not static, traditional systems tend to be slow to change and ill-equipped to propel a society into sustained growth. Today many of the poorer third-world countries depend on traditional economies.

Command—Command economies rely on a central authority, be it a dictator or democratically constituted government, to make all decisions about the economy.

Market—In a pure market system, there is no central authority, and custom plays very little role in this rather competitive market. Buyers and sellers decide what goods and services

Competency 2: Economics

CHAPTER 2

will be produced. Every consumer makes buying decisions based on his or her own needs, desires, and income. Individual self-interest rules over the good of others. Every producer decides for himself or herself what goods or services to produce, what the prices will be, which resources are used, and what production methods to use. Producers tend to be solely motivated by a desire for profit.

Mixed—A mixed economy contains elements from traditional, command, and market economies. Most countries have a form of mixed economy, although the mixture of tradition, command, and market sectors differs greatly. The U.S. economy has traditionally placed great emphasis on the market, although there is a large and active government (command) sector. The Soviet economy places main reliance on government to direct economic activity, but there is a small market sector.

Capitalism—The key characteristic of a capitalistic economy is that productive resources are owned by private individuals.

Socialism—This is a mixed economic system in which productive resources are all owned collectively by society, and thus, the allocation of them remains under the control of the government. Markets are used, however, to determine the price of goods and wages.

Planned—In a planned economy, the means of production are publicly owned with little to no private ownership. In these economies, instead of markets solving the basic economic questions, a central planning authority makes the decisions and decides what will be produced and how such production will occur.

COMPETENCY 2.3

Analyze the interaction of supply and demand in determining production, distribution, and consumption.

Sellers are on the supply side of a market, and buyers are on the demand side of a market. Both supply and demand reveal the interaction between the buyer, seller, and price. **Demand** is the relationship that shows how much someone will pay for something. Economists examine the demand relationship through the lens of prices and corresponding quantities that are demanded. **Supply** can also be framed in terms of a relationship between price and corresponding quantities that are produced.

A **demand relation** shows the quantity demanded at a particular price. Economists have a unique way of graphing demand relation. The supply-and-demand diagrams are done sideways, with the price put on the *y-axis* and the quantity on the *x-axis*. Demand graphs usually slope downward because people buy less when the price is high and more with the price is low. Supply graphs, on the other hand, usually slope up from left to right, as the higher a price is, the easier it is to make a profit selling a good on the market. High prices attract more sellers and induce an expansion of production.

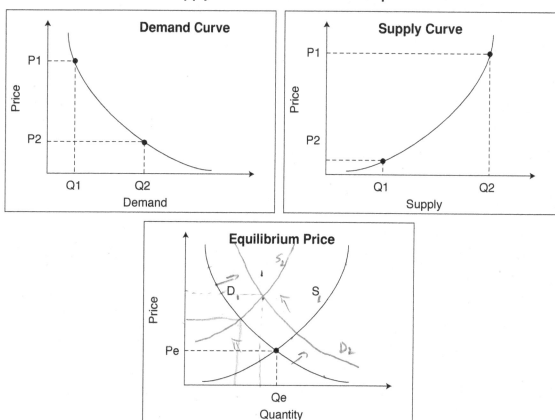

Figure 2.4
Supply-and-Demand Relationships

The intersection of the supply-and-demand curves is referred to as the **equilibrium** (e). The word "equilibrium" is synonymous with stable. The price and quantity in a market will frequently not be equal to the equilibrium; but if that is the case, then the market will be adjusting and, hence, not stable.

Market competition usually makes prices shift toward the equilibrium price. In turn, quantities supplied and demanded meet together at the equilibrium quantity. Both excess demand and excess supply put pressure on prices. Economists call the measure of the market's responsiveness of quantity to price as **elasticity**. If the quantity produced responds to changes in price, then demand is **elastic**; if quantity fails to respond to price change, then the demand is said to be **inelastic**. If the price is above or below the equilibrium price, it reveals a difference in quantity supplied versus quantity demanded. Such difference is termed **excess demand**. If prices rise above equilibrium, there is **excess supply**. An important caveat to consider is that when the price is low and there is excess demand, buyers cannot buy all that they want at the current price. Buyers begin to compete for more of these good deal products by offering higher prices. The higher prices might chip away at the buyer's good deal, but even the higher prices may still be considered bargains. But then sellers might realize that there is a lot of interest in their product and respond by raising prices. For the buyer, this is not a good thing at all. All it takes is a little competition among buyers to raise the market price.

When there is no excess demand or supply, the price stays stable. As such, markets usually do trend toward equilibrium. As supply goes up, the price goes down. When demand goes up, both the equilibrium price and quantity rise, too.

COMPETENCY 2.4

Analyze how macroeconomic factors (e.g., national income, employment, price stability) influence the performance of economic systems.

Macroeconomics is the study of the economy as a whole. Macroeconomists try to figure out how aggregate units affect a national economy. In an effort to forecast economic conditions and ascertain the health of an economy, macroeconomists focus on three things:

1. national output (measured by the **GDP—Gross Domestic Product**);
2. the role of inflation; and
3. unemployment.

National Output: GDP

GDP (Gross Domestic Product) is the most important and comprehensive economic indicator that macroeconomists look at to ascertain the well-being of an economy. GDP is defined as the total money value of final goods and services that a country produces over a given period of time, usually one year. The number represents a snapshot of the economy at a certain point in time. Since almost all that is produced in an economy gets bought and turned into income, economists also use GDP to measure a country's income.

One way of measuring GDP, and perhaps the most common way, is the **expenditures approach**. The expenditure approach looks at the amount of new goods and services purchased in a country for a given year. The idea is simply that what each sector in the country spends is equal to what they earn producing it.

A simple equation is used in the expenditure approach:

$$GDP = C + I + G + NX$$

This means that the total GDP is equal to the total amount of goods and services in one year (**consumption** = C) plus the total amount of investment items bought by businesses and individuals (**investment** = I) plus the amount of new goods and services bought by the government

(government **goods** = G), plus (NX = **net exports**), the difference between the goods bought by people outside of the country and the goods people in the country bought from outside of the country.

When an economy is functioning smoothly, the amount of national output produced (**aggregate supply**) is equal to the amount of national output purchased (**aggregate demand**). However, economies have different cycles—sometimes things are good and sometimes not so good. Market economies experience fluctuations of aggregate economic activity. There are four phases to this economic cycle:

1. **Boom**—an expansion of the economy that brings prosperity;

2. **Recession**—a contraction of the economy with a decline in GDP and a rise in unemployment;

3. **Trough**—a turning point in an economic cycle, a period in which there is a slide from the mean to the lowest point in a recession;

4. **Recovery**—a period in which there is a rise from the trough back to the mean and during which there is lessening unemployment and rising prices.

Unemployment and Inflation

Two other indicators that macroeconomists look to when trying to figure out the health of an economy are unemployment and inflation. Particularly during periods of trough and recovery, these two indicators become quite important, and they both have to do with spending. Inflation results from too much spending in an economy. This happens when buyers want to buy more than sellers can produce, and buyers bid up prices. Unemployment occurs when there is not enough spending in an economy. When sellers make too many goods and there are not enough buyers for those goods, there is a **surplus** situation that results in unemployment, as sellers have to lower their production and do so by laying off workers.

There are three types of unemployment:

- **Frictional unemployment** occurs when workers voluntarily move from one job to another with time in-between. Examples of frictional unemployment include high school or college graduates that enter the workforce; stay-at-home parents that return to the workforce; and individuals that move to another area and look for employment in the new location.

- **Cyclical unemployment** takes place when the economy falls as the result of a recession. Businesses often survive by laying off workers rather than cutting salaries and prices.

- **Functional unemployment** can occur in different ways. In the first type, there are more workers than available jobs. For example, a company might move manufacturing to countries where the cost of production is lower. Thus, the availability of jobs

Competency 2: Economics

in the company's home country in that industry is diminished. In the second type, worker skills are either not in demand or do not match industry needs. For instance, at one time, a high school education was the key to success in many careers. Changing times and increased technical industry demands may result in a demand for individuals with college or advanced degrees. Finally, functional employment results from seasonal work. For example, individuals who teach snow skiing would work in the winter months, but not in the summer months.

Essentially, unemployment and inflation are indicators of an economy's instability that result when there is an inequality between aggregate demand and aggregate supply. Unemployment tells macroeconomists how many people from the labor pool are unable to find work. When economies grow, the unemployment figures are low, as businesses need more people to work to keep up with the demand for goods and services.

Macroeconomists look at the **inflation rate**, or the rate at which prices rise, to determine whether the economy is growing at a healthy rate. An economy that grows too quickly and whose spending is too high has inflation—a period in which the prices rise too quickly because a monetary unit's value has decreased and the purchasing power of that monetary unit has lessened. In these cases, governmental intervention should happen to try to slow the economy and encourage less spending. Conversely, governmental action is also required when there is not enough spending in an economy, production slows, and unemployment rises. During these periods, governments try to stimulate the economy and encourage higher levels of spending. The result of that sort of intervention usually leads to higher levels of employment.

Governmental Economic Stabilization Tools

Governments have a few tools that they can use in order to stabilize their economies.

Fiscal Policy

One method is to try to control spending and unemployment by manipulating the levels of spending and taxes through two types of fiscal policies: expansionary fiscal policies or contractionary fiscal policies. **Expansionary fiscal policy** raises government spending and/or decreases taxes in order to increase spending. **Contractionary fiscal policy** decreases government spending and increases taxes in order to decrease spending in the economy.

Monetary Policy

The other tool that the governments can use to stabilize the economy is monetary policy. In the United States the **Federal Reserve System** (also called the Fed) implements monetary policy by changing the level of money in the banking system. The monetary policy actions of the Fed influence the availability and cost of both money and credit in the economy. Thus, they have a direct effect on prices, employment, and economic growth. As a result, Fed decisions wind up directly bearing upon the willingness of consumers and businesses to spend money on goods and services. So, Fed decisions can influence, either directly or indirectly, all levels of the economy. In order to influence the availability and cost of money and credit, the Fed uses three monetary policy tools:

1. open-market operations;

2. reserve requirements; and

3. the discount rate.

1. Open-Market Operations

The Fed's most flexible and often-used tool of monetary policy is its **open-market operations** for buying or selling government securities. Open-market operations refer to the Fed's buying or selling of U.S. Government bonds in the open market. The purpose is to influence the amount of reserves in the banking system and, consequently, the banking system's ability to extend credit and create money.

   a. **To expand the economy**—The Fed would buy bonds in the open market. For instance, if $50 million in bonds were purchased directly from commercial banks, the banks' balance sheet would look like this:

All Commercial Banks	
R + 50 million Bonds − 50 million	

Banks are now holding an additional $50 million in excess reserves that they can use to extend additional credit. To induce borrowers, banks are likely to lower interest rates and credit standards. As loans are made, the money supply will expand. The additional credit will stimulate additional spending, primarily for investment goods.

Alternatively, the $50 million in bonds could be purchased directly from private individuals. The private individuals would then deposit the proceeds in their bank accounts. After the money was deposited, the balance sheet of all commercial banks would look as follows:

All Commercial Banks	
R + 50 million	DD + 50 million

As above, the banks are now holding excess reserves they can use to extend credit. Lower interest rates, a greater money supply, and a higher level of total expenditure will result.

   b. **To contract the economy**—The Fed would sell bonds in the open market. If it sold $20 million in bonds directly to the commercial banks, the banks' balance sheet would change as follows:

Competency 2: Economics

All Commercial Banks

R + 20 million	
Bonds + 20 million	

In our example, the banks are now deficient in reserves. This means that if the individuals who have money in the bank all asked for it at the same time, the bank would not have enough to pay them. They need to reduce their demand deposit liabilities (money owed to depositors), and they will do so by calling in loans and making new credit more difficult to obtain. Interest rates will rise, credit requirements will be tightened, and the money supply will fall. Total spending in the economy will be reduced.

If the Fed sells the $20 million in bonds directly to private individuals, payment will be made with checks drawn against the private individuals' bank accounts. The banks' balance sheet will change as follows:

All Commercial Banks

R − 20 million	DD − 20 million

Again, in our example, banks are deficient in reserves. They are forced to reduce credit availability, which will raise interest rates, reduce the money supply, and lead to a drop in total spending.

Bonds are a financial instrument frequently used by government and business as a way to borrow money. Every bond comes with a **par value** (stated or face value), a **date to maturity** (ranging from 90 days to 30 years), a **coupon** (a promise to pay a certain amount of money each year to the bondholder until maturity), and a **promise** to repay the par value on the maturity date. The issuing government or business sells the bonds in the bond market for a price determined by supply and demand. The money received from the sale represents the principal of the loan, the annual coupon payment is the interest on the loan, and the principal is repaid at the date of maturity. There is also a secondary market in bonds.

2. Reserve Ratio

Reserve ratio is another type of policy that the Fed can use is in banking. The Fed can set the legal reserve ratio for both member and non-member banks. The purpose is to influence the level of excess reserves in the banking system and, consequently, the banking system's ability to extend credit and create money.

a. **To expand the economy**—The Fed would reduce the reserve requirement. Assume that the reserve requirement is 8%, and all banks are "all loaned up" at $500 million in loans. If the Fed reduces the reserve requirement to 6%, required reserves fall to $30 million, and there are immediately $10 million in excess reserves. Banks will lower the interest rates they charge and credit requirements in an attempt to make more loans. As the loans are granted, the economy's money supply and total spending will rise.

All Commercial Banks	
R 30 million	DD 40 million

b. **To contract the economy**—The Fed would raise the reserve requirement. Assume that the reserve requirement is 8%, and all banks are "all loaned up" at $500 million in loans.

All Commercial Banks	
R 50 million	DD 40 million

If the Fed raises the reserve requirement to 10%, required reserves rise to $50 million, and banks are immediately $10 million deficient in reserves. Banks will raise the interest rates they charge and impose credit requirements to reduce the amount of money borrowed. They may also call in loans. As the loans are reduced, the economy's money supply and total spending will fall.

3. Discount Rate

The third type of policy that the Fed can use is to control the discount rate. One of the responsibilities of the Fed is to act as a "lender of last resort" to banks. Member banks needing reserves can borrow from the Fed. The interest rate that the Fed charges on these loans is called the discount rate. By changing the discount rate, the Fed can influence the amount member banks try to borrow and, consequently, the banking system's ability to extend credit and create money.

a. **To expand the economy**—The Fed would lower the discount rate. A lower discount rate would make it less "painful" for member banks to borrow from the Fed. Consequently, they will be more willing to lend money and hold a low level of excess reserves. A lower discount rate would lead to lower interest rates and credit requirements, a higher money supply, and greater total spending in the economy.

b. **To contract the economy**—The Fed would raise the discount rate. A higher discount rate would make it more "painful" for member banks to borrow from the Fed. Consequently, they will be less willing to lend money and more likely to hold a high level of excess reserves. A higher discount rate would lead to higher interest rates and more stringent credit requirements, a lower money supply, and lower total spending in the economy.

Competency 2: Economics

Table 2.2
Monetary Policy Summary Table

Tool	Action	Effect on Interest Rates	Effect on Money Supply	Effect on Total Spending	Effect On GNP
Open Market Operations	Buy	Lower	Raise	Raise	Raise
Open Market Operations	Sell	Raise	Lower	Lower	Lower
Reserve Ratio	Raise	Raise	Lower	Lower	Lower
Reserve Ratio	Lower	Lower	Raise	Raise	Raise
Discount Rate	Raise	Raise	Lower	Lower	Lower
Discount Rate	Lower	Lower	Raise	Raise	Raise

COMPETENCY 2.5

Evaluate the roles of government, central banking systems, and specialized institutions (e.g., corporations, labor unions, banks, stock markets) in market and command economies.

Governmental Functions in Market and Command Economies

Market Economy

Governments have five functions in a market economy:

1. **Provide the economy with a legal structure and social framework:** Without a legal structure in place, an economy may collapse. Governments must ensure property rights; provide enforcement of contracts; and furnish regulations, legislation, and means to ensure product quality, define ownership rights, and enforce contracts. In the United States, several institutions combine to tackle this responsibility: the FDA (Food and Drug Administration), the Fed, and the SEC (Securities and Exchange Commission).

2. **Maintain competition:** In market economies there is the potential for large firms to achieve a **monopoly** and become the dominant or sole provider of a good or service or for a few companies to create an **oligopoly**. Both limit competition and make the market inefficient. Thus, the government needs to develop laws and regulations to maintain competition. Competition persuades producers and suppliers to react to price and consumer choice.

3. **Redistribute income and social welfare:** The government should provide protections for the people who do not have the skills or resources to earn a living in a market economy. Unfortunately, market economies leave many people vulnerable, and in order for society to function, market economies need to provide for those who cannot take care of themselves, so they need to provide relief to individuals who are poor, dependent, disabled, and unemployed. In the United States, Welfare, Social Security, Medicaid, and Medicare programs are examples of such programs. These programs are built on taxing those with larger incomes to help those in need through progressive taxes, in an effort to make tax policies and the after-tax distribution of income more fair. The United States employs other methods of redistribution, such as farm subsidies and low-interest college loans.

4. **Provide public goods and services that the markets do not:** The government must step in when markets cannot or will not provide the needed goods or the right quantity of goods and services. There are many types of goods and services that the markets do not provide and government picks up, like defense, security, police protection, judicial system, and sometimes education and health services if the market does not provide enough of them.

5. **Correct any market failures and promote growth and stability:** Governments employ as their arsenal various budget, fiscal, and monetary policies to promote macroeconomic growth and stability (e.g., increasing the GDP; fighting inflation and unemployment) and provide the economic conditions through which the marketplace of private enterprise can function efficiently. In the United States, the executive branch of government covers both taxing and spending through the Treasury Department. The Federal Reserve System controls interest rates, money supply, and reserve requirements.

Features of a Market Economy

Central Bank: The role of the central bank in a market economy is to oversee the stability of the banking system and conduct monetary policy in order to control inflation, unemployment, and to stimulate economic growth and function as a bank of last resort. In the United States, the Fed is the central bank.

Corporations: To a large degree, market economies are based on corporations, legal entities that have as their goal production of specific goods and services to make a profit. It is a major use of labor and resources. Corporations in a market economy compete with each other for profit. To get more investors in their company, owners of corporations sell pieces of ownership called **stock**. The people who own stock are called **shareholders** or **stockholders**. The size of their ownership is determined by the amount of stock in a company that they own. As part owners of a company, shareholders receive some of the profits from a company in the form of payments called **dividends**.

There are two types of stocks that are issued by corporations: private and public. Public stocks are traded freely in an open market called a **stock exchange**. With public stocks, anyone, if they

Competency 2: Economics

have the money to invest, can own a part of these corporations. Private corporations can issue stock and have shareholders. However, their shares are not traded in public stock exchanges.

The **stock market** is the epitome of the market economy, where transactions take place exclusively for the purpose of making money. A stock exchange is a place where stocks are traded. As more people buy a stock, its value increases. The primary goal of a buyer is to buy the stock at a low price and sell it at a high price. When a stock is sold at a price higher than when they bought it, the profit is called a **capital gain**.

Command Economy

In a command economy, the government regulates production. The economy is centrally planned, and the government controls all economic decisions. The government has the final authority on which goods and services are produced, how the finished products will be utilized, and who buys which goods and services, as well as the allocation of the revenues earned from their distribution. It sets actual wages and prices. The effort to control the many decisions that are needed to be made to control the economic activity of a country may be too complex to actually be effective in all areas. However, in most command economies, control revolves around the manufacture of the country's industrial goods. In these economies, the government usually owns and operates the production facilities and thus can regulate how much and what type of goods are produced. By controlling all elements of supply, the government in a command economy can ensure that their population has the goods it needs. Often the prices of the goods produced are regulated by the government in order to maintain balance in the economy. In addition, in command economies, the government makes sure that sufficient jobs exist and sets and enforces quality standards.

Command economies typically can boast of an efficient use of resources. Because they can control the rate of production, they also have the ability to adjust supply if it exceeds demand. As a result, inventories of finished goods are smaller, thus ensuring that the right number of goods is bought and sold and that products do not sell at a loss.

Although it might seem that command economies control the entire consumer market, that is not so, as not every type of consumer product is owned or heavily regulated by the central government. Some areas remain outside government regulation. For instance, command economies usually steer clear of markets like agriculture, much in the same way that the free enterprise systems do.

Characteristic Features of Command Economy:

- Traditionally rather stable and relatively immune to financial downturn and inflation
- Surplus production and unemployment rates remain relatively level
- Encourages investments in long-standing project-related infrastructures with promise of no recession threats

- Deliberate and planned approach to money making usually improves a country's economic conditions

- Emphasizes collective benefit, rather than the requirements of a single individual, through distribution of wages and bonuses on the basis of collective contribution

Command Economy: Specialized Institutions

In a command economy, the government sends directives to both state-owned and private enterprises with regard to production capacity, volume, and modes of production.

COMPETENCY 2.6

Analyze the features of global economics (e.g., exchange rates, terms of trade, comparative advantage, less developed countries) in terms of their impact on national and international economic systems.

World trade has increased globally and is an increasingly significant portion of the U.S. economy. The volume of world trade has increased tremendously since the end of World War II. The United States plays a major role in shaping this trade. Adam Smith's book *The Wealth of Nations* points out the advantages of specialization and international trade. They both increase production efficiency and allow greater total output than would otherwise be possible. Production possibilities tables allow us to quantify the efficiency gains of specialization. This is known as the principle of comparative advantage.

Comparative Advantage

The **principle of comparative advantage** says that trade should be based on the comparative opportunity costs between two countries. It basically states that whichever country can produce a good more cheaply should produce that good and should trade for some other good that the country cannot produce as cheaply. Even though one nation may enjoy absolute advantage over another in the production of goods, it serves both nations' best interests to seek the lower domestic opportunity cost for the less productive nation. So, with comparative advantage, theoretically at least, both nations gain from trading and there is a more efficient allocation of the world's resources as well as larger outputs.

Financing International Trade—Exchange Rates

When nations engage in trade with one another, they have to pay for the items. But the question is how to pay for these items when there are different national currencies involved. So, two nations have to exchange their currencies following an **exchange rate** rooted in the international currency market. For instance, an American firm that wants to export something to Brazil does not want to be paid in *riales* because that currency cannot be used in the United States. So, the importer must exchange its currency for U.S. dollars. This service is provided (for a fee) by major banks that have created currency exchanges.

In our example, over time, we might see that the U.S. exports cause an increased demand by Brazilians for U.S. dollars. The increased foreign demand for the U.S. dollar increases the supply of the foreign currency in exchange markets and the dollar appreciates. U.S. imports would increase the demand for the foreign currency and would increase the supply of U.S. dollars in exchange markets. So, the international exchange rates work much like the law of supply and demand as the exchange rates float.

There are two major types of currency exchange formats: floating and fixed—although a managed float is also an available option. At the end of World War II, 44 nations met and created the **Bretton Woods system**. The U.S. dollar served as the focal point of this system because the U.S. dollar became the reserve currency of the system. Countries bought and sold dollars to maintain their exchange rates. The value of the U.S. dollar was fixed at $35 per ounce of gold and was convertible on demand for foreigners holding U.S. dollars. The dollar became "as good as gold."

Two new organizations were also created at the Bretton Woods Conference: the **International Monetary Fund (IMF)** and the **World Bank**. The IMF was created to supervise the exchange-rate practices of member nations. It also was intended to lend money to nations that were unable to meet their payment obligations (that is, to do "bailouts"). IMF funds come from fees charged to the 178 member nations. The World Bank, funded through the sale of bonds, loans money to developing nations for economic development.

The Bretton Woods system dissolved in 1971 as the U.S. dollar came under devaluation pressure and gold drained from the nation's reserves.

In March 1973, a managed, floating exchange rate was established by the major industrial countries. Central banks of various nations have at times intervened to alter their nation's currency value. An example of this occurred in 1995 when the Fed and U.S. Treasury sold German *marks* and Japanese *yen* to increase the value of the dollar, which they believed had fallen excessively. The managed float has withstood severe economic upheavals, such as the OPEC oil crisis in 1973. Some nations, to maintain a more stable domestic currency, have "pegged" the value of their currency to a fixed rate with the U.S. dollar or another industrial nation's currency. An independent floating exchange rate would be subject to the laws of supply and demand in the currency marketplace

Balance of Payments

The **balance of payments** account refers to the sum of a country's transactions with other countries and is summarized in three main accounts: current, capital, and financial account balances. Today, most economists combine the capital and financial accounts (as they are similar in content) into the financial account.

The **current account** primarily tracks the import and export of goods and services but also includes net international transfer payments and net international factor income. If a nation imports more than it exports, it has an unfavorable balance of trade/current account deficit. If a nation exports more than it imports, it has a favorable balance of trade/current account surplus. The current account is as diagrammed here

Net investment income is net interest and dividends paid by foreigners to Americans. **Net transfers** consist of foreign aid, money sent to Americans or their families living overseas. The current account is often termed the "balance of trade," and the United States has run deficits in this account for decades. This trade deficit results because the United States imports more than it exports. The economic impact of trade deficits is an oft-debated topic. Is it good or bad for an economy? If a nation imports more than it exports, a net job increase in the foreign nation is created. If there is unemployment at home, it is difficult to justify this "exporting of jobs." If the demand for foreign goods and services must be paid for in the foreign currency, this causes a depreciation of the net importer's currency that at some point may reverse the trade imbalance. Also, if the foreign workers' wages are lower, this represents a deflationary effect.

The financial account records trade-in assets, such as gold, government securities, banking liabilities (deposits/loans), corporate securities, and fixed assets such as real estate. The official reserves account consists of the foreign currencies held by a nation's central bank. These reserves are increased or decreased in reaction to the balance of the current and capital account. If the balance is negative, a deficit is noted; if the balance is positive, a benefit is noted. Whether a deficit or surplus is good or bad depends on how the issue is resolved. The implications of trade deficits or surpluses can be complicated.

Developing Nations' Economies

Many economists will tell you that for the economy to work for one country, it must work (somewhat) well for all countries. Economic growth in developing nations is confronted with four entrenched obstacles:

- traditional attitudes and beliefs;

- continued rapid population growth;

- a misuse of resources (including capital flight—the legal or illegal export of currency or money capital from a nation by that nation's leaders); and

- trade restrictions.

COMPETENCY 2.7

Evaluate the functions of budgeting, saving, and credit in a consumer economy.

A **consumer economy** is the part of the economy that is centered on the consumer, rather than on the relationship between businesses. This is the part of the economy where we analyze individuals buying goods and services for their own use. The consumer economy urges the consumer to buy, buy, buy. But, an individual only has so much wealth. So, the consumer economy is driven by the availability of cheap credit. **Credit** is simply a promise to pay for goods or services that have already been provided. Individuals obtain this credit from banks and credit card companies who allow borrowers to pay back their loans over time. For giving people the privilege of credit, banks charge the consumer bank fees and interest on the balance of the loan. Banks use the money that they gain from lending out money to one person to finance their lending to another person.

There are positive and negative effects of credit. On the positive side, credit allows individuals to purchase really expensive items that they otherwise would never be able to afford if they had to pay outright, like homes and cars. On the negative side, credit creates debt. Consumers could use credit too much and wind up unable to make their payments. Moreover, with the addition of interest to the principle of the loan, consumers pay significantly more for these goods and services that they otherwise would have had they purchased it outright. Consumer debt becomes a problem for a larger economy when so many people are unable to pay their debt payments. Sometimes these loans are guaranteed by the U.S. government—in effect the public pays for it—and creditors can be paid if someone defaults on a loan; however, in some cases, consumers seek legal help for their overabundance of debt and file for bankruptcy. If too many consumers file for bankruptcy, then many creditors never get paid.

CHAPTER 3

Political Science

Political science is the organized study of government and the administration and control of its internal and external affairs. It borrows from the related disciplines of history, philosophy, sociology, economics, and law. Political scientists explore such fundamental questions as: *What are the philosophical foundations of modern political systems? What makes a government legitimate? What are the duties and responsibilities of those who govern? Who participates in the political process and why? What is the nature of relations among nations?* Political scientists use a wide variety of methods of investigation: qualitative, quantitative, historical comparative, interpretive, and critical lines of inquiry.

Principal Subfields of Political Science

At the present time, the study of political science in the United States is concerned with the following broad subtopics or subfields:

Political theory is a historical exploration of the major contributions to political thought from the ancient Greeks to the contemporary theorists. These theorists raise fundamental questions about the individual's existence and his or her relationship to the political community. **Political theory** also involves the philosophical and speculative consideration of the political world.

American government and politics is a survey of the origins and development of the political system in the United States from the colonial days to modern times, with an emphasis on the Constitution; various political structures such as the legislative, executive, and judicial branches; the federal system; political parties; voter behavior; and fundamental freedoms.

Comparative government and politics is a systematic study of the structures of two or more political systems (such as those of the United Kingdom and the People's Republic of China) to achieve an understanding of how different societies manage the realities of governing. Also considered are political processes and behavior and the ideological foundations of various systems.

International relations examines how nations interact with each other within the frameworks of law, diplomacy, and international organizations, such as the United Nations.

The Development of the Discipline of Political Science

Early History	Political science is a systematic study of government developed in the United States and in Western Europe during the nineteenth century as new political institutions evolved. Prior to 1850, during its classical phase, political science relied heavily on philosophy and utilized the deductive method of research.
Post-Civil War Period	The political science curriculum was formalized in the United States by faculty at Columbia and Johns Hopkins, who were deeply influenced by German scholarship on the nation-state and the formation of democratic institutions. Historical and comparative approaches to analysis of institutions were predominant. Emphasis was on constitutional and legal issues, and political institutions were widely regarded as factors in motivating the actions of individuals.
Twentieth Century	Political scientists worked to strengthen their research base, to integrate quantitative data, and to incorporate comparative studies of governmental structures in developing countries into the discipline. The American Political Science Association (APSA) was founded in 1903 to promote the organized study of politics and to distinguish it as a field separate from history. From the early 1920s to the present, political science has focused on the psychological analysis of the behavior of individuals and groups in a political context. Research has been theory-based, values-neutral, and concerned with predicting and explaining political behavior.

COMPETENCY 3.1

Identify the features and principles of the U.S. Constitution, including its amendments, the separation of powers, checks and balances, and federalism.

Features of the U.S. Constitution

Constitutional Foundations

The government of the United States rests on a written framework created to strengthen a loose confederation that was in crisis in the 1780s. The **Constitution** is a basic plan that outlines the structure and functions of the national government. Clearly rooted in Western political thought, it sets limits on government and protects both property and individual rights.

Historical Background

Following the successful revolt of the British colonies in North America against imperial rule, a plan of government was implemented that was consciously weak and ultimately ineffective, the **Articles of Confederation**. The Articles served as the national government from 1781–1787. The government under the Articles consisted of a **unicameral** (one house) legislature that was clearly subordinate to the states. Congressional representatives were appointed and paid by their respective state legislatures and their mission was to protect the interests of their home states. Each state, regardless of size, had one vote in Congress, as had been the case in the Continental Congress, which could request, but not require, states to provide financial and military support. Under the Articles of Confederation, the national government had the authority and responsibility to control foreign policy such as declaring war or making treaties, assess state contributions to the war effort, borrow and issue money, settle disputes between states, and admit new states to the Union.

Key weaknesses of the Articles included: its inability to levy taxes, draft troops, regulate interstate and foreign trade; its lack of a powerful or effective chief executive and a national court system; its rule that amendments must be approved by unanimous consent; and the inability of the government to make the states enforce legislation that they did not support. As a result, the government was rather weak and ineffective and seemed more like a confederation of sovereign states, rather than a united country.

Without a strong central government to rein these sovereign states in, the 1780s was a decade racked by internal conflict. The economy deteriorated as individual states printed their own currencies, taxed the products of their neighbors, and ignored foreign trade agreements. Inflation soared, small farmers lost their property, and states engaged in petty squabbles with one another. The discontent of the agrarian population reached crisis proportions in 1786 in rural Massachusetts when Revolutionary War veteran **Daniel Shays** led a rebellion of farmers against the tax collectors and the banks that were seizing their property. **Shays' Rebellion** symbolized the inability of the government under the Articles to maintain order. People began to realize that there was a need to create a national government that could replace the confederation of sovereign states. In response to the economic and social disorder and the dangers of foreign intervention, a series of meetings to consider reform and revision of the Articles of Confederation was held.

In 1787, the **Constitutional Convention** was convened in **Philadelphia** ostensibly to revise the ineffective Articles. Under the presidency of George Washington, representatives from every state except Rhode Island met and over four months drafted the **Constitution** that forms the foundation of our government today.

Philosophy and Ideology of the Founders

Among the 55 state representatives assembled at the 1787 Constitutional Convention were **James Madison**, who recorded the debate proceedings; **George Washington**, president of the body; **Gouverneur Morris**, who wrote the final version of the document and its famed preamble, "We the People of the United States, in order to form a more perfect union . . ."; and **Alexander Hamilton**, one of the authors of the *Federalist Papers* (1787–1788). This collection of essays, to which **Madison** and **John Jay** also contributed, expresses the political philosophy of the Founders and was instrumental in bringing about the ratification of the Constitution.

The **Founders** drew upon three important British documents as well as Enlightenment ideas gleaned from the philosophies of the seventeenth and eighteenth centuries in Western Europe. The **Magna Carta (1215)**, the **Petition of Right (1628)**, and the **Bill of Rights (1689)** promoted the principle of a limited government that resonated in the interests of the Founders. The framers of the Constitution also drew upon the ideas of Thomas Hobbes and John Locke who stressed that government had a social contract with the people it represented: if the government did not protect their interests, the people had a right to alter or abolish it. **Thomas Jefferson** incorporated Locke's doctrines in his **Declaration of Independence** (1776), with respect to a government's responsibility to protect the life, liberty, and property of its constituency. The Founders also drew upon **Montesquieu's** ideas about the necessity of separation of powers and checks and balances.

Debates and Compromises Among the Founders Regarding the U.S. Constitution

The Founders did not have an easy time agreeing on the nature of the new government, and much of the resulting Constitution actually comes out of the necessity of having to compromise interests. The first point of disagreement centered on the role of the executive. As many had experienced the problems associated with an authoritative monarchy, they were concerned about the problems caused by a strong and unchecked chief executive. Others argued that the weak presidency of the Articles of Confederation also led to problems, and this group wanted a strong central government. The compromise introduced the concept of **checks and balances** that would permeate the government, making sure that no one branch had unlimited or unchecked power. The compromise dictated that a president could have broad powers, but also that the president's term in office would be limited to a term of four years. The president would have the ability to control foreign policy and could veto Congressional legislation. Should the president commit and be convicted of a crime, Congress would have the power to impeach him. The power to make appointments to offices and to conclude treaties was also tempered as Congress was required to provide its consent.

Another major conflict occurred between the large and small states over the matter of representation. Small states did not accept the argument from large states that they should have more of a voice in government because they represented more people. The large states, led by Virginia, presented a plan calling for a strong national government with representation favoring the larger states (**Virginia Plan**) and the smaller states, which countered with the **New Jersey Plan**. The

Competency 3: Political Science

latter would have retained much of the structure of the Articles of Confederation including equal representation of the states in Congress. Connecticut offered a solution in the form of the **Great Compromise**. The compromise resulted in the division of Congress into two parts—the **Senate,** where all states would have equal voting power; and the **House of Representatives,** which would be determined in proportion to a state's population.

Slavery was an issue that pitted the interests of northern states against those of southern states. Delegates decided on the **Three-Fifths Compromise,** which decided that each slave was to count as three-fifths of a person for purposes of determining population count and with regard to direct taxation on states. Representatives also disagreed about the role of slavery in the new nation. The compromise was that slaves remained the property of their owners, whether or not they had fled to states where slavery was illegal. In a nod to the emergent abolitionist movement of the period as well as to the realization of how much the South thought it needed slavery for its economic survival, it was decided that for at least 20 years, no law that prohibited the importation of slaves could be passed.

The method to be used for the selection of a president was another area of conflict. Many of the Founders expressed concern over whether or not common people actually knew enough to vote for their leaders and feared that democracy might usher in a popular, but unqualified, ruler. So, the compromise introduced the idea of an **Electoral College** that actually elected the president. The framers of the Constitution decided that each state would have the same number of electors as it did senators and representatives.

The Founders were also concerned about the limits of state power and the extent of control that the federal government had on the states. The compromise worked out determined that all laws must conform to the Federal Constitution; however, all power not explicitly given to the federal government belonged to the states.

Washington, Franklin, and others who supported the adoption of the new constitution began to call themselves **Federalists,** while their opponents were called the **Anti-Federalists**. The Federalists, led by **Alexander Hamilton, James Madison,** and **John Jay** argued eloquently for the adoption of the Constitution. The Anti-Federalists, like **Henry** and **Sam Adams**, argued that the Constitution failed to uphold some of the basic rights for which the revolution had been fought. The Anti-Federalists believed that the Constitution would weaken the states, favor the wealthy, increase taxes, and diminish individual liberty. They objected in particular to the absence of a **Bill of Rights** or any written guarantee of certain basic rights and freedoms for all citizens. The voices of the anti-Federalists were heard when New York and Virginia were hesitant to ratify the new Constitution until the promise of a Bill of Rights convinced them to approve of it.

Basic Principles of the Constitution

The authors of the Constitution sought to establish a government free from the tyrannies of both monarchs and mobs. Two of the critical principles embedded in the final document, **federalism** and **separation of powers**, address this concern. The federal system established by the

Founders divides the powers of government between the states and the national government. Local matters, such as zoning issues, are handled by local governments; however, those issues that affect the general populace are the responsibility of the federal government. American federalism is defined in the **Tenth Amendment,** which declares: "The powers not delegated to the United States by the Constitution, nor prohibited by it to the States, are reserved to the States respectively, or to the people." In practice, the system may be confusing in that powers overlap (e.g., welfare) and, in those cases where there is a conflict, the federal government is supreme.

The principle of separation of powers is codified in **Articles I, II,** and **III** of the main body of the Constitution. The national government is divided into three branches that have separate functions (**legislative, executive,** and **judicial**). Not entirely independent, each of these branches can check or limit in some way the power of one or both of the others (**checks and balances**). This system of dividing and checking powers is a means for guarding against the extremes the Founders feared. Following are some examples of checks and balances:

- The legislative branch can check the executive by refusing to confirm appointments.
- The executive can check the legislature by vetoing its bills.
- The judiciary can check the legislature and the executive by declaring laws unconstitutional.

Additional basic principles embodied in the Constitution include:

- the establishment of a representative government (**republic**);
- the idea that government derives its power from the people (**popular sovereignty**), expressed in the **Preamble** to the Constitution, which opens with the words "**We the People**"; and
- the enforcement of government with limits (**rule of law**).

Overview of the Articles of the Constitution and the Amendments

Preamble

"We the People of the United States, in Order to form a more perfect Union, establish Justice, insure domestic Tranquility, provide for the common defense, promote the general Welfare, and secure the Blessings of Liberty to ourselves and our Posterity, do ordain and establish this Constitution for the United States of America."

Basically, the Preamble lists the reasons that the 13 colonies sought independence from England and establishes why this newly independent group of people believed they needed to have a Constitution in order to correct problems with the Articles of Confederation and to create a strong government that would protect and defend its people.

Competency 3: Political Science

Articles of the Constitution

The articles of the Constitution define the organization of the United States government and identify how the federal government interacts with states.

	Focus	Description
Article I	Legislative Branch	Establishes the Legislative Branch, the Congress, as a two-bodied entity comprised of the House of Representatives and the Senate that makes the laws for the United States; describes the qualifications for holding office and how the number of representatives and senators is determined for each state; defines roles and responsibilities for individuals in Congress; describes congressional responsibilities and limitations; identifies how bills become laws.
Article II	Executive Branch	Establishes the Executive Branch comprised of a president, vice president, cabinet, and departments that serve under each cabinet member. Describes the role, responsibilities, and limitations of the Executive Branch.
Article III	Judicial Branch	Establishes the Judicial Branch comprised of the Supreme Court and the lower courts which decide criminal and civil cases according to federal, state, and local laws; guarantees trial by jury in criminal case; identifies the type of cases that the Supreme Court must decide.
Article IV	State and Federal Rights	Identifies the states' powers to make and carry out their own laws; obligates states to respect the laws of other states and that "full faith and credit" shall be given to each state, which means that legal documents that are valid in one state must also be valid in others; requires states to work together in terms of extraditing suspects; sets up how new states are admitted to the Union and that new states may not trample over another states' borders; states that the Federal Government must make sure that each state has a republican or constitutional government and provide for the defense of each state against invasion or domestic unrest.
Article V	Amending the Constitution	Explains the process for amending the Constitution (approval of two-thirds vote of each house of Congress and three-fourths vote of the state legislatures).
Article VI	Supremacy Clause	Establishes that the Constitution and federal laws are the supreme laws of the land and are higher than state or local laws; requires individuals in Federal and state offices to swear an oath of allegiance to the U.S. and the Constitution.
Article VII	Ratifying the Constitution	States that 9 of the 13 states needed to ratify it in order for it to go into effect; the Constitution was presented to the Constitutional Convention on September 17, 1787, and 12 out of the 13 states approved it.

There are currently **27 Amendments to the Constitution.** The first ten amendments are listed as articles and were voted on and ratified together. These articles were added to the Constitution in order to gain the support of those who feared that the Constitution gave the Federal Government too much power. These first 10 amendments are known as the **Bill of Rights** and deal primarily with civil liberties and civil rights. James Madison is credited with writing a majority of them.

Amendment	Date Ratified	Focus
1	1791	Guarantees freedom of religion, speech, the press, and assembly and the right of individuals to petition the government to respond to grievances.
2	1791	Provides for the people's right to keep and bear arms in a regulated militia and states that this right cannot be infringed upon by the government.
3	1791	Gives people security from quartering troops in their homes during either war or peace without the consent of the owner.
4	1791	Protects the rights of an individual against unreasonable searches and seizures and states that the government must have probable cause and a search warrant must be issued before a legal search can commence.
5	1791	States that the government must provide **due process** before punishing a person; states that a person may not be held for a crime without being indicted; provides a person the **right against self-incrimination**; guarantees a person's right against double jeopardy.
6	1791	Provides, in criminal cases, for a person's right to a speedy and public trial and a trial by an impartial jury; establishes a right to legal counsel, that accused individuals be informed of the charges against them, be able to confront the witnesses against them, and be able to call witnesses on their behalf.
7	1791	Provides for the right of a jury trial of civil cases in federal court (where the amount is in excess of $20 (these types of trials are no longer heard in federal courts); and that no decision of a jury shall be overturned by any court in the United States except according to the rules of common law.
8	1791	States that excessive bails or fines cannot be imposed upon individuals and that **cruel and unusual** punishments cannot be imposed.
9	1791	Indicates that citizens and states have rights beyond those stated in the Constitution such that even rights not listed in the Constitution cannot be violated or abridged.
10	1791	Reserves powers not delegated to the United States by the Constitution to the states, or the people.
11	1795	Provides that states have a certain degree of sovereign immunity and that individuals may not sue states in federal courts.

Competency 3: Political Science

Amendment	Date Ratified	Focus
12	1804	Redefines the process of electing the president and the vice president such that both are chosen by the Electoral College and must be on the ballot together; also ensures that whoever runs as vice president must also be eligible to be president.
13	1865	Abolishes slavery and involuntary servitude except as punishment for a crime in which one has been convicted; bans slavery and involuntary servitude except as punishment for a crime in which one has been convicted.
14	1868	Provides equality for all citizens who are born in the United States or naturalized; confers state as well as national citizenship; states that the Fifth Amendment's protection of due process for individuals also extends to states rather than just the federal government; applies **"equal protection of laws"** which would become one of the focal points of the modern civil rights movements; allows for the reapportionment of the seats in the House of Representatives following a census and counts all persons, except for untaxed Native Americans; voids the three-fifths clause in Article 1 regarding population counts.
15	1870	States that all male U.S. citizens shall not be denied the right to vote, regardless of race, color, or previous condition of servitude. This cleared the way for male African-American former slaves to vote.
16	1913	Allows the Congress to pass direct taxes such as the income tax.
17	1913	Allows senators to be directly elected by voter; allows governor to fill state senator positions if a position opens during a term.
18	1913	Made the sale or manufacture and transport of alcohol illegal (also known as Prohibition); repealed by the Twenty-First Amendment in 1933.
19	1920	Guarantees that citizens shall not be denied the right to vote on account of sex; gives women the right to vote.
20	1933	Changes the inauguration date of the President from March 4 to January 20 and new terms of Senators and Representatives to January 3 in order to shorten the "lame-duck" session of Congress (session just after the November election and before the new president assumes office); also establishes how the death of a president before a swearing-in would be handled.
21	1933	Repeals the Eighteenth Amendment, making alcohol legal again (only time an amendment has been repealed); gave states the power to make laws about making, selling, and drinking alcohol.
22	1951	Limits presidential terms to two terms, or ten years in the case of a vice president who becomes president due to a president's death or removal.

Amendment	Date Ratified	Focus
23	1961	Gives U.S. citizens who live in the District of Columbia the right to vote for president; gave the District three electoral votes.
24	1964	Makes it illegal to use poll taxes as a way to deny voting rights.
25	1967	Outlines the order of succession to the presidency. If the president dies or cannot serve, the vice president takes office; if both the president and vice president die or cannot serve, the Speaker of the House assumes the presidency.
26	1971	Extends the right to vote to eighteen-year-old citizens (previously the age requirement was 21).
27	1992	Establishes the procedures for Congressional pay increases; pay increases must wait until after the next election to go into effect.

The Constitution reserves some powers to the Federal Government and some to the states. Some are concurrent powers that are shared by both federal and state governments.

Powers Reserved for the Federal Government	Powers Reserved for the States	Powers Shared by State and Federal Governments (Concurrent Powers)
— Regulate foreign commerce — Regulate interstate commerce — Mint money — Regulate naturalization and immigration — Grant copyrights and patents — Declare and wage war and declare peace — Admit new states — Fix standards for weights and measures — Raise and maintain an army and a navy — Govern Washington, D.C. — Conduct relations with foreign powers — Universalize bankruptcy laws	— Conduct and monitor elections — Establish voter qualifications within the guidelines established by the Constitution — Provide for local governments — Ratify proposed amendments to the Constitution — Regulate contracts and wills — Regulate intrastate commerce — Provide for education for its citizens — Levy direct taxes — Maintain police power over public health and safety — Maintain integrity of state borders	— Taxing, borrowing, and spending money — Controlling the militia — Acting directly on individuals

Competency 3: Political Science

COMPETENCY 3.2

Identify the functions of U.S. political institutions, including the executive, legislative, and judicial branches.

Structure and Functions of the National Government

The national government consists of the three branches: the legislative, executive, and judicial branches as outlined in the Constitution, as well as a huge bureaucracy comprised of departments, agencies, and commissions.

The Legislative Branch

Legislative power is vested in a **bicameral** (two-house) Congress, which is the subject of Article I of the Constitution.

The **expressed** or **delegated powers** of Congress are set forth in **Section 8 of Article I of the Constitution**. They can be divided into several broad categories including economic, judicial, war, and general peace powers.

Economic Powers	Judicial Powers	War Powers	Peace Powers
— to lay and collect taxes — to borrow money — to regulate foreign and interstate commerce — to coin money and regulate its value — to establish rules concerning bankruptcy	— to establish courts inferior to the Supreme Court — to provide punishment for counterfeiting — to define and punish piracies and felonies committed on the high seas	— to declare war — to raise and support armies — to provide and maintain a navy — to provide for organizing, arming, and calling forth the militia	— to establish rules on naturalization — to establish post offices and post roads — to promote science and the arts by granting patents and copyrights — to exercise jurisdiction over the seat of the federal government (**District of Columbia**)

The Constitution includes the so-called "**elastic clause**" that grants Congress **implied powers** to implement the delegated powers. In addition, Congress maintains the power to discipline federal officials through **impeachment** (formal accusation of wrongdoing) and removal from office. The House of Representatives has the power to charge officials (to impeach) and the Senate has the power to conduct the trials. The first impeachment of a president was that of Andrew Johnson. **Article V** empowers Congress to propose **amendments** (changes or additions) to the Constitution. A two-thirds majority in both houses is necessary for passage. An alternate method is to have amendments proposed by the legislatures of two-thirds of the states. In order for an amendment to become part of the Constitution, it must be **ratified** (formally approved) by three-fourths of the

FTCE Social Science 6–12

states (through their legislatures or by way of special conventions, as in the case of the repeal of Prohibition).

The Senate also has the power to confirm presidential appointments to the cabinet, federal judiciary, and major bureaucracies, and to ratify treaties.

Both houses of Congress are involved in choosing a president and vice president if there is no majority in the Electoral College. The House of Representatives votes for the president from among the top three electoral candidates with each state delegation casting only one vote. The Senate votes for the vice president. The Senate has exercised this power only twice, in the disputed elections of 1800 and 1824.

Article I, **Section 9** specifically denies certain powers to the national legislature. Congress is prohibited from suspending the right of **habeas corpus** (writ calling for a party under arrest to be brought before the court where authorities must show cause for detainment), except during war or rebellion. Other prohibitions include: the passage of export taxes, the withdrawal of funds from the treasury without an appropriations law, the passage of **ex post facto** laws (make past actions punishable that were legal when they occurred), and favored treatment of one state over another with respect to commerce.

The work of the Congress is organized around a committee system. The **standing committees** are permanent and deal with such matters as agriculture, the armed services, the budget, energy, finance, and foreign policy. Special or **select committees** are established to deal with specific issues and usually have a limited duration. **Conference committees** iron out differences between the House and the Senate versions of a bill before it is sent on to the president. One committee unique to the House of Representatives is the powerful **Rules Committee**. Thousands of bills are introduced each term, and the Rules Committee acts as a clearing house to weed out those that are unworthy of consideration before the full House. Constitutionally, all revenue-raising bills must originate in the House of Representatives. They are scrutinized by the powerful House **Ways and Means Committee**. Committee membership is organized on party lines with **seniority** being a key factor, although in recent years, length of service has diminished in importance in the determination of chairmanships. The composition of each committee is largely based on the ratio of each party in the Congress as a whole. The party that has a **majority** is allotted a greater number of members on each committee. The chairmen of the standing committees are selected by the leaders of the majority party.

The legislative process is complex. A **bill** (proposed law) can be introduced in either house (with the exception of **revenue bills**, which must originate in the House of Representatives). The bill is referred to the appropriate **committee** and then to a **subcommittee**, which will hold **hearings** if the members agree that it has merit. The bill is reported back to the **full committee**, which must decide whether or not to send it to the **full chamber** to be debated. If the bill passes in the full chamber, it is then sent to the **other chamber** to begin the process all over again. Any differences between the House and Senate versions of the bill must be resolved in a **conference committee** before it is sent to the **president** for consideration. Most of the thousands of bills introduced in Congress die in committee with only a small percentage becoming law.

Debate on major bills is a key step in the legislative process because of the tradition of attaching **amendments** at this stage. In the House, the rules of debate are designed to enforce limits necessitated by the size of the body (435 members). In the smaller Senate (100 members), unlimited debate (**filibuster**) is allowed. Filibustering is a delaying tactic that can postpone action indefinitely. **Cloture** is a parliamentary procedure that can limit debate and bring a filibuster to an end.

Constitutional qualifications for the House of Representatives state that members must be at least **twenty-five** years of age, must have been **U.S. citizens for at least seven years**, and must be **residents of the state** that sends them to Congress. According to the **Reapportionment Act of 1929**, the size of the House is fixed at **435** members. The number of representatives for each state varies and is based on the population of that state. They serve terms of **two years** in length. The presiding officer and generally the most powerful member is the **Speaker of the House**, who is the leader of the political party that has a majority in a given term.

Constitutional qualifications for the Senate state that members must be at least **thirty** years of age, must have been **U.S. citizens for at least nine years**, and must be **inhabitants of the state** that they represent. Each state has an equal number of senators: two per state. Senators are elected for terms of **six years** in length on a staggered basis so that one-third of the body is up for re-election in each national election. The president of the Senate is the **vice president**. This role is largely symbolic, with the vice president casting a vote only in the case of a tie. There is no position in the Senate comparable to that of the Speaker of the House, although the **majority leader** is generally recognized as the most powerful member.

The Executive Branch

The **president** is the head of the executive branch of the federal government. **Article II** of the Constitution deals with the powers and duties of the President or chief executive. Following are the president's principal **constitutional responsibilities**:

- serves as **Commander-in-Chief** of the armed forces;
- negotiates treaties (with the approval of two-thirds of the Senate);
- appoints ambassadors, judges, and other high officials (with the consent of the Senate);
- grants pardons and reprieves for those convicted of federal crimes (except in impeachment cases);
- seeks counsel of department heads (Cabinet members);
- recommends legislation;
- meets with representatives of foreign states;
- sees that laws are faithfully executed.

Despite the attempts by the Founders to set clear limits on the power of the chief executive, the importance of the presidency has grown dramatically over the years. Recent trends to reassert the preeminence of the Congress notwithstanding, the president remains the most visible and powerful single member of the federal government and the only one (with the exception of the vice president) elected to represent all of the people. The president's powers with respect to foreign policy are paramount. The president, as the commander-in-chief of the armed forces, can make battlefield decisions and shape military policy.

The most significant domestic tool that the president has is the budget, which the president must submit to Congress. Though Congress must approve all spending, the president has a great deal of power in budget negotiations. The president can use considerable resources in persuading Congress to enact legislation and the president also has opportunities, such as in the annual State of the Union address, to reach out directly to the American people to convince them to support presidential policies.

Presidents also possess the power to **veto** legislation. A presidential veto may be overridden by a two-thirds vote in both houses, but such a majority is not easy to build, particularly in the face of the chief executive's opposition. A **pocket veto** occurs when the president neither signs nor rejects a bill, and the Congress adjourns within ten days of his receipt of the legislation.

The fact that the president is the head of a vast federal bureaucracy is another indication of the power of the office. Although the Constitution makes no mention of a formal **Cabinet** as such, since the days of George Washington, chief executives have relied on department heads to aid in the decision-making process. Washington's Cabinet was comprised of the secretaries of **state**, **war**, and **treasury**, and an **attorney general**. Today there are 15 Cabinet departments, with **Homeland Security** being the most recently created post. The **Executive Office of the President** is made up of agencies that supervise the daily work of the government. The **White House Staff** manages the president's schedule and is usually headed by a powerful **chief of staff**. Arguably the most critical agency of the Executive Office is the **Office of Management and Budget**, which controls the budget process for the national government. Other key executive agencies include the **Council of Economic Advisors** and the **National Security Council**, which advises the president on matters that threaten the safety of the nation and directs the **Central Intelligence Agency**.

The **Constitutional Requirements** for the office of president and vice president are as follows: candidates must be at least **35** years of age, must be **natural born** citizens, and must have **resided in the United States for a minimum of 14 years**.

Article II provides for an **Electoral College** to elect the president and vice president. Each state has as many votes in the Electoral College as it has members of Congress, plus three additional electors from the District of Columbia—making a grand total of 538 electors. The Founders established the Electoral College to provide an **indirect** method of choosing the chief executive.

The Judicial Branch

Article III of the Constitution establishes the **Supreme Court** but does not define the role of this branch as clearly as it does the legislative and executive branches. Our contemporary judicial branch consists of thousands of courts and is, in essence, a dual system with each state having its own judiciary functioning simultaneously with a complete set of federal courts. The most significant piece of legislation with respect to establishing a network of federal courts was the **Judiciary Act of 1789**. This law organized the Supreme Court and set up the 13 **federal district courts**. The district courts have **original jurisdiction** (to hear cases in the first instance) for federal cases involving both civil and criminal law. Federal cases on appeal are heard in the **Courts of Appeal**. The decisions of these courts are final, except for those cases that are accepted for review by the Supreme Court.

The **Supreme Court** today is made of a **chief justice** and eight **associate justices**. They are appointed for life by the president with the approval of the Senate. In the early history of the United States, the Supreme Court was largely preoccupied with the relationship between the federal government and those of the states. In 1803, the process of **judicial review** (power to determine the constitutionality of laws and actions of the legislative and executive branches) was established under **Chief Justice John Marshall** in the case of *Marbury v. Madison*. This power has become the foundation of the American judicial system and underscores the deep significance of the courts in determining the course of U.S. history.

The Supreme Court chooses cases for review based on whether or not they address substantial federal issues. If four of the nine justices vote to consider a case, then it will be added to the agenda. In such cases, **writs of certiorari** (orders calling up the records from a lower court) are issued. The justices are given detailed briefs and hear oral arguments. Reaching a decision is a complicated process. The justices scrutinize the case with reference to the Constitution and also consider previous decisions in similar cases (**precedent**). When all of the justices agree, the opinion issued is **unanimous**. In the case of a split decision, a **majority opinion** is written by one of the justices in agreement. Sometimes a justice will agree with the majority but for a different principle, in which case he/she can write a **concurring opinion** explaining the different point of view. Justices who do not vote with the majority may choose to write **dissenting opinions** to air their conflicting arguments.

In addition to the Supreme Court, the federal District Courts, and the Courts of Appeal, several special courts at the federal level have been created by Congress. The **U.S. Tax Court** handles conflicts between citizens and the Internal Revenue Service. The **Court of Claims** was designed to hear cases in which citizens bring suit against the U.S. government. Other special courts include the **Court of International Trade**, the **Court of Customs**, and the **Court of Military Appeals**.

The Federal Bureaucracy

In addition to the President's Cabinet and the Executive Office, a series of independent agencies makes up the federal bureaucracy, the so-called "**fourth branch**" of the national government.

Most of these agencies were established to protect consumers and to regulate industries engaged in interstate trade. Others were set up to oversee government programs. From the time of the establishment of the Interstate Commerce Commission in 1887, these departments grew in number and influence. Late in the 1970s, the trend began to reverse, as some agencies were cut back and others eliminated altogether.

Among the most important of these powerful agencies are the **regulatory commissions**. The president appoints their administrators with the approval of the Senate. Unlike Cabinet secretaries and other high appointees, they cannot be dismissed by the chief executive. This system protects the independent status of the agencies.

Following are examples of some of the major regulatory agencies and their functions.

- **Interstate Commerce Commission:** Monitors surface transportation and some pipelines
- **Federal Reserve Board:** Supervises the banking system, sets interest rates, and controls the money supply
- **Federal Trade Commission:** Protects consumers by looking into false advertising and antitrust violations
- **Federal Communications Commission:** Polices the airwaves by licensing radio and television stations and regulating cable and telephone companies
- **Securities and Exchange Commission:** Protects investors by monitoring the sale of stocks and bonds
- **National Labor Relations Board:** Oversees labor and management practices
- **Consumer Product Safety Commission:** Sets standards of safety for manufactured products
- **Nuclear Regulatory Commission:** Licenses and inspects nuclear power plants

Another category of the "fourth branch" of government is made up of the **independent executive agencies**. These were created by Congress and resemble Cabinet departments, but without Cabinet status. Nonetheless they are powerful entities. Some of the key executive agencies include the Civil Rights Commission, the Environmental Protection Agency, and the National Aeronautics and Space Administration. The top level executives of these agencies are appointed by the president with the approval of the Senate.

Some of the independent agencies are actually **government corporations**. These are commercial enterprises created by Congress to perform a variety of necessary services. Their roots can be traced back to the **First Bank of the United States** established in 1791 by Secretary of the Treasury **Alexander Hamilton**. The **Federal Deposit Insurance Corporation** (FDIC), which insures bank deposits, is a more recent example. Under **Franklin Roosevelt's New Deal**, the **Tennessee Valley Authority** (TVA) was authorized to revive a depressed region of the nation. Today it oversees the

Competency 3: Political Science

generation of electric power throughout a vast region and maintains flood control programs as well. The largest and most familiar of the government corporations is the **United States Postal Service**.

The large and powerful federal bureaucracy shapes and administers government policy. It is inherently political despite occasional efforts throughout the years to maintain the integrity of the bureaucratic staff. Dating back to the administrations of **Andrew Jackson**, the practice of handing out government jobs in return for political favors (**spoils system**) had been the rule. The **Civil Service Act** (the **Pendleton Act**) was passed in 1883 in an attempt to reform the spoils system. Federal workers were to be recruited on the basis of merit determined by a competitive examination. Veterans were given preferential status. The Civil Service system was reorganized in the 1970s with the creation of the **Office of Personnel Management (OPM),** which is charged with recruiting, training, and promoting government workers. Merit is the stated objective when hiring federal employees. A controversial policy of the OPM is **affirmative action,** a program to help groups discriminated against in the job market find employment.

COMPETENCY 3.3

Identify the effects of voter behavior, political parties, interest groups, public opinion, and mass media on the electoral process in the United States.

Democracy is a political system in which the populace votes for leaders in free and fair elections. As a result, government is based on the consent of the governed. This requires active participation of the people to be informed citizens who understand key issues and vote in elections. Political parties form when individuals have similar views and values to promote those through candidates for election. Interest groups, as well as public opinion, also have viewpoints that they want candidates and voters to consider. Mass media, and now social media, report on these views through digital and print forms, which often shape thinking and voter behavior.

Political Parties

A **political party** is an organization comprised of people who hold similar ideas about government and seek to influence government by electing its members to public office. Political parties serve multiple functions:

- To recruit political leaders, provide a label for its candidates, and train them
- To integrate and mobilize citizens by organizing societal interests and providing voters with choices
- To articulate and aggregate interests and communicate popular preferences by building and aggregating support among broad coalitions of citizen interest groups
- To formulate public policy and structure public debate

- To structure political conflict and competition by integrating multiple conflicting demands into coherent policy

- To organize the process of government

- To link state governments to the national government

Political parties have three distinct elements:

- The party-in-the-electorate

- The party organization

- The party-in government (public officials and those who seek to be)

While certainly parties attract people with similar views, they also have a presence in the electorate that, over time, can alter people's beliefs and behaviors, so much so that political parties become defined by the ideas and behaviors of their members. As an organization, political parties have formal roles and structures that they follow in order to manage party affairs. As a government quasi-entity, political parties help shape institutions of government. Members of political parties elected to positions in state and federal executive and legislative branches tend to appoint members from their own political party to government positions.

While political parties today form a cornerstone of our civic society, this was not always the case. The Constitution does not mention political parties, and the Founders in general were opposed to them. Madison viewed political parties as "sinister interests" prone to undermining, perverting, or usurping the will of the majority; in 1796, George Washington warned in his **Farewell Address** of the "baneful effect" of the political party, which "agitates the Community with ill-founded jealousies and false alarms." Political parties were thought of as searching for profit, not providing for the common good.

Despite early concerns about the evil of political parties, two of President Washington's chief advisors, Thomas Jefferson and Alexander Hamilton, formed the first two parties. It is interesting to remember the Founders' fears of political parties in the light of politics today. Yet, the first two parties developed simultaneously with the organization of the new government in 1789. It was the initial conflict over the interpretation of the powers assigned to the new government by the Constitution that gave rise to the first organized American political parties. The Federalist Party evolved around the policies of Washington's Secretary of the Treasury, Alexander Hamilton. He and his supporters favored a "loose construction" approach to the interpretation of the Constitution. They advocated a strong federal government with the power to assume any duties and responsibilities not prohibited to it by the text of the Constitution. Federalists generally supported programs designed to benefit banking and commercial interests, and in foreign policy they were pro-British. The Democratic-Republicans, or Jeffersonian Republicans, formed in opposition to the Federalists. They rallied around Washington's Secretary of State, Thomas Jefferson. The Jeffersonians took a "strict constructionist" approach, interpreting the Constitution in a narrow, limited sense.

Competency 3: Political Science

Sympathetic to the needs of the "common man," the Democratic-Republicans were mistrustful of powerful centralized government.

By Washington's *Farewell Address* in 1796, the new political parties began to play an essential role in the presidential election and political parties played a central role in the election of 1796. Both the Federalists and the Democratic-Republicans put up candidates for the office. Shortly thereafter, however, the Federalist party began to lose steam, first with the 1800 election of Thomas Jefferson, then the 1804 death of the Federalist leader Alexander Hamilton following the famous duel with Aaron Burr. Jefferson's re-election in 1804, followed by another Democratic-Republican win with James Madison in 1808, caused the Federalist Party to wither away.

By the 1820s, the Democrats had splintered into factions led by **Andrew Jackson** (Democrats) and **John Quincy Adams** (National Republicans). The Jacksonians continued with Jefferson's tradition of supporting policies designed to enhance the power of the common man. Their support was largely agrarian. The National Republicans, like their Federalist predecessors, represented the interests of bankers, merchants, and some large planters. Eventually a new party, the **Whigs**, was organized from the remnants of the old Federalists and the National Republicans. The Whigs were prominent during the 1840s, but like their Democratic rivals, they fragmented during the 1850s over the divisive slavery issue. The modern **Republican Party** was born in 1854 as Whigs and anti-slavery **Democratic Party** came together to halt the spread of slavery. The Republicans built a constituency around the interests of business, farmers, workers, and the newly emancipated slaves in the post–Civil War era.

Although the two-party system is firmly established in the United States, over the years, "**third parties**" have left their marks. The national nominating conventions were introduced in the 1830s by the **Anti-Masonic Party** and were soon adopted by the Democrats and the Whigs. The **Prohibition Party** opposed the use of alcohol and worked for the adoption of the **Eighteenth Amendment**. In the 1890s, the **Populist Party** championed the causes of the farmers and workers and impacted the mainstream parties with its reform agenda. Among the Populist innovations were the **initiative petition** (a mechanism allowing voters to put proposed legislation on the ballot) and the **referendum** (allowing voters to approve or reject laws passed by their legislatures). The **Progressive** or **Bull Moose Party** was a **splinter party** (one that breaks away from an established party, in this case the Republican Party) built around the personality of Theodore Roosevelt. Another party formed around the personality of a forceful individual was the 1992 **Reform Party** of **H. Ross Perot**. Perot did not capture any electoral votes but garnered 19 percent of the popular tally. Other more recent parties include the Green Party, which championed environmental causes, and the Libertarian Party, which promotes civil liberties, non-interventionism, laissez-faire economics, and the abolition of the welfare state.

Today, political parties exert a variety of functions essential to the democratic tradition in the United States. Nominating candidates for local, state, and national office is their most visible activity. At the national level, this function has been diluted somewhat by the popularity of **primary elections** allowing voters to express their preference for candidates. Raucous conventions where party bosses chose obscure "**dark horse**" candidates in "smoke-filled rooms" are largely a thing of the past.

Political parties stimulate interest in public issues by highlighting their own strengths and maximizing the flaws of the opposition. They also provide a framework for keeping the machinery of government operating, most notably in their control of Congress and its organization, which is strictly along party lines. American political parties appear in theory to be highly organized. The geographic size of the country coupled with the federal system of government keep the parties in a state of relative decentralization. At the local level, the fundamental unit of organization is the **precinct**. At this level, there is usually a captain or committee to handle such routine chores as registering voters, distributing party literature, organizing "**grass-roots**" meetings, and getting out the vote on election day. **State central committees** are critical to the parties' fundraising activities. They also organize the state party conventions. There is great variety from state to state regarding the composition and selection of the state committees, which often formulate policies independent from those of the national committee. In presidential election years, the **national party committees** are most visible. They plan the **national nominating convention**, write the party **platforms** (summaries of positions on major issues), raise money to finance political activities, and carry out the election campaigns. Representatives from each state serve on the national committees, and the **presidential nominee** chooses the individual to serve as the **party chairperson**.

Political Beliefs and Characteristics of Citizens

The population of the United States, with its diverse components, is difficult to characterize with respect to political beliefs and attitudes and individual citizens tend to hold a variety, and often contradictory, set of beliefs about their government, leaders, and the political system. The process by which individuals form their political allegiances is called **political socialization,** and the culture that develops as a result of this is called **political culture**. **Cleavages**, or divides, often occur where society breaks into separate groupings of individuals. Examples of factors that create these groupings include family ties, race/ethnicity, gender, socioeconomic class, religion, education, and region. Political allegiances are also affected by advertising and media (e.g., radio, TV, movies, newspapers, blogs, social networking sites), which influence political opinion.

Despite the categorization of Americans as either **liberals** or **conservatives**, most studies indicate that individuals do not follow clearly delineated **ideologies** (firm and consistent beliefs with respect to political, economic, and social issues). The terms *liberal* and *conservative* with reference to the political beliefs of Americans are difficult to define precisely. Liberals tend to favor change and to view government as a tool for improving the quality of life. Conservatives, on the other hand, are more inclined to view both change and government with suspicion. They emphasize individual initiative and local solutions to problems. A puzzling reversal is seen in the attitudes of liberals and conservatives when confronting moral issues such as abortion and school prayer. Here conservatives see a role for government in ensuring the moral climate of the nation while liberals stress the importance of individual choice.

Competency 3: Political Science

The most basic way that citizens influence the electoral process in the United States is **voting**. Since the passage of the Twenty-Third Amendment in 1965, U.S. citizens, both male and female, who are 18 years old or older, are eligible to vote. The number of people, however, who actually choose to use their right to vote, is surprisingly few. Reasons for not voting range from a belief that an individual really cannot change anything, a belief that votes are not counted properly, difficulty among certain racial or ethnic groups in being able to cast their votes due to voter intimidation, lack of adequate numbers of voting machines, limited hours to vote, and misunderstandings about the voter registration process. Only about 57% of eligible voters actually voted in the 2008 Presidential Election. In Florida, for example, that number was only slightly higher, as 58% of eligible voters cast ballots.

Political Institutions and Special Interests

Interest groups

Interest groups have a strong hold on politics today. **Lobbyists** (individuals who try to influence legislation on behalf of a special interest) are an ever-growing part of today's politics. Interest groups are not exclusively found in the Senate, but since each state has only two senators, it is the place where lobbyists spend a lot of time and money when a bill needs to be defeated. American officials and political leaders are continually subjected to pressure from a variety of interest groups seeking to influence their actions. Such groups arise from bonds among individuals who share common concerns. Interest groups may be loosely organized (**informal**), with no clear structure or regulations. A good example of such an informal or ad hoc interest group was the "March of the Poor" on Washington, D.C., in 1963 to focus Congress's attention on the needs of the "underclass" in America. A group of neighbors united in opposition to a new shopping mall that threatens a wetland is an example of this type of group. Other interest groups are much more **formal** and permanent in nature. They may have suites of offices and large numbers of employees. Their political objectives are usually clearly defined. Labor unions, professional and public-interest groups, and **single-issue** organizations fall into this category. The National Rifle Association and the National Right to Life Organization are examples of single-issue pressure groups. Interest groups employ a variety of tactics to accomplish their goals. The concept of the **iron triangle** consists of the symbiotic relationship among Congress, federal agencies, and lobbyists. Lobbyists provide legislators with reports and statistics to persuade them of the legitimacy of their respective positions. Federal agencies use lobbyists and connections to influence legislation for continuation of funding. Congressional leaders receive agency support for the continuation or implementation of certain bureaucratic policies within their districts.

Lobbyists are required to register in Washington and to make their positions public. They are barred from presenting false and misleading information and from bribing public officials. Regulatory legislation cannot, however, curb all the abuses inherent to a system of organized persuasion.

One particularly controversial brand of pressure group is the **Political Action Committee (PAC)**. PACs were formed in the 1970s in an attempt to circumvent legislation limiting contributions to political campaigns. Critics see these interest groups as another means of diluting the influence individual voters may have on their elected officials. Some politicians refuse to accept PAC money.

Public Opinion and Media

Public opinion refers to the attitudes and preferences expressed by a significant number of individuals about an issue that involves the government or the society at large. It does not necessarily represent the sentiments of all or even most of the citizenry. Nonetheless, it is an important component of a democratic society.

The **media** is another element of political science in which influence has exploded with the appearance of the Internet and social media. A large segment of our society, our oldest citizens, grew up without, or with limited exposure to, television and depended instead on newspapers and radio for information on current events. Now, cable television's 24-hour news channels, YouTube, blogs, and other Internet news providers (many offering opinions disguised as news) have changed our perception of media's reach. In today's technological society, the influence of the **mass media** on public opinion cannot be overemphasized. Print and broadcast media have already demonstrated their ability to reach large numbers of people cheaply and efficiently. Now, electronic media join the ranks. These opinion shapers not only serve as watchdogs over governmental, business, and society's actions as they scrutinize questionable actions or behaviors; but they have also been accused of creating and manufacturing public opinion. In recent elections, the electronic media in particular have been criticized for oversimplifying complicated issues and reducing coverage of major events to brief sound bites. Both the print and broadcast media claim to present news in a fair and objective format, but both conservatives and liberals claim that coverage is slanted. **Paid political advertising** is another vehicle for molding public opinion. In this case, objectivity is neither expected nor attempted, as candidates and interest groups employ "hard-sell" techniques to persuade voters to support their causes.

Measuring the effects of the media on public opinion is difficult, as is gauging where the public stands on a given issue at a particular point in time. **Public opinion polls** have been designed to these ends. Pollsters usually address a **random sample** and try to capture a **cross section** of the population. Their questions are designed to elicit responses that do not mirror the biases of the interviewer or the polling organization. Results are tabulated and analyzed, and generalizations are presented to the media.

Although polls are more accurate today than in the past, they are still subject to criticism for oversimplifying complicated issues and encouraging pat answers to complex problems. Public opinion is constantly in a state of flux, and what may be a valid report today is passé tomorrow. Another criticism is that interviewees may not be entirely candid, particularly with respect to sensitive issues. They may answer as they think they should but not necessarily with full honesty.

Competency 3: Political Science

A type of election poll that has been the target of sharp criticism is the **exit poll** in which interviewers question subjects about their votes as they leave the polling places. These polls may be accurate, but if the media present the results while voting is still in progress, the outcome may be affected. Predicting the winners before voters throughout the country have had the opportunity to cast their ballots in a national election robs a segment of the electorate of the sense that its participation is of any consequence. In the 2000 election, exit polls led to confusion as Florida results were projected prematurely; the television networks vowed to be more careful.

Voter Apathy

In recent years, attention has focused on the problem of voter apathy. Despite efforts to extend suffrage to all segments of the adult population, participation in the electoral process has been on the decline. Several theories have been advanced to explain this trend. There is widespread belief that Americans are dissatisfied with their government and mistrust elected officials. Therefore, they refuse to participate in the electoral process. Some citizens do not vote in a given election, not because they are "turned-off" to the system, but because they are ill, homeless, away on business, or otherwise preoccupied on election day. College students and others away from their legal residences find registration and the use of **absentee ballots** cumbersome and inconvenient. Efforts were made in the 1990s to streamline the registration process with such legislation as the **"motor-voter" bill** that makes it possible for citizens to register at their local registries of motor vehicles.

While most attempts to explain voter apathy focus on negatives, some analysts disagree. They see disinterest in the ballot as a sign that the majority of Americans are happy with the system and feel no sense of urgency to participate in the political process.

Political participation is not limited to voting in elections. Working for candidates, attending rallies, contacting elected officials and sharing opinions about issues, writing letters to newspapers, marching in protest, and joining in community activities are all forms of political participation. While voter turnout has decreased in recent years, other forms of participation seem to be on the increase.

COMPETENCY 3.4

Identify the elements and functions of state and local governments in the United States.

The United States government divides authority and jurisdiction among national, state, and local governments. It comprises one national (federal) government, 50 state governments, more than 3,000 county governments, and over 85,000 local government units comprising over 19,000 municipalities, 16,000 township governments, 15,000 school districts, and 31,000 special districts.

The federal government is the largest body of government in the United States. It makes, enforces, and explains laws for the entire country. The Constitution functions as the foundation of all law for U.S. citizens and lays out the responsibility and structure of the federal government. The following are the specific powers that the Constitution delegates to the federal government:

- To regulate foreign commerce and interstate commerce
- To tax, borrow, and coin money; universalize bankruptcy laws
- To regulate naturalization and immigration
- To establish a postal service
- To grant patents and copyrights
- To establish courts
- To declare and wage war and to declare peace, and conduct relations with foreign powers
- To govern territories, admit new states, and govern Washington, D.C.
- To raise and maintain an army and a navy, and to define and punish felonies and piracy on the high seas
- To fix standards for weights and measures

There are some powers that the federal and state governments share: Both Congress and the states may levy taxes, borrow money, and charter banks and corporations. Both the state and federal governments may establish courts, make and enforce laws, and take private property for public purposes, as well as spend money to provide for the public welfare.

The **Tenth Amendment to the U.S. Constitution** reserves to the states **any power that the constitution does not give to the federal government and does not deny to the states.** In situations where both the states and Congress claim jurisdiction over an issue, the federal courts decide which claim is more valid. State governments have the following powers:

- To conduct and monitor elections
- To establish voter qualifications within the guidelines established by the Constitution
- To provide for local governments
- To ratify proposed amendments to the Constitution
- To regulate contracts and wills
- To regulate intrastate commerce
- To provide education for its citizens
- To levy direct taxes

Competency 3: Political Science

States may NOT:

- Issue paper money;
- Conduct foreign relations;
- Impair the obligations of contracts;
- Establish a government that is not republican in form—although the three-branch structure is not required;
- Legalize the ownership of one person by another (slavery) (Thirteenth Amendment);
- Determine qualifications for citizenship (Fourteenth Amendment);
- Deny the right to vote because of race, color, or previous condition of servitude (Fifteenth Amendment);
- Deny the vote to women (Nineteenth Amendment).

Today there are 50 states in the United States. Every state government is almost a mirror of the federal government in that each state has a constitution, elected officials, and governmental organization. The state constitutions may not disagree with the Constitution of the United States. Every state government also has three **branches**: the executive, the legislative, and the judicial. Laws passed by states cannot disagree with the federal Constitution. State laws apply only to the people that live in that state.

Every state has the responsibility to protect the lives of the people in that state. The state is responsible for transportation, education, and the laws of business in that state. State and local governments share responsibility for providing many important services that directly affect the daily lives of their residents. These include the following:

- Setting educational standards and establishing methods for funding public education
- Building and maintaining transportation networks
- Establishing state-sponsored colleges and universities
- Licensing and regulating businesses and professions
- Creating and overseeing nonfederal courts and the criminal justice system
- Issuing marriage licenses and driver's licenses
- Issuing and recording birth and death certificates
- Administering publicly funded health, housing, and nutrition programs for low-income and disabled residents
- Managing state parks and other lands for recreation and environmental conservation purposes
- Administering and certifying elections, including elections for federal officials

- Commanding the state National Guard, except when it is called to national service
- Regulating employment of children and women in industry
- Enacting safety laws to prevent industrial accidents
- Handling unemployment insurance
- Operating a state highway patrol

In the early nineteenth century, state governments were new and relatively weak entities. Their size alone made it difficult for them to adequately serve the needs of their largely rural populations, who tended to live far apart from one another. State governments found it difficult to provide adequate transportation and communication for their citizens. To manage these local needs more carefully, state governments turned to local governments. County governments began to spring up, becoming important sources of information and administration. In many rural towns, then as now, the county courthouse was the most prominent public building in the area. Because of this history of local governments acting as a liaison or even arm of the state government, both state and local governments have overlapping duties and responsibilities and they cooperate in some of the above services that they provide for their residents, from welfare to transportation.

Local governments may be considered creatures of state governments as they function as subordinate governmental bodies that exist in two tiers: counties, also known as boroughs in Alaska and parishes in Louisiana; and municipalities, or cities/towns. State governments have power over these local authorities as states can abolish a local government, merge it with another, or give it additional authority if they so choose. Local authority in counties, for instance, comes from state-approved charters that set up their county governments and state how they will function. County charters cannot disagree with their state's constitutions or the U.S. Constitution. Counties have a variety of powers. They determine the location of highways, are responsible for highway repair, provide relief for their poor, determine voting precincts and polling places, and organize school and road districts. In some states, counties are divided into townships.

Municipal governments are also called townships, boroughs, villages, cities, and townships. They are usually headed by a mayor or city manager, and are one of the smallest bodies of government. There are usually many cities in a county. Municipal governments have the power to levy taxes; to borrow; to pass, amend, and repeal local ordinances; and to grant franchises for public service corporations. The taxes collected pay for police, fire departments, parks, and other services. Like counties, municipal governments have charters that must be approved by the state government. City government is the closest form of government to the people. In some areas, there are even smaller township governments.

Municipalities generally take responsibility for parks and recreation services, police and fire departments, housing services, emergency medical services, municipal courts, transportation services (including public transportation), and public works (streets, sewers, snow removal, signage, and so forth). Whereas the federal government and state governments share power in countless ways, a local government must be granted power by the state. In general, mayors, city councils, and other governing bodies are directly elected by the people.

COMPETENCY 3.5

Analyze the guiding concepts, principles, and effects of U.S. foreign policy.

The Constitutional Framework for Foreign Policy

The Constitution lays out the institutional framework for foreign policy that places it under control of the federal government. The Founders divided responsibility for foreign affairs between the president and the Congress. The president, as the head of state, could appoint and receive ambassadors, sign treaties, and represent the United States abroad. Congress could declare war, but the president, as commander-in-chief, could actually wage the war. The president also had the authority to negotiate treaties that are then subject to the advice and consent of the Senate (two-thirds vote needed for approval). The president appoints key foreign policy and military officials as well as ambassadors, but the Senate must consent.

The Theoretical Framework of International Relations

The study of how nations interact with one another can be approached from a variety of perspectives, including the following:

- A traditional analysis uses the descriptive process and focuses on such topics as global issues, international institutions, and the foreign policies of individual nation-states.

- The strategists' approach zeroes in on war and deterrence. Scholars in this camp may employ game theory to analyze negotiations, the effectiveness of weapons systems, and the likelihood of limited versus all-out war in a given crisis situation.

- The middle range theorists analyze specific components of international relations, such as the politics of arms races, the escalation of international crises, and the role of prejudice and attitudes toward other cultures in precipitating war and peace.

- A world politics approach takes into consideration such factors as economics, ethics, law, and trade agreements and stresses the significance of international organizations and the complexities of interactions among nations.

The grand theory of international relations is presented by Hans J. Morgenthau in *Politics Among Nations* (1948). He argues for realism in the study of interactions on the international stage. Morgenthau suggests that an analysis of relations among nations reveals such recurring themes as "interest defined as power" and striving for equilibrium/ balance of power as a means of maintaining peace. The idealists assume that human nature is essentially good; hence, people and nations are capable of cooperation and avoiding armed conflict. They highlight global organizations, international law, disarmament, and the reform of institutions that lead to war.

An analysis of international politics can be conducted at various levels by looking at the actions of individual statesmen, the interests of individual nations, and/or the mechanics of a whole system of international players. In studying the rise of Nazism and its role in precipitating World War II, the individual approach would focus on Hitler, the state approach would treat the German preoccupation with racial superiority and the need for expansion, and the systemic approach would highlight how German military campaigns upset the balance of power and triggered unlikely alliances, such as the linking of the democratic Britain and the United States with the totalitarian Soviet Union in a common effort to restore equilibrium.

During the Revolutionary War, John Adams was directed by the Continental Congress to outline a plan for the new country's foreign policy. Adams, like many of the Founders, advocated free trade and the avoidance of political ties. The demands of war, however, made military aid from foreign states a necessity. France, who had struggled with Britain, gave aid to the Americans. In 1778, France and the North American colonies signed a military alliance, the first and only military alliance until the twentieth century. The nation's early leaders, having led a revolution against Great Britain, were generally opposed to alliances with European powers, having known and seen the effects of alliances in Europe that led to war for the last few hundred years.

When the first Congress met in 1789, foreign policy was not a primary concern of theirs. They felt that they did not need a big army to protect the new country, and they authorized an army to have only a maximum strength of 840 men. Most of the nation's military strength came from state militias. Their concerns with trade were also relatively mild, and early tariff laws kept tariffs low to keep trade free from government interference.

Isolationism and Non-Interventionism

One of the earliest guiding concepts and principles of U.S. foreign policy was that of **isolationism**. Isolationism is basically a policy of non-interventionist policy in terms of military intervention combined with a political policy of protectionism, which states that there should be legal barriers to control trade with other nation-states. **Non-interventionism** is a diplomatic policy, whereby a nation seeks to avoid alliances with other nations in order to avoid being drawn into a war that is not related to their own territorial defense. The difference between ideas of isolationism and non-interventionism is that isolationism includes isolating oneself from immigration and trade, and non-interventionism refers solely to military alliances and policies.

America has a long history of non-interventionism. In George Washington's 1796 *Farewell Address*, he laid the foundations for a non-interventionist policy when he cautioned that the United States should "steer clear of permanent alliances with any portion of the foreign world." With regard to Europe in particular, he stated that

> "the great rule of conduct for us, in regard to foreign nations, is in extending our commercial relations, to have with them as little political connection as possible. Europe has a set of primary interests, which to us have none, or a very remote relation. Hence she must be engaged in frequent controversies the causes of which

are essentially foreign to our concerns. Hence, therefore, it must be unwise in us to implicate ourselves, by artificialities, in the ordinary vicissitudes of her politics, or the ordinary combinations and collisions of her friendships or enmities."

Both Adams and Jefferson followed Washington's advice, with John Adams avoiding a war with France and Jefferson, stating in his inaugural address in 1801, that the United States should practice "peace, commerce, and honest friendship with all nations, entangling alliances with none." This idea was elaborated upon during James Monroe's administration in response to the new independence of the Spanish colonies in Latin America in the early 1800s with his **Monroe Doctrine** in 1823, which stated that the United States would not interfere in European affairs and it would oppose any European attempt to colonize the Americas. He stated that

"In the wars of the European powers, in matters relating to themselves, we have never taken part, nor does it comport with our policy, so to do. It is only when our rights are invaded, or seriously menaced that we resent injuries, or make preparations for our defense."

Monroe elaborated saying that if any country attempted to re-colonize Latin America, or if Russia attempted to move on the western coast of America, the United States would respond with force.

While Americans sought non-interventionist policies with regard to military intervention, it had a bit of a different attitude with regard to trade. Beginning in 1776, John Adams recommended the idea of **trade reciprocity**, which simply stated that the United States would treat foreign countries the same way that it was treated. Tariffs became one measure that the United States would reciprocate with and tariffs became a standard trade policy until the twentieth century.

American interests became more concerned with the doctrine of **Manifest Destiny** which sought to settle the continent coast to coast, arguing that the United States had a divine obligation to civilize the continent and control its riches. Some political scientists today assert that the policy the United States held against the Native Americans and the idea of Manifest Destiny were actually interventionist policies, and treatment toward the Native Americans and wars with them should be regarded as "foreign policy." It should be noted that while European states became preoccupied in the nineteenth century with grabbing territory overseas, the United States became more focused on expanding its territory in contiguous areas.

Throughout most of the nineteenth century, the United States did practice the idea of non-interventionism in global affairs. Toward the end of the nineteenth century, its involvement in world politics became more substantive as it sought to protect its imperialist and trade interests.

Expansionism and Unilateralism

The first significant foreign military intervention occurred in the **Spanish-American War** in which America occupied and controlled the Philippines. As a result of the war, the Philippines, Guam, American Samoa, and Puerto Rico became American territories, and the United States gained **hegemony** (dominance) over Cuba. In 1899, Filipinos revolted over American rule and the three-year-long war left nearly 4,500 American combat deaths, 16,000 Filipino combat deaths, and estimates of between 250,000 and one million Filipinos killed or died of disease or starvation during the long war.

With the Philippines as a U.S. territory, the United States became embroiled in conflict in Asia. The United States began to claim, what was referred to by John Hay, McKinley's Secretary of State, as **spheres of influence** in which the United States had to protect its interests. But, with the European powers carving out spheres of influence for themselves in China, the United States called for an **Open Door Policy** that would allow all nations equal trading access in China.

In 1904, after President Teddy Roosevelt sent the U.S. navy to Panama to help it throw off the yoke of Colombian rule and the United States started building the Panama Canal, Roosevelt issued his **Roosevelt Corollary** to the Monroe Doctrine. It stated that the United States would intervene in the domestic affairs of any weak or negligent state in the Caribbean or Central America to keep them free from outside forces that might seek to take them over. Under the Roosevelt Corollary, the United States sent military forces to Nicaragua, Haiti, the Dominican Republic, Cuba, Panama, and Mexico.

World War I and a Return to Isolationism from 1920–1941

Although World War I broke out in Europe in 1914, United States efforts to remain neutral succeeded for three years until it was forced into the war in April 1917 by the German policy of unrestricted submarine warfare. It entered the war in an effort to insure freedom of trade routes with Europe. During the war, the United States was not officially tied to the Allies by treaty but instead by military cooperation. By the end of the war, the United States had sent over five million men to serve in the aid of the Allies. By the end of the war, President Woodrow Wilson sought to enact his policy of **Fourteen Points** at the Versailles Peace Conference, and indeed, it did become the basis for postwar settlement.

One of the goals that Wilson advocated was the establishment of a **League of Nations** that would hopefully resolve all future conflicts before they caused another war. Unfortunately for Wilson, the Republican-controlled U.S. Senate refused to ratify the Treaty of Versailles, which had provided for the creation of a League of a Nations. Afterwards, the United States returned to an isolationist stance during the interwar period. The United States chose instead to make separate peace treaties with different European nations. While Wilson's Fourteen Points failed to gain support in the United States, his idea that people had the right to **self-determination** became a rallying cry for many under the thumb of British and French colonial rule in the Middle East and South Asia. Moreover, what is called **Wilsonianism**, the idea of spreading democracy and peace under American auspices, had a tremendous effect on American foreign policy. These efforts continued even with the 1928 passage of the **Kellogg-Briand Pact**, which was designed to outlaw war.

The United States returned to a policy of high tariffs and isolationism. Despite having such a mindset, the United States continued to develop economic ties with Europe, so much so that the

Competency 3: Political Science

Great Depression of 1929 had a direct effect on all of the key European economies. The United States was keenly aware of growing tensions in Europe and in vain tried to keep out of it. In response to the growing threat from Nazi Germany, Congress passed a series of neutrality acts from 1935–1937 that sought to keep the United States out of a European conflict. It was only after the outbreak of World War II in 1939 that President Franklin Roosevelt was able to shift American foreign policy to aid the Allies.

On June 10, 1940, President Roosevelt spoke at the University of Virginia in Charlottesville and outlined a shift in U.S. foreign policy from that of neutrality to **non-belligerency**. He stated that the United States would pursue "two obvious and simultaneous courses: we will extend to the opponents of force the material resources of this nation; and at the same time, we will harness and speed up the use of those resources in order that we ourselves in the Americas may have the equipment and training equal to the task of any emergency and every defense." He made it clear that the United States would gear up to be ready for war, should the need arise. In his State of the Union address in January 1941, Roosevelt spoke of the **Four Freedoms** that should be enjoyed by people everywhere in the world: the freedoms of speech and religion, and freedoms from want and fear. The passage of the **Lend-Lease Act** allowed the United States to assist countries whose defense was seen as vital to the United States by lending or leasing them war supplies, materials, or equipment.

World War II and the End of Isolationism, Unilateralism, and Strict Neutrality

With the Japanese attack on Pearl Harbor on December 7, 1941, the United States formally joined the war. The United States learned just how untenable the policy of isolationism was in modern world politics. The war created interesting alliances when the United States, Britain, and France joined with the Soviet Union—an alliance that lasted throughout the war but broke apart after Germany was defeated. The use of the atomic bomb to end the war changed the way that war was fought and set the stage for the Cold War that would follow.

Roosevelt was determined, even before war began, to help craft a peace that would best benefit the United States as a world power. FDR and the allies created the United Nations (UN) to guarantee the security of member nations and promote economic prosperity around the globe. The idea was to have an organization that would promote peace through understanding among nations. The agreement was that the five great powers—the United States, Great Britain, China, France, and the Soviet Union—would have permanent seats on the Security Council and could veto any action by the UN. They also created new economic organizations that would promote trade and economic growth, and would avert a repeat of the disastrous economic policies after World War I that led to yet another world war. Some of the institutions they created were the International Monetary Fund, the World Bank, and the General Agreement on Tariffs and Trade in an effort to regulate exchange rates, rebuild war torn economies, and lower trade barriers. These new institutions represented a shift in American strategy from isolation and unilateral action to engagement and multilateral action.

By the end of the war, the international order had changed and the United States rose to become the dominant economic power because it was unencumbered by the rebuilding efforts in Europe. The U.S. had an intact industrial base, a thriving economy, and a military power made stronger by its relationship with business in what Eisenhower would refer to as the "military-industrial complex."

Cold War (1945-1991)

U.S. foreign policy during this period can be divided into three parts: containment, détente, and unrestricted competition. Fissures in ideological stances among the allies increased steadily as the leader of the Soviet Union, Joseph Stalin, encouraged the spread of communism through eastern and central Europe. As this influence spread through eastern and central Europe after the Red Army liberated Eastern Europe, the British became a little concerned but could do nothing. When Stalin sought to gain influence in Greece and Turkey, the United States responded with its idea of a **containment policy**, a term coined by State Department staffer George Kennan. It was based on the premise that the United States must apply counterforce to any aggressive moves by the Soviet Union, and it was implemented in the **Truman Doctrine**. This began an attempt by the United States to craft its foreign affairs around the idea to resist communism and oppose the Soviet Union. The world became divided into two camps, one side led by the United States and the other by the Soviet Union. The Soviet Union created a political, military, and ideological barrier known as the Iron Curtain that separated it and its dependent eastern and central European allies from contact with the West and noncommunist areas. Eventually, a third group also emerged, led by the efforts of the Indian Prime Minister Jawaharlal Nehru and the **Non-Aligned Movement**. One of Truman's main initiatives was to get Congress to pass the **Marshall Plan**, a plan to pump billions of dollars into Western Europe to help rebuild it and its economies to make it strong enough to prevent communism. The Marshall Plan set up a new guiding principle for U.S. foreign aid to be used as a key element of American diplomacy. For the first time, the United States joined a military and political alliance in peacetime: the **North Atlantic Treaty Organization (NATO)**.

Another guiding principle that emerged during the Cold War was the **domino theory,** in which it was believed that if one region came under communist influence, then other nations in the area would follow. In an effort to prevent this, the United States limited trade and technology transfer and surrounded the Soviet Union and its allies with military forces and American allies.

Nuclear and military tensions continued to escalate with the Cuban Missile Crisis in 1962 when the USSR tried to put nuclear missiles in Cuba, merely ninety miles from U.S. soil. The confrontation between the two superpowers brought the world to the brink of nuclear war. Shortly after, both the USSR and the United States sought to find ways to limit the nuclear and military tensions between the two countries. The United States began to seek ways to limit the growth of nuclear weapons through test bans and nonproliferation treaties. Both sides also began to limit their own arsenals, and eventually arms control became arms reduction in the 1980s.

Competency 3: Political Science

One of the most striking applications of the domino theory was the U.S. intervention in Vietnam, where nationalist forces from the north, led by Ho Chi Minh, defeated French colonial forces at Dien Bien Phu in 1954. Vietnam was divided into a communist north and a capitalist south, with the promise of elections in two years that could unify the country. The elections never materialized, as the struggle between the two Vietnams intensified. Determined to halt the spread of communism, the United States supported the corrupt capitalist regime in the south. Beginning early in the Kennedy administration, first hundreds and then thousands of U.S. military "advisors" were sent to South Vietnam.

Both South Vietnamese Prime Minister Ngo Dinh Diem and President Kennedy were assassinated in November 1963 within a few weeks of each other. Lyndon Johnson assumed the U.S. presidency with public declarations of no desire to "widen" the war in Vietnam. Yet he convinced Congress to support a massive military buildup in Southeast Asia. The **Gulf of Tonkin Resolution,** passed by Congress in August 1964, provided President Johnson with broad legal authority to combat North Vietnamese aggression. In July 1965, Lyndon Johnson chose to Americanize the war by increasing U.S. combat strength in Vietnam from 75,000 to 125,000, with additional U.S. forces to be sent when requested by field commander General William Westmoreland. As Johnson wrote in his memoirs, "Now we are committed to major combat in Vietnam. We had determined not to let that country fall under Communist rule as long as we could prevent it."

By the early 1970s, the American military was mired in the Asian jungles, at a cost of billions of dollars and tens of thousands of lives. The U.S. national interest in the region was no longer clear, and the antiwar movement grew until the United States was completely split on the issue. Finally, a treaty with the North Vietnamese government allowed the United States to withdraw in 1973. The United States got involved in Vietnam for several reasons: to bail out the French colonial power, to promote "democracy," and, most of all, to contain communism. However, the U.S. understanding of the conflict was highly flawed. The South Vietnamese were not "democrats," the North Vietnamese were not controlled from Moscow and Beijing, and the war was mostly about nationalism and independence. By the time the United States extracted itself from Vietnam in 1973, there were more than 58,000 American dead and 300,000 wounded. The lying and deceit of the military and the Johnson administration had eroded trust in government. The war, and wars in general, became hugely unpopular, and many began to see the limits to the United States projecting its power over the rest of the world. The experience had a huge impact and continues to have an impact today. The credibility of much of the United States' foreign policy apparatus was undercut. The fiasco also led many citizens and leaders to question the role and effectiveness of U.S. foreign intervention. This debate continues today.

Détente and the End of the Cold War

In 1969, when President Nixon announced that the time for confrontation was over and a new era of negotiation was in order, American foreign policy began to take a new direction. The United States realized that it needed a new direction as the toll of continued competition with the Soviet Union and an escalating nuclear arms race was not in the best interests of the United States.

This competition had intensified since 1949, when the Soviet Union exploded their bomb. Under President Richard Nixon, **détente**, an easing of tensions between the United States and the Soviet Union, led to increased trade and cultural exchanges and, most importantly, to an agreement to limit nuclear weapons—the 1972 **Strategic Arms Limitation Treaty** (SALT I). In the same year, Nixon also began the process of normalizing relations with the People's Republic of China.

The culmination of détente was the achievement of the **Helsinki Accords** in 1975. The heads of government of virtually every European state, as well as Canada and the United States met in Finland. The Soviets hoped that the group in Helsinki would recognize their control of Eastern Europe and other conquered territories, and the Western powers wanted the USSR to agree to human rights and other protections for all citizens. Both got what they wanted. The inviolability of borders was made an important point in international law and human rights. Until the fall of the Berlin Wall and the reunification agreement in Germany, the Helsinki Accords were as close as we came to a European peace since the end of World War II.

In 1977, President Jimmy Carter expressed his desire to make human rights the cornerstone of his foreign policy. In 1979, the Iranian hostage crisis erupted and undermined Carter's domestic support. The Republicans charged that Carter and the Democrats had made America weak. Détente finally died when the Soviets invaded Afghanistan in 1979. Carter also promulgated the **Carter Doctrine**—that the Persian Gulf was an area of vital U.S. interest and the United States would fight to maintain its interests there.

The Soviet Union's invasion of Afghanistan resulted in an American-led boycott of the 1980 Summer Olympics in Moscow. Superpower rivalry continued for a time and particularly escalated with the election of Ronald Reagan to the presidency. When Ronald Reagan was elected, U.S.-Soviet relations deteriorated rapidly. He called the USSR an evil empire, stepped up defense spending, announced an activist foreign policy to be designed, once again, to contain Soviet expansion, and began funding the Afghan opposition. President Reagan actively supported anti-communist, anti-left-wing forces in both Nicaragua and El Salvador, which he considered client states of the "evil" Soviet Union. He increased American defense spending significantly during his first term. The Soviet Union simply could not match these expenditures. Faced with a serious economic crisis, in 1985, Soviet leader Mikhail Gorbachev instituted new policies called **glasnost** (openness) and **perestroika** (economic restructuring) that eased tensions with the United States. He announced a new way of thinking in foreign policy that renounced class struggle and the idea of confrontation as the sole way of dealing with other countries. Gorbachev and Reagan met at several summits. Gorbachev, in desperate need to reallocate his country's resources from military to domestic uses, kept up his spate of reforms and attempts at reducing tension. By the third summit meeting, the leaders seemed to have found a recipe for dealing with each other, and they signed an agreement to eliminate all intermediate-range nuclear forces in Europe. By the early 1990s, the Cold War had effectively come to an end. The Soviet Union ceased to exist with the independence of the Baltic States (Estonia, Latvia, and Lithuania), Ukraine, Belarus, Armenia, Georgia, and the Central Asian republics.

Competency 3: Political Science

Searching for a New World Order

The collapse of the Soviet Union did not mean an end to conflict around the world. The **Iron Curtain** fell when Eastern Europe rebelled in 1989, and the USSR acknowledged the independence of countries formerly in its Eastern European bloc. Communism was also rapidly collapsing in the Soviet Union itself. The Iraqi invasion of Kuwait in 1990 prompted the United States to put together an international coalition under the auspices of the UN that culminated in the brief Persian Gulf War in 1991. Both the UN and NATO were involved in seeking a resolution to the ethnic conflict in the former Yugoslavia. While the United States arranged a settlement in the region known as the **Dayton Accords** (1995), it did not prevent a new outbreak of fighting between Serbs and ethnic Albanians in the province of Kosovo. NATO aircraft bombed targets in Serbia, including the capital Belgrade, in response. This was the first time that NATO forces conducted combat operations in Europe.

Efforts of the United States to be the "world's policeman" led to the U.S. invasion of Kuwait and its war with Iraq under President George H. W. Bush. In 1990, when Iraq invaded Kuwait, the United States led a UN-approved operation to expel Iraqi troops from Kuwait. The operation was lauded as a great success, and President Bush's approval ratings skyrocketed. Shortly thereafter, the Soviet Union was wracked by a coup in August 1991, and then, the collapse of the USSR. The Cold War and Communism were gone.

War on Terrorism, 2001 to Present

After September 11, 2001, when more than 3,000 people were killed in terrorist attacks on New York City's World Trade Center, the Pentagon, and the related crash of a plane in Pennsylvania that did not reach its intended target, the United States responded by declaring a **"war on terrorism."** Part of President George W. Bush's approach was to create a new **Office of Homeland Security** that had Cabinet status. He declared war against the Taliban regime in Afghanistan, not because they had anything to do with the war but because they had harbored al-Qaeda, a terrorist organization claiming responsibility for the attacks. By the end of 2001, the Taliban regime had been overthrown and more than 17 countries had troops in Afghanistan.

The policies of the United States began to change from reactive strategies of containment and deterrence to a more proactive policy of preemptive military action under the **Bush Doctrine**. The United States found itself having to deal with new threats to U.S. security: terrorism, anti-Americanism, and the clash of civilizations. In March 2003, Bush launched a war in Iraq, arguing that Iraq was developing weapons of mass destruction, contrary to evidence from weapons inspectors and scholars of the region. The administration argued that Iraq was a safe haven for terrorists and asserted that the Iraq regime was connected to al-Qaeda without any direct evidence from intelligence or scholarly sources. While the UN did not approve of the invasion, a comparatively small coalition of countries launched an invasion, and Saddam Hussein was quickly overthrown. Coalition forces found no evidence of weapons of mass destruction. The Bush administration changed its justification for the war to the goal of promoting democracy in the Middle East. After Bush declared his "mission accomplished" and challenged militants in Iraq with a taunt to "bring 'em on," violence escalated. By the end of June 2007, more than 3,585 American soldiers had died, and civil war broke out in Iraq.

The 2008 election of Barack Obama to the U.S. presidency signaled that the feeling in the country had turned from praising the goals of the Bush Doctrine to looking for a new way. President Obama's unofficially named **Obama Doctrine** emphasized negotiation and collaboration over confrontation and unilateralism. President Obama and Russian President Medvedev reached agreements on both military and economic issues. Force, however, was still an option. In 2011, Osama Bin Laden, the founder of al-Qaeda responsible for the September 11 terrorist attacks, was killed by U.S. special forces in Pakistan. While Obama's second term continued the fight against the Islamic State of Iraq and the Levant (ISIL), also called the Islamic State of Iraq and Syria (ISIS), terrorism and its effects continued to spread throughout the world. Vladimir Putin was elected President of Russia in 2012. Under his leadership, Russia took over the Crimean peninsula of the Ukraine, which created the highest level of tension between the East and the West since the Cold War.

Overview of International Relations

International relations is a discipline inextricably linked to the field of foreign policy. **Foreign policy** involves the objectives nations seek to gain with reference to other nations, and the procedures they employ in order to achieve their objectives. The principal foreign policy goals of sovereign states or other political entities may include some or all of the following: independence, national security, economic advancement, encouraging their political values beyond their own borders, gaining respect and prestige, and promoting stability and international peace.

The foreign policy process represents the stages a government goes through to formulate policy and arrive at decisions with respect to courses of action. A variety of models have been identified in the process of creating foreign policy. The primary players (nations, world organizations, multinational corporations, and non-state ethnic entities such as the Palestine Liberation Organization) are often referred to as **actors**.

The **unitary/rational actor model** assumes that all nations or primary players share similar goals and approach foreign policy issues in like fashion. The actions players take, according to this theory, are influenced by the actions of other players rather than by what may be taking place internally. The rational component in this model is based on the assumption that actors will respond on the world stage by making the best choice after measured consideration of possible alternatives.

Maximizing goals and achieving specific objectives motivate the rational actor's course of action. The **bureaucratic model** assumes that, due to the many large organizations involved in

Competency 3: Political Science

formulating foreign policy, particularly in powerful nation-states, final decisions are the result of struggle among the bureaucratic actors. In the United States, the bureaucratic actors include the Departments of State and Defense, as well as the National Security Council, the Central Intelligence Agency, the Environmental Protection Agency, the Department of Commerce, and/or any other agencies and departments whose agendas might be impacted by a foreign policy decision. While the bureaucratic model is beneficial in that it assumes the consideration of multiple points of view, the downside is that inter-agency competition and compromise often drive the final decision.

A third model assumes that foreign policy results from the intermingling of a variety of political factors, including national leaders, bureaucratic organizations, legislative bodies, political parties, interest groups, and public opinion. The implementation of foreign policy depends upon the tools that a nation or primary player has at its disposal. The major instruments of foreign policy include diplomacy, military strength/actions, and economic initiatives.

Diplomacy involves communicating with other primary players through official representatives. It might include participation in conferences and summit meetings, negotiation of treaties and settlements, and the exchange of official communications. Diplomacy is an indispensable tool in the successful conduct of an entity's foreign policy.

The extent to which a player may rely on the military tool depends upon its technological strength, its readiness, and the support of both its domestic population and the international community. President George H. W. Bush's decision to engage in a military conflict with Iraq's Saddam Hussein in 1991 after Iraq's invasion of Kuwait, largely rested on positive assessments of those factors. Sometimes, the buildup of military capabilities is in itself a powerful foreign policy tool and thus a deterrent to armed conflict, as was the case in the Cold War between the United States and the Soviet Union.

Economic development and the ability to employ economic initiatives to achieve foreign policy objectives are effective means by which a principal player can interact on the international scene. The Marshall Plan, through which the United States provided economic aid to a ravaged Europe after World War II, could be viewed as a tool to block Soviet expansion as well as a humanitarian gesture. It was a tool to resurrect the devastated economies of Europe, which had been major trading partners and purchasers of U.S. exports before the war. Membership in an economic community, such as Organization of Petroleum Exporting Countries (OPEC) or the European Community (EC), can drive the foreign policy of both member nations and those impacted by their decisions.

The Modern Global System

International systems today evidence many of the global forces and foreign policy mechanisms formulated in Western Europe in the eighteenth and nineteenth centuries. Largely due to the influence of Western imperialism and colonialism, the less developed countries of modern times have, to a great extent, embraced ideological and foreign policy values that originated in Europe during the formative centuries. Such concepts as political autonomy, nationalism, economic advancement through technology and industrialization, and gaining respect and prestige in the international community move the foreign policies of major powers and many less developed countries as well.

Historical Context of the Modern Global System

The modern global system or network of relationships among nations owes its origins to the emergence of the nation-state. It is generally recognized that the **Peace of Westphalia** (1648), which concluded the Thirty Years War in Europe and ended the authority of the Roman Catholic popes to exert their political dominance over secular leaders, gave birth to the concept of the modern nation-state. The old feudal order in Europe that allowed the Holy Roman Emperor to extend his influence over the territories governed by local princes was replaced by a new one in which distinct geographic and political entities interacted under a new set of principles. These allowed the nation-states to conduct business with each other, such as negotiating treaties and settling border disputes, without interference from a higher authority. Hence, the concept of sovereignty evolved.

The eighteenth century in Europe was notable for its relatively even distribution of power among the nation-states. With respect to military strength and international prestige, nations such as England, France, Austria, Prussia, and Russia were on the same scale. Some of the former major powers, such as Spain, the Netherlands, and Portugal, occupied a secondary status. Both the major and secondary players created alliances and competed with each other for control of territories beyond their borders. Alignments, based primarily on economic and colonial considerations, shifted without upsetting the global system. Royal families intermarried, and professional soldiers worked for the states that gave them the best benefits without great regard for political allegiances. The nation-state of the eighteenth century was a relatively new phenomenon.

Military conflicts in the eighteenth century tended to be conservative, with the concept of the **balance of power** at play. Mercenaries and professionals controlled the action, mindful of strategic maneuvers to bring about victory. Wiping out the enemy was not the principal goal. Major upheavals were avoided through the formation of alliances and a high regard for the authority of monarchs and the Catholic Church. The eighteenth century has been dubbed the **"golden age of diplomacy"** because it was an era of relative stability in which moderation and shared cultural values on the part of the decision-makers were the rule.

Statesmen of the era traded territory with little consideration of ethnic loyalties. This style of diplomacy was irrevocably altered by the French Revolution and the Napoleonic Wars that saw **nationality** emerge as a rallying point for conducting wars and for raising the citizen armies necessary to succeed in military conflicts.

The trend was exacerbated in the mid-nineteenth century by the European drive for unification of distinct ethnic groups and the creation of the Italian and German nation-states. Structural changes in the process and implementation of international relations occurred in the nineteenth and twentieth centuries due to major political, technological, and ideological developments.

The twentieth century has seen a particularly impassioned link between nationalism and war. The scientific and industrial revolutions of the eighteenth century gave rise to advancements in **military technology** that in the nineteenth and twentieth centuries dramatically altered the concept and the conduct of war. Replacing the eighteenth century conservative, play-by-the-rules approach, was a new, fiercely violent brand of warfare that increasingly involved civilian casualties and aimed at utter destruction of the enemy. The World Wars of the twentieth century called for mass mobilization of civilians as well as of the military, prompting leaders to stir up nationalistic sentiments. The development of nuclear weapons in the mid-twentieth century rendered total war largely unfeasible. Nuclear arms buildup, with the goal of **deterrent capabilities** (the means to retaliate so swiftly and effectively that an enemy will avoid conflict), was viewed by the superpowers as the only safety net.

Another factor molding the structural changes in international relations that surfaced in the nineteenth and twentieth centuries was the **ideological component**. The French Revolution, anchored in the ideology of "liberty, equality, and fraternity," is viewed as the harbinger of future trends. Those conservative forces valuing legitimacy and monarchy fought the forces of the Revolution and Napoleon to preserve tradition against the rising tide of republican nationalism. Ideological conflicts became more pronounced in the twentieth century, with its binding "isms"—Communism, democratic republicanism, liberalism, Nazism, socialism—competing for dominance.

The Contemporary Global System

The values of the contemporary system are rooted in the currents of eighteenth- and nineteenth-century Europe, transplanted to the rest of the world through colonialism and imperialism. The forces of nationalism, belief in technological progress, and ideological motivations, as well as the desire for international respect and prestige, are evident worldwide. Principal players in Africa, Asia, Latin America, and the Middle East often dominate the diplomatic arena. The contemporary scene in international relations is comprised of a number of entities beyond the **nation-state**. These include: **non-state actors** or **principal players**, **non-territorial transnational organizations**, and **non-territorial intergovernmental** or **multinational organizations**.

Contemporary **nation-states** are legal entities occupying well-defined geographic areas and organized under a common set of governmental institutions. They are recognized by other members of the international community as sovereign and independent states. **Non-state actors** or **principal players** are movements or parties that function as independent states. They lack sovereignty, but they may actually wield more power than some less developed nation-states. The **Palestine Liberation Organization (PLO)** is an example of a non-state actor that conducts its own foreign policy, purchases armaments, and has committed acts of terror with grave consequences for the contemporary international community. The **Irish Republican Army (IRA)** is an example of a non-state actor that employed systematic acts of terror to achieve political ends, as is ISIS/ISIL, which does so currently.

Non-territorial transnational organizations are institutions such as the Catholic Church that conduct activities throughout the world but whose aims are largely nonpolitical. A relatively new non-territorial transnational organization is the **multi-national corporation (MNC),** such as General Motors, Hitachi, or Royal Dutch Shell. These giant business entities have bases in a number of countries and exist primarily for economic profit. Despite their apparent nonpolitical agendas, multinational corporations can greatly impact foreign policy, as in the case of the United Fruit Company's suspect complicity in the overthrow of the government of Guatemala in the 1950s. Initially, the MNC was largely an American innovation, but in recent years, Asian players, particularly the Japanese, have proliferated, changing the makeup of the scene.

An **intergovernmental organization**, such as the United Nations, NATO, or the EC, is made up of nation-states and can wield significant power on the international scene. While NATO is primarily a military intergovernmental organization and the EC is mainly economic, the UN is really a multipurpose entity. While its primary mission is to promote world peace, the UN engages in a variety of social, cultural, economic, health, and humanitarian activities. In the case of the European Union, the influx of refugees from other countries has created divides. Surging immigration is part of what drove Great Britain's 2016 vote to leave the European Union.

The contemporary global system tends to classify nation-states based on power, wealth, and prestige in the international community. Such labels as **superpower**, **middle power**, **small power**, and the like tend to be confusing because they are not based on a single set of criteria or a shared set of standards. Some countries may be strong militarily, as was Iraq prior to the Persian Gulf War, yet lack the wealth and prestige in the international community to classify them as super or secondary powers. Others, such as Japan, may have little in the way of military capabilities but have wide influence due to economic preeminence.

The **structure** of the contemporary global system during the Cold War was distinctly **bipolar**, with the United States and the Soviet Union assuming diplomatic, ideological, and military leadership for the international community. With the breakup of the Soviet Union and the reorganization of the Eastern bloc countries has come the disintegration of the bipolar system. Since the 1970s, when tensions between the United States and the Soviet Union eased, a **multi-polar system**, in which new alignments are flexible and more easily drawn, has been emerging.

President George H. W. Bush spoke of the **New World Order** at the end of the Cold War. This concept involves alliances that transcend the old bipolar scheme with its emphasis on ideology and military superiority and calls for multinational cooperation as seen in the Persian Gulf War. It also assumes greater non-military, transnational cooperation in scientific research and humanitarian projects. The multi-polar system is less cohesive than the bipolar system of the recent past and the orders of the distant past, such as the **hierarchical system** (one unit dominates) of the Holy Roman Empire or the **diffuse system** (power and influence are distributed among a large number of units) of eighteenth century Europe. A set of fundamental rules has long governed international relations and, though often ignored, is still held as the standard today. These rules include **territorial integrity**, **sovereignty**, and the **legal equality of nation-states**. However, in an age of covert operations, mass media, multinational corporations, and shifting territorial boundaries, these traditional rules of international conduct are subject to both violation and revision.

Competency 3: Political Science

International Law

The present system of international law is rooted in the fundamental rules of global relations: territorial integrity, sovereignty, and legal equality of nation-states. It embodies a set of basic principles mandating what countries may or may not do and under what conditions the rules should be applied.

Historical Context

Despite evidence that the legal and ethical norms of modern international law may have guided interactions among political entities in non-Western pre-industrial systems, contemporary international law emanates from the Western legal traditions of Greece, Rome, and modern Europe. The development of the European nation-state gave rise to a system of legal rights and responsibilities in the international sphere that enlarged upon the religious-based code of the feudal era. In medieval Europe, the church's emphasis on hierarchical obligations, duty, and obedience to authority helped shape the notion of the "**just war.**" **Hugo Grotius** (1583–1645), Dutch scholar and statesman, codified the laws of war and peace and has been called the "**father of international law.**"

A new era was launched in 1648, with the **Peace of Westphalia**, that promulgated the idea of the treaty as the basis of international law. Multilateral treaties dominated the eighteenth century, while Britain, with its unparalleled sea power, established and enforced maritime law. By the nineteenth century, advances in military technology rendered the old standard of the "just war" obsolete. Deterrents, rather than legal and ethical principles, provided the means to a relatively stable world order. The concept of **neutrality** evolved during this period, defining the rights and responsibilities of both warring and neutral nations. These restraints helped prevent smaller conflicts from erupting into world wars.

Contemporary International Law

In the twentieth century, international law has retreated theoretically from the tradition of using force as a legitimate tool for settling international conflicts. The **Covenant of the League of Nations** (1920), the **Kellogg-Briand Pact** (1929), and the **United Nations Charter** (1945) all emphasize peaceful relations among nations, but the use of force continues to be employed to achieve political ends. The **International Court of Justice**, the judicial arm of the United Nations, and its predecessor, the **Permanent Court of International Justice,** represent concerted efforts to replace armed conflict with the rule of law. Unfortunately, the World Court has proven to be ineffective. Nation-states are reluctant to submit vital questions to the Court, and there is a lack of consensus as to the norms to be applied. Members of the United Nations are members of the Court, but they are not compelled to submit their international disputes for consideration.

The UN Charter seeks to humanize the international scene in its admonition that all member nations assist victims of aggression. This approach negates the old idea of neutrality. It further dismisses the tradition of war as a legitimate tool for resolution of disputes between nation-states of equal legal status. Aggressive conflicts can be categorized as crimes against humanity, and individuals may be held personally accountable for launching them.

The concept of international law has been criticized on several fronts. The rise of **multiculturalism**, with its emphasis on multiple perspectives, has called into question the relevance of applying Western legal traditions to the global community. International law has been seen as an instrument of the powerful nations in pursuit of their aims at the expense of weaker nations. Strong nation-states are in a position to both enforce international law and to violate it without fear of reprisal. These observations have led some to conclude that international law is primarily an instrument to maintain the **status quo**.

International law can be effective if parties involved see some **mutual self-advantage** in compliance. **Fear of reprisal** is another factor influencing nations to observe the tenets of international law. **Diplomatic advantage** and **enhanced global prestige** may follow a nation's decisions to abide by international law. It can be argued that international law is valuable in that it seeks to impose **order** on a potentially chaotic system and sets expectations that, while not always met, are positive and affirming.

COMPETENCY 3.6

Compare various political systems in terms of elements, structures, and functions.

There are many forms of government and ways to categorize them. Political scientists tend to classify government based upon how power is distributed geographically, how and to what extent the legislative and executive branches of government interact with one another, and the size of the body that is governed.

One method of describing government is based on where supreme governmental authority lies: centralized, decentralized, or shared. Each way has its benefits and tradeoffs. In centralized systems, government can have more uniform policy, equity, and less conflict; however, decentralized systems are considered closer to the people, more responsive and flexible to meeting their citizens' needs, and open to innovation. There are three types of systems that fall under this category: unitary, con-federal, and federal systems of government. If all of the authority lies in a sole, central organization, it is called a **unitary** form of government. In unitary systems, because every citizen is entitled to the same rights and benefits, it is easier to maintain unity and to form a common national identity. These systems tend to run more smoothly because policy is easier to implement, and less effort is spent sorting out who should do what. They also have economic benefits because regulations seem to be more consistent, one product can be sold across a whole nation, and efficiencies of scale can be more easily capitalized upon.

In the **confederation (con-federal)** form of government, most of the power is allocated to regional governments who can defy the national government to whom they allow only a limited amount of power. The regional states therefore retain a significant amount of sovereignty and can

Competency 3: Political Science

veto any national-level policy. Before the Constitution, the United States had a con-federal system of government in which the states had significant powers. During the Civil War, the South also was a confederacy.

A **federal** government is the opposite of a confederation, as member states give up most of their power to a central government but retain some power as well. Power in this structure is viewed as being shared. Federal systems of government tend to work well in countries where variations in local conditions, economies, or cultures make it difficult to try to impose a single system. These systems also work with countries that have geographically diverse populations that make it difficult to impose rule from a single location as well as in capitalist countries where both people and businesses have the capacity to move if conditions do not favor them. Local governments must compete to keep people and jobs within their borders. The United States has a federal form of government where sovereignty is shared by the national government and the state governments.

Another way to define government is how the executive (law-enforcing) and legislative (law-making) branches interact. A **parliamentary** system of government is a fusion of the executive and legislative branches. In this system, the executive leader is referred to as the **prime minister** or **premier**. The executive in this form of government is not separated from the legislative branch but rather is a member of it who is elected by other members of the legislative branch to preside over it. Since the executive, or prime minister, is selected by Parliament, he or she is accountable to it. In these systems, if prime ministers lose a vote of confidence, they must resign and forfeit their positions so a new government can be formed. A strength of these systems is the idea that they deliver effective but responsible government. Because the prime minister has the confidence of the parliament, his or her legislative agenda can be more easily implemented. One problem with a parliamentary system is that it must rely upon catering to minority parties in order to gain power, and so many coalitions break down when only a handful of members disagree with an agenda.

Presidential systems of government are based on the strict application of the idea of **separation of powers**. In these systems, the executive, legislative, and judicial functions are divided into separate branches that retain equal amounts of power, and have a set of checks and balances that give each branch their own jurisdiction of power and limit the power of each. The United States has a presidential system, as the Founders were quite determined to avoid having a government that would give too much power to an executive branch. The executive branch in this form of government is, as the name suggests, a president. A weakness of the system is that because power is shared, if the parties in power in the executive and legislative branches are different, legislative agendas may be stymied by one party refusing to negotiate with the other.

Another way to define government is based on the number of decision makers who participate in government operations. If no one is making the decisions in government (everyone is free to do as he or she pleases), it is called **anarchy**. This political movement, often symbolized by a big black flag, believes in the elimination of the state, and instead advocates self-rule by free individuals in autonomous communities or **stateless societies**. While such societies may have been common among small prehistoric groups, the complexity of today's societies usually requires some sort of leadership. The more people within a society, the more individual differences and preferences create disputes and struggles for power, prestige, territory, physical goods, or other items. The term *stateless society* has another meaning. Some peoples of the world (e.g., Kurds, Palestinians) are a defined group without a physical area and leader to call their own. Such people become refugees and seek asylum and help from other countries either as groups or individuals. Depending on the number in the group, they may be viewed as an expense and a problem for the host nation.

If only one person has dominant power and makes all the decisions in government, it is called an **autocracy**. Usually autocracy refers to a government where power is controlled by a monarch, a political dictator, or a religious leader. For example, Adolf Hitler, the Führer (leader) of Nazi Germany, was a political dictator. The organization ISIS is led by a key religious terrorist leader who seeks to create an Islamic state.

In an **oligarchy**, political power rests with a small, elite group that makes all of the decisions in government. These systems tend to be exclusionary and do not allow new groups into it. An oligarchy may be a **competitive oligarchy,** and some have accused the United States of promoting an oligarchy. While oligarchies do share power, unlike a dictatorship, they actually have tended to arise almost as transitional governments that have come out of a dictatorship. A **plutocracy** is a type of oligarchy that has rule by only a few, super-wealthy individuals. A practical application of an autocracy and oligarchy occurs when autocrats need to surround themselves with loyal followers who will do their bidding, and so they must turn to an elite group of individuals to carry out their agenda. Autocrats have to be careful that their enforcers do not decide that they want more power and depose (i.e., murder) the autocrat.

A **polyarchy** is rule by many. Both oligarchies and polyarchies hold elections, contrary to autocracies, which do not. However, polyarchies tend to have more fair elections, but oligarchies tend to engage in a number of practices to limit their political opponents. Polyarchies have problems because they consist of a rule by a group with mass participation that must rely, however, on a leadership that is managed by competing elites. This means that, on the one hand, it is democratic, in that there is some choice and competition for power, but undemocratic in that mass participation is limited to only what the wealthy elites permit.

When everyone is given the opportunity to participate in government and power is distributed evenly and more widely diffused, it is called a **democracy**. In a **representative democracy**, people choose individuals to run the government and to make decisions for them. Voters indicate their approval or disapproval of their representatives through elections that are held for a set number of years, depending on the position. The United States is a representative democracy.

In a **communist** form of government, all goods and production are owned equally, and commonly under this form of government; there is no individual ownership.

A **socialist** form of government operates under the belief that the inequalities that exist in society are unjust and the government provides extensive social services to its citizens.

Competency 3: Political Science

A fourth way to define government is how the leaders get their positions. If the leader obtains his or her position by hereditary means, it is called a **monarchy**. A **constitutional monarchy,** such as exists in Great Britain today, has a monarch but also a government that is elected and a constitution that sets out how the government should function. If the leaders are elected as they are in the United States, it is called a **republic**.

A final method of defining government is based on whether there are effective constraints on the government. If there are effective constraints on the government, it is called a **constitutional** form of government. If there are no effective constraints on government, it is called a **dictatorship**. A dictatorship type of government actually is the oldest form of government as it does not require the permission of the people for an individual to take hold of the government. A dictator has absolute control over a government and is authoritarian in nature. Dictators often have complete control over their citizens' lives and can wield their power completely in order to exert their will. While dictatorships often have a military and bureaucracy, and sometimes a legislature, a dictator usually has complete discretion to direct and overrule their efforts. In dictator systems that are based on military power, the term **military dictatorship** is used.

An **authoritarian** government is one in which rulers can make decisions without consent of those they are governing. Many systems of government have provisions that allow, in times of national emergencies, for an executive to make decisions without consulting others. Sometimes martial law can be declared, national security decisions can be made, and emergency powers may be used. A **totalitarian** government is an extreme form of authoritarian government in which it endeavors to achieve complete conformity by all to the ideals of the state with no dissension tolerated.

Another way of looking at government is to examine the rights of its citizens. Historically, in **monarchies**, a majority of citizens did not have a voice in public life. Because citizens are not agents in public life, their main contribution is as a subject, not a citizen. Historically, political power was reserved to be the domain of a few aristocrats who controlled most of the land and the wealth. The hierarchical structure of the society mandated a system of authority and obedience to those in highest authority. Over time, nobles began to demand a greater role in society and eventually, in many monarchies, the king's power became restricted and political rights were extended to a greater number of people in a society. In a **Marxist** state, the citizen sacrifices the expense of the individual and his or her family for the greater good of the state. In a **democracy**, because everyone is involved in the political process, a citizen has the responsibility to pay attention to public issues, become involved in public life, vote, support public institutions that serve the common good, and obey the laws of the land.

FTCE Social Science 6–12

COMPETENCY 3.7

Analyze the key elements of U.S. citizenship, including rights, privileges, and responsibilities.

Civil Rights and Individual Liberties

Civil rights are those legal claims that individuals have to protect themselves from discrimination at the hands of both the government and other citizens. They include the right to vote, equality before the law, and access to public facilities. **Individual** or **civil liberties** protect the sanctity of the person from arbitrary governmental interference. In this category belong the fundamental freedoms of speech, religion, press, and rights such as **due process** (government must act fairly and follow established procedures, as in legal proceedings). The origin of the concept of fundamental rights and freedoms can be traced to the British constitutional heritage and to the theorists of the Enlightenment. Jefferson's **Declaration of Independence** contains several references to the crown's failure to uphold the civil rights that British subjects had come to value and expect.

When fashioning the Constitution, the Founders included passages regarding the protection of civil liberties, such as the provision in Article I for maintaining the right of **habeas corpus**. One of the criticisms of the Constitution lodged by its opponents was that it did not go far enough in safeguarding individual rights. During the first session of Congress in 1789, the first ten amendments (the **Bill of Rights**) were adopted and sent to the states for ratification. These amendments contain many of the protections that define the ideals of American life. The Bill of Rights was meant to limit the power of the federal government to restrict the freedom of individual citizens.

The **Fourteenth Amendment** of 1868 prohibits **states** from denying civil rights and individual liberties to their residents. The Supreme Court is charged with interpreting the law, particularly as it applies to civil rights. Not until the **Gitlow Case** in 1925 did the Supreme Court begin to exercise this function with respect to state enforcement of the Bill of Rights. States are now expected to conform to the federal standard of civil rights. The amendment that is most closely identified with individual liberty in the United States is the **First Amendment**, which protects freedom of religion, speech, press, assembly, and petition. The First Amendment sets forth the principle of **separation of Church and State** with its "free exercise" and "establishment" clauses. These have led the Supreme Court to rule against such practices as school prayer (*Engel v. Vitale*, **1962**) and Bible reading in public schools (*School District of Abington Township v. Schempp*, **1963**).

The **Fourth Amendment**, which outlawed unreasonable searches and seizures, mandates that warrants be granted only upon probable cause, and affirms the right of the people to be secure in their persons, is fundamental to the Court's interpretation of due process and the rights of the accused.

The **Fifth Amendment**, which calls for a grand jury, outlawed **double jeopardy** (trying a person who has been acquitted of a charge for a second time) and states that a person may not be

Competency 3: Political Science

compelled to be a witness against himself, is also the basis for Supreme Court rulings that protect the accused. Cruel and unusual punishments are banned by the **Eighth Amendment**. This clause has been invoked by opponents of capital punishment to justify their position, but the Supreme Court has ruled that the death penalty can be applied if states are judicious and use equal standards in sentencing to death those convicted of capital crimes. In the twentieth century, a major concern for litigation and review by the Supreme Court has been in the area of civil rights for minorities, particularly African-Americans.

When civil rights organizations such as the NAACP brought a series of cases before the courts under the equal protection clause of the **Fourteenth Amendment**, they began to enjoy some victories. Earlier, when the Supreme Court enforced its separate but equal doctrine in the 1896 case **Plessy v. Ferguson**, it did not apply the equal protection standard and allowed segregation to be maintained.

The Court reversed itself in 1954 in the landmark case **Brown v. Board of Education**, which ruled that separate but equal was unconstitutional. This ruling led to an end to most *de jure* (legally enforced) segregation, but *de facto* (exists in fact) segregation persisted, largely due to housing patterns and racial and ethnic enclaves in urban neighborhoods.

Landmark Supreme Court Cases

In addition to the previously cited Supreme Court rulings in civil rights and individual liberties cases, the following landmark decisions are notable for their relevance to the concepts of civil rights and individual freedoms:

- ***Dred Scott v. Sandford*** (1857)—ruled that as a slave, Scott had no right to sue for his freedom and further that Congressional prohibitions against slavery in U.S. territories were unlawful.

- ***Near v. Minnesota*** (1931)—barred states from using the concept of prior restraint (outlawing something before it has taken place) to discourage the publication of objectionable material, except during wartime or in the cases of obscenity or incitement to violence.

- ***West Virginia Board of Education v. Barnette*** (1943)—overturned an earlier decision and ruled that compulsory saluting of the flag was unconstitutional.

- ***Korematsu v. United States*** (1944)—upheld the legality of the forced internment of persons of Japanese ancestry during World War II as a wartime necessity.

- ***Mapp v. Ohio*** (1961)—extended the Supreme Court's exclusionary rule, which bars, at trial, the introduction of evidence that has not been legally obtained to state courts as well as federal courts. The Court has modified this ruling, particularly with reference to drug cases, so that evidence that might not initially have been obtained legally, but which would eventually have turned up in lawful procedures, can be introduced.

- *Gideon v. Wainwright* (1963)—ruled that courts must provide legal counsel to poor defendants in all felony cases. A later ruling extended this right to all defendants facing possible prison sentences.

- *Escobedo v. Illinois* (1964)—extended the right to counsel to include consultation prior to interrogation by authorities.

- *Miranda v. Arizona* (1966)—mandated that all suspects be informed of their due process rights before questioning by police.

- *Tinker v. Des Moines School District* (1969)—defined the wearing of black armbands in school in protest against the Vietnam War as "symbolic speech" protected by the First Amendment.

- *New York Times v. United States* (1971)—allowed, under the First Amendment's freedom of the press protection, the publication of the controversial Pentagon Papers during the Vietnam War.

- *Roe v. Wade* (1973)—legalized abortion so long as a fetus is not viable (able to survive outside the womb).

- *Bakke v. Regents of the University of California* (1978)—declared the university's quota system to be unconstitutional while upholding the legitimacy of affirmative action policies in which institutions consider race and gender as factors when determining admissions.

- *Hazelwood School District v. Kuhlmeier* (1988)—ruled that freedom of the press does not extend to student publications that might be construed as sponsored by the school.

- *Obergefell v. Hodges* (2015)—recognized the legality of same-sex marriages.

U.S. Citizenship Rights

Citizens of the United States enjoy all of the freedoms, protections, and legal rights that the Constitution promises. Some of the freedoms and rights protected in the Bill of Rights include:

- Freedom of Religion
- Freedom of Assembly
- Right to Keep and Bear Arms
- Freedom of Speech
- Freedom of the Press
- Protection for Those Accused of Crimes

Competency 3: Political Science

U.S. Citizenship Privileges

- Citizenship allows people to vote and participate in the representative democracy by voting for people who reflect their positions or views on public policy matters.

- Citizens are entitled to an American passport, and they enjoy the protection of the American government if they are persecuted by a foreign government.

- Citizens cannot be deported to another country.

- Citizens may sponsor friends or family who wish to apply for citizenship.

- Citizens are eligible for many welfare benefits, like food stamps or medical aid.

- Citizens can hold certain jobs that require candidates to be at least naturalized U.S. citizens. Only citizens may run as candidates in local, state, and federal elections and hold positions in government.

- Citizens have the right to leave the United States, and even live outside of it, without abandoning their citizenship.

Key Responsibilities of a U.S. Citizen

One of the key roles of citizens in the United States is to participate in civic life. The Constitution, while it does not explicitly list responsibilities, does assume some civil duties that are inherent in the Constitution.

- Citizens are presumed to obey the laws of the land in letter and spirit.

- Citizens must remain loyal to the United States.

- Citizens have a responsibility to serve as impartial jurors when called.

- Citizens have a responsibility to serve in the armed forces when called upon to do so.

- Citizens should participate in public life and must vote responsibly. Through voting, people have a voice in the government. This civic duty requires that citizens be informed about public issues, be aware of how their political leaders and representatives fulfill their responsibilities, understand the different views of the parties and candidates, and cast votes in elections.

- Citizens should engage in civic activity and participate in civil institutions, organizations, or charities.

- Citizens must pay taxes.

CHAPTER 4

World History

What is **history**? Is it really just an old recitation of facts and stories of the past? Today's historians consider history to be much more complex—both factual and interpretive, with more focus of differing perspectives and different "truths." In the past, history was taught as a series of dates, events, and activities of extraordinary individuals (in most cases, men). Teaching history this way did little to uncover the many facets of history and failed to develop students' understanding or use of the concepts that are fundamental toward understanding and analyzing historical events and phenomena. History teachers today approach the past with a more open eye, realizing that the experiences of class, gender, race, ethnicity, and age affect not only our understanding of what happened in the past, but also what the past was.

History is the study of the past through the use of material from both oral and written sources. It encompasses political, economic, social, and cultural aspects of the past. The term "history" is derived from the Greek word *historia*, which means "information" or "an enquiry designed to elicit truth."

While history often seems like a simple chronology of events, it is really a story of causes and effects. Thus, a primary focus in the study of history lies in trying to answer *why* something occurred. What were the reasons that an event happened? In the study of history, **causality** is the reason why something either changed or remained the same. Historians seek to define why and how a certain event happened: were the reasons evident or hidden? Theories of historical causation have dominated historical discourse since the time of Plato. **Conflict**, or the opposition of ideas, principles, values, or territorial claims occurs when ideas or people oppose one another and this can be the cause or effect of a historical event. Conflict may occur both within and between societies.

Historians use two types of sources: **primary sources** and **secondary sources**. The distinction between these is the author's proximity to an event. Primary sources consist of documents, oral histories, or physical objects that were created during the period being studied or immediately after it.

The idea is that the primary sources reflect an "insider's" understanding of an event, or "firsthand knowledge" of an event. Examples of primary sources are: original documents, diaries, personal narratives, speeches, government records, letters, interviews, autobiographies, pottery, buildings, clothing, novels, newspaper articles (written soon after an event), photographs, manuscripts, original theatrical or literary works, coins, stamps, and even tombstones. **Secondary sources** are one step removed from an event, and contain someone's impressions, judgments, and interpretations of primary material or an event. Secondary sources include history textbooks, journal articles, documentaries, books written about a period of time, encyclopedias, histories, and biographies. Whether approaching either a primary or secondary source, historians must learn how to properly analyze a document. Historians should consider how, when, and where a document was created, as it might have an effect on what was actually recorded. As all sources have bias, historians need to try to uncover how bias has affected the source. They should consider how close in time and location a source was created to a certain event. What was the intention of a document? Was it meant for private or public consumption?

Bias (prejudice or presupposition toward or against a person or idea) also affects historical accounts. Not only does every writer have bias, but also every historian. When historians look at primary source material, they must decide how the author viewed his or her material or situation. When historians consider a source, they bring in their own biases or predispositions to value certain pieces of information over another. Because bias exists, whether or not historians acknowledge it, the focus of historians on certain events, peoples, or ideas taints their material. Indeed, the very authenticity of "fact" remains rather problematic. Because bias is present in all sources, some sources might be considered more reliable than others. In addition, of course, each historian might have a different opinion based on his or her own biases about what is "reliable" or not.

Historical context is the political, economic, social, and cultural setting for a particular idea or event. Historians must look at context in order to better understand something in history and to situate an event or situation in its wider meaning. By looking at its historical context, a historian can ascertain how unique or ordinary an event or situation was in comparison to others; historical context gives the historian clues to the meaning of an event or person. One tool that historians use when examining historical context is its **chronology**. Chronology is the timeline of events, and time forms a reference point; however, the concept of time is a socially constructed category that defines time according to a particular group's understanding of it. Societies have used a variety of methods to refer to time: reigns of rulers, planting seasons, generations, and cosmic cycles of stars, planets, and the moon. Time has also been measured as occurring in terms of a key event. For example, the birth of Jesus was one of those key events with years measured as BC (before Christ) or AD (Medieval Latin phrase *Anno Domini*, which translates to "in the year of the Lord"). The terms BCE (Before the Common Era) and CE (Common Era) replaced the BC and AD labels. Both sets of terms mean exactly the same thing. For example, 1492 AD is the same as 1492 CE.

Trying to make sense of the past as a whole can be quite difficult for historians unless they break it up into periods that seem to make more sense. But **periodizing** the past is a rather political event, in which historians use their own biases or understandings to group the past into what

Chapter 4

Competency 4: World History

makes sense to them. Historians today should be more sensitive to periodization and more careful about referring to an era with a term that only makes sense according to one geographical area. For instance, the Victorian Era makes sense when looking at the reign of Queen Victoria in England, whereas it would not be appropriate to label the same time period in China as "Victorian."

COMPETENCY 4.1

Identify characteristics of prehistoric cultures and early civilizations (e.g., Mesopotamian, Egyptian, Indus Valley, Chinese).

The definitions of "history" versus "prehistory" are subjective and differ from region to region. While historians traditionally have looked at written sources, and humans have been around before writing began, historians in the nineteenth century developed different terms to describe pre- and post-writing eras. They began to refer to the period of time before the acquisition of writing as "prehistory," and the period of time after society began to write as the "historic" phase. The difference between history and prehistory, then, rests with the presence or absence of writing. Because writing appears in different places at different times, some places might be in the prehistoric phase, while others are in the historic phase. Historians of prehistory have to rely on the work of archaeologists who find and examine non-written records, pottery shards, buildings, tools, weapons, bones, and so on. Based on these artifacts, prehistory is considered to be the **Stone Age**.

Scientists estimate that Earth is approximately 4.5 billion years old. There is debate as to when humans first appeared, as well as from whom and what humans descended. Current terminology favors the use of the word **australopithecines** (southern ape-like creatures) as early human ancestors. In 1974, archaeologists discovered the bones of an australopithecine in Ethiopia and called her "Lucy." Lucy died more than three million years ago. She stood about three feet tall, walked on two legs, and lived in a family group. Walking upright enabled Lucy and other australopithecines to travel distances more easily, to carry food and children, and to keep away from threatening animals. These australopithecines also had developed an opposable thumb, meaning that the tip of the thumb is able to cross the palm of the hand. The opposable thumb was crucial for tasks like picking up small objects and making tools. While Lucy was the first australopithecine discovered, recent digs have found evidence of creatures like Lucy as old as 6 million years.

There are many theories about the origin of humans and how they evolved and spread from one area to another. Most of the theories suggest that about 100,000 years ago, there were a variety of hominids all over the world. For instance, *Homo sapiens* are largely believed to have lived in Africa and Southwest Asia, while *homo erectus* lived in Africa, and *homo Neanderthalensis* lived in Europe. Something changed, and these diverse groups became one group of *homo sapien sapiens*.

Two of the big schools of thought suggest that either hominids developed similarly at the same time in different locations, or that there is a single origin for humans. One theory, the **Multiregional Continuity Model**, suggests that *homo sapiens* evolved from a group of *homo erectus* who left Africa and dispersed all over the world. Over time, the *homo erectus* changed in some ways, but retained common characteristics in other ways—creating the division of people into different races that we see today. Another theory, the current leading theory, the **Out of Africa Model**, holds that modern humans developed only recently. This theory holds that *homo erectus* left Africa and mingled with other populations, but it was in Africa that *homo sapiens* developed and eventually took over all of the other hominids without interbreeding with them.

Archaeological and Historical Periods Chart

	Period	Years

Stone Age	Before 10,000 BCE
	10,000–8000 BCE
	8000–5500 BCE
	5500–4000 BCE
	4000–3000 BCE
		Paleolithic (Old Stone Age)
		Mesolithic (Middle Stone Age)
		Neolithic (New Stone Age)
		    Prepottery
		    Pottery Chalcolithic
		    (Copper Age)

Bronze Age	3000–2800 BCE 2800–2500 BCE 2500–2200 BCE 2200–2000 BCE 2000–1800 BCE 1800–1500 BCE 1500–1400 BCE 1400–1200 BCE	**Early Bronze Age** (EB) EB I EB II EB III EB IV **Middle Bronze Age** (MB) MB I MB II **Late Bronze Age** (LB) LB I LB II
Iron Age	1200–1000 BCE 1000–600 BCE	Iron I Iron II
Babylonian and Persian Periods	586–332 BCE	
Hellenistic Period	332–37 BCE	
Roman Period	37 BCE–325 CE	

Stone Age

The Stone Age describes the period of time in which humans made and used tools from stone. Historians divide the Stone Age into three periods: Paleolithic, Mesolithic, and Neolithic.

The **Old Stone Age** or **Paleolithic** (Greek for "old stone") period occurred 2.5 million years ago in Europe, Asia, and Africa until 10,000 BCE. This period marks the period of the emergence of the first hominids *homo sapiens*. In the most advanced parts of the Middle East and Southeast Asia, it ended about 6000 BCE, but it lingered until 4000 BCE or later in Europe, the rest of Asia, and

Competency 4: World History

Africa. The Stone Age in the Americas began when humans first arrived in the New World, some 30,000 years ago, and ended in some areas about 2500 BCE, at the earliest.

These Paleolithic peoples are characterized by the following:

1. Hunter-Gatherer
2. Highly mobile, nomadic with a large territorial range
3. Crude tools
4. Work divided along gender lines
5. Art
6. Use of fire to provide warmth and light

Paleolithic peoples did not know how to grow crops or raise animals and relied on hunting and gathering to take care of themselves. They lived in small bands of around 20 and needed a large area to support their food needs. As a result, they were nomadic and they followed animal migrations and vegetation cycles. Paleolithic peoples knew how to make tools and weapons that could have made them effective hunters. Tools and weapons that they did use were ground stone tools like chipped pebbles, stone flakes, needles, and harpoons. Work was divided primarily along gender lines. Men focused on activities like hunting, in which upper body strength was important, and women focused on gathering, cooking, and childbearing. During this time, Paleolithic peoples sought refuge in caves and other natural formations, as evidenced by paintings of animals on the walls of caves during this period. Around 500,000 years ago, people began to use fire to provide light and warmth in shelters and caves. Over time, people used fire to improve techniques of making tools and weapons.

The **Mesolithic** ("Middle Stone Age") period occurred from 10,000 to 8000 BCE. This era is shorter than either the Paleolithic or Neolithic time periods. Although relatively few artifacts have been found, it appears that people in this time developed smaller, more refined tools and started to develop agricultural practices.

Recent evidence has suggested that the **Neolithic Revolution**, rather than occurring in the later **Neolithic** age (New Stone Age), actually began much earlier, during the Mesolithic period. This revolution, perhaps one of the most significant turning points in all of history, was the shift from food-gathering to food-producing, or farming. This shift laid the foundations for the rise of civilizations. With the development of farming, humans began to turn away from a nomadic lifestyle and settle down in one place. The cultivation of crops on a regular basis made possible the support of larger populations, at first small villages and eventually larger towns. At the same time, people began to domesticate animals such as horses, dogs, goats, and pigs. Settling down in one location had both advantages and disadvantages. Farming and settled life brought a change in the way people related to each other. It also made people more susceptible to diseases, both in nature and animal-borne. Food supplies became less reliable because people depended on a small range of farmed foods. Their diet narrowed to what they could produce, rather than the wider variety of what they could gather. More problems arose because as these food producers settled down, they had to protect their food sources and devote considerable time to clearing and cultivating their land. As food supplies stabilized, people stayed in one place, and they also began to create more stable housing. During this period, there were small, widely dispersed settlements, but no cities.

During the **Neolithic Period** (8000 BCE to 3000 BCE) humans further domesticated plants and animals as the end of the Neolithic Revolution occurred. The following developments characterize the Neolithic period:

- Farming and agriculture
- New technologies
- Agricultural villages, rather than the previous nomadic way of living
- Early cities and villages
- Institutions such as family, religion, and state governments
- Crafts, such as pottery, knitting, spinning, and weaving
- Bronze Age tools, at the end of the period

During the Neolithic period, cities and villages began to develop, and a division of labor began to occur. This led to the development of crafts, such as pottery, knitting, spinning, and weaving; and a rise in trade among groups. Institutions also began to develop, such as the family, religion, and state governments. Between 4000 and 3000 BCE, writing developed. With the existence of written records, the Neolithic period ended and societies emerged with characteristics that enabled them to be considered civilizations. The first civilizations emerged in Mesopotamia and Egypt.

Bronze Age and Iron Age

Because of the varied times that these ages developed in different areas of the world, historians today do not tend to use "Bronze Age" or "Iron Age" to delineate the periods of history. Rather, the ages tend to blur into each other, depending on location.

River Valley Civilizations

As people moved away from nomadic life toward more communal living in towns, they advanced their farming and herding techniques and did not have to spend as much time growing food. As a result, people then turned toward other types of production, such as pottery and textiles, and in turn, **civilization**, during which the institutions of law, government, economic growth, military, and religion emerged. More complex societies developed around river valleys—around 6000 BCE in the Fertile Crescent, 4800 BCE in the Nile Delta in China, and 2500 BCE in India. All of these early communities had certain things in common that qualifies them as "early civilizations."

Competency 4: World History

One of the main things that early communities had in common was that they developed along rivers. Why rivers? Rivers provide people with the water they need for survival. They are also a good source of food, such as fish, and they also attract animals to them, thus providing people with another means of bolstering their food supply. Also, the lands around rivers tend to be quite fertile and full of nutrients left over by floods, making these lands good for agriculture. Rivers also provide a convenient means of transportation.

Main Characteristics of River Valley Civilizations

1. **Cities or large dense settlements:** Early civilizations arose from cultures that had been able to transition from producing small amounts of food to becoming proficient enough in farming to be able to produce enough food surpluses to sustain large populations. As they were able to do so, urban centers began to develop.

2. **Separation of population into specialized occupational groups:** Because food was more readily available, people now were free to do things other than activities that revolved around finding enough food to survive. All of the early civilizations turned to specialization of labor due to the availability of surplus agricultural resources. People could now turn to crafts, metallurgy, forestry, and so on. They could be artisans, merchants, healers, priests or provide other services.

3. **Social hierarchy, including an elite populace exempt from subsistence labor:** Another byproduct of developing specialized occupational groups was social stratification in which an elite class of warriors, priests, nobles, and royalty developed whose domination of lower social classes elements freed them from having to engage in everyday subsistence labor. The elites justified their existence by providing services to the entire population in the form of military protection, religious direction, political representation, legal authority, and social order.

4. **Elite able to extract taxes and tribute from lower classes:** Ruling elites imposed various forms of tribute and taxes like poll taxes, property taxes, income taxes, export duties, and sales taxes on lower social classes in the interest of the state. These resources were used to benefit the common good, such as offerings to the gods or the construction of urban defenses.

5. **Monumental public buildings:** All civilizations used the advantage of their large populations to engage in the construction of monumental buildings for the state. These buildings ranged from defensive city walls in Babylon and China to beautiful temples and palaces. Monumental public buildings not only furnished security and improved the quality of life for its inhabitants, but the character of the achievement tended to reflect the aspirations of a civilization, not to mention its level of cultural development.

6. **Writing:** All great civilizations developed a system of writing and record keeping.

7. **Long distance trade:** Trade with other distant civilizations provided diversity of thinking and introduction of new goods and materials.

8. **Rule of law:** Set policies and procedures define norms for social behavior for the good of the group.

9. **Non-kin-based community:** Individuals broadened their concept of a community with a common sense of purpose.

Mesopotamia

By around 3000 BCE, the first urban-agricultural societies began to emerge in Mesopotamia, which literally means "the land between two rivers" (the fertile land between the Tigris and Euphrates rivers). A series of ancient civilizations sprang up along these rivers—the Sumerians, Akkadians, Babylonians, and Persians.

The history and culture of Mesopotamian civilization is dependent on the ebb and flow of the Tigris and Euphrates rivers. This made life unstable, as flash floods and torrential rains could change the course of these rivers and destroy crops, livestock, and village homes. While the rivers constantly threatened the welfare of the towns, they were also beneficial to them: they nourished the soil, enabling the people to produce a surplus of food. Mesopotamian villages and towns eventually evolved into independent and nearly self-sufficient city-states, with little interest in unification with the other Mesopotamian city-states.

Sumer

Two of the earliest groups in the Mesopotamia region, the **Sumerians** and **Akkadians**, utilized the advantages that the rivers gave them. They built tremendous irrigation projects in an effort to control the water around them. Large projects such as the building of canals, dikes, drainage ditches, and reservoirs not only helped people regulate water and control flooding; they also required organization: people to assign jobs, allocate resources, and do the building. As a result, leaders emerged, government formed, and a civilization developed.

The most important of these peoples, the Sumerians who lived in southern Mesopotamia, were the first group to develop a system of writing. What began as a pictographic form of writing soon turned into **cuneiform** (wedge-shaped) writing. Unlike pictograms, cuneiform could convey concepts and sounds. The resulting writing system became so complicated that a new class formed: professional scribes who could master it. Scribal schools began to flourish throughout Sumer and became centers of culture and learning. They also developed cylinder seals that people would use to "sign" documents or to show ownership.

With these developments in writing, Mesopotamians made great advancements in other methods of learning: mathematics, medicine, and religion. Their math system was based on the number 60, and it is because of their system that we still divide an hour into 60 minutes and a circle into 360

Competency 4: World History

degrees. They also learned how to use geometry and to apply their knowledge to the construction of buildings and irrigation systems. Mesopotamians also understood multiplication and division, and developed a calendar based upon lunar phases. They also made many scientific advances. They invented the wheel and plow and learned how to use bronze to produce stronger tools and weapons. In medicine, evil spirits were believed to cause sickness, and treatment was by magic, prescription, and even basic surgery.

The Sumerian religion was **polytheistic** with the creation of gods and goddesses who represented almost everything in the cosmos. Their gods took the form of man and used nature to punish society. Society itself sought to appease the gods through public, state-organized religion that focused on temples maintained by priests. These step-shaped large temples that contained, at the heart of them, a pyramid shaped structure called a **ziggurat**. They typically were built in the center of Sumerian cities and were focal points of Sumerian life and religion. The priests were powerful members of Sumerian society and controlled some of their early governments. Because the farmers had believed that their crops depended upon the gods being pleased with them, they sought the priests to act as intermediaries with the gods. The priests, from the ziggurat, managed the irrigation systems, demanded portions of each farmer's crops as a tax, and ran the ziggurat like a city hall. The priests began to lose power when the society needed a military to protect it against invaders. These military leaders, in time, became full-time rulers, passing on their power to their sons after them and creating a series of city-states under the rule of **dynasties**.

The Mesopotamians created myths to explain the origins of the universe and mankind. They produced the first epic poem, ***The Epic of Gilgamesh***. The epic, written around 2700 BCE, tells us about the organization of Sumerian society. The epic tells the tale of the ruler of Uruk, Gilgamesh, and his friend Enkidu and explains the creation of the universe. It also details how Uruk and Enkidu perform heroic acts but how Enkidu eventually offends the gods and dies. The tales explore morality, immortality, loyalty, and friendship.

Sumerian society was made up of nobles, free clients, commoners, and slaves. The king was supreme and kingship was hereditary. The nobility—the king, his family, the chief priests, and high palace officials—controlled most of the wealth in land and held most of the power. The commoners were free and had a political voice. The Sumerian slave population included foreigners, prisoners of war, criminals, and debtors. Sumerian women could pursue most of the occupations of city life and could even become priests.

The Sumerian civilization looked, on the surface, like it had a good set-up. The Sumerians organized a government of city-states and developed educational and religious systems, but it was fatally flawed in where it chose to locate itself. The river valley had neither geographic protection nor predictable river flooding and proved vulnerable to a series of invasions from the Babylonians, Hittites, and Assyrians. By 1700 BCE, the civilization had been overthrown, but its conquerors adapted many of their predecessors' traditions and technologies.

Other Mesopotamian Regimes

North of Sumeria, another group, the **Akkadians**, led by **King Sargon I** about 2331 BCE, created a permanent army, attacked Sumer and all of northern Mesopotamia, in turn forming the world's first empire that stretched from the Mediterranean Sea to present-day Iran in the east. Sargon's empire would last about 140 years, until the advent of another empire that would come from Babylon. A group of Amorites, led by **Hammurabi**, united all of Mesopotamia under the **Babylonian Empire** in 1792 BCE. Hammurabi's greatest legacy was the code of laws that he put together known as the **Code of Hammurabi**. **Hammurabi's Code** created one of the world's earliest comprehensive law codes that, for the first time, was written for all to see. It had two notable features: it instituted different laws and punishments for rich and poor and for men and women and was based on the idea that the punishment should fit the crime. The Code also set up an important idea in Mesopotamian society—that government had a responsibility for what occurred in society and, if all else failed, it ultimately had to answer to the victim of a crime.

In 1595 BCE, an Indo-European tribe that had settled in Asia Minor (now Turkey), the **Hittites** sacked Babylon. The Hittites introduced iron tools into agriculture and war. Their success largely came through because they learned how to use iron in their weapons while their enemies used weapons made out of bronze, a much weaker element. The Hittites also used the horse-drawn chariot to beat their enemies. The Hittites remained a strong force in western Asia until about 1200 BCE and were ultimately defeated by the Lydians.

After the Hittite Empire fell, other groups emerged in the region. One of these was the **Assyrians**, a powerful people who relied chiefly upon its military strength and established its capital at **Nineveh**. Its army contained war chariots, foot soldiers, and a cavalry. They were masters at siege warfare, and used terror to control their enemies. The Assyrian system of government allowed kings to rule through local leaders who collected taxes, enforced laws, and raised troops. They constructed a system of roads that linked distant parts of their empire together.

The **Chaldeans** took advantage of a crumbling Assyria and took the old city of Babylon as their new capital. Their most famous ruler was **Nebuchadnezzar II** who fought the Egyptians and Jews, captured the Jewish capital of Jerusalem, and rebuilt Babylon into a city of splendor that featured the **Hanging Gardens of Babylon**, one of the Seven Wonders of the Ancient World. The Chaldeans made great advances in astronomy and charted the position of the stars as it related to political and weather events.

The **Phoenicians** built a wealthy trading society at the western end of the Fertile Crescent along the Mediterranean Sea in what today is Lebanon. The Phoenicians were great sailors who founded colonies along their large trade routes. One such colony was Carthage, which was to figure prominently later on. Their biggest legacy was the **Phoenician alphabet**, a writing system set up to help with trade. It was more flexible and easier to use than pictographs or cuneiforms. The Phoenician alphabet consisted of 22 letters, all of which were consonants. The Greeks would later take this alphabet and add vowels to it, and later it was modified further by the Romans into our modern alphabet.

Competency 4: World History

The earliest Hebrews lived in the area between Mesopotamia and Egypt in the second millennium BCE. While the origin of the Jews is uncertain, they migrated from Egypt into the Sinai Peninsula and Palestine. They were originally a nomadic people, but as cities grew and prospered, some Hebrews migrated to these cities. In the power vacuum created by the fall of the Hittite and Egyptian states, a Hebrew state emerged. The Hebrews encountered the Philistines, another ancient people who settled in Canaan. The Philistines enjoyed a definite advantage over the Hebrews, as they knew how to forge iron into swords and shields and used them in their ships and chariots. Over time, the Hebrews learned the secrets of smelting iron and could fight the Philistines on more equal terms. The Hebrews instituted **monotheism**, the worship of one God, Yahweh. This put them squarely at odds with their neighbors who prayed to multiple gods. Under Saul and David, the 12 tribes of Israel became united under a monarchy. David led the Jews to defeat the Philistines and to capture Jerusalem. There, King Solomon built a large temple in Jerusalem where it became the home of the Ark of the Covenant, which was considered the promise between God and the Hebrew people and demonstrated their unity. King Solomon eliminated the tribal division of Israel and instead placed it under 12 territorial districts. Upon Solomon's death, the kingdom was divided in two as the northern kingdom (Israel) was destroyed by the Assyrians in the eighth century BCE. The southern half became the center of Judaism with the capital in Jerusalem until the Babylonians destroyed it in 587 BCE. It was during this "Babylonian Captivity" that the exiles redefined their beliefs into the law of Yahweh and became known as Jews. About 50 years after the fall of Judah, the Persian king Cyrus the Great conquered Babylon in 539 BCE and allowed 40,000 Jews to return to Jerusalem to rebuild Solomon's Temple, which had been destroyed by the Babylonians. The walls of Jerusalem were rebuilt in 445 BCE.

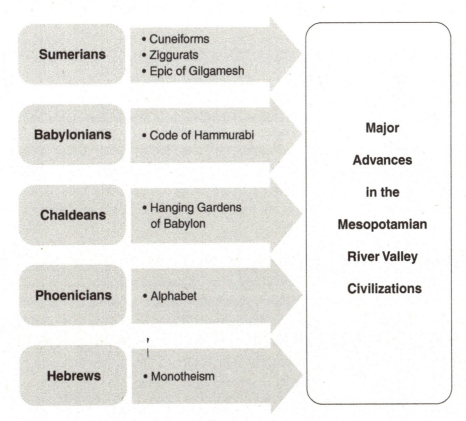

Egypt

The Nile River valley provided a home for Egypt. The civilization of the Nile Valley is usually broken up into five periods: the pre-dynastic period 4000–3100 BCE, **Old Kingdom** (2650–2200 BCE), the **Middle Kingdom** (2050–1570 BCE), the **New Kingdom** (1570–1090 BCE), and the **Third Intermediate Period** (1090–332 BCE). The Egyptian River valley shared many similarities with the Tigris-Euphrates Valley. The distance from Babylon in Mesopotamia to the Nile River Valley was about 750 miles—if one traveled by caravan, that is. This distance was close enough for the Egyptians and Mesopotamians to exchange some goods and customs, but it was far enough away that a distinct Egyptian civilization emerged. This civilization was deeply religious and united under a strong central authority, which they considered a divine king whom they called the pharaoh. Egyptians settled along the Nile River, an area of extremely rich soil made so by the predictable floods of the river each year that gave them a very stable agricultural cycle and helped them to compile ample food surpluses.

The Egyptians recognized two sets of geographical divisions in their country: Upper (southern) Egypt, which consisted of the narrow valley of the Nile; and Lower (northern) Egypt, which consisted of the triangular Delta region. This might seem odd, that the south is considered "upper" and the north "lower," but the names were given according to the direction that the Nile flows. Protected by the desert and a marshy, harbor-less seacoast and endowed with predictable river flooding that deposited fertile soil along the river banks each year, Egypt took advantage of its natural isolation and self-sufficiency to create a unique culture that depended little on its neighbors. The cities along the Nile were part of a single state that was first unified by about 3000 BCE, and continued that unification for the next 2,500 years.

The Egyptians established an effective government with a highly structured bureaucracy under the divine kings, the **pharaohs**. Egyptian society was less urban than Mesopotamian society and also less stratified. Peasants made up the majority of the population, slavery was limited, and women enjoyed more freedoms and legal protections than their Mesopotamian counterparts.

The stability that the pharaohs and the bureaucracy provided also enabled them to develop complex forms of art, religion, writing, and mathematics. The Egyptians spent considerable resources on preparing for the afterlife and glorifying both the living and dead pharaohs. To a large extent, these interests drove the developments of art, mathematics, science, and engineering with the construction of burial tombs for the pharaohs.

In Mesopotamia, the king was considered to have been appointed by the gods; however, in Egypt, the pharaoh was considered to actually be a god. It was the pharaoh, so believed the people, who actually made the Nile rise and fall each year, and with that, went the fortunes of the people. From his capital at Memphis, the god-king administered Egypt according to set principles called *ma'at*, embodying order, justice, and truth. The pharaoh did so with the help of the huge bureaucracies that he created to run the government. The leader of the bureaucracy was the **vizier**, a hereditary position that enabled the vizier to control all of the Egyptian bureaucracy. The Egyptians believed that in return for the pharaohs building and maintaining temples, the gods oversaw

Competency 4: World History

the welfare of the state and thus ensured the continuing pharaonic rule. The pharaoh had a similar obligation to the people in that he was obligated to rule in a benign and beneficent manner and to safeguard the people's welfare.

The political unification of Egypt began during the period of the Old Kingdom, a period of prosperity and cultural growth. Because the pharaoh was thought to be a god, religion and government were closely intertwined in the Old Kingdom, and Egypt was considered to be ruled by a **theocracy**.

The most dramatic symbols of the king's divinity were the **pyramids**. The pyramids were temples where the king would continue to be worshipped even after his death. They also illustrated the hierarchical structure of Egyptian society, of which the pharaoh was the capstone. Only princes, royal wives, and select officials were given the privilege of erecting a tomb beside the royal pyramids.

The pyramids played a political purpose as well. By carrying out an astonishingly large project focused on his person, the king made a statement about his power. The sheer size of the Great Pyramids at Giza demonstrated the pharaoh's ability to organize a vast labor force. Some suggest that the encampment of workers at Giza represented the largest gathering of human beings to that date.

The pharaoh's obligation was to rule over Egypt carefully. The Old Kingdom saw a huge bureaucracy develop that extended from the village to the district to the central administration to keep track of land, labor, products, and people, and—of course—the amount of taxes that everyone owed.

So, how did the Egyptians keep track of all of this? They depended on scribes and a system of writing called **hieroglyphics**. Literacy was a societal hallmark. The scribes worked on papyrus, made out of the papyrus reed that grew only in Egypt. Scribes also used their writing skills to develop literature, poetry, religious hymns, and instruction manuals.

Egyptian society was less urban than its Mesopotamian counterparts, but it was also less stratified to the degree that both men and women had remarkably equal legal rights. The social hierarchy demanded that the royal family ranked highest, followed by priests, administrators, regional governors, military commanders, and then free workers. The majority of the population was made up of peasants, and slavery was quite limited. Egyptian art and literature from this period display interest in maintaining social order and proper relations with the gods, and instructing high officials in appropriate behavior.

The Egyptian religion embodied a complex vision of the afterlife and much of the kingdom's wealth went for these religious purposes: preparing for the afterlife and glorifying the divine pharaoh. Egyptians believed in the afterlife and they made extensive preparations for safe passage to the new world and a comfortable existence once they arrived there. The Egyptian **Book of the Dead**, present in many excavated tombs, contained rituals and spells to protect the journeying spirit. The final and most important challenge was the weighing of the deceased's heart to determine whether or not the person lived a good life.

To serve their religious needs, Egyptians developed technologies that enabled them to construct monumental tombs and temples, and their interesting mummification made them well-schooled in chemistry and medicine. The wealthier you were, the more lavish your final resting place. Common people had to make do with simple pit graves or small mud brick chambers, and sometimes they were just wrapped up in linen and buried in the sand. The kings erected pyramids filled with treasures and curses and other magical precautions to foil tomb robbers, all to no avail; when archaeologists entered the tombs, they seldom discovered an undisturbed royal tomb. Mummies attracted a great deal of attention again in the nineteenth century when amateurs and professionals went in search of the royal tombs. Mummies were found, and it became quite fashionable in Europe to seek the medicinal advantage that ground-up mummies provided.

The government of the Old Kingdom collapsed around 2100 BCE. For almost 200 years, a series of problems, invasions, famine, and civil war dominated the region until about 2055 BCE, when a new dynasty rose to power as the **Middle Kingdom** with their capital at Thebes. The Middle Kingdom prided itself on the great defense that it provided. However, it fell to invaders called the **Hyksos**, around 1650 BCE from Syria. Some historians assert that climate change brought both the Old and the Middle Kingdoms down, for it altered the regular flood pattern of the Nile and caused the divine authority of the monarch to erode and brought civil war that destroyed the unity. It was not until nobles from Thebes emerged to overthrow the Hyksos that Egypt was once again united and thus ushered in the New Kingdom phase from 1570–1075 BCE.

The New Kingdom rulers realized that they needed to build up their military to keep Egypt safe from invaders. They created Egypt's first permanent army with foot soldiers, archers, and charioteers. The pharaohs also felt that they needed to extend their rule south in order to have a land barrier from troops coming from further afield. With the expansion of Egyptian rule, trade also increased.

One of the best-known pharaohs was a woman who took power around 1500 BCE, **Queen Hatshepsut**. When her husband died, she proclaimed herself ruler in the name of her young son. She realized some of the difficulties of a woman ruling, so she dressed like a man, even wearing the false beard that male pharaohs wore. Unlike other rulers, she spent her 22-year reign focusing more on trade and trading expeditions than war. She was reportedly murdered by her stepson, **Thutmose III**, who took over as ruler and destroyed all paintings and statues of his stepmother. He proved to be more interested in war than trade.

Another important ruler from the New Kingdom was **Akhenaton** (originally named Amenhotep IV) who ruled from 1363–1347 BCE. Akhenaton proclaimed that all of Egypt should worship only one god, the sun god **Aten**. He banned the worship of other gods and even ordered all other gods' images destroyed.

Egypt's brief experiment with monotheism did not last, as Akhenaton's successor, Tutankhamon, restored the worship of Egypt's traditional gods and moved the kingdom's capital back to Thebes. Under Ramses the Great (**Ramses II**), the Egyptians settled a conflict with the Hittites (Ramses married a Hittite princess), and he ruled for more than 60 years. The Egyptians regained Palestine but faced increasing invasions from the Kush and the Assyrians.

Religion retained its central place in New Kingdom society. The royal family in the New Kingdom built most of Egypt's magnificent temples, whose sculpted columns set a precedent for later Greek architecture. So intense were Egyptians' religious feelings that they threatened the stability of the New Kingdom in the fourteenth century BCE when the pharaoh Akhenaton reformed the official religion and created the cult of Aten and attempted to impose monotheism on the Egyptian population. The principal gods of Ancient Egypt were Amon and Re. During the Old and Middle Kingdoms, the priests began to combine them into a cult of Amon Re. The cult of Osiris also became important.

From the end of the **New Kingdom** until 12 BCE, Egypt and the entire Near East were greatly influenced by two migrations of Indo-Europeans that disturbed and remolded existing states. While Mesopotamia became unified under the Hittites, Egypt was first influenced by Hyksos and then by the introduction of monotheism by the pharaoh **Akhenaton**.

	Main Achievement	Importance
Early Egypt	Unification	Created civilization that would endure for centuries
Old Kingdom	Bureaucracy	Provided a framework for ruling Egypt
Middle Kingdom	Stability	Economic prosperity
New Kingdom	Created Empire	Increased trade

India

India's oldest civilization was unknown until, by accident, British engineers uncovered brick ruins as they were building a railroad in the mid-1800s close to a small modern city called Harappa; however, it wasn't until the 1920s that archeologists took an interest in the area and found the bricks to be 5000 years old. Thus, the **Indus Civilization** is sometimes called the **Harappa Civilization**. Unlike many other ancient civilizations, the Indus civilization had a nearly continuous history stretching over many centuries into the present, aided partly because the huge mountains north and west of the Indus River prevented the numerous invasions that Mesopotamia encountered. However, thanks to the **Khyber Pass** through the Hindu Kush Mountains, the civilization did have some trade contact with other lands, as material evidence points to trade contacts between Indus Valley cities and the resource-rich areas to the north and to Mesopotamia to the west. The Indus River civilizations are thought to have spanned a half million square miles, twice the size of the Egyptian and Sumerian civilizations.

The Harappa civilization shares many of the characteristics of the other ancient river valley civilizations; however, rather than building large monuments and tombs, the Harrapans were skilled builders who focused on more practical aspects of the city. They constructed high brick walls, arranged streets in a rectangular grid, and created sophisticated drainage systems that carried waste under the streets and outside the city walls. They also developed clay seals with inscriptions written in a highly sophisticated language that remains undeciphered.

Although the Indus River civilizations existed for thousands of years, they were eventually invaded around 1500 BCE by the Aryans, now referred to as **Indo-Iranian** or **Indo-Europeans**. The Aryans brought with them strong cultural traditions that still remain. The Aryans were taller, lighter skinned, and spoke a different language than the Indus. Although the Aryans conquered the Indus, they chose to live alongside them. The combination of the civilizations affected its development. The Indus had walled cities, trade networks, and a system of writing. The Aryans brought agriculture and a class system that determined one's role in society. The first Aryans arrived with a three-class system: priests, warriors, and peasants or traders, and added a new class of non-Aryan laborers and craftspeople. Although the Aryans lived with the Indus, they chose to limit their contact with non-Aryans. As a result, the class system became more rigid and divisive. It consisted of four groups that ranked people at birth according to family occupation, color, and ritual purity: priests, warriors, landowners and merchants, and peasants and laborers. These groups were further subdivided by castes of people who lived, worked, ate, and married within their group. People outside the system were referred to as the untouchables, consisting of those whose occupations as butchers, gravediggers, trash collectors, etc., were believed to have made a person physically and spiritually unclean and, thus, had none of the protections of caste laws. The idea was that even their touch would endanger the ritual purity of others. This system is known today as the caste system.

The Aryans spoke and wrote in a language called Sanskrit. One of the greatest contributions of this civilization is a treasure of literature. The most significant of these is sacred literature, the **Vedas**, consisting of four collections of prayers, magical spells, and instructions for performing rituals, all of which was to form the foundations for the Hindu religion. Much of what we know about the Aryans comes from the **Rigveda**, their collection of 1,028 hymns that presents their history in religious terms.

China

Even before the Sumerians settled in southern Mesopotamia, early Chinese cultures began farming settlements along the Huang He Valley (known as the Yellow River Valley) sometime around the eighth millennium BCE, and like that of India, has had a nearly continuous existence since then. Also, like many of the other civilizations, geography influenced its development. China's many rivers and mountains isolated China, and Chinese culture evolved with little outside influence.

In the North China Plain, as in the river-valley civilizations of Mesopotamia and Egypt, the presence of great, flood-prone rivers and the lack of dependable rainfall directed the formation of institutions capable of organizing and mandating large numbers of people to build and maintain irrigation systems. As in the other ancient river-valley civilizations, society became more complex as villages began to expand.

Competency 4: World History

According to legend, the first Chinese dynasty, the **Xia** (Hsia) dynasty, emerged along the Huang He Valley (Yellow River Valley). While much of what is known about this prehistoric dynasty might be legend, the formation of an authoritarian central government became a hallmark of Chinese civilization. The first historic dynasty, the **Shang**, controlled China for about 500 years from 1532–1027 BCE and was a central force in introducing irrigation and flood control systems in the Huang He Valley. Unlike the cities of the Indus Valley or Fertile Crescent, the major Shang cities were constructed of wood and were highly stratified. The major Shang city, Anyang, had higher classes living within the city walls in timber framed houses with walls of clay and straw, while the lower classes lived in hovels outside the city. The Shang had many accomplishments during their reign, such as the production of silk cloth, making pottery called kaolin, and bronze casting. They also developed a calendar and an original written language.

The Chinese rulers, like their Egyptian counterparts, used religion to bolster their position in society. The Shang rulers, for instance, served as intermediaries between the people of the kingdom and powerful and protective ancestors and gods. Like the Egyptians, the Shang ordered complex tombs built for their kings. These burial sites were designed and built during the king's lifetime; then when the king was buried, people were sacrificed to be buried with the king to assist him in the afterlife.

Also, like the Egyptians, the Shang engaged in massive building projects, which required them to be able to control large labor forces. The Shang, for instance, were known for surrounding their cities with tremendous earthen walls. These walls took a great number of men to build, likely more than 10,000, over a long period of time. The Shang rulers depended upon the development of a large bureaucracy to enable them to rule from the capital, recruit and manage the military, and collect taxes.

The Shang had limited contact with the rest of the world, although it did engage in long-distance trade with Mesopotamia. They developed an ethnocentric attitude and considered Shang China to be the center of the world. The central role of the family played an important part in Shang society. Usually multiple generations would live in the same household in a **patriarchal** structure that gave the most power to the eldest living male. Even when family members died, they continued to play a central role in day-to-day life, as one's ancestors were considered to be a family's intermediaries with the gods. In this way, ancestor worship and respect dominated family life.

Around 1100 BCE, the **Zhou** overthrew the Shang. The Zhou developed the concept of the ruler as the divine Son of Heaven who ruled in accord with the **Mandate of Heaven**. The basic idea of the Mandate was that if the gods were pleased with a ruler, wars would be won and harvests would be plentiful. However, if the opposite should happen, the people had a right to change the rulers. Carefully applying this Mandate of Heaven to their own ascension to rule, a new group on the scene, the Zhou, justified the removal of the Shang Dynasty.

The Zhou instituted many reforms and improvements. They started large water projects to control rivers and irrigation, established the manufacture and trade of silk, developed caravan routes across Central Asia, and established schools of ancient philosophy. Trade and crafts increased and social mobility and advancement occurred. Geographical expansion increased the available land for cultivation. A decentralized system of government divided the territory into 200 domains; however, this proved to be their undoing. A feudal system developed in which land was given to trusted nobles who provided loyalty and military service to the king and protection to the people. At first, the local lords submitted to the control of the Zhou rulers; however, over time, local lords became less dependent on the king. The regional lords later bound together, which led to a period of **Warring States** in which the old aristocracy was undermined by competition between the states and advances in military technology. As a result, regional lords became powerful and fought each other from 403 to 221 BCE.

As part of their quest for power, these lords sought out the advice of teachers and advisers. **Kongfuzi**, known in the West by the Latin form of the name **Confucius**, for instance, was one of the many teachers who answered the lords' pleas for advice and wisdom. The various philosophies that these teachers formulated became known as the **Hundred Schools of Thought**. Teachers tried to explain all things through the dual principles of yin and yang, as well as the five elements: water, fire, wood, metal, and earth. The ideas taught in the Hundred Schools of Thought influenced Chinese thought for centuries.

Confucius withdrew from public life after unsuccessful efforts to find employment. He gathered around himself a circle of students to whom he presented his wide-ranging ideas on morality, conduct, and government that were later written down by his followers in what we know today as the **Analects**. Confucius taught that the family was important to the state, that the values of the family applied to national life, and that only educated and virtuous people should enter government service. The perfect Confucian gentleman was a man of integrity, education, and culture who should use those qualities to serve his ruler. If Confucianism emphasized social engagement, its great rival, **Daoism**, taught that people should withdraw from the empty formalities and rigid hierarchy and distractions of Chinese society. For **Laozi**, who is credited with the foundational text of Daoism, the **Dao De Jing**, almost all purposeful actions are counterproductive.

COMPETENCY 4.2

Evaluate the influence of ancient civilizations (e.g., Greek, Roman, Indian, Chinese) on the evolution of modern civilization.

Greece—the Cradle of Western Civilization

European civilization was concentrated in and around the Aegean Sea and differed in several ways from the River Valley civilizations. This was due in large part to the fact that the Greek civilization did not have a river valley, nor plains, nor even a contiguous body of land to unify it. The Greeks did have a number of small islands that, while beneficial in terms of trade, were unable to support large populations. Consequently, the city-states that dominated ancient Greece were

Competency 4: World History

constantly looking for new land and new colonies in the Mediterranean. Such quests undoubtedly led to a tremendous amount of tension and conflict, both between and within the city-states as a result of the heated competition for limited resources. In its quest to gain territories and to establish spheres of influence, Greek influence came to dominate a significant part of the world. This domination was achieved chiefly through the activities of Alexander the Great, who ruled from 356 BC–323 BCE. His conquests spread Greek culture from the Aegean Sea to the Mediterranean Sea, then to North Africa, and then to India. The results of Greek culture flourished and propagated as its influence continued across both time and space. Today's world owes much to the Greeks.

The effects of ancient Greek language and culture on modern civilization are seen mostly in the sciences and the humanities, including mathematics, philosophy, naturalistic art, literature, rhetoric, Western-style warfare, architecture, religion, philosophy, government, sports, politics, theater, and education. The Greeks laid down the foundations for the way modern researchers approach studies of human behavior through the development of the disciplines of history and philosophy. Much of the understanding of other ancient civilizations is the result of the writings of ancient Greeks. And, thanks to the Muslims in the Middle East, the ideas of the ancient Greeks were preserved in their libraries whereas Europe eschewed that sort of learning and destroyed libraries. Greek philosophies of Aristotle, Plato, and Socrates continue to shape the ideas of generation after generation. In the field of sports, the ancient Greeks gave us the idea of athletic competitions including the Olympic Games, rewarding those who excelled on their own merit, rather than through family connections and corruption.

The works of ancient Greek writers are studied, read, acted, and produced today, and they make up a cornerstone of liberal arts education in the United States. In literature, the works from Greek tragedies like Sophocles, Euripides, Aeschylus, Greek epics (Homer), and Greek comedy (Aristophanes) are still studied. One of the most well known is Homer, whose epic poems *Iliad* on the Greek expedition against the Trojans and *Odyssey* about the adventures of Odysseus were important in defining Greek ideals.

The Greeks left their imprint on education. The Greek educational system featured activities such as educational competitions, mentor networks asking students questions (e.g., the Socratic Method), and emphasizing that strength of body was as important as strength of mind. Thus, the Greeks influenced the inclusion of physical education into school curriculum. Geometry, a standard subject in modern schools, also had its beginnings in Ancient Greece as the result of the work of the mathematician Euclid, who formed many geometric proofs and theories and discovered the value of *pi*.

Greek architecture's form and substance continues to be a cornerstone of architecture throughout the world to this day. Buildings in ancient Greece reflected their mathematical origins as buildings were believed to be the embodiment of perfect mathematical design: symmetrical and perfectly proportioned.

Democracy is, in large part, a Greek invention. Modern democracies are based largely on the Athenian form of direct democracy in which each citizen had a voice in government. Modern civilizations have used this philosophy as a basis for their own indirect democracies, where citizens elect officials who then make and enforce laws. One might also say that it was Greek democracy that paved the way for some of the freedoms that Western democracies pride themselves on, such as freedom of speech, freedom of the press, and freedom of movement. As a result, citizens of democracies can think critically and speak out without fear of antagonizing and without adverse personal or political repercussions.

However, the Romans get the credit for transmitting much of Greek influence throughout the West. The scholarship of Alexandria so impressed the Romans that they constantly strove to emulate the Greeks. They hired Greek tutors for their children, sought to master rhetoric in Greek style, and even considered Greek an important language for them to learn. The Romans adopted much of the Greek culture that they encountered as they took over Greek lands. In addition to borrowing many Greek artistic and educational ideas, Romans also adopted many Greek religious customs. A quick perusal of the Roman pantheon of gods and goddesses reveal that the Romans largely took the Greek gods and "Romanized" them for their own.

The study of Greek classics later formed the foundation of the Renaissance period when Europeans turned toward the classics for inspiration and knowledge. Even Reformation leaders considered a study of Greek to be essential. Greek art reached levels of excellence that were not reproduced until, arguably, the Renaissance when master painters in Southern Europe looked to ancient Greece for theme, styles, and techniques.

Greek influence on modern culture has not always been positive. Greek life was organized around the **polis**, the Hellenic city-state. Because geography of Greece with many small islands almost dictated this type of ruling system in with hundreds of poleis, each evoked a loyalty and attachment by its citizens that made the idea of dissolving one's own polis into a larger unit unthinkable. The result was twofold: both constant war among city-states, and extraordinary achievements in literature and art by writers and artists who recorded the events of war. So, the idea of unification bred both positive and negative results.

Because no single city-state could produce large numbers of men to fight on the battlefield, the Greeks constructed their society in a way that would make them more efficient than their foes. The institution of a slave economy freed up male citizens to, among other pursuits, make war. Although Greek slavery differed in some important aspects from the later Western version—Greek slavery was not based on race in the same way—it helped expand their economy and territory, and became an institution that the West would later emulate.

While the Greek society is championed for its development of democracy, not all people were able to participate in it. While Athenian citizenship was granted to adult males of native parentage, it also limited the freedom of women, immigrants, and slaves. These exclusions of parts of the populace from enjoying the benefits of democracy set the precedent for many of modern civilization's views about freedoms, rights, and privileges in society. In terms of sexism, the Greeks gave women almost no political, social, or economic rights, perhaps making it harder for women today to be treated equally. Women, like slaves, lacked the right of political participation in the city-state. Freeborn women were citizens, enjoying the protection of the laws as well as having recourse to the courts in property disputes, but they were not able to participate in the democracy. All women had to have male guardians to protect them physically and legally. Men restricted women's freedom of movement partly to reduce uncertainty about the paternity of their children and to protect their daughters' honor. To preserve her reputation and ensure the paternity of her children, an upper-class woman was expected to avoid close contact with men other than family members or close friends. Poorer women had a bit more freedom, as they had to work and did so often as small-scale merchants and craft producers. While ostensibly women were allowed to inherit land and control their own dowry, in practice, a woman was not allowed to control the land she inherited. Often, female heirs would be forced to marry the dead man's closest male relative to produce sons so that her inheritance would go to a male heir.

Roman Empire

The Roman Empire, like its Greek neighbors, had a tremendous influence on modern civilization. However, much of what is termed "Roman" may have come from the Greeks as well as the Etruscans, those who lived in the area before them and from whom the Romans borrowed much of their religious and social institutions. In fact, one of the hallmarks of Roman civilization was its ability to assimilate ideas and institutions not only from the past, but also from the areas that they conquered. They assimilated many of the customs of the ancient Etruscans, and then, like the Macedonians before them, also readily adopted the culture of Hellenic Greece. What emerged was a Greco-Roman culture that influenced art, law, architecture, language, government, and engineering.

From 1000 to 500 BCE, the Italian peninsula was dominated by three groups who inhabited the region and battled for its control: the Latins, Greeks, and Etruscans, and each seemed to influence the other.

The Latins were members of an Indo-European tribe of farmers and shepherds who wandered into the region and settled on both sides of the Tiber River in a region they called Latium. Between 750 and 600 BCE, they built the original settlement at Rome, a cluster of wooden huts atop Palatine Hill, one of the area's seven hills,

In about 616 BCE, the Etruscans emerged from northern Italy and brought their skill as metalworkers, jewelers, and engineers to the area. Romans borrowed much from the Etruscans, including their alphabet and number system, their type of government, gladiator games and chariot races, religious rituals believed to please the gods, styles of sculpture and painting, and building techniques, including that of the arch.

Aspects of social life were also borrowed from the Etruscans. Rome was composed of three tribes, which were further divided into clans composed of groups of families. In each of these divisions was a class of nobles and a class of commoners. The nobles, referred to as **patricians**, occupied some important positions in society: they were landowners who were also advisors to the king. Society was a patriarchal one in which the father of the family was responsible for protection and was the priest of his home. It was a patron-client society in which patrons had clients who they protected and whose own position in society was bolstered by the number of clients one had.

Romans also borrowed some ideas of government that they later implemented in their system, and which has been emulated by other modern societies. The early Etruscan kings were not hereditary ones; they were elected by the nobles. The Etruscan kings also had a council, or senate, composed of 30 senators who advised them. In 509 BCE, the Romans overthrew the last of the Etruscans and set up a new form of government called a *republic*, the word stemming from the Latin *res publica*, which means "public affairs." A republic is a form of government in which citizens vote on their leaders. The concept of leaders having a group of people that give them advice continues to be important throughout the civilizations that followed.

Although elements of continuity can be seen in the Roman Republic, the new form of government could also be considered a departure from the common experiences of ancient civilizations. Having begun as a monarchy, Rome expelled its king and established an aristocratic republic somewhat like the Greek *poleis*. The Romans, unlike the Greek democrats, extended citizenship to a large population, first throughout Italy and then across their entire empire. The Roman government seemed to work well because it included a system of checks and balances in which each government constrained the actions of others, with the objective that no one person or group would gain too much power.

The Romans shared their citizenship with those elites whom they conquered in order to guarantee loyalty and to strengthen Rome's grip on their territories. The Roman policy of assimilation and toleration enabled it to be successful in its early stages, similar to the Ottoman Empire that followed it. Romans looked to Greece not only for fighting techniques, but also for education and approaches to learning. Most upper-class Romans hired Greek tutors, and most educated Romans knew Greek as well as Latin.

Military victory brought economic and political change to the Romans, a change in lifestyle, and, in some views, general moral deterioration. In consolidating its power over huge territories, the Romans committed atrocities, enslaved whole peoples, and destroyed cities with little provocation. Also, as the military grew more powerful, foreign conquests created huge amounts of standing armies and veterans who needed to be occupied during times of peace. The trouble these groups wrought in Rome prompted many to urge expansion just to keep the soldiers busy and out of the affairs of Roman senators. As these military men grew powerful, turmoil between old and new elites loomed on the horizon. Military expansion produced economic change: rural Roman society moved from one of independent farmers to one in which slave labor became the primary means of the rural economy. By the end of the first century BCE, the slave population totalled about 2–3 million slaves. Most of the slaves were prisoners of war and conquered civilians.

In many ways, the Roman Empire remains the ideal upon which much of Western civilization, and certainly American civilization, has shaped itself. Because so much of the United States has been constructed on Roman foundations, a fascination with why Rome fell has occupied historians and political pundits alike. In an effort to avoid repeating the mistakes of the past, many historians and politicians examine the nature and extent of an empire in our increasingly global environment. Are we doomed to repeat the mistakes of the past? Are empires a thing of the past, or has the word "empire" just been replaced with the word "hegemony" (power) today?

Legacy of the Romans

What is the legacy that Rome offers? Do Roman ideas really form the foundation of Western society? The legacy of the Roman Empire can be seen today in language, law, government, architecture, urban and regional development, and in Christian churches.

Rome's language, Latin, was the official language of the empire. Until the seventeenth century, both Latin and Greek were considered standard courses for all educated Europeans. The Latin language was predominant in the Roman Empire and became the basis for Spanish, French, Portuguese, Romanian, and Italian—the Romance languages. These languages started out as frontier languages in which peoples tried to blend their language with that of the new rulers, and the results were really just different versions of "bad Latin" that later established themselves as bona fide languages. Latin also exerted its influence in areas that did not speak any romance languages, largely as a result of the influence of the Roman Catholic Church. Until the late 1900s, Latin served as the language of prayer in the Roman Catholic Church. Many English words, especially legal and medical terminology, have Latin roots.

Another legacy of the Roman Empire is the hundreds of towns that Rome founded and developed in the frontiers of their empire. These new towns served as their administrative centers and today provide the basic structure of cities around much of Europe and North Africa. Roman roads, 50,000 of them, connected the cities of the empire and formed the foundation for much of Europe's land transportation today. Roman development of a system of connected roads financed and controlled by the government also facilitated the Roman expansion. Today the Roman road system influences our state planning and even the construction of highway systems. The Romans created systems for water and sewage that made it possible for the cities to move further away from rivers and water settle the interiors of countries. Their development of concrete facilitated not only the building of the aqueducts, but also large buildings and structures.

Roman art and architecture has left an enormous imprint on modern design. The Roman influence led art to embrace realistic representations of people and move away from the idealized visions that the Greeks had provided. These realistic representations were found all over Rome, not just in the form of majestic statues, but also in graffiti that adorned public buildings. Graffiti became a form of criticism of public officials and societal issues, with which modern architecture is also inundated. The Roman legacy is found today in neoclassical architecture with the use of arches and vaults and in the Romanesque architectural style. Many of the Roman buildings served as models for buildings in the United States. For instance, Thomas Jefferson used the Roman Parthenon as his inspiration for the University of Virginia's Rotunda, and the U.S. Capitol Building also reflects basic tenets of Roman architecture. Roman inspiration is also seen in a basic component of modern urban civilization, the apartment.

Roman influence in science and engineering can also be felt today. While the Greeks had been more interested in new scientific research and were interested in knowledge for knowledge's sake, the more practical Romans were more interested in application of knowledge and in collecting and organizing information. **Galen**, a physician who lived in Rome in the 100s CE, wrote several volumes of medical knowledge; physicians up until the last century used his compendium of knowledge as a basic reference work. **Ptolemy** synthesized the knowledge of others into a single theory of astronomy that Earth was the center of the universe. As engineers, they applied the knowledge they gained from science to plan their cities, build water and sewage systems, and improve farming methods. For example, they constructed enormous buildings made possible by their developments in human-powered cranes that could lift up heavy blocks of stone and put them into place. Bricks were laid in a way in which no mortar was needed to hold the bricks together. They also used their engineering knowledge to construct bridges and roads that still survive today. Their contributions to urban planning can be felt today in most European cities that have elements of a grid system of roads that were originally planned by Roman engineers.

Modern literature, drama, and history writing owe great debts to Roman authors. For example, the technique of satire was developed from Roman authors. **Virgil**, **Livy**, **Plutarch**, and **Tacitus** gave us great themes for modern literature and theater, and Tacitus's history writing served as emulation for historians over the years.

Roman law inspired the formation and imposition of civil law, a form of law based on a written code of laws that we have today. The Romans, for instance, were the first to come up with the idea of "innocent until proven guilty" and that the burden of proof was on the accuser. They believed that people had rights guaranteed to them under the law. The civil law system was adopted by many countries in Europe after the empire fell. Centuries later, those nations carried their systems of laws to colonies in Africa, the Middle East, Asia, and the Americas. As a result, many countries in these regions have civil law systems that we have in place today.

Contemporary indirect democracies also owe a lot to Rome for the development of the government form. The social and political structure of Rome was much like that of the Greeks. The Romans had **patricians** (landowning nobles), **plebeians** (all other free men), and slaves. Roman government was organized as a representative republic. The main governing body was made up of two distinct groups: the Senate, which comprised patrician families, and the Assembly, initially made up of patricians but later opened up to plebians. The U.S. government today is a republican form of government. We even use some of the same terms (e.g., *Senate*) and structures (two chambers of Congress) that the Romans used.

Although the Romans tolerated Judaism, many Jews were discontented with Roman rule and hoped for a Messiah who would win their independence. In this setting, Jesus was born. His teachings, which formed the basis of the new religion of Christianity, spread among all people within the empire, not just Jews. The Romans persecuted the early Christians because the Christians refused to worship the emperor. Nevertheless, Christianity gained many followers and during the 300s CE, it became the official religion of the Roman Empire. As Roman rule became more decentralized and centers of Christianity sprang up in Byzantium and Alexandria, it greatly influenced the people there. The Roman Church used the Roman imperial administrative organization for its own uses and later became known as the Holy Roman Empire.

Competency 4: World History

Classical Civilizations of India: Mauryan Empire and Gupta Dynasty

India's Mauryan and Gupta civilizations contributed to modern civilization primarily through their development of trade, religions, mathematics, and science.

The Mauryan civilization arose around 321 BCE and lasted until about 180 BCE. The height of the civilization occurred during the reign of **Ashoka Maurya**. During his period, the Mauryan Empire became quite powerful due to its trade in silk, cotton, and elephants, and because of its military prowess. While the Mauryans were able to extend their influence considerably through these activities, Ashoka's reaction to a rather violent military victory actually made him renounce such activities and convert to Buddhism. As a result, his conversion helped the religion spread beyond India and into many parts of Southeast Asia.

After Ashoka's death in 232 BCE, the Mauryan Empire declined, and it was not until the appearance of the more decentralized and smaller **Gupta Empire** from 320 to 550 CE that advances in math and science made their mark on the civilizations that followed. One tremendous influence that contemporary civilization has from the Gupta mathematicians was the concept of zero and development of a decimal system that used the numbers 1 through 9. The numbers we use today come from Hindu-Arabic numerals that Indian scholars created and the Arabs brought to Europe. Astronomy developments were reflected in the work of the most famous Indian astronomer, **Aryabhata**, who correctly argued that Earth rotates on its axis and revolves around the sun. Aryabhata also knew that Earth was a sphere and calculated its circumference pretty accurately.

The Gupta Empire also influenced modern medicine. Indian doctors introduced the idea of inoculations: how to inject small amounts of viruses to protect people against disease. This has had a lasting effect on civilization, as now a simple inoculation can prevent a crippling or fatal disease. Indian doctors also contributed to surgical techniques, such as the way broken bones and wounds were treated.

During the Gupta Dynasty period, problems begin to erupt for women that resulted in women increasingly losing their rights, particularly after the issuance of **Manu's Laws**. During this period, Indian women lost the right to win or inherit property, participate in sacred rituals, and study religion, and were also forced to marry at quite young ages, as young as six or seven. This marked a tremendous change for women and one that contributed significantly to some of the problems modern women have had with regard to equal rights and protections across the globe.

Han China

China's **Han Dynasty** lasted about 400 years, from 206 BCE to 220 CE, and reached its height under the emperor **Wudi** who ruled from 141 BCE to 87 BCE. Under his rule, China extended its control to the north and west of China and even took Manchuria, Korea, and Vietnam. To strengthen China, Wudi promoted economic growth, set up new roads and canals, and instituted monopolies on salt, iron, and alcohol. He also took land away from large landowners and limited the power of merchants. Under his rule, many developments influenced the evolution of modern civilization.

The Han Dynasty made significant contributions to the development of technology during that era. Han Dynasty inventions included paper and rudimentary books, the dictionary, and the development of a common written language across China. Needless to say, the invention of paper affects almost every aspect of modern life today.

In farming, Han inventions included the iron plow and the wheelbarrow that enabled the Han to plow more land faster. Han inventions extended also to the seismograph, which measured Earth tremors. Han emperors were particularly concerned with these, as earthquakes were considered signs of the heaven's disapproval with them. In medicine, the Han made advances in acupuncture to control pain and cure disease.

Perhaps the Han Dynasty's greatest contribution was the development of a network of trade routes that extended throughout Asia and to the Mediterranean Sea. Chinese silk was the focus of early trading; however, eventually the route was used to transport a variety of goods as well as to transfer aspects of culture from one civilization to another. This route was used from about 114 BCE until the 1400s CE. Because silk was the original item that was traded, later historians described the network as the **Silk Road**, although that name was not applied during the use of the trading network.

Wudi developed a civil service system in which candidates had to pass exams in order to obtain jobs in the government. His bureaucracy of more than 130,000 people was designed so that only the best and the brightest would have jobs. Job applicants took formal exams in history, law, literature, and the texts of Confucius. While the exams were theoretically open to all, in reality, only the wealthy could afford the tutoring to pass the difficult exams.

The Han dynasty ultimately collapsed because of the high taxes required to keep the system going. The economic imbalance caused resentment and ultimately the end of the empire. Because a system of inheritance allowed for each son to acquire equal portions of his father's land, plots of land became smaller and smaller with each generation. As a result, it became difficult for owners of small plots to make a living and to pay their taxes. Large landowners did not have to pay taxes, so when their landowning increased, their tax decreased. As a result, the gap increased between rich and poor.

COMPETENCY 4.3

Identify the major contributions of African, Asian, and Mesoamerican societies before 1500 CE.

Africa

The most significant early civilization in Africa was Egypt, as previously discussed. This civilization was located in northern Africa, along the Mediterranean, north of the Sahara Desert. While Egypt was geographically a part of Africa, contemporary studies place it more within the context of the Middle East, rather than North Africa. As such, this section focuses on the other civilizations in Africa for this competency.

Before 1500 BCE, the peoples of these African civilizations left few written records, and historians rely on literature from travelers and traders to the region, art, artifacts, archeological discoveries, oral traditions, and other nontraditional historical sources. The village was the essential unit of political and economic life in the regions, and the chief or the elders exercised political control. The societies were matrilineal, which means that women played a crucial rule.

A variety of kingdoms, empires, and small city-states arose in Africa during this period. Three of the biggest issues that affected the development of African kingdoms were ecological change, the development of long-distance commerce (trade), and the spread of Islam.

Environmental change affected African society as it altered settlement choices and facilitated the decline of empires. The drying up of the Sahara, for instance, forced farmers to move away from what had once been lush green areas to other areas that did not suffer from such ecological change. As people migrated, they took their customs and agricultural methods with them and influenced others. Some environmental changes even led to the downfall of empires. For instance, Aksum's decision to cut down forests led to soil erosion and affected its ability to produce enough food to feed its people.

Trade determined the extent of contact with other civilizations in both East and West Africa. When societies trade with one another, not only are goods and monies exchanged, but also ideas, religions, and culture. Traders from Greece, India, and Southeast Asia landed on the east coast of Africa, and in exchange for their pottery, silk, cotton cloth, and wheat, they received luxury goods like ivory, gold, coconut oil, and slaves from the Africans. Traders brought with them new food for crops, like rice and bananas, that changed the eating habits of the Africans. Trade was also profitable for those who lived along trade routes. In West Africa, Muslim traders crossed the Sahara to exchange salt for gold, and those who lived in-between taxed all trade along the trade routes. While traders also brought with them new ideas and religions, these failed to have the lasting impact of the goods that traders brought with them.

Caravan routes connected the Mediterranean coast with Sudan, and shipping routes between the African coast and Yemen brought Islam into West Africa. With greater contact with Muslim traders, Africans began to convert to Islam. Because two of the Pillars of Islam mandate the giving of *zakat*, or charity, to others and to complete the hajj (trip to Mecca), new travel routes from Africa to Mecca opened up. Leaders who were eager to demonstrate their religiosity made pilgrimages to Mecca and distributed alms to people along the way. Some of these alms-giving resulted in the creation of new centers of learning and hospice along the hajj routes. Another benefit to the hajj expeditions was the exchange of ideas and people between those who had previously had little contact with one another. Despite conversions to Islam, many Africans did not forget their old practices or faiths and simply incorporated the new ideas into their belief system. As a result, while Islam was brought to the area by the traders, the practice and interpretation of it bore little resemblance to the original. In many ways though, it simply attests to the flexibility of the new religions and their ability to assimilate into new cultures.

In the areas south of Egypt and in the upper reaches of the Nile, two important African kingdoms developed. The **Kingdom of Kush** in the south of the ancient region known as **Nubia**, emerged independently of Egypt by 700 BCE. The **Kushites**, known as intermediaries between Egypt and East Africa, eventually became a distinct empire. The Nubian civilization was tremendously influenced by its interactions with its more complex and technologically advanced neighbors, the Egyptians. Much of their contact with one another centered on their trade relationship, for the Nubians supplied the Egyptians with a wide range of goods, from building materials, to slaves, to ivory and ebony wood. Not only did the Nubians have control of valuable resources like gold and precious stones, but, because of the location of the kingdom, they also served as middlemen for trade along the Upper Nile. Nubians profited by charging taxes on any goods that went through their land. By 1472 BCE, apparently the taxes became so high that Queen Hatshepsut of Egypt had five ships carried across the desert to avoid paying taxes!

During the New Kingdom period, the Egyptian government imposed Egyptian culture, language, and religion on the native population, and Nubian architecture came to be based on Egyptian models. But, in the eighth century BCE, the kingdom of Meroe emerged, and Nubia overtook their once-powerful neighbors and ruled all of Egypt for half a century. During this time, the Nubian rulers retained their Nubian names but imitated the style and traditions of the pharaohs. By the fourth century, though, power shifted south to the competing state of Axum and sub-Saharan African cultural influences replaced Egyptian ones.

Axum, located in modern-day Ethiopia, built its power from trade, especially in ivory and gold. Its trading routes extended into the Mediterranean and to the Red Sea areas, establishing contacts between the people and religions of those areas. Two sets of mass conversions impacted the development of Axum and its peoples. In the fourth century, Axum converted to Christianity, and in the seventh century, it converted to Islam. From Axum, Christianity spread throughout Africa. The peoples who lived on the **Swahili Coast of Africa** (East Africans), primarily Bantu-speaking peoples, also engaged in a significant amount of trade. In fact, their word for trader is "Swahili." The Swahili language today reflects some of the effects of the trade their peoples engaged in as the Swahili language is a mix of the original Bantu language with Arabic and Persian. Extensive trade of gold, slaves, rhinoceros horns, spices, and ivory with Muslims in exchange for cotton cloth, copper and brass, and iron tools began in the early tenth century and flourished. The wealth that this trade brought created powerful kingdoms along the coast that became wealthy trading centers and important cultural and political centers. Islam spread throughout the region as the ruling elites and merchant classes converted in order to facilitate some of their developing political and economic relationships. The trade linked the East African coast with India, China, and the Indies.

Kingdoms of Kush, Axum, and the Swahili Coast

Kush	Axum	Swahili Coast
• Trade	• Trade—ivory and gold	• Mix with Arab culture and language
• Tax collection on trade that passed through	• Spread Christianity and Islam	• Trade of gold, slaves, ivory throughout the Indian Ocean
		• Influence of Islam

Western Africa

Three of the most important empires in sub-Saharan Africa were the Soninke people of Ghana, Mali, and Songhai. Trade, specifically the gold trade, dominated economic activity and significantly influenced the social, political, and religious activities of the people who lived there. This was similar to the dominance of trade in the Kush, Axum, and Swahili Coast kingdoms discussed above. As Islam spread across North Africa in the seventh and eighth centuries, the African kingdoms became an important cog in the wheel of the Mediterranean economy. As people from south of the Sahara began to trade their goods for salt, they began to encounter Islamic traders who became interested in the goods that the West African peoples had—namely gold.

Located in present-day Ghana, the Soninke people thrived, ruled by their war chief that they referred to as a *ghana*. Muslim traders who visited the area referred to the whole region as Ghana. By the 700s CE, the Soninke were growing rich from taxing the trans-Saharan trade routes, particularly from the gold and salt that came through their country. Only the king had the right to own gold, and he limited the supply of gold in order to keep its price from falling. It was through traders that Ghana came into contact with Islam, which primarily attracted the rulers. These rulers tried to spread Islam beyond their court but had difficulty in doing so. Many of the upper classes, convinced that they needed to embrace Islam in order to appease the king, did observe Islam along with their former beliefs.

Among the upper classes, Islam's growth encouraged the spread of literacy and the Arabic language because to study the Qur'an, converts had to learn how to read and write Arabic. As literacy became more important, the ruling kings began to get assistance from a large bureaucracy composed of family members who filled needed posts.

By the thirteenth century the Kingdom of Mali was established. By 1235, the Kingdom of Mali had formed partly as a result of a shift of trade routes and the decline of the Ghana empire due to its numerous wars with Muslim empires to the north. The Kingdom of Mali rose to power built on the same territory Ghana had ruled 150 years earlier. Mali's first great leader, Sundiata, took over the Kingdom of Ghana and unified the area. He helped create his capital of Niani as an important center of commerce and trade. After Sundiata's death in 1255, some of Mali's rulers became Muslims, influenced by Arab traders in the region. They built mosques, attended public prayers, and supported the preaching of Muslim religious leaders. The most famous of them was Sundiata's grand-nephew, Mansa Musa. Mansa Musa was a skilled military leader who did a good job controlling the gold and salt trade. He kept up a large army of over 100,000 men. As a devout Muslim, his hajj in Mecca in 1324–1325 CE attracted quite a bit of attention as he brought 60,000 people with him. The people that the pilgrims met along the way were quite impressed with the entourage's lavish clothing and gifts. In fact, those on the pilgrimage gave away so much gold along their trip that the price of gold tanked. No doubt lured by the prospect of more gold, Mansa Musa's group attracted many artists, scholars, and architects along the way who returned with him to Mali and engaged in numerous projects in his empire, turning Mali's Timbuktu into a tremendous center of education, religion, and culture.

The Empire of Songhai emerged as a breakaway kingdom from Mali, as Mali declined after the death of Mansa Musa. During the fifteenth and sixteenth centuries, the Songhai Empire stood as one of the largest empires in the history of Africa. It had two important rulers. First, Sunni Ali, helped build the empire from a professional army that featured a riverboat fleet of war canoes and a mobile fighting force on horseback. In 1468, Sunni Ali captured Timbuktu. Sunni Ali's son lost power after a rebellion that was initiated by Muslims who were angry that he did not practice Islam faithfully. The leader of the revolt was a devout Muslim named Askia Mohammad. During his rule, he set up an efficient tax system, initiated political reform, and revitalized the area, turning it into a well-governed and thriving empire. He also created religious schools, and mosques, and opened his court to scholars and poets from all over the Muslim world.

The Kingdom of Benin also proved to be of tremendous import for the region. In the 1480s, Portuguese trading ships began to sail into Benin where they traded with Benin merchants for pepper, ivory, leopard skins, and slaves. This initiated European influence in the region during which they enslaved Africans, and seized and colonized the region. The coastal part was known as the "Slave Coast."

Competency 4: World History

Trading Empires of West Africa

Empire	Key Facts
Ghana	**Location:** Near Niger and Senegal rivers **Key cities:** Koumbi Saleh (capital) **Trade:** Controlled gold-salt trade routes **Religion:** Local beliefs, some Muslim influences
Mali	**Location:** Along upper Niger River **Key cities:** Niani (capital), Timbuktu **Trade:** Controlled gold-salt trade routes **Religion:** Islam and local beliefs
Songhai	**Location:** Near Niger River **Key cities:** Gao (capital), Timbuktu **Key rulers:** Sundiata; Mansa Musa **Trade:** Trans-Saharan trade that controlled gold-salt trade routes **Religion:** Islam, local beliefs

Common Characteristics of African Societies

There are some common characteristics of the West African societies:

- Each featured a trade-based economy and sought to control both salt imports from the north and gold purchases from the south.

- All of the governments in the region filled their coffers from taxes imposed on the buying and selling of salt, gold, and other goods.

- Islam was a unifying theme, as the ability to communicate in Arabic furthered the Arabic-centered trade, provided administrators, and stimulated intellectual life. Islam, as a cosmopolitan religion, found adherents mostly in the cities, while the countryside retained their traditional beliefs and gods.

- Due to extensive trade successes, many cities rose in the region to become centers of learning, trade, and politics. Similarly, a cultural gulf developed between urban and rural areas, reflecting the economic and political separations that arose as economic and political power moved to these powerful cities.

By the end of the fourteenth century, sweeping changes enveloped the area as it became primarily concerned with maintaining and expanding trade. Important new developments during the fifteenth century were the presence of ships along the Atlantic and Indian coasts carrying European traders and missionaries from Portugal, Holland, Spain, and England. Initially, Africans saw the Europeans as another set of traders and were eager to supply them with slaves, goods, and minerals. These European traders initially seemed content to establish trade and supply centers along the coast and made little effort to expand their influence. It would prove to be a temporary and illusory effort by the Africans to direct the nature and extent of the trade with their new partners.

Asian Societies

Chinese Societies

By 1500, China saw three important Chinese dynasties develop: the T'ang (618–907 CE), the Song (960–1279 CE), and the Ming (1368–1644). Achievements of this region have four key themes:

1. Triumphs and problems with the rise and spread of Buddhism
2. Intellectual and cultural achievements during the Tang and Song dynasties
3. Mongols and their achievements
4. Ming Dynasty and the closing of China to the West

Spread of Buddhism

The religion with the greatest impact on China was Buddhism. Buddhism first came to China during the Han era, but few Chinese adopted the religion at that time. By the Tang Dynasty, Buddhism was well established in China, as many of the Tang rulers were Buddhists and supported the religion. The period of time from 400 to 845 CE is referred to as the Age of Buddhism and as Buddhism spread during this period, the Buddhist monasteries became centers of learning and medicine.

In the mid 800s, the Age of Buddhism came to an end when the religion lost official favor as it incurred the wrath of the Tang emperor, Confucian scholars, and Daoists. The Tang emperor, Emperor Wuzong, viewed the growing power of Buddhist religious communities as threats and launched a violent campaign against them, destroying temples and texts, killing monks, and forcing 26,000 Buddhist monks and nuns to return to life outside the protection of the monasteries. Confucians saw the Buddhist dismissal of the pursuit of material accumulation as a drain on the treasury and the labor pool. The Daoists saw Buddhism as a rival religion that threatened to take over.

Sui Dynasty

The Sui Dynasty formed in 589 when a ruler named Wendi reunified China and built a centralized government. He initiated a series of reforms designed to improve government organization by creating a new legal code, restoring order, and reforming the bureaucracy. He also created policies to provide all adult males with land and to ensure the availability of grain for the people. The major accomplishment though was the building of the **Grand Canal**, a 1,000-mile waterway that linked the Yellow River with the Yangzi. The Grand Canal produced many economic benefits, but at a terrific human cost. Built in seven years, over 5.5 million people between the ages of 15 and 55 were pressed into service. Because these people were taken from their homes and fields reluctantly, as many as 50,000 police supervised the construction. Those who did not or could not work were flogged and chained. The economic toll on families was enormous, as not only were their men taken away from the family fields, but every fifth family had to provide one person who would supply and prepare food for the workers. Huge public works such as this often required this type of forced labor—it was not limited to the Chinese. The Sui Empire ended when a Sui general seized power and started the Tang Dynasty.

Tang

The Tang Dynasty ruled China from 618 CE until 907 CE, when it collapsed under the weight of an empire that had stretched its limits so much that local warlords were able to seize power. The Tang emperors presided over one of the most celebrated periods in Chinese history; however, they were not Chinese. They were of Turkish descent and brought with them the military and cultural practices of the nomads of Central and Inner Asia.

As China's Tang Dynasty gained more power, it became less welcome to outside ideas. In the beginning of the Tang Dynasty, China dominated East Asia: artistic creativity and the economy expanded, poetry flourished, and China enjoyed a golden age that made it the most sophisticated country in the world. But powerful states began to establish themselves along the border. As a society begins to feel the tension from their border areas, it tends to withdraw into itself, and the late Tang Dynasty was no exception. It became less eager to adopt music, craft, and art styles from distant lands. Instead, the late Tang Dynasty was more oriented toward the civil arts, and it welcomed into its midst men of literary talent from undistinguished families. It was also a time in which the Buddhist religion spread rapidly. Confucianism, too, was much stronger at the end of the Tang Dynasty, thanks to the intellectual flowering of the ninth century. During the Tang Dynasty, new technologies contributed significantly to the intellectual development of the period. Movable type, porcelain, gunpowder, and mechanical clocks were introduced. The Tang Dynasty was the great age of Chinese poetry. The *Complete Tang Poems* include more than 4,800 poems by 2,200 poets. Men who wanted to be seen as members of the educated elite had to be able to recognize lines quoted from earlier poets' works and write technically proficient poems at social occasions. The skill in composing poetry was so highly respected that it was tested in civil service examinations.

Song Dynasty

After the fall of the Tang Dynasty, warlords from several different ethnic identities fought for control of northern China, some of them establishing short-lived dynasties. For some reason, enormous amounts of people began to flee southward toward the Yangtze River, perhaps fleeing northern, Central Asian aggressors. This led to the formation of new power centers far away from the center. In time, the Song dynasty brought political and economic prominence to southern China; however, the cost to the peasant was steep. A change in the tax system left many peasants struggling for survival, and many went from owning land to renting or even becoming landless. As a result, people who used to exert a degree of independence became subject to wealthier people who lived in towns or cities.

The Song period saw the flowering of the **scholar-official class** that was certified through highly competitive **civil service** exams. In contrast to the exams during the Tang period, the Song Chinese scholar-official class was larger, better educated, and less aristocratic. The spread of printing had aided the expansion of the educated class. With the introduction of printing, the price of books lowered and more Song scholars could afford to buy books. Demand for books was fueled by the eagerness to compete in the civil service exams. The Song rulers looked to these exams as a way to identify capable men. The exams were given a measure of legitimacy as confidence increased in the objectivity of the examiners. The names of test-takers were replaced with numbers, and clerks recopied each exam so that the handwriting could not be recognized. While early in the eleventh century, fewer than 30,000 men took the initial exams; by the end of that century, nearly 80,000 took the test; and by the end of the dynasty, about 400,000 took the test. Because the number of available posts did not change, each candidate's chances of passing plummeted, reaching as low as 1 in 333 in some places. Men often took the exam several times and were, on average, about 30 years old when they passed.

China by the mid-fourteenth century was very different from the China of the Sui Dynasty because China's population had nearly doubled. More of the population lived in the south, which had become the undisputed economic center of China. China had become a more commercialized society, with a higher proportion of its farmers engaged in producing for the market, rather than subsistence farming. Yet some continuities remained. Because the civil-service exams continued to be used, education, and the public's commitment to it, expanded significantly and became a defining element in this culture.

Mongols

The Mongols were a nomadic people from Central Asia who raised sheep and horses and whose skill on horses and with archery gave them an enormous advantage over other peoples in the area. For centuries, Mongols were divided into separate clans, each led by a **khan**, who was chosen to lead based on his military and leadership skills. At the end of the twelfth century, a powerful khan named **Temüjin** began to conquer his rivals and unite various Mongol tribes. In 1206, he took the title **Genghis Khan**, which means "Universal Ruler." Genghis Khan used his military and organizational skills to unify the Mongol tribes and set the Mongols on a path to conquer an empire that ranged from the Pacific to Eastern Europe.

With a population of about two million and a highly mobile army of 130,000 cavalry, the Mongols forged their empire through superior military technology, innovative battle tactics, and what amounted to effective "PR." Tales of a few of their conquests so frightened their enemies that many cities just surrendered rather than have to face the Mongols on the battlefield. Certain military advancements made the Mongols' jobs much easier. For instance, Mongol horsemen could travel up to ninety miles a day, existing for the most part on dried beef and yogurt. They developed saddles and stirrups that enabled them to fire arrows accurately from horseback and could fire up to a range of 300 yards. Armies were well-organized, and spy networks provided reconnaissance before battles.

Competency 4: World History

After Genghis Khan's death, the empire was divided into **hordes**, or small independent empires. The Kipchak Empire (**Golden Horde**) conquered modern-day Russia and parts of central Asia; the Empire of Persia included the lands west of the Hindu Kush and south of the Caucasus Mountains and Oxus River; the Empire of Chaghatai included China; and the Empire of the Great Khan included Tibet, the Gobi Desert, and China where **Kublai Khan**, Genghis Khan's grandson, established the **Yuan** Dynasty. The Yuan Dynasty had numerous achievements that paved the way for tremendous successes for China:

- Peace and prosperity promoted population growth.

- The Grand Canal was extended to Beijing, a feat that enabled the growth of Kublai Khan's capital city and facilitated the rice trade from South China into the area.

- An 1,100-mile paved road was built, which facilitated trade and communication north to south and linked China to India and Persia.

- The dynasty implemented paper money, which further facilitated trade.

The Mongols also delved into India under **Timur the Lame**, or **Tamerlane**, to destroy the Delhi Sultanate for a few years. It would be a descendant of Timur, Babar, who would found the Mughal Empire there.

In spite of the Mongols' reputation, largely written by those they conquered since the Mongols were illiterate, the Mongols brought notable economic progress to much of the area over which they ruled. The empire was largely peaceful, as a vital component of the Mongols' rule was to encourage and protect trade along established trade routes. The period is referred to as the **Pax Mongolica**. It was a time of increased contact with Europe, and internal transportation and communication were improved. One of the trademarks of the Pax Mongolica was the spread and exchange of ideas made possible by the peace.

Ming Dynasty

In 1368, under the leadership of a peasant named Zhu Yuanzhang and a rebel army, the last of the Mongol emperors was overthrown. Zhu took the name **Hongwu**, which means "vastly martial" and founded the Ming Dynasty. With Hongwu and his Ming Dynasty (which means "brilliant"), power in China was once again given back to the native Chinese. During this time, peace prevailed, and Chinese culture grew and flourished. The Ming emperors were determined to eradicate anything from the Mongol past, and they did so by trying to reinvigorate Chinese culture and to recreate the splendors of past Han, Tang, and Song dynasties. In order to do so, they advocated a strong centralized government based on Confucian principles. With more power in their hands, the emperors were able to push their own agenda onto the whole of China.

Another characteristic of Ming civilization was that neo-Confucianism was restored as the government's official ideology. The Ming divided the Confucian Chinese society into four classes: the land-owning gentry and scholar-bureaucrats who administered the empire in the name of the emperor, peasants, artisans, and merchants. As part of this re-Chinafication process, the civil service exam was restored.

Japan

The Chinese civilization's influence on East Asia was important. It was their form of government, and not directly controlling areas of East Asia, that inspired emulation. Japan had a history largely determined by its geography because it was relatively isolated from the rest of East Asia. Located off the coast of mainland Asia and surrounded with mountains, made up of four main islands with great agricultural soil, Japan was well able to protect itself from serious invasions, and its contact with foreigners, even China, was relatively limited.

Early Japanese culture prior to 400 CE remains somewhat of a mystery. It was not until the fifth century that the emergence of an important family, called the Yamato Clan, emerged as leaders in the fifth century and continues to rule to this day. **Shinto**, "the way of the gods," became the religion in Japan where they worshiped the *kami*, nature and its forces, both seen and unseen. The goal under Shinto is to become part of the *kami* by following certain rituals and customs. The religion also encourages obedience and proper behavior. The Yamato clan claimed that the emperor was a direct descendant of the sun goddess, one of the main forces in the Shinto religion.

Japan's tenuous relationship with China resulted in periods in which contact with it resulted in Chinese influences making their way into Japan. In 522, Korean and Chinese Buddhist missionaries went to Japan and unwittingly ignited a fascination with all things Chinese. While Buddhism did spread quickly in Japan, many Japanese chose instead to blend elements of Buddhism into Shinto or just practice both simultaneously.

Another significant Chinese influence occurred when **Prince Shotoku** in the seventh century borrowed ideas for bureaucratic and legal reforms from the Tang Dynasty. While he didn't get to implement them, they were enacted after his death and referred to as the **Takia Reforms** (645 BCE). These reforms created a centralized government with a bureaucracy based on the Chinese systems and a tremendous land redistribution process began in which land was nationalized and then redistributed. Peasant farmers were given land in exchange for a payment of a land tax and rice; the aristocrats retained a large amount of tax-exempt land and control over government offices. The Japanese created a law code modeled on the one in China and borrowed styles of art, medical practices, scientific developments, a system of weights and measures, and a calendar from China. Two things, though, that the Japanese did resist were Confucianism and the civil service exam.

Feudal Japan

In 794, the capital was moved to **Heian**, which remained the capital until 1869 and today is called Kyoto. During this period, Chinese influence began to wane and the power of the Japanese aristocratic families increased. One of those families, the **Fujiwara**, intermarried with the emperor's family and eventually began to exert real power over the country. While the emperor did continue to rule, he became more of a figurehead and the Fujiwara exerted control of the Japanese government from the early ninth to the mid-twelfth centuries. Under the Fujiwara and during the **Heian period**, Japanese society experienced a golden age.

Japanese feudalism developed around the same time as Western Europe, and although there are some similarities, they developed independently. With power moving toward aristocratic families and away from the emperor, power became decentralized—particularly the further one got from the capital. Over time, great warrior landowners living at a distance from the capital started building up private armies for protection, as well as control. Farmers and small landowners began to beseech these private armies for protection and traded their land for it. As a result, these landowning heads of armies became even more powerful and were called **samurai**. Samurai were counterparts to the feudal barons in medieval Europe, only they were part warrior and part nobility. They had a code of conduct similar to the idea of chivalry in Europe. They, in turn, gave land to lesser samurai who operated more as hired guns for pay. Peasants and artisans worked in the fields and shops to support the samurai class. Just as in European feudalism, the hierarchy was bound together in a land-for-loyalty exchange.

In 1338, the Fujiwara were challenged by the Minamoto. After numerous battles and plotting, the emperor made Minamoto Yoritomo the title of great general, or **shogun**. The shogun became, like the Fujiwara before them, the real rulers of the country, leaving the emperor in place as a figurehead. The shogun, in effect, became a military dictator and had control over the military, military finances, the laws, courts, and appointments.

Mesoamerica

Much of what is known about Mesoamerican civilization differs substantially from the civilizations reviewed above. Rather than building their cities along river systems, the peoples of the Americas built their cities along lakes or small rivers. They did not use metals in their tools. Indeed, they hardly used metal at all, except for artwork and jewelry. They did not use wheels or animals for transportation, largely because there were no such animals that they could use. Llamas, however, were used to carry small loads here and there. For the most part, transportation of people and goods was done by land or canoe. Writing systems, except for the Maya and possibly the Olmec, were unknown.

Mesoamerican civilization was largely based on a relationship between the gods and the environment. At Teotihuacan, people worshipped many gods and constructed enormous pyramids devoted to the Sun, the Moon, and to Quetzalcoatl. Human sacrifice was viewed as a sacred duty and essential to the well-being of society.

The first distinct Mesoamerican culture was the **Olmecs**, which settled where Mexico is today, and lived from 1200 to 1400 BCE. Olmec society centered on a priestly elite and peasant farmers and succeeded in producing a large food supply and great stone buildings. Some of their other achievements include developing a system of writing in hieroglyphics that, unfortunately, no one can translate today, and a calendar based on their observations of the heavens. Archaeologists believe that the Olmec, for religious reasons, carved enormous heads weighing as much as 18 tons out of volcanic rock. This sort of large-scale artwork that required the transport of such large rock more than eighty miles away indicates that the Olmec must have had a rather sophisticated political and social organizational system and that they had technology that enabled them to carry out such transport. The Olmec civilization disappeared mysteriously around 200 CE.

Mayan

From about 300 BCE to 800 CE, the **Maya** peoples, whose descendants still dwell in the same area of the Yucatan peninsula of Mexico, Guatemala, and Belize, had to contend with a tropical climate and fragile soils. Mayan civilization developed around religious centers that became a collection of city-states that were ruled by one king. The Mayans who lived near cities controlled their environment by draining swamps and building elevated fields. As a result, they were able to produce enough food to feed their growing population. Their social structure was made up of priests, nobles, and warriors who did not work, a smaller merchant class, peasants, and slaves.

The Golden Age of Mayan civilization was from 500 to about 850 CE. During that time, the Maya developed not only tremendous cities but also a complex calendar system. Although many Mayans lived in small rural areas, cities were developed as ceremonial centers with impressive religious temples. Rulers served priestly as well as political functions. The Mayans divided their cosmos into three parts: the heavens above, humans existing in the middle, and the underworld below. The Mayan creation story holds that the gods created humans out of maize and water. They also believed that the gods controlled agricultural cycles in exchange for sacrifices and bloodletting rituals. Much of their religious beliefs were concerned with the organization of time. If they failed to perform certain ceremonies at certain times, death would surely follow. This focus prompted the Mayans to become extremely particular about their calendar, which was based on a number structure of 20. The Mayans also created a system of time that was among the most accurate of its day. Mayan warfare also revolved around religious significance in that a certain number of days of religious ritual would precede a battle. One characteristic of Mayan warfare was that it was centered around the acquisition of slaves, rather than land. The slaves were used in large-scale building projects and in agricultural production. War and disagreements between the various city-states meant that they were often at war with one another and that there were many people who were slaves or who became sacrifices.

For reasons unknown, the Mayan civilization collapsed beginning about 850 CE as the people began to abandon their cities. Leading reasons seem to be environmental degradation and overuse of land, political dissension and unrest, natural disaster, and outside invaders.

Chapter 4

Competency 4: World History

The Aztecs

The **Aztec** confederation that arrived in central Mexico around the start of the 13th century was built on a policy of territorial expansion and was based on war, human sacrifice, and the veneration of women. Because war was used as a means to solidify their rule, Aztec rulers frequently went to war, promoting divine mandates, seizing land and peasants, and profiting in the spoils of war.

Despite the focus on war, women also held substantial power in Aztec society. Women dominated the household and markets, served as teachers and priestesses, and were seen as the founders of royal lineages. They built their capital at Tenochtitlan, which is modern-day Mexico City.

Despite having an empire that reached 12 million people at one point, the Aztecs did not use a bureaucratic form of government. By and large, they allowed people to govern themselves as long as they paid tribute. Roads were built to connect their vast empire and to make it easier for them to collect taxes or tributes. Because of the improved road systems, ideas and technology transferred from both the conquerors as well as the conquered.

Farming was done on artificial islands called Chinampas. From the peoples they conquered, the Aztecs borrowed architectural techniques, the calendar, and a writing system, as well as from their social system, their religion, and many of their arts and crafts. The Aztec emperor held absolute power and was usually elected by the priestly and warrior elite. The emperor's word was law, and he was treated like a god. As such, he was considered head of state, commander-in-chief of the military, and head priest.

The Aztecs were polytheistic, and priests used a sophisticated calendar to determine the feast days of each god. Priests also sought to predict the future by reading signs, and they sometimes ordered human sacrifice to appease the gods. These human sacrifices were most often people at the social margins of society, recent criminals, or slaves. It is estimated that tens of thousands of men and women were killed annually, and the Aztecs used this form of terrorism to control the people. The Aztec civilization ended partly because of rebellions and partly due to the arrival of the Spanish conquistadors in 1519.

The Incas

In the Andean regions of Peru, the **Incas** flourished from about 1200 CE until the 1500s CE. The Incan Empire was the largest in pre-Columbian America and possibly the largest empire in the world in the early 1500s. Unlike the Aztecs who practiced human sacrifice, the Inca method of control was not terrorism, but rather imperial unification over the almost 2,000 miles of territory that it covered. Like the Aztecs, the Inca emperor exercised total power and presided over a well-organized empire. The Incas forced their conquered peoples to adopt the Inca religion, language, and dress. Their accomplishments included an excellent system of roads, tremendously large-scale irrigation works, terraced hillsides to control erosion and grow crops, and an effective bureaucracy. Inca society was highly regimented, but the state took care of the poor and the aged.

Incan society divided itself into clans that were expected to provide labor and goods to their chiefs and to manage the exchange of goods. Trade became the primary means of interaction and unification among communities. Each community produced goods that suited its locale: coastal regions produced maize, fish, and cotton; mountain valleys produced quinoa, potatoes, and tubers; higher elevations contributed wool and metal; and the Amazonian region provided cocoa, medicines, and fruits. Communications between parts of the empire were made possible by an elaborate network of roads and bridges. Because the Incas lacked a written language, they kept records by using the *quipu*, a knotted string in which the knots were tied in certain ways to mean certain ideas. The Inca also developed a sort of pony express system of communication in which stations were set up every two miles and runners would deliver messages along the route. It proved to be an effective means of communication for people who lacked a written language.

The Incan society was polytheistic and the emperor was considered the child of the sun god, who was at the center of the state religion. Incan religion had a strong moral aspect, emphasizing rewards for good behavior and punishments for bad behavior. Their emperors were mummified after death and were considered the intermediaries between the gods and their people. Incan rulers, because they were considered gods, only married their sisters (with few exceptions) to keep their bloodlines pure. In order for an emperor to ensure his place in the afterlife, he had to secure new land, and so the empire was always in a state of expansion.

COMPETENCY 4.4

Identify the major contributions of the Middle Ages, the Renaissance, and the Reformation period to Western civilization.

Middle Ages

The Middle Ages is a dynamic period during which the idea of Europe as a distinct cultural unit emerged. During late antiquity and the early Middle Ages, political, social, economic, and cultural structures were profoundly reorganized. Roman imperial traditions gave way to those of the Germanic peoples who established kingdoms in the former Western Empire. The Middle Ages period can be divided into three parts: Lower Middle Ages: 500–1000 CE; High Middle Ages: 1000–1250 CE; and Late Middle Ages: 1250–1500 CE. Each part made major contributions to Western civilization.

Lower Middle Ages: 500–1000 CE

The Lower Middle Ages began after the fall of the Roman Empire, which had left a vacuum in many areas of life. The Roman Catholic Church provided a basis for social unity and contributed, in part, to events in the Carolingian Renaissance: Schools, development of manorial and feudal systems, the Crusades. These, in turn, contributed to the rise of European monarchies.

Competency 4: World History

Contributions of the Catholic Church

Monasticism and Monasteries: Monks took on important roles during this time, primarily serving as protectors of a tremendous collection of learning—as monks tended to be one of the few members of European society who could read and write. Many monasteries contained libraries and places where they copied books and compiled illuminating manuscripts of various works, most notably religious texts, and preserved some of the books and texts from the ancient Greeks and Romans. The monasteries acted as schools for the upper classes and were sometimes inns, hospitals, or places of refuge in times of war. Monks, like St. Patrick and St. Boniface, also served as missionaries to the "barbarians" and spread the influence of the Catholic Church throughout Europe, eventually making it the major religion of the area. Monasteries also became important reservoirs for horticultural and agricultural skills. Monks were experts with herbs and cultivated their own grains, vegetables, and orchards. From their horticultural activities, the monks collected and developed many medicines. Many unique plants would be kept in monasteries and would become important later, during the Renaissance.

Integration of the Church into the Feudal System: The feudal system was a trademark of medieval Europe, and the Church played an important role in it. The church controlled about one-third of all the lands in Western Europe tax-free, and the members of what the French would refer to as the "First Estate" had enormous amounts of wealth and power throughout the period. Some of the Church's excesses would be exactly what people would rebel against later, during the Reformation and the French Revolution. The Church demanded tithes from the people who lived in Christendom—a tax of one-tenth of one's assets that would be payable to the Church.

Romanesque Architectural Style: The practice of using rounded arches, barrel vaults, thick walls, buildings with dark, simplistic interiors and small windows, usually at the top of a wall, typified the architectural style of churches found throughout Europe.

Contributions of the Carolingian Renaissance

Creation of schools: In an effort to reform the church, Charlemagne, King of the Franks, instituted clerical schools and created centers of learning that combined church and education. Students in these schools studied religion, music, grammar, and other subjects. Charlemagne invited scholars from all over Europe to come teach and study. The lasting contribution from this system would be the distribution of knowledge throughout Europe, not only because of this scholarly exchange but also because the scholars in their free time copied the ancient texts from Charlemagne's massive collection and sent the texts all over Europe. This enabled many valuable works from the ancient world to be preserved.

Carolingian miniscule: This was the creation of a uniform writing style with capital and small letters as well as spacing so that the Roman alphabet could be read more easily. This advancement became a standard in all of the languages of Western civilization.

Feudalism: This decentralized political, economic, military, and social system of personal ties and obligations bound vassals to their lords. The nature of feudalism varied in different areas and changed over time. But at its base were serfs—peasants who were bound to the land. They worked on the lord's property three or four days a week in return for the right to work their own land.

Manorialism: Manorialism was an economic system in which large estates, granted by the king to nobles, encompassed self-sufficient villages populated by serfs. By 800 CE, about 60 percent of Western Europe was *enserfed*, meaning that there was a contractual agreement between lords, who provided justice and protection, and serfs, who provided their labor for a fixed amount of time each year. Large manors might incorporate several villages. The lands surrounding the villages were usually divided into long strips with common land between strips. Ownership was divided among the lord and his serfs. A long-term effect of feudalism and manorialism was agricultural surpluses. Surpluses meant that some members of the society were relieved from agricultural production and could move into other specialized areas. As a result, craftspeople emerged, and towns and cities grew. With increased crafts, Europeans began to trade more with others, and these skilled craftspeople began to earn extra money. This led to the development of a banking system and eventually a "middle class."

High Middle Ages: 1000–1250 CE

The High Middle Ages were marked by economic and territorial expansion, demographic and urban growth, the emergence of national identity, and the restructuring of secular and ecclesiastical institutions. It was the era of the Crusades, Gothic art and architecture, the papal monarchy, the birth of the university, the recovery of ancient Greek thought, and the soaring intellectual achievements of St. Thomas Aquinas (ca. 1224–1274). During this period, the principle of common law was established in England by Henry II who also created the idea of a grand jury and trial by jury. The agreement known as the Magna Carta signed by English King John provided a foundation for the future U.S. Constitution, as well as constitutions in other countries. Society during the High Middle Ages separated into three distinct classes: clergy, who were in charge of spiritual matters; nobility (landowners), whose job was to protect their subjects; and the Third Estate, which consisted of everyone else—middle class, peasants, serfs, and slaves.

The Magna Carta

While earlier kings of England—Henry I, Stephen, and Henry II—had issued charters making promises or concessions to their barons, the kings were not threatened, and the agreements were broadly phrased. But new taxes on the barons and a weakened position by the crown resulted in the barons demanding their "rights."

Although written in stages, the Magna Carta starts with a preamble and contains several sections. These included the following: assertion of a "free church," feudal law, rights of sub-tenants, reform of the law and of justice, control of behavior of royal officials, and stipulations of what would occur if the king failed to adhere to the agreement. Language found in the United States Constitution, as well state constitutions, can be traced to the Magna Carta, which was signed by King John in 1215.

Gothic Architectural Style

The Gothic style of architecture featured pointed arches, high narrow vaults, thinner walls than the earlier Romanesque style, flying buttresses, and elaborate, ornate, airier interiors with stained glass windows. Over time, Gothic cathedrals became more than places of worship, as the Church sponsored artists and sculptors to decorate them with their work. Much of the development of art during this period centered on religion.

Town Growth

Advances in technology and agriculture (e.g., heavier plow, horse collar, and three-field system of farming) increased productivity, which increased population and resulted in subsequent growth in towns. But towns need protection, which contributed to the development of weaponry (e.g., axes, pikes, and two-edged swords) that could be used on horseback. A middle class of **burghers** (wealthy merchants who lived within the town) and **bourgeoisies** (townspeople who were neither nobles nor peasants) formed.

Crusades

The increased authority of the papacy and the relative decline in the power of the emperor became clear in the emergence of the Crusades as a major preoccupation of Europe. Although the capture of Jerusalem (1099) and the establishment of a Latin kingdom in Palestine were offset by disasters and quarrels, the papacy gained greatly in prestige and strengthened its position in relation to the emperor and Germany, which had avoided participation in this first of many crusades. For more than two centuries, the Crusades remained a powerful movement headed by the pope. Numerous crusades were waged in the Holy Land, and the crusading ideal was applied to military and religious campaigns in Spain and Eastern Europe. Later popes launched Crusades against heretics and opponents of papal authority and sanctioned the emergence of military orders. The Crusades thus reflected the widespread devotion to the church and to its leader, the pope. However, one benefit of the Crusades was the expansion of trade routes across the Mediterranean. As a result of these, with more contact with people outside of Europe, ideas and thinking expanded and people actually began to question old ways of thinking. The Church responded by clamping down on what was termed **heresies**.

Scholasticism

As people expanded their way of thinking, more institutions began to develop to explore ideas; these **universities** inspired a greater movement to study some of the ideas and advances made in the Muslim cultures, ideas from law, science, philosophy, and medicine. As more of the texts from the ancient world that had been housed in the Muslim world for centuries made their way to Europe, the ideas of Aristotle, Ptolemy, and other Greeks were brought back to Europe to be studied.

Late Middle Ages: 1250–1500 CE

In some ways, the Late Middle Ages represents a time of contrast. Prosperity and growth in Europe slowed. Famines and plagues, including **Black Death**, decimated populations, killing one-third to one-half of the people in Europe. This resulted in social unrest and uprisings, including an end to the feudal system due to a lack of a labor force. Rivalries within the Catholic Church caused dissention and factions, and the **Inquisition** resulted in the persecution of individuals who were considered to be heretics. Thomas Aquinas asserted that faith and reason were not incompatible. On the other hand, arts and sciences flourished as printing was invented and information spread more easily. A new **guild** system created a developmental path for artisans to gain skills. This resulted in not only quality-controlled merchandise and controlled prices, but also the beginnings of unions.

The end of the period became an **Age of Discovery** in which Columbus traveled to the Americas and Vasco da Gama became the first to sail directly from Europe to India.

The Renaissance (1500s–1800s)

The Renaissance, which means "rebirth," emphasized new learning, including the rediscovery of much classical material and new art styles. Italian city-states, such as Venice, Milan, Padua, Pisa, and especially Florence, were the home to many Renaissance developments, which were limited to the rich elite.

Conditions that led to the Renaissance

- Crusades and new trade routes gave Europeans contact with more advanced civilizations, inspired new ways of thinking.
- Because of scandals that occurred, the Church lost much of its power, and people began to doubt its ultimate authority.
- With increased trade, and growth of middle classes, new ways of thinking emerged that reflected more desires for worldly goods and less concern about life in the hereafter.
- Competition among wealthy patrons led to developments in education and art, since wealthy people battled each other through sponsorship of scholars and artists.

Chapter 4

Competency 4: World History

Humanism

Humanism was a new philosophy that defined the Renaissance. It consisted of four main aspects:

1. Admiration and emulation of the Ancient Greeks and Romans
2. Philosophy of enjoying this life, instead of just waiting for the next one
3. The glorification of humans and the belief that individuals can do anything
4. The belief that humans deserved to be the center of attention

As intellectuals delved more into the writings and ideas of the ancient Greeks and Romans, they were struck with the ancients' complete lack of preoccupation with ideas of salvation and afterlife that had dominated medieval thoughts and had resulted in societies becoming less concerned with improving their living conditions. Most humanists were actually religious. The main difference between the beliefs of the church and of the humanists was that the humanists believed that this life was important and should be enjoyed, and that human accomplishments in the scholarly, artistic, and political realms should be celebrated; the church did not agree, and felt that people should focus on awaiting the afterlife instead. Although Humanism was a movement chiefly found among intellectuals, it had a huge impact on the age. Though many believe that Humanism replaced religion in the Renaissance; in reality, the two coexisted. One impact of Humanism that has dominated Western ideas even today is the concern and focus on the individual and individuality, and a subsequent lessening of the import or authority of institutions.

Literature, Art, and Scholarship

Humanists, as both orators and poets, were inspired by and imitated works of the classical past. They contributed to literature, art, and scholarship of the time. The literature was more secular and wide-ranging than that of the Middle Age and included Dante's *Divine Comedy*. But it was **Gutenberg's** invention of the printing press that had the most impact and encouraged authors to write in their own common languages rather than in the classical languages of Greek and Latin. As a result of the printing press, literature was available to more people, which spread the ideas of the Renaissance.

Artists also broke with the medieval past, in both technique and content. Renaissance art sometimes used religious topics but often dealt with secular themes or portraits of individuals. Oil paints, chiaroscuro, and linear perspectives produced works of energy in three dimensions. Paintings tended to have more detailed backgrounds, were more realistic, and were more geometrically precise. Subjects also tended to show more emotion than in the paintings of earlier artists. **Leonardo da Vinci** (1452–1519) produced numerous works, including *The Last Supper* and *Mona Lisa*. **Michelangelo** (1475–1564) produced masterpieces in architecture, sculpture *(David)*, and painting (the Sistine Chapel ceiling). His work was a bridge to a new, non-Renaissance style called Mannerism. Raphael (1483–1520) used his mastery of perspective and ancient styles to produce works of harmony, beauty, and serenity, and to convey a sense of peace. **Titian** (1479–1576) was a painter who painted scenes of luxury in such a vivid, immediate way that his paintings seem real to the viewer.

Renaissance scholars were more practical and secular than medieval ones. Manuscript collections enabled scholars to study the primary sources and to reject all traditions that had been built up since classical times. Also, scholars participated in the lives of their cities as active politicians. **Machiavelli** (1469–1527) was one of the most famous scholars. His work *The Prince* is amoral in tone and describes how a political leader could obtain and hold power by acting only in his own self-interest.

The Reformation

The Reformation destroyed Western Europe's religious unity and introduced new ideas about the relationships between God, the individual, and society. Its course was greatly influenced by politics and led, in most areas, to the subjection of the church to the political rulers. It also divided the Western Church into two halves: Catholicism and Protestantism.

Long-Term Causes of the Reformation

- Growth in the power of the secular king and the decrease in the power of the Pope
- Popular discontent with the empty Church rituals
- Movement towards more personal ways of communicating with God
- Fiscal crisis in the Church that led to corruption and abuses of power

Short-Term Causes of the Reformation

- **John Wycliffe** and his supporters, the Lollards, argued for a simplification of Church doctrine and a lessening of priests' power and questioned the idea of transubstantiation.
- **Jan Hus** was burned at the stake in 1415 after he argued that the priests weren't a holy group, questioned transubstantiation, and said that the priest and the people should all have both the wine and the bread. His followers fought and won against the emperor, who let them set up their own church.
- **The Avignon Exile and Great Schism** both undermined the power and prestige of the Church and made many people question the absolute power of the Papacy.
- **The printing press** enabled quick distribution of ideas from those dissatisfied with the church, and now people could read the Bible for themselves and make up their own minds about truths.

Competency 4: World History

Key Reformers

Martin Luther (1483–1546) was a German who led the Protestant Reformation. He could not reconcile the problem of the sinfulness of the individual with the justice of God. During his studies of the Bible, Luther came to believe that personal efforts—good works, such as a Christian life and attention to the sacraments of the church—could not "earn" the sinner salvation, but that belief and faith were the only way to obtain grace. By 1515, Luther believed that "justification by faith alone" was the road to salvation. This called into question many of the basic tenets of the Catholic Church. So, in 1517, Luther nailed **95 theses**, or statements, about indulgences, or the cancellation of a sin in return for money, to the door of the Wittenberg church, and challenged the practice of selling indulgences. At this time, he was seeking to reform the church, not divide it. In 1519, Luther presented various criticisms of the church and was driven to say that only the Bible, not religious traditions or papal statements, could determine correct religious practices and beliefs. In 1521, Pope Leo X excommunicated Luther for his beliefs. Luther's followers split from the Catholic Church to form the Protestant tradition.

In 1536, **John Calvin** (1509–1564), a Frenchman, arrived in Geneva, a Swiss city-state which had adopted an anti-Catholic position. He left after his first efforts at reform failed. Upon his return in 1540, Geneva became the center of the Reformation. Calvin's analysis of Christianity had a universal appeal. Calvin emphasized the doctrine of predestination (God knew who would obtain salvation before those people were born) and believed that church and state should be united. Calvinism triumphed as the majority religion in Scotland, under the leadership of John Knox (ca. 1514–1572), and in the United Provinces of the Netherlands. Puritans in England and New England also accepted Calvinism.

English attempts at reformation differed from the rest of Europe. Rather than individuals taking the lead, personal and political decisions by the rulers determined much of the course of the Reformation. In 1533, **Henry VIII** became infatuated with Anne Boleyn and was denied an annulment of his marriage by the Catholic Church. However, Protestant beliefs and practices made little headway during Henry's reign, as he accepted transubstantiation, enforced celibacy among the clergy, and otherwise made the English church conform to most medieval practices. Under Edward VI (1547–1553), son of Henry VIII who succeeded to the throne at age 10, the English church adopted Calvinism. Clergy were allowed to marry, communion by the laity expanded, and images were removed from churches. Doctrine included justification by faith, the denial of transubstantiation, and only two sacraments. Some reformers wanted to purify (hence their name, the "Puritans") the church of its remaining Catholic aspects. The resulting church was called Anglican. It was Protestant in doctrine and practice but retained most of the physical possessions, such as buildings, and many of the powers of the medieval church, such as church courts.

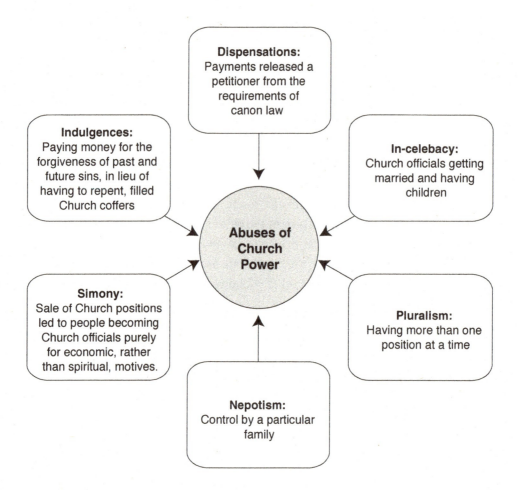

The Counter-Reformation

The Counter-Reformation brought changes to the portion of the Western church that retained its allegiance to the pope. Ignatius of Loyola (1491–1556), a former soldier, founded the Society of Jesus in 1540 to lead the attack on Protestantism. Jesuits became the leaders of the Counter-Reformation. The Sack of Rome in 1527, when soldiers of the Holy Roman Emperor captured and looted Rome, was seen by many as a judgment of God against the lives of the Renaissance popes. In 1534, Paul III became pope and attacked abuses while reasserting papal leadership.

The Wars of Religion (1560–1648)

The period from approximately 1560 to 1648 witnessed continuing warfare, primarily between Protestants and Catholics. In the latter half of the sixteenth century, the fighting was along the Atlantic seaboard between Calvinists and Catholics; after 1600, the warfare spread to Germany, where Calvinists, Lutherans, and Catholics fought.

Competency 4: World History

- **The Catholic Crusade:** The territories of **Charles V**, the Holy Roman Emperor, were divided in 1556 between Ferdinand, Charles's brother, and Philip II (1556–1598), Charles's son. Ferdinand received Austria, Hungary, Bohemia, and the title of Holy Roman Emperor. Philip received Spain, Milan, Naples, the Netherlands, and the New World. It was Philip, not the pope, who led the Catholic attack on Protestants. Spain dominated the Mediterranean following a series of wars led by Philip's half-brother, Don John, against Moslem (largely Turkish) forces. Don John secured the Mediterranean for Christian merchants with a naval victory over the Turks at Lepanto off the coast of Greece in 1571. Portugal was annexed by Spain in 1580 following the death of the king without a clear successor. This gave Philip the only other large navy of the day, as well as Portuguese territories around the globe.

- **England and Spain:** England was ruled by two queens, **Mary I** (reigned 1553–1558), who married Philip II, and then **Elizabeth I** (reigned 1558–1603), while three successive kings of France from 1559 to 1589 were influenced by their mother, **Catherine de' Medici** (1519–1589). Mary I sought to make England Catholic. She executed many Protestants, earning the name "Bloody Mary" from opponents. Mary married Philip II, king of Spain, and organized her foreign policy around Spanish interests. They had no children. Elizabeth I, a Protestant, achieved a religious settlement between 1559 and 1563 that left England with a church governed by bishops and practicing Catholic rituals but maintaining a Calvinist doctrine. Catholics participated in several rebellions and plots. **Mary, Queen of Scots**, had fled to England from Scotland in 1568 after alienating the nobles there. In Catholic eyes, she was the legitimate queen of England. Several plots and rebellions to put Mary on the throne led to her execution in 1587. Elizabeth was formally excommunicated by the pope in 1570. In 1588, as part of his crusade and his effort to stop England from supporting the rebels in the Netherlands, Philip II sent the Armada, a fleet of more than 125 ships, to convey troops from the Netherlands to England as part of a plan to make England Catholic. The Armada was defeated by a combination of superior English naval tactics and a wind that made it impossible for the Spanish to accomplish their goal. A peace treaty between Spain and England was signed in 1604, but England remained an opponent of Spain.

- **The Thirty Years' War:** Calvinism was spreading throughout Germany. The Peace of Augsburg (1555), which settled the disputes between Lutherans and Catholics, had no provision for Calvinists. Lutherans gained more territories through conversions and often took control of previous church-states—a violation of the Peace of Augsburg. A Protestant alliance under the leadership of the Calvinist ruler of the Palatinate opposed a Catholic League led by the ruler of Bavaria. Religious wars were common. The war brought great destruction to Germany, leading to a decline in population of perhaps one-third, or more, in some areas. Germany remained divided and without a strong government until the nineteenth century. The Catholic crusade to reunite Europe failed, largely due to the efforts of the Calvinists. The religious distribution of Europe has not changed significantly since 1648. Nobles, resisting the increasing power of the state, usually dominated the struggle. France, then Germany, fell apart due to the wars. France was reunited in the seventeenth century. Spain began a decline that ended its role as a great power of Europe.

COMPETENCY 4.5

Identify the social, cultural, political, and economic characteristics of African, Asian, and Eastern European societies from 1500 to 1900.

Africa

Social

By far the biggest social impact in Africa during this period was the emergence of the slave trade, which depopulated tremendous areas throughout Africa. Typically, the Atlantic slave trade sought men, and the Eastern slave trade to the Islamic empires sought women. It is estimated that between 1500 and 1900, more than 12 million Africans were taken just in the Atlantic slave trade alone, and perhaps as many as 50 million were taken altogether. The effects on the various societies were tremendous and are still being felt today as the continent still struggles to recover from almost 400 years of losing its strongest men and women. When many of the able-bodied people from ages 18–40 are removed from a civilization, it affects the civilization in numerous directions—economically, socially, culturally, and politically.

Portugal was one of the first European countries to plunder the African continent in search of slaves. The Portuguese first targeted Northern Mauritania in 1444 and eventually moved their way down the western coast of Africa. The Dutch, French, Spanish, and British soon followed in their footsteps.

As the profit from Africans selling Africans into slavery was tremendous, many Africans engaged in the trade. Slavery itself was not a new concept in Africa, and most families actually had slaves in them. Because private land ownership was largely absent during this time, slaves were one of the few forms of wealth-producing property that Africans could possess. But slavery within African societies was different from the Atlantic Slave Trade experiences. In Africa, usually slaves were taken in times of war; they were allowed to marry and have children; and they were treated well within the household. In an effort to get more slaves to sell to the white slave sellers, more societies launched wars deeper and deeper within the African continent in order to meet the demand.

Slave exports helped create a number of large and powerful kingdoms that relied on a constant warfare to generate the great numbers of human captives required for trade with the Europeans. For example, the Yoruba kingdom of Oyo on the Guinea coast, founded sometime before 1500, used its rather large army and iron technology to capture tremendous numbers of slaves and sell them. In the nineteenth century, the kingdom of Dahomey, in what is now the Republic of Benin, became a major slaveholder. The Kongo also became big slave exporters, starting their relationship with the Portuguese as early as 1483. The Kongo exported slaves and ivory in exchange for European luxury goods and guns. The Kongo developed in what would become a typical pattern for those African countries who engaged in the trade. Over time, as the Kongo sought to find more and more slaves to trade, the country focused itself on trying to find slaves. As a result, productive workers were removed from the area and an economy developed that was dependent upon slavery. Over time, the Kongo became more dependent upon the Portuguese and was unable to provide basic necessities for itself. The Portuguese desire for slaves undermined the authority of the kings of the Kongo and the state gradually declined. Eventually, war broke out and the kingdom was mostly destroyed. The Asante Kingdom on the Gold Coast of West Africa also became a major slave exporter in the eighteenth century.

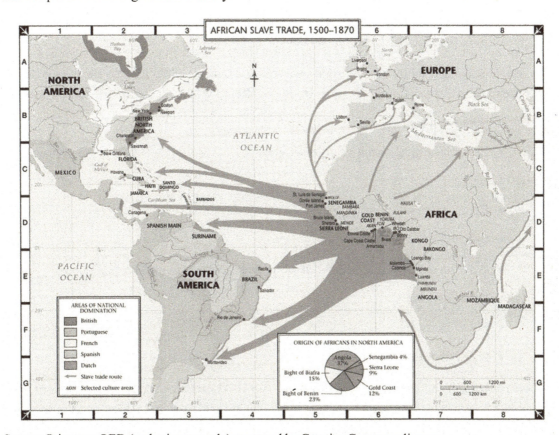

Source: Princeton QED (qed.princeton.edu) governed by Creative Commons license.

The slave trade had many social effects on Africa:

- Africa was seen as a cheap source of labor.

- The loss of so many able-bodied men from Africa made it rather easy for the continent to be colonized, as Africa's ability to defend itself was compromised.

- In areas where the majority of individuals that were taken as slaves were men, women were thrust into roles previously occupied by the men. Because there were so few men, polygamy increased dramatically.

- Little development or modernization took place.

- In an effort to meet the demands of the slave trade, laws were changed that made crimes punishable by slavery.

- Populations in the cities decreased as people fled cities to avoid being captured. Without cities, civilization begins to suffer.

- Contact with the outside world became quite limited as slave-traders no longer brought with them new ideas or technologies.

- Racism took hold, largely to justify and perpetuate the exploitation of Blacks, who were portrayed as lesser human beings.

A second major social influence on Africa was religion, and all of the African societies had religious systems. Those that followed "African Traditional Religion" had the following commonalities:

- Belief in a supreme God
- Belief in several divinities or lesser gods
- Belief in ancestors
- Belief in life after death
- Belief in reincarnation
- Belief in the power of the spoken word, like incantations and songs
- Belief in prayers
- Belief in sacrifice
- Roles of priests, holy men, seers, and spirit mediums

As slave-traders and others from the East and the West came to Africa, other religions also found homes in Africa as Christianity, Islam, and Judaism flourished in different parts of the continent.

Cultural

African music took a central role in almost all African societies. There was music for almost all occasions—work, naming ceremonies, marriages, funerals, etc.

African art was inspired by religion, kingship, and personal beautification. Traditionally art was made for the upper classes and royalty, but in the 1500s–1900s, it became accessible to all. Some of the art forms included specialized wood, bronze, brass and stone sculptures, painting of homes, body adornments, charms, and amulets.

Competency 4: World History

Political

Both internal and external forces affected political development throughout the African continent.

Internally, there was a rise of empires and nation-states:

- Ghana, Mali, and Songhai
- Kanem, Bornu, and Hausa States
- Ife, Oyo, Benin, Dahomey, Asante, and Kongo

Europeans came to Africa for the three G's: God, Gold, and Glory. While the Europeans benefited greatly, this was disastrous for the continent. Trade in gold, ivory, and pepper increased, and the slave trade developed. South Africa and Mozambique began to have substantial European influence. Forts and castles were constructed to protect the newcomers and their interests. Benin slipped into corruption and decay. The introduction of European weapons changed the balance of power that previously existed.

Economic

During this time period, pastoral and agricultural economies developed, which successfully supplied the food needed for the population. In time, surplus food enabled a market economy to develop.

Manufacturing also began to develop. Some of the main manufacturing that occurred were tanning from hides and skins, metallurgy, and textile manufacturing.

The slave trade shifted the existing trade routes within Africa, causing earlier profitable trading patterns and routes to disappear.

Asia

An important development during the early modern years was the development of the Gunpowder Empires. During this period, huge empires developed that were able to grow in part because of their adaptation of gunpowder for use by their armies. The Mongol invasions were significant because their knowledge of firepower and arms made those who were wiped out marginal. The Mongols also brought something called *yasa* law (secular law) and imposed it on the communities they conquered, and which the Ottomans later adopted as well. Both the Ottomans and Safavids also benefited from the introduction of gunpowder, guns, and canons and used them to gain a technological advantage over the Europeans. The Ottomans, Safavids, Mughals, and rulers of China and Japan were able to capitalize on that power, and so began a period in which they were able to assume a great deal of political power, build opulent cities, and flourish in the arts.

Ottoman Empire

Social

The social structure of the Ottoman Empire consisted of a cosmopolitan, heterogeneous mix of peoples from many races, religions, ethnicities and who had different languages. The Ottoman Empire sought to erase some of these differences and get people to think of themselves as "Ottoman." The inability of the Ottoman Empire to do this in the wake of increasing nationalism in the nineteenth century eventually led to its dismantling, the emergence of "Turkism," and the eventual formation of the Republic of Turkey after World War I.

The Ottoman Empire emerged from small tribal groups that had come from Central Asia and had been one of the Seljuk Turks tribes. Eventually, small princedoms began to be grouped under the rule of one state and thus began a process of absorptions that attracted more warriors. In 1326, the Osman and his army captured Bursa and used it as a base to set up the capital of the burgeoning empire. In 1453, under Mehmed the Conqueror, the Muslims defeated the Byzantine Empire and captured Constantinople. They made Constantinople their capital city and with that began their multi-cultural approach to rule that featured the tactics of assimilation, toleration, and accommodation. They allowed Christian and Jewish subjects there to continue to practice their religion and organized them into different legally-recognized groups that enabled them a certain amount of internal autonomy to retain their religious authorities, administer justice in matters of personal law (like marriage, inheritance, etc.), and regulate their own economic, social, and legal affairs. Non-Muslims did have a degree of freedom in that they did not have to serve in the military. They were allowed to practice their own religion in freedom, but they did have to pay taxes. Muslims did not have to pay taxes, but they did have to serve in the military.

There were two main social groups in the Ottoman society: the ruling class and the subjects. Total loyalty and devotion to the sultan and the Ottoman State were the chief requirements for someone to belong to the ruling class. Since this was the only determining line between the ruling class and the subjects, there was a lot of mobility in the social structure. There were four main groups in the ruling class. First was the palace section, which provided leadership with the sultan at the head of the class. Then there was the military, the Janissaries, who protected the empire and expanded into new areas. Next was the treasury, in charge of taxes. Finally, there was the religious section with the religious scholars who made sure that the **Shari'ah**, Muslim religious law, was followed. The religious section included mosques and schools. Ottoman subjects were largely divided according to occupation groups. Peasants farmed the land that was leased to them by the government; artisans crafted and were organized into craft guilds; merchants traded goods; and pastorals were divided into clans led by a hereditary chief.

One issue that the Ottomans had to resolve was not only how to expand, but how to continue to expand and meld these areas into the Ottoman Empire. One tactic that they used was the slave system. The system, however, was quite unlike the slave system of the Americas. The Ottoman slave system allowed for slaves to be educated and trained and to accumulate money and power. They found their slaves primarily in two places: the Balkans and the Caucuses. Boys periodically

Competency 4: World History

were taken from Christian villages and moved to various parts of the Ottoman Empire where they would work in a variety of fields. In the sorting process, the Ottomans would use a science called **phrenology**, where they determined a boy's capabilities through an examination of the bumps on his head. The lucky few would be taken to Istanbul, converted to Islam, trained, educated, and then entered into service as **Janissaries**, the military arm of the Ottoman Empire. Female slaves, who typically came from the Caucasus region, were brought to serve in domestic settings. Some female slaves were brought into the Sultan's harem where they would undergo vigorous education and training in the hope of being married to an Ottoman official. Only very few were ever chosen to be the sexual partners of the Sultan.

Women did not have as much access to public power as men did; however, women in elite households, especially those in the Sultan's household, could be rather powerful political figures. Women could hold and inherit property, conduct business, run charitable foundations, and defend their interests in Islamic courts.

Cultural

Coffeehouses were a center of male public life. They were places where men could drink coffee and also trade news and gossip, as well as see entertainment by storytellers and musicians. The bathhouse also served a vital function in Ottoman society, being a place where ideas could be exchanged and alliances forged. Women in particular used the bathhouse as a place to arrange marriages, heal rifts between families, and conduct business.

Under **Suleiman the Magnificent**, from 1520–1566, Ottoman culture reached its zenith as he poured money into public construction and financed learning institutions and the arts. Architects, most notably **Sinan**, a Janissary of Armenian descent, built magnificent mosques and palaces, bridges, and other public buildings throughout Anatolia. During this time, there were great literary and artistic achievements that rivaled the achievements of the European Renaissance.

Political

As head of the Ottoman empire, the Sultan (which means "power holder") had immense power, issued all laws, and made all major decisions. He did, however, have numerous advisors, mostly gained from the Janissaries. Typically, the Sultan's sons would be sent away at a young age to the provinces and given an area to rule. This period acted as a training ground for them, as they, with their mother's help, would have to amass a retinue of advisors and learn how to rule. There was no system of primogeniture as there was in Europe. Instead, the next Sultan was chosen based on which son was closest in proximity to the capital at the time of the ruler's death, or by fratricide (a son's ability to eliminate/kill all of his brothers). Another important power-holder in the Ottoman Empire was the **valide sultan**, or the Sultan's mother. She was in charge of reproductive politics, as she decided who could be the sexual partners of the Sultan. She was in charge of the enormous budget of the Harem, doled out all payments to the women of the Harem, and was in charge of the training of the next sultan.

A hallmark of Ottoman society was that it was a partial **meritocracy**. Individuals with talent received preferential treatment. The early Ottomans drew significantly upon both Jewish and Christian talent, often raising them ahead of Muslim Turks due to their performance rather than their religion or connections.

A turning point in Ottoman history was the **Treaty of Karlowitz** by which the Ottomans had to give up some claims to Hungary and Transylvania and which was thought by some to usher in the "decline." The empire went through a period of restructuring in the nineteenth century where the minorities gained more freedoms in an effort to keep them from wanting to break away from the Empire. Restructuring ultimately did not work, as the Ottoman Empire fell victim to both European nationalism, as well as crafty European bankers all too willing to help finance Ottoman modernization efforts and who ultimately bankrupted the empire.

Economic

Artisans in urban areas were organized into **guilds** that helped to regulate membership and set standards of production that resulted in Ottoman goods being of high quality. Guilds also had social functions as well. They took care of sick or injured members and facilitated care of widows. In festivals, guilds would take part in grand processions that would demonstrate the mastery of their craft.

China

During this period, the Ming Dynasty ruled until 1644, followed by the Qing (or Manchu) Dynasty, which ruled until 1912.

Ming Dynasty

The Ming had increasingly isolated themselves from Chinese life, ruling through eunuch servants and administrators. By closing itself off, the dynasty also chose not to develop a shipping industry, and its navy was effectively inoperable. With no one to protect them, the Chinese suffered tremendously from pirates and smugglers on China's eastern coast, and the government could not respond quickly or well. These problems continued when a series of famines struck China in the early seventeenth century. The government failed to organize effective relief efforts and the peasants revolted.

The Ming Dynasty closed China to foreigners. Foreigners were allowed in some restricted areas but were monitored closely. Chinese merchants were not encouraged to trade overseas. This resulted in a slow loss of the technical superiority that China had possessed. By the end of the Ming Dynasty, China no longer could compete with Europe.

Competency 4: World History

Social

The Ming focused on eradicating anything foreign from Chinese society and returned to traditional values. The family was a central institution in Chinese society, and renewed attention to it drove Ming social developments. Sons continued to be preferred over daughters, and women's lives centered around home activities, such as raising children, maintaining the household, and controlling home expenses. Some women, however, did work as midwives, textile workers, and performers.

The patriarchal family took center stage in Chinese society. The Confucian ideal of filial piety was applied both to the patriarch of the family and to the emperor. The father was venerated as the head of the household, and all male ancestors were worshipped.

Cultural

Education centered on preparation for the civil service exams. Local education flourished and enabled rural and urban poor a chance to take the exams.

Economic

The dynasty attempted to prop up the economy by changing paper money into a system based on silver currency. But when the American silver flooded the market, it caused tremendous inflation in China.

Merchants were at the bottom of Ming society as they were seen as people who did not actually produce anything but profited from the work of others. They were seen as supporting foreigners and almost engaging in robbery.

Political

Prior to the Ming Dynasty, the government consisted of a central administrative system known as the Three Departments and Six Ministries. The Ming administration had a single department called the Secretariat, which managed the Six Ministries. In the early part of the dynasty, power was decentralized. Government officials were often sent to the provinces to serve as governors and by the end of the dynasty government officials often oversaw two or more provinces.

Qing (Manchu) Dynasty

The Qing Dynasty began as a Manchurian chieftain who, as the result of inter-tribe feuding, gained control and renounced the Ming Dynasty. Mongols and Han Chinese ultimately joined the cause to overcome the Ming Dynasty. The Manchurians were not ethnically Chinese. Rather, the Qing chose to remain an ethnic elite and forbade interaction with the Chinese—making it actually illegal for the Chinese to learn the Manchu language, to marry a Manchu, or to migrate to the Manchu homeland. The Manchurians only comprised about 3 percent of the population in China and were unable to run the government by themselves. They opened positions to only the best and the brightest of Chinese. Although the highest offices were reserved for the Manchu, it was Chinese officials who, in nonmilitary positions, mostly presided over the Manchu outside of the capital. In many provincial government positions, a system of dual appointments was used—with the substantive work being done by the Chinese appointee and the Manchu there to ensure the Chinese loyalty to Qing rule. Realizing that it would be senseless to impose a new system on the Chinese, many of the Ming institutions were retained. For instance, the emperors continued to uphold Confucian court practices and presided over temple rituals.

Social

The Qing social hierarchy consisted of privileged classes, commoners, and the lowest of the low. The privileged classes consisted of the emperor, scholar bureaucrats, and landowners. There were three groups that comprised the commoner group: peasants (they were the most numerous), artisans and workers, and merchants (ranked at the bottom in terms of social rank, but in terms of wealth they were quite high). The lowest of the low included actors, beggars, and prostitutes.

Cultural

The Manchu emperors supported Chinese literary and historical projects of enormous scope, and much of China's ancient literature was protected because of these Manchu projects. A proliferation of books resulted from the invention of woodblock printing. Producing more books, led to high literacy rates and a more educated and reflective population. Traditional opera, drama, literature, and artistic techniques reached new heights. Of particular interest were themes devoted to Chinese historical topics and heroes. The emperors studied and understood Confucianism and patronized Confucian schools and academies, opened up a National library, and had an encyclopedia of Chinese history and thought written.

Economic

Qing emperors looked after people's welfare and promoted agriculture. During the rule of Qianlong, the sixth emperor of the Qing dynasty, the economy was doing so well that tax collection was cancelled four times! Agricultural production increased during Qianlong's reign, and New World crops made their way to China's shores. These new crops, including sweet potatoes, were quite effective and they, along with new techniques for irrigation and fertilizers, resulted in food surpluses, which resulted in a healthier and larger population.

Political

The basis for Manchu power was twofold: military strength and the corrupt, ineffective government left by the Ming Dynasty. The Qing dynasty's quest for political and social control discouraged technological innovation from outside China because it was feared that this would cause unsettling change and could incite riots. As a result, the more the Qing resisted foreign improvements, the more likely they were to lose the technological war between the two. Over the nineteenth century, the Chinese lost more and more ground to the Europeans whose Industrial Revolution catapulted them into a significantly advanced era. The Qing may have been right to be wary of the effect of foreign interaction, because as soon as they did open the gates, however minutely, the British began to ply the Chinese with opium and caused tremendous problems that eventually resulted in the **Opium War**, where Britain was angry that the Chinese did not want opium distributed on their soil. The Opium War with Britain lasted from 1838–1842, and the Chinese fell to the gunpowdered steamboats that the British used to attack the Grand Canal. As a result of a series of defeats, China had to enter into what is referred to as the "unequal treaties" in which they had to cede Hong Kong, open their ports to European commerce and residence, allow Christian missionaries on their soil, legalize the opium trade, and not issue any more tariffs on British imports to China. As a result, by 1900, 90 Chinese ports were under foreign control, foreign merchants were controlling China's economy, Christian missionaries were converting Chinese, and foreign gunboats were patrolling China's waters. Eventually, the **Boxer Rebellion** was launched by an anti-foreign society called the Society of the Righteous and Harmonious Fists who tried to rid China of the "foreign devils." The rebellion was crushed.

Russia

The history of Russia begins about 882 with the founding of the first united East Slavic state. Over time the Russian culture became a mix of Slavic and Byzantine cultures. Russia disintegrated when Mongols invaded and overtook the country from 1237–1240, killing about half the population. Russia fell under Tatar rule in 1242, which ruled a large part of Russia for two centuries, resulting in Russia becoming increasingly isolated during that time.

In the fourteenth century, the Russian princes of Muscovy began to gain power as the Mongol power started to decline. In 1480, **Ivan III**, known as Ivan the Great, refused to pay tribute to the Mongols and declared Russia free of Mongol rule. He focused on expanding territory and declared himself *tsar* (also spelled "czar"), the Russian word for emperor or Caesar. Ivan then went about legitimizing his rule. He married a Byzantine princess to give legitimacy to his connection to the Orthodox Church, acquired symbols of imperial rule—such as putting an imperial eagle onto his coat of arms—and created a genealogy that creatively traced his family's origins back to the Roman Caesars. He and his grandson, Ivan IV (Ivan the Terrible), both wielded absolute power and used their power to expand Russia eastward. By the mid-1500s, Ivan the Terrible had centralized power over the entire Russian sphere and ruled ruthlessly.

After Ivan IV's death in 1584, Russia's feudal lords battled over who should rule the empire. This is a period from 1604–1613 that historians have named the **Time of Troubles**, when "pretenders" who took the throne would be killed one after the other.

In 1613, **Mikhail Romanov** was elected tsar and thus began the rule of the **Romanov Dynasty**. Under Mikhail Romanov, Russia extended its empire to the Pacific. Romanov continued Westernization.

Peter I reigned from 1682–1725 and was one of the most extraordinary people in Russian history. Peter built up the army through conscription and a 25-year term of enlistment. He gave flintlocks and bayonets to his troops instead of the old muskets and pikes. Artillery was improved and discipline enforced. By the end of his reign, Russia had a standing army of 210,000, despite a population of only 13 million. The tsar ruled by decree. All landowners owed lifetime service to the state, either in the army, the civil service, or at court. In return for government service, they received land and serfs to work their fields. Conscription required each village to send recruits for the Russian army. By 1709, Russia manufactured most of its own weapons and had an effective artillery.

After a series of largely ineffective rulers, Catherine II "the Great," (reigned 1762–1796) continued the Westernization process begun by Peter the Great. The three partitions of Poland, in 1772, 1793, and 1795, respectively, occurred under Catherine II's rule. Russia also annexed the Crimea and warred with Turkey during her reign.

Social and Economic

- Russian nobles dominated society and always posed an underlying threat to those in power. Attempts were periodically made to limit their power.

- Ivan IV set up an advisory council of merchants and lower-level nobles in an attempt to lessen the power of the nobles.

- Between 1484 and 1505, Ivan IV created a feudal system in which about 23,000 soldiers were given estates in return for military service. In contrast to what was accepted practice throughout Europe, he gave land to people not connected with the aristocracy: about 60 percent of his new estate holders were just regular soldiers. Land parcels on these lands were rented to serfs in return for their labor and service to the vassal. What soon transpired was that these peasants were turned into serfs who became tied to the land, unable to flee.

- By the end of the seventeenth century, 20,000 Europeans lived in Russia, developing trade and manufacturing, practicing medicine, and smoking tobacco, while Russians began trimming their beards and wearing Western clothing.

Cultural

- The Russian Orthodox Church dominated society.

- Ivan III declared Moscow as the center of the Eastern Orthodox Church, "the third Rome."

Competency 4: World History

- The adoption of Byzantine terms, rituals, title, and emblems provided legitimacy for Ivan III's rule.

- In 1649, three monks were appointed to translate the Bible for the first time into Russian. The Old Believers refused to accept any Western innovations or liturgy in the Russian Orthodox Church and were severely persecuted as a result.

Political

- Rule was by the tsar, who was an autocrat. Government officials and nobles acted under government authority, but there was no representative body.

- Under Ivan III and Ivan IV, Russia's territory expanded, using much the same rationale as other European conquerors in the new worlds: the new lands were empty, expansionary aims were beneficial to the natives, and expansion was ordained by God. Peasants were offered freedom from their feudal lords if they agreed to settle in the east. The only issue was that they would have to settle it themselves. These peasant-soldiers became known as **Cossacks** and they expanded Russian territory from the sixteenth to eighteenth centuries into Siberia in the north and in the south to the Caspian Sea. As Russian tsars developed more advanced technology of firearms, the Russians were able to conquer the native tribes of Siberia.

- Under Ivan IV (Ivan the Terrible), a secret police was created, a force of 6,000 men who dressed in black and rode black horses and rode through the empire punishing anyone who spoke out against the tsar or his policies. Ivan IV launched several killing sprees, perhaps influenced by his spiraling mental condition, against the people of Novgorod, who he suspected wanted to separate from Russia. Ivan IV's murder of his son, the sole heir to the crown, caused the **Time of Troubles** and left Russia without a monarch after the death of Ivan IV. This period is noted for being one of the reasons Russia lagged behind Western Europe.

COMPETENCY 4.6

Evaluate the significant scientific, intellectual, and philosophical contributions of the Age of Reason through the Age of Enlightenment.

The **Enlightenment** and the **Age of Reason** are two names given to the predominant intellectual movement of the eighteenth century that sought a distinct break with the past. It was an intellectual movement among the upper and middle class elites. It involved a new secular worldview that explained the world and looked for answers in terms of reason rather than faith, and in terms of an optimistic, natural, humanistic approach, rather than a fatalistic, supernatural one.

In the past, some kind of a religious perspective had always been central to Western civilization. The philosophical starting point for the Enlightenment was the belief in the autonomy of human intellect apart from God. The most basic assumption was faith in reason rather than faith in revelation.

The Enlightenment believed in the existence of God as a rational explanation of the universe and its form; "God" was a deistic Creator who made the universe and then was no longer involved in its mechanistic operation. That mechanistic operation was governed by "natural law." The Enlightenment believed in a closed system of the universe in which the supernatural was not involved in human life, in contrast to the traditional view of an open system in which God, angels, and devils were very much a part of human life on Earth.

The intellectuals of the Enlightenment, called **philosophes**, began to question the traditions of society and to look at the universe in a scientific, critical light. During the Enlightenment, all the trademark aspects of European society were exposed to criticism and analysis through reason. No institution was spared, for even the church itself was attacked by the cynical philosophes. Though the Enlightenment began as a movement that only reached the intellectual elite of society, its repercussions would eventually reach and have a big impact on society as a whole.

The philosophes as a whole saw their societies emerging from the darkness of superstition, ignorance, and intolerance—much of what they associated with the Medieval Catholic Church and with Feudal monarchy. They believed that for man to continue to advance, people had to develop their powers of reason and leave behind emotion, superstitious belief, blind faith, autocratic and arbitrary rule in administration and government, and cultural heritage. They argued for the development of universal, cross-cultural, shared expressions of human action. They thought that if people started thinking similarly, sharing ideas, and focusing on the merits of those ideas, people's basic goodness would come out; then the world would be a better, more peaceful place, organized and tended to by ideas and the people who had them. As a result, the world would rid itself of fanatical wars fought in the name of religion, persecution of so-called heretics and other free spirits, rule of absolute monarchs and privileged aristocrats, and general ignorance and backwardness of a population that had been kept in the dark by worldly and spiritual authorities for too long. Other ills of society, like slavery, would be abolished; torture and cruel punishment would be removed from judicial systems; and freedom of conscience would be enhanced by the separation of churches and state. Progress was the banner under which societies would abandon their benighted old ways and usher in a liberated and altogether happier future.

Competency 4: World History

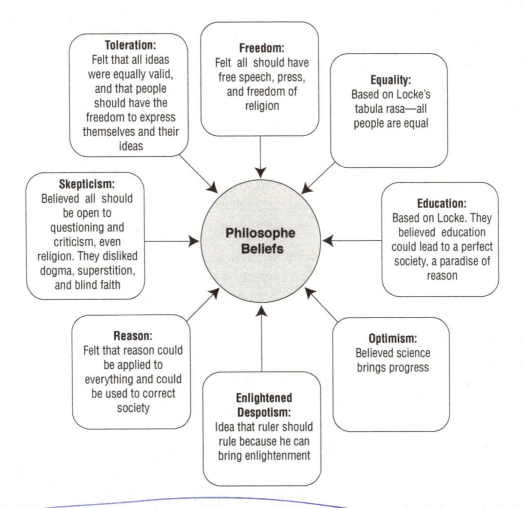

Rationalists stressed deductive reasoning or mathematical logic as the basis for their **epistemology** (source of knowledge). They started with "self-evident truths" from which they constructed a coherent and logical system of thought. For example, **René Descartes** (1596–1650) sought a basis for logic and thought he found it in man's ability to think. "I think; therefore, I am" was his most famous statement. **Benedict de Spinoza** (1632–1677) developed a rational pantheism in which he equated God and nature. He denied all free will and ended up with an impersonal, mechanical universe. **Gottfried Wilhelm Leibniz** (1646–1716) worked on symbolic logic and calculus and invented a calculating machine. He, too, had a mechanistic world and lifeview and thought of God as a hypothetical abstraction rather than a persona.

Empiricists stressed inductive observation—the "scientific method"—as the basis for their epistemology. For example, **John Locke** (1632–1704) pioneered the empiricist approach to knowledge and stressed the importance of environment in human development. He classified knowledge as (1) according to reason, (2) contrary to reason, or (3) above reason. Locke thought reason and revelation were both complementary and from God. **David Hume** (1711–1776) was a Scottish historian and philosopher who began by emphasizing the limitations of human reasoning and later became a dogmatic skeptic. He was the one who raised the argument about the tree falling in the forest. **Voltaire** (1694–1778) was often regarded as the leading figure of the Enlightenment.

A talented writer and social critic who poked fun at almost every facet of society, Voltaire stood for many of the ideals of the period. He helped popularize science for his 1738 work, in which he helped make Newton's discoveries understandable. He absolutely hated religion because of the intolerance that it bred, and he felt religion should be a private matter. Voltaire faced persecution and censorship, and as a result, he was a dedicated advocate of intellectual and religious freedom. **Diderot** (1713–1784) was most famous for his *Encyclopedie*, which classified all human knowledge from the most common to the most complex. The aim of the book was to "change the general way of thinking." Despite being banned throughout Europe, Diderot's masterpiece was still distributed and had a great impact on the intellectuals of Europe. **Baron de Montesquieu** (1689–1755) was a writer who believed that societies and political institutions could be studied scientifically, and that a balanced government with checks and balances would work.

The "**Counter-Enlightenment**" is a comprehensive term encompassing diverse and disparate groups who disagreed with the fundamental assumptions of the Enlightenment and pointed out its weaknesses. For example, Roman Catholic Jansenism in France argued against the idea of an uninvolved or impersonal God and Hasidism in Eastern European Jewish communities, especially in the 1730s, stressed a joyous religious fervor in direct communion with God.

The Elite Culture of the Enlightenment

During the Enlightenment, a new form of elite culture took hold throughout Europe, crossing national and linguistic boundaries, united in their use of French, feelings of cosmopolitanism, and distinctly separate from the majority of people.

Europe's elite began to travel around the continent. They visited cultural centers and cities, as well as the ancient monuments of antiquity. Cities became ideal tourism spots for these elite, featuring new amenities like streetlights and public transportation. New public spaces, like coffee houses and theaters, that centered around a spread of ideas, were places where people could meet and talk about ideas. The elite also met in salons and academies, both of which helped spread ideas and unite people. There, people could dispute their ideas and come up with new ones.

A **republic of letters** began to develop in which journals and newspapers circulated among the elite. Though the republic was limited to the educated, all classes and backgrounds could join in. Publishing increased tremendously and people began to read more. Traveling libraries were developed, as were journals and, most importantly, newspapers. There were new employment opportunities in bookselling and publishing, as well as the smuggling of so-called bad books, which ranged from Voltaire to pornography (i.e., anything that was banned).

Art, Literature, and Music

The art of the Enlightenment consisted of two competing styles: **Rococo** and **Neoclassicism**. Rococo was the art of the nobility and emphasized the airy grace and refined pleasures of the salon and the boudoir: very pretty and bright with swirling pastel colors. It sought to make a break with

Competency 4: World History

the heavy, Baroque past and emphasized lightness and airy movement. Famous Rococo painters were Francois Boucher and Fragonard. **Neoclassicism**, on the other hand, favored line over color, and was all about drama, tension, emotion, content, and an imitation of ancient style. The philosophes loved the Neoclassicist works for they favored themes that the philosophes liked.

Literature during the Enlightenment took center stage. The first modern **novel** was developed by Englishmen Samuel Richardson and Henry Fielding. The novel emerged as a new form of writing in which a story was told and characters were presented in a realistic social context filled with everyday problems. **Satire** was also perfected during the Enlightenment by brilliant writers such as Jonathan Swift and Voltaire. Also, during this time, **romantic poetry** was born. Earlier poetry followed strict rules and was not very emotional, but in the Enlightenment, writers like William Wordsworth and Friedrich von Schiller took poetry into new directions—so new, in fact, that it turned into a new style, Romanticism. Johann von Goethe, whose masterpiece was *Faust*, was a romantic poet who came to embody the entire period.

Music during the Enlightenment also shifted away from the dramatic organ and choral music of Bach and Handel and toward the lighter and more elegant work of Hayden, Mozart, and Beethoven. Particular attention was paid to the symphony, and these composers left their indelible stamp on it.

COMPETENCY 4.7

Identify the causes, effects, events, and significant individuals associated with the Age of Exploration.

The Age of Exploration

Overseas exploration, begun in the fifteenth century, expanded. Governments supported such activity in order to gain wealth and to preempt other countries. This age has three parts:

1. Discovery: refers to the era's advances in geographical knowledge and technology

2. Reconnaissance: preliminary exploration

3. Expansion: migration of Europeans to other parts of the world

Causes

A variety of factors explain why the Age of Exploration happened when it did and where it did. While ideas about the Middle East, India, and China certainly had made their way to Europe before this period, the exploits of Christian Crusaders from the eleventh to thirteenth centuries enhanced curiosity about the region, its people, its scientific and technological advancements, as well as it spices and other goods. This curiosity created an interest in developing more regular trade with the East. Trade opportunities, however, were stymied as Europeans were limited largely to trade across land, and trade between Europe and Asia only occurred through middlemen. These middlemen varied; sometimes they were Ottomans, sometimes Mongols, and most recently Venetians. Each time a good passed through a foreign land, it was subject to taxes, and each time it passed through the hands of an individual trader, the price of the goods increased in order to allow for sufficient profit. By the time goods made their way to Europe, they had been taxed quite heavily. Europeans became anxious to find a way around the middlemen, make their own deals in Asia, and transport the goods themselves. Spain and Portugal, recognizing they both had easy access to the sea, set their sights on finding an easier and faster route to India.

The Renaissance, Reformation, and Age of Exploration happened around the same time, so many of the ideas of one impacted the other. The Renaissance prompted searches for new knowledge, and adventurism ignited dreams about the possibilities of what lay beyond the shores of the Atlantic and Mediterranean seas. The Reformation infused a new spirit for missionaries, particularly those from Portugal and Spain, to find new souls to convert.

Political centralization in Spain, France, and England might also help explain their outward push as the government had more control of its resources to organize and develop incentives, funds, and opportunities for traders to expand their markets and the commercial revolution that made Europe eager for more markets for their products. Later, the Industrial Revolution would prompt Europe to look elsewhere for raw materials and a market for their finished goods. Portugal led the way in the initial stages of exploration primarily because it was strategically situated near the coast of Africa, had long-standing trade relations with Muslim nations, and was led by a royal family that supported exploration, **Prince Henry the Navigator**.

Prince Henry was a key contributor to the age. In 1415, he had joined in the Portuguese attack on Ceuta in North Africa. There the Portuguese found lots of exotic spices and precious metals, along with new opportunities to spread Christianity. Prince Henry returned to Portugal intent on trying to expand Portugal's shipping reaches. Knowing the limits imposed by the current technology, he started a school devoted to navigation. Many of the advances occurred primarily as a result of Prince Henry's new school, which that contained a shipyard attached to the school as a ready experimental lab with which to facilitate nautical innovation. This created a maritime revolution that sparked advances in technology like the astrolabe, and the magnetic compass. Better maps and improvements in shipbuilding opened the minds of the Portuguese and Spanish to the possibilities of long-distance sea travel that had seemed rather risky and impossible earlier. The Portuguese sailed their ships further and further down the coastline of Africa and established trading posts along the way. It would be twenty years after Prince Henry's death that some of the dreams he had would be realized when Bartolomeu Dias passed the tip of Africa and, eleven years later, when Vasco da Gama would sail to India.

While the above reasons account for why countries might be interested in exploration, there were also reasons why individuals might be interested in leaving the comforts of "civilization" to venture into the unknown. Some of the individual reasons for individual explorers to be interested in exploration may be summed up as the three G's: God, Gold, and Glory.

Competency 4: World History

1. God: The crusading zeal that had inspired Europeans centuries before to look outward to other non-Christians also influenced the people of the sixteenth century who were out for more people to convert to Christianity. Realizing that they had already failed in their attempts to convert Muslims, they looked for new converts.

2. Gold: Economics and politics also spurred exploration. After the Reconquista, many men found that their economic and political choices were limited, so they looked for commerce in other places.

3. Glory: Many individuals explored for adventure.

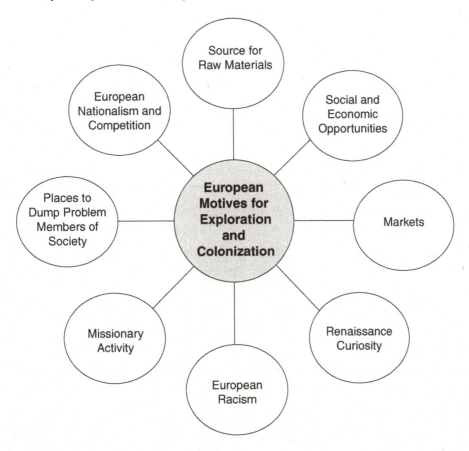

Effects

The effects of the Age of Exploration were also multi-variable, depending on time and place. Typically, historians focused on the benefits of exploration and conquering new lands without looking at what happened to the peoples that they conquered; however, there were both positive and negative effects for the conquerors as well as the conquered.

One unintended benefit of European exploration to the Americas was the transfer of horses. During the conquistadors' expeditions into the Southwest, some horses escaped and formed large herds on the Great Plains. Within a few generations, Native Americans in the Great Plains region became experts on horseback, expanding their hunting and trading capabilities and dramatically transforming Native American culture. Another good result of exploration, at least in terms of the Europeans, was that European life expectancy increased back in Europe because of the availability of new foodstuffs that contained some essential vitamins that had been missing from the European diet. As a result, population soared in Europe. Growth of foreign trade also developed, primarily in England. England's biggest export, wool, was taken up by other countries who were eager to tap into England's "monopoly."

Another mixed result was the **Columbian Exchange** that happened as a consequence of the Spanish and the Portuguese entry into the New World. New foods, resources, and animals were transferred between Europe and the Americas, resulting in massive changes for both regions. However, more dubious things were exchanged as well with this new pattern of trade—diseases, weapons, and people. War, slavery, and starvation claimed many lives, but disease, especially smallpox, had the most devastating effect. In Mexico, the native population plummeted from 25 million in 1519 to 2 million by 1600. European settlement physically displaced numerous tribes, setting in motion the sad fate of Native Americans throughout American history. The economy suffered because it could not meet the demand.

Some contend that the effects of exploration on the native peoples of the New World cannot be underestimated. In what really was genocide, the Native Americans suffered at the hands of each of the European groups who came to their lands. The biggest consequence was the diseases that spread. The number of Indians who died from European diseases was so great that the Spanish and Portuguese had a problem with labor supply. Their solution to this problem was to bring their own labor with them—and thus began the **Atlantic Slave Trade**. The Europeans saw several advantages in using African slaves for their labor. Most of the Africans had some immunity to the mosquitoes found in the Americas, and so they, unlike the Europeans, were resistant to the diseases that went along with mosquitoes. Africans also were well-versed in farming, and so they had the skills to help cultivate crops. They also did not know the land where they were going to, so the slaves would have little opportunity to flee—they would be stuck there. In 370 years, the Atlantic Slave Trade transported more than 9 million slaves, who made it to the shores of the Americas (20 percent of slaves died along the way). In what came to be called the Triangular Trade System, Africans were sent to the Americas, merchants bought coffee, sugar, and tobacco, and then they sold the goods to Europe. Another triangular trade had merchants selling Africans for sugar and then selling them to American rum producers.

With so much trade going on between Europe and the Americas, new ways of thinking about such trade developed. The English developed the ideas of **mercantilism**, which essentially was a system of economic regulations aimed at increasing the power of the state. Central to this idea was that a country needed to maintain a balance of trade with other countries. In order to do that, it needed raw materials and the colonies provided a great place for the acquisition of raw materials. So, another effect of the Age of Exploration was the development of colonies and **mercantilism**. Mercantilism was a system of economic regulations aimed at increasing the power of the state. Central to this idea was that a country needed to maintain a balance of trade with other countries.

Competency 4: World History

Main Events Early in the Age of Discovery

- In 1488, Portugal financed the voyage of Bartolomeu Dias.

- In 1497, Vasco da Gama rounded the Cape of Good Hope, explored the east African kingdoms, and then went all the way to India where he established trade relations.

- In 1492, Columbus "discovered" the New World when he landed at Hispaniola and thought he had arrived in India. When he returned for a second trip, he brought an army for conquest.

- In 1494, the **Treaty of Tordesillas**: In an effort to settle a dispute between the Spanish and the Portuguese over who should get which territory, Pope Alexander VI (a Spaniard, actually) set up a Line of Demarcation that would separate the territories of the world between the two largest Catholic powers, the Spanish and the Portuguese. The Portuguese at the time were more concerned about preserving their spice trade in the east, and so they willingly gave the Spanish the New World territories, with the exception, of what would be Brazil (this is why the Brazilians speak Portuguese and the rest of South America speaks Spanish).

Significant Individuals

Portugal

- Prince Henry the Navigator (1394–1460) supported exploration of the African coastline, largely in order to seek gold.

- Bartolomeu Dias (1450–1500) rounded the southern tip of Africa in 1487.

- Vasco da Gama (1460–1524) reached India in 1498 and, after some fighting, soon established trading ports at Goa and Calicut.

- Albuquerque (1453–1515) helped establish an empire in the Spice Islands after 1510.

- Pedro Cabal (1467–1520) sighted Brazil and defeated Arabs in the Indian Ocean.

- Amerigo Vespucci: First to announce that the "New World" was not Asia, but rather a continent; cartographers began to call the New World "America" in honor of him.

Spain

- Christopher Columbus (1451–1506), seeking a new route to the (East) Indies, "discovered" the Americas in 1492.

- Ferdinand Magellan (1480–1521) circumnavigated the globe in 1521–1522.

- Conquests of the Aztecs by conquistadors Hernando Cortés (1485–1547), and the Incas by Francisco Pizarro (ca. 1476–1541), enabled the Spanish to send much gold and silver back to Spain.

- Vasco Núñez de Balboa (1475–1517) crossed the Isthmus of Panama, first European to see the Pacific Ocean.

Other Countries

England

- In the 1490s, the Cabots, John (1450–1498) and Sebastian (ca. 1483–1557), explored North America.

- After 1570, various Englishmen, including Francis Drake (ca. 1540–1596) led English "sea dogs" against Spanish shipping around the world.

- Sir Martin Frobisher (1535–1594): northeastern Canadian coast

- Sir Walter Raleigh (1552–1618): Roanoke Settlement

France

- Jacques Cartier (1491–1557) explored parts of North America for France in 1534.

- Samuel de Champlain (1567–1635) and the French explored the St. Lawrence River, seeking furs to trade.

- Giovanni da Verrazzano (1480–1527) explored the northern Atlantic coast of modern-day U.S.

Dutch

The Dutch established settlements at New Amsterdam and in the Hudson River Valley. The Dutch founded trading centers in the East Indies, the West Indies, and southern Africa.

Competency 4: World History

COMPETENCY 4.8

Assess the social, political, and economic effects of the Industrial Revolution.

The Industrial Revolution describes a time of transition when machines began to significantly displace human and animal power in methods of producing and distributing goods, and an agricultural and commercial society converted into an industrial one. The Industrial Revolution began in the mid-1700s and by the mid-1800s industrialism had swept across Europe west to east, from England to Eastern Europe. Few countries purposely avoided industrialization, because of its promised material improvement and national wealth. The economic changes that constitute the Industrial Revolution have done more than any other movement in Western civilization to revolutionize Western life.

Although Europe and Great Britain were at the center of the industrial revolution, other countries also contributed. Countries that were colonies of European nations played a part. For example, the British East India Company had a major influence on India during the Industrial Revolution. Prior to that time period, India had been a major source of raw cotton and an important exporter of textiles. However, British control reversed that. The East India Company taxed India. Funds obtained by the taxes were then used to expand the company. The company further seized cotton crops in India for production in Great Britain. The finished textile products were brought back to India, but without duties or tariffs. By the end of the Industrial Revolution, India was buying a large portion of Great Britain's textile market.

Roots of the Industrial Revolution can be found in the following events:

1. the Commercial Revolution (1500–1700), which spurred the great economic growth of Europe and brought about the Age of Discovery and Exploration, which in turn helped to solidify the economic doctrines of mercantilism;

2. the effect of the Scientific Revolution, which produced the first wave of mechanical inventions and technological advances;

3. the increase in population in Europe from 140 million people in 1750, to 266 million people by the mid-part of the nineteenth century (more producers, more consumers);

4. the political and social revolutions of the nineteenth century, which began the rise to power of the "middle class," and provided leadership for the economic revolution.

The Commercial Revolution started in the textile and metallurgical industries because those industries lent themselves to mechanization and mass production. Coal replaced wood as an energy source, which increased coal mining and resulted ultimately in the invention of the steam engine and the locomotive. The factory system, which had been created in response to the new energy sources and machinery, was perfected to increase the output of manufactured goods.

Social Effects

The Industrial Revolution spurred the growth of cities, as the new factories acted as magnets, pulling people away from their rural roots and beginning the most massive population transfer in history. Cities tended to develop in favorable locations, near resources such as coal, iron, water, and railroads and, as the result of **urbanization**, the numbers of cities in Europe increased more than 700 percent over 100 years; however, urbanization had its drawbacks as too many people came to cities, which had neither the infrastructure nor the jobs to support them. Public sanitation and public health were in short supply, and diseases such as typhoid and cholera broke out. Another effect of industrialization and the creation of factories was pollution. Chimneys, bridges, and factory smoke blocked out most of the light in towns, layers of ash covered the streets, and burning coal produced a lot of dirty, black smoke that surely had an effect on the health of the people. The result of infrastructure problems like bad sewage, air and water pollution, and diseases resulted in higher infant mortality rates and shorter life expectancy in urban areas. Housing was often limited and families sometimes had to live in rooming houses.

The Industrial Revolution also brought changes in social hierarchies. The upper class started to consist more of very rich industrial and business families who then married into noble families to give themselves "old-world" authority as well. Upper middle classes consisted of lawyers and doctors (business people and professionals). Lower middle classes consisted of teachers, office workers, shop workers, and clerks. The lower classes were made up of factory workers and peasants.

Economic Effects

The most obvious effect of the Industrial Revolution is that goods were produced more efficiently. This resulted in an increased supply of goods, and along with that the price of goods decreased. With the lowering of prices for goods, there was more consumer demand for goods. As a result, more factories were created to keep up with consumer demand.

The Industrial Revolution created a new type of wealth, no longer based on land, but on the ownership of factories and machinery. The emergence of a new group of capitalists who financed and profited from industrialization began to emerge. These early entrepreneurs had to find two kinds of capital to finance their operations: long-term capital to expand present operations, and short-term capital to purchase raw materials, maintain inventories, and pay wages to their employees. While industrialists met their long-term capital needs through mortgages, short-term capital for raw materials and maintaining stock was accommodated by extending credit to the manufacturers by the producers or dealers. Often, a supplier of raw materials waited from 6 to 12 months for payment of his goods, after the manufacturer was paid for the finished product.

A transportation revolution ensued in order to distribute the productivity of machinery and deliver raw materials to the eager factories. This led to the growth of canal systems, the construction of hard-surfaced "macadam" roads, the commercial use of the steamboat (demonstrated by Robert Fulton, 1765–1815), and the railway locomotive (made commercially successful by George

Competency 4: World History

Stephenson, 1781–1848). A subsequent revolution in agriculture made it possible for fewer people to feed the population, thus freeing people to work in factories, or in the new fields of communications, distribution of goods, or services like teaching, medicine, and entertainment.

The payment of wages was not an easily solved problem. Payment systems often were designed at the expense of the worker. Some employers staggered the days on which they paid their employees; others paid employees in script. Some paid a portion of their workforce early in the day, allowing them to shop for household needs. When the money had circulated through the shopkeepers back to the employer, another portion of the workforce was paid. All of these methods proved to be unacceptable. One outcome of this need to finance short-term capital came from new, private banks that catered to industrialists. Unfortunately, many of these banks failed as they were unable to meet the demands of the factory economy. A banking system was eventually set up to distribute capital to areas where it was needed, drawing it from areas where there was a surplus.

Industrialization brought about the rise of big business. With big business came the need to invest large amounts of money and the quandary of where to find it. Many businesses turned to selling stocks or shares of their business to investors. This added investment of capital enabled businesses to expand and delivered tremendous profits to investors and owners.

In terms of economics, the emergence of the **factory system** not only changed how work was organized but also what work meant. No longer was skilled craftsmanship valued; now the main motive was how to reduce work to its simplest repetitive motions in order to produce output faster, but not necessarily better. Assembly line work revolutionized the work experience on an individual level and ultimately resulted in an almost dumbing down and de-skilling of the workforce.

Cities made the working class a powerful force by raising consciousness and enabling people to unite for political action and to remedy economic dissatisfaction. The Industrial Revolution created a unique new category of people who were dependent on their job alone for income, a job from which they might be dismissed without cause. Until 1850, workers as a whole did not share in the general wealth produced by the Industrial Revolution. Conditions would improve as the century wore on, as union action combined with general prosperity and a developing social conscience to improve the working conditions, wages, and hours first of skilled labor, and later of unskilled labor.

However, with the new industrial age, a new quantitative and materialistic view of the world took hold. This caused the need for people to consume as much as they could. A concerted effort was undertaken to change fundamental values to encourage **consumption**, as it was the lifeblood of an industrialized and capitalistic society. Rather than practicing the good old concepts of thrift and staying out of debt, the Industrial Revolution pushed people to consume! The economics of the society depended on people buying goods. If too few goods were purchased, then factory orders would fall and people would be laid off from work. A sure way to prevent economic ruin was to convince people to be intensive and insatiable consumers, buying things they never even knew they needed. To encourage such consumption, the **advertising industry** was created, which sought to use any technique necessary to get people to feel they needed to purchase goods, and to convince them that they should even throw away still functioning items in order to get the "latest, improved" models. Such techniques worked and increased consumer demand. To keep up with and track the demand, there were improvements all along the supply chain, including transportation, warehousing, shipping, and record-keeping. These developments led to bigger department stores, chain markets, and later mail-order catalogs, such as the Sears catalog, to move goods rapidly from the shelves of stores to the hands of consumers. The need to pay for all of these goods, especially when money was tight, sparked the development of credit services, credit and charge cards, lay-away plans, and even pay-over-time deals.

The standards of living increased, although unequally applied. Consumption increased with a new materialistic view of the world. As the society became one based on consumption, more money was needed in order to survive. Most families did not have enough money with just the parents working, so small children too were sent to work in factories. For fewer people lived on the farms where only certain types of food grew; in the cities, people had access to a variety of foods and so their diets improved, as did their health.

Political Effects

The Industrial Revolution coincided with the advent of imperialism. Industrial technology had consequences that not only supported and prompted Europeans to look beyond their borders but also facilitated it. The European countries that had already gone through industrialization had better and cheaper weapons and were able to use their weapons, or the threat of them, to conquer people who did not have access to that same technology. In addition, countries needed a steady supply of raw goods as well as a market to sell the goods once they were manufactured. Colonies would prove wonderful opportunities to do both. The industrial imperialists turned to two areas of the world—Africa and Asia—where they saw big markets and easy access to them.

The Industrial Revolution also led to the creation of new social and political ideologies. **Adam Smith** in his ***Wealth of Nations*** argued that economic prosperity and fairness in a country is best achieved through private ownership. Smith introduced the concept of the **invisible hand** that stated that if all individuals follow their own self-interests, it would be for the economic good of everyone, since everyone will do what they do best. He felt that individuals should own the means of production and sell their goods on an open and free market where demand, not the government, controlled prices and availability. When governments removed themselves completely from regulation, he called it ***laissez-faire*** economics. The industrialists embraced his ideas because for them, it ensured more profit and less government regulation. Others were not convinced and took quite different positions. Jeremy Bentham argued that the government should manage the economy and address social problems. Malthus argued that the reason for poverty is overpopulation, which can be addressed by delayed marriages and abstinence instead of government involvement. Robert Owen and Charles Fourier theorized the concept of **utopian socialist societies** without capitalists. **Karl Marx** pointed out that factory workers were exploited under capitalism, not just because of individual malfeasance, but also because there were inherent flaws in the system. He noted that the working class could and would eventually revolt and take over the means of production. Once class structure was overturned and the instruments of power that conspired against the workers on

Competency 4: World History

behalf of the rich were overturned, then the workers' lives would improve. Marx's ideas sparked not only the foundation of **socialism** and **communism** but also movements that began to demand reform and improvement in the lives of workers. In fact, the hard working conditions and bad economic life led to various protests and riots by the workers and eventually led to the formation of trade unions and "benevolent societies" that tried to protect worker rights.

There were some good political effects of the Industrial Revolution as it resulted in the extension of the right to vote to the middle class and then, eventually, to all members of society; it helped push the idea of public education to meet the needs of an industrialized society; and it helped develop tools of mass media, beginning with print media.

COMPETENCY 4.9

Identify the causes, effects, events, and significant individuals associated with the Age of Revolution.

Revolutions (1775–1848)

The Age of Revolution might be considered products of the Enlightenment, where the values of freedom, equality, and sovereignty created a shift in understandings about the roles and functions of people, religion, and the state. No longer did people consider their rulers all-powerful beings who had a Divine Right to rule. Now, with Enlightenment, people believed that just rule comes only from a ruler whose power came from the constituents. What is significant about this Age of Revolution is the seeming idea that these pressures for change existed throughout the world, each one inspiring the other to revolt. Challenges to governmental authorities inside one nation seem to provide inspiration across borders. This series of revolutions spread throughout the world:

- North America: Colonists sought freedom from Britain in the quest for enlightenment values of freedom, equality, and popular sovereignty.

- France: Inspired by events in North America, they abolished their monarchy, church, and aristocracy and established a republic built on equality and popular sovereignty.

- Colonies in Latin and South America fought for their freedom against French and Spanish rule.

The French Revolution I (1789–1815)

Radical ideas about society and government developed during the eighteenth century in response to the success of the "scientific" and "intellectual" revolutions of the preceding two centuries. Armed with new scientific knowledge of the physical universe, as well as new views of the human capacity to detect "truth," social critics assailed existing modes of thought governing political, social, religious, and economic life.

The rising expectations of "enlightened" society were demonstrated by the increased criticism directed toward government inefficiency and corruption and toward the privileged classes. The clergy (**First Estate**) and nobility (**Second Estate**), representing only two percent of the total population of 24 million, were the privileged classes and were essentially tax exempt. The remainder of the population (**Third Estate**) consisted of the middle class, urban workers, and the mass of peasants, who bore the entire burden of taxation and the imposition of feudal obligations. As economic conditions worsened in the eighteenth century, the French state became poorer, and totally dependent on the poorest and most depressed sections of the economy for support at the very time this tax base had become saturated.

The Revolution of the Third Estate overcame the monarchy and created a republic. Eventually, **Napoleon Bonaparte** spread these revolutionary ideas as he conquered much of Europe to create an empire that was, for a time, the largest empire since Roman times. However, French-ruled peoples viewed Napoleon as a tyrant who repressed and exploited them for France's glory and advantage, and enlightened reformers believed Napoleon had betrayed the ideals of the Revolution. Napoleon was ultimately defeated by a combination of several factors: his inability to conquer England, economic distress, war with Spain, and the invasion of Russia. He was exiled to the island of Elba, but returned to try to seize power from French King Louis XVIII. He lost the battle of Waterloo in 1815 and was exiled as a prisoner of war to the South Atlantic island of St. Helena.

The French Revolution was a key event in history because it formed the foundation for other reforms and revolution. As a result, the modern world that came of age in the eighteenth century was characterized by rapid revolutionary changes, which paved the way for economic modernization and political centralization throughout Europe.

The Post-War Settlement: The Congress of Vienna (1814–1815)

The **Congress of Vienna** met in 1814 and 1815 to redraw the map of Europe after the Napoleonic era and to endeavor to preserve the future peace of Europe. The Vienna settlement was the work of representatives of the four nations that had done the most to defeat Napoleon: England, Austria, Russia, and Prussia. The "Quadruple Alliance" of these countries provided for concerted action to arrest any threat to the peace or balance of power.

Europe was spared a general war throughout the remainder of the nineteenth century. But the failure of the statesmen who shaped the future in 1814–1815 to recognize the forces, such as nationalism and liberalism, unleashed by the French Revolution, only postponed the ultimate confrontation between two views of the world—change and accommodation, or maintaining the status quo.

1848 Revolutions

The year 1848 is considered the watershed of the nineteenth century. The revolutionary disturbances of the first half of the nineteenth century reached a climax in a new wave of revolutions that extended from Scandinavia to southern Italy, and from France to central Europe. Only England and

Competency 4: World History

Russia avoided violent upheaval. The issues were substantially the same as they had been in 1789. What was new in 1848 was that these demands were far more widespread and irrepressible than ever. The accumulation of domestic economic and population crises seemed to build up enough pressure that contention spread easily and found long standing, highly repressive, and seemingly powerful governments as their targets. Industrialization's exploitation of workers, the shifting of society away from skilled to unskilled labor increased people's irritation and angst. At the same time, advances in education and the appearance of liberal policies in the United States, England, Belgium, and Switzerland led to a gradual spread of reformist ideas and values, which contrasted sharply with the absolutist monarchies in power. Generally speaking, the 1848 upheavals shared the strong influences of romanticism, nationalism, and liberalism, as well as a new factor of economic dislocation and instability. Revolutions in countries like France, Italy, Austria, and Prussia tended to occur in governments where there was widespread distrust and fear coupled with rising food prices and unemployment. In the end, the revolutions did not succeed, owing partly to divisions within the revolutionary ranks and also because the old governments refused to give in.

Other factors contributed to revolution. For example, middle-class predominance within an unregulated economy continued to drive liberals to push for more government reform and civil liberty. They enlisted the help of the working classes to put more pressure on the government to change, and they demanded more rights. Financial crises and investment failures caused by a downturn in the commercial and industrial economy prompted an economic slowdown. As a result, businesses failed, wages decreased, and unemployment increased. Living conditions in cities deteriorated and poor harvest and crop failures caused food shortages and higher prices. Large increases in world population exacerbated the problems. Rulers and governments were not prepared to address these new economic and industrialism challenges. Feelings of nationalism among European minorities as well as pre-1848 tensions sparked discontent and anger, especially in repressive countries. Other ideological perspectives such as liberalism, democracy, and socialism also fueled dissent.

Although none of the revolutions succeeded, they had a lasting impact. The failures of restoration and the power of political ideas fostered social change. Peasants realized that they had more power than they thought, and rulers realized that they needed to be more attentive to the people's wishes. Liberals learned that they needed educated, literate citizens in order to run a constitutional government. They saw that the masses might have demands that conflicted with their own. As a result, the educated liberals had to reevaluate their goals and how much they should buy into a system with which they disagreed. The left became quite bitter and hardened by the failures of 1848. They turned to more militant means to achieve their ends, even becoming willing to use terror, violence, and assassination to achieve their goals. The conservative elite began to realize that while using brute force is a good temporary measure to secure power, it was not a good, long-term response to revolutionary fervor, as it would only increase opposition and resentment. There was a realization that it would be better to have liberal concessions to keep radical voices marginalized so they would not gain more power. Everyone realized that revolutions needed power and armies to back them up, but that, nevertheless, nationalism was a powerful new force in politics. Nationalist groups realized that there was indeed reason to fear both groups within their own country as well as outside of it. So, nationalist fervor continued to mount and created more fissures within the society and would weaken many of these new, tenuous governments. More power was given to the **Realism** movement where art and literary forms of expression focused more on real life and portrayals of poverty, oppression, and injustice.

COMPETENCY 4.10

Evaluate the impact of imperialism and nationalism on global social, political, geographic, and economic development.

In the early days of history, people identified themselves as part of a family, a tribe or, as civilization developed, a village, city, social class, religious affiliation, or other ideology. But as borders became more defined, groups were identified in terms of a sense of **nationalism**, which describes both the attitude that members of a nation have when they care about their national identity and the actions that the members of a nation take when seeking to achieve or sustain self-determination. **Imperialism** is the desire to extend a country's control to other areas through military domination or negotiation with other controlling countries. The areas under another country's control were called **colonies**.

Impact of Nationalism on Global Social, Political, Geographic, and Economic Development

Nationalism has had an enormous influence on world history. The quest for national supremacy has inspired millennia of imperialism and colonization, while struggles for national liberation have resulted in many revolutions.

In modern times, the **nation-state** has become the dominant form of societal as well as political organization. For example, when immigrants came to the United States and gained citizenship, their identity often became that of an American more than what had been their ethnic background. In the latter half of the century, many people returned to a sense of ethnic as well as national identity, describing themselves as Irish-Americans, African-Americans, Italian-Americans, and so on. At times, nationalism has resulted in a kind of us-versus-them, xenophobic attitude in which ethnic minorities were seen to be threats and faced discrimination and persecution as a result.

Nationalism fed into country-wide economies rather than economies centered in smaller units. Threats to the economy were seen as threats to the nation. Other countries sometimes used adverse economic tools such as embargoes, blockades, and sanctions to deter trade with a country in hopes of gaining concessions from it.

Politically, nationalism was promoted by the government as a unifying force. Symbols, music, flags, creeds, and narratives were adopted as signs of national affiliation and patriotism. And the spirit of nationality dampened the efforts of revolutionaries. Nationalism powerfully affected social

Competency 4: World History

as well as political development. Authors and intellectuals began to write and discuss identity as a nation. Individuals began to see themselves are part of a much greater whole. Education, literacy, and communication were seen as strategies that would inform people and result in a stronger nation. But when nationalism turns ugly, the results can be war, military conflict, and even genocide. Nationalism was a powerful force behind the world wars of the twentieth century and wars that continue to be fought today. It can be said that in human history, there have been very few, if any, times when war was not being waged somewhere on the globe. In today's world of terrorism, the concepts of war and genocide are no longer found only within nation-states, making the elimination of war and genocide even more of a challenge.

Impact of Imperialism on Global Social, Political, Geographic, and Economic Development

Imperialism differs from **colonialism**. Colonialism is the official government rule of one state over the other; imperialism is when one country exerts cultural or economic influence over another without having governmental institutions act for them; in practical terms, imperialism also is the perpetuation of the influence of a colonial empire over a country, even when it no longer has sovereignty over it. For example, the United States exerts an imperial influence over much of the world, as its popular culture and economics influence a great percentage of it; however, the United States' role as a colonial enterprise is much more limited. Countries under imperial domination do retain a degree of autonomy and self-determination, while their counterparts under colonial control do not.

By 1914, most of the world was under formal European control. Such domination not only resulted in a remarkable transformation in the relationship between Europe and the wider world but also brought up the question of whether or not this was a good idea. There are two sides to this:

(1) Was Western intervention a boon, bringing technological development, liberal politics, and social reform, or

(2) Was Western intervention a bust, destroying the world for the sake of filling their own pockets and partaking of guilty pleasures, creating tremendous political instability, poverty, social divisiveness, and eroding the chances of these nations to thrive in the modern world as independent nations?

The impact of Western imperialism had and continues to have a dramatic, transforming, and disruptive impact on the societies of Africa, Asia, the Americas, and the Pacific. In fact, only a few non-industrialized regions were able to withstand the aggressive agendas of the West. Most significantly, it undermined civilizations, even putting an end to some of them. Indigenous civilizations of the Americas, like the Aztecs and Incans, were decimated and so seriously undermined that the region still feels the effects of it today. The forced migration that occurred through the African slave trade radically changed the landscape not only of Africa, but also the Americas. Lasting effects of racial oppression continue. The economic toll that the Western economic exploitation had world-wide as they plundered the colonial world was unequaled. The imposition of the West's "liberal" forms of government and reforms actually unraveled political and social structures in Africa and Asia to such an extent that they never recovered.

Colonizers tended to assume that because they may have had technological superiority over the places they colonized, they also had racial, cultural, and religious superiority as well. What resulted were beliefs of environmental determinism that assumed that the reason why certain peoples were "behind" in terms of technology could be traced to climactic and racial reasons. What resulted was colonial behavior and thought that emanated from a physical mapping of the world, visually separating colonized and colonizer into "them" and "us." A geographical result of colonialism on geographical development was the imposition of borders that bore little resemblance to "natural" borders or to political borders that had existed prior to colonial rule. The carving up of the Ottoman Empire, the Middle East, and South Asia into areas designed to maximize benefits for the former colonizers rather than the inhabitants created numerous conflicts that are still being felt today. For example, the modern political boundaries in West Africa are based upon linguistic, political, and economic contrasts that resulted from colonial policies in the region, rather than "on the ground" realities. The use of techniques like partition as parting gifts to countries at the end of colonial rule fashioned new countries that had little bearing on the political realities of the area, and doomed them to a history of conflict not only within their borders, but beyond them as well.

The economic consequences of empire varied depending on the nature and the extent of the imperial relationship. When imperialism involved demographic displacement, colonial peoples experienced catastrophic results with huge losses of people, lands, and resources that continue to be felt today. In other places, we see mixed results. In the early modern trading empires, certain colonial peoples benefited from the new trade relationships that were established with Europeans that changed or bolstered their positions within their own societies. Other societies, like China during the Opium Wars, wanted to restrict trade. Some consequences of imperialism were the transfers of tools and technologies and also the exchange of animals and plant species (along with diseases). For instance, Australia benefited from the introduction of sheep, and Native Americans made effective use of the horse.

COMPETENCY 4.11

Analyze the causes and effects of political transformations and military conflicts in the twentieth century.

The rise of nationalism, colonialism, and imperialism in the nineteenth century set the stage for political transformations and military conflicts in the twentieth century. These included World War I, the Russian Revolution, and World War II.

World War I (WWI)

Causes

The match that set off a world war was the **assassination of Archduke Franz Ferdinand** at Sarajevo on June 28, 1914, and Austria-Hungary declared war against Serbia. By the first week of

Competency 4: World History

August, Germany had declared war on Russia and France and formed an alliance with the Ottoman Empire. When Germany crossed the border of Belgium, Great Britain declared war on Germany. However, many other preceding factors contributed to the war.

For example, a variety of attitudes had developed among many of the European world powers. Serbia was extremely nationalistic. Germany sought world power status. France wanted revenge over losing two territories to Germany. Britain was fighting imperialist issues and emergent nationalism in its colonies. This was compounded by the alliance system (**Triple Alliance** of Germany, Austria-Hungary, and Italy and the **Triple Entente** of Britain, Russia, and France), which separated Europe into two armed camps, sparking rivalry between the powers and increases in defense funding. Although these alliances were defensive in nature, they meant that any conflict between two countries involved the other countries.

Effects

At the beginning of the war, the European countries that were immediately engaged in the war imagined that the war would be short and end in glorious victory. But the war lasted four years, and by the end, it had been fought around the world in Africa, the Mid-East, and Asia, as well as in Europe, on land and on sea. The United States tried to remain neutral but was pulled into the war when a German U-boat sank British liner the *Lusitania*, which was carrying 128 American passengers. After the war, colonies that supported Europe during the war, like India, and protectorates, like Egypt, thought they would be rewarded for their support. When that did not occur, nationalism continued to rise and some of the colonies demanded independence. Empires declined, and in some cases, collapsed. Some monarchies (e.g., Germany and Russia) became republics. Before the war, Europe contained 19 monarchies and 3 republics, yet only a few years after the war, they had 13 monarchies, 14 republics, and 2 regencies. Because boundaries in the Middle East had redrawn following the war, the introduction of new states and leaders gave rise to long-term crises and problems that continue today.

The world recognized the need for a global body to promote international peace and security, which resulted in the League of Nations. The idea for the league came from U.S. President Woodrow Wilson; however, the United States Congress did not ratify the proposal to join the league. Still, the U.S. position in the world rose.

The war had huge human costs. By the end of the war, more than 70 million military personnel, including 60 million Europeans, had been mobilized. More than 9 million combatants and 7 million civilians died in the war. In terms of social changes, women had to take over the roles of men in businesses and communities during the war. With the numbers of men who were injured or did not survive, women's new roles continued, to some degree. Women acquired the right to vote throughout most of the countries in Europe. People developed more interest in socialism, and there was increased involvement of government in society. The status of working classes improved.

Economically, industrialization and mass-mechanization needed for the war effort continued after the war and even increased with more attention to research and development, especially in the areas of chemicals, armaments, communication, and transportation. But property damages were quite heavy and war strained the resources of each country to the maximum. War debt resulted in uncontrollable inflation across Europe and the world's financial center shifted from England to the United States.

The **Treaty of Versailles** that marked the end of the war had deleterious effects on the post-war environment as it caused hostilities and resentment that helped set the stage for World War II. Germany was singled out for harsh treatment and was forced to sign a humiliating treaty accepting blame for causing the war and ordered to pay compensation for it. Germany also lost territory to Italy and France. The German government was not well-liked by the citizens of Germany. Many former members of the military remained openly hostile with and sought revenge.

Russian Revolution

The **Russian Revolution** actually refers to two revolutions that took place in Russia in 1917. Within a year, the Russian empire had collapsed, been replaced by a provisional government, and was then replaced with a **Bolshevik (Communist)** government. The revolutions resulted in the abdication of Tsar Nicholas and a turn toward a socialist/communist government.

Causes

Although many aspects of World War I contributed to the Russian Revolution, events prior to the war also contributed. In 1894, Nicholas II had become the Tsar of the Russian empire, an autocratic ruler who was known as Nicholas the Bloody as the result of anti-Semitic massacres, violent suppressions of the people, and execution of political opponents. Upper classes and educated classes resented Tsar Nicolas's autocracy and the regime was seen as corrupt. The people believed he was responsible for Russia's defeat in the Russo-Japanese war. Tsar Nicholas approved the Russian mobilization of troops, which led to Germany declaring war on Russia in 1914 as part of World War I.

World War I took a tremendous toll on Russia. So many men joined or were forced to join the army (15 million) that there were insufficient numbers to run the factories and farms. This led to widespread shortages of basic food. Working conditions in the factories deteriorated so badly that workers rioted and engaged in strikes to try to get better wages as well as improved health and safety conditions. Tsar Nicolas responded to worker strikes with violence, which only caused more strikes, including strikes by transportation workers that further paralyzed the country. Prices soared as availability of goods plummeted. There were food shortages and a threat of famine in the big cities.

Military morale was extremely low. By October 1916, Russia had lost between 1.6 and 1.8 million soldiers, and an additional 2 million were taken prisoners of war, and 1 million were missing. Mutinies occurred as soldiers lacked food, shoes, and weapons. Tsar Nicholas was blamed for the poor condition of the army, as well as his handling of the war. As a result, there was an increase in radical socialist parties dedicated to overthrowing both Tsarism and (eventually) capitalism.

Vladimir Lenin led the October Revolution. Lenin based his ideology on the work of Karl Marx. This fostered the spread of communism in the twentieth century.

Effects

The Russian revolution changed Russia—and the world. Russia and autocratic rule gave way to the Soviet Union and establishment of a socialist/communist government. As a result, society, government, and the economy completely transformed. Although Russia withdrew from World War I, it emerged as a world power and communism began to spread around the world. The countries and leaders of the world began to be divided into communist and capitalist camps.

World War II (WWII)

World War I had been described as "the war to end all wars." However, that was not to be. Issues and problems continued to develop. World War II formally began in 1939 and became a battle of two opposing military alliances: the Allies and the Axis. More than 100 million individuals in more than 30 countries were directly involved in the war; however, the war and its repercussions were greater than that.

Causes

No single issue or event caused World War II. Rather, unresolved problems left over from World War I, new global issues, and the effects of the Russian Revolution impacted the world in a variety of ways.

Part of the world experienced a kind of boom in the 1920s following World War I in Western society and culture in the United States, Canada, and much of Europe. Industrial growth was widespread and consumer demand increased. Large-scale use of new forms of transportation (personal automobiles, aviation) and communication/media (radio, motion pictures, telephones, advertising) grew exponentially. The United States became the dominant player in world finance. Meanwhile, Germany struggled under the financial and other burdens imposed by the Treaty of Versailles. When Germany could no longer pay reparations, the U.S. proposed the **Dawes Plan** in which Wall Street stock markets invested heavily in Germany. But in 1929, Wall Street stock markets crashed, and the entire world was thrust into an economic depression.

Germany continued to suffer in other ways under the conditions of the Treaty of Versailles. Not only were they financially punished, but they also felt humiliated by the terms of the treaty. Their military was restricted and some of their land had been given to other countries. This, combined with the Great Depression, created an environment for a rise of German nationalism and emergence of the Nazi Party. In 1939, the Nazis, under the leadership of new Chancellor Adolf Hitler, built up the military, which gave Germany increased pride. Hitler ordered troops into the Rhineland, made alliances with Italy's Mussolini and Japan to form the Axis powers, and marched into Austria. Within the Axis powers, fascism—which glorified the military, denounced international organization and cooperation, and considered war an accepted means for achieving national goals—became a dominant ideology. Hitler responded to world concern about his expansionist moves, by replying that he had no more interest in expansion; however, he then demanded the Sudetenland and invaded first Czechoslovakia and then Poland.

In order to make up for the harshness of the Treaty of Versailles, Britain Prime Minister Neville Chamberlain thought that if the world gave into some of Hitler's demands, he would be appeased. Hitler's response was to invade Czechoslovakia. Chamberlain acquiesced and said Britain would only step in if Hitler invaded Poland. Hitler invaded Poland, and Great Britain and France declared war on Germany two days later. The Poland invasion marks what is considered to be the official start of World War II.

The Empire of Japan was already at war with China and, as the result of Japan's alliance with Germany, Japan became part of the greater war. The United States stayed out of the war until December 7, 1941, when the Japanese attacked Pearl Harbor in Hawaii.

Effects

The effects of World War II were larger and more widespread than World War I, and impacted more people. The old great powers of the world declined in influence. Many of the European empires began to de-colonize, and remaining colonies demanded independence. Third World nationalist movements emerged. The Russian army had built up to fight against Germany, and by the end of the war, the Russian army occupied most of Eastern Europe. As the result of American war efforts and victories, the United States increased in influence. Thus, the United States and the Union of Soviet Socialist Republics (USSR) became the world's two superpowers. This led to the bipolarization of Europe and the beginning of the Cold War, in which both superpowers endeavored to gain bigger and better weapons and increase their influence across the globe. The Space Race between the United States and the USSR began as part of this effort for control and dominance. Although the concept for the **United Nations** first appeared in 1942, the United Nations was formally chartered in 1945 to act on world issues such as peace and security, human rights, and international law.

Millions of people were killed, injured or left homeless in Europe. Infrastructure, homes, and businesses were destroyed, which resulted in mass dislocation, resettlement of people, and financial struggle, for both individuals and countries as a whole. The **Nuremberg war trials** tried former Nazi leaders for crimes against humanity carried out in the systematic murder of millions of Jews and others in the **Holocaust**. Postwar Germany was divided into four zones of occupation, each controlled by one of the victorious powers. Japan was in ruins from extensive bombing and from the U.S. nuclear attack. War trials for military leaders were also held in Japan, which was temporarily placed under U.S. rule; however, the Japanese emperor retained the crown.

The war, while terrible, had some positive outcomes. New technology developed during the war to fight diseases would sharply lower mortality rate and increase population growth. Computer technologies got their start in World War II. Technological developments during war had a significant impact—for instance, the English developed radar, which paved the way for television. This

Competency 4: World History

led to additional progress in computers and electronics. Women that became part of the workforce during World War II found a new voice and wanted to continue to have a place outside as well as inside the home. This sparked other changes and over time, women gained additional rights as the result. Finally, the development of the atomic bomb changed the nature of future wars. While other countries gained nuclear capabilities over time, nuclear capabilities also required that nations and their leaders make better choices in order to avoid nuclear war. America's gearing up for the Second World War resulted in a boom for the economy and there were labor shortages rather than unemployment. American GIs (soldiers) returned home, and many attended college on the GI Bill. The people in the United States were not only more prosperous, but they were becoming better educated. Soldiers returning to America resulted in the boom of babies born from 1946 to 1964. The individuals who were of age to be part of the war were often referred to as "the greatest generation." Their large numbers of postwar offspring were known as "baby boomers" who became the largest generation of individuals born in the United States.

COMPETENCY 4.12

Analyze major contemporary global political, social, economic, and geographic issues and trends.

Globalization has many definitions and many perspectives, but is not a new concept—it has been happening for thousands of years. Basically, behind the definition of globalization is the notion that no one nation stands by itself, for the world really is a place in which we see the interaction and integration of people, governments, and businesses with people of other nations through trade and investment. Globalization challenges the idea that a state's influence stops at its borders, which really are just human designations of where a country should stop.

Globalization has increased in scope and diversity. In the past few decades, the flow of information and technology between and among peoples has spurred increases in cross-border trade, as goods and services are distributed more quickly than ever before. As a result, the world seems more connected in its day-to-day operations than previously. Such interaction has its effects on all aspects of life—environmental, cultural, political, economic, and social. Technology allows anyone to interact with people in nations that were once only known through photographs, maps, books, encyclopedias, and personal anecdotes.

Two principal factors drive globalization today: economic policies and technology. In terms of economic policies dictating the extent and direction of global interaction, the adoption of free-market economic systems throughout the world has resulted in new international opportunities for trade and investment. Eliminating trade and political barriers resulted in expansion of foreign markets and a re-honing of domestic ones. It is this constant integration with the world beyond one's borders that has made both countries and businesses realize that they need to have a carefully crafted international business and financial structure in place in order to meet needs. The other driver in globalization is technology, which has dramatically transformed the economic life of individuals, companies, and nations. Today's technologies facilitate communication across the world, allow international financial transactions with a flick of a switch, and provide opportunities to collaborate with partners all over the world.

Globalization, however, is not without its detractors. Opponents of globalization have argued that the hold that multinational corporations now have over the world has been at the expense of local enterprise, development, culture, and the common people. Resistance to globalization has pushed such movements as "buy local," "sustainability efforts," and calls for increased attention to regulation of these megalith corporations. Environmentalists express concern about the destruction of resources, like the rainforest, to meet the temporary needs of these corporations.

Below are some big issues that are happening today. The best way to become familiar with the latest on any of these issues is to pick up some copies of reputable, thoughtful newspapers and/or magazines and read about current thought and developments on any of the following topics. By no means is this an exhaustive list.

Political

- Clash of Civilizations: Inter-religious conflict, especially the tensions between Islam and Christianity
- Terrorism and the Rule of Law
- Ability of nations to fit into an increasing global world that emphasizes internationalism
- Role of the United Nations and NGOs
- Palestinian-Israeli Conflict
- Change in the world's power structure—emergence of China and India
- Widening of the gap between political views on the right and left
- Global terrorism, rise of fears, unrest, and War on Terror
- International cybersecurity issues including hacking of political figures, parties, and countries; cyber-fraud and misuse of social media to affect public opinion
- Wars in the Middle East
- "Axis of Evil" countries and the demonizing of others
- Controversies about genocide—who defines it, where is it happening, when should other countries intervene?
- Peacekeeping missions
- Conflicts and lack of cooperation among major U.S. political parties.

Competency 4: World History

Social

- Women, children, and family issues
- Sex trade, national and international
- Growing distrust and discontent by various groups such as racial/ethnic groups, LGBT, gender, socioeconomic classes, professional
- Role of the media, especially social media, with implications for school issues such as cyber-bullying, misuse of social media by adolescents, identity issues, plagiarism, and so on.
- Health crises and ethical questions of who should receive health care and who pays
- Concern about immigrants and other newcomers in a community

Economic

- Current global economic crises and their causes and consequences
- Successes and stresses of global economic development
- Global poverty and hunger
- Reform of World Bank and the International Monetary Fund, focusing particularly on international coordination of macroeconomic policy
- Global economic imbalances and their effects on the U.S. dollar
- Monetary integration in Europe and elsewhere
- Trade reform
- Development gap and ways of closing it
- Intellectual property rights in an increasingly technological and global world

Geographic

- Impact on environmental disasters like oil spills
- Impact of global climate change
- Mass migrations by refugees and demographic challenge to assimilate or reject them
- Global environmental crisis
- Genetic engineering of food and the future
- Creation of sustainable societies

COMPETENCY 4.13

Identify major world religions and ideologies.

Religion is defined as belief in, worship of, and communication with a deity or supernatural being. Religions have developed and continued for different reasons. Sometimes geography plays a role, and individuals become familiar with and join religions that are practiced by the family or that are within a reasonable geographic distance. Religions often focus on social or ethical norms as well as worship. Religions differ in beliefs, rituals, practices, history, structure, and format.

Judaism

Judaism is a religion whose adherents are called Jews. It is referred to as an Abrahamic religion because it traces its roots to God's covenant with Abraham. Judaism has several basic tenets: (1) There is one God who created the world. He is omnipotent, omniscient, and omnipresent. (2) Yahweh chose the Hebrew people to be "His people." (3) Yahweh entered into a covenant with the Hebrews in which he promised Abraham to take care of the Children of Israel forever in return for their obeying him fully. The covenant set out standards of behavior that the Jews were obliged to obey. The commandments that Yahweh gave the Jews are the structure of religious practice and daily life. If either a person or a community goes against Yahweh's commandments, then they and/or the community have committed a sin. (4) Jews are to conduct themselves ethically and treat others well. (5) Group worship and prayer are essential elements of a Jewish life. There are three basic branches of Jewish belief and practice: **Orthodox** Judaism, which conducts worship only in Hebrew and interprets Jewish law strictly and literally; **Reform** Judaism, which has a more liberal interpretation of legal and religious doctrines; dietary laws are not traditionally observed; and **Conservative** Judaism, which combines doctrinal reform with traditional observance.

Christianity

Christianity is an Abrahamic religion which began as a Jewish reform movement based on the premise that **Jesus of Nazareth** (first century CE) was the Messiah (Liberator) who would free the Jews from any foreign domination. The historical Jesus attracted followers during his three years of preaching, performing miracles, and teaching others about the Word of God in and around the area of Galilee and northwest Palestine. He welcomed sinners, other castoffs from society, and women into his band of followers, which shocked contemporaries and religious leaders of the time. He fought against what he saw as the corruption of Jewish society and the commercialization of the temple. Jesus urged people to look beyond the material world, focus on the spiritual, and asserted that there would be a life after death in the Kingdom of Heaven that was far better than the material world. Jewish society did not embrace Jesus' teachings and scoffed at the idea that he was the Messiah, someone they expected would be rich, powerful, and would have an army to support him. Jesus' teachings struck fear not only in Jewish power-holders, but also among the occupying Romans who saw him as a potential political threat. Jesus was captured, tortured, and crucified.

Christians believe that Jesus' miracle days were not over with his death, as three days after his death, he rose from the dead, spent forty days with his disciples, and then ascended into heaven. Much of what is known about Jesus is recorded in the New Testament by some of the disciples of Jesus who spread the word about his life, death, and resurrection. Saul of Tarsus (10–67 CE), later called Paul, transformed Christianity from a small Jewish reform movement into a separate religion and helped spread the word across the Roman Empire. Paul believed he was chosen by God to convert non-Jews, or Gentiles. Paul taught that Jesus had advocated a completely new way of believing in God, and that rather than being a splinter movement off of Judaism, it was a whole new religion. Over time, a variety of forms of Christianity developed, including Roman Catholicism, Eastern Orthodoxy, Protestantism, and many others. The particular form generally determines what rituals and sacraments are practiced (e.g., communion, baptism, marriage).

Christians believe that Jesus is the Son of God who died on the cross to save humankind. The Christian scripture consists of two major parts of the Bible: the Old Testament, basically Jewish scripture; and the New Testament, chief of which are the four Gospels. It is from the Gospels that the life and teachings of Jesus are revealed. The basic tenets of Christianity are (1) there is one God who is omniscient; (2) Jesus Christ is the Son of God and died for the sins of humankind; (3) The Trinity—God the Father, God the Son, and God the Holy Spirit—all work together and separately to address the needs of humankind.

Buddhism

The historical Buddha was born Prince Siddhartha Gautama to a wealthy Kshatriya family in the Himalayan foothills of a border region between India and Nepal in the 500s BCE. Siddhartha came to believe that there were major phases in life that everyone would go through: old age, sickness, and death, and that only living the life of a religious person was redeemable. He resolved to try to find a way to keep people from falling victim to age and sickness. So Siddhartha decided to spend his life searching for "truth." He wandered through the forests of India for several years searching for enlightenment. He tried many ways to become enlightened: starvation, studying with gurus, and other tactics—yet none worked. Out of frustration, he turned to meditation, which eventually led to enlightenment, and from then on he was known as the **Buddha**, the Enlightened one. He resolved to spread the lessons he learned to others. He taught that life's suffering could be avoided through the "Middle Way," a life of moderation. Buddha is not a god, and the practice of Buddhism has three tenets: (1) to lead a moral life; (2) to be mindful and aware of thoughts and actions; and (3) to develop wisdom and understanding.

After the Buddha's death, his disciples gathered together to compile his teachings, but there were different opinions on the correct teachings and practices. Despite some shared beliefs, several different types of Buddhism emerged.

Confucianism

The era between 600 and 300 BCE in China is called the era of a **Hundred Schools**. During this time, Chinese philosophers were contemplating moral, political, and theological ideas. The most famous of these Chinese philosophers is **Confucius** (551–479 BCE) who lived during the time when the **Zhou Dynasty** was being torn apart by warring lords. Confucius thought that the turbulence in society was happening because of a disappearance of love and respect. He thought that by restoring respect for tradition, society would once again become stable and orderly. Confucius believed that questions about religion, afterlife, and spirits were beyond the capacity of human reason. His philosophy was of an ethical nature, and his teachings were essentially an ethical system for people to follow. He believed that the best government was one filled with educated and conscientious people and that men of talent were better than those of birth. His idea of a meritocracy and for governments to select those of talent was later reflected in the institution of the Chinese civil service exam and the creation of **bureaucracy**.

After Confucius's death, his sayings were compiled by disciples into a book called the *Analects*. The *Analects* form the foundation of the Chinese philosophy of Confucianism, which developed a code of ethics, morality, and way of life that should form the basis not only of a ruler's actions, but also those of society in general. It remained a philosophy until about the first century CE, when it began to take on aspects of a religion.

Confucius believed that a moral society was ruled by hierarchical relationships among family members. The main idea here is something called "filial piety." Confucius believed that social order, harmony, and good government could be restored in China if Chinese society were organized around five basic relationships that were based upon the family: 1) ruler and subject, 2) father and son, 3) husband and wife, 4) older brother and younger brother, and 5) friend and friend. He thought that even rulers should practice these traits and in return, the subjects of a ruler would be loyal.

Islam

Islam traces its roots to the prophet Abraham, as does Judaism and Christianity. The Jews recount that Abraham married Sarah, who bore Isaac, who was the father to Jacob and Esau, and from Jacob came the twelve tribes of Israel. The Muslims acknowledge that the tribes spring from Abraham's relationship with Hagar who had Ishmael, from whom the twelve Arabian tribes emerged. In the Arabic language, *islam* means "submission," which in a religious context means submission to God. A person who submits is called a "*Muslim*" (the prefix "mu" is "one who").

In 570 CE, Muhammad was born in Mecca, a trading crossroads and pilgrimage spot in Arabia. Islam spread significantly, primarily because of its birth in a trading post among merchants who travelled far and wide and who could export the religion easily. Moreover, because traders came through who practiced a great many religious beliefs, the effect on early Islam was tremendous. Despite this, most of the people in the region were not Christians or Jews, and most practiced some form of polytheism. When Muhammad was 25, he married Khadija, a wealthy widow who was

Competency 4: World History

about fifteen years older. As the husband of a wealthy woman, Muhammad was freed from a life of work. He chose to focus on spiritual endeavors and often went to retreats outside Mecca. While at one of the retreats, Muhammad received a message from the Archangel Gabriel that told him to "recite" everything Gabriel said. These revelations, which would continue over the next twenty-three years, from the Archangel Gabriel were believed to be God's message to humanity through his final prophet, Muhammad. The resulting text is the Qur'an (sometimes spelled "Koran"). With its beautiful poetic language and lofty expressions, it is considered a miracle, something beyond Muhammad's education and experience because he was illiterate. Muslims believe that these revelations were corrections to previous Abrahamic revelations. Muslims believe that Gabriel delivered God's message to Muhammad and that Muhammad was simply God's messenger. Muslims do not believe that Muhammad himself was divine. The Qur'an names many Jewish and Christian prophets in it and accepts many Jewish and Christian traditions. The Qur'an names twenty-five prophets, including Abraham, Moses, Jesus, as well as Muhammad. While the Qur'an says that the earlier prophets were true, it also says that their messages were corrupted over the years. Muslims believe that the Torah and the Bible are both the Word of God, and that Jews and Christians are Ahl al-Kitab, or peoples of the book, and as such, are to be protected. Muslims believe that God's message to Muhammad restored the purity of the original messages. Because the Qur'an is believed to be God's final word, Muslims do not accept the existence of any prophets after Muhammad. The basic tenant of Islam is that there is only one God (Allah).

Islam advocates the following moral principles: to stay away from alcohol, pork, and gambling; to practice charity, patience, and humility; to forgive enemies; and to avoid greed, lying, and malice. There are five pillars of Islam, which define what it means to be a Muslim and how one should practice Islam:

1. To be a Muslim, one does not need a long conversion process, but one simply has to say the *Shahadah*, or bear witness that "there is no God but Allah, and that Muhammad is his Messenger." This declaration of the faith must be uttered publicly at least once in a Muslim's lifetime, although most Muslims recite it daily.

2. The *Salat* (Prayer): Muslims may pray anywhere—in the middle of an airport, a busy shopping mall, in school, in the street, etc. All they need to do is to find the direction of Mecca and pray toward it.

3. *Zakat* (Alms): Muslims believe that all things belong to God, and that humans hold wealth in trust for him. For that reason, Muslims believe wealth should be distributed throughout the community of believers. Additional charity work is also encouraged.

4. *Sawm* (Fasting): During the month of Ramadan, the ninth month in the lunar Islamic calendar, Muslims fast between dawn and dusk in order to commemorate the month in which the revelations from the Archangel Gabriel began. The end of Ramadan is celebrated by the **Eid al-Fitr**, one of the major festivals on the Muslim calendar.

5. *Hajj* (Pilgrimage to Mecca): All Muslims are required to make one pilgrimage to Mecca in their lifetimes, provided they are physically and financially able to do so.

Islam was considered a rather progressive religion at the time, appealing to women and minorities because it treated them better than other religions did at the time. Women were given the right to earn their own living, choose their own marriage partners, and to own and dispose of their personal property and earnings as they wished. The roles of men and women may be different, but these roles are seen as complementary, each as important as the other's.

When Muhammad died in 632 BCE, he had not designated a successor. Some Muslims, who became known as Shi'ites, believed that the successor should be a member of Muhammad's family. Other Muslims, who became known as Sunnis, believed the successor should be the oldest and most venerated of the Muslim community. This created a divide in Islam, which continues to this day and remains a source of war between the two factions.

Islam proved to be a religion that was quite conducive to rapid expansion. It was easy to learn and practice—one just needed to know the six basic principles and the five pillars. There was no priesthood, so one could practice it everywhere. Islam promoted equality, so many were attracted to it because it improved their status in society. Non-Muslims welcomed Muslim rule because they were not treated badly, nor were they forced to convert. It was easily portable because no equipment was needed and easily spread along trade routes. Islam included the idea of jihad, a defensive idea that said one should always strive to perfect oneself (lesser jihad), but also, when attacked or threatened, one was allowed and expected to defend oneself (greater jihad).

Hinduism

Hinduism differs from other religions in that it is not a uniform, organized belief system but more of a set of related traditions that reflect common themes such as devotion to God or gods, the duties of family life, and concentrated meditation. Hindus may have different rituals, beliefs, and philosophies. As a result, generalizing about what it means to be a Hindu is complex. All Hindus do not believe in the same deity. Some worship Shiva, Vishnu, or some other deity. Others look within themselves to the divine Self. Most Hindus recognize that Brahman is the unifying principle and Supreme Reality behind all that exists.

Hinduism is the oldest major religion, dating back approximately four thousand years. As such, no specific founder or date of origin is associated with Hinduism. The writers of most Hindu sacred texts are also unknown. Believers regard Hinduism as eternal ("sanatana"). Although the authority of the *Vedas* (a collection of ancient sacred texts from the Vedic religion) and the Brahmans (the priestly class) is accepted and respected, some Hindus reject the authority of one or both.

Westerners often learn about Hinduism from religious movements (e.g., New Age) or the incorporation of beliefs (e.g., yoga) in mainstream approaches to wellness and spirituality. The diversity and acceptance of beliefs within Hinduism is often an appealing alternative to traditional world religions.

CHAPTER 5

U.S. History

COMPETENCY 5.1

Evaluate the impact of the Age of Exploration on the Americas.

Although the Vikings had arrived in North America approximately 500 years earlier, the Age of Exploration describes a time in which Europe first "discovered" and explored the new world. Governments supported such activity in order to gain wealth and to preempt other countries. Explorers were often motivated by one or more of the three Gs: God, Gold, or Glory. This era is marked by three phases: discovery, preliminary exploration, and expansion as Europeans migrated to the Americas. Spain, Portugal, England, and France played the greatest roles in this age.

Spanish and Portuguese Beginnings

Italian explorer Christopher Columbus believed he could find a route to the East by sailing west. He asked for support from the King of Portugal, cities in Italy, and the King of Spain without success. Finally, King Ferdinand of Spain changed his mind and in 1492, sponsored the voyage in which Columbus discovered the "New World" of the Americas. With the support of the Spanish king, Columbus made three additional trips to the Americas where he explored islands in the Caribbean and finally landed on the mainland of South America. On one of his return voyages to Spain, Columbus stopped in Portugal and described what he had found to Portuguese King John II, who was also interested in exploring and claiming territories in the new world. In an effort to settle a dispute between the Spanish and the Portuguese over who should get which territory, Pope Alexander VI (a Spaniard, actually) set up a Line of Demarcation that would separate the territories of the world between the two largest Catholic powers, the Spanish and the Portuguese. This was the **Treaty of Tordesillas.** The Portuguese at the time were more concerned about preserving their spice trade in the east, and so they willingly gave the Spanish the New World territories, with the exception of what would be Brazil (this is why the Brazilians speak Portuguese and the rest of South America speaks Spanish).

English and French Beginnings

In 1497, Italian **Giovanni Caboto** (known in history by his English name of **John Cabot**) sailed under the sponsorship of the king of England in search of a Northwest Passage (a water route to the Orient through or around the North American continent). He became the first European since the Vikings more than four centuries earlier to reach the mainland of North America, which he claimed for England. Beginning in 1534, **Jacques Cartier** (1491–1557), authorized by the king of France, mounted three expeditions to the area of the St. Lawrence River, which he believed might be the hoped-for Northwest Passage. He explored up the river as far as the site of present-day Montreal.

Impact on the Americas

The insatiable European appetite for expansion of its trade, the search for new commodities, the desire to build empires, and the use of slave labor to extract the wealth from their new land greatly affected not only the lands they conquered but also many other areas of the world. Spain deliberately destroyed the native, wealthy, and perhaps rather oppressive empires in America, only to substitute their own brutal rule in their stead. As Spain expanded its areas of control, it forced elements of Spanish culture onto weakened populations, including new religion, new languages, new power structures, new political and sexual cultures, and new attitudes toward the role of women in society. Europeans took over areas perceived to be "stateless" in which local rule was deemed illegitimate. They ethnically cleansed the areas of the local inhabitants and set off economic and political changes that permeated indigenous societies throughout the continent.

In the West Indies, a pattern would be set that would be followed throughout the conquistador period. Priests forced many natives to become Christians or else perish at the hands of the army's sword. Native people were enslaved to toil in mines and on plantations. On the Taino Islands, for instance, when the Spanish arrived, there were between 1 and 2 million residents. Within 50 years, there were only 500 natives left. The Spanish looked to Africa to find laborers, and from 1518 to the mid-1800s, the Spanish brought millions of slaves to the Americas.

While the Spanish did introduce new animals to the Americas—including horses, sheep, cattle, and pigs—the conquistadores destroyed at least two great civilizations, the Aztecs and the Incas. The effects on Mexico were devastating as it went from a population of 25 million people to 1 million in only 100 years.

When the Portuguese settled in Brazil, they, like the Spanish, forced people to give up their religion and convert to Christianity. They forced people to work on sugar plantations. So many people died because of diseases that the Europeans brought with them for which the natives had no immunity, that the Portuguese were left needing laborers to extract the resources from their newly conquered land. So, starting in the mid-1500s, they turned to West Africa, where they bought

Competency 5: U.S. History

slaves and transported them to work in Brazil. This forced migration of Africans to Brazil changed the racial landscape of the Americas.

Europeans in North America took similar measures against the native populations. They wiped out from 50% to 90% of the native populations through war, exposure to disease and new germs, and slavery.

Economic Impact:

- Economic growth was rapid with an increase in business and trading.
- Vast amounts of gold and silver were removed from the Americas and redistributed to Europe and across the globe.
- Prices of goods rose due to inflation and mercantilist economic policies.
- Capitalism emerged as the dominant economic system.

Social Impact:

- The rising middle class benefited from new economic and social opportunities.
- Power and wealth were concentrated in the hands of a relatively few white people of European descent.
- A strict economic and social hierarchy developed.
- The foundation was laid for continued economic and social issues to develop.
- Millions of Africans were brought to the New World as slaves.
- The slave system altered how and where land was developed, and destroyed lives.
- Native populations were decimated by disease, malnutrition, war, and forced labor.
- The blending of indigenous populations with Europeans and Africans resulted in new cultural and racial groups, and a blending of cultures.

Political Impact:

- New forms of political systems and control were developed, which placed the Native Americans on the outside or bottom of the systems.

Cultural Impact:

- Christianity spread throughout the Americas.
- Christian missionaries worked to convert the native populations and set up schools.
- The Catholic Church became dominant in many colonial regions.

- Christianity was blended with traditional beliefs and practice.

- Animals from Europe brought to the Americas, like horses and cattle, changed both transportation and food sources.

- New plants and crops were exchanged.

COMPETENCY 5.2

Analyze the social, cultural, political, and economic development of the Americas during the colonial period.

The Colonial World

People came to the New World for a wide variety of reasons: some came to make a profit for both themselves and the financiers of their trip, some out of a desire for religious freedom, and some for adventure. By and large, the colonization of the Americas hinged on four major factors:

- the universal economic theory at the time, **mercantilism**, which held that colonies exist for the economic benefit of the mother country and are useless unless they help to achieve profit;

- the rivalry of three major nations—England, France, and Spain—that dictated and greatly influenced the nature and the development of each of the colonies;

- the geography; and

- the native population in the area.

While the European countries each had their individual approaches toward exploration and colonization, there were also some shared characteristics.

Spain's New World ventures focused primarily on South America, Central America, Mexico, and the American Southwest. For the Spanish conquistadores, the king remained the source of all authority. When disputes arose between explorers, or explorers wanted to gain some authority in the lands they conquered, they had to go back to the Spanish king to ask for his permission or help. The Spanish wanted, above all else, gold. They were also a strongly Catholic regime that quickly brought in priests to convert the native peoples. The Spanish wreaked havoc on indigenous societies, decimating all facets of their civilization, and were exceedingly cruel to their laborers.

France's experiences in the New World were more limited, focusing on North America. In 1608, Samuel de Champlain established a trading post in Quebec, from which the rest of what became New France eventually spread. French exploration and settlement spread through the Great Lakes region and the valleys of the Mississippi and Ohio rivers. French settlements in the Midwest were generally forts and trading posts serving the fur trade. Their relations, for the most part, were friendly with the Indians they encountered. The economic systems they put in place were joint stock companies.

In 1609, Holland sent Englishman Henry Hudson to search for a Northwest Passage. In this endeavor, Hudson discovered the river that bears his name and made trade arrangements with the Iroquois for furs. In 1624, Dutch trading outposts were established on Manhattan Island (New Amsterdam) and at the site of present-day Albany (Fort Orange). The Dutch were not interested in forming a colony in the New World; their interests remained purely economic. As traders, they were interested in procuring some of the resources from the country.

When the English finally began colonization, commercial capitalism in England had advanced to the point that the English efforts were supported by private rather than government funds, allowing English colonists to enjoy greater freedom from government interference. Five of the original thirteen colonies had originated due to the financing of corporations: Virginia, Plymouth, Maryland, South Carolina, and North Carolina were all corporate in origin. A capitalistic economy emerged with small farmers, artisans, merchants, and aristocrats working for profit. In time, some Americans created commercial monopolies that needed a constant source of dependent labor to augment their wealth.

Two groups of merchants gained charters from James I, Queen Elizabeth's successor. One group was based in London and received a charter to North America between what are now the Hudson and the Cape Fear rivers. The other was based in Plymouth and was granted the right to colonize in North America from the Potomac to the northern border of present-day Maine. They were called the Virginia Company of London and the Virginia Company of Plymouth, respectively. They were joint-stock companies that raised their capital by the sale of shares of stock. The Virginia Company of London settled **Jamestown** in 1607. It became the first permanent English settlement in North America. During the early years of Jamestown, the majority of the settlers died of starvation, various diseases, or hostile actions by Native Americans. The colony's survival remained in doubt for a number of years. Impressed by the potential profits from tobacco growing, King James I was determined to have Virginia for himself. In 1624, he revoked the London Company's charter and made Virginia a royal colony. This pattern was followed throughout colonial history; both company colonies and proprietary colonies tended eventually to become royal colonies.

Many Englishmen came from England for religious reasons. For the most part, the Englishmen fell into two groups, **Puritans** and **Separatists**. Though similar in many respects to the Puritans, the Separatists believed the Church of England was beyond saving and so felt they must separate from it. Led by William Bradford (1590–1657), a group of Separatists departed in 1620, having obtained from the London Company a charter to settle just south of the Hudson River. Driven by storms, their ship, the **Mayflower**, made landfall at Cape Cod in Massachusetts. This, however, put them outside the jurisdiction of any established government; and so, before going ashore, they drew up and signed the *Mayflower Compact*, establishing a foundation for orderly government based on the consent of the governed. After a number of years of hard work, they were able to buy out the investors who had originally financed their voyage and thus gain greater autonomy.

The Puritans were far more numerous than the Separatists. Charles I determined in 1629 to persecute the Puritans aggressively and to rule without the Puritan-dominated Parliament. In 1629, the Puritans chartered a joint-stock company called the Massachusetts Bay Company. The charter neglected to specify where the company's headquarters should be located. Taking advantage of this unusual omission, the Puritans determined to make their headquarters in the colony itself, 3,000 miles from meddlesome royal officials.

Puritans saw their colony not as a place to do whatever might strike one's fancy, but as a place to serve God and build His kingdom. Dissidents would only be tolerated insofar as they did not interfere with the colony's mission. One such dissident was **Roger Williams**. When his activities became disruptive, he was asked to leave the colony. He fled to the wilderness around Narragansett Bay, bought land from the Indians, and founded the settlement of Providence (1636).

Another dissident was **Anne Hutchinson**, who openly taught things contrary to Puritan doctrine. She was banished from the colony. She also migrated to the area around Narragansett Bay and with her followers founded Portsmouth (1638). In 1663, Charles II, having recently been restored to the throne, moved to reward eight of the noblemen who had helped him regain the crown by granting them a charter for all the lands lying south of Virginia and north of Spanish Florida. The new colony was called Carolina, after the king. In 1664, Charles gave his brother James, Duke of York, title to all the Dutch lands in America, provided James conquered them first. New Amsterdam fell almost without a shot and became New York.

North American Colonies

The colonies were generally divided into three regions: New England, Middle Atlantic, and Southern. Each region seemed to have a distinct culture and attitudes toward religion, politics, and economic interests. The geography of each region also contributed to the region's unique characteristics, which reflected its origins.

New England Colonies

The New England colonies, consisting of Massachusetts, Rhode Island, Connecticut, and New Hampshire, enjoyed a much more stable and well-ordered society than did the Chesapeake colonies of Maryland and Virginia. Puritans placed great importance on the family, which in their society was highly patriarchal. Puritans also placed great importance on the ability to read, since they believed everyone should be able to read the Bible. As a result, New England was ahead of the other colonies educationally, and it enjoyed widespread literacy. Since New England's climate and soil were unsuited to large-scale farming, the region developed a prosperous economy based on small farming, home industry, fishing, trade, and shipbuilding. Boston became a major international port.

Southern and Chesapeake Colonies

Beginning around 1650, British authorities began to take more interest in regulating American trade for the benefit of the mother country. A key idea that underlay this policy was the concept of **mercantilism**. Each nation's goal was to export more than it imported (i.e., to have a "favorable balance of trade"). To achieve their goals, mercantilists believed economic activity should be regulated by the government. Colonies could fit into England's mercantilist scheme by providing staple crops, such as rice, tobacco, sugar, and indigo, and raw materials, such as timber, that England would otherwise have been forced to import from other countries. Parliament passed a series of Navigation Acts (1651, 1660, 1663, and 1673) to help accomplish these goals.

Tobacco, first planted by the Europeans in 1611, proved to be the commodity crop that the mercantilist enterprise had been searching for, as Europeans on the continent clamored for it. As a result, in the 1620s, there was a tremendous boom in tobacco export, so much so that the colony of Virginia quickly grew into a full-sized settlement that included men, women, and children. In fact, there was so much planting of the crop that the tobacco quickly exhausted the soil. As colonists expanded to sow more tobacco seed, the Powhatan tribe became so unsettled by the rapid expansion that on March 22, 1622, the Indians attacked and killed almost a quarter of the inhabitants in the settlements. This did not sit well with King James I, who already was unhappy with the lack of profit that the Virginia Company was making. He disbanded the company and made Virginia a royal colony. He started the headright system in 1617 as a means to get more Europeans to come to the New World and grow tobacco. The deal was that every new person would get fifty acres of land. Because not many people had the funds to pay for their trip over, wealthy planters would offer to pay people's way, provided they gave the land to the planter and agreed to work as an indentured servant for a period of time, after which they would be given a little plot of land of their own.

During the first half of the seventeenth century, Blacks in the Chesapeake area made up only a small percentage of the population and were treated essentially as indentured servants. Between 1640 and 1670, this status gradually changed, and Blacks came to be seen and treated as lifelong chattel slaves whose status would be inherited by their children. By 1750, they composed 30% to 40% of the Chesapeake population. While North Carolina tended to follow Virginia in its economic and social development (although with fewer great planters and more small farmers), South Carolina developed a society even more dominated by large plantations and chattel slavery.

Middle Atlantic Colonies

Pennsylvania was founded as a refuge for **Quakers**. One of a number of radical religious sects that had sprung up about the time of the English Civil War, the Quakers held many controversial beliefs. They believed all persons had an "inner light," which allowed them to commune directly with God. They therefore placed little importance on the Bible. They were also pacifists, and they declined to show customary deference to those who were considered to be their social superiors.

Delaware, though at first part of Pennsylvania, was granted a separate legislature by William Penn. Until the American Revolution, Pennsylvania's proprietary governors also functioned as governors of Delaware. Eighteenth-century America's population continued to grow rapidly, both from natural increases due to prosperity and a healthy environment and from large-scale immigration, not only of English but also of other groups such as Scots-Irish and Germans.

By the end of the first century of European colonization in America, the colonists had created strong governments, developed a wide variety of agricultural and industrial activities, and established complex societies. By 1732, the colonies had created three types of governments:

- **Royal colonies,** where the English monarch controlled the colonies and appointed governors and their councils to run them.

- **Proprietary colonies,** where landowners determined the direction of government.

- **Corporate colonies,** where corporations and their stockholders determined the direction of the government and economy.

By the mid-1700s, all thirteen colonies had become royal colonies. As the colonies became royal colonies, their economic activity began a transformation, moving from a focus on farming to a focus that included **household manufacturing,** in which families produced articles for their own use, and some **commercial industries for profit**, including fishing, lumbering, shipbuilding, flour milling, and iron manufacturing. All of the industries were able to take advantage of the cheap and abundant natural resources and did not have to expend much capital.

By the end of the seventeenth century, the colonies already had become a diverse place with people of varying political, cultural, socio-economic, religious, and racial backgrounds; however, some of these differences resulted in conflicts over the decades. Some of these tensions existed primarily in the way that European colonists treated the varying nations of American Indians throughout North, Central, and South America. Unlike the English, the Spanish and French included Native Americans in the social and economic lives of their communities—although unequally. The English purposefully excluded Indians from their social, economic, and political lives. The Quaker communities, on the other hand, exhibited tolerance.

Economic Changes During the Eighteenth Century

Compared to the economic environment in Europe, which was suffering the effects of war and inflation, the British colonists had a higher standard of living than their European counterparts. By the eighteenth century, colonists typically engaged in four types of work:

1. **Agricultural**: The main way they earned their livings was through different types of farming. Plantation farming was based upon commercial single-crop commodities; commercial farming was when people on smaller farms would raise crops, not for just their own sustenance, but to sell in the market; and self-sufficient family farming was where people grew crops to satisfy their own needs and use any surplus to buy goods or pay their taxes.

2. **Craftsmen**: Men who had gone through some sort of training as an apprentice would often work as craftsmen in trades such as blacksmiths, coopers, weavers, carpenters, and shipwrights.

3. **Mercantilists**: In trading, merchants would buy and sell goods they themselves did not make in order to make a profit.

4. **Service provision**: Other people offered services in communities, like butchers, market workers, doctors, and hair cutters.

Because of the emergence of more specialized industry, three types of classes characterized colonial society:

1. **Rural landowners:** Southern plantation owners who invested in land, slaves, buildings, lands, tools, and seeds

2. **Merchants:** traders and sellers of goods and services

3. **Wage earners:** wage earners who invested in industrial stock or various enterprises

By the end of the eighteenth century, the gulf between the rich and poor had widened considerably. In Boston and Philadelphia, the top 10% owned more than 60% of the wealth.

Table 5.1
American Colonies

	Northern Colonies: Massachusetts Bay Colony; Rhode Island, Connecticut, New Hampshire, Maine	Mid-Atlantic Colonies: New York, New Jersey, Pennsylvania, Delaware
Type of Colonies	Small towns were the center of governments; typically started as royal colonies	Proprietary colonies established during the reign of Charles II (Restoration Colonies). Charles distributed land to his loyal followers and also used the colonies as a means to get rid of "problem" populations within England, like the Quakers
Economy	• Manufacturing, fishing, shipbuilding, lumbering, fur trading, commerce, small family-run farms. • Most of the food was grown at home, that which was not was imported from England. • Self-sufficient farms. • Exported corn and wheat industry. • Profited from triangular trade with Africa and West Indies	• Part industrial, part agricultural; fur trade. • Farms were larger than those in New England. • Grew wheat, rye, and barley and was the "Bread Basket of the Colonies" • Raised livestock. • Factories produced iron, paper, and textiles. • Considerable trade with England.
Social Structure	Population largely homogenous, white, Puritans	Gentry Middling sort (farmers, shopkeepers, teachers)
Religious Factors	People were considered, at least in the eyes of God, to be relatively equal. Pilgrims in Mass. sought religious freedom. Rhode Island passed laws of religious toleration. Religions: Puritans dominated New England	Quakers in Pennsylvania sought religious freedom—no army or war; greater toleration. Religions: Dutch Reformed and Presbyterian dominated
Motivations for Settling	Many sought to practice their own religion free of interference from government	Sought religious freedom (in Pennsylvania) and to make money. Many of those who came for the economic opportunities did not bring their families with them and so they eagerly worked hard
Who Settled	Primarily British Puritans	Dutch, English, Swedes, Germans, and French, so there was an emphasis on cultural diversity from the beginning. Many artisans and indentured servants came as well.

Competency 5: U.S. History

	Chesapeake Colonies: Virginia and Maryland	Southern Colonies: North and South Carolinas, Georgia
Type of Colonies	• Virginia founded by the London Company for profit in 1607; later became a royal colony. • Maryland was a proprietary colony founded by the Calvert family.	• Restoration colonies • Georgia founded as a buffer between English colonies and Spanish Florida
Economy	• Single crop economies—money crops—rice, indigo, cotton, and tobacco. • Slaves formed a large part of the workforce on plantations. • Maintained close ties to England as South provided raw materials in exchange for European goods. • Had large debt to English merchants and bankers.	• Single-crop economies—money crops—rice, indigo, cotton, and tobacco • Slaves formed a large part of the workforce on plantations. • Maintained close ties to England as South provided raw materials in exchange for European goods. • Had large debt to English merchants and bankers.
Social Structure	Socially stratified— • Plantation owners at the top—wealthy owned many slaves and dominated economic, political, and social spheres • Small landowners (few owned slaves) • Tenant farmers: worked on others' land, paid rent, some worked as overseers • Slaves: Lowest	Socially stratified— • Plantation owners at the top—wealthy owned many slaves and dominated economic, political, and social spheres • Small landowners (few owned slaves) • Tenant farmers: worked on others' land, paid rent; some worked as overseers • Slaves: lowest
Religious Factors	• Maryland passed laws of religious toleration. • Religion: Anglican (Church of England) dominated (except Maryland was Catholic)	• Religion: Anglican dominated
Motivations for Settling	• Mostly out to make money • Maryland founded as haven for Catholics	• Mostly out to make money and as a long-term venture, so they brought their families with them.
Who Settled	Primarily British: Adventurers and younger sons of aristocracy attracted to southern colonies; indentured servants worked on plantations to pay for their passage; criminals came to escape the death penalty (and chose colonies instead); as indentured servant numbers declined, slavery rose.	Primarily British: Adventurers and younger sons of aristocracy attracted to southern colonies; indentured servants worked on plantations to pay for their passage; criminals came to escape the death penalty (and chose colonies instead); as indentured servant numbers declined, slavery rose.

Colonial Societies During the Eighteenth Century

Most of colonial society could fit into one of these five types of societies:

1. **Colonial Farming Societies.** The bulk of the people who lived in the colonies lived on small, family-run, and self-sufficient farms. This included most who lived in the New England and Southern colonies, as well as many of those in the Middle Colonies.

2. **Urban Seaport Societies.** Big cities developed along the Atlantic Seaboard and became major seaports and commercial centers like Boston, New York, Newport, Philadelphia, and Charleston. Wealthy merchants and traders had become quite powerful.

3. **Frontier Societies.** As the next generation of colonists moved westward to find new, cheap land, they had to "rough it," living with bare necessities and creating their own environment. Much like the same issues that the first Europeans faced when they landed on American shores, frontier societies had to create every element of their society. However, unlike the early colonists, the frontier societies did not have a strong community presence, due to how spread out everyone was and the lack of organized law and order, community institutions, or organized churches. As a result, the frontier lands were considered difficult places to live. Frontier societies faced increasing conflict with those back East, as the frontier people felt that they were not being treated equally. They protested that they were not given adequate protection from Indian attacks or equal representation in government assemblies, and that the East purposely did not provide courts for the frontier. The frontier societies claimed that some of these grievances could be traced to ethnic and economic differences between them and Eastern society. The frontier population was decidedly "foreign"—meaning of German and Scots-Irish descent, and tended to consist of self-sufficient farmers or commercial farmers whose security was rather tenuous.

4. **Plantation/Slave Societies.** This was a highly stratified society in which social mobility did not occur.

5. **Native American Societies.** European settlers engaged in a massive attempt to wipe the Indian peoples off of their lands. In 300 years, the Native American population declined from 10 million to about 1 million. Many of those tribes that had close contact with Europeans suffered much the same fate as their South American counterparts, as more than 50% caught diseases. As tribes were dispossessed of their lands, they moved westward in search of freedom.

Social Changes During the Eighteenth Century

Changes in colonial society occurred on a number of levels: population growth, ethnic diversity, increasing importance of cities, creation of urban elites, rising levels of consumption, and the growth of a stronger internal economy.

- Population changes skyrocketed, as there were about 650,000 new immigrants, including about 325,000 slaves who came unwillingly. By the second half of the century, there were significant differences and stratification in terms of colonists' social and economic lives. There was enormous population growth, expanding from 300,000 people in 1700 to 2.5 million by 1775.

- The ethnic and linguistic composition of the immigrants also changed. Not only were more West Africans of various ethnic and linguistic groups coming as slaves, but also there were changes among Europeans, too, as more Scots-Irish and German immigrants flocked to America.

- Cities contained 20% of the population (10% higher than in 1700); there were four main cities in the colonies: Boston, New York, Philadelphia, and Charleston.

- Social and economic stratification intensified after 1750.

- Aristocratic plantation owners in the South had the most wealth and influence.

- Lawyers, merchants, officials, and clergymen dominated the North.

- Yeoman farmers constituted the majority of the population, and they owned land.

- Lesser tradesman, manual workers, and hired hands usually did not own land.

- Indentured servants and slaves were at the lowest level of society. About 20% of the population were slaves.

- A revitalization of religious beliefs and practice, often known as the **Great Awakening**, spread in the 1730s–1740s in the Southern and Middle colonies, as a reaction against established churches.

- Colonial press developed.

Figure 5.1
Population of the New England Colonies, 1620–1750

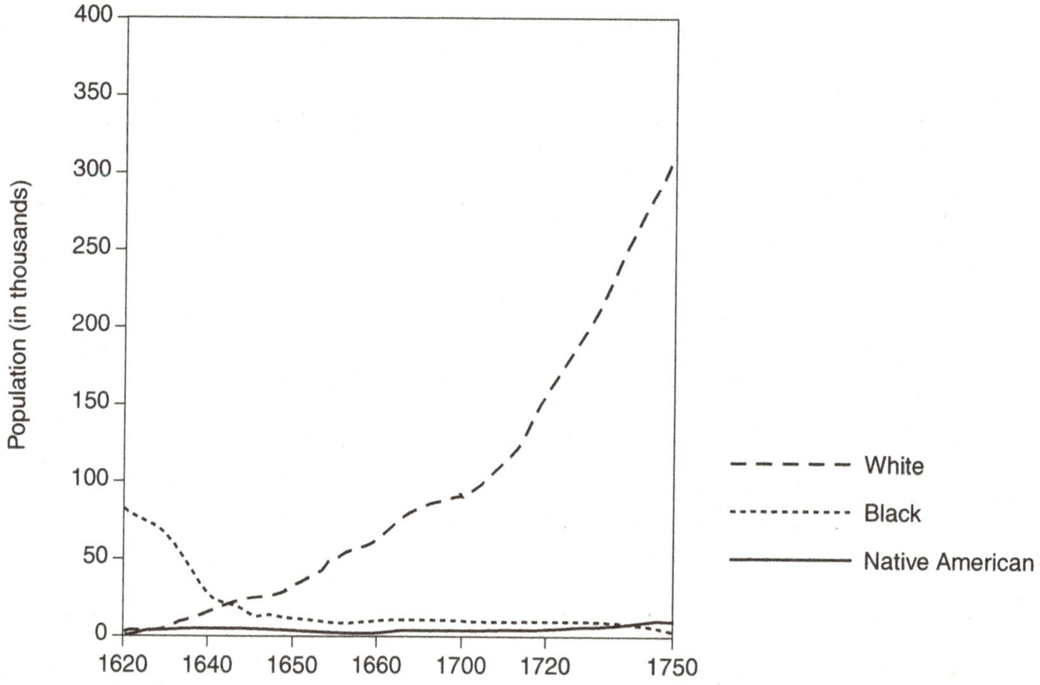

(Line graph showing population in thousands from 1620 to 1750, with lines for White, Black, and Native American populations. The White population rises steeply to about 300,000 by 1750; Native American population starts near 80,000 in 1620 and declines sharply; Black population remains low throughout.)

© 2003 Facts On File, Inc.

COMPETENCY 5.3

Identify the causes, significant individuals, and effects of the events associated with the Revolutionary era.

Albany Plan of Union

In 1754, representatives of seven colonies and 150 Indians met in Albany, New York, to gain the allegiance of the Iroquois Confederacy and to provide a system for the collective defense of the colonies in the face of the coming war with France. After renewing the alliance with the Iroquois, who promised to continue to protect the English from attacks by the French-supporting Hurons, Benjamin Franklin proposed the **Albany Plan of Union**. This plan provided for an intercolonial government that would regulate dealings with the Native Americans, organize and run a colonial army, manage the public lands, legislate, and supervise the collection of taxes for a common defense fund. England rejected the proposal because they felt that a union of the colonies would make them too unmanageable. The colonies also rejected the Albany Plan because they did not want to relinquish any of their powers to a grand council, particularly the right to tax. Franklin's annoyance at the lack of support was reflected in his published cartoon in which he drew a snake broken into pieces, with the inscription below: "Join, or Die." The drawing was based on the popular belief that a snake that had been cut in half would come to life again if the pieces were joined before sunset. This rejection of the Albany Plan foreshadowed what would happen later in colonial affairs and the issues that would arise in future intercolonial gatherings like the First and Second Congress. Had the Albany Plan passed, it could have rendered the American Revolution unnecessary. This also proved to be the last attempt to devise an intercolonial union.

Figure 5.2

By Benjamin Franklin
Cartoon in the *Pennsylvania Gazette* May 9, 1754

The Seven Years' War and the Treaty of Paris, 1763

While conflict and tensions between the French and English over colonial supremacy over North America had been going on for many decades, in the early 1750s, tensions came to a head as England and France both vied for land in the Ohio River Valley. English troops under the command of a rather inexperienced George Washington marched to oust the French by force. The French led a force of 600 troops against Washington, forcing him to surrender. Thus began the French and Indian War, also known as the **Seven Years' War**, a war that actually lasted nine years. It is also called the **French and Indian War**, because the French and Indians fought on the same side. The war was one of several skirmishes for empire between the British and the French (which happened all over the world, notably in India). Some historians have referred to this as the first world war.

There were three phases of fighting during the Seven Years' War:

Phase 1: 1754–1756, characterized by limited nature of the war, being confined to the North American continent.

Phase 2: 1756–1757, when the war spread to the West Indies, India, and Europe. Still, much of the fighting continued to be in North America. **William Pitt**, the British Secretary of State, directed the war effort and issued orders to the colonists. He ordered British commanders to forcibly enlist colonists to serve and to seize needed supplies from them. These measures led to a struggle between the colonists and the British that hampered the war effort.

Phase 3: 1758–1763: By 1758, some of the problems that had plagued the British started to resolve. Pitt relaxed some of his measures and gave more troops to the colonies, leading the British to regain some military successes. The Fall of Quebec in September 1759 helped the British to convince the French to surrender in 1760. A peace treaty, however, was not signed until 1763.

During the war, British-colonial tensions increased, as anti-British feelings in the colonies found their voice. The colonists and the British had very different fighting styles and tactics. The colonials used guerilla tactics, and the British marched in formation. The colonial militias who helped fight for the British remained under their own command, despite British insistence that they remain under British authority.

Britain imposed new taxes, as they were deeply in debt because of the war and thought that Americans should share the cost of the war. The colonists did not want to pay higher taxes to pay for the cost of the war. The British felt that they had been fighting for the defense of the colonists, and that such ungrateful responses were unjustified. The new British king, **George III**, and his Prime Minister, **George Grenville**, also considered that the tax burden that the colonists had to bear was considerably less than that of taxpayers back in England, so they did not believe it was too harsh of a burden.

As a result of the British victory in the French and Indian War, France lost its foothold in the New World. The **Treaty of Paris (1763)** made them relinquish their New World possessions, including Canada. They also agreed to get out and stay out of India, which made Great Britain the supreme military power in that part of Asia. Because Spain had fought on the side of France, it gained and lost in this treaty. Spain lost Florida to England, but gained all French land west of the Mississippi. In addition, as compensation for Spain's loss of Florida to England, Spain was awarded the Louisiana territory.

At the end of the war, Britain had mixed emotions about the war. While they were grateful that they now had a larger and safer empire, they also had accumulated significant debt. The colonists' protests against paying that debt resulted in growing feelings of contempt for the colonists. British attempts to force the colonists to pay for the war and to recoup their financial losses by levying taxes wound up only sparking colonial anger and fueling revolutionary fervor. For the colonies, the war had united them against a common enemy for the first time. It also created long-standing anger against the British, who were viewed as overly harsh and whose disdain for the colonists created even more resentment.

Another effect of the war was that the English raised the price of goods that they sold to the Indians and stopped paying rent on their western forts. In response, the Ottawa leader, Pontiac, united an unprecedented amount of tribes due to concern about the spread of colonists and their culture, and attacked colonial outposts in the Ohio valley. The attacks and the wars are referred to as **Pontiac's Rebellion** or **Pontiac's Uprising**. Although the British ultimately prevailed, how they handled the conflict provoked further resentment among the colonists. In response to Pontiac's Rebellion and the attacks, the British issued the **Proclamation of 1763**, which drew a line west of the rivers running through the Appalachians and said that the colonists were not allowed to settle past that line, in order to avoid further conflicts with the Indians. While this improved relations between the British and the Native Americans, it worsened the relationship between the British and the colonists. The problem was that the colonists had already expanded beyond the Ohio River Valley and encroached on Indian lands. Settlers were annoyed by the proclamation and viewed it as unwarranted British interference. It also can be viewed as the first in a series of new efforts by the British to control the colonists more tightly, the end of **salutary neglect**, and the beginning of the road to revolution. It also led to French support of the American colonies during the upcoming revolution, as France wanted its own measure of revenge against the British.

Grenville Acts

From 1763–1765, British Prime Minister Grenville led the charge to extract more taxes from the colonists. He put forth four pieces of legislation that would be sources of great discontent for the colonists: the **Sugar Act (1764)**, the **Currency Act (1764)**, the **Quartering Act (1765)**, and the **Stamp Act (1765)**.

Sugar Act

This established new taxes aimed at deterring molasses smugglers by *lowering* the duty on molasses, sugar, textiles, coffee, and indigo coming into the colonies from the West Indies. American colonists did not think it was fair that they should be taxed in the same manner as those who lived in England, particularly as they had no representation in Parliament. Cries of **"no taxation without representation"** filled town halls and public gatherings. Colonists were upset that any violators would be tried in vice-admiralty courts, where judges could issue verdicts and there would be no deliberation of a jury. Colonists felt this overstepped British authority over them and violated their rights as Englishmen.

Currency Act

The British felt that the colonial currency fluctuated too much to the detriment of the British. This act forbade the colonies from issuing money, as it ruled that colonial currency could not be used for trade. Colonists were angered that their money had no value.

Quartering Act

Britain decided that it could save money if the cost for housing and feeding British troops in America was the responsibility of the Americans. Thus, this act forced colonial assemblies to raise taxes to provide housing and provisions, like bedding, cooking utensils, firewood, beer, cider, and candles for 10,000 new British troops in barracks near colonial centers. Colonists questioned why troops were being sent over now, after the cessation of war with France. This law was expanded in 1766 and required the assemblies to billet all British soldiers residing in their borders in taverns and unoccupied houses.

The reaction of the colonists was largely negative. The colonists generally preferred to rely on militia units rather than formal armies because it was cheaper. Militiamen could be called for service during a particular crisis and then disbanded when the fighting was concluded, without the colonists having to pay for long-term provisioning. Colonial assemblies fretted about the cost of expenses for an army that they did not feel they particularly needed. The French were no longer a threat by the mid-1760s, and many believed Britain had ulterior motives for keeping a large contingent in the colonies. It is plausible that England may have considered that it would need an army to force unpopular policies and laws on the colonists.

Stamp Act

This direct, internal tax was a broad-based tax that required the use of stamped paper for all legal documents, licenses, diplomas, almanacs, pamphlets, newspapers, and playing cards. The presence of the stamp on the paper indicated that the tax had been paid in sterling, the "official" currency, and not colonial currency. Funds from the tax were to be used to help pay for the provisioning of British soldiers in the colonies. There was little that could be done in the colonies for which they would not need to pay tax. The Stamp Act made colonists realize that this tax was likely only the beginning, and that many more taxes would follow. They felt that the tradition of self-taxation was being unjustly taken away from them by Parliament. So, reaction to this tax was more forceful than any protest that preceded it.

The tax united some of the most powerful and articulate members of colonial society, lawyers, clergymen, journalists, and businessmen, who deluged the public with pamphlets and argument against the tax. James Otis's pamphlet, *The Rights of the British Colonies Asserted and Proved*, decried the unconstitutionality of the taxation without representation. He argued that because colonists did not elect members to Parliament, Parliament had no right to tax them; therefore, the colonists did not have to pay them. The British ignored the plea in the pamphlet, asserting that according to the principles of **virtual representation**, Parliament members represented all subjects of the Empire, regardless of who actually voted for them. As such, the colonists had no authority to challenge the Parliament.

Opposition to the tax increased. In Boston and New York, mobs burned the customs officers in effigy, tore down a customs house, and almost destroyed the governor's mansion. They sought to intimidate potential tax agents into not performing their duties—and it worked. By the time the law was to go into effect, no duty collectors were willing to perform their job. Patriotic societies, known as **Sons of Liberty**, were formed to organize colonial resistance to the taxes. Merchants agreed not to import any British goods, and the Sons of Liberty exerted pressure on them to abide by that decision. The boycott so affected British merchants that they put pressure on Parliament to repeal the act, and they did so in 1766. In addition, George III replaced Prime Minister Grenville with Lord Rockingham, who oversaw the repeal and also put forth the **Declaratory Act,** which, as a face-saving gesture, stated that the British government had a right to tax and legislate in the colonies.

Townshend Acts (1767)

After William Pitt replaced Lord Rockingham as prime minister, he became too ill to govern effectively. Charles Townshend became the Minister of the Exchequer and the dominant figure in colonial affairs. Determined to settle the issue of imperial finance, Townshend drafted the **Townshend Acts,** external taxes that issued levies on all lead, paint, paper, glass, and tea that was not produced in North America, which the colonists were only allowed to buy from Great Britain. These were aimed to pay the salaries of all government officials stationed in the colonies. One tactic the colonists had used before when they were protesting taxes was to refuse to pay the officials—so, this tax aimed to remedy this situation. Anyone who refused to pay this was also sent to the vice-admiralty courts, which would also be paid for from the taxes created from the Townshend Acts. One of the Townshend Acts, the **New York Restraining Act**, suspended the New York legislature for failing to comply with the law requiring the colonists to provide for British troops.

Colonists protested that Parliament did have the right to regulate colonial trade, but not to raise revenue. There were repeated calls for protest and unity among the colonies to repeal the measures. Rallies were held that sought the support of all people, not just the elites. As a result, the rallies were more unnerving for the British, as they were significantly larger and more threatening. A second import boycott was led by the **Daughters of Liberty,** who encouraged women to take up the cause and make their own goods, rather than buy British-made goods. By 1770, the Townshend Duties, with the exception of the tea tax, were repealed.

Boston Massacre

As part of the Townshend Acts, the British sent 4,000 troops to Boston, a city of only 16,000 people, to help enforce customs duties collections. Tensions between the troops and the townspeople flared, even more so when the soldiers competed for second jobs with the colonists. On one occasion, on March 5, 1770, a riotous crowd of about 60 Bostonian laborers and seamen shouted insults and threw rock-filled snowballs at a detachment of soldiers who were guarding the customs house. The redcoats fired into the crowd, killing five townspeople and wounding six others. The angry citizens, led by Samuel Adams, demanded the removal of the British troops. In the trial that followed, in which Samuel's cousin, John Adams, defended the soldiers in court, the soldiers were found not guilty.

Concerned about an uprising that could get out of control, the governor ordered the soldiers out of the city and the colonists considered it a victory. Although the majority of colonists considered the mob actions inflammatory and did not support the rabble-rousers, news of the "massacre" spread throughout the colonies and aroused hatred everywhere. The event became used as propaganda, much like the picture below, in order to arouse public indignation against the British.

Paul Revere's print of "The Bloody Massacre perpetrated in King Street" in Boston, March 5, 1770 was advertised in Boston's newspapers. Termed the "Bloody Massacre," it sought to stir up colonial hatred of the British government.

Tea Act

The British granted concessions to the financially floundering East India Company, which had 18 million pounds of unsold tea sitting in their warehouses in India, which allowed the company to ship tea directly to the colonies, rather than only by way of Britain. The result would be that East India Company tea, even with the tax, would be cheaper than smuggled Dutch tea. The colonists would, it was hoped, buy the tea, tax and all. The East India Company would be saved, and the Americans would be tacitly accepting Parliament's right to tax them. The net result would have been cheaper tea for the colonists; however, there was a proviso—only British agents could sell the tea, cutting out local North American merchants. Americans responded by angrily opposing yet another tax upon them which created tensions at colonial ports. Some ship captains saw the potential for trouble and did not land. In other ports, angry mobs forced ship owners to burn the ship and tea cargo.

Boston Tea Party

In response to the Tea Tax, pro-British Governor Thomas Hutchinson (1711–1780) of Boston forced a confrontation by ordering Royal Navy vessels to prevent the tea ships from leaving the harbor. After 20 days, this would, by law, result in the cargoes being sold at auction and the tax paid. During the night of December 16, 1773, about 50 Bostonians disguised as Mohawks boarded the ships sitting in Boston Harbor, loaded down with tea, and dumped 342 chests (worth £10,000 pounds in the British currency of the day) into the harbor. Other ports "restaged" the Tea Party in order to inflame public opinion and garner more support for those opposed to the British. The British responded with the **Coercive Acts** (also called the **Intolerable Acts**).

Intolerable Acts (1774)

The British Parliament moved quickly to punish Massachusetts for the Boston Tea Party and to reassert its authority over the colonies. Although some people had reservations about the effect of the acts in the colonies, Parliament passed a series of acts that the colonists called "intolerable." However, the acts prompted feelings of sympathy among the other colonies and moderates for what was happening in Massachusetts, fostered unity among the colonies against British rule, and pushed many moderates into the radical camp. Most significantly, it spurred the summoning of the **First Continental Congress** in 1774.

- The **Boston Port Act** closed the port of Boston to all but essential trade (firewood and food) until local citizens agreed to pay for the lost tea (they would not). They sought to set an example for the other colonies.

- The **Massachusetts Government Act** tightened control over the Massachusetts government and its courts, destroyed all colonial power in the legislature, greatly increased the power of Massachusetts's royal governor at the expense of the legislature, and limited town meetings.

- The **Administration of Justice Act** provided that royal officials accused of crimes in Massachusetts could be tried elsewhere, where chances of acquittal might be greater. Therefore, any soldier who killed colonists would be granted extraterritoriality.

- The **Quartering Act** allowed the new governor, General Thomas Gage (1721–1787), to quarter his troops anywhere, including unoccupied private homes.

First Continental Congress (September 5, 1774–October 26, 1774)

In response to the Intolerable Acts, all of the colonies, except Georgia, decided to meet for seven weeks in order to formulate a united protest of the Intolerable Acts. Their goals were to enumerate American grievances, find a strategy to resolve them, and to come up with a document that firmly outlined what the colonial relationship was with the royal government, without severing their ties to it. Many of the prominent figures of the era were in attendance: George Washington, Samuel Adams, John Adams, Patrick Henry, and John Jay.

The First Continental Congress agreed on the following:

- The colonists would obey Parliament only when they thought it was best for both sides. This was a major break with British tradition and proved to be a huge step towards independence. They also stated they would start a total economic boycott (non-importation, non-exportation, and non-consumption accords) and petition King

George III with a *List of Grievances* at the same time. They formed the **Continental Association** to help organize this boycott.

- Elected committees called **committees of observation** would enforce the boycott, attack dissention and become *de facto* governments. They would endeavor to convince people that they had different interests than England, and as such, were not "English," but "American." The committeemen became leaders of the revolution and gained power as time went on.

- The colonies had the right to tax and legislate themselves.

- The colonies had the right to mobilize a colonial militia and raised a defensive force of 20,000 **Minutemen** to be ready in minutes, just in case they needed them.

The Committees of Observation expanded their powers and coordinated all acts of insubordination in the colonies. The British underestimated the First Continental Congress and decided to teach the colonists a military lesson. They sent troops to Massachusetts, which was officially declared to be in a state of rebellion. Orders were sent to General Gage to arrest the ringleaders of the resistance, or failing that, to provoke any sort of confrontation that would allow him to turn the British military loose on the colonists.

Battles of Lexington and Concord (April 19, 1775)

General Gage dispatched 800 of his British troops to confiscate weapons that they believed were held in Concord. **Paul Revere** heard about this and sounded his alarm for the minutemen to get ready. They confronted the British in Lexington and the minutemen suffered eighteen casualties—eight colonists were dead and ten were injured. The minutemen retreated, and the British went on to Concord. At Concord, the British were met with even more resistance from the Massachusetts militia, and the British suffered many more casualties than did the colonists. The ability of the colonists to resist the British caused the Battle at Concord to be referred to as "the shot heard 'round the world." For the year following the Battle at Concord, the Americans besieged Boston, where the British had retreated.

Second Continental Congress (May 10, 1775)

The Second Continental Congress convened just weeks after the battles of Lexington and Concord, when the Congress was called to prepare the colonies for war and became the main intercolonial government. Congress was divided into two main factions: mostly New Englanders who leaned toward declaring independence from Britain and individuals mostly from the Middle Colonies who were not yet ready to go that far. Nonetheless, they authorized printing American paper money, created Washington's Continental Army, and offered to end armed resistance if the King would withdraw troops and revoke the Intolerable Acts. In July, the King rejected the Olive Branch Petition and Parliament passed the Prohibition Act that outlawed British trade with the colonies and instructed the Royal Navy to seize any American ships that were engaged in trade.

Competency 5: U.S. History

Declaration of Independence

The Declaration of Independence was primarily the work of Thomas Jefferson (1743–1826) of Virginia. It was a restatement of political ideas by then commonplace in America and showed why the former colonists felt justified in separating from Great Britain. The Declaration of Independence was formally adopted by Congress on July 4, 1776, when twelve colonies, except for New York, voted for it.

The primary importance of the Declaration was its statement of principle (life, liberty, and pursuit of happiness) and the explanation that government was based on the consent of the people. The Declaration articulated the colonies' grievances against the Crown and recognized both individual liberty and the government's primary responsibility—to serve the people. After the Declaration was signed, there was no turning back—because the delegates had committed treason. This Declaration stated that the colonies were free and independent entities, absolved of all allegiance to England. It made official what had already been happening, and the revolution was in full swing.

Treaty of Paris (September 3, 1783)

Benjamin Franklin, John Jay, and John Adams negotiated peace with the British in Paris. The resulting treaty formally recognized the independence of the United States. It stipulated the following:

1. Britain and the major European powers recognized that the United States was an independent nation.
2. Private British creditors would be free to collect any debts owed by U.S. citizens.
3. Congress was to recommend that the states restore confiscated loyalist property.
4. American fishing rights were established along the Grand Banks of Newfoundland.

In the Treaty of Versailles, signed at the same time, Britain made peace with France and Spain, and the Spanish regained Florida. All land between the Appalachians and the Mississippi River was ceded to the new American republic—and Britain promised to withdraw its garrisons throughout the territory without attempting to secure the land rights of its Indian allies. However, the new nation had accumulated massive debt during its War of Independence (although some had been taken on by France)—more than $11 million in national debt, and state debts of more than $65 million.

COMPETENCY 5.4

Identify the causes, significant individuals, and effects of the events associated with the Constitutional era and the early republic.

After the collapse of British authority in 1775, it became necessary to form new state governments. By the end of 1777, ten new state constitutions had been formed. Most state constitutions included bills of rights—lists of things the government was not supposed to do to the people.

In the summer of 1776, Congress appointed a committee to begin devising a framework for a national government. The end result preserved the sovereignty of the states and created a very weak national government. **The Articles of Confederation** provided for a unicameral Congress in which each state would have one vote, as had been the case in the Continental Congress. Executive authority under the articles would be vested in a committee of thirteen members, including one member from each state. In order to amend the Articles, the unanimous consent of all the states was required.

The Articles of Confederation government was empowered to make war, make treaties, determine the amount of troops and money each state should contribute to the war effort, settle disputes between states, admit new states to the Union, and borrow money. But it was not empowered to levy taxes, raise troops, or regulate commerce. Ratification of the Articles of Confederation was delayed by disagreements over the future status of the lands that lay to the west of the original 13 states. Maryland, which had no such claim, withheld ratification until, in 1781, Virginia agreed to surrender its western claims to the new national government.

The United States Constitution (1787–1789): Development and Ratification

As time went on, the inadequacy of the Articles of Confederation became increasingly apparent. It was decided in 1787 to call for a convention of all the states to meet in Philadelphia for the purpose of revising the Articles of Confederation. The men who met in Philadelphia in 1787 were remarkably able, highly educated, and exceptionally accomplished. For the most part, they were lawyers, merchants, and planters. Though representing individual states, most delegates thought in national terms. George Washington was unanimously elected to preside, and the enormous respect that he commanded helped hold the convention together through difficult times.

The delegates shared a basic belief in the innate selfishness of man, which must somehow be kept from abusing the power of government. For this purpose, the document that they finally produced contained many checks and balances, designed to prevent the government, or any one branch of the government, from gaining too much power.

Benjamin Franklin played an important role in reconciling the often-heated delegates, and in making various suggestions that eventually helped the convention arrive at the "Great Compromise," proposed by Roger Sherman (1721–1793) and Oliver Ellsworth (1745–1807). **The Great**

Compromise, also called **The Connecticut Compromise**, provided for a presidency, a Senate with all states represented equally (by two senators each), and a House of Representatives with representation according to population.

Another crisis involved North-South disagreement over the issue of slavery. Here also a compromise was reached. Slavery was neither endorsed nor condemned by the Constitution. Each slave was to count as three-fifths of a person for purposes of apportioning representation and direct taxation on the states (the **Three-Fifths Compromise**). The federal government was prohibited from stopping the importation of slaves prior to 1808.

The third major area of compromise was the nature of the presidency. The result was a strong presidency with control of foreign policy and the power to veto Congress's legislation. Should the president commit an actual crime, Congress would have the power to impeach him. Otherwise, the president would serve for a term of four years and be re-electable without limit. As a check on the possible excesses of democracy, the president was to be elected by an **electoral college**, in which each state would have the same number of electors as it did senators and representatives combined. The person with the second highest total in the electoral college would be vice president. If no one gained a majority in the electoral college, the president would be chosen by the House of Representatives.

The new Constitution was to take effect when nine states, through special state conventions, had ratified it. As the struggle over ratification got under way, those favoring the Constitution astutely named themselves **Federalists** (i.e., advocates of centralized power) and labeled their opponents **Anti-federalists**. By June 21, 1788, the required nine states had ratified, but the crucial states of New York and Virginia still held out. Ultimately, the promise of the addition of a bill of rights helped win the final states. In March 1789, George Washington was inaugurated as the nation's first president.

Few Anti-federalists were elected to Congress, and many of the new legislators had served as delegates to the Philadelphia Convention two years before. George Washington received virtually all the votes of the presidential electors, and John Adams received the next highest number, thus becoming the vice-president. After a triumphant journey from Mount Vernon, Washington was inaugurated in New York City, the temporary seat of government (April 30, 1789).

James Madison was given the task of writing what would become the Bill of Rights: ten amendments that were ratified by the states by the end of 1791. The first nine spelled out specific guarantees of personal freedoms, and the Tenth Amendment reserved to the states all those powers not specifically withheld or granted to the federal government. The **Judiciary Act of 1789** provided for a **Supreme Court** with six justices, and invested it with the power to rule on the constitutional validity of state laws. It was to be the interpreter of the "supreme law of the land." A system of district courts was set up to serve as courts of original jurisdiction, and three courts of appeal were established.

Congress established three departments of the **executive branch**—state, treasury, and war—as well as the offices of attorney general and postmaster general.

COMPETENCY 5.5

Evaluate the impact of westward expansion on the social, cultural, political, and economic development of the emerging nation.

In just a five-year period, the United States increased its size by a third. It annexed Texas in 1845 and received half of the Oregon territory from the British. As a result of the U.S.-Mexico War, the United States acquired California, Nevada, Utah, and parts of Arizona, Colorado, New Mexico, and Wyoming. But such rapid expansion was not without its issues: conflicts intensified between North and South over whether or not slavery should be allowed in the new territories. Decisions about how and when to broaden the U.S. borders had been evolving since its origins. It had taken American colonists 150 years just to push as far west as the Appalachian Mountains and another 50 years just to push the frontiers to the Mississippi River.

Deciding where the western borders of the United States would be proved to be a thorny issue that played out over the course of the nineteenth century when the concept of **Manifest Destiny** typified American ideas about the West. Before that, however, there needed to be an understanding or policy about how territories would become states. The **Northwest Ordinance of 1787** set up a three-step process for statehood that centered on the numbers of people settled and the establishment of a constitution:

> **Step 1** The first step for a new state would be to settle 5,000 male landowners and write a temporary constitution. Then it could have a territorial legislature to manage local issues.
>
> **Step 2** The second step would be to settle 60,000 male landowners and write a state constitution.
>
> **Step 3** The third step would be to have Congress approve the constitution and its statehood.

Treatment of the Native Americans who lived in much of this land was not taken into consideration. The Native Americans protested, and war between the United States and various Native American tribes ensued.

Although the term "Manifest Destiny" was not actually coined until 1844, the belief that the American nation was destined to eventually expand all the way to the Pacific Ocean, and to possibly embrace Canada and Mexico, had been voiced for years by many who believed that American liberty and ideals should be shared with everyone possible, by force if necessary. The rising sense of nationalism that followed the War of 1812 was fed by the rapidly expanding population, the reform impulse of the 1830s, and the desire to acquire new markets and resources for the burgeoning economy of "Young America." The completion of America's continental borders from the Atlantic to the Pacific was facilitated by policymakers who tackled the situation through purchase, diplomacy, legal appropriation, or war.

Competency 5: U.S. History

Americans did purchase a great part of the land. The **Louisiana Purchase of 1803,** bought when Napoleon was gearing up for war in Europe and was reeling from revolution in Haiti, offered the whole territory, not just New Orleans as was initially thought, for the price of $15 million. Thomas Jefferson was uncertain of the legality of the purchase, as there was nothing in the Constitution that mentioned purchasing land, but he did so anyway, lest Napoleon change his mind. The **Gadsden Purchase of 1853** enabled the United States to buy the 29,640-square-mile area from Mexico for $10 million. The area today forms southern Arizona and southwestern New Mexico. The United States also bought **Alaska** from Russia for $7 million in 1867.

Americans also used diplomatic relations and war to negotiate for land in the West. After the War of 1812, the United States and Britain decided that they would both occupy Oregon. The **Adams-Onis Treaty of 1819** had not only gained Florida from Spain, but also set the northern boundary of Spanish possessions near the present northern border of California. The territory north of that line and west of the vague boundaries of the Louisiana Territory had been claimed over the years by Spain, England, Russia, France, and the United States. By the 1820s, all of these claims had been yielded to Britain and the United States. The United States claimed all the way north to the 54°40′ parallel. Unable to settle the dispute, they had agreed on a joint occupation of the disputed land. In the 1830s, American missionaries followed the traders and trappers to the Oregon country. They began to publicize the richness and beauty of the land. The result was the "Oregon Fever" of the 1840s, as thousands of settlers trekked across the Great Plains and the Rocky Mountains to settle the new Shangri-La. In 1846, with the Oregon Treaty, the United States agreed to a compromise with Great Britain. By the terms of the treaty, they agreed that the U.S.-Canada boundary east of the Rockies, the 49th parallel, was extended westward to the Pacific, in return for the United States accepting Vancouver Island as a British territory.

Another result of the 1812 war was that it removed Great Britain as a potential ally of the Native Americans, so now the United States was free to appropriate lands from the Native Americans without thinking twice about it. When he was a general under President Monroe, Andrew Jackson received permission to invade Spanish Florida in an "unofficial war" that resulted in Spain ceding Florida in the Adams-Onis 1819 treaty.

The United States also gained Texas and California through its war with Mexico. Texas had been a state in the Republic of Mexico since 1822, following the Mexican Revolution against Spanish control. The new Mexican government invited immigration from the north by offering land grants to Stephen Austin (1793–1836) and other Americans. By 1835, approximately 35,000 "gringos" were homesteading on Texas land. The Mexican officials saw their power base eroding as the foreigners flooded in, so they moved to tighten control through restrictions on immigration and through tax increases. The Texans responded in 1836 by proclaiming independence and establishing a new republic. The ensuing war was short-lived. The Mexican dictator, **Antonio López de Santa Anna** (1794–1876), advanced north and annihilated the Texan garrisons at the Alamo and at Goliad. On April 23, 1836, **Sam Houston** (1793–1863) defeated Santa Anna at San Jacinto, and the Mexicans were forced to let Texas go its way.

Houston immediately asked the American government for recognition and annexation, but President Andrew Jackson feared the revival of the slavery issue. He also feared war with Mexico, and so he did nothing. When the next U.S. president, Martin Van Buren, followed suit, the new republic sought foreign recognition and support, which the European nations eagerly provided, hoping thereby to create a counterbalance to rising American power and influence in the Southwest. France and England both quickly concluded trade agreements with the Texans. After a great deal of maneuvering and politicking, Texas was admitted into the Union in 1845. Mexico protested the admission of Texas into the United States, a protest that the United States saw as reason to send troops into Texas.

The Mexican-American War lasted two years and ended with the signing of the **Treaty of Guadalupe-Hidalgo** in 1848. The United States had succeeded in winning the war and, with the Treaty of Guadalupe-Hidalgo, succeeded in fulfilling its Manifest Destiny. The treaty itself represented U.S. expansionist goals. Bankrupt from the war, Mexico agreed to $15 million as payment for the vast land. In addition, the United States agreed to forgive all Mexican debts. A few years later, it was discovered that the boundary information in the Treaty of Guadalupe-Hidalgo was inaccurate. Diplomatic tension followed. In 1853, the United States negotiated with Mexico to resolve the boundary dispute that resulted at the termination of the Mexican War, and to purchase the land in question. In what became known as the **Gadsden Purchase**, the United States paid $10 million for a strip of territory south of the Gila River in what is now southwestern New Mexico and southern Arizona. The district of New Mexico had, like Texas, encouraged American immigration. Soon that state was more American than Mexican. The Santa Fe Trail, running from Independence, Missouri, to the town of Santa Fe, created a prosperous trade in mules, gold, silver, and furs, which moved north in exchange for manufactured goods. American settlements sprung up along the route.

The U.S. war with Mexico raised a number of thorny issues that would continue to plague the Americans for decades to come. Americans had precipitated this war for territorial gain, an issue that flatly contradicted what it had fought for just decades earlier. The war also gave practical battle experience and tactical experience to young officers and soldiers who, fifteen years later, would form the nuclei of the Union and Confederate armies. It also gave the Americans the false understanding that war was short and quick, which doubtlessly affected the bravado with which they threw around the threat of war and fighting.

Advocates of the war with Mexico cheered the victory of a new Protestant democratic civilization against a corrupt Catholic quasi-tyranny. They also championed it as the final piece in the puzzle of the United States' quest for Manifest Destiny—spanning the country from shore to shore. Opponents of the war—and there were many, among them John Quincy Adams, Ralph Waldo Emerson, Henry David Thoreau, and the young Abraham Lincoln—regarded it as a blatant, cold-blooded act of robbery by which a large, powerful nation set out to steal half of the territory of a smaller, weaker, innocent neighbor. Conspiracy theorists opined that the war was a proslavery conspiracy designed to secure territories receptive to slavery and could easily tip the balance in favor of the slave states. *Control of Federal policy/laws, direction of country*

Competency 5: U.S. History

The issues revealed by the war and attempts to justify it only grew more complex and problematic over the next few years. It helped to frame the context of American public life for the next twenty years. The land hunger that drove the Mexican War and inspired the Treaty of Guadalupe-Hidalgo spurred American settlements and diplomatic saber-rattling elsewhere on the continent, most notably in the Pacific Northwest. Under the slogan "54°40′ or fight," American claims to that region—not only present-day Washington, Idaho, Montana, and Oregon, but also large parts of Canada—led to a series of diplomatic clashes with Great Britain. But the British were far stronger than the Mexicans were, and diplomacy averted a full-scale war between the United States and Britain.

Anti-Expansionists

Not everyone appreciated the idea of the United States expanding from sea to sea. Many argued that it was unconstitutional and dangerous (as treaties with the Indians would be broken, giving rise to an increase of attacks in the West), and it could lead to war with Mexico, as well as produce a nation too large to govern. Other protests revolved around the idea of slavery. Abolitionists worried that expansion would lead to more slavery, which would impede the new manufacturing industry.

Social

Expansion westward seemed perfectly natural to many Americans in the mid-nineteenth century. Many considered it their duty to extend their liberty to new realms, to spread their wonderful government from sea to shining sea. At the heart of Manifest Destiny was the pervasive belief in American cultural and racial superiority. Native Americans had long been perceived as inferior, and efforts to "civilize" them had been widespread since the days of John Smith and Miles Standish. With religious fervor spiking because of the **Second Great Awakening**, many sought to apply this movement to a need to spread the word of God to the Native Americans. Many settlers believed that God had shined his blessing on the American nation, and it was the duty of Americans, as Christians, to spread the word of God to the Native Americans, whom they considered heathens.

A utopian sense of purpose and opportunity affected Americans, who considered the opportunity to civilize the West and spread their government to the region would justify any misdeeds that had to happen along the way. Permeating society was the belief that by civilizing the "noble Savage," forcing them to become "humanized," "civilized," and "Christianized" by adopting the behaviors, dress, and beliefs of white American society, then the Native Americans would be "saved." Those who stood in the way of such progress deserved to be eliminated. What was viewed as "progress" for the white man was considered a disaster by the Native Americans, who suffered through physical, spiritual, and mental attacks, and then displacement.

Opportunity also lured people to move westward. The government extolled the virtues of the West and arranged programs to sway people into leaving the East and moving to new land. News of gold and other valuable minerals being found in the West, coupled with government programs that could help people acquire and hold land, caught the public's attention, and many Easterners flocked to the West. They left the comforts of the East, supported by their belief that as individuals, they had a right and duty to move westward, and that by doing so, they were fulfilling a national duty of Manifest Destiny.

Economic

Economic interests were some of the chief motivators of westward expansion. The desire for more land brought aspiring homesteaders to the frontier. When gold was discovered in California in 1848, the number of migrants increased even more. Regional approval for westward expansion resulted from each region believing that westward expansion could solve some of their problems. Northerners felt that the wide expanse of the West could resolve a pressing issue of urban overpopulation and economic instability. The South argued that expansion would free up a lot of land for agriculture and manufacturing, which would help the stability of the economy. Both regions realized that as the United States expanded, hopefully reaching the Pacific Coast, the railroad would take a more central role in the U.S. economy. By extending the railroads, new trade could be created within the United States, and would also provide access to the Pacific Ocean trade. Having more land also gave the United States more trading power with countries such as Asia, and the manufacturing that developed in the West made America more efficient and self-reliant. The settlers could obtain or make many goods that had previously been obtained only by trade with other countries.

Cultural

Expanding the boundaries of the United States was, in many ways, a cultural war as well. The desire of Southerners to find more lands suitable for cotton cultivation would eventually spread slavery to these regions. North of the Mason-Dixon Line, many citizens were deeply concerned about adding any more slave states. Manifest Destiny touched on issues of religion, money, race, patriotism, and morality. These clashed in the 1840s as a truly great drama of regional conflict began to unfold.

Political

While Manifest Destiny united many Americans with a shared belief that God had a grand mission for them, it also divided them. As the United States acquired more territory during the first part of the nineteenth century, the issue of slavery and where it would be permitted began to divide the country. Increasingly through this period, many Southerners and some Northerners wanted slavery to exist everywhere in the United States, including in the new territories added to the country. Many other Americans did not want slavery to expand at all, and some wanted slavery to be prohibited across the entire nation. Eventually, these tensions would lead to the American Civil War.

COMPETENCY 5.6

Identify the social, cultural, political, and economic characteristics of the antebellum period.

Political

Between 1819 and 1860, critical issues emerged in the United States that would serve as the foundation of crises that would explode in the United States in the 1850s and 1860s. The period immediately following the War of 1812 witnessed a high tide of nationalism and unity, but just underneath the surface lurked issues such as federal versus states rights, an issue that had never been resolved. Attendant to that concern was another critical issue—the extension of slavery in the western territories—and this pitted the North against the South. The **Compromise of 1820** had settled this issue for nearly thirty years by drawing a dividing line across the Louisiana Purchase that prohibited slavery north of the line, but permitted slavery south of it.

The seizure of new territories from Mexico reignited the issue of the expansion of slavery. California adopted a constitution that prohibited slavery and applied for statehood in 1849. Some members of Congress were unwilling to admit California as a free state and were concerned about other issues, such as the movement to end slavery in the District of Columbia and the emergence of personal liberty laws in the North that barred courts and police from returning runaways to the south. Furthermore, there were several other territories such as New Mexico, Oregon, and Utah, which had applied for statehood. The Union had fifteen free and fifteen slave states in 1849, but the admission of these Western states threatened to upset the balance. Southern representatives brought up the idea of secession, while state legislatures in the North passed resolutions demanding that slavery be prohibited in the Western territories.

The **Compromise of 1850** attempted to settle the problem by admitting California as a free state, but allowing slavery in the rest of the area acquired from Mexico; and the abolition of slave trade, but not slavery, in the District of Columbia. The idea that averted an immediate crisis was found with the introduction of **popular sovereignty** that allowed individuals living within a territory or state to decide the slavery issue for themselves, rather than Congress making the decision for them.

Enactment of the **Fugitive Slave Law** as part of the Compromise of 1850 exacerbated sectional tensions. Northerners resented the new act that enabled Southerners to travel freely within the North and seize individuals who they claimed were fugitives, including some free African-Americans and a number of escaped slaves who had been living in the North for several months and, in some cases, years. The South was angered by Northern attempts to prevent the Fugitive Slave Act from being enforced by the passage of state laws that barred the deportation of slaves, despite the federal act authorizing Southern agents to retrieve runaway slaves.

The question of slavery in the territories exploded once again when the senator from Illinois, Stephen A. Douglas, in an effort to get a transcontinental railroad built so that it would run through his home state, proposed that Kansas and Nebraska territories be opened to white settlement and that the status of slavery be decided according to the principle of popular sovereignty. Douglas reasoned that if territory north of the 36°30′ line were admitted to the Union, it would strengthen his argument that the railroad should be built in the North. The resulting **Kansas-Nebraska Act of 1854** left the fate of slavery up to residents without specifying when and how they were to decide. The act also repealed the Missouri Compromise, further destabilizing the political situation. The Kansas-Nebraska Act convinced many Northerners that the South wanted to open all federal territories to slavery and brought into existence the **Republican Party**, committed to excluding slavery from the territories. In addition, many Northern states passed **personal liberty laws** that required a trial by jury for all who were accused of being fugitive slaves, and guaranteed them the right to have an attorney. Southerners were naturally furious at this deliberate weakening of the Fugitive Slave Law.

Sectional conflict was intensified by the Supreme Court's **Dred Scott decision**, which declared that Congress could not exclude slavery from the western territories. Dred Scott, a Missouri slave, had sued his owner for his freedom after his owner took him to a free state. Scott won his case, but then lost on appeal, and so the case went to the Supreme Court in 1857. Normally, the Supreme Court stayed out of slavery controversies and let the state courts decide outcomes. But this time, the Supreme Court did take on the case and Scott lost. The Court stated that Scott was not a citizen, so he could not sue in federal courts. The Court also stated that residency in a free state did not make one free; moreover, the Court decided that Congress did not have the power to regulate slavery in the territories. This decision nullified the Missouri Compromise and the Kansas-Nebraska Act as well. The Dred Scott decision meant that slavery essentially could be anywhere in the United States and its territories, and it became a turning point in the impending crisis between North and South. The ruling did not prevent individual states from passing anti-slavery laws or measures enforcing them, but it did make it clear that the federal government could not act on or enforce such laws due to the designation of slaves as property. The ruling seemed to weaken the ability of any state to prohibit slavery since the federal government would not intervene and it caused outrage in the North, while Southerners considered it to be a major step forward since it upheld their argument that slaves were property.

The last incident that divided the Union and provoked the secession crisis was the election of Abraham Lincoln in the 1860 Presidential election. The deep divisions within the major parties and the United States led to the election of Lincoln, who received only 40% of the popular vote. Lincoln had engaged Stephen A. Douglas in a number of debates during the Illinois state race and, although he lost the state race, he gained considerable attention. Lincoln had little political experience and was opposed to the expansion of slavery. The South viewed Lincoln as an abolitionist and a direct threat to the Southern way of life. Immediately following the election of Lincoln, South Carolina began to discuss secession from the Union. Southern states had long maintained that they had the right to nullify acts of Congress and even withdraw voluntarily from the Union without approval from the federal government, if they had sufficient cause or grievances.

Competency 5: U.S. History

It did not take long for South Carolina to pass a bill of secession, and six other states followed its lead and voted themselves out of the Union. These six states were Mississippi, Florida, Alabama, Georgia, Louisiana, and Texas. These six states would form the Confederate States of America, and Jefferson Davis was chosen to be the president of the "nation." As President Buchanan was leaving office, he told Congress that states did not have the right to secede, but that the federal government did not have the right to use force to prevent them from doing so. Attempts to negotiate failed, and the situation was unresolved when Lincoln arrived for his inauguration. Lincoln made it clear that he considered secession to be insurrection and stated that the federal government should take all actions necessary, including force, to protect forts and property in the South and to put an end to insurrection.

Social and Cultural Characteristics

The white South's social structure was much more complex than the popular stereotype of proud aristocrats disdainful of honest work, and ignorant, vicious, exploited poor whites. The old South's intricate social structure included many small slave owners and relatively few large ones. Large slaveholders, the **planters,** were extremely rare. In 1860, only 11,000 Southerners, three-quarters of 1% of the white population, owned more than fifty slaves; a mere 2,358 owned as many as 100 slaves. However, although large slaveholders were few in number, they owned most of the South's slaves. More than half of all slaves lived on plantations with twenty or more slaves, and slave ownership was relatively widespread. In the first half of the nineteenth century, one-third of all southern white families owned slaves, had owned them, or expected to own them. Slave owners were a diverse lot. A few were African-American, mulatto, or Native American; one-tenth were women; and more than one in ten worked as artisans, businesspeople, or merchants, rather than as farmers or planters. Few led lives of leisure or refinement.

The average slave owner lived in a log cabin rather than a mansion and was a farmer rather than a planter. The average holding varied between four and six slaves, and most slaveholders possessed no more than five. White women in the South, despite the image of the hoop-skirted Southern belle, suffered under heavier burdens than their northern counterparts. They married earlier, bore more children, and were more likely to die young. They lived in greater isolation, had less access to the company of other women, and lacked the satisfactions of voluntary associations and reform movements. Their education was briefer and much less likely to result in opportunities for independent careers.

The plantation legend was misleading in still other respects. Slavery was neither dying nor unprofitable. In 1860, the South was richer than any country in Europe except England, and it had achieved a level of wealth unmatched by Italy or Spain until the eve of World War II.

During the antebellum period, a wave of social reform swept the United States. Many of the reform movements that resulted grew out of the **Second Great Awakening**, which, like the original Great Awakening, was a period of revival that spread throughout the country and sparked an intense period of evangelicalism throughout the South and the West. It preached religious conversion and that the Second Coming was near, and encouraged people to speed the process and fight evil present in the United States through social reform. A number of reform movements sprang up throughout the country targeting alcohol and poverty as social evils. Women, in particular, were drawn to this movement and were targeted as well, creating the emergence of an ideology called the Cult of True Womanhood (also known as the Cult of Domesticity).

Society in America was in flux in the early nineteenth century. Not only was the new nation going through all the pangs of emerging out of colonialism into full-fledged self-rule, but also tremendous sweeping movements of immigration, industrialization, urbanization, and westernization all affected life at home. The composition of the population of the United States was changing, as immigrants from Ireland and Germany flooded the country, introducing new cultures to the mix. White, middle-class, native-born men left their home businesses and set off to work in new factories, stores, and offices. Although middle-class white women became more rooted in the home, working-class and farm white women left their homes and communities to work in growing factories, thus bringing up a whole host of new problems that women faced as they worked in the man's domain. Changes did not just affect white women, but also slave women who found their lives and family life disrupted once again. The surge in demand for Deep South cotton combined with a stagnant economy in the northern part of the South prompted mass translocation of slaves from the Upper South to the Lower South, in the process ripping apart families and selling them to Southern cotton plantation owners hundreds of miles away.

In this rapidly changing society, Americans clung to what they thought would be an area of stability: the family. The belief that men and women belonged in separate, but complementary, domains took hold and it was considered that women, due to their gentle, sensitive, and emotional souls, belonged to the private sphere, in the home, where they would provide a haven for their husbands and children who were no doubt suffering from the rigors of industrialization and capitalism. What emerged was something referred to as the cult of true womanhood that defined how women, true women, were supposed to act and acknowledged that a true woman's goals should be twofold: marriage and motherhood. The ideology of true womanhood was perpetuated through print culture, religion, and discourse, which both empowered and confined women. It expanded access and elevated the importance of women's education, because it emphasized that women needed more schooling in order to raise their sons to be good citizens and to influence their husbands. This reasoning opened one profession deemed suitable for females: teaching. By the 1840s, women used this ideology to create a nascent women's rights movement.

Women in particular jumped on the bandwagon and embraced the idea of reforming different elements of society. Revival meetings and reform societies offered women unique opportunities for participation in public life and politics. One area that women successfully targeted was the temperance movement that sought to reduce alcohol consumption. Inspired by religion, as well as the effects alcohol had on family life and the workplace, **Temperance Societies** sprang up that encouraged people to sign pledges not to drink, and, in some places, pushed for **prohibition**. The movement did result in a sharp decline in alcohol consumption. The group also targeted gambling, and by 1860, every state had laws that outlawed lotteries on the books. After an 1830 report on the prevalence of prostitution in New York City, women formed **The Female Moral Reform Society** in 1834 that sought to eliminate prostitution and to help rehabilitate those women who were caught in its web. Other reform societies emerged that targeted problems in penitentiaries, orphanages, and asylums, under the idea that society had an obligation to provide for those unable to take care of themselves.

Another movement that came out of a reform-minded culture was the creation of utopian groups. The **Shakers** split from the Quaker groups and built communes where they could share work and all of the good things that came out of it. They had some progressive ideas about life and granted near equal rights to women. However, their numbers never took off as they also practiced celibacy. One experimental community was **Brook Farm,** which was dedicated to another group of reformists, mainly intellectuals who were writers and philosophers, called the **Transcendentalists,** who believed that humans shared aspects with God. This meant that ultimately, if guided properly, man could attain perfection. Some well-known Transcendentalists were **Nathaniel Hawthorne, Ralph Waldo Emerson, Henry David Thoreau,** and **Elizabeth Peabody**.

Before the 1830s, abolition movements were dominated by free Blacks, and gained only sporadic and few white supporters, save for a few movements, like the Quakers, who believed slavery should end because it was morally wrong, and the **American Colonization Society,** that sought to transfer free slaves and ship them back to Africa. Prominent Black support did come from free slaves such as **Frederick Douglass, Harriet Tubman, and Sojourner Truth**. With increased radicalization of the abolitionists combined with a similar entrenchment of the South on the issue, slavery began to take center stage, particularly in combination with Westward expansion and decisions about what to do about new states. Slave resistance also became more of an issue. Some slaves chose indirect means of resistance, like slowing down their work pace or sabotaging work. The idea of an **Underground Railroad** also became an important cultural concern.

Economic

There were several characteristics of the U.S. economy during the antebellum period that had an effect on later events.

1. The South continued to be primarily agrarian and slow to industrialize while the North had moved more into manufacturing.

2. Economic power had shifted more from the Upper South to the Lower South, as cotton became more important to the lower Southern antebellum economy and upper Southern tobacco slid into a free-for-all. With the invention of the **cotton gin** by Eli Whitney, cotton cultivation spread everywhere throughout the South. Initially there was tremendous demand for Southern cotton, both from the Northern mills and English textile mills, but the South became dependent on the availability of cotton around the world, particularly in far flung parts of the British Empire such as India. Any downswing in price resulted in an economic adjustment for the entire South. The idea that **"Cotton is King"** took hold, and by 1860, cotton production exploded in the South and comprised

57% of all U.S. exports. The spread of cotton also increased the spread of slavery. From 1820–1840, around 2 million people from various places in Africa were moved or sold to others in the Gulf States region of the United States.

3. The availability of transportation continued to be more limited in the South than in the North and posed more problems for the Southerners in terms of getting their goods to the market or ports. During this period, there were calls for government-led internal improvements, such as the construction of canals and a national railroad.

4. The period also saw the emergence of more protective tariffs that sought to increase the appeal of American goods by increasing the duty for imported goods.

COMPETENCY 5.7

Identify the causes, significant individuals, and effects of the events associated with the American Civil War and Reconstruction eras.

Causes of the Civil War ("The War of Northern Aggression")

Growth of Sectionalism. Differences between the Southern plantation cotton economy and the Northern industrial economy resulted in differences in income levels and economic attitudes that manifested themselves in considerations of race and culture. The South, a more remote agrarian lifestyle that used slaves, was not as used to variations of culture experienced by individuals in the North who lived in cities and worked together in factories. In many ways, the North was more self-sufficient than the South.

Unfair Taxation. The development of the North and South into different types of economies caused also polarization. The South preferred to trade with England rather than the North. It would send cotton to English mills and buy European goods in return. By the early 1800s, the Northern politicians pushed through heavy taxes on European goods so Southerners would be forced to buy goods from the North instead. The South perceived this as blatantly unfair and as a tax directed at them.

States versus Federal Rights. Unresolved issues of state versus federal authority festered as Southern states argued that they should have the right to decide if they wanted to accept certain federal legislation, such as slavery or taxation. The Southern states asserted that they had the right of **nullification** by which they could rule federal acts void. The federal government refused to allow nullification, and proponents of federal rights, primarily Northerners, argued that nullification was a dangerous precedent that would just make the country weaker and more open to takeover or dissolution.

Competency 5: U.S. History

Growing Controversy between Proslavery versus Anti-Slavery Proponents. Each time the United States gained more territory, there were disagreements over whether or not the new state should allow slavery. The vociferousness of these disagreements was a little odd, as the average U.S. citizen in both the North and the South did not own slaves. Even so, the politicians became interested in slaves and the concept of slavery. The North viewed it as a moral issue, and the South viewed slavery as an economic issue.

Growth of the Abolitionist Movement. Feelings in the North intensified with the passage of the Fugitive Slave Act, the Dred Scott Case, the publication of Harriet Beecher Stowe's *Uncle Tom's Cabin*, and John Brown's Raid. Religious and reform groups and media campaigns targeted the immorality of slavery.

The 1860 Election of Abraham Lincoln. The run-up to the election caused political rifts within the Whig party, which resulted in its dissolution. The Southern members joined the Democratic Party and the Northerners joined the Republican Party. In the razor-thin 1860 Presidential election, Abraham Lincoln defeated three candidates—Stephen A. Douglas (Northern Democrat), John C. Breckinridge (Southern Democrat), and John Bell of the Constitutional Union party. Before Lincoln was sworn in, South Carolina seceded from the Union and six other states joined it.

The Civil War and Reconstruction (1860–1877)

Hostilities Begin

On **December 20, 1860,** South Carolina passed a secession ordinance and shortly thereafter, Mississippi, Florida, Alabama, Georgia, Louisiana, and Texas seceded as well. By **February 1861,** the **Confederate States of America** was formed in Alabama. In his inaugural address, Lincoln urged Southerners to reconsider their actions, but warned that the Union was perpetual, states could not secede, and that he would therefore hold the federal forts and installations in the South. Only two remained in federal hands: Fort Pickens, off Pensacola, Florida; and **Fort Sumter**, in the harbor of Charleston, South Carolina. Lincoln soon received word from Major Robert Anderson, commander of the small garrison at Fort Sumter, that supplies were running low. Desiring to send in the needed supplies, Lincoln informed the governor of South Carolina of his intention, but promised that no attempt would be made to send arms, ammunition, or reinforcements unless Southerners initiated hostilities.

Confederate General P.G.T. Beauregard, acting on orders from Confederate President Davis, demanded Anderson's surrender. Anderson said he would surrender if not resupplied. Knowing supplies were on the way, the Confederates opened fire at 4:30 a.m. on **April 12, 1861**. The next day, the fort surrendered. The day following Sumter's surrender, Lincoln declared an insurrection and called for the states to provide 75,000 volunteers to put it down. In response to this, Virginia,

Tennessee, North Carolina, and Arkansas declared their secession. The remaining slave states, Delaware, Kentucky, Maryland, and Missouri, wavered but stayed with the Union.

Advantages of the Confederacy and the Union

The North enjoyed several advantages over the South. It had overwhelming preponderance in wealth and was vastly superior in industry, giving them vast resources to draw upon. The North also had an advantage of almost three to one in manpower whereas over one-third of the South's population was composed of slaves, whom Southerners would not use as soldiers. Unlike the South, the North received large numbers of immigrants during the war. The North retained control of the U.S. Navy, and thus, would command the sea and be able to blockade the South. Finally, the North enjoyed a much superior system of railroads.

The South also had some advantages. It was vast in size, making it difficult to conquer. Its troops would be fighting on their own ground, a fact that would give them the advantage of familiarity with the terrain, as well as the added motivation of defending their homes and families. Its armies would often have the opportunity of fighting on the defensive, a major advantage in the warfare of that day.

At the outset of the war, the South drew upon a number of highly qualified senior officers, such as **Robert E. Lee, Stonewall Jackson,** and **Jeb Stuart.** By contrast, the Union command structure was already set when the war began and, thus, was hampered by the lack of new ideas and initiatives (particularly as many of the great senior officers had joined the South). Jefferson Davis had extensive military and political experience, while Lincoln was much superior to Davis as a war leader, showing firmness, flexibility, mental toughness, great political skill, and, eventually, an excellent grasp of strategy.

Progress of the War

At a creek called **Bull Run** near the town of Manassas Junction, Virginia, the Union Army met a Confederate force on July 21, 1861. In the **First Battle of Bull Run** (called First Manassas in the South), the Union army was forced to retreat. The reaction among the Union officials was to embark on a series of commander changes throughout 1861–1862, hoping to turn back the Southern troops. Some victories, such as at the **Battle of Antietam**, the bloodiest battle in the Civil War where a total of 31,000 men perished from each side, gave the North a bit of confidence, but was not enough to make the North confident in its military leadership. Nevertheless, after claiming the Battle of Antietam a victory, Lincoln issued the **Emancipation Proclamation,** which took effect on **New Year's Day, 1863,** freeing all of the slaves in the areas of rebellion.

As the war dragged on, the greater population and material advantages of the North became a significant factor. The blockade and Union victories that gave them control of the Mississippi allowed Union forces to divide the South in half and to interrupt the South's trade and supply lines. The Union had a better Navy, and in addition to blocking Southern ports, also shelled land forts and took part in joint Army and Navy actions. The one battle between the newly constructed Union

Competency 5: U.S. History

ironclad ship, **The Monitor**, and the Confederate ironclad ship, **The Virginia**, demonstrated the superiority of the Union Navy even though neither side actually won the battle between the two ships.

Furthermore, several key Confederate officers were severely injured or killed. The replacement of the North's largely ineffective McClellan only made an impact when he was permanently removed from the command of the Army in favor of **Ulysses S. Grant**. After 1863, the Union was able to go on the offensive and invade the South. **Vicksburg** and **Gettysburg** were besieged and ultimately fell to the Union. Lincoln's **Gettysburg Address** stressed the honor of the dead on both sides and the need to bind up the wounds of a nation. This conciliatory attitude, as well as his determination to readmit the Southern states as quickly as possible, would be reflected in his **Ten Percent Plan**.

The final Union campaign consisted of a series of coordinated offensives in the South. Sherman's "March to the Sea" created a path of destruction and aroused bitter feelings in the South that would not end with the war. The final Confederate collapse was only a matter of time. Grant cut off all supplies to Lee and the Army of Northern Virginia, which had withdrawn to the area around Richmond; on April 9, 1865, Lee surrendered at **Appomattox Court House**. Other Confederate armies still holding out in various parts of the South surrendered over the next few weeks. Lincoln did not live to receive news of the final surrenders. On April 14, 1865, he was shot in the back of the head while watching a play in Ford's Theatre in Washington.

The Ordeal of Reconstruction

Reconstruction began well before the fighting of the Civil War came to an end. The North was concerned with four basic issues: who the local rulers would be for the South and what role would they have; should governmental control of the South be in the hands of the President or Congress; issues with the freedom of former slaves; and should they reestablish the old system that had been in place, or build something anew so that these problems would not happen again. There were two main views about these problems, one that rested with the executive branch, Lincoln, and another with the legislative, basically the Radical Republicans in Congress. Lincoln favored leniency and the Radical Republicans favored revenge.

To restore legal governments in the seceded states, Lincoln developed a policy called the **Ten Percent Plan** that made it relatively easy for Southern states to enter the collateral process. Lincoln's plan stipulated that Southerners, except for high-ranking rebel officials, could take an oath promising future loyalty to the Union and acknowledge the end of slavery. When the number of people who had taken this oath within any one state reached 10% of the number who had been registered to vote in 1860, a loyal state government could be formed. Tennessee, Arkansas, and Louisiana formed loyal governments under Lincoln's plan but were refused recognition by a Congress dominated by Radical Republicans.

Radical Republicans such as **Thaddeus Stevens** of Pennsylvania believed that Lincoln's plan did not adequately punish the South, restructure Southern society, or boost the political prospects of the Republican Party. Instead, the radicals in Congress drew up the more stringent **Wade-Davis Bill,** which required a majority of individuals who had been alive and registered to vote in 1860 to swear an "iron-clad" oath stating that they were loyal and had never been disloyal. Under these terms, no confederate state could have been readmitted unless African-Americans were given the vote. Until a majority of individuals took the oath, the state could not send representatives to Congress. Lincoln killed the bill with a "pocket veto," and the radicals were furious. When Lincoln was assassinated, the radicals rejoiced, believing that Vice President Andrew Johnson would be less generous to the South, or at least easier to control. However, Johnson, although having pledged earlier to be harsh with the South, changed his mind and embraced Lincoln's Ten Percent Plan to be more lenient with the Southern states. His plan was not totally magnanimous, however.

His plans for reconstruction waffled a bit. First he stated that certain Southerners, like officers, officials, and members of the planter class whose property was worth more than $20,000, were not allowed to take the oath of loyalty and had to apply personally to the president for a pardon. But this policy lacked teeth as Johnson proceeded to grant thousands of pardons, which then allowed the previous social and governmental power brokers in the South to remain there. After only eight months, Johnson declared that Reconstruction was over and former Confederates could return to Congress in December 1865. Congress, on the other hand, was agitated by Johnson's overtures to the South and decided to refuse to admit ex-Confederates to its ranks. Congress justified their position by arguing that the Constitution gave them, not the president, the power to admit new states.

Thirteenth and Fourteenth Amendments and Congressional Reconstruction

Tensions between Congress and Johnson continued to build, and Congress decided to embark on their own reconstruction plans. The **Thirteenth Amendment,** officially ending slavery, had already been passed. After Johnson's succession to the presidency, Congress passed a Civil Rights Act and extended the authority of the Freedmen's Bureau. Johnson vetoed both bills, claiming they were unconstitutional, but Congress overrode the vetoes. Congress then approved the **Fourteenth Amendment** and sent it to the states for ratification in June 1866. The Fourteenth Amendment defined citizenship and forbade any states to deny various rights to citizens. Any state that denied the vote or other rights to eligible citizens, including African-Americans, would have their representation in Congress reduced. The Amendment also prohibited the paying of any Confederate debts and made former Confederates ineligible to hold public office. Johnson tried to block the Fourteenth Amendment throughout the country, urging Southern state legislatures to vote against it and organizing a National Union Convention in the North to do the same.

In response to Johnson's machinations, Congress embarked on some manipulating of their own with the passage of a series of **Reconstruction Acts,** which would give Union generals control of military districts in the South and supervision of elections. They also forced states to ratify the Fourteenth Amendment, to make changes to their state constitutions, and to submit them to Congress for approval. Johnson continued to work against Congressional policies so they fought back by passing the Tenure of Office Act that was passed over Johnson's veto. This act forbade Johnson from dismissing his cabinet members without permission of Congress. In particular, they limited Johnson's power over the army by forcing him to issue orders through Grant, who in turn was not allowed to be dismissed without Congressional approval. Congress also passed this measure in order to protect the Secretary of War, Edwin M. Stanton, who was the last radical Republican cabinet member still in office. In response, Johnson issued orders to commanders in the South that limited their powers, removed some of the best officers, and then, as a last straw, dismissed Stanton in order to test the constitutionality of the Tenure of Office Act. Before the matter could be taken up in court, Congress responded by impeaching Johnson but was one vote shy of removing him from office. Johnson remained in office but offered little resistance to the Radical Republicans during his last months in office.

The Election of 1868 and the Fifteenth Amendment

In 1868, the Republicans nominated for president Ulysses S. Grant, who had no political record and whose views—if any—on national issues were unknown. The narrow victory of even such a strong candidate as Grant prompted Republican leaders to decide that it would be politically expedient to give the vote to all Blacks, in the North as well as the South. For this purpose, the **Fifteenth Amendment** was drawn up and submitted to the states. Ironically, the idea was so unpopular in the North that it won the necessary three-fourths approval only with its ratification by southern states. Though personally of unquestioned integrity, Grant naïvely placed his faith in a number of thoroughly dishonest men. His administration was rocked by one scandalous revelation of government corruption after another.

Many of the economic difficulties that the country faced during Grant's administration were caused by the necessary readjustments from a wartime economy back to a peacetime economy. The central economic question was deflation versus inflation, or more specifically, whether to retire the un-backed paper money, greenbacks, printed to meet the wartime emergency, or to print more.

Early in Grant's second term, the country was hit by an economic depression known as the **Panic of 1873**. Brought on by the over-expansive tendencies of railroad builders and businessmen during the immediate postwar boom, the Panic was triggered by economic downturns in Europe and more immediately, by the failure of Jay Cooke and Company, a major American financial firm.

The Panic led to clamor for the printing of more greenbacks. In 1874, Congress authorized a small new issue of greenbacks, but it was vetoed by Grant. Pro-inflation forces were further enraged when Congress demonetized silver in 1873, going to a straight gold standard. Silver was becoming more plentiful due to Western mining and was seen by some as a potential source of inflation. Pro-inflation forces referred to the demonetization of silver as the "Crime of '73." In the election of 1876, the Democrats campaigned against corruption and nominated New York Governor **Samuel J. Tilden**, who had broken the Tweed political machine of New York City. The Republicans passed over Grant and turned to Governor **Rutherford B. Hayes** of Ohio. Like Tilden, Hayes was decent, honest, in favor of hard money and civil service reform, and opposed to government regulation of the economy. Tilden won the popular vote and led in the electoral vote 184 to

165. However, 185 electoral votes were needed for election, and 20 votes, from the three Southern states still occupied by federal troops and run by Republican governments, were disputed. A deal was made whereby those 20 votes went to Hayes in return for removal of federal troops from the South. Reconstruction was over.

Consequences of Reconstruction

Reconstruction had effectively ended. The struggle between the President and the Congress and between the North and the South had finally ended, but the impact of both the war and the efforts to restore the Union would continue to exert an influence on the development of the United States. The Union had been preserved, but at what cost, and to what extent, was the nation that emerged after 1877 fundamentally different from the one that had gone to war in 1861?

The abolition of slavery led to real changes in the lives of former slaves, but it did not end their economic dependence on Southern whites, nor did it end discrimination in the South. African-Americans after the Civil War were able to marry and divorce, and hundreds published letters and ads seeking loved ones from whom they had been separated as a result of the internal slave trade. African-Americans immediately began to form their own schools and churches. The restrictions that forbade slaves from learning to read and write in the old slave codes were now nullified, and former slaves emphasized the importance of education, especially for children. Former slaves also began to leave white churches and form their own church communities, which often had distinctive elements such as music or dance as part of the service. African-Americans also gained control over their time and their movements, but in terms of their economic status, little had changed. The failure of the government to provide former slaves with land or other economic opportunities meant that many Blacks ended up renting land or sharecropping from their former masters. White southerners could no longer exercise complete control over former slaves—for instance, many African-American males refused to allow their wives to work for whites—but they could demand a large portion of their crop as rent payment. Whites could also charge African-Americans high prices for seed and other supplies that had to be purchased from stores owned by whites.

Despite these efforts by conservative Southerners, the new Southern Republican party came to power in the constitutional conventions of 1868–1870, and as a result, the new Southern state constitutions were more democratic. Initially both Blacks and Republicans were elected to serve in the new governments.

Reconstruction laws encouraged investment and industrialization, though, while it helped in some areas, it also increased corruption. The question of land redistribution was very important to Blacks but was not paid adequate attention by Republicans. The effects on the Southern economy were terrible. Government industrialization plans geared toward helping the South industrialize did not work well. High tax rates turned public opinion against reconstructionists whose governments had to raise taxes substantially to pay for the Civil War damage.

Reconstruction transformed Southern society and culture and increased divisions within the population. The first division was between those who supported and those who disagreed with

Competency 5: U.S. History

Reconstruction. Opponents called Southerners who cooperated with Reconstruction proponents or who joined the Republican Party **scalawags**. The Northerners who ran such programs were referred to as **carpetbaggers** and were considered to be greedy, corrupt businessmen trying to take advantage of the South. The influx of these Northern "carpetbaggers" to the South resulted in the Republican Party gaining power in the South and passing some civil rights laws like ones that legalized interracial marriage and that allowed Black students to attend schools. In many of the state senates, Blacks gained positions of power.

The rapid cultural and economic changes occurring in the South resulted in racial tensions, as former slaves also faced campaigns of terror and intimidation by white Southerners who wanted to keep them in their place in society, sabotage Black civil rights, and persuade them not to try to exercise their right to vote. The **Ku Klux Klan** targeted all of those who supported Reconstruction—Black and white. They often attacked and murdered scalawags and leaders of all races, community activists, and teachers. In response to the violence in the South, Congress passed the **Enforcement Acts** and an **Anti-Klan Law** that made actions against the civil rights of others to be criminal offenses. The laws had little impact and Klan violence continued.

Eventually, the North lost interest in trying to enforce the laws and measures designed to advance civil rights for Blacks. As a result, many of the civil rights laws were overturned and conditions worsened for Blacks in the South. In 1883, a rewrite of the Fourteenth Amendment declared that Congress only had the power to outlaw public rather than private discrimination. The *Plessy v. Ferguson* case ruled that state-mandated segregation was legal as long as there were "separate but equal" facilities. In response to this case, Southern states introduced **Jim Crow Laws** designed to segregate whites from African-Americans.

It was not just in the South that African-Americans encountered discrimination and hostility, although the worst abuses did take place in the South. All in all, Reconstruction was a mixed bag, but in terms of achieving equality within the United States, it was clearly a failure.

COMPETENCY 5.8

Evaluate the impact of agrarianism, industrialization, urbanization, and reform movements on social, cultural, political, and economic development in the late nineteenth and early twentieth centuries.

Agrarianism

After the Civil War, aside from some cotton mills and a few tobacco-processing plants in the South, the vast majority of Southerners remained farmers. In the post-war era, individual farmers had a difficult time in the South as many were forced to sell their land if they could not pay their debts. Wealthy landowners swooped in and took over farms. Landless farmers were forced into **sharecropping** in which people who were unable to pay their debts had to promise to pay it with their crops—the **crop lien** system was designed to keep the poor in constant debt as their crops would rarely be worth enough money, so they would borrow more money. Huge interest rates on their loans forced these sharecroppers to continually borrow more and more money and promise more and more crops, essentially keeping both Black and white sharecroppers in a different type of slavery—one that lacked any sort of social safety net. Economic problems also intensified in both the South and the Midwest as Southern yeoman farmers were forced into growing cotton rather than their own food, making them at the mercy of cotton merchants and unable to sustain themselves. In the Midwest, dropping prices and rising technology resulted in increases in production that resulted in a tremendous oversupply of their products.

Farmers tried to deal with their mounting debts, and so they supported ways to increase the money supply, which they reasoned would make payments easier. They knew that it would cause inflation, which would make the farmers' debts worth less money, and they thought that the banks would not be as interested in pursuing them. The farmers advocated using silver, rather than gold, as the banking standard because they thought it would be advantageous for them to do so. With the support of Western miners along with the farmers in the South and Midwest, they felt that they could come out ahead.

The result of a lot of this economic and social pressure was that farmers decided to form agrarian cooperative organizations that would protect them from outside interests. In the 1870s, farmers in the Midwest, South, and Texas formed a network of **Granges** that not only addressed economic issues of farmers but also social and educational issues. The Grange Movement, which by 1875 had more than 1 million members, sought to allow farmers to buy machinery and sell crops as a group and therefore reap the benefits. They tried to lobby for legislation, notably what became referred to as the **Granger Laws** that sought to address some of the problems of railroad exploitation that farmers faced trying to get their goods to market. Eventually, the Granger Laws were ruled unconstitutional and Congress passed the **Interstate Commerce Act of 1887,** which sought to address the same issues. The Grange movement eventually died out due to lack of funds. They were replaced by **Farmers' Alliances** in the 1890s. One movement started in Texas, and then another formed in the Midwest—both alliances sought to group farmers together to combat the effects of railroad and industrial exploitation of farmers. The Farmers' Alliances were more political and less social than the Grange movements had been. They ran for political office, eventually controlling eight state legislatures and in the 1890s had 47 representatives in Congress. The Farmers' Alliances pushed the **Subtreasury Plan** to help farmers by having the federal government keep crops until prices rose and to finance low-interest loans to farmers.

Divisions within the Northern and Southern sections of the Farmers' Alliance prompted the formation of a third party in Omaha in 1882, the **People's Party,** which became the political arm of the Populist Party. The People's party put up a candidate for the 1892 election under a platform called the **Omaha Platform,** which called for government ownership of utilities, railroads, and the telegraph, government-sponsored farm loans, a graduated income tax, shorter workdays, direct election of U.S. senators, abolition of the National Bank, government-operated postal savings banks, restriction of undesirable immigration, abolition of the Pinkerton detective agency, gener-

Competency 5: U.S. History

ous coinage of silver, and a single term for the president and vice-president. Although its candidate lost, the party did receive 1 million votes and gained a few Congressional seats, enough to put their interests in the public spotlight.

Ten days after President **Grover Cleveland** took office in 1883, the country entered a four-year financial crisis. Several major corporations went bankrupt, 16,000 businesses disappeared, the stock market crashed, banks began to fail, and by 1895, unemployment reached a staggering 3 million. Populist cries to enlarge the money supply grew considerably, and progressive parties gained in popularity. By 1896, the Populists backed the Democratic candidate William Jennings Bryan against the Republican **William McKinley**. Bryan ran on his call for **free silver**. In a famous speech that he gave called the **Cross of Gold** speech, he argued that although increasing the money supply would be an inflationary move, it would loosen the Northern banking hold on the rest of the country and no longer would big business be able to "press down upon the brow of labor this crown of thorns" nor "crucify mankind upon a cross of gold." Despite gaining a lot of political fervor during the election, Bryan lost, partly because the Populists were unable to court the interests of the urban classes and convince them of the benefits of a silver standard. McKinley, upon his election, quickly passed the **Gold Standard Act** that required all paper money be backed by gold—a rather fortuitous move because, with the discovery of gold in Alaska, the economy improved.

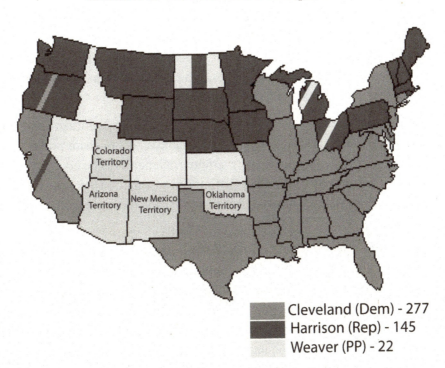

Figure 5.3
Election of 1892 Electoral College Results

Industrialization

Between 1860 and 1900, the United States became the world's leader in manufacturing through capital accumulation, natural resources, especially in iron, oil, and coal, and new inventions. Industrialization was also advanced by an abundance of labor supplemented by massive immigration, transport, and communications. The telephone was introduced by Alexander Graham Bell in 1876. The development of the modern steel industry introduced by Andrew Carnegie, the invention of the first incandescent light by Thomas Edison, and George Westinghouse's discovery of how to use alternating current and transformers to transmit electricity over long distances further stimulated industrial growth. Henry Ford experimented with the internal combustion engine and figured out how to mass-produce cars for mass consumption with the formation of the Ford Motor Company in 1903. A few individuals, such as John D. Rockefeller, who came to control 95% of all U.S. oil refineries by 1877, became extremely wealthy, but the mass of workers who were employed by the rising number of factories had a difficult time earning enough to feed and clothe their families. The benefits of these new inventions were transmitted throughout the United States thanks to the efforts of the railroad industry, which not only opened up the West but also aided in the development of other industries.

With the development of more technologies that enabled businesses to produce better and faster, industry had to struggle more to make profits. In order to make sure they could sell their goods, prices had to remain low, production had to expand, and wages were kept as low as possible. In order to do this, many small businesses went out of business as they failed to meet loan payments or effectively regulate their business and keep production up to economies of scale. As a result, businesses began to consolidate in order to remain viable. More and more businesses merged which only led to greater economies of scale and led to corporate **consolidation**. Some of the consolidating techniques that companies used were:

- **Pools**—These were essentially "Gentlemen's Agreements" between companies that set limits on production and created agreements to share profits. They did not last very long because they required companies to be honest with one another and proved to be rather detrimental to small businesses and farmers. The **Interstate Commerce Act of 1887** made these pools illegal among railroads.

- **Trusts**—Originated by John D. Rockefeller, trusts relied on the idea that one company could control another by forcing it to yield control of its stock to the bigger company's board of trustees. One type of trust was pioneered by Rockefeller when he used a method of **horizontal integration** to build Standard Oil. Horizontal integration created monopolies within a particular industry. Rockefeller used horizontal integration to take over oil refineries in the United States through either legally buying out smaller companies or destroying them through cutthroat competition or pooling agreements. Antitrust legislation later eliminated the use of horizontal integration.

Competency 5: U.S. History

Holding Companies—This occurred when a corporation could hold enough stock in various companies to have a controlling interest in the production. This method of **vertical integration** allows other companies to survive, although it might buy out all of the factors in production. One example of this was Gustavus Swift, who took over the stockyards, slaughterhouses, processing, and packaging plants in the meat industry but still allowed other companies to compete with his meat-packing empire. Andrew Carnegie also did this with the steel industry.

Numerous problems resulted from corporate consolidation of power. The banking system became more fragile as bigger businesses became their lifeblood. If a major business failed, bank failures soon followed. As a result, the United States suffered financial instability throughout the late nineteenth and early twentieth centuries. Monopolies also created a class of extremely powerful men who believed in **laissez-faire economics,** whose hallmark was not only that there was no room in the market for government intervention but also that **Social-Darwinism** supported their ideas—for only the fittest companies should and would survive in the market, and state intervention or regulation was futile. As conditions worsened for the "average worker" and small businessman, public resentment increased and the government did respond with various attempts at limiting the power of these strong businesses and powerful businessmen.

Conditions in factories were often appalling, and the rise of the Union movement was partly a response to the dangerous working conditions, low pay, and lack of job security. Mechanization of industry brought enormous changes for workers. No longer were workers their own bosses; they now had to report to others. Specialization and routinization of work in mass-production assembly lines resulted, over time, in a lessening of skill among workers. Efforts to increase worker efficiency led to more and more attempts to regulate and control workers' lives outside of work. Wages for male workers were lowered and jobs for men were eliminated as factory owners found out that they could employ women and children and pay them even lower wages. Pressure to speed up production at the expense of safety and health resulted in a more dangerous workplace.

Management used various methods to force people to stay in their jobs without complaint. When workers went on strike, businesses paid people called "scabs" to come in and take over their jobs. They launched all-out PR campaigns to discredit any striking workers. They also used Pinkerton agents to infiltrate unions and as guards to keep suspected unionists and strikers out of factories. Other techniques were employing lockouts, blacklisting of workers, yellow dog contracts that made, as a condition of employment, a worker agree not to join a union, court injunctions, and boasting of open shops, which did not make joining a union a condition of employment.

Workers, struck by the widespread misery that was infecting cities, sought to unite to seek changes. Labor unions formed to counter poor treatment of workers. Many in government, the courts, and business considered labor unions to be radical organizations and were not receptive to their demands. One of the first national labor unions was the **Knights of Labor,** founded in 1869 by a Philadelphia tailor, Uriah Stephens, and who led a series of strikes under the leadership of **Terrence Powderly** in the 1880s. The Knights organized skilled and unskilled workers to join it. The basic ideology of the Knights of Labor was that they wanted to get rid of capitalism and instead have a cooperative workers' alliance that would allow workers to work for themselves. The Knights advocated an eight-hour work day, abolition of child and prison labor, equal pay for men and women, safety codes in the workplace, prohibition of contract foreign labor, a federal income tax, government ownership of railroad and telegraph lines, and abolition of the National Bank. Originally disdainful of strikes as they favored arbitration, they increasingly advocated violence to meet their goals. As a result, the popularity of the Knights began to decline and unions became more associated with violence and political radicalism.

The formation in 1886 of the **American Federation of Labor** (AFL) led by **Samuel Gompers** sought to take the Labor Movement in a different direction. Gompers believed that it would be best to focus on issues of higher wages and shorter workdays. Gompers avoided the sort of rhetoric associated with the Knights of Labor that had attracted anarchists to it and instead included only skilled laborers. The AFL sought to avoid party politics and was formed as a confederation of trade unions that represented skilled workers in matters of national legislation. They maintained a national strike fund to support striking workers, engaged in a PR campaign that wrapped trade unions up in evangelical rhetoric and boasted of its moral imperatives, mediated disputes between labor and management, and pushed for closed shops that barred employment to non-union workers. Another organization soon emerged, the **Industrial Workers of the World,** referred to as the **Wobblies,** that sought to unite all workers and felt that the only way to make sure workers were treated fairly was to overthrow capitalism with violence.

Notably, there were two groups consistently excluded from union membership: women and immigrants. Unions felt that women, immigrants, and African-Americans would compete for jobs and would endanger workers' well-being. In 1903, the **Women's Trade Union League** was founded and tied some of the travails of women in the workplace to the lack of suffrage.

Industrialization did have some good benefits to society as it spread technology and goods to formerly isolated communities. Income levels rose as did employment levels, leading to growth in the commercial society. Higher life expectancies resulted from improved access to medical care and varied diets. Flush toilets, processed and preserved foods, ready-made clothing, department stores, print culture, and advertising all became familiar components of daily life thanks to industrialization. Despite the drawbacks, industrialization enabled the United States to emerge as a major power.

Urbanization

Rapid urbanization, the process by which an increasing portion of the population moved to the cities and suburbs as a result of industrialization, migration, and corporate incentives, became another hallmark of the era. Cities, where most factories were located, became dirtier and less healthy environments. These were often impersonal metropolises that were divided into business, residential, social, and ethnic centers, rather than the old types of cities where people tended to have merged sectors. For example, the emergence of the Boston to Washington area as a series of cities that provide common needs—like centers of banking, commerce, media, academics, and immigration—functioned almost like one gigantic city, referred to in hindsight as a **megalopolis.**

Advances in **mass transportation** like railroads, streetcars, and subways not only facilitated transportation of goods but also people to cities. Cities expanded, and the construction of newer neighborhoods meant people could move between the inner core of the city and the outer core, or the suburbs. What resulted from this development was a sort of stratification of society as class distinctions began to emerge from where people lived, as opposed to just what occupation they held. Many immigrants who arrived after 1880 tended to be from Southern and Eastern Europe, and settled in the inner core of the cities. Many of the new immigrants began to settle in **ethnic neighborhoods** in **tenement housing**, which were multi-family urban houses (a simultaneous housing also developed that targeted wealthier urbanites, **row houses** which were single-family dwellings that shared walls with other houses). While some of these new neighborhoods experienced severe overcrowding and squalid conditions, they also provided opportunities for some—namely women—who were able to find work outside the home, albeit at reduced wages.

Increased urbanization also provided opportunities for some select men who sought to facilitate the needs of these new urban residents who were having trouble contending with problems of housing, transportation, water, and sanitation, in return for political favor. These **political bosses** did help the poor find homes and jobs, get citizenship and voting rights, and build parks, roads, and sewage lines. But, they did so through **graft** and **kickbacks,** and created **political machines,** the most famous of which was led by **Boss Tweed of Tammany Hall in New York City.** A whole host of problems developed that inspired reform movements to try to tackle some of the growing problems of urban life.

Reform Movements

Middle-class organizations, largely run by women, targeted the urban poor for their reform efforts. They lobbied local governments for building safety codes, better sanitation, and public schools. The **Settlement House Movement** focused on building community centers in slum neighborhoods. **Jane Addams** was one of the most influential members of the movement and along with **Ellen Gates Starr** founded **Chicago's Hull House** to provide English lessons for immigrants, day care for working mothers, and playgrounds for children. She also cultivated notions of social responsibility for the urban poor and inspired the formation of other settlement houses so that by 1910, there were over 400 settlement houses nationwide.

Efforts also targeted the political realm, focusing on the evils of political machines and patronage. **Thomas Nast**, a political cartoonist, helped arouse public outrage against Boss Tweed, who was eventually found guilty of corruption and sentenced to jail. After an all-out political brawl, the **Pendleton Service Act of 1883** created the bipartisan Civil Service Commission that made appointments to federal jobs a meritocracy awarded to candidates based on their performance on examination rather than through their political connections.

Women's suffrage became an important political issue during this period, led by **Susan B. Anthony** who sought to get Congress to amend the constitution and permit women to vote. By 1890, while suffrage had yet to make it to national consideration, the **American Woman Suffrage Association**, which had targeted state constitutions, had given women the right to vote on school issues. It was not until 1920 and the **Nineteenth Amendment** that women were given the right to vote.

COMPETENCY 5.9

Evaluate the impact of immigration on social, cultural, political, and economic development in the late nineteenth and early twentieth centuries.

Immigration had a tremendous effect on the cities during the Gilded Age of the late nineteenth and early twentieth centuries, as it proved to be one of the great ages of immigration in American history. Between 1870 and 1920, approximately 20 million Europeans arrived in the United States in search of a better life, trying to escape families, land shortages, and religious or political persecution. But in many ways, this immigration differed from previous immigrations in that the immigrants were refugees from the ailing empires of Austria-Hungary, Russia, Italy, and Germany. Greeks, Slavs, Armenians, and Jews rounded out the new group of immigrants that came to the United States in the 1890s. One reason for this influx of immigration simply was because travel was easier. With the development of large ocean-going steamships and the time cut down to only three weeks for trans-Atlantic voyages, the appeal of making the move to America increased, and the cost for such a trip dropped considerably. Moreover, the rise of American industries and the growth of the railroad system created thousands of jobs that acted as powerful inducements to those wanting to venture to the United States to try their luck.

Most of these "new" European immigrants settled in the Northeast, dominated by Irish and Italians, and the Midwest, dominated by Germans. While the West also experienced an influx of European immigrants, it mostly attracted immigrants from China. Lured by the prospect of earning money by working on the expanding western railroad system, many Chinese immigrants settled in California.

Problems attendant to the numbers of new immigrants were that cities needed to have resources available to take care of the new people. The floods of immigrants that poured into the nation's largest cities wound up swamping the cities' resources of housing and employment. The living conditions in the urban areas where most immigrants settled were horrendous. Tenement buildings were crowded, lacked windows, did not have indoor plumbing or water, and sanitation was lacking. Cholera and typhoid diseases were prevalent due to the lack of adequate medical care, limited access to safe drinking water, horse manure and garbage piled up on the streets, and sewage flowing through open gutters. Massive fires that occurred in almost every major city provided another frequent problem. Crime intensified as gangs formed, political corruption ran amok, theft

Competency 5: U.S. History

was prevalent, and alcoholism took a grip on many new immigrants depressed at what the "land of opportunity" actually provided them.

In response to growing alarm at urban immigrants' living and working conditions, social reformers began to organize public and private relief programs and to pursue attempts to establish legal standards for housing and working conditions. These scattered reform efforts were among the seeds of a much larger, more comprehensive series of reform movements that soon came to dominate American life. They chiefly targeted improving sanitation and health concerns. Moreover, an **Americanization Movement** designed to teach immigrants the skills they needed to assimilate into American culture dominated attempts by reform organizations seeking to help these new citizens. Some of these programs were government funded and taught immigrants citizenship skills, "American cooking," and social etiquette.

Not all immigration was encouraged. Although immigration was one of the primary forces that shaped the country, Americans were not overly enthused about immigration and did not hail its virtues. In fact, the emergence of a new idea called **nativism** became more prominent where there was overt favoritism towards native-born Americans. Immigrants became viewed as potential threats to the American way of life. Native-born white Americans feared that newcomers would not only do much better than they would, but might even do so well that native-born Americans would possibly be excluded from reaping the benefits of any economic or social success. Anti-immigrant feeling was linked rather closely to religious, ethnic, and racial prejudices of the late nineteenth century. Americans seemed to fear that the "new immigrants" would not fit into the **melting pot** and take on the new blended identity of Americans in which merged people shed the languages and customs of their national origin to embrace their new American identity. Some, though, were worried that immigrants from despotic monarchies would dilute or pollute American democracy. They felt that these immigrants could not understand democracy and would take enormous educational resources away from native-born children and instead devote precious resources toward the futile democratic training of these immigrants. These fears had little basis in reality. Indeed, for millions of immigrant children, school became their primary contact with America, and they all too willingly shed their own identity in an effort to Americanize and fit in with their peers.

This also was the first great period of Asian immigration to America, mostly from China, but with a trickle of immigrants from Japan and Korea as well. However, anti-Asian feeling in the western United States arose, likely born out of fears that native-born workers would lose their jobs to Chinese immigrants who willingly accepted lower wages. Such anti-Asian sentiment resulted in a series of acts that targeted these groups specifically. In 1882, Congress passed the **Chinese Exclusion Act** that banned entry for ten years to all Chinese except those who were more valued, like students, teachers, merchants, government officials, and tourists. In 1892, the ban was extended for another ten years. In 1902, the immigration of Chinese immigrants was restricted indefinitely and not repealed until 1943. In 1906, waves of anti-Chinese aggression that filled the streets became extended to Japanese and other Asian peoples. Attacks weren't limited to just physical assaults: local government entities began imposing their own measures designed to give Asian immigrants the message that they were unwelcome. The San Francisco Board of Education segregated Japanese children by putting them in separate schools. Japan protested the treatment of its emigrants and President Theodore Roosevelt worked out a deal called the 1907–1908 **Gentlemen's Agreement** by which Japan agreed to limit the number of unskilled workers they sent to the United States in exchange for repeal of the San Francisco segregation order.

At the start of the 1920s, the United States started setting limits and quotas to restrict immigration. The **Quota Act of 1921** set immigration quotas based on national origins and discriminated against the "new immigrants" who came from southern and eastern Europe. The Act imposed a cap of 3% of the number of immigrants from any country living in the United States. These limits were set to reduce the "foreign influence" in the country. The **Immigration Act of 1924** further restricted immigration by reducing the 1921 cap from 3% to 2%. The **National Origins Act of 1929** put quotas on immigration in proportion to the origins of Americans in 1920.

COMPETENCY 5.10

Identify the causes, significant individuals, and effects of the events associated with the World War I era.

American foreign policy continued to remain committed to the **Monroe Doctrine**, which asserted that America would intervene anywhere in the Western Hemisphere where it felt its interests or security was at stake. It resolved to stay out of Europe's disputes. When **Woodrow Wilson** won the presidency in 1912, he seemed to advocate what the public wanted with regard to the simmering tensions in Europe—the United States should just stay out of it.

When World War I broke out in Europe, Wilson issued a proclamation of American neutrality which called for Americans to treat all of those fighting in the war fairly and without favoritism. Wilson had opined that America might be the new world arbiter of international disputes and urged Americans to be neutral in thought as well as in action. However, Americans, despite proclamations of neutrality as the best course for America, were not neutral at all. America was a rather ethnically diverse country and people took sides according to their ethnic origins—German-Americans supported the Germans, British-Americans supported the British, and the Irish, as they did not like the British, supported the Germans as well. Economic ties with the British continued according to international law, which stated that neutral countries could trade with countries on both sides of the conflict and that any attempt to stop such trade was also legal and could be done through blockade. Wilson himself shared ideological similarities with the British and believed that the British were the ones best able to promote his brand of **Wilsonianism** that consisted of ideas of democracy, internationalism, American exceptionalism, and diplomacy. Moreover, many of Wilson's advisors openly favored the Allies. A series of events occurred that made Wilson reconsider his position of neutrality:

Blockades made it difficult for America to continue to deal with both sides of the war. England was able to effectively stop American ships from trading with the Germans. The British impounded and confiscated U.S. vessels, but in an effort not to anger U.S. merchants, paid for the confiscated merchandise. The Germans attempted to counter the blockade with **submarines** or **U-boats**. By using the U-boats, the Germans had a problem in that they could not, as stipulated by international law, warn civilian vessels of an impending attack. Even though the Germans warned Wilson that they would attack any U.S. civilian ship as it might contain wartime materials, Wilson was adamant that the Germans respect international law.

Sinking of the Lusitania. In May 1915, the British passenger liner *Lusitania* on a voyage from New York to Liverpool was sunk by a German submarine, killing 1,198 passengers, among them 128 Americans. Unbeknownst to the passengers, the ship had been loaded up with hidden arms and munitions destined for the British war effort. The action provoked condemnation of the Germans by the Americans and for a while, the Germans responded by limiting their use of submarine warfare. **Secretary of State William Jennings Bryan**, a pacifist, believed that Americans should be forbidden from traveling on belligerent ships and that contraband should not be allowed on passenger ships. Wilson disagreed and insisted that the Germans should stop their submarine warfare. Bryan resigned rather than insisting on questionable neutral rights. In 1916, the Germans sank another passenger liner, the *Arabic*. In response, Congress debated the **Gore-McLemore Resolution,** which attempted to do just what Bryan had advocated, but the resolution never passed. Wilson, in response, asked Congress to put the military into a state of preparedness for war, just in case it was needed. After another U-boat attack on *The Sussex* on March 24, 1916, Wilson threatened Berlin with severing diplomatic relations and the Germans promised not to do it again.

Two incidents elevated tensions between the United States and Germany. Germany announced on January 31, 1917, that it would sink all ships, belligerent or neutral, without warning in a large war zone off the coasts of the Allied nations in the eastern Atlantic and the Mediterranean. Wilson broke diplomatic relations with Germany on February 3, and the Germans responded by sinking several American ships during February and March.

The British intercepted a secret message from the German foreign secretary, Arthur Zimmermann, to the German minister in Mexico, and turned it over to the United States on February 24, 1917. The **Zimmermann Telegram** included a German proposal that, in the event of a war between the United States and Germany, Mexico should attack the United States. After the war, the territories lost in the Mexican-American War—Texas, New Mexico, and Arizona—would be returned to Mexico. The telegram also suggested that Germany would help Japan, too, if they went to war with America. When the telegram was released to the press on March 1, many Americans became convinced that war with Germany was necessary. Wilson first asked Congress for "armed-neutrality," but anti-war Senators filibustered the plan and so Wilson called the Congress into a special session and declared war on Germany on April 6.

During the War

After the declaration of war, the United States realized that their 120,000-man army had little experience and was not ready for war. The government embarked on a series of measures to make sure that it would win the war. Congress passed the **Selective Service Act** to require all males between the ages of 21 and 30 to register. By the end of 1918, more than 24 million American men had registered for the draft, 4.8 million had served in the war, 2 million had seen active combat, 400,000 African-Americans had served in segregated units, and 15,000 Native Americans had served as scouts, messengers, and snipers in non-segregated units. Most of those drafted were white, poorly educated Americans in their early twenties.

Government power expanded significantly during the time America was involved in the war. It took control of the telephone, telegraph, and railroad, and added a new bureaucracy to handle it. It created the **War Industries Board** to liaison with big business to meet government needs. The board coordinated all facets of the economy, both industrial and agricultural production, to guarantee and standardize the quality of goods. It created the **Food Administration** led by Herbert Hoover to promote "victory gardens" as well as set prices and regulated the distribution of food during the war. The War Industries Board also set up the **Railroad Administration and Fuel Administration** to regulate each industry and to ration gasoline throughout the country.

The government also took advantage of the wartime situation to put some restrictions on civil liberties. Anyone who refused to support the war was targeted. Unfortunately, some groups, particularly those of German descent, were also persecuted and even killed during anti-German hysteria that developed during the war. The Government chimed in on public fears by passing two acts, the **Espionage Act of 1917** and the **Sedition Act of 1918.** The Espionage Act of 1917 provided for fines and imprisonment for persons who made false statements that aided the enemy, incited rebellion in the military, or obstructed recruitment or the draft. Printed matter advocating treason or insurrection could be excluded from the mails. The Sedition Act of May 1918 forbade any criticism of the government, flag, or uniform, even if there were not detrimental consequences, and expanded the mail exclusion. The laws were applied in ways that trampled on civil liberties. The Espionage Act was upheld by the Supreme Court in the case of *Schenck v. United States* in 1919. The opinion, written by Justice Oliver Wendell Holmes, Jr., stated that Congress could limit free speech when the words represented a "clear and present danger," and that a person cannot cry "fire" in a crowded theater. The Sedition Act was similarly upheld in *Abrams v. United States* a few months later.

World War I: The Military Campaign

The American force of about 14,500, which had arrived in France by September 1917, was assigned a quiet section of the line near Verdun. When the Germans mounted a major drive toward Paris in the spring of 1918, the Americans experienced their first important engagements. In June, they prevented the Germans from crossing the Marne at Chateau-Thierry and cleared the area of Belleau Woods. In July, eight American divisions aided French troops in attacking the German line between Reims and Soissons. The American First Army, with over half a million men under Pershing's immediate command, was assembled in August 1918, and began a major offensive on the southern part of the front on September 12. Following the successful operation, Pershing began a drive against the German defenses between Verdun and Sedan, an action called the Meuse-Argonne Offensive. He reached Sedan on November 7. During the same period, the English in the

Competency 5: U.S. History

North and the French along the central front also broke through the German lines. The fighting ended with the armistice on November 11, 1918.

Wartime Social Trends

Large numbers of women, mostly white, were hired by factories and other enterprises in jobs never before open to them. When the war ended, almost all returned to traditional "women's jobs" or to homemaking. Returning veterans replaced them in the labor market. The labor shortage opened industrial jobs to Mexican-Americans and African-Americans. **W.E.B. DuBois**, the most prominent African-American leader of the time, supported the war effort in the hope that the war would make the world safe for democracy and bring a better life for African-Americans in the United States. About half a million rural Southern African-Americans migrated to cities, mainly in the North and Midwest, to obtain employment in war and other industries, especially in steel and meatpacking. In 1917, there were race riots in 26 cities in the North and South, with the worst in East St. Louis, Illinois.

In December 1917, a Constitutional amendment to prohibit the manufacture and sale of alcoholic beverages in the United States was passed by Congress and submitted to the states for ratification.

Peacemaking (1918–1920)

From the time of the American entry into the war, Wilson had maintained that the war would make the world safe for democracy. He insisted that there should be peace without victory, meaning that the victors would not be vindictive toward the losers, so that a fair and stable international situation in the postwar world would ensure lasting peace. In an address to Congress on January 8, 1918, he presented his specific peace plan in the form of the **Fourteen Points**. The first five points called for open rather than secret peace treaties, freedom of the seas, free trade, arms reduction, and a fair adjustment of colonial claims. The next eight points were concerned with the national aspirations of various European peoples and the adjustment of boundaries. The fourteenth point, which he considered the most important and had espoused as early as 1916, called for a "general association of nations" to preserve the peace.

Wilson decided that he would lead the American delegation to the peace conference, which opened in Paris on January 12, 1919. In doing so, he became the first president to leave the country during his term of office. In the negotiations, which continued until May 1919, Wilson found it necessary to make many compromises in forging the text of the treaty. Following a protest by 39 senators in February 1919, Wilson obtained some changes in the **League of Nations** structure to exempt the Monroe Doctrine and domestic matters from League jurisdiction. Then, on July 26, 1919, he presented the treaty with the League within it to the Senate for ratification. Almost all of the 47 Democrats supported Wilson and the treaty, but the 49 Republicans were divided. About a dozen were "irreconcilables" who thought that the United States should not be a member of the League under any circumstances. The remainder included 25 "strong" and 12 "mild" reservationists who would accept the treaty with some changes. The main objection centered on Article X of the League Covenant, where the reservationists wanted it understood that the United States would not go to war to defend a League member without the approval of Congress.

On September 3, 1919, Wilson set out on a national speaking tour to appeal to the people to support the treaty and the League and to influence their senators. He collapsed after a speech in Pueblo, Colorado, on September 25, and returned to Washington, where he suffered a severe stroke on October 2, which paralyzed his left side. He was seriously ill for several months and never fully recovered. The treaty failed to get a two-thirds majority either with or without the reservationists. Many people, including British and French leaders, urged Wilson to compromise with the reservationists, including the issue of Article X. Many historians think that Wilson's ill health impaired his judgment, and that he would have worked out a compromise had he not had the stroke. The Senate took up the treaty again in February 1920, and on March 19, it was again defeated both with and without the reservationists. The United States officially ended the war with Germany by a resolution of Congress signed on July 2, 1921, and a separate peace treaty was ratified on July 25. The United States did not join the League.

Domestic Problems and the End of the Wilson Administration

In January 1919, the **Eighteenth Amendment** to the Constitution prohibiting the manufacture, sale, transportation, or importation of intoxicating liquors was ratified by the states, and it became effective in January 1920. The Nineteenth Amendment providing for women's suffrage, which had been defeated in the Senate in 1918, was approved by Congress in 1919. It was ratified by the states in time for the presidential election of 1920.

Americans feared the spread of the Russian Communist revolution to the United States, and many interpreted the widespread strikes of 1919 spurred by inflation as Communist-inspired and the beginning of the revolution. Bombs sent through the mail to prominent government and business leaders in April 1919 seemed to confirm their fears, although the origin of the bombs has never been determined. The anti-German hysteria of the war years was transformed into the anti-Communist and anti-foreign hysteria of 1919 and 1920, and continued in various forms through the 1920s. In 1919, J. Edgar Hoover was selected to head a new Intelligence Division in the Justice Department to collect information about radicals.

White hostility based on competition for lower-paying jobs and a pattern of perceived Black encroachment into neighborhoods led to race riots in 25 cities in 1919, with hundreds killed or wounded and millions of dollars in property damage. The Chicago riot in July was the worst. Fear of returning African-American veterans in the South led to an increase in lynchings from 34 in 1917 to 60 in 1918 and 70 in 1919. Some victims were veterans still in uniform.

COMPETENCY 5.11

Identify social, cultural, political, and economic developments (e.g., Roaring Twenties, Harlem Renaissance, Great Depression, New Deal) between World War I and World War II.

The United States retreated into isolation after World War I. The Senate refused to ratify the Versailles Peace Treaty and signed a separate peace with Germany and Japan. In another embarrassing move, the United States also refused to join the League of Nations—the same league whose creation came out of an idea proposed by the U.S. president, Woodrow Wilson. The U.S. ended the concept of free and open access to immigration. Until 1914, more than 1.2 million people had immigrated to the United States. But once the 1920s immigration restrictions were in place, the overall total of immigrants per year was limited to about 160,000, and each country had a fixed number of immigrants. The United States turned inward, and such a move proved to be a good thing. The 1920s became known as the **Roaring Twenties**, a time when America was reveling in its prosperity, enjoying the fruits of its inventions, beginning its love affair with the automobile as by 1929, 1 out of every 5 residents owned a motor vehicle, and soon, the post–World War I United States was one of the richest nations in the world.

The Roaring Twenties (1920–1929)

Economic Developments

The economy remained the story of the 1920s, both for its highs and for its lows.

Some of the big developments in the period were as follows:

- **Initial Recession Followed by Recovery:** Following the war, with the return of the soldiers looking for jobs, the U.S. economy began to slide into a recession. By 1922, not only had the economy recovered, but the nation also began to grow and prosper. Recovery proved to be rapid, except for farmers who were finding it impossible to meet and beat worldwide competition.

- **Retreat from Regulation:** After the war, regulatory institutions were quickly dismantled and government, which had already been working with businesses through the War Industries Board during the war, became more **pro-business** than ever.

- **Emergence of Welfare Capitalism:** Support of organized labor declined and membership declined from 5 million to 3.5 million nationwide. Strikes over unfair wages or unsafe working conditions resulted in federal troops being called in to suppress the strikes. Businesses, in an effort to keep unions out, developed **welfare capitalism** in order to persuade workers not to join unions and instead enjoy new benefits offered by their places of employment, like pension plans, profit sharing, stock purchase plans, and insurance. Welfare capitalism seemed to have worked as long as prosperity continued. As such, the 1920s prosperity wrought a fast erosion in union membership. Women, African-Americans, and immigrant workers remained at the bottom of any scale.

Corporate Consolidation: Without regulation, more mega-companies formed during the 1920s with a trend toward corporate consolidation. In most fields, an oligopoly of two to four firms dominated. For example, in the automobile industry, Ford, General Motors, and Chrysler produced 83% of the vehicles in 1929. Government regulatory agencies such as the Federal Trade Commission and the Interstate Commerce Commission were passive and generally controlled by individuals from the business world.

Lobbying: Special interest groups began to band together to affect federal legislation.

Mass Consumption: The speed with which materialism spread throughout the United States was breathtaking. Due to technological breakthroughs, especially the ability to electrically wire households, there were more and new products on the market, and people wanted them. Automobiles, washing machines, refrigerators, electric irons, electric and gas stoves, and other inventions made living much easier and improved the quality of life. Mass-produced articles like clothing and food became more affordable. As Americans craved these new goods, many sought to buy them on credit. A new type of credit called **installment credit** let purchasers spread payments out over time for some of these new household goods. These new household inventions resulted in new ways of thinking about domestic work, which was now cut down considerably with new products that could perform tasks in a fraction of the time it used to take.

Economic Polarization among Various Classes Reached New Heights: By 1929, the richest 1% in America held 45% of the wealth. The rising gap between the rich and the poor caused many to think that perhaps America was moving in the wrong direction.

Bank Consolidation: There was also a trend toward bank consolidation. Because corporations were raising much of their money through the sale of stocks and bonds, the demand for business loans declined. Commercial banks then put more of their funds into real estate loans, loans to brokers against stocks and bonds, and the purchase of stocks and bonds themselves.

Political Developments

The Roaring Twenties saw three presidents—**Warren G. Harding**, **Calvin Coolidge**, and **Herbert Hoover**—all firmly pro-business Republicans who surrounded themselves with advisors who thought similarly.

Competency 5: U.S. History

Warren G. Harding: Harding, a handsome and amiable man of limited intellectual and organizational abilities, who had spent much of his life as the publisher of a newspaper in the small city of Marion, Ohio, was elected in 1920. He recognized his limitations and surrounded himself with advisors whom he trusted would help him but who proved to be mostly corrupt. The Teapot Dome Scandal began in 1921 when Secretary of the Interior Albert B. Fall secured the transfer of several naval oil reserves to his jurisdiction. In 1922, he secretly leased government oil reserves at Teapot Dome in Wyoming to oilmen in return for $400,000 in bribes. Harding's Veteran's Bureau chief was caught stealing Bureau funds, and the Attorney General was found to have been engaging in influence peddling. Harding died in office in 1923 and Vice President Calvin Coolidge became president.

Calvin Coolidge: Known as "Silent Cal," Coolidge really did not do much except to continue Harding's conservative economic policies, lower income-tax rates, reduce debt, build roads, and seek to prohibit government interference with business. He ran in 1924 on the platform "Coolidge Prosperity" against the Progressive **Robert M. La Follette,** who had started his own party and who railed against monopolies, and called for the nationalization of railroads and the direct election of the president.

Herbert Hoover: Coolidge did not seek another term, and the convention quickly nominated Herbert Hoover, the secretary of commerce, for president. The platform endorsed the policies of the Harding and Coolidge administrations. Hoover, an Iowa farm boy and an orphan, graduated from Stanford University with a degree in mining engineering. He became a multimillionaire from mining and other investments around the world. After serving as the director of the Food Administration under Wilson, he became Secretary of Commerce under Harding and Coolidge. He ran against New York Governor Alfred E. Smith, a Catholic and an anti-prohibitionist, who controlled most of the non-Southern delegations. Southerners supported Hoover's nomination with the understanding that the platform would not advocate repeal of prohibition. Hoover believed that cooperation between business and government would enable the United States to abolish poverty through continued economic growth. The main thing that he ended up dealing with was the Depression.

Social Developments

With consumerism and modernization, people migrated to the cities, where manufacturing jobs were more readily available. By 1920, for the first time, a majority of Americans (51%) lived in an urban area with a population of 2,500 or more. A new phenomenon of the 1920s was the tremendous growth of suburbs and satellite cities, which grew more rapidly than the central cities. Streetcars, commuter railroads, and automobiles contributed to the process, as well as the easy availability of financing for home construction. The suburbs had once been the domain of the wealthy, but the technology of the 1920s opened them to working-class families.

The principal driving force of the economy of the 1920s was the automobile. Automobile manufacturing stimulated supporting industries such as steel, rubber, and glass, as well as gasoline refining and highway construction. During the 1920s, the United States became a nation of paved roads. The Federal Highway Act of 1916 started the federal highway system and gave matching funds to the states for construction. The car made Americans take to the roads and allowed people to move further away from city centers, thus starting a whole new area of living called **suburbia**. By 1929, out of the 100 million people who lived in the United States, more than 23 million had cars.

Traditional American moral standards regarding premarital sex and marital fidelity were widely questioned for the first time during the 1920s. The automobile, by giving people mobility and privacy, was generally considered to have contributed to sexual license. Birth control, though illegal, was promoted by **Margaret Sanger** and others and was widely accepted. Divorce laws were liberalized in many states at the insistence of women. Domestic service was the largest job category. Most other women workers were in traditional female occupations such as secretarial and clerical work, retail sales, teaching, and nursing. Rates of pay were below those for men. Most women still pursued the traditional role of housewife and mother, and society accepted that as the norm.

The migration of southern rural African-Americans to the cities continued, with about 1 million moving during the 1920s. By 1930, about 20% of American Blacks lived in the North, with the largest concentrations in New York, Chicago, and Philadelphia. While they were generally better off economically in the cities than they had been as tenant farmers, they generally held low-paying jobs and were confined to tiny, segregated areas of the cities. A native of Jamaica, **Marcus Garvey** (1887–1940) founded the **Universal Negro Improvement Association**, advocating African-American racial pride and separatism rather than integration, and called for a return of African-Americans to Africa. In 1921, he proclaimed himself the provisional president of an African empire, and sold stock in the Black Star Steamship Line, which would take migrants to Africa. The line went bankrupt in 1923, and Garvey was convicted and imprisoned for mail fraud in the sale of the line's stock and then deported. His legacy was an emphasis on African-American pride and self-respect.

Increased life expectancy and a decreasing birth rate also posed some problems for Americans. Although they lived better and longer due to advances in nutrition and sanitation, they also had fewer children. With fewer children and people living longer than before, old-age pensions became an important issue.

Cultural Developments

The 1920s witnessed the birth of new forms of mass culture and new opportunities for leisure time for Americans. As a result, there were new forms of entertainment and culture. The **movies** became an important part of American culture. Sports also took center stage, especially baseball, and players like Babe Ruth were idolized by millions. Sports figures and movie stars became larger-than-life celebrities.

Prohibition did not prevent people from going to **speakeasies** to drink alcohol. Prohibition did bring all sorts of problems to the country as some groups, like organized crime, found ways to continue the supply of alcohol to a population who still seemed to want it.

Many writers of the 1920s were disgusted with the hypocrisy and materialism of contemporary American society and were disillusioned by World War I. Often called the "Lost Generation," many of them, such as novelists Ernest Hemingway and F. Scott Fitzgerald and poets Ezra Pound and T. S. Eliot, moved to Europe where they wrote about America from afar. Common literary themes reflected some of the anxiety about the changes that were happening: alienation, hypocrisy, conformity, etc. In their writings, they lambasted the narrow-minded, small-town values of pre-War America and waxed on about the evils associated with the materialistic business culture of the 1920s.

The twenties also inspired new styles from talented artists like **Georgia O'Keeffe** in painting, **Aaron Copland** and **George Gershwin** in music, and **Frank Lloyd Wright** in architecture.

African-Americans flocked to Harlem where a movement sprang up in the largest Black neighborhood of New York City. Theaters, cultural clubs, and newspapers celebrated Black culture. Writers of the **Harlem Renaissance,** such as poet **Langston Hughes** and novelist **Zora Neale Hurston,** explored the Black experience in America. A major part of the Harlem Renaissance was the proliferation of **jazz,** which owed a lot to Black culture and music, and featured improvisation and free-spiritedness. Jazz became emblematic of the Roaring Twenties, so much so that the period is also referred to as the **Jazz Age**. Jazz became hugely popular in the cities, and its best-known musician of the era was **Louis Armstrong**. Many whites were attracted to the vibrant movement and provided some financial support. However, this support was tepid, as whites may have wanted to experience the carefree vivaciousness offered by the Renaissance and join in celebrating the "African-ness" of American Black culture, but many did not want to hear about real problems facing Black America.

The youth of the era, particularly urban, middle-class, college students, rejected the values that their parents had about sex, dress, public behavior, and religion. The generation flirted with all sorts of temptations that their parents had forbidden—they drank bootleg liquor, went to jazz clubs, dated, and partied through the night. Women also embraced this new era as they challenged ideas about how women should act in public. The **flapper** characterized the free-spiritedness of the era and welcomed in a whole new world for women who now had obtained the right to vote. Flappers illustrated a marked change from women in the past—no longer corseted and shrouded in long, heavy, drab dresses, these women sported makeup (previously associated with only prostitutes and actresses) highlighted by their ruby-red lips, short dresses, flesh-colored silk stockings, bobbed hair, and strings of pearls. They exploded all sorts of ideas about how women should behave in public: they drank, smoked, and danced provocatively.

There was conservative backlash to the freedoms offered by the Roaring Twenties. People who dwelled in rural areas often felt threatened by the changes happening in society. The return of the **Ku Klux Klan,** this time to the Midwest where it soon spread to the South, grew to more than

5 million members and targeted not only Blacks, but Catholics, Jews, immigrants, and anyone who deviated from their understanding of acceptable behavior and native, white, Protestant supremacy. They used vigilante justice, terror, and political pressure to achieve their aims.

While the KKK may have taken fears about "the other" to the extreme, there were other examples of racism deemed more "socially acceptable" and government-approved. Immigrants were specifically targeted by the government, which started issuing immigration quotas for certain immigrants. The **Sacco-Vanzetti Case** illustrated the growing concern about immigrants. Sacco and Vanzetti were two Italian immigrant anarchists who were arrested on charges of murder. Despite there being no real evidence tying them to the crime, they were convicted and executed in 1927.

Religious fundamentalism grew in the 1920s, perhaps out of sincere alarm at the flapper movement and general *carpe diem* attitude of the *bon vivants* of the day. The clash between religion and science led to the **Scopes Monkey Trial,** which dealt with a teacher, John Thomas Scopes, who broke a Tennessee law that forbade teachers from teaching evolution. The attorneys for the case, the civil liberties lawyer **Clarence Darrow** for the defense, and **William Jennings Bryan** for the prosecution, battled in a courtroom some of the conflicts that were happening throughout the country: how to reconcile tradition with progress. Scopes wound up being convicted and had to pay a small fine, but Bryan, who in his arguments posited that the Bible was error-free, found himself not knowing what was in it. As a result, Bryan looked foolish, and he, along with the fundamentalist movement and the entire South, became targets of ridicule in the press.

The Great Depression and the New Deal (1929–1941)

Political and Economic Developments

Reasons for the Depression

Stock prices increased throughout the decade. The boom in prices and volume of sales was active after 1925 and intensive during 1928–1929. Nine million Americans invested in the market and many, seeking quick profits, had borrowed money to buy stocks on margin. Margin buyers bought stock by putting 10% down and borrowing 90% of it through a broker's loan, using the stock that they were buying as collateral. All was good, as long as prices continued to rise. Careful investors, realizing that stocks were overpriced, became concerned about the health of the market and began to sell to take their profits. During October 1929, prices declined as more stock was sold. On **Black Thursday**, October 24, 1929, almost 13 million shares were traded, a large number for that time, and prices fell precipitously. As normally happened when the price of a stock fell more than 10%, the lender sold the stock for whatever it would bring, and thus further depressed prices. When this process started in late October, the forced sales brought great losses to the banks and businesses that had financed the broker's loans, as well as to the investors. Investment banks tried to boost the market by buying, but on October 29, **Black Tuesday**, the market fell about 40 points, with 16.5 million shares traded. Prices continued to drop all the way through mid-November when stocks eventually lost more than 70% of their value.

Competency 5: U.S. History

While the **Stock Market Crash of 1929** certainly took its toll on the American economy, a crash in the market does not necessarily result in a depression. There were a number of contributing factors that led to the Great Depression:

- **Overproduction/Underconsumption:** In order to finance their businesses and grow and produce under ideas of **economies of scale,** companies expanded to such a degree that they had to keep producing more and cutting wages in order to keep their profits up. Many companies, in their efforts to expand quickly, got loans to keep themselves afloat. In many cases, they lied or exaggerated their assets to banks who wound up empty-handed when corporations defaulted on their loans. Additionally, companies cut wages to save money. But that reduced people's ability to buy goods. As a result, companies had a hard time unloading their merchandise and created large inventories. By 1929, those at the lower end of the economic scale could not buy goods, and those at the upper end had cut back on purchases as well.

- **Bank Failures:** During the 1930s, more than 9,000 banks failed and the lack of insurance on bank deposits meant that people lost their money when a bank failed. Banks that did survive were unwilling to lend, and as a result, the economic situation worsened and a potential means of recovery was eliminated.

- **Lack of Recovery in Farming:** The farm economy, which involved almost 25% of the population, had never recovered from the post-war recession. Farmers continued to see a decline in prices, faced a return of foreign competition, and were often unable to repay their debts.

- **International Trade Difficulties:** European economies, already burdened with World War I debt repayments, were unable to buy U.S. goods that already had high tariffs on them.

- **Government Policies:** Government policies, with their hands-off approach to regulation of industry, had encouraged easy credit with discounted rates that proved to be harmful to the economy.

During the early months of the depression, most people thought it was just an adjustment in the business cycle that would soon pass. As time went on, the worst depression in American history set in, reaching its bottom point in early 1932. As banks crashed and drought conditions affected the Midwest, people lost their money, jobs, and then homes. The homeless built shantytowns referred to as **Hoovervilles** in all of the major cities. As farm prices dropped even lower, and drought conditions turned the Great Plains area into a giant **Dust Bowl,** many left their farms and homes to move westward, in search of a better life.

Hoover's Depression Policies

At first, Hoover was encouraged not to embark on any federal relief programs, as it would undermine the American ideal of **rugged individualism.** Later, as it became apparent that this was not just a momentary dip in the economy, he attempted to get companies to voluntarily promise not to lower wages anymore and to maintain employment. He also asked state and local governments to step in and provide relief efforts. His plan did not work because businesses did not cooperate, and local and state governments could not keep up with the demand for aid. Eventually he tried some other ideas in an effort to boost the economy.

- **The Agricultural Marketing Act:** Passed before the market crash, this law created the Federal Farm Board. It had a revolving fund of $500 million to lend agricultural cooperatives to buy commodities, such as wheat and cotton, and hold them for higher prices.

- **The Hawley-Smoot Tariff:** This law increased duties on both agricultural and manufactured imports to extremely high rates in order to protect American trade. It had the reverse effect, and it worsened the economy as it completely killed off any foreign trade.

- **The Reconstruction Finance Corporation (RFC):** The RFC loaned money to railroads, banks, and other financial institutions. It prevented the failure of basic firms, on which many other elements of the economy depended, but was criticized by some as relief for the rich.

- **The Federal Home Loan Bank Act:** This law created home-loan banks, to make loans to building and loan associations, savings banks, and insurance companies to help them avoid foreclosures on homes.

Election of 1932

The Republicans renominated Hoover while the Democrats nominated **Franklin D. Roosevelt,** governor of New York. As Hoover reeled from the problems of the Depression, another event also plagued him. In June 1932, just when Congress was getting ready to deliberate about a bill that would give World War I veterans an early bonus payment of benefits, 10,000 impoverished World War I veterans and their families marched on Washington in support of the bill. When the bill was defeated, about 3,000 of these **"bonus marchers"** stayed in Washington to protest. They set up camp in a portion of the city in the Hoovervilles, and some squatted in empty government buildings throughout the summer. In July, Hoover ordered the army to remove the bonus marchers, but **General Douglas MacArthur** went overboard and used the army to march on the veterans. Armed with tear gas, bayonets, and tanks, they attacked the protesters, burned down their makeshift shacks, and in the process killed 100 people, including two babies who suffocated from exposure to the tear gas. The attack on the veterans resulted in widespread condemnation of the administration and seemed to symbolize Hoover's response to any crisis: odd and ineffective. It also killed any chance he may have had for reelection.

Roosevelt, on the other hand, seemed prepared and eager to attack some of the problems that the country faced. In order to find a good platform, Roosevelt gathered a "brain trust" of lawyers and university professors. Together, they decided that the way to end the Depression was for the government to regulate business and restore purchasing power to the masses by cutting production. They believed this would lead to rising prices and rising wages and made sense according to the economic principle of **economics of scarcity**. Roosevelt also believed in direct unemployment relief and repealing prohibition. So, although he called for a cut in spending, Roosevelt communicated optimism and easily defeated Hoover, with over 57% of the popular vote.

The First New Deal

In February 1933, before Roosevelt took office, Congress passed the **Twenty-First Amendment to repeal prohibition** and sent it to the states. In March, the new Congress legalized light beer. The amendment was ratified by the states and took effect in December 1933. When Roosevelt was inaugurated on March 4, 1933, the American economic system seemed to be on the verge of collapse. Roosevelt assured the nation that "the only thing we have to fear is fear itself," called for a special session of Congress to convene, and asked for "broad executive powers to wage war against the emergency." Two days later, he closed all banks and forbade the export of gold or the redemption of currency in gold.

The special session of Congress passed a great body of legislation that left a lasting mark on the nation. The period has been referred to as the **"Hundred Days."** Historians divided Roosevelt's legislation into the **First New Deal (1933–1935)** and a new wave of programs beginning in 1935 called the **Second New Deal**.

Name of Policy, Agency, or Act	Abbrev.	Year Enacted	Problem to Solve	Significance
Agricultural Adjustment Act	AAA	1933	Farmers still having difficulty.	Protected farmers from price drops by providing crop subsidies in exchange for an agreement to reduce production by up to one-half. The money to pay for the subsidies came from a tax on the processing of the commodities. Farm prices increased, but tenants and sharecroppers were hurt when owners took land out of cultivation. Was a public relations disaster for the New Deal as so many in the country were going hungry at the time. The law was repealed in January 1936 on the grounds that the processing tax was not constitutional.
Beer-Wine Revenue		1933		After the repeal of Prohibition with the Twenty-First Amendment, Congress imposed new taxes on the sale of wine and beer.
Civilian Conservation Corps	CCC	1933	Unemployment rate was 25% in 1933, which meant that 16 million Americans were jobless.	Between 1933–1941 over 3 million young men ages 18–25 went to work camps to perform reforestation and conservation tasks all over the country. Planted nearly 3 billion trees to reforest America. Removed surplus of workers from cities, provided healthy conditions for boys, gave each boy $30 a month of which $25 was required to be sent home to their families.
Civil Works Administration	CWA	1933	Unemployment still high.	Provided public works jobs at $15/week to 4 million unemployed workers to take on temporary and makeshift jobs like sweeping streets. Brought much criticism, and the experiment was terminated in April 1934.

Competency 5: U.S. History

Name of Policy, Agency, or Act	Abbrev.	Year Enacted	Problem to Solve	Significance
Emergency Banking Relief Act		1933	Lack of confidence in the banking system.	First day of the special session of Congress passed this act, which provided for de facto 100% deposit insurance. It also put unsound banks under the purview of the Treasury Department and granted special government seals to those who were deemed sound. The bill was passed before a four-day Bank Holiday that Roosevelt instituted in order to give his plan time to work. In his first **Fireside Chat**, he told everyone that it was safe to put their money back into reopened banks. To everyone's relief, when the banks reopened for business on March 13, depositors stood in line to redeposit money. This resulted in a tremendous boost on the stock market as the exchange recorded the largest one-day percentage price increase ever. This ended the run on banks.
Emergency Farm Mortgage Act		1933	Stop farm foreclosures from taking place.	Provided funds to protect farmers in danger of foreclosure.
Frazier-Lemke Farm Bankruptcy Act		1934		Allowed farmers to defer foreclosure on their land while they obtained new financing, and helped them to recover property already lost through easy financing.
Federal Emergency Relief Act	FERA	1933	Millions of Americans had been unemployed for years, and local relief agencies could no longer help them.	Distributed $500 million to state and local relief agencies to provide relief to citizens in their communities. Constructed over 5,000 public buildings and 7,000 bridges, organized adult literacy programs, financed college education for poor students, and set up day-care centers for low-income families.
Federal Housing Act	FHA	1934		Insured long-term, low-interest mortgages for home construction and repair.

Name of Policy, Agency, or Act	Abbrev.	Year Enacted	Problem to Solve	Significance
Glass-Steagall Act (also called, the Banking Act of 1933)	FDIC	1933	Concern about bank failures and lack of public confidence in the banking system.	Created federally insured bank deposits ($2,500 per investor at first) to prevent bank failures. Established the Federal Deposit Insurance Corporation (FDIC) to insure individual deposits in commercial banks, and separated commercial banking from the more speculative activity of investment banking.
Home Owners Loan Corporation		1933	Prevent home foreclosures.	Gave authority to borrow money to refinance home mortgages and prevent foreclosures. Lent more than $3 billion to more than one million homeowners.
National Industrial Recovery Act	NIRA	1933	American factories had decreased their production levels and factories were stagnant. The goal was to increase the productivity of industry but at the same time protect it from overproduction and unstable prices.	This law was viewed as the cornerstone of the recovery program. It sought to stabilize the economy by preventing extreme competition, labor-management conflicts, and overproduction. A board composed of industrial and labor leaders in each industry or business drew up a code for that industry, which set minimum prices, minimum wages, maximum work hours, production limits, and quotas. Created National Recovery Administration (NRA) to regulate business through the establishment of fair competition, production codes, limiting production, instituting minimum wages, and permitting collective bargaining of workers and the right for them to join unions. Granted immunity from antitrust prosecutions for major industries.
Public Works Administration	PWA	1933		Received $3.3 billion appropriation from Congress for public works projects. Undersecretary of Interior **Harold Ickes** spent $4 billion on construction of 35,000 projects like dams, bridges, office buildings, highways, schools, and hospitals.

Competency 5: U.S. History

Name of Policy, Agency, or Act	Abbrev.	Year Enacted	Problem to Solve	Significance
Securities and Exchange Commission	SEC	1934		Regulated stock market and restricted margin buying. Set up commission to supervise stock exchanges and punish fraud in securities trading.
Tennessee Valley Authority	TVA	1933	Unemployment in the TVA region gave rise to an attempt to revitalize the economy there.	Roosevelt's first major experiment in regional public planning. Federal government built a series of 20 dams in 40,000 square miles to prevent flooding, soil erosion, improve navigation, and generate and sell hydroelectric power. It also manufactured nitrates for fertilizer, conducted demonstration projects for farmers, engaged in reforestation, restocked bodies of water with fish, and provided jobs, all in an effort to rehabilitate the area and enrich the land. First public competition with private power industries. One problem is that it unintentionally flooded some farmland.
Truth in Securities Act		1933	Designed to eliminate fraud in the stock market.	Declared that companies that deceived their stockholders could be sued. Required that full information about stocks and bonds be provided by brokers and others to potential purchasers.

The economy improved, but did not recover. The gross national product (GNP), money supply, salaries, wages, and farm income rose. Unemployment dropped from about 25% of nonfarm workers in 1933 to about 20.1%, or 10.6 million, in 1935.

Many people began to complain about Roosevelt's policies. Conservatives felt that there was too much regulation, taxation, and government spending. They opposed the higher tax rates and complained that relief programs stymied American self-interests in lifting themselves up and thwarted their individualism. Leftists complained that the AAA policy of letting food go to waste when people were starving was immoral. They also felt that government policies were still geared too much toward helping business rather than punishing them for the greed that got the country in this position.

The Second New Deal

Roosevelt launched a second series of legislative initiatives aimed at continuing to tackle the problems of the economy and to make more inroads into recovery.

Name of Policy, Agency, or Act	Abbrev.	Year Enacted	Problem to Solve	Significance
National Youth Administration	NYA	1935		Established as part of the WPA to provide part-time employment to more than 2 million college and high school students and youth not in school who lacked jobs.
Rural Electrification Administration	REA	1935	Rural areas of the United States lacked access to electricity as only 1 in 10 in the rural areas had it.	Encouraged farmers to join cooperatives to bring electricity to farms in rural areas not served by private companies. Used money to run power lines, wire homes and barns, and to lend to rural cooperatives to build power plants. Despite its efforts, by 1940, only 40% of American farms were electrified.
Social Security Act		1935	No safeguards to protect the elderly.	Established a retirement plan for persons over age 65, which was to be funded by a tax on wages paid equally by employee and employer. The first benefits, ranging from $10 to $85 per month, were paid in 1942. Another provision of the act had the effect of forcing the states to initiate unemployment insurance programs. It also provided aid to blind, deaf, disabled, and dependent children as well as those injured in industrial accidents.
Soil Conservation Act		1936	Stop erosion from the drought created in the Dust Bowl area.	Encouraged farmers to change farming practices to reduce run-off and soil erosion. Subsidized farmers to stop producing soil-depleting crops.
Works Progress Administration	WPA	1935	Unemployment still as high as in 1934, 10 million Americans still unemployed.	Created as a result of the **Emergency Relief Appropriations Act of April 1935.** Funds of 4.8 billion used to employ 8.5 million workers in construction and other jobs, but more importantly provided work in arts, theater, and literary projects. The WPA employed people from the relief rolls for 30 hours of work a week at pay double the relief payment but less than private employment. Was able to stimulate local economies and beautify cities.
Wagner Act	NLRB	1935		Allowed workers to join unions and outlawed union-busting tactics by management.

Competency 5: U.S. History

CHAPTER 5

The Last Years of the New Deal

Frustrated by a conservative Supreme Court that had overturned much of his New Deal legislation, Roosevelt proposed to Congress the **Judicial Reorganization Bill**, which would allow the president to name a new federal judge for each judge who did not retire by the age of 70½. The appointments would be limited to a maximum of fifty, with no more than six added to the Supreme Court. He also tried to increase the size of the court from nine to fifteen justices, but Congress rejected the measure. The president was astonished by the wave of opposition from Democrats and Republicans alike, but he uncharacteristically refused to compromise. In doing so, he lost the bill, as well as control of the Democratic Congress, which he had dominated since 1933. Nonetheless, the Court changed its position, as Chief Justice Charles Evans Hughes and Justice Owen Roberts began to vote with the more liberal members.

Most economic indicators rose sharply between 1935 and 1937. Roosevelt decided that the recovery was sufficient to warrant a reduction in relief programs and a move toward a balanced budget. The budget for fiscal year 1938 was reduced from $8.5 billion to $6.8 billion, with the WPA experiencing the largest cut. During the winter of 1937–1938, the economy slipped rapidly and unemployment rose to 12.5%. In April 1938, Roosevelt requested and received from Congress an emergency appropriation of about $3 billion for the WPA, as well as increases for public works and other programs. In July 1938, the economy began to recover, and it regained the 1937 levels in 1939.

Social Dimensions of the New Deal Era

Unemployment for African-Americans was much higher than for the general population, as they were pushed deeper into poverty and segregation. Before 1933, they were often excluded from state and local relief efforts. Racism itself made their lives more difficult. The **Scottsboro Trial** in 1931 revealed the uneven hand of justice, as after nine Black teens were arrested for throwing white homeless men off of a train, they were then accused and convicted by a white jury of rape. Although the Supreme Court intervened, they were still imprisoned. Organizations like the **Brotherhood of Sleeping Car Porters** and the militant **Harlem Tenants League** fought for civil rights and attacked discrimination.

With Roosevelt's election, African-Americans generally switched to the Democratic side, mainly because of the relief programs. More African-Americans were appointed to government positions by Roosevelt than ever before, but the number was still small. Despite some of these advances, Roosevelt seems to have given little thought to the special problems of African-Americans, and he was afraid to endorse legislation such as an anti-lynching bill for fear of alienating the Southern wing of the Democratic Party.

Black protest at the apparent unequal treatment in welfare programs that often wound up excluding Blacks from receiving aid finally reached a head. In 1941, in a **March on Washington Movement**, the leader of the porters union planned a huge march. Afraid that the march would lead to riots, FDR promised to outlaw discrimination in war industries in exchange for a cancellation of the march. In Executive Order No. 9902 on June 25, 1941, in exchange for the cancellation of the march, FDR established the Fair Employment Practices Committee (FEPC).

Native Americans also suffered from the unequal distribution of federal aid during the Great Depression. In 1929, a Supreme Court ruling stated that landless tribes could not receive federal aid. These Native Americans had to wait until 1931 when Congress repealed the Dawes Act of 1887 by passing the **Indian Reorganization Act of 1934.** The law restored tribal ownership of lands, recognized tribal constitutions and government, and provided loans to tribes for economic development.

Mexican-Americans were not allowed to receive aid as no government programs addressed the needs of migratory farm workers. It was not until 1937 when the government set up the **Farm Securities Administration** that any aid to those in migratory labor camps was received.

Labor Unions

Labor unions lost both members and influence during the 1920s and early 1930s. The National Industrial Recovery Act gave them new hope when it guaranteed the right to unionize, and during 1933, about 1.5 million new members joined unions. The passage of the **National Labor Relations Act** resulted in a massive growth of union membership, but at the expense of bitter conflict within the labor movement. The American Federation of Labor was made up primarily of craft unions. Some leaders wanted to unionize the mass-production industries, such as automobiles and rubber, with industrial unions. In November 1935, John L. Lewis and others established the Committee for Industrial Organization to unionize basic industries, presumably within the AFL.

President William Green of the AFL ordered the CIO to disband in January 1936. When the rebels refused, they were expelled by the AFL in March 1937. The insurgents then reorganized as the independent **Congress of Industrial Organizations (CIO)**. During its organizational period, the CIO sought to initiate several industrial unions, particularly in the steel, auto, rubber, and radio industries. In late 1936 and early 1937, it used a tactic called the sit-down strike, with the strikers occupying the workplace to prevent any production. By the end of 1941, the CIO was larger than the AFL. Union members comprised about 11.5% of the work force in 1933 and 28.2% in 1941.

COMPETENCY 5.12

Identify the causes, significant individuals, and effects of the events associated with the World War II era.

Belief that the United States should stay out of foreign wars and problems reappeared in the 1920s and 1930s. Most Americans believed that U.S. entry into World War I had been a mistake and that the United States should not become embroiled in international war again. When the **Nye Commission** issued its report revealing American arms manufacturers had lobbied for World War I,

Competency 5: U.S. History

bribed officials, and were currently supplying Fascist governments with weapons, the public declared that involvement in European wars was destructive for America. As tensions gathered in Europe, Congress passed a series of **Neutrality Acts** that reflected the antiwar sentiments.

The Neutrality Acts:

The Johnson Act of 1934: This law prohibited any nation in default on World War I payments from selling securities to any American citizen or corporation.

The Neutrality Act of 1935: On outbreak of war between foreign nations, all exports of American arms and munitions to them would be embargoed for six months. In addition, American ships were prohibited from carrying arms to any belligerent, and the president was to warn American citizens not to travel on belligerent ships.

The Neutrality Act of 1936: The laws gave the president authority to determine when a state of war existed, and prohibited any loans or credits to belligerents.

The Neutrality Act of 1937: The laws gave the president authority to determine if a civil war was a threat to world peace, and whether it was covered by the Neutrality Acts. It also prohibited all arms sales to belligerents, and allowed the **cash-and-carry** sale of nonmilitary goods to belligerents.

The Neutrality Act of 1939: Roosevelt officially proclaimed the neutrality of the United States. The Democratic Congress, in a vote that followed party lines, then passed a new Neutrality Act allowing the cash-and-carry sale of arms and short-term loans to belligerents, but forbidding American ships to trade with belligerents or Americans to travel on belligerent ships.

The American Response to the War in Europe

While the United States was proclaiming its neutrality, it simultaneously began to develop contingency and preparatory plans just in case they would be needed. After all, American neutrality before the First World War did not weather the whole war. Roosevelt created the **War Resources Board** to develop a plan for industrial mobilization in the event of war and established the **Office of Emergency Management** to centralize mobilization activities.

There was a high level of public interest in what was happening in Europe, and more Americans than ever spoke out on foreign policy, mainly due to the accessibility of information via the radio and the ethnic origins of many recent immigrants. Almost all Americans recognized Germany as a threat. They were divided on whether to aid Britain or to concentrate on the defense of America. The **Committee to Defend America by Aiding the Allies** and the **America First Committee**, which opposed involvement, were both formed in 1940. Over time, especially when the fall of France in June 1940 heightened concerns, Americans began to change their minds and talk more about America entering the war.

Congress approved the nation's first peacetime draft, the **Selective Service and Training Act** in 1940. Roosevelt determined that to aid Britain in every way possible was the best way to avoid war with Germany. As Britain ran out of money to buy new war supplies, Roosevelt signed a **Destroyers for Bases Agreement** to give Britain 50 old American destroyers in return for a 99-year lease on air and naval bases in British territories in Newfoundland, Bermuda, and the Caribbean.

Roosevelt had become so concerned about U.S. involvement in the war that after Hitler invaded France in 1940, and a takeover of England was in the cards, Roosevelt decided to run for an unprecedented third term, breaking a tradition that had existed since George Washington. He won.

American Involvement with the European War

Roosevelt turned the United States into an "arsenal of democracy" with the **Lend-Lease Act.** The act was pro-active in its objective, much like, as Roosevelt opined, "helping to put out the fire in your neighbor's house before your own house caught fire and burned down." This act allowed the United States to lend armaments to Britain, who no longer could afford to buy them, in exchange for goods and services after the war. In effect, the Lend-Lease Act ended the pretense of American neutrality. Roosevelt started the American Neutrality Patrol in which the U.S. Navy would search out, but not attack, German submarines in the western half of the Atlantic and warn British vessels of their location. Germany, cognizant that America was no longer neutral, had its U-boats torpedo the merchant ship the *SS Robin Moor* that sailed under the U.S. flag, outside of the war zone. The president declared a state of unlimited national emergency.

Germany invaded Russia in June 1941. American Marines occupied Iceland, a Danish possession, in July 1941 to protect it from seizure by Germany. Roosevelt and British Prime Minister Winston Churchill met on a battleship in Newfoundland and issued the **Atlantic Charter** that outlined their wartime goals, which included disarmament, self-determination, freedom of the seas, and guarantees of each nation's security, despite the fact that the United States was not yet in the war. Congress eliminated the cash-and-carry policy and allowed the United States to ship munitions to Britain on armed merchant ships. In November, the United States extended lend-lease assistance to the Russians.

Considering all of the activity that was happening between the United States and Germany in the European theater, it seems odd that the direct attack on American soil came from Japan and not from Germany.

Competency 5: U.S. History

The Road to Pearl Harbor and War

After Germany, Japan and Italy became allies in 1940, the United States reconsidered its dealings with Japan. It embargoed all aviation gasoline, fuel, and metal with Japan. This posed a great threat to Japan, which relied on foreign imports and needed the oil for its war machine. A year later, as Japan, which occupied French Indochina and seemed an unstoppable force in the Pacific, the United States ended trade altogether with Japan. In October 1941, a new military cabinet headed by General Hideki Tojo took control of Japan. The Japanese secretly decided to make a final effort to negotiate with the United States and to go to war if no solution was found. A new round of talks followed in Washington, but neither side would make a substantive change in its position.

The Japanese gave final approval on December 1 for an attack on the United States. They planned a major offensive to take the Dutch East Indies, Malaya, and the Philippines in order to obtain the oil, metals, and other raw materials they needed. At the same time, they would attack Pearl Harbor in Hawaii to destroy the American Pacific fleet to keep it from interfering with their plans. The United States, meanwhile, had broken the Japanese diplomatic codes and knew that trouble was imminent—they just did not know where the attack would occur. Between December 1 and December 6, 1941, it became clear to U.S. leaders that Japanese task forces were being ordered into battle. American commanders in the Pacific were warned of possible aggressive action there, but not forcefully. On Sunday, December 7, 1941, Japanese planes attacked the American fleet in Pearl Harbor. Two U.S. battleships were sunk, six were damaged and out of action, three cruisers and three destroyers were sunk or damaged, and a number of lesser vessels were destroyed or damaged. All of the 150 aircraft at Pearl Harbor were destroyed on the ground. Worst of all, 2,323 American servicemen were killed and about 1,100 wounded. The Japanese lost 29 planes, five midget submarines, and one fleet submarine.

On December 8, 1941, Roosevelt asked Congress for a declaration of war on Japan. Congress complied, albeit with one dissenting vote. Three days later, Germany and Italy declared war on the United States. Great Britain and the United States then established the Combined Chiefs of Staff, headquartered in Washington, to direct Anglo-American military operations. On January 1, 1942, representatives of twenty-six nations met in Washington, D.C., and signed the **Declaration of the United Nations**, pledging themselves to the principles of the Atlantic Charter and promising not to make a separate peace with their common enemies.

The Home Front

As had happened during other periods of crisis, the federal government acquired and exercised more power. During the war, the size of the government more than tripled. It established a few key agencies that enabled it to mobilize men and war supplies more effectively.

War Production Board (WPB)—The WPB was established in 1942 to convert the economy from a civilian basis to a wartime economy. The WPB allowed the government to mobilize industry toward the war effort in return for guaranteeing them lucrative profits. The board regulated the use of raw materials, helped allocate scarce materials, limited the manufacture of civilian goods so that more military goods could be produced, and was in charge of handing out military production contracts.

- **National War Labor Board**—Created out of the **Labor Disputes Act of 1943**, not only mediated labor-management disputes, but controlled the government takeover of businesses deemed necessary to national security.

- **Office of Price Administration**—Created in 1942, the OPA imposed price controls to stem inflation. It also established **rationing** on almost all consumer goods through local **War Price and Rationing Boards**.

- **Office of War Information**—Created in 1942, this office encouraged support on the home front by putting out propaganda pieces about the war. Hollywood joined in and created numerous films to boost the morale of troops overseas and to shore up stateside support.

Social Changes at Home

The war brought numerous changes on the Home Front, as it affected almost every aspect of daily life, creating new tensions and exacerbating old ones, providing new opportunities for some and closing the door to others.

One effect of the war was migration of Americans to centers of war production. As jobs opened and new industries developed that were geared to the war effort, people flocked to them. Many people left rural areas in the South and moved to the cities in the North and West. In the war-industry cities, housing shortages exacerbated conditions in fragile cities that were suffering from overcrowding. Urban slums grew and conflict between older residents and newcomers resulted in a proliferation of gang-related troubles. Race riots also became more frequent as more African-Americans entered new cities where only few had existed previously.

The war also changed the roles of women and the family in American society. More than 6 million women entered the paid labor force to meet war-industry needs; about 1 million worked in the aerospace industry alone, and more than 300,000 enlisted in the armed forces. By 1945, women constituted more than one-third of all employed workers. Images of **Rosie the Riveter** plastered throughout American society exemplified the millions of women who joined the workforce in previously male-dominated occupations. Considered to be vital to the nation's war effort, these women were considered temporary workers who did not have to be paid the same as male workers. Moreover, the women were expected to maintain their home responsibilities as well. This proved to be a bit difficult as women were forced to leave their children, often young, at home alone while they worked their shifts in the factories. The result was a breakdown in the family and a rise in juvenile delinquency. During this period, perhaps as a result of the wartime strains, marriages, births, and divorces soared.

Competency 5: U.S. History

African-Americans struggled in the war to fight against America's enemies, as well as to fight for equality at home. A planned march on Washington was canceled when Roosevelt signed an executive order that created the **Fair Employment Practices Committee** and prohibited discrimination in defense industries and government agencies. In addition, the NAACP and the Congress of Racial Equality campaigned for civil rights for African-Americans during the war. Once the war began, labor shortages forced factory owners to employ African-Americans, so much so that participation in the defense industry jumped from 3% to 9% of workers. In addition, more than 1 million African-Americans served in the armed forces, though usually in segregated units that were commanded by white officers. Few of these would see combat service, with the exception of the **Tuskegee Airmen,** and most of these units were in supply and transportation divisions. The U.S. army would not be desegregated until 1948. Despite these difficulties, African-Americans were given greater opportunities and political power because of their experiences during the war.

Government attacks on civil liberties during the war resulted in the abhorrent treatment of Japanese-Americans during it. Following the attacks on Pearl Harbor, prejudice and attacks on Japanese-Americans erupted. The U.S. government exacerbated the situation by viewing all people of Japanese descent as potential enemy agents. They uprooted more than 112,000 Japanese-Americans, more than two-thirds of whom had been born in the United States and had U.S. citizenship, and placed them in internment camps far away from the Pacific Ocean where there was a fear that a Japanese invasion would take place. None of those who were interned were ever convicted of any collusion with Japan. Most of those who were interned lost their homes and their possessions. The Supreme Court upheld the evacuation and internment of these Americans, building on an earlier case in 1919, *Schenck v. United States*, which stated that a citizen's civil liberties could be restricted during times of war. It was affirmed in **Korematsu v. United States** (1944), which stated that even though compulsory evacuation of large groups from their homes was abhorrent, when U.S. shores were threatened by hostile forces, "the power to protect citizens must be commensurate with the threatened danger."

As the war inched its way to a conclusion, the Allies met to discuss what the fate would be in Europe. They embarked on a series of key conferences to hash out what the postwar world would look like.

The first meeting occurred in the Soviet Union's embassy in Tehran, Iran, from November 28 until December 1, 1943, with Roosevelt, Stalin, and Churchill meeting in what came to be called the **Tehran Conference.** They discussed war strategy and the opening of a second front, as well as what the fate of Eastern Europe would be after the war. Stalin left the conference upset with what he saw as lackluster seriousness in fighting Germany. A decision was made at the conference to invade France, and the Soviets agreed to help in the war against Japan as soon as Germany was defeated.

The **Yalta Conference** was the second meeting attended personally by Stalin, Churchill, and Roosevelt. It was held in Crimea, USSR, and lasted from February 4–11, 1945. A plan to divide Germany into zones of occupation was formally accepted with the addition of a fourth zone taken from the British and American zones for the French to occupy. Berlin, which lay within the Russian Zone, was also divided into four zones of occupation.

The third summit meeting of the Big Three took place at **Potsdam** outside Berlin after the end of the European war but while the Pacific war was still going on. The conference began July 17, 1945, with Stalin, Churchill, and the new American President Harry Truman attending. The meeting did not go very well, as the United States and the Soviet Union strongly disagreed over what would happen in Germany and Eastern Europe. However, they did agree that Germany should be disarmed, its war industries should be dismantled, all Nazis should be removed from government, and that war crimes trials would be held. The **Potsdam Declaration** called for immediate Japanese surrender and hinted at the consequences that would ensue if it were not forthcoming. While at the conference, American leaders received the news of the successful testing of the first atomic bomb in the New Mexico desert, but the Japanese were given no clear warning that such a destructive weapon might be used against them.

On August 6, 1945, the atomic bomb was dropped by a single U.S. plane on Hiroshima, and an entire city disappeared, with the instantaneous loss of 70,000 lives. In time, many other persons died from radiation poisoning and other effects. Since no surrender was received, a second bomb was dropped on Nagasaki, obliterating that city. Even the most fanatical of the Japanese leaders saw the scale of death and destruction, and surrender came quickly. The only departure from unconditional surrender was to allow the Japanese to retain Emperor Hirohito, but only with the proviso that he would be subject in every respect to the orders of the occupation commander. The formal surrender took place September 2, 1945, in Tokyo Bay on the deck of the battleship *Missouri*, and the occupation of Japan began under the immediate control of the American commander, General Douglas MacArthur.

COMPETENCY 5.13

Identify the causes, significant individuals, and effects of the events associated with domestic and foreign affairs during the Cold War era.

The Emergence of the Cold War and Containment

Some of the following contributed to much of the rivalry that developed between the USSR and the United States and became the "third-world war" of the twentieth century:

- **Power Vacuum:** Following the collapse of Germany and Japan and Europe's preoccupation with rebuilding its countries, there was a vacuum of power, and questions remained about how and where rebuilding would occur and who would have what role in the old Axis countries.

- **Decolonization:** With the disintegration of the British and French empires outside of Europe, the United States and the USSR competed to gain both military bases and markets in the new countries.

Competency 5: U.S. History

Failure of Diplomacy: As both the United States and the USSR always thought they each had the "right" ideology, each had little regard toward appeasing the other.

U.S. Strategic and Economic Needs: The United States wanted to continue expanding its markets through an activist foreign policy.

Truman's Tough Style: Truman's diplomatic style was not appreciated by the Soviets. When Roosevelt died in April 1945, the Soviet Union knew little about Truman, other than that he said to the press in June 1941 when the United States was debating which side of the war it would join: "If we see Germany is winning, we ought to help Russia, and if Russia is winning, we ought to help Germany and that way let them kill as many as possible. . . ." In April 1945 when the Soviet Foreign Minister V. M. Molotov met with Truman for the first time at a brief meeting at the White House on the way to attend the UN conference in San Francisco, Truman reportedly gave Molotov a tongue-lashing and Molotov stormed out of the meeting. Hostility between the two intensified at the conference when the Soviets thought the United States would form a bloc of anti-Soviet nations. In retaliation, Truman ended the lend-lease program to the Soviets and condemned the Soviets for taking over Eastern European countries. Truman's advisor, Secretary of State Byrnes, advocated a "get tough" stance with the Soviets and urged Truman to lord the news of the U.S. atomic bomb over the Russians at the Potsdam conference in order to frighten them into compliance with the U.S. agenda. This tactic annoyed the Soviets.

Atomic Diplomacy: The USSR was annoyed that the United States was trying to scare them into concessions because of the U.S. monopoly on the atomic bomb. When Truman refused to give the bomb over to an international institution unless all of the world's fissionable materials were also given to an agency, the Soviets surmised that the United States would continue to force their agenda on the world unless another country developed a weapon as well. The Soviets reinvigorated their campaign to develop an atomic bomb.

U.S. Suspicion of Soviet Intentions: The United States obsessed over what the USSR had the potential to do, not what the reality was. The United States despaired and then geared up for a fight whenever the USSR sought interests in another country.

U.S. concerns began when the Communist government took over Poland and then Hungary and Czechoslovakia, areas that had been under its control during the end of World War II. The U.S. reaction was that the Soviet Union was trying to take over the world, and the result was a prolonged **cold war** in which both sides used mythological overtones of good versus evil to portray their conflict.

The failure of the Western powers and the Soviet Union to come to any agreement at Potsdam on which areas of influence each would possess or what new political alliances would form led the

United States and the West to give up on the idea that Communism and democracy could co-exist in the same space. Instead, the United States felt that if they could not co-exist or eliminate Communism, then they needed to **contain** it. In 1946, **George Kennan**, the American *chargé d'affaires* in Moscow, spelled out the idea of containment in a confidential cable to the State Department. Kennan outlined Soviet policy and intimated that the USSR intended to obliterate the West and capitalism. In March, Churchill's **"Iron Curtain"** speech solidified opposition to Soviet encroachments in Europe.

As part of the containment policy, the United States invested in areas at risk for Soviet takeover. Chief among the targets was Europe, and Secretary of State **George C. Marshall** proposed that the United States provide economic aid to help rebuild Europe. Congress passed the European Recovery Program, also known as the **Marshall Plan**, which provided more than $12 billion in aid to Europe. Money was also offered to Eastern Europe and the Soviet Union, but they did not take it.

Throughout the **Cold War,** competition between the two world powers would be played out in other countries. In 1947, civil war in Greece created a dynamic where the West was on one side and the Soviets were on another. When Great Britain notified the United States that it could no longer support the Greek government against the Communist insurgents, Truman asked Congress for $400 million in military and economic aid for Greece as well as for neighboring Turkey, which was also in danger. In what became known as the **Truman Doctrine**, he argued that while the United States would not initiate a war with the Soviet Union, it would support free peoples in countries that were resisting Communism.

After the United States, France, and Great Britain announced plans to create a West German Republic out of their German zones, the Soviet Union in June 1948 blocked surface access to Berlin. The U.S. then instituted the **Berlin Airlift** to transport supplies to the city until the Soviets lifted their blockade in May 1949. The crisis in Berlin prompted the formation in April 1949 of **NATO (North Atlantic Treaty Organization),** which was signed by the United States, Canada, Great Britain, and nine European nations. They pledged that an attack against one would be considered an attack against all. The Soviets formed the **Warsaw Treaty Organization** in 1955 to counteract NATO. Shortly after the creation of NATO, the Soviets exploded their first atomic bomb in 1949.

These events prompted the creation of the **National Security Agency (NSA)** and the **Central Intelligence Agency (CIA)**. The NSA consists of the U.S. president's advisors who provide information and counsel on national security and foreign policy matters. The mission of the CIA is to collect and analyze intelligence in order to prevent attacks on the United States, preempt threats to the United States, and safeguard secrets that keep the United States safe. The CIA was also given responsibility for covert actions and espionage that would provide intelligence and protect the interests of the United States. The Soviet Union had a military agency—the **KGB**—with a similar mission and goals. The KGB provided internal security of the USSR and acted as a form of secret police that combatted nationalism in Soviet states as well as any dissent and anti-Soviet activities. Like the CIA, the KGB gathered intelligence and counterintelligence through espionage and covert actions.

If the U.S. problems with the Soviet Union in Europe were not enough, it received a shock when China's Chiang Kai-shek's Nationalist government, to whom the United States had given more than $2 billion in aid between 1945 and 1948, lost out against **Mao Zedong's** Communist insurgents. Once Mao took office, the United States refused to enter into any diplomatic relations, which pushed Mao into dealing with the Soviet Union and Stalin, whom Mao already did not like. It would not be until 1979 that the United States would formally recognize the People's Republic of China.

The conflict with Communism resulted in mass hysteria in the United States and the start of a second **Red Scare**, just as Americans had faced after World War I. In order to counteract charges that liberal Democrats were soft on Communists, the Truman Administration set up **Loyalty Boards** to investigate the loyalty of all 3 million federal government workers in an effort to locate any security risks. Federal administrators—not judges—ran the hearings without having to bother with rules of evidence, testifying under oath, and with no penalty for perjury. These boards kept trial-like transcripts, however, and regularly leaked their results to the press. For many citizens, persons named as suspected members of the Communist Party were considered guilty of treason. The Loyalty Boards could not imprison people; they could only fire them. But anyone who was fired was **blacklisted**. To make matters worse, the Truman Justice Department compiled lists of organizations that opposed American foreign policy. Since American foreign policy was essentially anti-Communist, any one or any group who opposed U.S. actions was considered Communists. The Attorney General's office circulated membership lists of such disfavored groups.

This bred a whole atmosphere of fear within American society. Anyone who was found to have what was perceived at the time as "weakness" (e.g., previous associations with "known Communists," alcoholics, or homosexuals) was dismissed from the government without a hearing. **Alger Hiss,** a former State Department diplomat who served as Roosevelt's advisor at Yalta, was accused of disloyalty by Whittaker Chambers, a confessed Soviet spy, who asserted Hiss had given him classified documents. Hiss sued Chambers for libel and was even defended by Truman. Ultimately, in 1950, Hiss was convicted not of espionage, but of perjury. Democrats, many of whom supported Hiss, were seen as being soft on Communism. After Hiss, Americans began to fear that there were enemies in the United States, just waiting to get them and destroy the country.

The House of Representatives created the **House Un-American Activities Committee** and launched an investigation into purported Communist influence in the movie business. They targeted writers, directors, actors, and studio executives, brought them in to testify, and then inquired whether they "were now, or had ever been, a member of the Communist Party." The movie industry, worried about what effect this would have on their own profits, launched their own Communist hunt and brought in ex-FBI agents to clean up the studios. Agents made lists of anyone who had suspicious political beliefs and many of these individuals were blacklisted and did not work for the studios again. Some writers, however, worked under known *nom de plumes* and were able to continue to work, albeit quietly.

U.S. Senator Joseph McCarthy delivered speeches about the Communist influence that had wormed its way through the U.S. government. He declared that he had a list of more than 200 Communists who were currently in the State Department. He led a campaign of innuendo that destroyed the lives of thousands of innocent people. He held years of hearings in an effort to root out Communists. Those who were subpoenaed were forced to confess to associations with Communists.

Industries created blacklists that prevented people on the lists from working. But when McCarthy accused the Army of harboring Communists and started a televised series of **Army-McCarthy Hearings**, McCarthy had gone too far. The Army fought back, with the help of **Edward R. Murrow**'s CBS television show, and McCarthy was made to look foolish. In 1954, he was censured by the Senate for his activities. Finally, the public turned against him, and the era of McCarthyism ended.

In 1950, Julius and Ethel Rosenberg and Harry Gold were charged with giving atomic secrets to the Soviet Union. The Rosenbergs were convicted and executed in 1953. By 1950, after the double shock of the Soviets exploding the atomic bomb and the Chinese takeover by the Communist Party, the Truman administration decided that it needed to take the worldwide lead in resisting Communism. In April 1950, it issued a report, **NSC-68**, that stated the United States should stop Communism wherever it occurred, regardless of strategic or economic value to the United States. This led to a major expansion of American military power along with increased defense spending. It also dictated the U.S. response to Communism, played a role in U.S. participation in the Korean and Vietnam wars, and explained how the United States would view any country that tried to gain its independence from colonial powers if they turned to the Soviet Union for help.

Efforts to contain the spread of Communism led the United States into the **Korean War**. When North Korea invaded South Korea, President Truman committed forces commanded by General MacArthur, but under United Nations auspices. The UN forces (mostly American) drove the battle north of the 38th parallel, which divided North and South Korea. Chinese troops attacked MacArthur's forces pushing them south of the 38th parallel, but the UN forces eventually recovered their offensive momentum. In June 1953, an armistice was signed, leaving Korea divided along virtually the same boundary that had existed prior to the war.

Cold War under President Eisenhower

The Eisenhower administration basically kept Truman's policies toward the Communists, but called the policy "liberation" rather than containment with the idea that perhaps the U.S. would free Eastern Europe from Soviet control. Eisenhower's policy was termed New Look and suggested that should there be war, it would not be conventional, but rather massive retaliation with nuclear weapons. The fear of massive retaliation was meant to deter Soviet action that would put such an attack in motion. Confrontations with the Soviets often went to the edge of war, an approach called **brinksmanship**. The Eisenhower administration popularized the **domino theory** that if one nation fell to Communism, then nations around it would also fall like dominos.

There was, however, a fatal flaw in Eisenhower's doctrine of massive retaliation, as it left the United States without any option other than nuclear war to combat Soviet aggression. In 1956, when the Soviet Union put down a democratic uprising in Hungary, the United States could not provide assistance, because Eisenhower knew that such a move would turn the Cold War into a nuclear war over an inconsequential issue. So, he realized that in addition to his liberation and massive retaliation policies, he also needed to work quietly in a more indirect manner in order to control the Communist menace. He used the CIA to plant fake stories in newspapers, train foreign military officials, and launch a variety of covert operations to subvert any governments around the world considered "too friendly" to the Communists. The Eisenhower administration also tried to spread American culture and thereby discontent in the USSR through the United States Information Agency, which funded the **Voice of America**. There was also Radio Free Europe and Radio Liberty, funded by the CIA, which sent anti-Soviet messages around the world.

Between this atmosphere and Eisenhower's policies, Cold War tensions remained high throughout the 1950s. When Joseph Stalin died in 1953, there was hope that relations between the United States and the USSR would improve. However, this hope was short-lived. While the new Soviet leader, Nikita Khrushchev, offered the idea of peaceful coexistence among nations with different philosophies of government and economics, he became more aggressive with Eastern bloc countries who wanted to use the idea of "peaceful coexistence" to break free of Soviet control. When the Soviets crushed these rebellions, relations between the United States and the USSR worsened. Soviet advances in science, like the explosion of the hydrogen bomb, development of the first Inter-Continental Ballistic Missile (ICBM), and launching *Sputnik* into space, created enormous anxiety within the Eisenhower administration, as well as a determination to win the space race with the creation of **NASA** (**National Aeronautics and Space Administration**).

Other key events under the Eisenhower Administration that affected the Cold War included:

Khrushchev's Ultimatum (1958): The USSR employed their own attempt at brinksmanship when they expressed anger about bombers that the United States had in West Germany. The Soviets announced that unless talks began immediately on German reunification and disarmament, they would recognize East German control of all of Berlin. The United States did not respond, and the Soviets backed down.

U-2 Incident (1960): The Soviet Union shot down an American **U-2 spy plane**, but Eisenhower and the U.S. government initially **denied** that the United States was flying any U-2 missions over the Soviet Union. However, when the USSR produced the captured **American** pilot, the United States had to admit its involvement. Eisenhower refused to apologize or promise to suspend future spy missions against the USSR.

Eisenhower Doctrine: In order to protect American oil interests in the Middle East, Eisenhower announced the **Eisenhower Doctrine**, which stated that the United States would provide military and economic assistance to any Middle Eastern countries that resisted Communist insurgents. This resulted in a variety of actions in the Middle East. Prior to the official Eisenhower Doctrine, the United States ordered a CIA-orchestrated coup in Iran, which resulted in the re-installation of Mohammed Reza Pahlavi as Shah. This would prove to be an enormous long-term mistake that severely damaged the U.S. reputation in the region. This American-supported coup is referred to as one of the reasons for the anti-American movement in the Middle East.

Suez Crisis: The U.S. also offered foreign aid to countries to get them to comply with what the United States wanted and to turn away from the Soviet Union. But, in Egypt, U.S. funding for the Aswan Dam project that was supposed to provide electricity and additional farming land in Upper Egypt fell through. Egypt turned to the Soviets for aid and then seized the British-controlled Suez Canal—which had fallen under British control after Egypt's declaration of bankruptcy. Great Britain and France asked Eisenhower for military assistance to retake the canal, but Eisenhower refused. This forced the two powers to join with **Israel** and invade the **Suez** in 1956. Fearing that such an invasion would force the Egyptians into the arms of the Soviets, Eisenhower condemned the attack on Egypt and exerted heavy diplomatic and economic pressure on the aggressors. Unable to sustain the action in the face of U.S. disapproval and financial pressures, they all withdrew, Egypt retook the canal, and the Soviets built the Aswan Dam.

American Intervention in the Third World: With the fall of Britain's and France's colonial empires, many of the new countries were reluctant to become pawns in the Cold War. They became more intent on cementing their own nationalist struggles for power and doing what they needed to do as "new" nations, free of colonial control. The United States tried to expand its influence in these areas in controversial ways:

- **Guatemala** (1951): Leftist leader **Jacobo Arbenz Guzmán** was elected President and decided to expropriate all of United Fruit's (big U.S. company) unused land. United Fruit officials claimed Guzmán was a Communist, which led to the generation of a CIA plot to overthrow him. In 1954, CIA-supported troops drove Guzmán from power, and the new pro-U.S. regime returned the land before a huge civil war erupted. The coup drew enormous amounts of criticism around the world and severely damaged U.S.-Latin America relations.

- **Cuba** (1959): The **Cuban Revolution** erupted when Fulgencio Batista was ousted and **Fidel Castro** took control. Castro was anti-American and confiscated a lot of U.S. business interests there. Washington responded by cutting purchases of Cuban sugar. Castro responded by nationalizing all of the U.S. companies there, and asking the Soviets for loans to pick up the trade slack left by the Americans. Eisenhower broke off diplomatic relations with Cuba.

- **Indochina**: Nationalists under the leadership of Ho Chi Minh had sought independence from France. Ho turned to the Soviet Union in the 1950s after U.S. officials rebuffed his earlier requests for help in securing independence. The USSR supplied money and arms to Ho, which forced Eisenhower to support the other side, the French colonial regime, in order to contain the USSR. The U.S. poured in money to try to control Communism. This laid the foundation for U.S. troop involvement in the Vietnam War.

Competency 5: U.S. History

Cold War in the 1960s under the Kennedy Administration

John F. Kennedy was elected President of the United States in 1960, winning over candidate Richard Nixon. At the age of 43, Kennedy was the youngest president to be elected to office. (Note: Theodore Roosevelt was technically the youngest president at age 42; however, Roosevelt became president after the assassination of William McKinley.) Coming out of the postwar years, President Kennedy was a young war hero. He and his family were symbolic of the younger, more modern era of the early 1960s. Indeed, Kennedy and Nixon participated in the first-ever televised presidential debates. Nixon came into the debate as the frontrunner because he had been vice-president under Eisenhower for eight years; however, he refused to wear stage makeup and looked haggard onscreen. In contrast, Kennedy looked youthful and energetic. Poll numbers began to shift, and Kennedy ultimately won the election.

Under Eisenhower, the CIA had begun training some 2,000 Cuban exiles for an invasion of Cuba to overthrow Fidel Castro, the left-leaning revolutionary who had taken power in 1959. On April 19, 1961, this force invaded at the **Bay of Pigs** but was pinned down and forced to surrender. Some 1,200 men were captured. President Kennedy was left with an embarrassing situation, and the Soviets were antagonized.

In August 1961, Khrushchev closed the border between East and West Berlin and built the Berlin Wall. The Soviet Union began testing nuclear weapons in September 1961. Kennedy then authorized resumption of underground testing by the United States. By 1961, both the USSR and the United States had invested huge amounts of money in nuclear weapons, as an attempt to maintain parity with each other's stockpiles, and because they believed that such stockpiles served as a means of deterrence. With ever-expanding nuclear stockpiles, both realized it was not good enough just to have the weapons; the weapons had to be put in places where they could be launched. The United States put missiles in Turkey, and the Soviets put missiles in Cuba. U.S. spy planes and satellite pictures revealed the Soviet military bases and missiles in Cuba. This discovery resulted in the **Cuban Missile Crisis** in which Kennedy used brinksmanship to avoid a nuclear war with Russia. He instituted a naval quarantine of Cuba, went on national TV and issued an ultimatum for missiles to be removed. Khrushchev denounced the blockade and readied Soviet missiles for launch. The U.S. forces were placed on highest alert and were ready to "push the button." Kennedy and Krushchev reached a secret agreement: the Soviet Union would remove missiles if the United States agreed not to attack Cuba and removed its missiles from Turkey. As the American public did not know about the missiles in Turkey, when the crisis was averted, it was assumed that it was because Kennedy had forced the Soviets to back down and that the United States had won. Recent scholarship has suggested otherwise and holds that it was Krushchev who actually was the hero in the crisis.

Krushchev and Kennedy were startled by how close they came to nuclear war, and they set up a hotline between the two nations. This marked a shift in Cold War policy, away from direct confrontation and toward negotiation, in a new phase called **détente**, which, however, was not articulated as such until the Nixon administration. In 1963, both nations agreed to a treaty banning atomic tests in the atmosphere and the oceans.

It was also in the early 1960s that American containment policy shifted from heavy reliance on nuclear weapons to more conventional notions of warfare in pursuit of a more **"flexible response"** to the spread of Communism. Kennedy and his Defense Secretary, **Robert S. McNamara,** crafted the flexible response doctrine that would enable the United States to combat Soviet forces around the world through a variety of means, money, troops, CIA coups, or, as a last resort, nuclear weapons. Kennedy first applied his new doctrine to **Vietnam**, where U.S. funding of the corrupt South Vietnamese regime offended most South Vietnamese. The United States realized that money alone would not solve the issue, so, in an effort to prevent Communist-backed insurgents from taking control of South Vietnam, Kennedy decided to send 15,000 troops to Saigon as **"military advisors."** With that, the United States became more deeply embroiled in the conflict, which turned into a costly mistake that would involve the U.S. through the next two presidencies. In 1963, President Kennedy was assassinated in Dallas, Texas, and Lyndon Johnson became president. In 1965, President Johnson committed more combat troops to Vietnam and announced that it was his intention to defend South Vietnam "whatever the cost or whatever the challenge."

The United States ultimately fought a bloody and costly war in Vietnam that poisoned U.S. politics and wreaked havoc with its economy. When Richard Nixon was elected President in 1968, the Nixon administration inherited the conflict and it was not until 1973 under the guise of a peace agreement that the United States left South Vietnam in what many regarded as a "loss" for the United States.

Cold War and Détente in the 1970s and 1980s

Nixon's approach to the Cold War was reflected in two ideologies that he had. Together, Nixon and Kissinger came up with the term **détente,** which called for countries to respect each other's differences and to cooperate more closely with one another. Détente ushered in a relaxation of tensions that would last until the Soviet Union's invasion of Afghanistan in 1979. Moreover, Nixon issued his **Nixon Doctrine,** which announced that the United States would withdraw from its overseas troop commitments and instead rely on alliances with local governments to check the spread of Communism.

As proof in the thaw of tensions between Communists and the United States, Nixon travelled to Communist China, a country which the United States had earlier refused to recognize. Nixon's trip eased tensions with China and opened the door to trade relations with it. It also enabled Nixon to play his friendship with the Chinese off the Soviets—as China and the Soviet Union, the world's two largest and most powerful Communist countries, hated one another.

Richard Nixon ran for reelection in 1972 and was elected in a landslide victory; however, Nixon and some of his aides were implicated in a break-in of the Democratic national party offices at the Watergate offices and other "dirty tricks," including bugging of offices. **Watergate** became synonymous with political scandal at the highest level of office. Several of his aides ultimately went to prison for their roles in the break-in. Although Nixon initially denied knowledge of the "dirty tricks," he was ultimately linked to **Watergate**. Facing possible impeachment and conviction,

Competency 5: U.S. History

Nixon resigned the Presidency in 1974. He was later pardoned by his successor, Gerald Ford. However, one of the biggest outcomes of Watergate was the effect it had on people's perceptions of honesty and ethics in government.

By the end of the 1970s, however, the chance for an extended thaw utterly vanished when the 1979 Soviet invasion of Afghanistan significantly soured U.S.-Soviet relations. Seeking to place a greater emphasis on human rights in his foreign policy, Carter angrily denounced the incursion and boycotted the 1980 Olympics.

With the election of Ronald Reagan, who spoke of waging war with the Communists wherever they may be, relations with the Soviet Union worsened. In order to back up his threat, he dramatically increased military spending in the early 1980s. He backed up his military spending with harsh rhetoric when he called the Soviet Union "**the evil empire.**"

In 1985, **Mikhail Gorbachev** became head of the Soviet Union and change was in the air. Gorbachev believed that for the USSR to survive, he needed to engage in a series of reforms. His package of liberal reforms was referred to as **perestroika,** and he embarked on an opening of relations with the West, a policy called **glasnost.** By the time Reagan left the White House, tensions between the Soviet Union and the United States were quite warm. Despite improved East-West relations, however, Gorbachev's reforms were unable to prevent the collapse of a system that had grown rigid and unworkable. By most measures, the Soviet economy had failed to grow since the late 1970s, and much of the country's populace had grown weary of the aged Communist hierarchy. In 1989, the spontaneous destruction of the Berlin Wall signaled the end of Soviet domination in Eastern Europe, and two years later, the Soviet government itself fell from power. This marked the end of the Cold War, a period that had lasted for 46 years.

COMPETENCY 5.14

Identify the causes, significant individuals, and effects of the events associated with movements for equality, civil rights, and civil liberties in the nineteenth and twentieth centuries.

Civil Rights

Civil rights are legal claims to protect individuals from discrimination at the hands of both the government and other citizens. Civil rights include the right to vote, equality before the law, and access to public facilities. **Individual** or **civil liberties** protect the sanctity of the person from arbitrary governmental interference. In this category belong the fundamental freedoms of speech, religion, press, and rights such as **due process** (government must act fairly and follow established procedures, as in legal proceedings).

1877–1900: Reconstruction and Its Failures

Many people think the campaign for civil rights started between the 1950s and 1970s; however, it actually began during Reconstruction in the 1860s and 1870s. After the Civil War, Congress realized that it needed to protect former slaves. It passed a series of civil rights laws, and the states ratified three amendments to the Constitution to protect former slaves. But, that did not work. A combination of events resulted in many of the former slaves being unable to take advantage of their newfound freedom. Most former slaves were held in a sort of economic bondage as sharecroppers who worked for underhanded white landowners, subject to **Jim Crow** laws that kept them in inferior positions throughout the South. The battle for civil rights during Reconstruction involved the following:

Emancipation Proclamation, 1863: Lincoln's proclamation freed African-Americans in rebel states.

Thirteenth Amendment: emancipated all U.S. slaves, wherever they were.

Civil Rights Act of 1866: enabled Blacks to file lawsuits against whites, and to sit on juries. To safeguard these rights permanently, states ratified the **Fourteenth Amendment** and enfranchised Black men with the **Fifteenth Amendment**.

Ku Klux Klan Act of 1871: outlawed racial terrorism.

Civil Rights Act of 1875: prohibited racial discrimination in most public places, but was declared unconstitutional by a Southern-backed Supreme Court in 1883.

Fourteenth Amendment, defined citizenship; however, the Supreme Court held that it did not protect Blacks from discrimination by privately owned businesses, and that they would have to seek equal protection from the states, not the federal government.

Black Codes and **Jim Crow** laws: Local statutes that "kept Blacks in their place" and made loitering, unemployment, indebtedness, voting, and having sex with white women illegal offenses for Blacks. The **Grandfather Clause** was one of these laws passed in many Southern states. It created new requirements to vote, including literacy tests, payment of poll taxes, and residency and property restrictions. Individuals whose ancestors (grandfathers) had the right to vote before the Civil War, or as of a particular date, were exempt from the requirements. Voting officials could "waive" the requirement, if warranted. The intent and effect of these laws were to prevent poor and illiterate African-American former slaves and their descendants from voting. Poor and illiterate whites were often seen to present a case that "warranted" waiving of the requirement, and they were thus allowed to vote. This was one of many examples of how racism became legal. These and other codes gave impetus to groups like the KKK to terrorize Blacks. This was exacerbated after the

Supreme Court's 1896 decision in **Plessy v. Ferguson** that set up the "separate but equal" premise that would be used to make life difficult for Blacks.

- **Freedmen's Bureau** was formed by radical Republicans to redistribute confiscated Southern plantation lands to Blacks in order to put them on more equal footing with white farmers. Congress also sent federal troops into the South to help Blacks register to vote.

1877–1900: Significant Individuals

Ignored for the most part by white progressives after the Civil War, Blacks realized that they needed to better articulate their needs and provide a vision for their struggle. There were two approaches, characterized by **Booker T. Washington** and **W.E.B. DuBois**.

Booker T. Washington: a former slave, represented a rural point of view that embraced ideas of accommodation, rather than aggression. Harboring no illusions that white society would accept Blacks any time soon, he urged Blacks to strive for economic independence. He reasoned that the best way to do that was through self-help and hard work. To that end, he founded a vocational and technical college in Alabama for Blacks, called the **Tuskegee Institute**. In 1895, Washington argued in his "Atlanta Exposition," a famous speech delivered in Atlanta, Georgia, that social equality and political rights would come only if Blacks first became self-reliant and improved their financial footing. In time, he believed, white Americans would eventually respect them. He pleaded for **accommodation** and he refused to press for immediate equal rights, believing pragmatically that it was too soon to do so. He did push for an end to segregation and supported organizations bent on securing political rights for more Blacks.

W.E.B. DuBois: The other point of view, which tended to represent a more urban view, was that accommodation would doom Blacks to poverty and second-class citizenship. Dubois felt that Blacks should not have to tolerate white domination and should immediately fight for their social and political rights. He called on Blacks to develop a **Black consciousness** that would be distinct from that of whites and would emanate from an understanding of Black history, art, music, and religion. In 1905, DuBois founded the **Niagara Movement,** which called for federal legislation to protect racial equality and for full rights of citizenship. Two years later, in conjunction with white liberals, DuBois headed the **National Association for the Advancement of Colored People (NAACP),** which advocated an end to discrimination. His quest proved to be so strenuous that he eventually left the United States and moved to Africa.

1900–1950: Early Twentieth Century Roots of the Civil Rights Era

National Business League (NBL): founded in 1900 by Booker T. Washington in the spirit of accommodation and his belief that Blacks should "pull themselves up by their own bootstraps" through manual education and Black capitalism. The NBL was meant to encourage Blacks to accept segregation, start their own businesses, and frequent establishments owned by Blacks.

NAACP: Formed in 1909 by W.E.B. DuBois and other biracial activists, the NAACP's goal was to educate whites on the need for racial equality, while also trying to gain more political and legal rights for Blacks. It tackled the Supreme Court's "separate but equal ruling" and launched desegregation suits in many different states. The NAACP also worked for anti-lynching laws, as lynchings, public whippings, tarring and feathering, and other KKK-inspired tortures had reached an all-time high in the mid-1920s, and the urgency of the NAACP's intervention rose as well.

Harlem Renaissance: Considered the first important movement of Black artists and writers in the United States, Black artists and writers flocked to the largest Black neighborhood of New York City to promote W.E.B. DuBois's idea of cultivating "Black consciousness" in order to achieve equality. Middle-class Black artists and intellectuals flocked to the area and to some of the writing centers that DuBois started. These writers, like Zora Neale Hurston and Langston Hughes, sought to develop an appreciation and recognition of Black culture. They also pushed the idea of the "New Negro," which would be someone who would provide a new vision of the Black American, not one viewed as inherently inferior or conform to degrading Black stereotypes, but one independent of white stereotypes and who was militant, self-assertive, and proud of his or her race.

Missouri ex rel. Gaines v. Canada, 1938: The Supreme Court ruled that states that provide a school for white students needed to provide an in-state school for Blacks as well. They ordered that the University of Missouri had to build an entirely new law school for Blacks, or integrate them into the existing all-white school. This case marked the beginning of the Supreme Court's reconsideration of the "separate but equal" standard. Although the Court did not strike down segregation, it did state that if there were just one school available, then members of both races could attend it.

Tuskegee Airmen: An elite all-Black bomber unit in World War II which challenged stereotypes that Black men lacked intelligence, skill, courage, and patriotism. *Fighter, escorted bombers P-51 Mustang*

Congress of Racial Equality (CORE): Launched peaceful protests in order to gain sympathy from white Americans.

Competency 5: U.S. History

President's Committee on Civil Rights: Truman established this committee in 1946 to push for anti-lynching laws in the South and to try to register more Black voters. Although symbolically powerful, the committee had little practical influence.

***Morgan v. Virginia* (1946):** Eleven years before Rosa Parks would refuse to move to the back of the bus, 27-year-old Irene Morgan was jailed for refusing to give up her bus seat to a white person. Thurgood Marshall, chief counsel for the NAACP at the time, took up Morgan's case. Marshall chose to argue the case not under the Equal Protection clause of the Fourteenth Amendment, but rather under the Interstate Commerce clause in the Constitution. The Supreme Court ruled that segregated interstate buses were illegal because they put an "undue burden on interstate trade and transport." This struck down laws requiring segregation, but only in instances where interstate transportation was concerned.

Executive Order 9981: Truman ordered the desegregation of the armed forces in 1948.

***Sweatt v. Painter* (1950):** Heman Marion Sweatt filed this lawsuit when he was denied admittance into the University of Texas Law School in 1946 because he was an African-American. Thurgood Marshall and the NAACP took his case. As the case went through the court system, Texas built an all-Black law school in a different part of the state, thinking this satisfied the requirements of *Missouri ex rel. Gaines v. Canada*. But, the Supreme Court ruled that the new school was not really equivalent to the University of Texas because, as in the cases of graduate schools, there is something more important for a school than just to have four walls. In this case, the Supreme Court stated, quantitative differences in facilities and intangible factors, such as its isolation from most of the future lawyers with whom its graduates would interact, made the two schools incomparable. The Court ruled that the Equal Protection Clause of the Fourteenth Amendment mandated that Sweatt be admitted to the previously all-white university law school. This decision made it clear that segregation was doomed.

***McLaurin v. Oklahoma State Regents* (1950):** Another case that Thurgood Marshall argued resulted in the Supreme Court ruling that an institution of higher learning could not differentiate treatment to a student based on race.

1950–1968: Civil Rights Era

The NAACP fought throughout the 1940s and 1950s against segregation. Their efforts, slowly chipping away at the policy through the efforts of chief counsel Thurgood Marshall, would finally result in a tremendous verdict in ***Brown v. Board of Education of Topeka* (1954),** which would result in an overturning of ***Plessy v. Ferguson (1896)***, the late nineteenth-century case that had originated the "separate but equal" standard. This gave momentum to a vibrant Civil Rights Movement.

Brown v. Board of Education of Topeka (1954): The Supreme Court agreed to hear five cases regarding public school desegregation filed under the collective name of "Brown" on behalf of Linda Brown, a Black school-aged child. The NAACP, led by Thurgood Marshall, used sociological and psychological research to argue that school segregation created feelings of inferiority among the students and thereby provided an inherently unequal education that denied kids equal protection under the law. The Supreme Court, after six months of deliberation, returned a unanimous decision that "separate educational facilities are inherently unequal" and ordered schools to desegregate. As no time frame was issued, Southern states plodded slowly on any desegregation effort. In 1955, the Supreme Court ruled in ***Brown v. Board II*** that they needed to desegregate "with all deliberate speed," but Southern schools resisted.

Reaction to the Brown decision was problematic. Southern states chose to make schools private and have students pay tuition in order to avoid desegregation. Some states closed schools rather than desegregate. President Eisenhower did not support the decision, calling Chief Justice Earl Warren's appointment the worst mistake he ever made. Eisenhower opposed rapid change and objected to compulsory federal segregation laws. Federal agencies hindered desegregation, the FBI was obstructionist, and the Departments of Agriculture and Housing permitted segregation in their policies. Southern congressmen signed the **Southern Manifesto** that called *Brown* a "clear abuse of judicial power." In **Little Rock, Arkansas,** in 1957, the governor of Arkansas called out the National Guard to prevent Black students from enrolling in a Little Rock high school. Mobs joined in, and the situation became dangerous. Eisenhower did not want to get involved, but he did not want the publicity of mobs running amok in the streets of Little Rock. So, he reluctantly sent in 10,000 National Guardsmen and 1,000 army paratroopers to ensure the students' safety, enforce the desegregation order, and enable African-Americans to enroll in the local high school. In response, schools there, and in Virginia, which was facing a similar court order, were closed for the following two years to avoid desegregation. The school closings created a crisis in the South with groups organizing **Save Our Schools** (S.O.S.) campaigns who wanted schools to remain open and traditionalists who did not.

Blacks responded to both the momentum that the *Brown* decision gave them as well as to the alarming white response by engaging in their own activism. The first major mass Black activist movements came with bus boycotts. On December 11, 1955, in Montgomery, Alabama, **Rosa Parks**, a Black woman, refused to give up her seat on a city bus to a white passenger and was arrested. Under the leadership of **Martin Luther King, Jr.**, an African-American pastor, they formed the **Montgomery Improvement Association** and African-Americans of Montgomery organized a bus boycott that lasted for a year, until in December 1956, the Supreme Court refused to review a lower court ruling that stated that separate but equal was no longer legal.

Sit-ins characterized the next phase in the Civil Rights Movement. Blacks started a campaign of sit-ins, peaceful, massive, and nonviolent protest, which was met with violent reaction by Southern whites, who attacked the nonviolent protesters on a regular basis. On February 1, 1960, upon being denied service, four African-American students staged a sit-in in the "whites only" section of a Woolworth's lunch counter in Greensboro, North Carolina. Even though they were refused service, the four men sat at the counter until the store closed. The next day, the four men returned along with more than two dozen others who sat down and remained quietly at the counter until the store closed. More and more students flocked to Woolworth's throughout the day and each day thereafter, numbering in the hundreds. Although the students temporarily disbanded to negotiate a settlement, the Greensboro sit-in resumed the following spring when local business leaders refused to cave in to the protesters' demands. Blacks continued to boycott segregationist stores such as Woolworth's until merchants finally conceded and desegregated the lunch counters.

The sit-in movement quickly spread throughout North Carolina and into Virginia and South Carolina. The sit-in movement consisted largely of Black college students who were young, well educated, and upwardly mobile, but who were upset because, despite their education, there were few opportunities for them to enter the job force. While the sit-in movement itself was spontaneous, as it became more successful, civil rights leaders started to organize the protests. Eventually, the sit-ins inspired thousands elsewhere in the South and led to the formation of the **Student Nonviolent Coordinating Committee (SNCC)**. The SNCC attempted to orchestrate more sit-ins, but when that idea failed, they decided to take their operations to rural areas where they would work to organize rural voting efforts for Blacks. Their organization grew over time, and their numbers swelled largely because they maintained a clean reputation, free of violence (although this was not always successful). They set up a **Voter Education Project** and remained aloof from the more flashy civil rights leaders like Martin Luther King, Jr., who they viewed as swooping into an area, grabbing headlines, and swiftly moving on. They also grew distrustful of the federal government and its inability or refusal to help protect the SNCC from violence. The SNCC gradually became more radical and started to demand changes in the federal system. Other civil rights organizations criticized the SNCC because they feared that the provocative sit-ins would destroy all of the work they had done over the years. Many all-Black schools punished and expelled SNCC members. Despite the disapproval from Black sources, many whites who had read about the sit-ins and the harassments that the protesters endured supported and sympathized with the students.

Congress of Racial Equality (CORE): Led by James Farmer, CORE, originally a mainly white, middle-class group, underwent a membership change as more Blacks joined. Like the SNCC, CORE focused on helping local people in the Deep South. SNCC concentrated on efforts in Alabama and Mississippi and CORE focused on Louisiana.

Freedom Rides (1961): CORE organized a biracial **Freedom Ride** of seven Black and six white people who boarded interstate buses to travel through the South in an effort to desegregate bus terminals, as was required by federal law. They hoped that media attention and the likely arrests and public harassment that followed would force President Kennedy to intervene. In May 1961, Blacks and whites boarded buses in Washington, D.C., and traveled across the South to New Orleans to test federal enforcement of regulations prohibiting discrimination. They faced only mild opposition until they met a mob of white supremacists ten days later in Alabama. The mob, likely composed of KKK members, firebombed the bus and assaulted the Freedom Riders on board, nearly killing two of them. Once the Freedom Riders arrived in Birmingham, another mob attacked them while police just watched. Wounded and unsuccessful, the riders returned to the North and let the SNCC Freedom Riders take over. These new riders encountered severe opposition in Montgomery, Alabama, where yet another mob carrying iron pipes attacked the students. Police eventually arrested the SNCC Freedom Riders on charges of disturbing the peace. The Freedom Riders were put in small, windowless jail cells and were mistreated. Just as the protesters had hoped, the mob violence and police inaction in Birmingham and Montgomery outraged President Kennedy and were a major embarrassment for the U.S. government. In response, Kennedy sent 400 federal agents to prevent further violence in Montgomery and pushed the **Interstate Commerce Commission** to clarify its regulations regarding segregation on interstate buses. The success of the CORE and SNCC Freedom Rides prompted chapter organizations to sponsor their own rides in the Deep South throughout the 1960s.

Birmingham, Alabama (1963): In April 1963, Martin Luther King, Jr., and the Southern Christian Leadership Conference (SCLC) helped launch a series of nonviolent demonstrations in Birmingham, considered one of the most segregated cities in America, to desegregate public facilities. The activists organized boycotts and sit-ins to goad white residents and city officials into reacting. Birmingham was committed to its policy of segregation. The Police Commissioner personally supervised efforts to break up the marches by using police dogs, tear gas, clubs, electric cattle prods, and fire hoses to break up the demonstrations. The attacks on the demonstrators were televised and raised concerns about the issue. Demonstrations in other cities across the country were held in support of the Birmingham demonstrators. Alas, Birmingham remained unmoved. King, in a bold and perhaps reckless move, allowed hundreds of high school children to join the marches, calling it a **children's crusade**. Connor ordered the police to treat the children just like the adult marchers. The police department had a difficult time using violence against the little children. King himself was arrested again, and in jail, he took the opportunity to write his influential "Letter from a Birmingham Jail," in which he explained the Civil Rights Movement to his many critics. The letter was published and circulated throughout the country. The violence in Birmingham prompted the Justice Department to negotiate a settlement between the SCLC and city officials. The SCLC agreed to end the boycotts and protests, but only after local merchants promised to hire more Blacks and the city promised to enforce desegregation. Segregationists, however, protested the agreement and initiated a new wave of violence, and 3,000 army troops were sent to restore order. The events that took place in Birmingham and the resulting agreements changed the Civil Rights Movement in two major ways. First, they mobilized the moderate majority of Northern and Southern whites against segregation. Second, the Birmingham campaign marked the first time poorer Southern Blacks began demanding equality alongside the lawyers, ministers, and students. The majority of Blacks wanted immediate access to better jobs, housing, and education, and they wanted the country in general to be desegregated.

March on Washington (1963): The SCLC, NAACP, SNCC, and CORE organized the largest political rally in American history to convince Congress to pass the president's new civil rights bill. On August 28, 1963, more than 250,000 Blacks and whites marched down the Mall in Washington, D.C., and gathered peacefully in front of the Lincoln Memorial for the **March on Washington**. There, Martin Luther King, Jr., delivered his famous **"I have a dream" speech**, which outlined the visions of the Civil Rights Movement and called for racial equality. The march marked one of the last moments of harmony in the Civil Rights Movement.

Competency 5: U.S. History

Civil Rights Act of 1964: The 1964 Civil Rights Act outlawed racial discrimination by employers and unions, created the **Equal Employment Opportunity Commission (EEOC)** to enforce the law, and eliminated the remaining restrictions on Black voting. This is widely considered to be the most comprehensive piece of civil rights legislation and is the basis of all discrimination suits today. The law prohibited discrimination in employment as well as in public facilities. Civil rights leaders hailed the act as the most important victory over racism since the civil rights bills passed by Radical Republicans during Reconstruction. One interesting aspect of the Civil Rights Act of 1964 was that it outlawed not only racial discrimination, but also discrimination on the basis of color, nationality, religion, and gender. Conservative Southerners had actually had gender equality written into the document in the hope that it would kill the bill before it even got out of committee. However, conservatives lost their gamble, and the act passed with the gender provisions, boosting the growing **feminist movement** and protecting millions of working women.

Mississippi Freedom Summer (1964): The SNCC started working in Mississippi where white and Black college students worked together to integrate Southern communities. Their goals for the summer were to expand Black voter registration in the state, to organize a legally constituted "Freedom Democratic Party" that would challenge the whites-only Mississippi Democratic party, to establish "freedom schools" to teach reading and math to Black children, and to open community centers where indigent Blacks could obtain legal and medical assistance. The SNCC believed that if Black students were beaten or killed in demonstrations, it would mean little to the North. But if Northern white kids were hurt or killed, then the cause would be better publicized and they could gain more Northern support. In Philadelphia, Mississippi, three workers—one Black and two white—were killed. While six white men were accused of the murders, no one was tried for murder in state court. The men were tried for civil rights violations in federal court, and the county sheriff and two deputies were found guilty and sentenced to jail. Violence erupted against the participants and local Blacks on a massive scale—homes were bombed and burned.

Twenty-Fourth Amendment (1964): This amendment outlawed federal poll taxes as a requirement to vote in federal elections. This helped both poor whites and Blacks in the South.

March on Selma: The last great effort by the SNCC was to organize the 1965 march on Selma; however, the NAACP and the SCLC came in and took over the effort. The violence the marchers encountered exceeded all that had gone before. Sheriff Jim Clark and the Alabama State Patrol led brutal attacks against the marchers. Two Northern whites were murdered while participating in the march. The events were captured on national TV and helped convince Congress to pass the **1965 Voting Rights Act**. While the march was successful, it split the Civil Rights Movement apart.

Voting Rights Act of 1965: This law focused on those states that denied Blacks the right to vote, despite being given suffrage by the Fifteenth Amendment. It banned literacy tests as a prerequisite for voting and sent thousands of federal voting officials into the South to supervise Black voter registration. As a result, the Black voter registration rate jumped dramatically, in some places from less than 10% to more than 50%.

Emergence of the Militant Movement: With the increasing violence that activists were facing, outrage grew in the Black community, as did the perception that perhaps nonviolent protest was not so effective after all. **Malcolm X,** a minister of the **Nation of Islam,** urged Blacks to claim their rights "by any means necessary." Slowly, the SNCC and CORE also changed their ideas about integration and embraced a more separatist radical program of **Black Power**. In 1966, **Stokely Carmichael** called for the Civil Rights Movements to be "Black-staffed, Black-controlled, and Black-financed." He argued that Blacks needed to help their own communities and not rely on white aid. He argued that integration only siphoned the top Black leaders into the white system, so perhaps it was not such a good idea. Later, he moved on to the Black Panthers, self-styled urban revolutionaries based in Oakland, California. Other leaders, such as H. Rap Brown, also called for Black Power. On April 4, 1968, Martin Luther King, Jr., was assassinated in Memphis by James Earl Ray. Riots in more than 100 cities followed.

Watts Riots (1965): In August 1965, in the Watts district of Los Angeles, riots broke out and 34 people were killed and 1,000 wounded. Many observers were puzzled why Blacks would do this after finally achieving the Civil Rights Act of 1964. Rioters responded that the acts were wonderful; however, they did little to help the condition of the people living in the inner cities, scarred by high unemployment, substandard housing, and inadequate schools. After the riots, Martin Luther King moved to Chicago to get Blacks there to join nonviolent protests.

Black Panthers: Formed by Bobby Seale, Eldridge Cleaver, and Huey Newton, the Black Panthers became a paramilitary unit that would act as a police force in the ghettoes. Confrontation between the Panthers and the police led to shootouts and the disappearance of the SNCC and CORE influence and authority.

End of an Era: The Civil Rights Movement reached an impasse in 1968 when the movement realized that many problems remained that would require an overhaul of American society to fix—something most were not willing to do. Riots continued across the nation. When King was assassinated, riots in more than 100 cities broke out, with scores killed and thousands injured.

1900–1968: Significant Individuals

Marcus Garvey: A native of Jamaica, Garvey moved to Harlem and founded the U.S. chapter of the **Universal Negro Improvement Association (UNIA)**. He advocated African-American racial pride and separatism, rather than integration, and called for a return of African-Americans to Africa. In 1921, he proclaimed himself the provisional president of an African empire and sold stock in the Black Star Steamship Line that would take migrants to Africa. The line went bankrupt in 1923, and Garvey was convicted and imprisoned for mail fraud in the sale of the line's stock, and then deported. His legacy was an emphasis on African-American pride and self-respect.

A. Philip Randolph: President of the National Negro Congress; threatened FDR with a march on Washington if the federal government did not pass civil rights legislation.

Competency 5: U.S. History

Thurgood Marshall: The future first African-American on the Supreme Court was the chief counsel of the NAACP. Marshall won landmark victories in Supreme Court cases that helped tear down segregation statutes.

Martin Luther King, Jr.: As president of the Montgomery Improvement Association, King had led the year-long bus boycott, and his galvanizing speeches put him on the national stage as a voice of the Civil Rights Movement. King based his arguments on the belief that people had a duty to obey moral laws, even if they conflicted with man-made laws. He adopted a strategy of nonviolence (perhaps inspired by the nonviolent practices of the Indian activist Mahatma Gandhi), and argued that violence should never be used to support moral law. He believed that the best way to attack segregation and racism was by using **creative tension,** which makes people think about the concepts. For the most part, King was able to open doors for African-Americans to mainstream society. Peaceful massive resistance characterized the movement in its early stages. King was assassinated in 1968.

John F. Kennedy (JFK): With the help of Black voters, Kennedy was elected as the thirty-fifth president of the United States in 1960; however, his support of the Civil Rights Movement for the first two years of his administration was limited because he was trying to work the southern Congressional leaders who opposed civil rights initiatives. Kennedy had a change of heart and mind after the violent treatment of the Birmingham demonstrators in 1963. He had plans to push stronger civil rights legislation through Congress, but was assassinated in 1963 in Dallas, Texas.

Robert F. Kennedy: Robert Kennedy served as Attorney General during his brother's presidential administration. Robert Kennedy was a major proponent of civil rights and influenced both his brother's perspective and actions. After President Kennedy's assassination, Robert Kennedy served as a U.S. Senator and ran to be the Democratic nominee for president of the United States in 1968. He continued to be an active and vocal supporter of civil rights and social justice. He was assassinated in 1968.

Lyndon B. Johnson: Johnson was Kennedy's vice president who became the thirty-sixth president of the United States when Kennedy was assassinated. Johnson was a key supporter of civil rights legislation, and Congress passed the Civil Rights Act of 1964 and the Voting Rights Act of 1964 during his administration. Johnson also declared "War on Poverty" based on statistics that showed that almost 20% of the U.S. population was living in poverty. This spawned the development of numerous economic programs that expanded the federal government's role in education and health care. This included the Social Security Act to fund Medicaid and Medicare, Head Start for preschool children, the Food Stamp Program, and the Elementary and Secondary Education Act (which lives as on today's Every Student Succeeds Act).

Malcolm X: Originally born Malcolm Little, Malcolm X changed his last name to "X" to honor the heritage and identity of Black lives lost as the result of slavery. In contrast to the nonviolent approach of Martin Luther King, Malcolm X advocated a more militant and independent approach termed the Black Power movement. Malcolm X converted to Islam while in prison, and after making a holy pilgrimage to Mecca, he changed his militant views and worked with leaders of nonviolent movements to achieve racial integration. Malcolm X was assassinated in 1965.

Women's Rights Movement

Passage of the Fifteenth Amendment ensured voting rights for all citizens of the United States, regardless of race or color; however, women's right to vote was not mentioned. To test the issue, Susan B. Anthony voted in 1872 for Ulysses S. Grant, only to be arrested a few weeks later and convicted of illegal voting. Anthony was inspired to draft what became the Nineteenth Amendment, known as the Susan B. Anthony Amendment. The major issues in the Women's Rights Movement can be separated largely into "pre-suffrage" and "post-suffrage."

Timeline of Women's Suffrage in the United States

Women Lose the Right to Vote at the Beginning of the United States

1637   Anne Hutchinson was convicted of sedition and expelled from the Massachusetts colony for her religious ideas and outspoken behavior.

1776   Abigail Adams wrote her husband, John Adams, who was meeting with Thomas Jefferson about the Declaration of Independence, and asked him to "remember the ladies and be more generous and favourable to them than your ancestors. If particular care and attention is not paid [us], we are determined to foment a rebellion, and will not hold ourselves bound by any laws in which we have no voice." However, the Declaration's wording specified that "all *men* are created equal."

1777–1807   Women lose the right to vote in all states. The states of New York, Massachusetts, New Hampshire, and New Jersey, which had previously allowed women to vote, rescinded those rights.

1787   U.S. Constitutional Convention placed voting qualifications in the hands of the states.

Women's Movement and Abolitionist Movement Combine

1830s   Formation of female anti-slavery associations.

1836   Grimké sisters, Angelina and Sarah, began public speaking careers that tied the anti-slavery movement to the Women's Rights Movement. Angelina appealed to Southern women to speak out against slavery. Sarah was eventually silenced by male abolitionists who considered her public speaking a liability.

Competency 5: U.S. History

1840   World Anti-Slavery Convention in London. Lucretia Mott, Elizabeth Cady Stanton, and other women were barred from participating in the World Anti-Slavery Convention in London as the result of their gender. This snub led them to decide to hold a women's rights convention when they returned to America.

Women Organize and Target Suffrage

1844   Female textile workers in Massachusetts organized the first permanent labor association for working women, the **Lowell Female Labor Reform Association,** and demanded a ten-hour workday.

1848   July 19–20, 300 attended the first **Women's Rights Convention in Seneca Falls, New York**. Equal suffrage was proposed by Elizabeth Cady Stanton. After two days of discussion and debate, sixty-eight women and thirty-two men signed a Declaration of Sentiments, which outlined the main issues and goals for the emerging women's movement. A set of twelve resolutions was adopted calling for equal treatment of women and men under the law and voting rights for women.

1849   Harriet Tubman escaped from slavery, and over the next ten years she led many slaves to freedom by the Underground Railroad. Elizabeth Blackwell graduated from Geneva College with the first medical degree awarded to a woman.

1850   A women's rights convention was held in April in Salem, Ohio, and men were not allowed to speak at it. The first national women's rights convention was held in October in Worcester, Massachusetts, and attracted more than 1,000 participants. This marked the beginning of annual women's rights conventions that were held from 1850–1861.

1865–1870   Southern white women created Confederate memorial societies to help preserve the memory of the "Lost Cause." This activity propelled many white Southern women into the public sphere for the first time. During this same period, newly emancipated Southern Black women formed thousands of organizations aimed at "uplifting the race."

1866   Susan B. Anthony and Elizabeth Cady Stanton formed the **American Equal Rights Association**, founded to push for universal suffrage and civil rights for all Americans, irrespective of race, color, or sex. Lucretia Mott was elected president.

1867   Fourteenth amendment passed Congress, defining citizens as "male." This was the first use of the word "male" in the Constitution. Kansas held a state referendum on whether or not to give the right to vote to Blacks and/or women. Despite Stone, Anthony, and Stanton's campaign all over the state, suffrage for both Blacks and women lost.

Suffrage Movement Divides Over Black vs. Women's Suffrage

1868 — Passage of the Fourteenth Amendment extended to all citizens the protections of the Constitution against unjust state laws. This amendment was the first to define "citizens" and "voters" as "male." The Fifteenth Amendment also passed, giving the vote to Black men. Women petitioned to be included but were turned down. In New Jersey, 172 women attempted to vote; their ballots were ignored. Stanton and Anthony launched their women's rights newspaper, **The Revolution**, in New York City. Anthony organized the **Working Women's Association**, which encouraged women to unionize themselves to work collectively for higher wages and shorter hours.

1869 — Frederick Douglass and others backed down from women's suffrage to concentrate on the fight for Black male suffrage. In May, the women's rights movement split over disagreements about the Fourteenth Amendment and the Fifteenth Amendment. The more radical New York-based National Woman Suffrage Association formed in May with Elizabeth Cady Stanton as president. The primary goal of the NWSA was an amendment to the Constitution giving women the right to vote. In November, a more conservative organization, the American Woman Suffrage Association, which was based in Boston, was founded by Lucy Stone, Henry Blackwell, and Julia Ward, with Henry Ward Beecher as president. On December 10, the Wyoming territory passed the first women's suffrage law since 1807.

Civil Disobedience and State Suffrage

1870 — The Fifteenth Amendment that granted suffrage to former male African-American slaves, but not to women, was ratified without the support of the NWSA, who opposed the amendment because of its omission of women's suffrage. Frederick Douglass broke with the organization as a result. Utah territory granted women's suffrage.

1870–1875 — Several women attempted to use the Fourteenth Amendment in the courts to secure the vote or the right to practice law but they all were unsuccessful.

1871 — The Anti-Suffrage Society was formed.

1872 — Susan B. Anthony and supporters were arrested for attempting to vote for Ulysses S. Grant in the presidential election. Anthony's sisters and eleven other women were held for $500 bail. Anthony herself was held for $1,000 bail. At the same time, Sojourner Truth appeared at a polling booth in Battle Creek, Michigan, demanding a ballot; she was turned away.

1874   In *Myner v. Happerstett*, the U.S. Supreme Court decided that citizenship does not give women the right to vote, and that women's political rights are under the jurisdiction of each individual state. The **Woman's Christian Temperance Union** (WCTU) was founded, which later became an important force in the fight for women's suffrage. One of the most vehement opponents to women's enfranchisement was the liquor lobby, which feared women might prohibit the sale of liquor if they gained the right to vote.

1878   A Woman Suffrage Amendment was introduced in the U.S. Congress. The wording was the same that would be used in 1919.

1886   Suffrage amendment reached the U.S. Senate floor, and was defeated two to one.

1890   The NWSA and the AWSA were reunited to form NAWSA–National American Woman Suffrage Association, under the direction of Elizabeth Cady Stanton. The focus turned to working state by state to obtain voting rights for women. The Progressive campaign propelled thousands of college-educated white women and a number of women of color into lifetime careers in social work and made women an important voice to be reckoned with in American politics. Wyoming joined the union as the first state with voting rights for women.

1893   After a vigorous campaign led by Carrie Chapman Catt, Colorado men voted for women's suffrage. Other states soon followed suit: 1896: Utah and Idaho; 1910: Washington; 1911: California; 1912: Oregon, Kansas, and Arizona; 1913: Alaska and Illinois; 1914: Montana and Nevada; 1917: New York; 1918: Michigan, South Dakota, and Oklahoma.

1896   The **National Association of Colored Women** was formed, bringing together more than 100 Black women's clubs and included Mary Church Terrell, Ida B. Wells-Barnett, Margaret Murray Washington, Fanny Jackson Coppin, Frances Ellen Watkins Harper, Charlotte Forten Grimké, and Harriet Tubman.

Suffrage Comes to Fruition

1903   The **National Women's Trade Union League** (WTUL) was established to advocate for improved wages and working conditions for women.

1907   Harriet Stanton Blatch, Elizabeth's daughter, formed the Equality League of Self Supporting Women, which became the Women's Political Union in 1910. She introduced the English suffragists' tactics of parades, street speakers, and pickets.

1911   In New York City, 3,000 marched for suffrage. The **National Association Opposed to Woman Suffrage** (NAOWS) was organized and supporters included distillers and brewers, urban political machines, Southern congressmen, and corporate capitalists—like railroad magnates and meat-packers—who supported the "antis" by contributing to their "war chests."

1912   Teddy Roosevelt's Progressive Party included women's suffrage in its platform.

1913   A women's suffrage parade on the eve of Wilson's inauguration was attacked by a mob. Hundreds of women were injured, but no arrests were made. **Alice Paul** and **Lucy Burns** formed the **Congressional Union** to work toward the passage of a federal amendment to give women the vote. The group was later renamed the **National Women's Party (NWP)** and used civil disobedience, including hunger strikes and picketing the White House, to publicize the suffrage cause.

1916   Alice Paul and others broke away from NASWA to form the National Woman's Party. **Margaret Sanger** opened the first U.S. birth control clinic in Brooklyn, New York. Although the clinic was shut down ten days later and Sanger was arrested, she eventually won support through the courts and opened another clinic in New York City in 1923.

1920   The **Nineteenth Amendment**, called the **Susan B. Anthony Amendment**, was ratified by Tennessee on August 18. It became law on August 26. Its victory accomplished, NAWSA ceased to exist, but its organization became the nucleus of the **League of Women Voters**.

1923   The National Woman's Party first proposed the **Equal Rights Amendment** to eliminate discrimination on the basis of sex. It has never been ratified.

Post-Suffrage—Women's Movement and Equal Rights

Birth Control, Equal Pay, and Feminism

1921   **Margaret Sanger** founded the **American Birth Control League**, which evolved into the **Planned Parenthood Federation of America** in 1942.

1935   **Mary McLeod Bethune** organized the **National Council of Negro Women**, a coalition of Black women's groups that lobbied against job discrimination, racism, and sexism.

1960   The Food and Drug Administration approved **birth control pills**.

1961   President Kennedy established the **President's Commission on the Status of Women** and appointed Eleanor Roosevelt as chairwoman. The report recommended instituting fair hiring practices, equal pay, paid maternity leave, and affordable child care.

Competency 5: U.S. History

1963 — **Betty Friedan** published *The Feminine Mystique*, which articulated the dissatisfaction felt by middle-class American housewives with the narrow role imposed on them by society. Congress passed the **Equal Pay Act**, making it illegal for employers to pay a woman less than what a man would receive for the same job.

1964 — **Title VII of the Civil Rights Act** barred discrimination in employment on the basis of race and sex. At the same time, it established the **Equal Employment Opportunity Commission (EEOC)** to investigate complaints and impose penalties.

1966 — The **National Organization for Women (NOW)** was founded by a group of feminists, including Betty Friedan. NOW promoted child care, abortion rights, and the ERA.

1969 — California became the first state to adopt a **"no fault" divorce law**, which allowed couples to divorce by mutual consent.

1971 — *Ms. Magazine* was first published as a sample insert in *New York* magazine; 300,000 copies were sold out in eight days. The first regular issue was published in July.

1972 — The **Equal Rights Amendment (ERA)** was passed by Congress and sent to the states for ratification. Originally drafted by Alice Paul in 1923, the amendment read: "Equality of rights under the law shall not be denied or abridged by the United States or by any State on account of sex." The amendment died in 1982 when it failed to achieve ratification by a minimum of 38 states. **Title IX of the Education Amendments** banned sex discrimination in schools. As a result of Title IX, the enrollment of women in athletics programs and professional schools increased dramatically.

1973 — *Roe v. Wade* established a woman's right to legal abortion, overriding the anti-abortion laws of many states.

1978 — The **Pregnancy Discrimination Act** banned employment discrimination against pregnant women. Under the Act, a woman cannot be fired or denied a job or a promotion because she is or may become pregnant, nor can she be forced to take a pregnancy leave if she is willing and able to work.

1981 — **Sandra Day O'Connor** became the first woman to serve on the Supreme Court.

1994 — The **Violence Against Women Act** tightened federal penalties for sex offenders, funded services for victims of rape and domestic violence, and provided for special training of police officers.

1996   In *United States v. Virginia*, the Supreme Court ruled that the all-male Virginia Military School had to admit women in order to continue to receive public funding. It held that creating a separate, all-female school would not suffice.

2006   The Supreme Court upheld the ban on the "partial-birth" abortion procedure. The ruling, 5–4, which upholds the **Partial-Birth Abortion Ban Act**, a federal law passed in 2003, was the first to ban a specific type of abortion procedure. Writing in the majority opinion, Justice Anthony Kennedy said, "The act expresses respect for the dignity of human life." Justice Ruth Bader Ginsburg, who dissented, called the decision "alarming" and said it was "so at odds with our jurisprudence" that it "should not have staying power."

2008   **Hillary Clinton** entered the race to become the Democratic nominee for president, hoping to be the first woman nominated by a major political party. Although she lost the nomination, President Obama appointed her Secretary of State.

2016   Hillary Clinton ran as the Democratic nominee for president, the first woman ever nominated for president by a major political party; however, she lost the presidential race to Republican **Donald Trump,** who was elected as the forty-fifth president of the United States.

COMPETENCY 5.15

Identify the causes, significant individuals, and effects of the events associated with contemporary domestic and foreign affairs.

Domestic Issues

In 2016, the chief domestic issues that the United States is facing are the economy, financial reform, housing reform, environmental disasters, and racial unrest.

Current issues

        College Costs: Rising college costs and the inability of middle-class Americans to shoulder those costs has ignited discussion about where this will eventually lead. With the current state of the economy and the inability of new graduates to find jobs that pay enough for them to pay off college loans, the nation is facing the prospect of a declining percentage of college graduates among its adult population.

        Cyberterrorism: Because people around the world now use the Internet for communication, social interaction, and financial transactions, a great deal of personal information is potentially available to hackers or terrorist attack. Stolen information can result in identify theft and disclosure of information vital to the protection of the United States.

Gun Control: Concerns about the proliferation of guns, easy access to buying them at gun shows, permits to conceal these weapons, who should not be permitted to buy them, and training associated with gun ownership continue to be questions that are debated, particularly in the West.

Immigration: Problems around the world, especially in countries with potential terrorist influences, have created hundreds of thousands of refugees with no place to go. Americans fear that if the immigrants come to America, the United States could have more terrorist attacks. The same sort of fears expressed during the height of the immigration boom in the late nineteenth and early twentieth centuries continue to reveal themselves.

Poverty in the United States: The gap between rich and poor continues to widen. All of the issues attendant to the poor—housing, health care, and schooling, for example—will receive new focus. Faith-based initiatives were highlighted as a way to address growing poverty.

Public Education: A multistate effort of education standards reform, dubbed Common Core State Standards, set out to encourage a higher degree of critical thinking in the classroom. But the new standards also stirred debate. Battle lines were drawn over issues ranging from teacher accountability to concerns over student performance on new assessments.

Technology Use: Technology has transformed life in the twenty-first century. Almost anything—school, shopping, social media, gaming—can be done on the Internet; however, this transformation sometimes results in an overdependence on technology to the detriment of individuals and, possibly, society. Technology has created a **digital divide** between individuals who do and do not have access to technology. People can become so attached to technology that they text while driving and cause accidents. They can communicate online, but not face-to-face. Predators and others can pretend to be other people and entice or bully others.

Foreign Issues

China: A trade imbalance with China continues to concern economists.

Climate Change: Coming up with a worldwide agreement on whether or not climate change is occurring, and what we should do about it remains a topic of discussion and sometimes pointed exchange. The Obama administration opened the door to wide-ranging discussions about global warming and climate change.

Development: Policy about when and how to help out which foreign countries, particularly in a time of economic difficulty in the United States, which has its own infrastructure issues, remains a concern among foreign aid workers.

Israel: The U.S.-Israel relationship continues to be dominated by the broad issues of Arab-Israeli and Palestinian-Israeli peace. According to a U.S. State Department Bureau of Near Eastern Affairs fact sheet, U.S. efforts to reach a Middle East peace settlement hinge on UN Security Council Resolutions 242 and 338 and "have been based on the premise that as Israel takes calculated risks for peace, the United States will help minimize those risks."

North Korea: North Korea has nuclear capabilities; therefore, the United States has approached it differently, for example, than it has nations that are believed to be seeking nuclear capabilities. North Korea has also isolated itself, diplomatically and economically, from most of the world, with the exception of China.

Russia: Relations with Russia have waxed and waned over the years. The recent exchange of spies between the two countries may have an effect on relations in the future.

War on Terror: The War on Terror continues to dominate U.S. foreign and domestic policy. In early 2017, the Trump administration's efforts to tighten border security stirred debate over the effects of what president Trump termed "extreme vetting."

COMPETENCY 5.16

Identify key individuals, events, and issues related to Florida history.

Although Florida was the twenty-seventh state to be admitted to the Union on March 3, 1845, Florida has the oldest surviving European place-name in the United States. Spanish conquistador and explorer Juan Ponce de León arrived around what is now St. Augustine on Easter Sunday, 1513. Ponce de León was impressed with the beautiful plant life. He named the land *Florida*, the Spanish phrase for *Feast of the Flowers*, in honor of the day and the flowers he saw. However, Ponce de León and his expedition were not the first humans to be in what he called *Florida*. That distinction belongs to the Native Americans who were already living there.

Archeologists believe that Paleo-Indians first arrived in what is now Florida more than 14,000 years ago and lived in small groups around sources of fresh water. As the climate changed over time, the groups began to form larger and separate settlements and tribes. Tribes in northern Florida and the panhandle were more agricultural and grew maize. Tribes in other areas of the state depended more on hunting, fishing, and gathering. At one time, dozens of tribes existed in Florida; however, the fate of indigenous peoples in North America, South America, and Central America was also the fate of the Native Americans of Florida. Most perished from diseases introduced by the Europeans or warfare with Europeans who came to Florida.

Competency 5: U.S. History

Indians

The first Floridians were Indians. In North Florida, the **Apalachee** lived in the Tallahassee Hills beginning around 1000 CE. Prior to European contact, there were probably at least 50,000–60,000 Apalachees who lived in widely dispersed villages. They were considered, among other Indian tribes, to be an advanced civilization, as they were prosperous, well-organized, and fierce warriors. Their civilization seemed more developed than the others, as they had ballgames, ceremonial mounts, and a rigid feudal system. After the Spanish arrival in 1528, led by explorer Pánfilo de Narváez and later Hernando de Soto, the Apalachee attacked the Europeans. The advanced weapons used by Europeans overwhelmed the Apalachee, and they suffered from losses in battle as well as diseases carried by the Europeans. The Apalachee rulers, finally understanding the Spanish demands for conversion to Catholicism, did convert between 1633 and 1635. But it was not enough to keep the peace with Europeans, and in the early 1700s, the British attacked them, and killed and enslaved many. Some of the Apalachee migrated north to Creek territory, and others moved to Louisiana.

The **Timucuans** lived between the Aucilla River and the Atlantic Ocean down to the Tampa Bay. They were farmers who lived in independent villages and survived on farming and hunting small game. Typical Timucuan villages had groups of small huts protected by a circular wall of tree trunks. They practiced a rigid feudal system, and each Indian's occupation was determined by birth. Males typically were warriors and hunters, although potters and canoe makers also had high status. Women and children did most of the planting and harvesting of food. From 1649 through 1656, the Timucuan suffered both from attacks by the English and other Indian troops as well as being ravaged by smallpox. Some scholars think that the few remaining Timucuans merged with the Seminole tribe.

The **Calusa**, a name which means "fierce people," lived on the southwest coast of Florida and controlled most of southern Florida. They were good sailors with a reputation as good warriors. Their villages were typically built on stilts and had roofs but no walls. Their houses were made of huge mounds of shells, and they dug deep moats around their villages to protect them from invaders. They did not farm but were accomplished at fishing. They are known as the "Shell Indians" because they used shells for just about everything: tools, utensils, hunting, fishing, jewelry, and ornaments. It is suspected that the Calusa died out after being raided and sold as slaves by enemy tribes from Georgia and South Carolina, and the remaining ones were victims of smallpox and measles transmitted by the Spanish.

The **Tocobaga** Indians lived in small villages at the northern end of Tampa Bay from 900 to the 1500s. Each village was situated around a public area that was used as a meeting place. The houses were generally round and built with wooden poles that were topped with a roof made up of palm thatches. Their main source of food was shellfish, manatees, and small game. They died out about a hundred years after Pánfilo de Narváez, a Spanish explorer, arrived there in 1528, due to both Spanish attacks and disease.

The **Tequesta** settled in South Florida near Biscayne Bay in the present-day Miami area. Like other tribes in South Florida, the Tequesta were hunters and gatherers. The men often ventured out to the ocean in canoes to catch their food: sharks, sailfish, porpoises, sting rays, and manatee. Women and children would gather food in shallow waters, including clams, conches, oysters, and turtle eggs. While they also gathered nuts, berries, and small game, their food supply was more difficult to obtain, which may be one reason why they never expanded. Like the other Indian tribes, their encounters with the Europeans spelled their doom.

Florida of the Conquistadores

Ponce de Leon is considered to be the European founder of Florida. In 1513, he landed near present-day St. Augustine and continued up the coast of Florida until he reached the Calusa Indians. The Indians frightened the Spanish, who returned to their ships and set sail. Eight years later, Ponce de Leon returned with 500 men to build a colony. Upon landing, however, he and his men were again attacked by the Calusa, and de Leon was mortally wounded.

In 1528, another attempt was made by the Spanish to tame Florida. **Pánfilo de Narváez** arrived near Tampa Bay with a large army. A flaw in communication left de Narváez and his 300 soldiers and forty horses stranded. His ship, which contained all of his food and supplies, landed at a different spot from where it had been told to land. Narváez and his men waited and waited for the ship, and for an entire year, the ship's captain went up and down the coast searching for Narváez. Meanwhile, Narváez and his men were getting nervous, hungry, and sick, and had been attacked by the Apalachee over and over again. After about a month of waiting, he and his men went to a bay on the Gulf, built five barges out of pine trees, and used their shirts to make sails. In September 1528, Narváez and approximately 240 men set sail towards a Spanish settlement in Mexico on homemade barges. Unfortunately, a violent storm capsized their barges, and many, including Narváez, died. About 100 made it to an island off Texas. By spring, Narváez's provost, Nuñez de Cabeza de Vaca, and the few men who were still alive set off to walk to Mexico City. Seven years later, four of them, including de Vaca, eventually arrived there.

Hernando de Soto was given "La Florida" by King Carlos V in 1536. De Soto, deeply in debt when he left Spain in 1538, thought he would regain his fortune by finding gold in "La Florida." His expedition, unlike the ones before him, was relatively well-stocked with priests, women, horses, mules, war dogs, and pigs. On May 25, they made landfall in the Tampa Bay area and found a survivor from Narváez's expedition. **Juan Ortiz** had been living as an Indian since he was left behind and was able to work as both a guide and a translator for de Soto. As de Soto's expedition moved inland, however, they encountered resistance and fought with the natives. His brutal treatment of those he met—enslaving, mutilating, and executing those in his path—proved to be his undoing, as the Indians began to fight back. By the spring of 1540, de Soto and his army, never finding the gold they were seeking, left and went to explore Georgia, North Carolina and South Carolina, Tennessee, and Alabama. In 1542, as he headed across the Mississippi River into Arkansas, he became ill and died of a fever.

Competency 5: U.S. History

Florida of the French

The French Protestants, called **Huguenots**, sought to establish France as a mercantile power. Many of them were merchants and sailors. Their leader, Admiral Gaspard de Coligny, convinced Charles IX that France's future success as a nation depended upon competing with Spain and Portugal for the American colonies.

In 1562, **Jean Ribault** was sent from France to Florida to explore the area and begin a new colony. Ribault sailed with three ships that carried 100 Huguenots. He landed at St. Johns River and built a stone monument to mark his visit and claim the area for France. Afterwards, he continued to what is now South Carolina, where the Huguenots built a fort and named it Charlesfort, in honor of their king. Before long, the supplies began to dwindle, so Ribault sailed back to France. When he arrived, religious conflict had broken out in France, so he went to England to ask Queen Elizabeth to fund his trip. She had him arrested for establishing a French colony in Spanish territory, and he was put in a London prison. During this time, Ribault's lieutenant, **Rene Laudonnière**, was sent to rescue Charlesfort. He led an expedition of Huguenot colonists who established a colony called Fort Caroline in present-day Jacksonville. Initially, he established good relations with the Timucuan Indians. Supplies ran short, and the French colony was unable to get food from the natives. Some of the colonists no longer believed in Laudonnière's leadership. They stole boats and sailed south to become pirates and raid Spanish treasure ships. Most of the colonists at Fort Caroline decided to go home to France. The French colony was in trouble. Ribault, newly released from prison, planned to rescue and take control of Fort Caroline. Meanwhile, a Spanish explorer named **Pedro Menendez de Aviles** arrived in Florida. Menendez was ordered to get rid of the French, so he built his own fort at St. Augustine, marched on Fort Caroline, and later killed Ribault. Laudonnière, who was wounded in the attack, managed to escape to France.

Florida of the Spanish

Pedro Menendez de Aviles was sent to drive out the French colonists. He had eleven ships and brought more than 2,000 sailors, soldiers, and their families to Florida. When he built the fort at St. Augustine, he included watchtowers and forts to keep track of impending European vessels. As Florida's first Spanish Colonial Governor charged with making sure that all of Florida stayed under Spain's control, he established outposts up and down the coast and built more watchtowers at Cape Canaveral and Biscayne Bay. Menendez then sent two ships of settlers to what is now Parris Island, South Carolina. In 1569, more settlers arrived there, and the town began to bloom. They named their town Santa Elena, and it became the capital of Spanish Florida. Unlike those who had come before him, Menendez sought to have a good relationship with the Indians. He signed a treaty with the Calusa Indians to trade gold for food and other supplies his troops needed to survive. As part of the desire for "God, Gold, and Glory," Menendez focused on converting the Native Americans to Catholicism. All of the ships coming from Spain contained priests who, in many cases, became missionaries. Menendez went back to Spain to collect more settlers, but he died in 1574 before he could return to Florida.

Florida was part of the huge and complex Spanish empire, and was a Royal colony, like all Spanish colonies. As such, it was the lawful property of the Crown, and all appointments and decisions were made by the King and his advisors. The Spanish Empire was divided into two districts, New Spain and Peru. Florida was a province of New Spain. The colony was headed by a **governor** who was responsible for the welfare of all of the colonists. The governor served as general of the army and his primary duty in that regard was to protect St. Augustine. As the chief politician, the governor administered the law, acted as chief justice of the court, and settled small disputes. As a businessman, he was in charge of the colony's budget. As the chief in charge of the missionary effort, he was diplomat to the Indians, welfare director for the poor, construction engineer for the colony's defense, and religious leader. Florida governors served for five years if they came from Europe, and three if they came from another colony. Governors were required to post one-half of their earnings in bonds to pay for any heavy fines they may accrue. Near the end of their term of office, the Spanish Crown would send undercover agents to evaluate the governor and his colony.

Spanish Florida's greatest threat came from England, which had begun to invade Florida's mission system as early as 1658. St. Augustine was raided in 1665 and 1668. Governor James Moore of South Carolina attacked the Spanish in 1722 with an army of about 1,200 militia. More attacks followed as the Spanish mission system completely deteriorated. In 1740, Georgia's Governor James Oglethorpe organized a huge colonial militia to destroy St. Augustine, but the mission failed.

Florida: The British Period

In 1763, with the Treaty of Paris that marked the end of the French and Indian War, France gave up its land in North America and Spain gave Florida to the British. The British then divided Florida into two territories: East Florida and West Florida.

East Florida, bordered by the Apalachicola River, the Gulf of Mexico, and the Atlantic Ocean, chose St. Augustine as its capital. The first governor of East Florida, James Grant, remained on good terms with the Seminole Indians and had a flourishing trade with them. He also encouraged settlers in the other British colonies to come to Florida and settle there. Advertisements in London promised 20,000-acre lots to any group who wanted to settle in Florida. The rule was that individual holders could have 100 acres each. Former British soldiers were given 100 acres of land, and each of their family members was given 50 acres. Along with the British came slavery, and it was the slaves who largely built the colony. They cleared land, built homes, and introduced crops to the area, including citrus fruit, sugar cane, rice, cotton, and indigo. Western Florida had Pensacola as its capital and consisted of the land between the Mississippi River and the Apalachicola River (in modern-day terms, that included Alabama, Mississippi, and Louisiana). It had some disadvantages, as it was filled with pine trees and sand and was not as good for farming.

During the American Revolution, Florida remained loyal to the British, and even invited Loyalists to come live there when things became a little tense in the Northern colonies. In 1779, while the British were preoccupied with the American Revolution, Spain invaded Florida and regained control over it; after the revolution, the entire Floridian area was given to Spain.

The Seminole Wars and Transfer to the United States

Following the War of 1812 between the United States and Britain, American slave owners came to Florida in search of runaway African slaves and Indians. These Indians, known as the **Seminole**, and the runaway slaves had been trading weapons with the British throughout the early 1800s and had supported Britain during the War of 1812. From 1817–1818, the U.S. Army invaded Spanish Florida and fought against the Seminole and their African-American allies. Collectively, these battles came to be known as the **First Seminole War**.

Americans reacted to these confrontations by sending Andrew Jackson to Florida with an army of about 3,000 men. Jackson was successful in his attacks and left many dead and dying Seminole behind in their destroyed villages. He went on to attack Spanish settlements and captured Spanish forts at St. Marks and Pensacola. Spaniards began to realize that they could no longer keep their territory. They had been unable to bring settlers to Florida, and it was beginning to be a drain. Meanwhile, Spain knew that the United States was interested in the region because it would benefit their attempt to use the Mississippi River as a major trading location. Spain negotiated the **Adams-Onis Treaty**, which gave Florida to the United States and nullified the $5 million debt Spain owed to the United States. Florida now belonged to the United States. Andrew Jackson, in charge of setting up Florida's government, quickly divided Florida into two parts called counties. The area that had been West Florida became Escambia County, and what was once East Florida became St. Johns County. Jackson established county courts and mayors in the cities of St. Augustine (East Florida) and Pensacola (West Florida). Afterwards, Jackson left Florida and empowered **William Pope Duval** to lead Florida as governor. Florida became an official territory on March 30, 1822.

As settlement increased, pressure grew on the U.S. government to remove the Native Americans from their lands in Florida. To the chagrin of Georgia landowners, the Seminole harbored and integrated runaway Black slaves, and clashes between whites and Native Americans grew with the influx of new settlers.

Northern settlers were moving to Tallahassee, a Seminole settlement; but these settlers often clashed with the Seminole. In an effort to end these conflicts, the governor asked the Seminole to move. The Seminole refused. In 1823, it became necessary for the governor to offer the Seminole a treaty, which was called the **Treaty of Moultrie Creek**. This treaty required the Seminole to give up their land and move south. It also made them agree to discontinue hiding runaway slaves. The Seminole were given 4 million acres of land in the area south of present-day Ocala. The area that they were given was called a **reservation**. This reservation, however, did not meet their needs.

In 1829, President Jackson worked to have the **Indian Removal Act** made into a law. The Seminole were offered lands west of the Mississippi. Their leaders went to look at it, were persuaded to sign a treaty, did so, and then went back home and said they had been tricked. They refused to leave.

A warrior named **Osceola** led the Seminole in a surprise attack against the Americans. At the Dade Massacre, Osceola and his men killed more than 100 Americans. The United States sent in more troops, and fighting between the two went on until 1842, with the Seminole getting pushed further and further south. Osceola died on August 14, 1842, by which time the United States had spent between $20–$40 million on the war.

On March 3, 1845, Florida became the twenty-seventh state of the United States of America.

Florida in the Civil War

In 1845 when Florida became a state, the population was approximately 140,000. Of these, 63,000 were African-Americans, most of whom were slaves. Florida also had its share of free Blacks, who were descendants of Spanish citizens of African ancestry. When Florida became a state, it was a slave state.

Following Abraham Lincoln's election in 1860, Florida joined other Southern states in seceding from the Union. Secession took place January 10, 1861, and after less than a month as an independent republic, Florida became one of the founding members of the Confederate States of America. Because Florida was an important supply route for the Confederate Army, Union forces operated a blockade around the entire state. Union troops occupied major ports such as Cedar Key, Jacksonville, Key West, and Pensacola.

After Florida joined the other Confederate states and seceded from the Union, Confederate soldiers demanded that the Union soldiers stationed at **Fort Pickens** surrender. The Union soldiers refused to leave the fort, and a battle between the two lasted until the early part of 1862. Finally, the Confederate troops withdrew and the Union occupied Pensacola for the rest of the war. On February 20, 1864, the largest Civil War battle in Florida occurred near Lake City. It was called the **Battle of Olustee,** and it took the Confederacy six hours to win it. The Union Army sought to cut off Confederate supply lines. Confederate troops under the command of General Joseph Finnegan blocked the Union advance and sent them back toward Jacksonville. Almost 3,000 of the 11,100 who fought the battle were killed. Another large battle in Florida took place near Tallahassee, which resulted in Tallahassee being the only Confederate capital east of the Mississippi River that was not seized by Union troops. Major General John Newton landed U.S. Navy ships at the mouth of St. Marks River. They had trouble getting up the river, so the soldiers marched northeast to Tallahassee. A small Confederate militia group burned a bridge in their path so that the Union soldiers could not cross the river. The Union soldiers pressed on, and the two groups met at the Natural Bridge, a place where the river goes underground for a short distance. The Confederates were able to protect the natural crossing and push the Union soldiers back. The Union soldiers quickly retreated to their ships.

An estimated 16,000 Floridians fought in the Civil War. Most were in the Confederacy, but approximately 2,000 joined the Union army. Some Floridians didn't want to fight for either side, so they hid out in the woods and swamps to avoid being drafted. The Floridian soldiers were organized into eleven regiments of infantry, two cavalry, and numerous small units. Florida employed some groups dubbed the **Cow Cavalry** to protect the small towns and cattle ranches in the inner part of Florida. Numerous small battles occurred, and the Cow Cavalry met challenges. The group also helped keep the Confederate army supplied with food from Florida. With the war nearing its end, the Florida governor, John Milton, who had earlier declared that he would prefer death over having to rejoin the Union, saw the writing on the wall and killed himself on April 1, 1865. Florida was ordered to surrender just a few weeks later, on April 26. On May 10, 1865, Union Brigadier General Edward McCook and his staff entered Tallahassee and established federal control and authority over Florida. On May 20, the formal transfer of power began, and slaves were freed in Florida.

Florida under Reconstruction

After meeting the requirements of Reconstruction, including ratifying amendments to the U.S. Constitution, Florida was readmitted to the United States on July 25, 1868.

Florida had not suffered much damage during the war, and it became a popular tourist destination when railroads expanded into the area. Railroad magnate **Henry Plant** built a luxury hotel in Tampa, which later became the campus for the University of Tampa. **Henry Flagler** built the **Florida East Coast Railway** from Jacksonville to Key West and constructed numerous luxury hotels along the route, including in the cities of Saint Augustine, Ormond Beach, and West Palm Beach.

In February 1888, Florida had a special tourist: **President Grover Cleveland**, accompanied by his wife and members of his staff. He visited the Subtropical Exposition in Jacksonville where he gave a speech supporting tourism to the state; then he took a train to Saint Augustine, met Henry Flagler, and then continued by train to Titusville, where he boarded a steamboat and visited Rock Ledge. On his return trip, he visited Sanford and Winter Park.

Florida during the Booming Years

The 1920s were a prosperous time for much of the nation. Florida's new railroads opened up large areas to development, spurring a **Florida land boom**. Investors, mostly from outside Florida, raced to buy and sell rapidly appreciating land in new communities, such as Miami and Palm Beach. Most of the people who bought land in Florida did so without stepping foot in the state, by hiring people to speculate and buy the land for them. By 1925, the market ran out of buyers to pay the high prices, and soon the boom became a bust. The **1926 Miami hurricane** further depressed the real estate market. Florida also was able to take advantage of the railroads to boost its **citrus industry**. Citrus fruits became the staple of the Florida economy.

Florida in the Great Depression and the New Deal

The Great Depression arrived in 1929, but by that time, economic decay already consumed much of Florida. Roosevelt's New Deal helped Florida when the Civilian Conservation Corps, or CCC, employed about 40,000 boys and cut down millions of trees to build fire lines. They also planted 13 million trees, created many of the state parks and wildlife preserves, built federal buildings and schools, and rebuilt the Overseas Railroad connecting Miami to Key West. This line would serve to bring tourism to Key West.

Florida's first theme parks emerged in the 1930s, including **Cypress Gardens** (1936) near Winter Haven and **Marineland** (1938) near Saint Augustine.

Florida During World War II

The military took advantage of Florida's warm climate and vacant land and throughout the 1930s built 172 military installations, including 40 airfields. By 1942, America's training facilities in Florida were so overcrowded that they had to take over many hotels and motels throughout Florida. Some places were used as barracks and others as makeshift hospitals for injured military personnel sent home from overseas.

Off the coast of Florida, German U-Boats sank more than 24 ships and many burning ships could be seen from many areas along the coast. In late February 1942, German spies came on shore near Jacksonville with a plan to blow up railroad lines, but they were caught before they had a chance to accomplish their mission.

After this incident, the **Civil Air Patrol** was organized in March 1942, to protect the coasts of Florida. Dubbed the "Mosquito Fleet," they helped protect the coastlines of Florida and eliminated the threat from submarines.

Florida and Space

Because of Florida's low latitude, it was chosen in 1949 as a test site for the country's nascent missile program. **Patrick Air Force Base** and the **Cape Canaveral** launch site began to take shape in the 1950s. By the early 1960s, the space race was in full swing and generated a huge boom in the communities around Cape Canaveral. Fully engaged in a space race with the Soviet Union, Cape Canaveral became a centerpiece not only in the science program but also as a part of foreign policy.

In 1958, the **National Aeronautics and Space Administration**, NASA, was created to conduct space operations. Kennedy's 1961 pledge that the United States would "put a man on the moon" before the end of the decade fueled interest and funding to NASA's space program. On February 20, 1962, **John Glenn** became the first American to go into orbit. In 1963, NASA acquired almost 90,000 acres on Merritt Island near the Cape, which became the headquarters of the American space industry. In that complex, the astronauts were trained and the space rockets were built. When President Kennedy was assassinated later in the year, the Cape's name was changed to Cape Kennedy, but it was later changed back to Cape Canaveral. However, the complex was renamed the **Kennedy Space Center**. The space program continued to expand with the Apollo Program. The Apollo Program finally fulfilled the promise made by Kennedy when, on July 20, 1969, **Neil Armstrong** stepped on the surface of the moon and said, "That's one small step for man, one

Competency 5: U.S. History

giant leap for mankind." Visits to the moon continued as NASA continued to redesign itself and its mission. The space shuttle program began in the 1970s, flourished in the 1980s, and made Florida once again the center of attention as this new spacecraft concept made space travel less of a dream and more of a reality. Attending launches became an exciting experience for Floridians and other Americans. Throughout the state, people could stand outside their homes and watch the shuttle go into space.

Florida, Disney, and Tourism

Walt Disney chose central Florida as the site of his planned **Walt Disney World Resort** in the 1960s and began purchasing land.

In 1971, the first component of the resort, the Magic Kingdom, opened and began the dramatic transformation of the Orlando area into a resort destination with a wide variety of theme parks. Besides Disney World, the Orlando area today features Universal Orlando, Sea World, and the Orlando Eye. The economic windfall that came with Disney created many side industries and made tourism one of the top industries in the state.

CHAPTER 6

Social Science

COMPETENCY 6.1

Identify social science disciplines (e.g., anthropology, psychology, sociology).

Social science is a collection of disciplines concerned with the study of human aspects of the world. It emerged as a separate field in the middle of the nineteenth century. Each of these disciplines draws upon empirical, quantitative, and qualitative methods to understand it. While each of the social sciences explores one line of inquiry with regard to humans, each also borrows or acquires knowledge from another field. In this respect, no social science discipline can be completely studied in isolation. The social science disciplines include the following fields of study:

- **Anthropology** has been called "the most scientific of the humanities, and the most humanistic of the sciences." Anthropology is a science of the entire panorama of humankind, from human origins to contemporary life. Anthropology's holistic perspective requires that anthropologists study all facets of society and culture, including tools, techniques, traditions, language, beliefs, kinships, values, social institutions, economic mechanisms, cravings for beauty and art, and struggles for prestige. Anthropology describes the impact of humans on other humans. There are four major fields within the discipline: archaeological, biological, linguistic, and sociocultural anthropology. Anthropologists conduct field-based research and also use archival investigations and laboratory analyses. Some anthropologists use **ethnography** to study a particular culture. They involve themselves as participant observers, conducting their study from the viewpoint of that culture. They live for an extended time in the culture and interact as a member of it; they also systematically collect data and make observations, which they later describe. Ethnography provides an "insider's view" of

307

the experience of the culture, rather than a view of the culture based on the observations of individuals within the culture.

- **Civics** is the branch of political science that examines civic affairs and the rights and duties of citizenship. It focuses on the role of citizens in a government.

- **Economics** is the social science that studies how people choose to use limited or scarce resources to obtain maximum satisfaction of unlimited wants. It looks at the production, distribution, and consumption of goods and services. Macroeconomics is the study of the economy as a whole. Some of the topics considered include inflation, unemployment, and economic growth. Microeconomics is the study of the individual parts that make up the economy, such as households, business firms, and government agencies. Microeconomics emphasizes how these units make decisions, as well as the consequences of the decisions.

- **Education** is the social science field concerned with the pedagogy of teaching and learning.

- **Geography** is the study of Earth's surface, including such aspects as Earth's climate, topography, vegetation, and population. It is a spatial discipline, one in which geographers preoccupy themselves with how to organize space. There are four main branches of geography: human, physical, regional, and topical/systematic. Geographers may specialize in a variety of subfields that break off of the four branches of geography, but all of them have as their focus the spatial perspective. **Population geography** is a form of geography that deals with the relationships between geography and population patterns, including birth and death rates. **Political geography** deals with the effect of geography on politics, especially on national boundaries and relations between states. **Economic geography** is a study of the interaction between the Earth's landscape and the economic activity of the human population.

- **History**, derived from the Greek word *historia*, which means "information" or "an inquiry designed to elicit truth," is the study of political, economic, social, and cultural aspects of the past through the use of material, oral, and written sources. One line of inquiry that historians follow is to examine how the past affects our views of the present. Likewise, historians today acknowledge that the experiences of class, gender, race, ethnicity, and age affect not only our understanding of what happened in the past, but also what the past was. Historians use almost all of the social science fields to round out their understanding of what happened in the past and how we should interpret it today.

- **Political science** is the study of the principles of government, the manner in which government conducts itself, how we identify ourselves as citizens of a particular nation, how we participate in our political structure and how it affects us, and what motivates us to affiliate ourselves with certain points of view or parties. Political science reveals the relationships underlying political events and conditions.

Competency 6: Social Science

- **Sociology** is the study of human interaction, specifically how groups influence individual values, norms, and sanctions. Because individuals belong to multiple groups, each whose values, behaviors, and sanctions are not static and are socially constructed, sociologists examine the rules and processes that bind and separate these individuals and groups. Sociologists then study a range of human social relationships, social interaction, and culture, from how two people interact, to how nations and corporations interact with one another. Sociologists are especially interested in customs, traditions, and values that emerge from group experience and in the way the groups are affected by the customs, traditions, and values. Sociologists tend to draw heavily from the other social science disciplines of anthropology and psychology.

- **Psychology** is the scientific and systematic study of mental processes and/or behavior. Psychologists study directly observable behaviors that may include talking, eating, and acting a certain way. They also study things that cannot be so readily observed, like dreams, thinking, emotions, and the way physiology impacts behavior. There are a variety of subfields in psychology that include specialties in these areas: clinical, counseling, school, industrial-organizational, experimental, social, developmental, and psychometric.

COMPETENCY 6.2

Identify social science concepts (e.g., culture, class, technology, race, gender).

In order to effectively teach social studies, teachers need to understand and use the concepts and themes of social studies. A **concept** is an abstract product gleaned from analysis and synthesis of facts and experiences, rather than a simple, straightforward definition that can be memorized. Concepts are also dynamic constructs; they can expand as students grow and incorporate new experiences into their existing conceptual frameworks.

There are several ways to organize and identify key social studies concepts. The National Council for the Social Studies (NCSS) calls the main concepts "thematic strands" (*found at http://www.socialstudies.org/standards/strands*). The NCSS suggests that these concepts consist of the following:

- Culture
- Time, Continuity, and Change
- People, Places, and Environments
- Individuals, Groups, and Institutions
- Power, Authority, and Governance
- Production, Distribution, and Consumption

- Science, Technology, and Society
- Global Connections
- Civic Ideals and Practices

The problem with this approach is that it looks at social studies concepts as ideas that do not have wider explanations or theories, and it does not use multiple social science disciplines to further develop an idea. For example, in teaching about continuity and change, ideas within that theme (e.g., reform, revolution, progress) would also need to be addressed.

Another way to organize social studies concepts is by discipline, and to look at some of the major ideas on which each discipline tends to focus. Below, you will find brief definitions of some of the major social science concepts arranged by discipline.

History

Arts and Ideas: Societies have used various forms of art, such as dance, music, visual arts, literature, and theater, to express their beliefs, identity, and philosophical ideas. Art and ideas unite and motivate societies. Art may reflect conflict, celebratory occasions, or other events that define and/or divide a society.

Belief Systems: Religious, political, and philosophical systems help organize societies, and also shape the way societies act and react to both internal and external situations. For example, religious beliefs have informed art, war, and legal systems, and have shaped political, cultural, and social identities.

Change: The basic alterations and transitions in things, events, and ideas.

Conflict: A clash of ideas, interests, beliefs, agendas, objectives, or wills that results from forces that have incompatible ideas.

Choice: The ability, right, or power to select from a range of alternatives.

Continuity: How things remain the same.

Culture: The patterns of civilization, achievements, and customs of the people of a particular time and place and how they transmit these ideas to succeeding generations.

Diversity: Understanding, respecting, and appreciating others and oneself, as well as learning how to relate to those qualities and conditions that are different from our own. Diversity celebrates differentiation in kind and degree within language, cognitive style, disability, gender, education, socioeconomic class, geographic background, language, physical appearance, religion, sexual orientation, and other human characteristics and traits.

Competency 6: Social Science

Empathy: One's ability to understand others by thinking of how one would act if one were in the same situation.

Identity: The state or condition of being a certain thing. Identity plays a central role in history in terms of cultural, social, and political identity. To a large degree, identity may be constituted both internally and externally. Identity, or the perception of self and nation, plays a significant part in the formation and interpretation of history.

Interdependence: Reliance upon others in mutually beneficial interactions and exchanges.

Imperialism: The system and pursuit of empire through a process of accumulation and acquisition of land, resources, labor, and profits. Imperialism relies on an ideology that suggests certain people need domination or assistance in becoming civilized.

Migration: The voluntary and/or involuntary transport of peoples, goods, and ideas from one place to another. Migration has transformed and defined empires and nations, altering the social, political, and cultural landscape.

Movement of People and Goods: The constant exchange of people, ideas, products, technologies, and institutions from one region or civilization to another that has existed throughout history.

Nation-state: A political entity that provides a sovereign territory for a specific nation in which people are tied together through their citizenship (which might be linked to common language, ethnicity, race, ancestry, culture, etc.).

Nationalism: At its most basic, nationalism means the common identity for groups of humans. Nationalism may reflect the feelings of pride in and devotion to one's country. It also could mean the desire of a people to control their own government, free from foreign interference or rule.

Science and Technology: Technological development from the creation of tools and fire to space exploration has shaped not only a country's military, economy, and social culture, but also how it relates to the environment and belief systems.

Society: The complex pattern of political, economic, cultural, and social relationships that bind people to a society. The establishment of social classes affects not only the customs and norms of a society but also the way it organizes itself politically, militarily, and economically.

Urbanization: Movement of people from rural to urban areas.

Geography

The essential elements of geography:

The World in Spatial Terms: Geography maps the relationships between people, places, and environments by structuring the knowledge of them into real and mental maps, and then conducting a spatial analysis of that information. So, maps become a primary tool that geographers use in order to present, acquire, process, and decipher information in spatial terms.

Places and Regions: Place and region are basic units of geography. Geographers examine the physical and human characteristics of places to understand how places work. They also trace people's perceptions of areas, how people create their own mental regions that come from their own view of the world, and how these perceptions or biases are created and organized.

Physical Systems: Physical processes shape Earth's surface and interact with plant and animal life to create, sustain, and modify ecosystems. This element of geography looks at environmental phenomena and the interaction through ecosystems, renewable resources, and the water cycle.

Human Systems: People are central to geography in that human activities help shape Earth's surface and the human settlements and structures that are part of Earth's surface, and humans compete for control of Earth's surface. This element looks at characteristics, distribution, and migration of human populations. It also tries to find patterns—in culture, economic interdependence, human settlement, conflict, and cooperation—and determine how these patterns influence people's relationship with each other and the Earth.

Environment and Society: Humans modify Earth's environment through their actions. Such actions happen largely as a consequence of the way people value or devalue the Earth's resources.

The Uses of Geography: Geography informs people about the relationships they have between place and environments over time. This element explores how humans modify the physical environment, how physical systems affect human systems, and how the changes occur in the meaning, use, distribution, and importance of resources.

Environment: The surroundings, including natural elements and elements created by humans.

Geography and Environment: The elements of nature (heat, cold, rain, snow, etc.) undoubtedly influence the way and extent to which a society develops. People's attempts to modify their environment and adapt both themselves and the environment to meet their needs shape the course of human history. The geography and environment of a people impact their political, cultural, economic, social, and religious beliefs and the way that they organize themselves.

Competency 6: Social Science

Economics

Needs and Wants: Needs are essential goods and services that people need to survive, such as food, clothing, and shelter; whereas, the goods and services that people would like to have to improve their lives are wants, such as education, fancy clothing, health care, gym memberships, and entertainment.

Economic Systems: The way that a society allocates available resources and creates new ones shape the development of economic systems. Economic systems, from the simple bartering system to the more complex development of global capitalism, have shaped political and social systems. The development, exchange, and expansion of goods, markets, products, and ideas influence historical events both within and between societies.

Factors of Production: Resources necessary for production, like land, labor, capital, and enterprise.

Scarcity: Economic conflict when people have unlimited wants and needs, but limited resources.

Science and Technology: The tools and methods used by people to get what they need and want.

Civics

Justice: The fair, equal, proportional, or appropriate treatment rendered to individuals in interpersonal, societal, or governmental interactions.

Citizenship: Membership in a community (neighborhood, school, region, state, nation, or world) gained by meeting the legal requirements of national, state, or local governments with its accompanying rights, responsibilities, and dispositions.

Political Systems such as monarchies, dictatorships, and democracies address certain basic questions of government, such as: What should a government have the power to do? What should a government not have the power to do? A political system also provides for ways that parts of that system interrelate and combine to perform specific functions of government.

Power: The ability of people to compel or influence the actions of others. "Legitimate power is called authority."

Government: Organization, agency, and institutions through which a political unit exercises authority, controls and administers public policy, directs and controls the actions of its members, and develops and maintains lawmaking and law enforcement.

Government and Civics: The way that societies are governed and the authority by which to govern remains a central theme of historical inquiry.

Civic Values: Those principles that serve as the foundation for our democratic form of government. These values include justice, honesty, self-discipline, due process, equality, majority rule with respect for minority rights, and respect for self, others, and property.

Human Rights: Those basic political, economic, and social rights that all human beings are entitled to, such as the right to life, liberty, and the security of person; and a standard of living that is adequate for the health and well-being of himself and of his family.

COMPETENCY 6.3

Analyze the interrelationships between social science disciplines.

People are complex. Since social science involves society and people within the society, an almost infinite number of relationships can exist among the social science disciplines. For example, what relationships might exist between education and economics? Economics might determine the kind of education a person receives. Education might affect the amount of money a person can earn and how that person spends that money on needs and wants. A community's education level might affect the kinds of businesses that it attracts. Fewer businesses in a community mean that there is less tax money to support education. If there are few good employers, people have less opportunity to get a good job and pay income taxes that support education. Should schools provide additional services (food, clothing, health care) for children from lower-income families?

Adding other disciplines to the discussion increases the complexity. How does psychology interrelate with economics and education? Do the behaviors of people with high incomes and education differ from the behaviors of those who have lower incomes and education? How do people view others with varying levels of income or education? What about political science? Is there a relationship between political views and education, or between political views and economic level? How do people with one political perspective feel about others?

COMPETENCY 6.4

Interpret tabular and graphic representations of information related to the social sciences.

A **table** is a visual arrangement of data or information for identification of facts, trends, and comparisons. In the social sciences, tables often illustrate the results of research and data analysis. Tables can differ significantly in variety, structure, flexibility, notation, representation, and use. There is always a title for the table that tells you what the subject is—this should give you a frame of reference for the information within it. A table contains an ordered arrangement of rows and columns, and one of them, at least, should have a row and/or column devoted to the **header**, which displays the names or labels for the content. Make sure on the exam that you identify the header

Competency 6: Social Science

so you can better interpret and understand the information you are being asked to analyze. The information in a table is organized in rows and columns, usually two or more of each. The columns run vertically, and the rows are in the horizontal position.

The table below (Table 6.1) is a partial display of a complex table of population data from the United States Census Bureau. Of import in reading the table is the parenthetic notation "numbers in thousands" in the title and the reference numbers in superscript in the title and the data. Any analysis of the data would require the discussion of the numbers in the context of thousands. For instance, the total number of people under discussion, both men and women, is 299,106,000, or 299 million, 106 thousand people. In addition, analysis of the table information would take into account the inclusion of armed forces personnel and their families on post, whether overseas or stateside (footnote 1) and the definition of Hispanic (footnote 2).

Table 6.1
Population by Sex, Age, Hispanic Origin, and Race: 2008

(Numbers in thousands. Civilian non-institutionalized population[1])

Sex and age	Total Hispanic		Hispanic origin and race[2]							
			Total		Non-Hispanic					
					White alone		All other races			
	Number	Percent	Number	Percent	Number	Percent	Number	Percent	Number	Percent
Both sexes	299,106	100.0	46,026	100.0	253,079	100.0	196,768	100.0	56,312	100.0
Under 5 years	20,902	7.0	5,014	10.9	15,888	6.3	11,210	5.7	4,678	8.3
5 to 9 years	20,018	6.7	4,336	9.4	15,682	6.2	11,283	5.7	4,400	7.8
10 to 14 years	20,038	6.7	3,986	8.7	16,052	6.3	11,641	5.9	4,410	7.8
15 to 19 years	21,314	7.1	3,799	8.3	17,515	6.9	12,813	6.5	4,702	8.3
20 to 24 years	20,529	6.9	3,617	7.9	16,912	6.7	12,742	6.5	4,170	7.4
25 to 29 years	21,057	7.0	4,275	9.3	16,782	6.6	12,544	6.4	4,238	7.5
30 to 34 years	19,089	6.4	3,861	8.4	15,227	6.0	11,307	5.7	3,920	7.0
35 to 44 years	42,132	14.1	6,904	15.0	35,228	13.9	27,046	13.7	8,182	14.5
45 to 54 years	43,935	14.7	4,887	10.6	39,048	15.4	31,331	15.9	7,717	13.7
55 to 64 years	33,302	11.1	2,792	6.1	30,510	12.1	25,409	12.9	5,101	9.1
65 to 74 years	19,588	6.5	1,530	3.3	18,058	7.1	15,226	7.7	2,832	5.0
75 to 84 years	12,913	4.3	791	1.7	12,122	4.8	10,616	5.4	1,505	2.7
85 years and over	4,289	1.4	234	0.5	4,055	1.6	3,600	1.8	455	0.8

1 Plus armed forces living off post or with their families on post.
2 Hispanic refers to people whose origin is Mexican, Puerto Rican, Cuban, Spanish-speaking Central or South American countries, or other Hispanic/Latino, regardless of race.
Source: U.S. Census Bureau, Current Population Survey, Annual Social and Economic Supplement, 2008. Internet release date: September 2009.

FTCE Social Science 6–12

Information graphics or infographics are graphic visual representations of information, data, or knowledge. These graphics present complex information quickly and compactly. You might see them used in subway maps (as in the London Underground map displayed below), journalism, signs, education, and technical manuals. These are usually good ways to communicate difficult concepts that people would become lost in if they were written out in text format.

**Figure 6.1
London Underground Map**

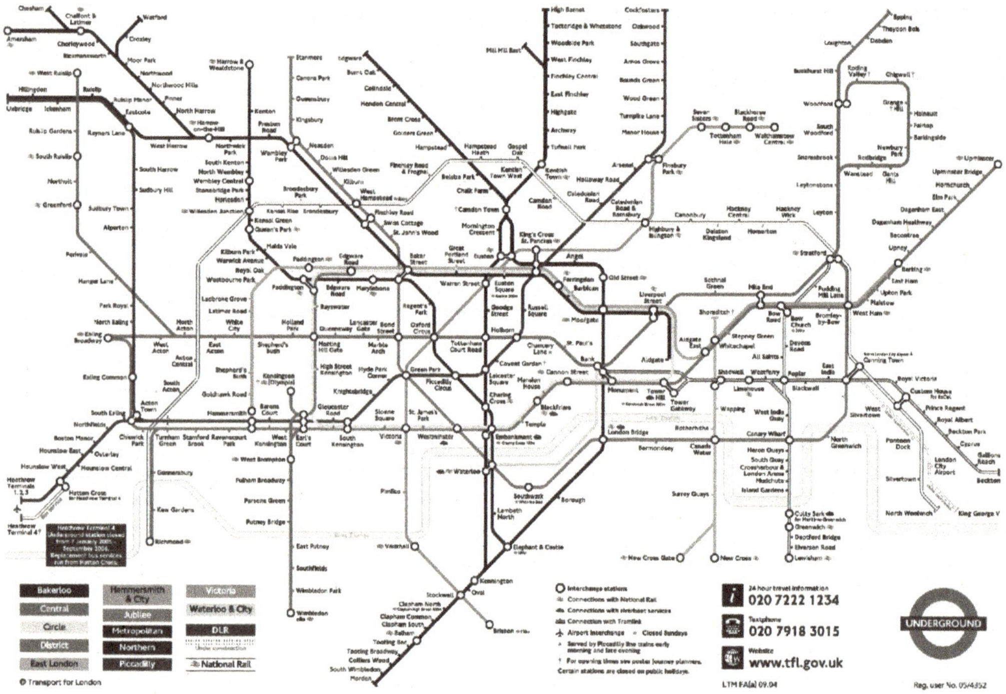

COMPETENCY 6.5

Identify appropriate strategies, methods, tools, and technologies for the teaching of social science.

Considering the breadth of state social studies standards that students are expected to know each year, teaching social science today mandates that teachers *avoid* teaching the subject as "just another long parade of facts." Teachers must provide learning experiences that result in meaningful learning by having students relate the facts and concepts that they learn to their understanding about how the world works. Content, therefore, should be integrative, and lessons should enable students to learn actively. Students have to make connections to the material and between the material that they are taught, not only in one year, but in year after year. The goal of Florida's social science curriculum is to enable students to acquire the knowledge, skill, and judgment to

Competency 6: Social Science

learn independently; to engage students as citizen actors so that they can engage in civic life in an intelligent and responsible manner, and to make decisions about local, national, and international issues; to appreciate and use historical and cultural resources, such as historic sites, museums, parks, libraries, and multimedia information sources to enrich their lives and expand their understanding of the social sciences throughout their lives. Some of the strategies, methods, tools, and technologies below can help in the teaching of social science.

The Florida Department of Education defines Florida's CPALMS (Curriculum Planning and Learning Management System; *http://www.cpalms.org/Public/*) as an online toolbox of information, vetted resources, and interactive tools that helps educators effectively implement teaching standards. It provides excellent content and ideas for teaching and learning by subject area. It also provides resources for students and parents to use.

Strategies and Methods to Teach Social Science

Develop Metacognition: Students need to be taught how to think about thinking. This involves awareness and control of cognitive processes. Students need to find methods that help improve their organizational capabilities so they can learn (i.e., having a physical or digital folder to put work in, using a graphic organizer before writing, having an agenda book to note all of their assignments in, knowing how to organize files and content online). There are a variety of ways to develop metacognition in students:

- *Explain strategies that a student can use:* Detail, out loud, how one might solve a problem, organize an essay, or prepare for a test.

- *Clarify why particular strategies are helpful and useful:* Help students develop **conditional knowledge** by letting them know what works, when, and why.

- *Clarify and model thinking and fix-up strategies:* Show students how you learn something, and then learn something together. It helps to verbalize what you are thinking and how to solve a problem. Students benefit by seeing you make errors along the way and use a fix-up strategy (e.g., rereading; read ahead for clarification; check for meaning of words in context, make connections with what is already known) to repair understanding.

Help students to come up with their own plan to use metacognition to ask and answer the following questions:

- What do I already know or understand about this subject, topic, or issue?

- Do I understand what I am supposed to know?

- Do I know where I can find some information to add to my knowledge?

- How much time will it take me to learn this new knowledge?

- What are some strategies and tactics that I can use to learn more about this?

- Did I understand what I just heard, read, or saw?
- How will I know if I am learning this new knowledge too quickly, too slowly, or just right?
- How can I spot a mistake if I make one?
- How should I revise my plan to learn this new knowledge if what I am doing is not working?

Activate Prior Knowledge: Learning happens when new information is added to old information and ideas. Some ways to activate prior knowledge are:

Brainstorming: This can be done in groups or individually.

Pre-reading or Surveying: Examining the learning outcomes, terms, major and minor headings prior to reading helps students determine what they already know about a topic.

Direct Instruction: Provide instruction direction, as in a lecture, explaining a new skill, providing baseline information, or modeling a thinking process.

Promote Critical Thinking: Thinking is interesting. Memorization is boring. Social studies is the story of people and their lives. The students of today will be part of the story of tomorrow. When students experience social studies as a real-world, authentic process that involves and affects their lives on a daily basis, they will find it more engaging than dates and facts about people, times, and places to which they have no connections.

- **Higher-Order Questioning:** Questions shape thinking. Bloom's Taxonomy and Webb's Depth of Knowledge are two methods teachers can use to plan and structure thinking.

Bloom's Taxonomy is a hierarchy of thinking skills originally developed by Benjamin Bloom in the 1950s, and revised in the 1990s. The old version emphasized thinking as a product, while the new version focuses more on thinking as an active process. Additionally, the revised version switches the top two levels. In teaching social studies, a teacher's focus should be on higher levels. Examples of lower-level questions would be *What are the first ten amendments to the Constitution called?* or *What is the capital of Florida?* Questions that include basic facts but focus on more higher-level thinking might be *How might the United States be different without the Bill of Rights?* or *What geographic conditions contributed to the selection of Tallahassee as the capital of Florida?*

Also, in the 1990s, Norman Webb created the Depth of Knowledge (DOK) Model to help analyze the thinking expectations for standards, assessments, and curricular activities. Like Bloom's Taxonomy, the DOK model can be used to help teachers identify questions that encourage higher levels of thinking.

Competency 6: Social Science

BLOOM'S COGNITIVE TAXONOMY

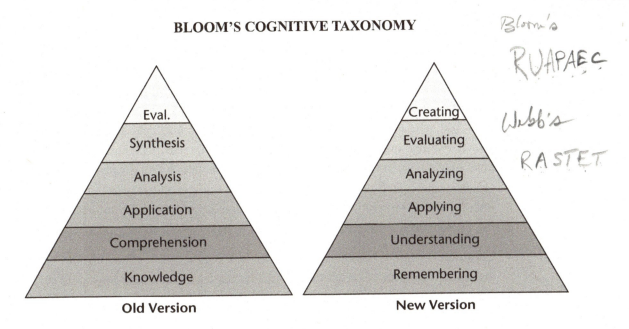

Old Version | New Version

Webb's Depth of Knowledge Model

Extended Thinking Making connections among concepts, high cognitive demands, complex reasoning. Create an ad campaign that would convince people to support a new tax to prevent beach erosion.
Strategic Thinking Reasoning (e.g., planning, sequencing, identifying more than one reasonable approach). Why is it important to reduce erosion on Florida's coastlines?
Skill/Concept Using or applying facts or concepts, two or more steps. What weather and land conditions contribute to erosion?
Recall/Reproduction Remembering factual information or procedures. Example: What is *erosion*?

- **Collaborative Processes:** Having students work together to solve a problem, present an idea, or develop a project builds skills that are helpful in a democracy. Collaborative work can help students retain information better, and it teaches them how to work with others. Collaborative and reflective discussions in both face-to-face and digital formats are ways to promote critical thinking and engagement.

- **Inquiry Teaching:** Teach students how to use the scientific method of inquiry by having them ask and answer key issues. Teaching inquiry involves the following steps: identify and clarify an issue; propose a hypothesis; locate, collect, and organize the data or evidence information they receive; evaluate, interpret, and analyze the data; then, finally, draw inferences and conclusions about the data and use this information to make generalizations. This way, students generate their own knowledge.

- **Problem-Solving through Inductive and Deductive Reasoning:** The underlying processes for problem-solving involve the teaching of facts, concepts, and generalizations. Reasoning inductively is using known facts to come to a generalization or conclusion. Reasoning deductively takes the opposite approach by starting with a generalization, and then identifying the details or facts from it. Concepts rely on facts, but facts are meaningless unless they relate to concepts and generalizations. Generalizations organize and summarize information obtained from an analysis of facts. While a generalization contains a broad assertion, a fact is only a truth about a particular incident. Students use facts, concepts, and generalizations in the process to finding solutions to problems, rather than memorization of isolated information. Case studies and webquests can be used to foster problem-solving skills.

- **Community-Based Instruction:** This method uses real-life situations and settings to explain a concept or enrich curriculum. Examples include field trips, field studies, mentoring/apprenticeships, and service learning.

Tools and Technologies to Teach Social Sciences

Fortunately for social studies teachers, many aspects of the social studies curriculum lend themselves quite well toward the integration of technology in the classroom. Using Florida State Standards as your guide, you can use some of the following applications of technology in your classroom to make it come alive for the students:

Web 2.0 Tools: Web 2.0 tools are online tools with which users create and share content. While most people might think of them in terms of social media, they can also include information curation (e.g., Storify), role play (e.g., Fakebook), infographics (e.g., Piktochart), quiz generators (Quizlet; Kahoot), digital sticky notes (e.g., Zazzle) concept mapping (Bubble.us) and more (see *http://webtools4u2use.wikispaces.com/*). These tools allow students to engage directly with content in digital formats.

Virtual Environments and Simulations: Virtual displays from museums around the world (e.g., Library of Congress (*https://loc.gov/*); United States Holocaust Museum (*https://www.ushmm.org/information/exhibitions/online-exhibitions*), as well as simulations, such as Oregon Trail (*https://archive.org/details/msdos_Oregon_Trail_The_1990*) or Annenberg Classroom (*http://www.annenbergclassroom.org/page/all-games-and-interactives*) help students make events from the past, present, or hypothetical come alive. Simulations help them engage in problem-solving in real-world contexts.

Presentations: Teachers can use **PowerPoint** effectively (not a lot of words on a slide, and good use of graphics and images) to bolster lectures, and students can learn how to use them to consolidate and present their own research papers. **Prezi** offers another type of presentation tool to excite student learning.

Competency 6: Social Science

VoiceThread allows the teacher or student to add comments in a variety of modes, including text, audio, and video.

Spreadsheets: Programs such as Microsoft Excel allow students to collect, organize, manipulate, and display data and information.

Atlases and Maps: Tools like Google Earth can display places around the world in multiple ways which allow students to answer questions about geography, mapping, and history.

Digital Projects: The Internet allows students to conduct research: accessing databases of journals and newspapers, sifting through information, verifying content, and citing information.

COMPETENCY 6.6

Evaluate examples of primary (e.g., letters, photographs, political cartoons) and secondary (e.g., historical texts, encyclopedias) sources.

Historians use two types of sources: primary sources and secondary sources. The distinction between these two types of sources is the author's proximity to an event. Primary sources are documents, oral histories, or physical objects that were created during the period being studied or immediately after it. The idea is that the primary sources reflect an insider's understanding of an event, or "firsthand knowledge" of an event. Examples of primary sources are: original documents, diaries, personal narratives, speeches, government records, letters, interviews, autobiographies, pottery, buildings, recordings of the event, clothing, novels, newspaper articles (written soon after an event), photographs, manuscripts, original theatrical or literary works, coins, stamps, and even tombstones.

Secondary sources are one step removed from an event, and they contain someone's impressions, judgments, and interpretations of primary material or an event. Secondary sources include: history textbooks, journal articles, documentaries, books written about a period of time, encyclopedias, histories, and biographies.

Whether approaching either a primary or secondary source, historians must learn how to properly analyze a document. Historians should consider how, when, and where a document was created, as it might have a tremendous effect on what was actually recorded. As all sources have bias, historians need to try to uncover how bias has affected the source. They should consider how close in time and location to a certain event a source was created. What was the intention of a document? Was it meant for private or public consumption?

Because bias is present in all sources, some sources might be considered more reliable than others. In addition, of course, each historian might have a different opinion based on his or her own biases about what is "reliable" or not. This process can pose some thorny questions, such as: Is an eyewitness to an event more or less reliable? Could eyewitnesses have been so consumed with emotion that their view or understanding of an event was skewed? Should the historian rely on a source that was meant for public consumption, or instead one that was more private? Which would be more truthful?

To make matters even more confusing, sometimes secondary sources are also primary sources. For instance, if you were writing a paper looking at how a particular author has written history, that author's history books would then become your primary sources. The designation of whether a source is primary or secondary is largely determined by how the author intends to use the source.

Practice Test 1

FTCE Social Science 6–12

Also available at the REA Study Center (www.rea.com/studycenter)

This practice test is also offered online at the REA Study Center. Since the FTCE Social Science 6-12 exam is administered on computer, we recommend that you take the online version of the test to receive these added benefits:

- **Timed testing conditions**—Gauge how much time you can spend on each question.

- **Automatic scoring**—Find out how you did on the test, instantly.

- **On-screen detailed explanations of answers**—Learn not just the correct answers, but also why the other answer choices are incorrect.

- **Diagnostic score reports**—Pinpoint where you're strongest and where you need to focus your study.

ANSWER SHEET FOR PRACTICE TEST 1

1. Ⓐ Ⓑ Ⓒ Ⓓ
2. Ⓐ Ⓑ Ⓒ Ⓓ
3. Ⓐ Ⓑ Ⓒ Ⓓ
4. Ⓐ Ⓑ Ⓒ Ⓓ
5. Ⓐ Ⓑ Ⓒ Ⓓ
6. Ⓐ Ⓑ Ⓒ Ⓓ
7. Ⓐ Ⓑ Ⓒ Ⓓ
8. Ⓐ Ⓑ Ⓒ Ⓓ
9. Ⓐ Ⓑ Ⓒ Ⓓ
10. Ⓐ Ⓑ Ⓒ Ⓓ
11. Ⓐ Ⓑ Ⓒ Ⓓ
12. Ⓐ Ⓑ Ⓒ Ⓓ
13. Ⓐ Ⓑ Ⓒ Ⓓ
14. Ⓐ Ⓑ Ⓒ Ⓓ
15. Ⓐ Ⓑ Ⓒ Ⓓ
16. Ⓐ Ⓑ Ⓒ Ⓓ
17. Ⓐ Ⓑ Ⓒ Ⓓ
18. Ⓐ Ⓑ Ⓒ Ⓓ
19. Ⓐ Ⓑ Ⓒ Ⓓ
20. Ⓐ Ⓑ Ⓒ Ⓓ
21. Ⓐ Ⓑ Ⓒ Ⓓ
22. Ⓐ Ⓑ Ⓒ Ⓓ
23. Ⓐ Ⓑ Ⓒ Ⓓ
24. Ⓐ Ⓑ Ⓒ Ⓓ
25. Ⓐ Ⓑ Ⓒ Ⓓ
26. Ⓐ Ⓑ Ⓒ Ⓓ
27. Ⓐ Ⓑ Ⓒ Ⓓ
28. Ⓐ Ⓑ Ⓒ Ⓓ
29. Ⓐ Ⓑ Ⓒ Ⓓ
30. Ⓐ Ⓑ Ⓒ Ⓓ
31. Ⓐ Ⓑ Ⓒ Ⓓ
32. Ⓐ Ⓑ Ⓒ Ⓓ
33. Ⓐ Ⓑ Ⓒ Ⓓ
34. Ⓐ Ⓑ Ⓒ Ⓓ
35. Ⓐ Ⓑ Ⓒ Ⓓ
36. Ⓐ Ⓑ Ⓒ Ⓓ
37. Ⓐ Ⓑ Ⓒ Ⓓ
38. Ⓐ Ⓑ Ⓒ Ⓓ
39. Ⓐ Ⓑ Ⓒ Ⓓ
40. Ⓐ Ⓑ Ⓒ Ⓓ
41. Ⓐ Ⓑ Ⓒ Ⓓ
42. Ⓐ Ⓑ Ⓒ Ⓓ
43. Ⓐ Ⓑ Ⓒ Ⓓ
44. Ⓐ Ⓑ Ⓒ Ⓓ
45. Ⓐ Ⓑ Ⓒ Ⓓ
46. Ⓐ Ⓑ Ⓒ Ⓓ
47. Ⓐ Ⓑ Ⓒ Ⓓ
48. Ⓐ Ⓑ Ⓒ Ⓓ
49. Ⓐ Ⓑ Ⓒ Ⓓ
50. Ⓐ Ⓑ Ⓒ Ⓓ
51. Ⓐ Ⓑ Ⓒ Ⓓ
52. Ⓐ Ⓑ Ⓒ Ⓓ
53. Ⓐ Ⓑ Ⓒ Ⓓ
54. Ⓐ Ⓑ Ⓒ Ⓓ
55. Ⓐ Ⓑ Ⓒ Ⓓ
56. Ⓐ Ⓑ Ⓒ Ⓓ
57. Ⓐ Ⓑ Ⓒ Ⓓ
58. Ⓐ Ⓑ Ⓒ Ⓓ
59. Ⓐ Ⓑ Ⓒ Ⓓ
60. Ⓐ Ⓑ Ⓒ Ⓓ
61. Ⓐ Ⓑ Ⓒ Ⓓ
62. Ⓐ Ⓑ Ⓒ Ⓓ
63. Ⓐ Ⓑ Ⓒ Ⓓ
64. Ⓐ Ⓑ Ⓒ Ⓓ
65. Ⓐ Ⓑ Ⓒ Ⓓ
66. Ⓐ Ⓑ Ⓒ Ⓓ
67. Ⓐ Ⓑ Ⓒ Ⓓ
68. Ⓐ Ⓑ Ⓒ Ⓓ
69. Ⓐ Ⓑ Ⓒ Ⓓ
70. Ⓐ Ⓑ Ⓒ Ⓓ
71. Ⓐ Ⓑ Ⓒ Ⓓ
72. Ⓐ Ⓑ Ⓒ Ⓓ
73. Ⓐ Ⓑ Ⓒ Ⓓ
74. Ⓐ Ⓑ Ⓒ Ⓓ
75. Ⓐ Ⓑ Ⓒ Ⓓ
76. Ⓐ Ⓑ Ⓒ Ⓓ
77. Ⓐ Ⓑ Ⓒ Ⓓ
78. Ⓐ Ⓑ Ⓒ Ⓓ
79. Ⓐ Ⓑ Ⓒ Ⓓ
80. Ⓐ Ⓑ Ⓒ Ⓓ
81. Ⓐ Ⓑ Ⓒ Ⓓ
82. Ⓐ Ⓑ Ⓒ Ⓓ
83. Ⓐ Ⓑ Ⓒ Ⓓ
84. Ⓐ Ⓑ Ⓒ Ⓓ
85. Ⓐ Ⓑ Ⓒ Ⓓ
86. Ⓐ Ⓑ Ⓒ Ⓓ
87. Ⓐ Ⓑ Ⓒ Ⓓ
88. Ⓐ Ⓑ Ⓒ Ⓓ
89. Ⓐ Ⓑ Ⓒ Ⓓ
90. Ⓐ Ⓑ Ⓒ Ⓓ
91. Ⓐ Ⓑ Ⓒ Ⓓ
92. Ⓐ Ⓑ Ⓒ Ⓓ
93. Ⓐ Ⓑ Ⓒ Ⓓ
94. Ⓐ Ⓑ Ⓒ Ⓓ
95. Ⓐ Ⓑ Ⓒ Ⓓ
96. Ⓐ Ⓑ Ⓒ Ⓓ
97. Ⓐ Ⓑ Ⓒ Ⓓ
98. Ⓐ Ⓑ Ⓒ Ⓓ
99. Ⓐ Ⓑ Ⓒ Ⓓ
100. Ⓐ Ⓑ Ⓒ Ⓓ
101. Ⓐ Ⓑ Ⓒ Ⓓ
102. Ⓐ Ⓑ Ⓒ Ⓓ
103. Ⓐ Ⓑ Ⓒ Ⓓ
104. Ⓐ Ⓑ Ⓒ Ⓓ
105. Ⓐ Ⓑ Ⓒ Ⓓ
106. Ⓐ Ⓑ Ⓒ Ⓓ
107. Ⓐ Ⓑ Ⓒ Ⓓ
108. Ⓐ Ⓑ Ⓒ Ⓓ
109. Ⓐ Ⓑ Ⓒ Ⓓ
110. Ⓐ Ⓑ Ⓒ Ⓓ
111. Ⓐ Ⓑ Ⓒ Ⓓ
112. Ⓐ Ⓑ Ⓒ Ⓓ
113. Ⓐ Ⓑ Ⓒ Ⓓ
114. Ⓐ Ⓑ Ⓒ Ⓓ
115. Ⓐ Ⓑ Ⓒ Ⓓ
116. Ⓐ Ⓑ Ⓒ Ⓓ
117. Ⓐ Ⓑ Ⓒ Ⓓ
118. Ⓐ Ⓑ Ⓒ Ⓓ
119. Ⓐ Ⓑ Ⓒ Ⓓ
120. Ⓐ Ⓑ Ⓒ Ⓓ

PRACTICE TEST 1

Questions: 120*
Time: 2 hours and 30 minutes

1. The two components of a climate graph are
   A. the amount of precipitation and temperature of an area over time.
   B. temperature highs and lows for a specific date of the year.
   C. the amount of rain expected in the tourist seasons.
   D. predicted rain and temperature for tomorrow.

2. What is true of the equator?
   A. It is also called the prime meridian.
   B. It is equidistant from the poles.
   C. It is perpendicular to lines of latitude.
   D. It is an example of a relative location.

3. Adam Smith's book *Wealth of Nations* focused on
   A. how the U.S. became a successful world power after World War II.
   B. financial planning.
   C. the market economy.
   D. small businesses.

4. A demand deposit at a commercial bank is
   A. a liability to both the depositor and the bank.
   B. an asset to the bank and a liability to the depositor.
   C. neither an asset nor a liability.
   D. an asset to the depositor and a liability to the bank.

5. The purpose of the Truman Doctrine was to
   A. aid the economic recovery of war-torn Europe.
   B. prevent European meddling in the affairs of South American countries.
   C. aid countries that were the targets of Communist expansionism.
   D. expand the Monroe Doctrine to include Eastern Asia.

---

* This practice test presents slightly more items than you are likely to see on test day. The actual test contains approximately 100 questions. You will only learn exactly how many questions you will get after you take the FTCE tutorial and sign the non-disclosure agreement on test day.

Practice Test 1

6. The Soviet leader whose policies of *glasnost* and *perestroika* encouraged the fall of communism in the Eastern bloc was

    A. Brezhnev.

    B. Khrushchev.

    C. Stalin.

    D. Gorbachev.

7. Which of the following statements best describes conditions in Africa before the European Age of Exploration?

    A. African cultures left a wealth of writings that archeologists use to identify significant events before 1500.

    B. Ghana was central to the trans-Saharan trade in gold and salt.

    C. Africa was isolated from other countries and had little contact from people outside of Africa.

    D. Christianity spread through Africa.

8. What form of government ruled Russia prior to the Revolution of 1917?

    A. democracy

    B. autocracy

    C. theocracy

    D. oligarchy

9. Renaissance Humanism was a threat to the Church because

    A. Humanists were starting their own religions.

    B. most Humanists were atheists.

    C. few Humanists learned to read and were unable to participate in religious services.

    D. Humanists emphasized life in the present rather than in the afterlife.

10. Which of these empires or kingdoms was part of the Islamic world?

    A. Ghana

    B. Sumer

    C. Mesopotamia

    D. Phoenicians

11. In the late Middle Ages, which system provided opportunities for craftspeople to pass on their skills to others who were apprentices until they gained expertise?

    A. guild

    B. manorialism

    C. feudal

    D. inquisition

12. What prompted the formation of the League of Nations?

    A. Multinational companies formed in the late twentieth century needed oversight.

    B. An organization was needed that could promote international peace and security following World War I.

    C. The Allies and Axis powers needed an organization to negotiate peace at the end of World War II.

    D. Countries that joined the European Union required a single entity to coordinate resources.

13. What is the Out of Africa model?

    A. a map of overland trade routes from Europe to Africa prior to 1500

    B. a description of how Africans were captured for the slave trade in the nineteenth century

    C. a theory for the origin of humans

    D. an artifact that is believed to be the earliest form of cuneiform from Mesopotamia

14. Which of the following was developed by the Ancient Greeks?

    A. hieroglyphics

    B. cuneiform

    C. democracy

    D. Latin

15. Germany's invasion of which country prompted the British to declare war on Germany in 1914?

    A. the Rhineland

    B. Belgium

    C. Sudetenland

    D. Austria

Practice Test 1

16. Which of the following terms is closely related to *autocracy*?

    A. democracy

    B. capitalism

    C. despotism

    D. theocracy

17. Article 1 of the U.S. Constitution creates

    A. a bicameral legislature.

    B. a unicameral legislature.

    C. the presidency.

    D. the judicial branch.

18. Which statement best describes the foreign policy of the United States during the Cold War?

    A. The United States had a policy of noninvolvement in Latin America.

    B. The United States intervened in another country's affairs if it prevented a country from falling under Communist control.

    C. The United States had few investments in Latin America during this time.

    D. The United States refused to support abusive regimes in Latin America, the Middle East, and the Philippines.

19. Which historical movement can be identified with Martin Luther?

    A. the Protestant Reformation

    B. the Scientific Revolution

    C. the Renaissance

    D. the Enlightenment

20. Which of the following statements about the Han Dynasty is true?

    A. The Han Dynasty created a system of trade routes that became known as the Silk Road.

    B. The Han Dynasty ended before the birth of Christ.

    C. The Han relied on Buddhism as the philosophical basis for government.

    D. China was relatively unsophisticated during the Han Dynasty, with little poetry or writings.

21. What was an outcome of the Industrial Revolution?

    A. a decrease in consumption of material goods

    B. a focus on craftsmanship

    C. an increase in agrarian living

    D. the birth of the advertising industry

22. Adolf Hitler became chancellor of Germany in 1933. What was one of his first official acts?

    A. He began building up Germany's army and weapons.

    B. He established government policies to ease the effects of the Great Depression.

    C. He established alliances with Italy and Czechoslovakia.

    D. He met with France and Britain to work out treaties.

23. Which of the following characterizes Paleolithic peoples?

    A. They were agrarian and grew crops.

    B. They used simple tools made of iron and wood.

    C. They did not know how to create fire for warmth or cooking.

    D. They were highly nomadic.

24. What would have been a logical outcome of the Americanization Movement in the late 1800s and early 1900s?

    A. Women gained the right to vote.

    B. The United States became increasingly more isolationist.

    C. Companies refused to hire individuals who had not become U.S. citizens.

    D. Immigrants learned what it meant to be an American.

25. In its decision in the case of *Plessy v. Ferguson*, the Supreme Court held that

    A. separate facilities for different races were inherently unequal and therefore unconstitutional.

    B. no slave could be a citizen of the United States.

    C. separate but equal facilities for different races were constitutional.

    D. imposition of a literacy test imposed an unconstitutional barrier to the right to vote.

Practice Test 1

26. A person who believed in Manifest Destiny in the 1800s would most likely want to
    A. preserve the environment.
    B. respect the rights of others.
    C. acquire more land and power.
    D. rule foreign countries.

27. What was an effect of the slave trade on Africa?
    A. Existing trade routes were strengthened.
    B. Africa was viewed as less important in terms of colonization.
    C. Contact with the outside world increased as the result of trading.
    D. Women took over roles previously occupied by men, and, because there were so few men, polygamy increased.

28. During the Enlightenment, Rococo and Neoclassicism can be classified as
    A. philosophies.
    B. styles of art.
    C. examples of the Republic of Letters.
    D. music styles.

29. Which of the following occurred in the same time period?
    A. Reformation and Age of Reason
    B. Age of Exploration and Industrial Revolution
    C. Renaissance and Middle Ages
    D. Renaissance, Reformation, and Age of Exploration

30. Which of the following is considered the cradle of Western civilization?
    A. Rome
    B. Greece
    C. Egypt
    D. Sumer

31. Which of the following would be considered a primary source in researching the factors that influenced U.S. involvement in the Korean War?

    A. A newspaper article about Veterans Day, published in 2001.

    B. A biography of Harry S. Truman by David McCullough, published in 1993.

    C. A journal article about the beginning of the Korean War by a noted scholar.

    D. The personal correspondence of a military man stationed with the 5th Regimental Combat Team (RCT) in Korea.

32. The first religious development to have an impact throughout colonial America was the

    A. establishment of religious toleration in Maryland.

    B. spread of Quaker ideas from Pennsylvania.

    C. Reformation.

    D. Great Awakening.

33. What was a weakness of the Articles of Confederation government?

    A. It had a bicameral legislative body.

    B. It did not have the power to declare war.

    C. The central government was weak.

    D. A simple majority (seven of the thirteen colonies) was needed to approve amendments.

34. The Marshall Plan

    A. ended the Cold War.

    B. granted British control over Palestine after World War I.

    C. ended the conflict in Korea.

    D. gave Western Europe billions to rebuild after World War II.

35. An economy in which productive resources are owned by private individuals is described as

    A. command.

    B. socialist.

    C. traditional.

    D. capitalistic.

Practice Test 1

36. What might be seen as the advantage of a command economy?

    A. It is familiar because it is based on tradition.

    B. It emphasizes collective benefit over individual benefit.

    C. Corporations compete with each other for profit, which is then paid to stockholders in the form of dividends.

    D. A central bank oversees the stability of the banking system and conducts monetary policy in order to control inflation and unemployment, and to stimulate economic growth.

37. What is true of the Bretton Woods system?

    A. It is a way to categorize types of economies.

    B. It involved international exchange of currencies.

    C. It is a way to regulate credit.

    D. It is a practical application of the Production Possibilities Frontier Curve.

38. A society must decide which and how many goods and services it should produce; how it should produce these goods and services; and how the goods and services should then be distributed among the people. These address the concept of

    A. technical efficiency.

    B. opportunity costs.

    C. macroeconomics.

    D. scarcity.

39. Which of the following involve the interaction between the buyer, the seller, and price?

    A. microeconomics; macroeconomics

    B. recession; recovery

    C. expansionary fiscal policy; contractionary fiscal policy

    D. supply; demand

40. *Sociology* is defined as

    A. the science of humankind.

    B. the study of how individuals become members of groups and move between groups, and how being in different groups affects individuals and the groups in which they participate.

    C. the study of Earth and its features.

    D. the study of the interpretation of the past and how it affects our view of the present.

41. The research method that involves a social scientist living among and interacting with the people being studied is known as

    A. quantitative research.

    B. experimentation.

    C. case study.

    D. participant observation.

42. According to the table below, what can you infer from the data about children from single-parent families in Florida?

    Florida Children from Single-Parent Families, 2008

    Scale: 5%–80%

Ethnic Group		
Non-Hispanic White	28%	
Black or African American	61%	
Asian and Pacific Islander	17%	
Hispanic or Latino	37%	

    A. In 2008, most children from single-parent families were Hispanic or Latino.

    B. The proportion of American Indian children from single-parent families is the lowest.

    C. The percentage of children from Asian single-parent families is higher than the percentage of non-Hispanic white children from single-parent families.

    D. The percentage of African American children from single-parent families represents the largest group of children from single-parent families.

43. Miss Bailey teaches sixth-grade social studies with twenty-five students of various achievement levels. She is starting a unit on the history of their local community and wants to stimulate the students' thinking. She also wants to encourage students to develop a project as a result of their study. Which type of project would encourage the highest level of thinking by the students?

    A. Giving students a list of questions about people, dates, and events, then having them put the answers on a poster, with appropriate pictures, to display in class

    B. Giving students questions to use to interview older members of the community, then having them write articles based on the interviews and publish them in a booklet

    C. Asking students to research the influence of the past on the present community, then asking students to project what the community might be like in 100 years and create a model to show what they think

    D. Using archived newspapers to collect data, then having them draw a timeline that includes the major events of the community from its beginning to the current date

Practice Test 1

44. Longitude and latitude are examples of which theme of geography?

    A. location

    B. place

    C. region

    D. movement

45. Economics is a science that deals with

    A. money and its uses.

    B. scarce resources and their allocation.

    C. the examination of balancing scarce resources with unlimited wants.

    D. market and planned economies.

46. One of the first political parties was the Federalist Party. Its founder stated the following: *Constitutions should consist only of general provisions; the reason is that they must necessarily be permanent, and that they cannot calculate for the possible change of things.*
    Who was the founder, and why did he make this statement?

    A. Thomas Jefferson; supported a strict and permanent interpretation of the Constitution

    B. Alexander Hamilton; argued for general interpretation of the Constitution

    C. George Washington; as the first president of the United States, favored Constitutional permanence based on the calculations of his cabinet

    D. Benjamin Franklin; as someone who signed the Declaration of Independence, favored change

47. Which amendment reserves to the states any power that the Constitution does not give to the federal government and does not deny to the state?

    A. Third Amendment

    B. Fifth Amendment

    C. Ninth Amendment

    D. Tenth Amendment

48. The term *periodization* is used

    A. to track economic trends.

    B. to place a historical event into a chronological context.

    C. in political science to study elections.

    D. in geography to study time zones.

49. The religion that most influenced the development of sub-Saharan Africa before the Age of Exploration was

    A. Christianity.
    B. Hinduism.
    C. Judaism.
    D. Islam.

50. The Monroe Doctrine stated that the United States

    A. was not concerned with the type of government other countries might have.
    B. was concerned only with the type of government that the countries of the Western Hemisphere might have.
    C. would not tolerate any new European colonization in the New World.
    D. claimed the Western Hemisphere as its exclusive zone of influence.

51. Mr. King has asked his students to visualize the Americas prior to the Age of Exploration and to describe what they see. Which student has an accurate "picture" based on history?

    A. Viola said, "I imagine a prosperous and healthy Aztec civilization."
    B. Joe said, "I see Native Americans riding horses."
    C. Carmen said, "I picture herds of cattle in what is now Florida."
    D. Jasmine said, "I visualize early American colonies developing on the East coast."

52. What caused Benjamin Franklin to draw the following cartoon?

    A. Males in the American colonies hesitated to join the militia.
    B. England disapproved of the Albany Plan of Union.
    C. Franklin wanted the colonies to reunite with Great Britain.
    D. France did not initially support American independence from England.

Practice Test 1

53. The purpose of the grandfather clause and literacy tests, used in the Southern states in the late 1800s and early 1900s, was to prevent

    A. illiterate and poor white people from voting.

    B. recent immigrants from voting.

    C. Black people from running for public office.

    D. Black people from voting.

54. What change to European governments came to characterize the time period 1750–1800 as the Age of Revolution?

    A. Monarchies were replaced by republics and democracies.

    B. Democratic governments evolved into socialist governments.

    C. Aristocracies became more powerful.

    D. Monarchies returned to power in most European nation-states.

55. What was a net result of the Eighteenth Amendment?

    A. All Americans were eligible to vote.

    B. Prohibition created major organized-crime activity in the United States.

    C. The Great Depression was eased.

    D. Presidents were limited to two terms of four years each.

56. What led to a large wave of Cuban immigration into southern Florida in the 1950s?

    A. The Cuban Missile Crisis

    B. The Cuban Revolution of 1959

    C. The Korean War

    D. Opportunities with the space industry in Florida

57. The concept of *culture* includes all of the following EXCEPT

    A. personal values.

    B. religious beliefs.

    C. styles of dress.

    D. individual intelligence.

58. Ms. Cole teaches civics. She asked her students to write an essay based on the following prompt:

    Which of the amendments in the Bill of Rights has had the most effect on your life? Why?

    According to Bloom's Taxonomy, at what level is this activity?

    A. comprehension

    B. synthesis

    C. strategic thinking

    D. evaluation

59. Which of the following impacted Africa the most between 1500 and 1900?

    A. the Renaissance

    B. the development of trade routes for the transportation of gold, ivory, and spices

    C. slave trade

    D. the Reformation

60. Phyllis Johnson is a middle-school social studies teacher who has chosen human diversity as the topic for a lesson unit. She has decided to approach the topic by asking students to engage in introspective activities. On the day she introduces the topic to the class, she asks the students to brainstorm a list of the different things they like about themselves. Then, she asks them to write two paragraphs in class describing their personal strengths in terms of (a) their classroom behavior, and (b) their behavior or relationships with others outside class. By asking her students to brainstorm different personal characteristics, Ms. Johnson is promoting her students' cognitive development by helping them

    A. activate prior knowledge as a basis for understanding new concepts.

    B. demonstrate their ability to write personal narratives.

    C. practice their grammar and sentence structure.

    D. develop positive self-esteem by identifying their assets and skills.

61. The next lesson in Ms. Johnson's unit will incorporate library research using print and digital sources. Before students go to the library, Ms. Johnson provides a list of questions to focus their thinking. The list includes the following questions: *What do I already know or understand about this subject, topic, or issue? Do I understand what I am supposed to do for the project? What are some strategies and tactics that I can use to learn more about this at the library? Did I understand what I just heard, read, or saw?* These questions help students develop

    A. organizational skills.

    B. literal thinking.

    C. metacognitive thinking.

    D. academic skills.

62. Ms. Johnson has created a kind of noncompetitive "bingo game" for her students to play. The game board looks like a bingo grid, and the goal is for each student to have all of the blocks completed. Some of the items in the blocks are things that can be observed (had blue eyes; is wearing green, is left-handed); and some of the items are things that cannot be observed (was born in a different state/country, plays a sport, plays a musical instrument, likes to read, had a pet). The students mingle and try to find individuals that exemplify one of the items. When that occurs, the individual signs that box on the "bingo card." One of the rules is that a student can only have one signature per person. The students complete the activity. Ms. Johnson has signs on opposite sides of the room. One sign is YES and the other sign is NO. She goes through each item and asks students to move to the side of the room that reflects their response. For example, all of the individuals with blue eyes would move to the YES side and everyone else would move to the NO side. This activity exemplifies

   A   problem-based learning.

   B. critical thinking.

   C. active learning.

   D. extended thinking.

63. After the bingo game, Ms. Johnson shows her students two terms and definitions: *Surface culture*, aspects of a culture or person that can be observed; and *deep culture*, aspects of a culture or person that are not known by observing. She asks the students if they think that they would have more in common with those who have the same surface culture traits or those who have the same deep culture traits. This question encourages students to think

   A. creatively.

   B. inductively.

   C. deductively.

   D. collaboratively.

64. Ms. Johnson gave her students the following assignment: *Write a one-page essay that describes the difference between surface culture and deep culture. Include a minimum of three examples other than those from the bingo game.* At what Bloom's Level is this assignment?

   A. application

   B. synthesis

   C. comprehension

   D. recall

65. The four main branches of geography are
    A. topical, political, relative, and absolute.
    B. systemic, topical, political, and regional.
    C. human, systemic, physical, and regional.
    D. physical, relative, political, and absolute.

66. Geographers use which of the following to analyze how places relate, including movements such as travel, migration, and the transmission of information?
    A. vernacular regions
    B. spatial interaction
    C. friction of distance
    D. space-time compression

67. The Enlightenment is also known as
    A. The Age of Discovery.
    B. The Age of Exploration.
    C. The Age of Revolution.
    D. The Age of Reason.

68. An *oligopoly* is
    A. a market form in which a market or industry is dominated by a small number of sellers.
    B. a government led by a small group of individuals who rule a country together.
    C. a black market.
    D. great for consumers.

69. Mr. Harrison asked his students to provide an example of an agent of erosion. Which student has the best response?
    A. George: dunes
    B. Leslie: a river
    C. Tamara: a drumlin
    D. Jacob: plate tectonics

Practice Test 1

70. *Human geography* is best defined as the study of

    A. where and why human activities are located.

    B. where and why natural forces occur as they do.

    C. populations and birth rates.

    D. human conflicts.

71. What is true of mixed economies?

    A. In a mixed economy, productive resources are owned by private individuals; however, what is produced is traded in traditional ways without the use of currency.

    B. Mixed economies are least stable.

    C. A mixed economy is sometimes called a traditional economy.

    D. The economies of most countries are mixed, with varied proportions of command, capitalist, and traditional economies.

72. In the 1790s political conflict between Thomas Jefferson and Alexander Hamilton, Jefferson would have been more likely to

    A. take a narrow view of the Constitution.

    B. favor Britain over France in the European wars.

    C. favor the establishment of a national bank.

    D. win the cooperation of Presidents George Washington and John Adams.

73. *GDP, inflation rates,* and *unemployment rates* are most related to

    A. macroeconomics.

    B. aggregate demand.

    C. microeconomics.

    D. aggregate supply.

74. The *Federalist Papers* were signed by "Publius." The consensus among scholars says the papers were written by

    A. Alexander Hamilton, James Madison, and John Jay.

    B. Thomas Jefferson, Alexander Hamilton, and George Washington.

    C. James Madison, George Washington, and John Calhoun.

    D. Alexander Hamilton, James Madison, and three others.

75. Which country and contribution are correctly matched?

    A. Kingdom of Kush—Code of Hammurabi

    B. Greece—Socratic Method

    C. China—the concept of pi

    D. Rome—the Magna Carta

76. Which of the following best defines the term *prehistoric*?

    A. prior to the use of fire

    B. prior to the use of tools

    C. prior to the appearance of the written word

    D. during the age of the dinosaur

77. Which of the following stated that in addition to intervention in the Americas, the United States would intervene to keep weak or negligent countries in the Caribbean or Central America from being taken over by outside forces? The Roosevelt Corollary to the

    A. Constitution.

    B. Truman Doctrine.

    C. Marshall Plan.

    D. Monroe Doctrine.

78. In 1950, a small neighborhood developed in a rural area of Orange County, Florida. By 1980, it had grown to be 4,000 homes; by the year 2000, there were 25,000 homes. There are currently 56,000 homes, and the area has decided to incorporate into a city with a governing body. Which of the following determines how a city charter would be sought?

    A. Local governments are chartered according to their state's constitution.

    B. Local governments apply to the federal government for a charter.

    C. States are divided into counties, and local governments are authorized by the counties.

    D. Local governments simply write a constitution and notify the next largest government entity of their existence.

79. Which of the following is a multi-disciplinary study of how social and environmental change occurs in the context of power relations, social structures, economic issues, and human–environment interactions?

    A. environmental determinism

    B. political ecology

    C. spatial interaction

    D. cultural diffusion

Practice Test 1

80. Ms. Vinton's class is studying the flora of Florida. What are they studying?

    A. plants

    B. soil composition

    C. rural areas

    D. sources of fresh water

81. Mr. Hilton's class is studying religion and is reviewing through the use of a Jeopardy game. The answer is: Yahweh. What is the correct question?

    A. What are the sacred writings of Buddha?

    B. Whom do Jews worship?

    C. Where did Confucianism originate?

    D. What is another name for Mecca?

82. Mr. Gomez often uses the inquiry method in teaching high school geography. What would you expect to see in his classroom?

    A. Students using the scientific method to identify how erosion affects specific beaches in Florida.

    B. Students working together to answer extended-thinking questions about global warming, based on Webb's Depth of Knowledge.

    C. Students participating in a service learning project to inform members of the community in ways to conserve water.

    D. Students playing a Jeopardy game to review terms.

Questions 83 and 84 refer to the following graph:

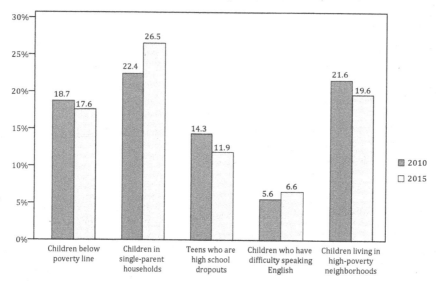

83. According to the graph, from 2010 to 2015, which of the following was true?

    A. The number of teens who dropped out of high school increased.

    B. The number of children who have difficulty speaking English increased.

    C. The number of children living below the poverty line increased.

    D. The number of children living in high-poverty neighborhoods increased.

84. According to the graph, the number of children who have difficulty speaking English increased from 2010 to 2015 from 5.6 percent to 6.6 percent. Which of the following can be inferred from the graph?

    A. The percentage of children living below poverty is related to the percentage of children living in high-poverty neighborhoods.

    B. Teens who are high school dropouts are most likely from single-parent households.

    C. Children living in single-parent households are the same children who have difficulty speaking English.

    D. A large percentage of children living in high-poverty neighborhoods live in single-parent households.

85. The first permanent European settlement in North America was

    A. New Orleans, in what is now Louisiana.

    B. Santa Fe, in what is now New Mexico.

    C. St. Augustine, in what is now Florida.

    D. Jamestown, in what is now Virginia.

Practice Test 1

86. Which of the following associated with President Johnson's administration?

    A. Bay of Pigs

    B. Watergate

    C. Cuban Missile Crisis

    D. the War on Poverty

87. Both the Compromise of 1820 and the Compromise of 1850 involved

    A. treaties with France and England.

    B. how to move American Indians to reservations.

    C. union demands in new industries.

    D. the balance of new territories or states that permitted slavery.

88. Which individual would have been most likely to benefit most from Granger Laws and the Interstate Commerce Act of 1887?

    A. a former slave in Mississippi

    B. a farmer in the Midwest

    C. a miner in Pennsylvania

    D. a supporter of Prohibition in New York

89. What did the Civil Rights Act of 1964 accomplish?

    A. It prohibited discrimination for reason of color, race, religion, sex, or national origin in places of public accommodation covered by interstate commerce.

    B. It desegregated public schools for the first time.

    C. It provided access to health care, food, and other support as part of the "War on Poverty."

    D. It created a system of assimilation for undocumented immigrants.

90. Caroline is taking a World History class and is learning about early world civilizations. Her teacher has asked her students to write about a topic that they have studied, and to interview someone who works in a profession related to the topic. Caroline has decided to write about the Code of Hammurabi. Whom should she interview?

    A. Kim Gray, a physician

    B. Jeremy Phillips, a teacher

    C. Joan Hernandez, a lawyer

    D. Alonzo Franks, an architect

91. What is the purpose of the "elastic clause" in the Constitution?

    A. It provides flexibility for the president to act during times of war.

    B. It allows the Supreme Court to consider controversial cases when needed.

    C. It describes the fluid nature of the checks and balances within the three branches of government.

    D. It grants Congress implied powers to implement the delegated powers.

92. Adam Smith in his book *The Wealth of Nations* introduced the idea that if all individuals follow their own self-interests, it will be for the economic good of everyone, since everyone will do what they do best. What did Smith call this concept?

    A. the invisible hand

    B. communism

    C. a command economy

    D. survival of the fittest

93. The Paleolithic, Mesolithic, and Neolithic periods are part of which geological age?

    A. Copper

    B. Bronze

    C. Iron

    D. Stone

94. A *philosophe* in the Age of Enlightenment would have most likely supported

    A. religious dogma.

    B. elimination of rulers.

    C. realistic pessimism that things would improve.

    D. critical thinking by the masses.

95. W.E.B. DuBois is best known for starting which of the following?

    A. the Harlem Renaissance and the Congress of Racial Equality (CORE)

    B. the Civil Rights Act of 1964 and the Equal Employment Opportunity Commission

    C. the Tuskegee Airmen and the Voter Education Project

    D. the Niagara Movement and the NAACP

Practice Test 1

96. England and other European nations formally recognized the independence of the United States in the 1783

    A. Mayflower Compact.

    B. Treaty of Paris.

    C. Treaty of Versailles.

    D. Constitution of the United States.

97. Who is most likely to have been a "bonus marcher" during Hoover's administration?

    A. impoverished World War I veterans

    B. AFL-CIO workers

    C. African Americans under the leadership of W.E.B. DuBois

    D. individuals who wanted to repeal Prohibition

98. What issue was the focus of the Thirty Years' War?

    A. religion

    B. nationalism

    C. imperialism

    D. class warfare

99. Ms. Green has asked the children in her class to identify fauna in their environment. Which child has correctly identified fauna?

    A. Marcus said he saw cumulus clouds in the sky after lunch.

    B. Jon said he saw a squirrel in a tree.

    C. Trina said she found three kinds of sedimentary rock on the school grounds.

    D. Kate said she saw a retention pond on her way to school.

100. A country's national output is termed

    A. macroeconomics.

    B. the Gross Domestic Product.

    C. the Federal Reserve System.

    D. the currency exchange rate.

101. What are the four phases in a market economy cycle?

    A. consumption, scarcity, equilibrium, surplus

    B. boom, recession, trough, recovery

    C. production, expansion, contraction, reduction

    D. competition, redistribution, collective benefit, comparative advantage

102. Which is the best way to describe the GNP?

    A. total goods and services

    B. total national production

    C. greater national production

    D. government natural production

103. A headline reads: "Auto sales decline and the steel industry suffers a slump; steelworkers laid off." This type of unemployment can best be characterized in economic terms as

    A. frictional.

    B. functional.

    C. total.

    D. cyclical.

104. Who serves as the president of the Senate?

    A. the Majority Leader

    B. the Vice President of the United States

    C. the senator with the greatest seniority

    D. the Speaker of the House

105. Including the Chief Justice, how many justices serve on the Supreme Court?

    A. 13

    B. 9

    C. 11

    D. 7

106. Which of the following is the *best* choice as the major cause of the Great Depression?

    A. military unrest in Europe

    B. the Cold War

    C. extensive stock market speculation

    D. weak unions

107. Which event would have been of most interest to Margaret Sanger?

    A. California became the first state to adopt a "no fault" divorce law in 1969.

    B. The Eighteenth Amendment went into effect in 1920.

    C. The Food and Drug Administration approved birth control pills in 1960.

    D. Bonus marchers protested in 1932.

108. The Truman Doctrine was issued in response to the threat of

    A. communist expansion in Greece and Turkey.

    B. the Red Army in Central Europe.

    C. communist North Korean invasion of South Korea.

    D. communist threat to South Vietnam.

109. Lisa's great-grandfather worked for an automobile manufacturer in the late 1930s. He was most likely a member of which of the following?

    A. SNCC

    B. EEOC

    C. CIO

    D. CCC

110. Which court case reversed the concept of "separate but equal"?

    A. *Plessy v. Ferguson*

    B. *Schenck v. United States*

    C. *Brown v. Board of Education of Topeka*

    D. *Morgan v. Virginia*

111. A U.S. senator does not want there to be a vote on a specific issue, so she filibusters. What parliamentary procedure will end the filibuster?

    A. adjournment

    B. cloture

    C. intervention by the Speaker of the House

    D. a presidential override

112. What would have been a *polis* in ancient Greece?

    A. the Aegean Sea

    B. an epic written by Homer

    C. a wealthy landowner

    D. Athens

113. What is the historical significance of the cities of Hiroshima and Nagasaki?

    A. As the result of mass migrations from those cities, a "gentlemen's agreement" between Japan and the United States limited the number of unskilled workers Japan sent to the United States.

    B. Hiroshima was the center of an Asian civilization that was eventually destroyed by the people of Nagasaki.

    C. That was where the first atomic bombs were dropped.

    D. Both cities were key locations in the Mongol civilization.

114. What was accomplished by the Selective Service Act?

    A. Prohibition was repealed.

    B. Women got the right to vote.

    C. Men between the ages of 21 and 30 had to register for the draft.

    D. Congress passed the Civil Rights Act of 1964.

115. President Woodrow Wilson's *Fourteen Points* was

    A. a recommendation for restricting the flow of immigrants into the United States during the first part of the twentieth century.

    B. an Executive Order which denied civil rights to African Americans during the Harlem Renaissance.

    C. a plan for peace following World War I.

    D. a speech supporting prohibition.

116. What is the effect of *Engel v. Vitale* (1962) on today's schools?

    A. Principals cannot search school lockers without cause.

    B. Prayer is not allowed in schools.

    C. Segregated schools were outlawed.

    D. Students with disabilities have civil rights that permit them access to the same kind of education as students who do not have disabilities.

117. Which of the following reasons was the immediate cause of the United States entering into World War II?

   A.   Nazi Germany sank American supply ships.

   B.   Japan attacked the U.S. naval base at Pearl Harbor.

   C.   Italy and Germany declared war on the United States.

   D.   The Archduke of Austria was assassinated.

118. Which of the following best characterizes the methods of the Reverend Dr. Martin Luther King, Jr.?

   A.   peaceful protests of segregation

   B.   a series of petitions to Congress calling for correction of racial abuses

   C.   armed violence against police and troops

   D.   a series of speaking engagements in Northern cities in hopes of pressuring Congress to take action

119. Who would have a capital gain?

   A.   Mr. Kent wins a governor's election and will move to the state capital.

   B.   Mrs. Corvin's students made above average progress on the state exams in math.

   C.   Ms. Wilson sells her stock in a company and makes a profit.

   D.   A city's population increases by over 10% from one census period to the next.

120. What part of the Constitution addresses *popular sovereignty*?

   A.   Article 1

   B.   The Bill of Rights

   C.   Amendments 1–5

   D.   Preamble

PRACTICE TEST 1 ANSWER KEY

Question	Answer	Field	Competency
1	A	Geography	Competency 1.4
2	B	Geography	Competency 1.1
3	C	Economics	Competency 2.6
4	D	Economics	Competency 2.4
5	C	Political Science	Competency 3.5
6	D	World History	Competency 5.13
7	B	World History	Competency 4.3
8	B	World History	Competency 4.11
9	D	World History	Competency 4.4
10	A	World History	Competency 4.3
11	A	World History	Competency 4.4
12	B	World History	Competency 4.11
13	C	World History	Competency 4.1
14	C	World History	Competency 4.2
15	B	World History	Competency 4.11
16	C	Political Science	Competency 3.6
17	A	Political Science	Competency 3.2
18	B	Political Science	Competency 3.5
19	A	World History	Competency 4.4
20	A	World History	Competency 4.2
21	D	World History	Competency 4.8
22	A	World History	Competency 4.11
23	D	World History	Competency 4.1
24	D	U.S. History	Competency 5.9
25	C	U.S. History	Competency 5.7
26	C	U.S. History	Competency 3.5

Practice Test 1 Answer Key

Question	Answer	Field	Competency
27	D	World History	Competency 4.5
28	B	World History	Competency 4.6
29	D	World History	Competency 4.7
30	B	World History	Competency 4.2
31	D	U.S. History	Competency 5.13
32	D	U.S. History	Competency 5.2
33	C	Political Science	Competency 3.1
34	D	U.S. History	Competency 5.13
35	D	Economics	Competency 2.2
36	B	Economics	Competency 2.5
37	B	Economics	Competency 2.6
38	D	Economics	Competency 2.1
39	D	Economics	Competency 2.3
40	B	Social Science	Competency 6.1
41	D	Social Science	Competency 6.1
42	D	Social Science	Competency 6.4
43	C	Social Science	Competency 6.5
44	A	Geography	Competency 1.1
45	C	Economics	Competency 2
46	B	Political Science	Competency 3.3
47	D	Political Science	Competency 3.2
48	B	World History	Competency 4
49	D	World History	Competency 4.3
50	C	Political Science	Competency 3.5
51	A	U.S. History	Competency 5.1
52	B	U.S. History	Competency 5.3
53	D	U.S. History	Competency 5.7
54	A	World History	Competency 4.9

Question	Answer	Field	Competency
55	B	Political Science	Competency 3.1
56	B	U.S. History	Competency 5.13
57	D	Social Science	Competency 6.1
58	D	Social Science	Competency 6.5
59	C	World History	Competency 4.3
60	A	Social Science	Competency 6.5
61	C	Social Science	Competency 6.5
62	C	Social Science	Competency 6.5
63	B	Social Science	Competency 6.5
64	A	Social Science	Competency 6.5
65	C	Geography	Competency 1
66	B	Geography	Competency 1.1
67	D	World History	Competency 4.6
68	A	Economics	Competency 2.5
69	B	Geography	Competency 1.2
70	A	Geography	Competency 1
71	D	Economics	Competency 2.2
72	A	Political Science	Competency 3.3
73	A	Economics	Competency 2.4
74	A	Political Science	Competency 3.1
75	B	World History	Competency 4.2
76	C	World History	Competency 4.1
77	D	Political Science	Competency 3.5
78	A	Political Science	Competency 3.4
79	B	Geography	Competency 1.3
80	A	Geography	Competency 1.1
81	B	World History	Competency 4.13
82	A	Social Science	Competency 6.5

Practice Test 1 Answer Key

Question	Answer	Field	Competency
83	B	Social Science	Competency 6.4
84	A	Social Science	Competency 6.4
85	C	U.S. History	Competency 5.16
86	D	U.S. History	Competency 5.14
87	D	U.S. History	Competency 5.6
88	B	U.S. History	Competency 5.8
89	A	U.S. History	Competency 5.14
90	C	World History	Competency 4.1
91	D	Political Science	Competency 3.2
92	A	World History	Competency 4.8
93	D	World History	Competency 4.1
94	D	World History	Competency 4.6
95	D	U.S. History	Competency 5.14
96	B	U.S. History	Competency 5.3
97	A	U.S. History	Competency 4.11
98	A	World History	Competency 4.4
99	B	Geography	Competency 1.1
100	B	Economics	Competency 2.4
101	B	Economics	Competency 2.4
102	A	Economics	Competency 2.4
103	D	Economics	Competency 2.4
104	B	Political Science	Competency 3.2
105	B	Political Science	Competency 3.2
106	C	U.S. History	Competency 5.11
107	C	U.S. History	Competency 5.11
108	A	U.S. History	Competency 5.13
109	C	U.S. History	Competency 5.11
110	C	U.S. History	Competency 5.14

Question	Answer	Field	Competency
111	B	Political Science	Competency 3.2
112	D	World History	Competency 4.2
113	C	U.S. History	Competency 5.11
114	C	U.S. History	Competency 5.10
115	C	U.S. History	Competency 5.10
116	B	Political Science	Competency 3.7
117	B	U.S. History	Competency 5.12
118	A	U.S. History	Competency 5.14
119	C	Economics	Competency 2.5
120	D	Political Science	Competency 3.1

PRACTICE TEST 1 SELF-ASSESSMENT GUIDE

Knowledge of Economics —/16

3	4	35	36	37	38	39	45	68	71	73

100	101	102	103	119

Knowledge of Geography —/10

1	2	44	65	66	69	70	79	80	99

Knowledge of Political Science —/19

5	16	17	18	33	46	47	50	55	72	74

77	78	91	104	105	111	116	120

Knowledge of Social Science —/14

40	41	42	43	57	58	60	61	62	63	64

82	83	84

Knowledge of U.S. History —/28

24	25	26	31	32	34	51	52	53	56	85

86	87	88	89	95	96	97	106	107	108	109

110	113	114	115	117	118

Knowledge of World History —/33

6	7	8	9	10	11	12	13	14	15	19

20	21	22	23	27	28	29	30	48	49	54

59	67	75	76	81	90	92	93	94	98	112

DETAILED EXPLANATIONS FOR PRACTICE TEST 1

1. **A**

    Climate can be displayed on a graph. A climate graph contains two pieces of information about an area: the amount of rainfall and the temperature over time. Both (B) and (C) include only one of the pieces of information. Option (D) describes future rain and temperature rather than rain and temperature over time.

2. **B**

    The equator is the line of latitude that is halfway (equidistant) between the North Pole and the South Pole. It is not a meridian (A). Because it is a line of latitude, it is parallel, not perpendicular to lines of latitude (C). The equator is an absolute location, not a relative location (D).

3. **C**

    Adam Smith's book *Wealth of Nations* addressed the market economy rather than the U.S. as a world power (A), financial planning (B), or small businesses (D).

4. **D**

    By definition, a deposit at a bank is placed on the bank's books as a liability, as this is money that is owed by the bank to the depositor. The deposit is an asset to the depositor, as it represents value owned by the depositor. Options (A), (B), and (C) do not reflect that relationship.

5. **C**

    The purpose of the Truman Doctrine was to aid countries that were the targets of Communist expansionism. It did not address European post-World War II economy (A), meddling of Europe into South American countries (B), or an expansion of the Monroe Doctrine to Eastern Asia (D).

6. **D**

    Gorbachev was the Soviet leader from 1985–1991. He was the last president of the Soviet Union. His policies of *glasnost* ("openness") and *perestroika* ("restructuring") contributed to the end of the Cold War. Brezhnev (A), Khrushchev (B), and Stalin (C) were Soviet leaders prior to that time.

7. **B**

    Ghana was central to the trans-Saharan gold and salt trade. African cultures left few, not many, written records prior to 1500 (A). Many trade routes passed through Africa, so it was not isolated from others (C). Islam, not Christianity, spread through Africa (D).

Detailed Explanations for Practice Test 1

8. **B**

   The rule of Nicholas II of Russia was an autocracy because it was an absolute monarchy. In a democracy (A), the people rule. A god rules in a theocracy (C), with the human ruler seen as the representative of the god. A small group of people rule in an oligarchy (D).

9. **D**

   Renaissance Humanism was a threat to the Church because of its focus on life in the present. People were less likely to follow church dogma in order to reach the afterlife. Humanists did not start their own religions (A) and were not generally atheists (B). The invention of the printing press increased available written materials and people were more, not less, likely to be able to read (C).

10. **A**

    Ghana was a part of the Islamic world between 1500 and 1900 CE. The Sumer (B), Mesopotamian (C), and Phoenician (D) civilizations existed prior to the development of Islam as a religion.

11. **A**

    In the late middle ages, a guild system created a developmental path for artisans to gain skills. This resulted in quality-controlled merchandise and controlled prices, but also the beginnings of unions. Manorialism (B) was an economic system in which large estates, granted by the king to nobles, encompassed a self-sufficient village and were populated by serfs. In feudalism (C), a decentralized political, economic, military, and social system of personal ties and obligations bound vassals to their lords. The inquisition (D) resulted in the persecution of individuals who were considered to be heretics.

12. **B**

    Following World War I, the world recognized the need for a global body to promote international peace and security, which resulted in the League of Nations. Multinational companies did not need oversight (A). The League of Nations formed after World War I, not World War II (C). The League of Nations included countries other than those in Europe (D).

13. **C**

    The current leading theory of human development is the Out of Africa model that holds that modern humans developed only recently. This theory holds that although as *homo erectus* left Africa and did mingle with other populations, it was in Africa that *homo sapiens* developed and eventually took over, without interbreeding, all of the other hominids. The Out of Africa model is not a map of trade routes (A), related to the capture of individuals who became slaves (B), or an artifact related to cuneiform (D).

14. **C**

    The concept of democracy originated with the Greeks. The Egyptians used hieroglyphics (A) as a form of writing, and the Sumerians developed cuneiform (B). Latin (D) was the language used by Romans.

15. **B**

    The British declared war in World War I when Germany invaded Belgium, not the Rhineland (A), Sudetenland (C), or Austria (D).

16. **C**

    Another related term for *autocracy*, more commonly used in the past, is *despotism*, or rule by a despot. A democracy (A) is rule by the people. Capitalism (B) is not a kind of rule, but an economic system. Theocracy (D) is a form of rule in which a deity is the authority, usually administered by priests.

17. **A.**

    Our federal system of government includes a bicameral legislature—the Senate and the House of Representatives—established in Article 1 of the Constitution. The United States does not have a unicameral legislature (B). The role of the president (C) is described in Article II. The role of the judicial branch (D) is described in Article III.

18. **B**

    During the Cold War, the U.S. foreign policy was to intervene in another country's affairs if doing so prevented that country from falling under Communist control. The other statements (A, C, D) do not describe the U.S. foreign policy at that time.

19. **A**

    Martin Luther was the leader of the Protestant Reformation. He is not associated with the Scientific Revolution (B), the Renaissance (C), or the Enlightenment (D).

20. **A**

    The Han Dynasty's greatest contribution was the development of a network of trade routes that extended throughout Asia, and to the Mediterranean Sea. Although Chinese silk was the focus of early trading, the route was used to transport a variety of goods, as well as to transfer aspects of culture from one civilization to another. Because silk was the original item that was traded, later historians described the network as the Silk Road although that name was not applied during the use of the trading network. The Dynasty did not end until about 220 CE, well after the birth of Christ (B). Buddhism was introduced into China during the Han Dynasty, but it did not form the basis of the government (C). During the Han Dynasty, China was a sophisticated country whose inventions included paper and rudimentary books, the development of a common written language, and the dictionary (D).

Detailed Explanations for Practice Test 1

21. **D**

    The industrial age encouraged a new quantitative materialism that focused on the need for people to consume as much as they could. Advertising was a new industry that focused on wants rather than needs. Thus, consumption increased rather than decreased (A). Since more items were mass-produced, there was less emphasis on the work of skilled craftspeople (B). Because of industrialism, fewer people were needed to produce food, so agrarian living decreased rather than increased (C).

22. **A**

    Following his ascension to chancellor in January 1933, Adolf Hitler almost immediately began secretly building up Germany's army and weapons stockpile. In 1934, he increased the size of the army, commissioned the construction of warships, and created a German air force. Compulsory military service was also introduced. He did not create government policies to ease the effects of the Great Depression (B). Although Hitler ultimately established an alliance with Italy, he invaded Czechoslovakia (C). He did not meet with France and Britain to form treaties (D).

23. **D**

    Paleolithic peoples were nomadic since they had little choice but to follow animal migrations and vegetation cycles. They did not know how to grow crops or raise animals (A), so they relied on hunting and gathering for their needs. Paleolithic peoples did know how to make tools and weapons from stone, but not from wood and iron (B). Work was divided primarily along gender lines, where men hunted and women used fire for cooking (C).

24. **D**

    As a result of the influx of immigrants to the U.S. in the late 1800s and early 1900s, the Americanization Movement was designed to teach immigrants the skills they needed to assimilate into American culture. Some of these programs were government-funded and taught immigrants citizenship skills, "American" cooking, and social etiquette. It did not involve women's suffrage (A), an isolationist perspective on the part of the U.S. (B), or refusals to hire immigrants who had not become U.S. citizens (C).

25. **C**

    In *Plessy v. Ferguson* (1896), the Supreme Court upheld "separate but equal" facilities. *Brown v. Topeka Board of Education* (1954) overturned this ruling and said that separate facilities were inherently unequal (A). The ruling that no slave could be a citizen of the United States was the 1857 case, *Dred Scott v. Sandford* (B). Various Supreme Court decisions in the 1950s, 1960s, and 1970s dealt with literacy tests as requirements for voting (D).

26. **C**

    The Manifest Destiny of the United States was a common perspective during the nineteenth century that the United States was destined to expand from coast to coast. Manifest Destiny did not involve the environment (A), respect for rights (B), or rule of foreign countries (D).

27. **D**

    The slave trade removed a large number of able men from Africa. As a result, women took over many of the roles that men had previously held, and polygamy increased. The slave trade did not affect trade routes (A). Since there were fewer men to defend African countries, other countries looked to Africa for colonization (B). Populations in the cities decreased as people fled cities to avoid being captured. Without cities, civilization begins to suffer. Contact with the outside world became quite limited as slave-traders no longer brought with them new ideas or technologies (C).

28. **B**

    Rococo and Neoclassicism were styles of art of the Enlightenment, rather than philosophies (A) or styles of music (D). Rococo was the art of the nobility and emphasized the airy grace and refined pleasures of the salon and the boudoir: very pretty and bright with swirling pastel colors. It sought to make a break with the heavy, Baroque past and emphasized lightness and airy movement. Neoclassicism favored line over color and was all about drama, tension, emotion, content, and an imitation of ancient style. A Republic of Letters (C) was part of the Enlightenment; it included letters, as well as journals and newspapers that circulated among the elite. Though the republic was limited to the educated, all classes and backgrounds could join in. Publishing increased tremendously, and people began to read more.

29. **D**

    The Renaissance, Reformation, and the Age of Exploration happened around the same time, and many of the ideas of one impacted the others. The Renaissance prompted searches for new knowledge, and adventurism ignited dreams about the possibilities of what lay beyond the shores of the Atlantic Ocean and the Mediterranean Sea. The Reformation infused a new spirit for missionaries, particularly those from Portugal and Spain, to find new souls to convert. The Reformation started in the 1600s and preceded the Age of Reason, which began in the 1700s (A). The Age of Exploration began in the fifteenth century, and the Industrial Revolution began in the mid-1700s (B). The Renaissance occurred around 1500 CE and followed the period of the Middle Ages (500 CE–1500 CE) (C).

30. **B**

    Greece was the most sophisticated society of the ancient world and is considered the cradle of Western civilization in that it contributed many concepts that have influenced Western culture (e.g., architecture, government, education, literature, mathematics). The Roman civilization (A) adopted many of the characteristics of Greece. While Egypt (C) and Sumer (D) were important early civilizations, they did not have the same impact on Western civilization that Greece had.

Detailed Explanations for Practice Test 1

31. **D**

    Personal correspondence is a primary source. Articles (A), biographies (B), and journal articles (C) are secondary sources.

32. **D**

    The Great Awakening was the first religious development to have an impact throughout colonial America. Neither religious tolerance in Maryland (A) nor the spread of Quaker ideas from Pennsylvania (B) had a widespread impact. The Reformation (C) was a movement in Europe during the 1500s.

33. **C**

    The Articles of Confederation government lacked a strong central government. The Articles of Confederation used a unicameral legislature, not a bicameral legislature (A). It did give the government the power to declare war (B). Amendments required unanimous approval by the states (D).

34. **D**

    After World War II, the European Recovery Plan, better known as the Marshall Plan, put more than $13 billion into Western Europe's economies to help rebuild Europe. It was also designed to help prevent the spread of communism. The Cold War began at the end of World War II and continued for forty-six years (A). The Marshall Plan occurred after World War II, not World War I (B). It did not involve the Korean War (C).

35. **D**

    An economy in which private individuals own productive resources is capitalistic. In a command economy, a central authority such as a dictator or democratically constituted government, makes all decisions about the economy (A). In a socialist economy, productive resources are owned collectively by society; however, the allocation of resources remains under the control of the government (B). A traditional economy usually relies on custom/tradition to determine production and distribution questions (C).

36. **B**

    The advantage of a command economy is that it emphasizes collective benefit over individual benefit. A command economy is not based on tradition (A). Corporations are not competitive in a command economy (C). A central bank is a feature of a market, not a command, economy (D).

37. **B**

    At the end of World War II, forty-four nations met and created the Bretton Woods system. The U.S. dollar served as the focal point of this system because the U.S. dollar became the reserve currency of the system. Countries bought and sold dollars to maintain their exchange rates. The Bretton Woods system is not a system for categorizing economies (A), a way to regulate credit (C), or a practical application of the Production Possibilities Frontier Curve (D).

38. **D**

Scarcity involves choices that are made when either purchasing or producing goods. Technical efficiency (A) is also called productive efficiency and is achieved when a society produced the greatest quantity of goods and services possible from its resources at a minimum cost, thus using fewer resources and increasing production quantities. This reduces scarcity. An opportunity cost is the loss of potential gain from other options when one option is chosen (B). Macroeconomics is the study of the economy as a whole (C).

39. **D**

Demand is the relationship that shows how much someone will pay someone else for something. Supply is the relationship between price and corresponding quantities that are produced. Thus, both involve buyer, seller, and price. Microeconomics is the study of the individual parts that make up the economy (e.g., households, business firms, and government agencies), and it particularly emphasizes how these units make decisions and what the consequences of these decisions are; macroeconomics is the study of the economy as a whole, including topics such as inflation, unemployment, and economic growth (A). Recession and recovery are two phases of the economic cycle (B). Expansionary fiscal policy and contractionary fiscal policy are tools the government uses to affect change in the economy (C).

40. **B**

Sociology, simply defined, is the study of how individuals become members of groups and move between groups, and how being in different groups affects individuals and the groups in which they participate. Anthropology is the study of humankind (A). Geography is the study of the Earth and its features (C). History is the study of the interpretation of the past and how it affects our view of the present (D).

41. **D**

Participant observation involves a researcher interacting with and observing the personal lives of the research subjects. Quantitative research (A) refers to the systematic investigation of observable events using statistical, mathematical, or computational techniques. Experimentation (B) describes a formal study in which a variable is manipulated to determine effects. A case study (C) is a report of an individual, group, or situation that was studied over time.

42. **D**

According to the graph, single-parent African-American families made up the largest percentage of single-parent families in Florida in 2008. In 2008, the percentage of children from single parent families was not Hispanic or Latino (A). There is no information about American Indian children (B). The percentage of Asian single-parent families is lower than the percentage of non-Hispanic white children (C).

Detailed Explanations for Practice Test 1

43. **C**

    Asking students to make a prediction and create a model is at the synthesis or extended level of thinking. Choices (A) and (D) are at the comprehension level. Choice (B) is at the application level.

44. **A**

    Longitude and latitude are part of the location theme of geography. Place (B) includes human interaction and culture. Region (C) groups areas by common physical characteristics or human characteristics. Movement (D) involves human characteristics.

45. **C**

    This answer is the simple definition of *economics*. Economics is the social science that examines how people choose to use limited or scarce resources to obtain maximum satisfaction of unlimited wants. Money and its uses (A), scarce resources and their allocation (B), and types of economies (D) are all factors within economics.

46. **B**

    Interpretation of the Constitution was a key difference between the Federalists, led by Alexander Hamilton, who argued for a loose interpretation. The party was not founded by Thomas Jefferson (A) who supported a more restricted interpretation of the Constitution, George Washington (C), or Benjamin Franklin (D).

47. **D**

    The Tenth Amendment reserves to the states powers that the Constitution does not give to the federal government or deny to the states. The Third Amendment (A) addresses no quartering of soldiers. The Fifth Amendment (B) focuses on the right to due process of law, and the freedom from self-incrimination and double jeopardy. The Ninth Amendment (C) describes other rights of the people.

48. **B**

    Periodization is a term used in history to study events in context. An example is the use of the term *Victorian era,* which describes a time relevant to Great Britain, to discuss an event in China that occurred at the same time. Periodization does not involve economics (A), political science (C), or geography (D).

49. **D**

    Islam spread in Africa starting in the seventh century, and influenced the cultures of Ghana, Mali, and other African states, including Sub-Saharan Africa. The other religions—Christianity (A), Hinduism (B), and Judaism (C)—did not have strong influences on the Sub-Saharan cultures.

50. **C**

The Monroe Doctrine held that the United States would not tolerate any new European colonization in the New World. The United States did desire to see republican governments instituted in countries all over the world, but would intervene only to prevent new European colonization in the New World, not existing colonization. The Monroe Doctrine did not address concern with the governments of other countries generally (A) or specifically in the Western Hemisphere (B), and it did not claim the Western Hemisphere as its exclusive zone of influence (D).

51. **A**

Prior to the Age of Exploration, the Aztec civilization was prosperous and healthy. As the result of disease and destruction brought by European explorers, the Aztec civilization was decimated. Horses (B) and cattle (C) were brought to the Americas during the Age of Exploration. The Age of Exploration preceded the development of the American colonies (D).

52. **B**

Benjamin Franklin proposed the Albany Plan of Union, which provided for an intercolonial government that would regulate dealings with the Native Americans, organize and run a colonial army, manage the public lands, legislate, and supervise the collection of taxes for a common defense fund. England rejected the proposal because it felt that a union of the colonies would make them too unmanageable. The colonies also failed to support it because they did not want to relinquish any of their current powers. Franklin's annoyance was reflected in the publishing of his cartoon in which he drew a snake broken into pieces with the inscription, "Join, or Die." The cartoon did not address enlistment in the militia (A). Franklin did not want the colonies to reunite with Great Britain (C). The cartoon did not address French support of the American Revolution (D).

53. **D**

Laws implementing the grandfather clause and literacy tests were specifically created to prevent Black people from voting. The grandfather clause stated that if your ancestors (grandfathers) were able to vote prior to 1867, then you could vote. Since most Black people had been slaves, that was not possible. There was generally a provision that the voting official could waive the requirement, if warranted. This loophole allowed illiterate and poor white people the right to vote (A). Immigrants who have not become citizens are never allowed to vote (B). While other laws may have prevented Black people from running for office (C), that was not the intent of the grandfather clause.

54. **A**

The Age of Revolution was the time period about 1750–1800 during which most European countries changed their government from monarchies to forms of government in which the people had more of a voice. The Age of Revolution specifically includes the American Revolution and the French Revolution. Democracies that did exist did not evolve into socialist governments (B). Autocracies became less, rather than more, powerful (C) and monarchies were not returned to power (D).

Detailed Explanations for Practice Test 1

55. **B**

    The Eighteenth Amendment made the sale of alcohol illegal, which led to a burgeoning bootlegging industry in which organized crime played a major role. The amendment was repealed by the Twenty-first Amendment in 1933. The Eighteenth Amendment did not address voting (A). It was passed in 1919 prior to the start of the Great Depression (C). The Twenty-Second Amendment addressed presidential term limits (D).

56. **B**

    The Cuban Revolution of 1959 led to a large wave of Cuban immigration into southern Florida, which transformed Miami into a major center of commerce, finance, and transportation. The Cuban Missile Crisis occurred in 1962 (A). The Korean War began in 1950 and ended in 1953, but was not related to Cuban immigration into southern Florida (C). The space industry in Florida was not the driving force that attracted Cubans to the United States (D).

57. **D.**

    Culture consists of the shared products of human interaction, both material and nonmaterial, and includes values (A), beliefs (B) and fashion customs (C). An individual's intelligence is the result of personal development and genetic inheritance. Because intelligence may vary greatly among individuals, it is not shared among members of a society and is not a factor of culture.

58. **D**

    The prompt *(Which of the amendments in the Bill of Rights has had the most effect on your life? Why?)* is at the evaluation level because it requires students to make a judgment. Comprehension (A) would focus on understanding of the amendments of the Bill of Rights. Synthesis (B) requires the development of something new and unique. Strategic thinking (C) is part of Webb's Depth of Knowledge, not Bloom's Taxonomy.

59. **C**

    The development of trade routes occurred prior to 1500 CE (B), so the slave trade had the greatest effect between 1500 and 1900 because it decimated the population of Africa. The Renaissance (A) and Reformation (D) were movements primarily in Europe.

60. **A**

    Introspective activities, such as brainstorming, help students to connect new information to previously learned information, an important cognitive process. While brainstorming can provide students with ideas for writing, it does not contribute to writing skill development (B). Brainstorming could provide opportunities to practice grammar and sentence structure (C) or improve self-esteem (D), but that is not its purpose.

61. **C**

    Thinking about what is known and unknown is metacognitive thinking. Literal-level questions focus on factual information (B). While the question prompts may contribute to the development of organizational skills (A) or indirectly impact academic skills (D), that is not their purpose.

62. **C**

    The bingo activity requires students to read, write, speak, listen, and move. Students are not solving a problem (A). They are gathering and displaying the answers to factual questions, which does not involve critical (B) or extended thinking (D).

63. **B**

    Reasoning inductively is using known facts to come to a generalization or conclusion. Reasoning deductively takes the opposite approach by starting with a generalization and then identifying the details or facts from it (C). Students are not asked to think of new solutions (A), nor are they working together (D).

64. **A**

    Since students are asked to provide different examples, they are using the concept in a different way: the application level. They are not asked to create anything new (B), and their thinking is beyond basic understanding (C) and remembering what was said (D).

65. **C**

    Geography can be divided into four main branches: (1) human, which focuses on the study of humans and the cultures they create; (2) physical, which focuses on the physical environment of Earth; (3) regional, which focuses on areas of Earth that are similar by examining them in terms of their commonalities; and (4) topical or systemic, which considers systematic studies of climate, landforms, economics, and culture. The concepts (e.g., political, relative, absolute) in the other options (A, B, D) relate to the study of geography, but are not the four main branches.

66. **B**

    Spatial interaction usually includes a variety of movements such as travel, migration, transmission of information, journeys to work or shopping, retailing activities, or freight distribution. Vernacular regions (A) are those loosely defined by people's perception (e.g., the Midwest, the Middle East). The boundaries of a perceptual region are determined by people's beliefs, not a scientifically measurable process. Friction of distance (C) is the degree to which distance interferes with an interaction. Space-time compression (D) is a sense of accessibility and connectivity that results in the perception that humans in distant places are closer together. For example, prior to the development of airplanes, traveling from the East Coast to the West Coast of the United States required an arduous journey of weeks or months. Today we can take a nonstop flight of a few hours to reach that destination. The physical distance hasn't changed, but our perception of the distance has.

Detailed Explanations for Practice Test 1

67. **D**

    The Enlightenment is also called the Age of Reason because this eighteenth-century movement involved a new secular worldview that explained the world and looked for answers in terms of reason rather than faith, and in terms of an optimistic, natural, humanistic approach rather than a fatalistic, supernatural one. Thus, they were "enlightened." The Age of Discovery (A) and Age of Exploration (B) preceded the Age of Reason. The Age of Revolution (C) was a product of the Age of Reason.

68. **A**

    An oligopoly is a market form in which a market or industry is dominated by a small number of sellers. A government led by a small group of ruling individuals (B) is an oligarchy. A black market (C) occurs when buyers and sellers are trading in illegal goods. An oligopoly is bad for consumers (D).

69. **B**

    Agents of erosion include streams (running water), mass movements, glaciers (moving ice), wind, and wave action. A river is an example of running water. Dunes (A) are one of the byproducts of interaction between natural processes that interacted to produce sediments. A drumlin (C) is formed from a glacier. Plate tectonics (D) is not a form of erosion.

70. **A**

    Human geography is the study of people's patterns and their processes in relation to the Earth's patterns and processes. (B) is too narrow in that it does not include human processes. (C) and (D) are also too narrow, although all given choices are a part of human geography.

71. **D**

    A mixed economy contains elements from traditional, command, and market economies. The economies of most countries are some form of mixed economy, although the proportions of tradition, command, and market economies differ greatly. Choice (A) does not reflect the characteristics of a mixed economy. Mixed economies are not necessarily unstable, depending on the mix of elements (B). Mixed economies are not the same as traditional economies (C).

72. **A**

    Jefferson would have been more likely to take a narrow view of the Constitution, whereas Hamilton had a broad and permissive view. Hamilton, rather than Jefferson, favored Britain over France (B), favored the establishment of a national bank (C), and won the cooperation of Presidents Washington and Adams (D).

73. **A**

GDP, inflation rates, and unemployment rates relate to the economy as a whole and are thus part of macroeconomics. Aggregate demand (B) is the amount of national output purchased. Microeconomics (C) focuses on the individual parts (e.g., households, business firms, and government agencies) of the economy and emphasizes how these parts make decisions as well as the consequences of those decisions. Aggregate supply (D) is the amount of national output produced.

74. **A**

Alexander Hamilton wrote fifty-two of the papers; James Madison, twenty-eight; and John Jay, the remaining five. Thomas Jefferson and George Washington were not involved (B). John Calhoun, a U.S. senator and eventually vice-president, was not born until 1782, and thus was only a child when the Federalist Papers were published (C). The Federalist Papers were written by three people, not five (D).

75. **B**

Socrates was a philosopher in Greece who developed a questioning style known as the Socratic Method. The Code of Hammurabi (A) was developed as part of the Babylonian Empire. The concept of *pi* originated in Greece (C). The Magna Carta was an English document (D).

76. **C**

Prehistory refers to time prior to the development of writing, rather than the use of fire (A), tools (B), or dinosaurs (D).

77. **D**

The key to this response is in the phrase "intervention in the Americas" because the Monroe Doctrine stated that the United States would oppose any European attempt to colonize the Americas. The Constitution (A) is the document that describes the fundamental principles by which the United States is governed. The Roosevelt Corollary preceded both the Truman Doctrine (B) and the Marshall Plan (C), so it could not have been based on either.

78. **A**

A local government is chartered according to its state's constitution. Just as the policies enacted by the state government must not conflict with federal law, a local government is subject to the legal environment created by the state's constitution and statutes. Local governments are not chartered by the federal government (B) or by counties (C). Notification to the next largest government agency does not result in a charter (D).

Detailed Explanations for Practice Test 1

79. **B**

    Political ecology is defined as a multi-disciplinary study of how social and environmental change occurs in the context of power relations, social structures, economic issues, and human–environment interactions. Environmental determinism (A) suggests that an area's physical characteristics, like climate, impact how people develop over time. Spatial interaction (C) describes how places interact through movement. Cultural diffusion (D) is an aspect of movement that focuses on how ideas, innovation, and ideology spread from one area to another.

80. **A**.

    Flora are plants. They are not related to soil composition (B), rural areas (C), or sources of fresh water (D).

81. **B**

    The God worshipped by the Jews was called Yahweh. Yahweh is not the name of sacred Buddhist writings (A), a place where Confucianism originated (C), or another name for Mecca.

82. **A**

    The scientific method is a form of inquiry. Question answering (at any level) is not necessarily inquiry (B). While service learning could involve inquiry, the task as stated does not involve inquiry (C). Playing a Jeopardy game is not a form of inquiry (D).

83. **B**

    In 2010, 5.6% of the children had difficulty speaking English; by 2015, the percentage had increased to 6.6%. The other factors—teen dropouts (A), children living below the poverty line (C), and children living in high-poverty neighborhoods (D)—decreased.

84. **A**

    It can be inferred that the children living below the poverty line are a large percentage of those children living in high-poverty neighborhoods, where 20% or more of the population is below the poverty line. However, none of the other correlations mentioned can be inferred from the data: Teens who are high school dropouts are most likely from single-parent households (B); children living in single-parent households are the same children who have difficulty speaking English (C); or a large percentage of children living in high-poverty neighborhoods live in single-parent households (D).

85. **C**

    In 1562, French Huguenots established a short-lived colony at Port Royal, South Carolina, and, two years later, at Ft. Caroline, Florida. In response to these attempted French colonies, the Spanish established an outpost in 1565 in present-day Florida. This Spanish settlement, St. Augustine, became the first European town in the present-day United States. New Orleans (A) was founded in 1716 and Santa Fe (B) was established in 1610. The first permanent English settlement in North America was Jamestown, founded in 1607 (D).

86. **D**

President Lyndon B. Johnson was a proponent of Civil Rights and, realizing that many Americans did not have adequate food or housing, declared a "War on Poverty." The Bay of Pigs (A) and Cuban Missile Crisis (C) were associated with the administration of President John F. Kennedy. Watergate (B) was the event that eventually caused President Richard Nixon to resign from the presidency.

87. **D**

Slavery was an issue that cropped up as the colonies fought for independence and continued to be an issue through the mid-1800s as the country wrestled with admitting new states and territories. While treaties (A) were an issue, they were not a focus of the Compromise of 1820 and the Compromise of 1850. Relocating American Indians (B) to reservations became a concern in the 1820s under the administration of President James Monroe. Union demands (C) were not a concern until the mid-1800s.

88. **B**

The Grange Movement, with more than 1 million members, sought to allow farmers to buy machinery and sell crops as a group and therefore reap the benefits. They tried to lobby for legislation, notably what became referred to as the Granger Laws, that sought to address some of the problems of railroad exploitation that farmers faced trying to get their goods to market. Eventually, the Granger Laws were ruled unconstitutional, and Congress passed the Interstate Commerce Act of 1887 that sought to address the same issues. Granger laws did not specifically apply to slaves (A), miners (C), or Prohibition supporters (D).

89. **A**

The Civil Rights Act of 1964 prohibited discrimination for reason of color, race, religion, sex, or national origin in places of public accommodation covered by interstate commerce, that is, restaurants, hotels, motels, and theaters. Besides dealing with the desegregation of public schools, the act, in Title VII, forbade discrimination in employment. Title VII also prohibited discrimination on the basis of sex. In 1965, the Voting Rights Act was passed, placing federal observers at polls to ensure equal voting rights. The Civil Rights Act of 1968 dealt with housing and real estate discrimination. *Brown v. Board of Education* overturned *Plessy v. Ferguson* in 1954, declaring that separate but equal facilities were inherently unequal; however, integration of schools did not occur immediately (B). The Civil Rights Act of 1964 did not address inequalities as part of the War on Poverty (C), or the rights of undocumented citizens (D).

90. **C**

The Code of Hammurabi was a body of legal codes proclaimed by Hammurabi, King of Babylon from 1792 BCE–1750 BCE. Therefore, the best person for Caroline to interview would be Joan Hernandez, a lawyer. While she could interview a physician (A), teacher (B), or architect (D) about the effects of laws in their professions, their views would not represent legal thought and expertise.

Detailed Explanations for Practice Test 1

91. **D**

    The Elastic Clause empowers Congress to make laws that are necessary and proper for carrying out its powers. The clause is not related to presidential actions during times of war (A), the Supreme Court (B), or the checks and balances among the three branches of government (C).

92. **A**

    Adam Smith's concept was termed "the invisible hand." The other responses do not reflect the concept described in *The Wealth of Nations*.

93. **D**

    Throughout the immense time span of the Stone Age, vast changes occurred in climate and in other conditions affecting human culture. Humans themselves evolved into their modern form during the latter part of it. The Stone Age has been divided accordingly into three periods: the Paleolithic, Mesolithic, and Neolithic. The word part *–lith* means rock or stone. There was no "Copper Age" (A). The Bronze (B) and Iron (C) ages occurred later.

94. **D**

    The philosophes were the intellectuals of the Enlightenment. They called into question the traditions of society and supported looking at the universe in a scientific, critical light. During the Enlightenment, all the trademark aspects of European society were exposed to criticism and analysis through reason; therefore, a philosophe would have supported critical thinking. A philosophe would not have supported religious doctrine (A), elimination of rulers (B), or pessimism (C) without application of reasoning.

95. **D**

    W.E.B. DuBois was an African-American leader in the early part of the twentieth century. He called on Blacks to develop a Black consciousness that would be distinct from that of whites, and would emanate from an understanding of Black history, art, music, and religion. DuBois founded the Niagara Movement, which called for federal legislation to protect racial equality and for full rights of citizenship. Two years later, in conjunction with white liberals, DuBois headed the National Association for the Advancement of Colored People (NAACP) that advocated an end to discrimination. The Harlem Renaissance describes a time period in the 1920s marked by African-American cultural, social, and artistic achievements, and CORE was led by James Farmer (A). The Civil Rights Act of 1964 was signed by President Lyndon Johnson and it created the Equal Employment Opportunity Commission (B). The Tuskegee Airmen were a World War II group of African-American pilots, and SNCC set up the Voter Education Project (C).

96. **B**

In 1783, Benjamin Franklin, John Jay, and John Adams negotiated peace with the British in Paris. The resulting treaty was called the Treaty of Paris and formally recognized the independence of the United States by Britain and major European powers. The Mayflower Compact, signed on the *Mayflower* ship by Puritan colonists from England, was the first written framework of government for what is now the United States (A). The Treaty of Versailles was signed at the same time as the Treaty of Paris; however, it was between Great Britain and the countries that had supported American independence: France, Spain, and the Dutch Republic (C). The Constitution of the United States describes the national framework of government (D).

97. **A**

Ten thousand impoverished World War I veterans and their families marched on Washington in support of a bill that would have provided them with early bonus payment of benefits. The bill was defeated, and about 3,000 of these "bonus marchers" stayed in Washington to protest. While the AFL was formed in 1886, the CIO was not formed until 1935, two years after Hoover left office (B). Though the Harlem Renaissance occurred within the timeframe of Hoover's administration, it had no connection to bonus marchers (C). Prohibition began well before Hoover's administration (D).

98. **A**

The Thirty Years War (1618–1648) was fought between the Catholic Holy Roman Empire and some of the German Protestant States. It did not involve nationalism (B), imperialism (C), or class warfare (D).

99. **B**

Since fauna are animals, Jon provided the correct response when he said he saw a squirrel in a tree. Fauna do not relate to clouds (A), types of rock (C), or bodies of water (D).

100. **B**

Gross Domestic Product (GDP) is defined as the total money value of final goods and services that a country produces over a given period of time, usually one year. The number is like a snapshot of the economy at a certain point in time. Macroeconomics (A) is more broad than the GDP and is defined as the study of the economy as a whole and includes topics such as inflation, unemployment, and economic growth. The Federal Reserve System (C) implements monetary policy by changing the level of money in the U.S. banking system. The currency exchange rate (D) describes the way in which international countries are able to trade goods and services.

101. **B**

The four phases of a market economy cycle are boom, recession, trough, and recovery. The terms in the other options are related to economics, but are not the four phases of a market economy.

Detailed Explanations for Practice Test 1

102. **A**

    GNP is the gross national product and is defined as the total goods and services produced by the nation in a given year. Choice (B) is only partially correct because services are not specified. Choices (C) and (D) are not economic terms.

103. **D**

    Cyclical unemployment occurs when the economy falls as the result of a recession. Businesses often survive by laying off workers rather than cutting salaries and prices. Frictional unemployment (A) occurs when workers voluntarily move from one job to another with time in-between. Functional unemployment (B) takes several forms, including more workers than available jobs, lack of demand for skills, workers with skills that do not match industry needs, and seasonal employment/unemployment. *Total unemployment* (C) is not an economic term.

104. **B**

    The Vice President serves as the president of the Senate. That position is not given to the Majority Leader (A), the senator with the greatest authority (C), or the Speaker of the House (D).

105. **B**

    Nine justices serve on the U.S. Supreme Court.

106. **C**

    The stock market crash, which was precipitated by extensive speculation, was a major cause of the Great Depression. Military unrest in Europe (A) was not a factor. The Cold War (B) began after World War II and, thus, could not have contributed to the Great Depression. Weak unions (D) did not contribute to the Great Depression.

107. **C**

    Margaret Sanger opened the first U.S. birth-control clinic in Brooklyn, New York, in 1916; therefore, approval of birth control pills logically would have been something she would have supported, rather than divorce laws (A), prohibition (B), or bonus marchers (D).

108. **A**

    Throughout the Cold War, competition between the two world powers would be played out in other countries. In 1947, civil war in Greece created a dynamic where the West was on one side and the Soviets were on the other. Truman asked Congress for $400 million in military and economic aid for Greece, as well as neighboring Turkey, which was also in danger. In what became known as the Truman Doctrine, he argued that while the United States would not initiate a war with the Soviet Union, it would support free peoples in countries that were resisting communism. While the Red Army is a term often used to describe Soviet or Chinese forces, that was not the impetus for the Truman Doctrine (B). The Truman Doctrine preceded the invasion of North Korea into South Korea (C) and the communist threat to Vietnam (D).

109. **C**

During its organizational period, the CIO (Congress of Industrialized Organizations) sought to involve several industrial unions, particularly in the steel, auto, rubber, and radio industries. SNCC (Student Nonviolent Coordinating Committee) (A), formed in the 1960s, did not involve labor unions. The EEOC (Equal Employment Opportunity Commission) (B), which formed after the Civil Rights Act of 1964, was not a labor union. The CCC (Civilian Conservation Corps) (D) was a Depression-era work program in which men worked in camps to perform reforestation and conservation tasks.

110. **C**

Brown v. Board of Education of Topeka reversed the "separate but equal" concept that had been decided in the *Plessy v. Ferguson* case; therefore, option (C) is correct and option (A) is incorrect. *Schenck v. United States* (B) upheld the Espionage Act which authorized fines and imprisonment for persons who made false statements that aided the enemy, incited rebellion in the military, or obstructed recruitment or the draft. In *Morgan v. Virginia* (D), the Supreme Court ruled that segregated interstate buses were illegal as they put an "undue burden on interstate trade and transport." This struck down laws requiring segregation, but only in instances where interstate transportation was concerned.

111. **B**

Cloture is a parliamentary procedure that can limit debate and bring a filibuster to an end. Adjournment (A) ends a meeting or session. The Speaker of the House (C) has no authority to rule on Senate operations or policies. The president cannot override Senate debate or end a filibuster (D).

112. **D**

A *polis* in ancient Greece was a city-state; therefore, Athens is the correct response. *Polis* is not a body of water (A), a kind of writing (B), or a person (C).

113. **C**

The United States detonated atomic bombs over the Japanese cities of Hiroshima and Nagasaki, which ended World War II. Hiroshima and Nagasaki were not migration centers to the United States (A). Hiroshima was not the center of a civilization (B). These were not cities in the Mongol civilization (D).

114. **C**

The Selective Service Act was passed in order for men to be registered for the draft prior to World War II. The Selective Service Act did not address prohibition (A), women's voting rights (B), or civil rights (D).

Detailed Explanations for Practice Test 1

115. **C**

President Woodrow Wilson presented his peace plan in the form of the *Fourteen Points*. The first five points called for open, rather than secret, peace treaties, freedom of the seas, free trade, arms reduction, and a fair adjustment of colonial claims. The next eight points addressed the national aspirations of various European peoples and the adjustment of boundaries. The last point called for a "general association of nations" to preserve the peace. The Fourteen Points did not address immigration (A), civil rights (B), or prohibition (D).

116. **B**

The *Engel v. Vitale* decision stated that prayer would not be allowed in schools. It did not address searches (A), segregation (C), or the civil rights of students with disabilities (D).

117. **B**

Many factors contributed to the U.S. decision to enter World War II, including the fact that Nazi Germany was sinking American supply ships because the United States was providing financial and military support to the Allied troops (England, France, China, and Russia). The immediate cause, however, was Japan's attack on the U.S. naval base at Pearl Harbor, Hawaii, without a declaration of war or any warning that hostilities were being commenced. The day after the attack, December 7, 1941, President Franklin Roosevelt went before the U.S. Congress and asked for a formal declaration of war with Japan in retaliation. President Roosevelt never asked Congress to declare war with Italy or Germany (A). Instead, three days after December 7, Italy and Germany declared war on the United States (C). The assassination of the Archduke of Austria (D) triggered World War I.

118. **A**

Dr. King's methods were characterized by nonviolent defiance of segregation. While King and/or his supporters might make speeches or send petitions, civil disobedience gave his movement its urgency. His methods were not characterized by governmental petitions (B), or armed violence (C), nor were speaking engagements (D) specifically part of Dr. King's plan—even though he was a gifted speaker.

119. **C**

Capital gain involves financial profit, so making a profit from the sale of stock would result in a capital gain. Elections (A), student grades (B), or population (D) do not result in capital gain.

120. **D**

The Preamble of the Constitution addresses popular sovereignty, or the idea that government derives its power from the people. Article 1 of the Constitution addresses the role and responsibilities of the Legislative Branch (A). The Bill of Rights (B) consists of the first ten amendments to the Constitution and civil liberties and civil rights. Amendments 1–5 are part of the Bill of Rights (C).

Practice Test 2

FTCE Social Science 6–12

Also available at the REA Study Center (www.rea.com/studycenter)

This practice test is also offered online at the REA Study Center. Since the FTCE Social Science 6-12 exam is administered on computer, we recommend that you take the online version of the test to receive these added benefits:

- **Timed testing conditions**—Gauge how much time you can spend on each question.

- **Automatic scoring**—Find out how you did on the test, instantly.

- **On-screen detailed explanations of answers**—Learn not just the correct answers, but also why the other answer choices are incorrect.

- **Diagnostic score reports**—Pinpoint where you're strongest and where you need to focus your study.

ANSWER SHEET FOR PRACTICE TEST 2

1. Ⓐ Ⓑ Ⓒ Ⓓ
2. Ⓐ Ⓑ Ⓒ Ⓓ
3. Ⓐ Ⓑ Ⓒ Ⓓ
4. Ⓐ Ⓑ Ⓒ Ⓓ
5. Ⓐ Ⓑ Ⓒ Ⓓ
6. Ⓐ Ⓑ Ⓒ Ⓓ
7. Ⓐ Ⓑ Ⓒ Ⓓ
8. Ⓐ Ⓑ Ⓒ Ⓓ
9. Ⓐ Ⓑ Ⓒ Ⓓ
10. Ⓐ Ⓑ Ⓒ Ⓓ
11. Ⓐ Ⓑ Ⓒ Ⓓ
12. Ⓐ Ⓑ Ⓒ Ⓓ
13. Ⓐ Ⓑ Ⓒ Ⓓ
14. Ⓐ Ⓑ Ⓒ Ⓓ
15. Ⓐ Ⓑ Ⓒ Ⓓ
16. Ⓐ Ⓑ Ⓒ Ⓓ
17. Ⓐ Ⓑ Ⓒ Ⓓ
18. Ⓐ Ⓑ Ⓒ Ⓓ
19. Ⓐ Ⓑ Ⓒ Ⓓ
20. Ⓐ Ⓑ Ⓒ Ⓓ
21. Ⓐ Ⓑ Ⓒ Ⓓ
22. Ⓐ Ⓑ Ⓒ Ⓓ
23. Ⓐ Ⓑ Ⓒ Ⓓ
24. Ⓐ Ⓑ Ⓒ Ⓓ
25. Ⓐ Ⓑ Ⓒ Ⓓ
26. Ⓐ Ⓑ Ⓒ Ⓓ
27. Ⓐ Ⓑ Ⓒ Ⓓ
28. Ⓐ Ⓑ Ⓒ Ⓓ
29. Ⓐ Ⓑ Ⓒ Ⓓ
30. Ⓐ Ⓑ Ⓒ Ⓓ
31. Ⓐ Ⓑ Ⓒ Ⓓ
32. Ⓐ Ⓑ Ⓒ Ⓓ
33. Ⓐ Ⓑ Ⓒ Ⓓ
34. Ⓐ Ⓑ Ⓒ Ⓓ
35. Ⓐ Ⓑ Ⓒ Ⓓ
36. Ⓐ Ⓑ Ⓒ Ⓓ
37. Ⓐ Ⓑ Ⓒ Ⓓ
38. Ⓐ Ⓑ Ⓒ Ⓓ
39. Ⓐ Ⓑ Ⓒ Ⓓ
40. Ⓐ Ⓑ Ⓒ Ⓓ
41. Ⓐ Ⓑ Ⓒ Ⓓ
42. Ⓐ Ⓑ Ⓒ Ⓓ
43. Ⓐ Ⓑ Ⓒ Ⓓ
44. Ⓐ Ⓑ Ⓒ Ⓓ
45. Ⓐ Ⓑ Ⓒ Ⓓ
46. Ⓐ Ⓑ Ⓒ Ⓓ
47. Ⓐ Ⓑ Ⓒ Ⓓ
48. Ⓐ Ⓑ Ⓒ Ⓓ
49. Ⓐ Ⓑ Ⓒ Ⓓ
50. Ⓐ Ⓑ Ⓒ Ⓓ
51. Ⓐ Ⓑ Ⓒ Ⓓ
52. Ⓐ Ⓑ Ⓒ Ⓓ
53. Ⓐ Ⓑ Ⓒ Ⓓ
54. Ⓐ Ⓑ Ⓒ Ⓓ
55. Ⓐ Ⓑ Ⓒ Ⓓ
56. Ⓐ Ⓑ Ⓒ Ⓓ
57. Ⓐ Ⓑ Ⓒ Ⓓ
58. Ⓐ Ⓑ Ⓒ Ⓓ
59. Ⓐ Ⓑ Ⓒ Ⓓ
60. Ⓐ Ⓑ Ⓒ Ⓓ
61. Ⓐ Ⓑ Ⓒ Ⓓ
62. Ⓐ Ⓑ Ⓒ Ⓓ
63. Ⓐ Ⓑ Ⓒ Ⓓ
64. Ⓐ Ⓑ Ⓒ Ⓓ
65. Ⓐ Ⓑ Ⓒ Ⓓ
66. Ⓐ Ⓑ Ⓒ Ⓓ
67. Ⓐ Ⓑ Ⓒ Ⓓ
68. Ⓐ Ⓑ Ⓒ Ⓓ
69. Ⓐ Ⓑ Ⓒ Ⓓ
70. Ⓐ Ⓑ Ⓒ Ⓓ
71. Ⓐ Ⓑ Ⓒ Ⓓ
72. Ⓐ Ⓑ Ⓒ Ⓓ
73. Ⓐ Ⓑ Ⓒ Ⓓ
74. Ⓐ Ⓑ Ⓒ Ⓓ
75. Ⓐ Ⓑ Ⓒ Ⓓ
76. Ⓐ Ⓑ Ⓒ Ⓓ
77. Ⓐ Ⓑ Ⓒ Ⓓ
78. Ⓐ Ⓑ Ⓒ Ⓓ
79. Ⓐ Ⓑ Ⓒ Ⓓ
80. Ⓐ Ⓑ Ⓒ Ⓓ
81. Ⓐ Ⓑ Ⓒ Ⓓ
82. Ⓐ Ⓑ Ⓒ Ⓓ
83. Ⓐ Ⓑ Ⓒ Ⓓ
84. Ⓐ Ⓑ Ⓒ Ⓓ
85. Ⓐ Ⓑ Ⓒ Ⓓ
86. Ⓐ Ⓑ Ⓒ Ⓓ
87. Ⓐ Ⓑ Ⓒ Ⓓ
88. Ⓐ Ⓑ Ⓒ Ⓓ
89. Ⓐ Ⓑ Ⓒ Ⓓ
90. Ⓐ Ⓑ Ⓒ Ⓓ
91. Ⓐ Ⓑ Ⓒ Ⓓ
92. Ⓐ Ⓑ Ⓒ Ⓓ
93. Ⓐ Ⓑ Ⓒ Ⓓ
94. Ⓐ Ⓑ Ⓒ Ⓓ
95. Ⓐ Ⓑ Ⓒ Ⓓ
96. Ⓐ Ⓑ Ⓒ Ⓓ
97. Ⓐ Ⓑ Ⓒ Ⓓ
98. Ⓐ Ⓑ Ⓒ Ⓓ
99. Ⓐ Ⓑ Ⓒ Ⓓ
100. Ⓐ Ⓑ Ⓒ Ⓓ
101. Ⓐ Ⓑ Ⓒ Ⓓ
102. Ⓐ Ⓑ Ⓒ Ⓓ
103. Ⓐ Ⓑ Ⓒ Ⓓ
104. Ⓐ Ⓑ Ⓒ Ⓓ
105. Ⓐ Ⓑ Ⓒ Ⓓ
106. Ⓐ Ⓑ Ⓒ Ⓓ
107. Ⓐ Ⓑ Ⓒ Ⓓ
108. Ⓐ Ⓑ Ⓒ Ⓓ
109. Ⓐ Ⓑ Ⓒ Ⓓ
110. Ⓐ Ⓑ Ⓒ Ⓓ
111. Ⓐ Ⓑ Ⓒ Ⓓ
112. Ⓐ Ⓑ Ⓒ Ⓓ
113. Ⓐ Ⓑ Ⓒ Ⓓ
114. Ⓐ Ⓑ Ⓒ Ⓓ
115. Ⓐ Ⓑ Ⓒ Ⓓ
116. Ⓐ Ⓑ Ⓒ Ⓓ
117. Ⓐ Ⓑ Ⓒ Ⓓ
118. Ⓐ Ⓑ Ⓒ Ⓓ
119. Ⓐ Ⓑ Ⓒ Ⓓ
120. Ⓐ Ⓑ Ⓒ Ⓓ

PRACTICE TEST 2

Questions: 120*
Time: 2 hours and 30 minutes

1. Ms. Bateman is grading economics papers. Lindsey has written a paper about the pure market system. Which sentence in Lindsay's paper is incorrect?

    In a pure market system, there is no central authority. Custom plays a large role in this rather competitive market. Buyers and sellers decide what goods and services will be produced. Every consumer makes buying decisions based on his or her own needs and desires and income. Individual self-interest rules over the good of others. Producers tend to be solely motivated by a desire for profit.

    A. Producers tend to be solely motivated by a desire for profit.
    B. Individual self-interest rules over the good of others.
    C. Every consumer makes buying decisions based on his or her own needs and desires and income.
    D. Custom plays a large role in this rather competitive market.

2. *Plate tectonics* is a set of related concepts that describe how the Earth's crust works. Which of the following statements is true?
    A. Earthquakes can occur when plates collide.
    B. According to tectonic plate theory, the continents have become stationary plates and the plate movement occurs only under the ocean floor.
    C. Plate movement influences hurricanes.
    D. Plates are affected by gravity and ocean tides.

3. In the United States, which of the following powers is reserved only for the states?
    A. Raise and maintain an army and navy
    B. Grant copyrights and patents
    C. Ratify proposed amendments to the Constitution
    D. Regulate naturalization and immigration

4. The principle of "popular sovereignty" was
    A. applied as part of the Missouri Compromise.
    B. a central feature of the Kansas-Nebraska Act.
    C. a key issue for the United States in entering World War I.
    D. resolved issues remaining from the Albany Plan of Union.

---

* The actual test contains approximately 100 questions. You will only learn exactly how many questions you will get after you take the FTCE tutorial and sign the non-disclosure agreement on test day.

Practice Test 2

5. Which of the following was a major tipping point in John F. Kennedy's 1960 presidential election victory over Richard Nixon?
    A. Americans' deep and growing dissatisfaction with the Eisenhower Administration
    B. Kennedy's better showing in nationally televised debates
    C. Kennedy's record as a congressman and U.S. senator
    D. Nixon's failure to serve in the armed forces during the Second World War

6. Which of the following series is in correct chronological order?
    A. French and Indian War, Revolutionary War, War of 1812
    B. Revolutionary War, War of 1812, French and Indian War
    C. War of 1812, French and Indian War, Revolutionary War
    D. War of 1812, Revolutionary War, French and Indian War

7. Ms. Alvarez has collected a variety of print and media resources for the students to use in their research. Which of the following would be the best way to motivate students to research the questions they have prepared?
    A. The teacher should assign two to three questions to each student so that all the questions are covered.
    B. The teacher should allow students to select the questions they would like to research.
    C. The teacher should select three key questions and assign them to all the students.
    D. The teacher should assign one topic to each student, then provide the students with additional information.

8. Serena takes digital notes in class using an iPad. If you were to review her notes over the first semester, you would see the following terms: *environment, human systems, physical systems,* and *environment and society*. What course is Serena most likely taking?
    A. Civics
    B. Geography
    C. History
    D. Economics

9. Victor is working on a project for his geography class. He has collected data about his school's building. He has the following information: There are 40 classrooms in the building.

   5 are used for math only.

   5 are used for language arts only.

   20 are used for multiple subjects.

   2 are used for music only.

   1 is used for physical education only.

   2 are used for art only.

   5 are used for science only.

   5 are used for social sciences only.

   What type of graphic would be the best for Victor to use in displaying his data?

   A. scatter plot

   B. line graph

   C. area chart

   D. pie chart

10. What commonality was shared by the three Kingdoms of Kush, Axum, and the Swahili prior to 1500 CE?

    A. They had a common African religion.

    B. The kingdoms had been British colonies prior to becoming independent kingdoms.

    C. The kingdoms were ruled by three brothers of a dynasty.

    D. All three were countries whose economies were based on trade.

11. The author of *The Wealth of Nations* was

    A. Adam Smith.

    B. James Madison.

    C. Benjamin Franklin.

    D. Thomas Jefferson.

12. Kevin lost his job in an automobile plant because the company began using robots for welding on the assembly line. Kevin plans to go to technical school to learn how to repair microcomputers. The type of unemployment Kevin is faced with is

    A. functional.

    B. educational.

    C. cyclical.

    D. frictional.

13. Which religion and sacred writings are correctly matched?

    A.   Hinduism, *Vedas*

    B.   Islam, *Analects*

    C.   Judaism, *Gospels*

    D.   Buddhism, *Qur'an*

14. What was the focus of Mayan cities?

    A.   Ceremonial centers

    B.   Governmental headquarters

    C.   Central marketplaces

    D.   Festivals and celebrations

15. A promise to pay for goods or services that have already been provided is called

    A.   credit.

    B.   a bond.

    C.   interest.

    D.   a liability.

16. Which of the following is true about a monopoly?

    A.   Consumers can be sure they are paying a fair price.

    B.   A single company dominates the industry.

    C.   There are multiple sellers protected by government regulation.

    D.   Competition drives down prices.

17. Alexander Hamilton wrote many of *The Federalist Papers*. As part of one, he stated the following:

    IT HAS been already observed that the federal government ought to possess the power of providing for the support of the national forces; in which proposition was intended to be included the expense of raising troops, of building and equipping fleets, and all other expenses in any wise connected with military arrangements and operations. But these are not the only objects to which the jurisdiction of the Union, in respect to revenue, must necessarily be empowered to extend. It must embrace a provision for the support of the national civil list; for the payment of the national debts contracted, or that may be contracted; and, in general, for all those matters which will call for disbursements out of the national treasury. The conclusion is, that there must be interwoven, in the frame of the government, a general power of _____, in one shape or another.

    What is the best word to fill the blank in the last sentence?

    A. public defense

    B. taxation

    C. governance

    D. civilians

18. The underlying issue that led to the outbreak of war between the United States and Japan in 1941 was

    A. Japanese aid to the Germans in their war against Britain.

    B. the U.S. desire to annex various Pacific islands held by Japan.

    C. the Japanese attack of Pearl Harbor.

    D. American resentment of Japanese trading policies and trade surpluses.

19. Which of the following was NOT included in the basic beliefs most of the Founders held that led them to view political parties as dangerous to a stable government?

    A. Parties created and exploited conflicts that undermined consensus on public policy.

    B. Parties were instruments by which a small and narrow interest could impose its will on society.

    C. Parties provide only a general understanding of where the candidate stands.

    D. Parties stifled independent thought and behavior.

20. Which of the following statements is true of the Silk Road?

    A. The Silk Road was developed during the Ming Dynasty.

    B. The Silk Road was a system of trade routes that existed for the purpose of trading in silk and many other commodities.

    C. The Silk Road was a system of waterways that enabled traders to move from country to country as smoothly as silk.

    D. The Silk Road was originally developed for military use and defense.

21. Which of the following is an example of a civil liberty?

    A. A family can attend the church of their choice.

    B. A business gives employees a bonus at the end of the year.

    C. A man yells "Fire!" in a movie theater, although there is no fire.

    D. The government provides crop subsidies to farmers.

22. The Inductive/Discovery Approach can be best used to teach

    A. generalizations and facts in social science.

    B. the order of the Bill of Rights.

    C. historical events.

    D. metacognitive thinking.

23. Why did the framers of the Constitution design the system of checks and balances?

    A. To maintain parity of power between the branches of government

    B. To minimize foreign intervention

    C. To help maintain the financial stability of the new government

    D. To set the foundation for a national bank

24. How many Senators serve in Congress?

    A. The number varies by state, depending on the population of the state

    B. 51: two from each state and one from Washington, D.C.

    C. 435

    D. 100

25. Which of the following individuals meets the requirements to be the president of the United States?

    A. James S. is a 60-year-old veteran who served in the Vietnam War. He is married and has four children. He has a successful law practice in Washington, D.C. He is a naturalized citizen.

    B. Faith J. is 30 years old. Both of her parents worked for the government and she was the youngest member of the legislature of her state. She is not married and has an undergraduate degree in psychology.

    C. Carl K. is 37 years old. He was born in the United States; however, his father was in the military and Carl spent the first 18 years of his life living in various bases in Europe and Asia. Carl attended college at the University of Tennessee and then joined the military. He served as an intelligence agent in Iraq for 8 years. When Carl completed his military service, he moved to New Mexico. Karl is not married.

    D. Maria N. is a forty-year-old physician from Florida. Her parents are from Puerto Rico. She was born in Orlando and moved to Miami when she was 12. After completing medical school, she started a medical practice in Tallahassee. Maria is divorced with two children.

26. For what length of term are Supreme Court Justices appointed?

    A. 6 years

    B. 1 year, renewable annually

    C. life

    D. 10 years

27. In terms of the economy, the "4 Es" (Allocative Efficiency, Productive Efficiency, Full Employment, Equity) are

    A. ways for society to use existing resources to reduce scarcity and obtain the maximum satisfaction possible.

    B. strategies used by the Federal Reserve to avoid a stock market crash.

    C. techniques used by capitalists in a traditional market to stabilize prices.

    D. principles used in a command economy to maximize control.

28. In terms of technical efficiency, which of the following correctly identifies the number of cars and motorcycles that can be produced, according to the graph below?

    A. 9 cars and 9 motorcycles

    B. 7 cars and 4 motorcycles

    C. 9 cars and 4 motorcycles

    D. 4 cars and 10 motorcycles

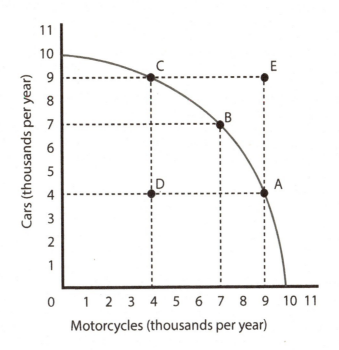

29. The major responsibility of the Federal Reserve is to

    A. implement monetary policy.

    B. control government spending.

    C. regulate commodity prices.

    D. help the president run the executive branch.

30. GDP can be defined as the value of

    A. all final goods and services produced in an economy in a given year.

    B. the federal budget minus expenditures and plus income taxes.

    C. national income earned by consumers, producers, and exporters.

    D. national debt owed to other countries.

31. Which of the following founders was one of the authors of the Federalist Papers and wrote the Bill of Rights?

    A. Alexander Hamilton

    B. James Madison

    C. John Jay

    D. Thomas Jefferson

32. *Ethnography* is defined as

    A. the study of the cultures of prehistoric peoples.

    B. a systematic description of a human society from the perspective of a researcher who lives and interacts with members of the culture over time.

    C. an interpretive explanation of human behavior.

    D. experimental research with individuals that focuses on racial and ethnic differences.

33. Mrs. Joffrion teaches Civics. Her class has been discussing the rights and responsibilities of citizenship. She has assigned an essay for students to complete:

    Imagine that you have your own country and are creating your own government. Based on the rights and responsibilities of American citizens, what three rights and/or responsibilities of American citizens would also be important in your country? Why? What additional right or responsibility would you create for your citizens? Why?

    In terms of Webb's Depth of Knowledge, what would be the level of this assignment?

    A. skill/concept

    B. synthesis

    C. evaluation

    D. extended thinking

34. Which college student organization or entity would logically have been formed as the result of *Title IX of the Education Amendments*?

    A. a peace and justice organization

    B. co-ed residential halls

    C. a women's swim team

    D. an organization for LGBT students

35. The Bill of Rights

    A. delegated to the federal government all the rights not given to the states.

    B. established a viable two-party political system.

    C. was written to overcome concerns about federalism.

    D. are also called the Articles of the Constitution.

Practice Test 2

36. What is considered an important movement of Black artists and writers?
    A. Roaring Twenties
    B. Harlem Renaissance
    C. Lost Generation
    D. Jazz Age

37. What was the result of the Eighteenth Amendment?
    A. All Americans became eligible to vote.
    B. Prohibition heightened criminal activity.
    C. The Great Depression was eased.
    D. Presidents were limited to two terms of four years each.

38. The place where supply and demand curves intersect is called
    A. the equilibrium.
    B. the standard of equity.
    C. a mixed economy.
    D. technical efficiency.

39. McCarthyism in the 1950s was an attempt to reveal
    A. communist infiltration in the United States government.
    B. corruption in the Roosevelt administration.
    C. misuse of corporate funds for political purposes.
    D. the dangers of nuclear energy.

40. Which of the following associations is accurate?
    A. Franklin D. Roosevelt and the New Deal
    B. Adolf Hitler and economic prosperity
    C. Black codes and freedom for slaves
    D. Charles de Gaulle and the Tehran Conference

41. In 1492, Christopher Columbus's voyage took nearly 40 days to cross the Atlantic Ocean, a trip that would take a modern ship less than one week. This difference best reflects the geographic concept of

    A. distance decay.

    B. uneven development.

    C. stimulus diffusion.

    D. space-time compression.

42. Which of the following New Deal programs was designed to reduce unemployment?

    A. Agricultural Adjustment Act

    B. National Industrial Recovery Act

    C. Glass-Steagall Act

    D. Civilian Conservation Corps

43. Which of the following accurately describes an impact of nationalism on a country?

    A. Economies are concentrated in smaller units and are, therefore, more diverse.

    B. A spirit of nationalism encourages the efforts of revolutionaries who want change.

    C. Nationalism encourages a multicultural approach and embraces new immigrants as individuals who will contribute new and different ideas and values.

    D. Nationalism promoted by the government is a unifying force.

44. What is true of *globalization*?

    A. It has a common definition set by the United Nations.

    B. The recommendation to "buy local" is just another way of saying that what was once global is now local.

    C. Both technology and changes in world economies have impacted globalization.

    D. Globalization recognizes the importance of each country's borders as limits.

45. Which article and its focus are correctly matched?

    A. Article III, Executive Branch

    B. Article I, Legislative Branch

    C. Article V, Ratifying the Constitution

    D. Article VII, Supremacy Clause

Practice Test 2

46. *Government by the many* is called a(n)
    A. democracy.
    B. oligarchy.
    C. monarchy.
    D. anarchy.

47. An example of relative location is
    A. regional geography.
    B. 28 North Main Street in Williamsport, Pennsylvania.
    C. the corner of 57th and 5th in Manhattan.
    D. the house across from the Mayfair Shops on Florida Ave., in Miami.

48. Which of the following represents monetary policy geared to increase the supply of money?
    A. The purchase of bonds by the Federal Reserve Bank
    B. The sale of bonds by the central bank
    C. An increase in reserve requirements
    D. An increase in the discount rate

49. The U.S. economy is growing too fast. What can be done to contract it?
    A. The Fed can buy bonds in the open market.
    B. The government can decrease spending and increase taxes.
    C. The Fed can reduce the reserve requirement for banks.
    D. The Fed can lower the discount rate for banks.

50. John lives in a country in which the government regulates production and controls all economic decisions. The government owns and operates the manufacture of industrial goods and regulates the kind and quantity of goods that are produced. Prices are also controlled. John's country uses which economic model?
    A. authoritarian
    B. traditional
    C. command
    D. mixed

51. Which historical figure was most likely to be an *empiricist*?

    A. Diderot, author of *Encyclopedie*, which classified all human knowledge from the most common to the most complex.

    B. Genghis Khan, ruler of the Mongols

    C. Samuel Richardson, author of the first modern novel

    D. Pope Alexander VI, who settled territorial disputes with the *Treaty of Tordesillas*.

52. The period early in the development of human cultures, before the use of metals, is called (the).

    A. Ancient Times

    B. Stone Age

    C. Horse Age

    D. Bronze Age

53. A *philosophe* of the Age of Enlightenment was most likely to be a(n)

    A. priest

    B. merchant

    C. warrior

    D. intellectual

54. To regain admission to the Union during the period of Reconstruction, most states of the former Confederacy were required to

    A. grant Black people all the civil rights that Northern states had granted them before the war.

    B. ratify the Fourteenth Amendment.

    C. ratify the Sixteenth Amendment.

    D. provide free land and farming tools for the recently freed slaves.

55. Which of the following regions was most heavily represented among immigrants to the urban areas of the United States after 1890?

    A. Southern and Eastern Europe

    B. South America

    C. Asia

    D. Africa

Practice Test 2

56. Which of the following historical figures was a major contributor to the Age of Exploration and is identified with the country he sailed for?

    A. Christopher Columbus, Great Britain

    B. Prince Henry the Navigator, Portugal

    C. John Cabot, Norway

    D. Jacques Cartier, Spain

57. In the early years of self-government the United States implemented a national government based on the Articles of Confederation. What was one of the Articles' key weaknesses?

    A. The chief executive role was too powerful.

    B. Amendments had to be approved by only half of the states.

    C. The legislature was bicameral

    D. There was no national court system.

58. The primary colonial objection to the Stamp Act was that

    A. it was an internal tax, whereas Americans were prepared to accept only external taxes.

    B. it was the first tax of any kind ever imposed by Britain on the colonies.

    C. the proposed tax rates were so high that they would have crippled the colonial economy.

    D. it had not been approved by the colonists through their representatives.

59. Which of the following is part of the hydrologic cycle?

    A. rain

    B. animals

    C. plants

    D. earthquakes

60. What was unique about the Hammurabi Code?

    A. It was the earliest-known example of a ruler proclaiming publicly to his people an entire body of laws.

    B. It was written in books that citizens could reference.

    C. It established a legislature to create laws.

    D. It was the first body of laws based on the principle of human rights.

61. Which of the following individuals participated in the Protestant Reformation?

    A. René Descartes

    B. Mary, Queen of Scots

    C. Machiavelli

    D. John Calvin

62. _____ graphs usually slope downward because people buy less when the price is high and more when the price is low.; and _____ graphs usually slope up from left to right, as the higher a price is, the easier it is to make a profit selling a good on the market.

    A. command, market

    B. microeconomics, macroeconomics

    C. frictional, functional

    D. demand, supply

63. What factors would a macroeconomist examine in order to gauge the health of an economy?

    A. the mix of traditional, command, and market components

    B. consumption and investment

    C. unemployment and inflation

    D. equity and equilibrium

64. What was true of the Roman Empire?

    A. The strength of the Roman Empire came from centuries of peace that resulted from isolating itself from other countries.

    B. The empire promoted equality among all classes with little differentiation among individuals from different socioeconomic groups.

    C. Romans spoke a common language: Italian.

    D. The Roman government included a system of checks and balances, which prevented any one person or group of people from gaining too much power.

Practice Test 2

65. The eighth-grade students in Ms. Alvarez's class are studying Native Americans. Ms. Alvarez wants to strengthen her students' ability to think critically and work collaboratively. She also wants to provide opportunities for the students to use a variety of print and media resources during this unit of study. Ms. Alvarez plans to begin the unit by leading the class in a brainstorming session. Which of the following criteria should guide Ms. Alvarez as she leads the brainstorming session to formulate questions to guide their research?

    A. The questions should emphasize the content presented in the available print materials.

    B. The questions should focus on student perceptions of Native Americans.

    C. The questions should emphasize thinking skills such as comparison, analysis, and evaluation.

    D. The questions should focus on how to do research.

66. Mrs. Carson's class has collected samples of soil from various locations in the community. They are comparing samples and hypothesizing how each soil type might have formed. The focus of the study would be described as

    A. lithospheric.

    B. atmospheric.

    C. biospheric.

    D. hydrospheric.

67. Which of the following is NOT an assumption of the Production Possibilities Frontier Curve model?

    A. Society is capable of producing only two goods, e.g., guns and butter.

    B. At a given point in time, society has a fixed quantity of resources.

    C. All resources are used in their most productive manner.

    D. Demand for goods increases as the price and supply increase.

68. A bank is deficient in its reserves. What could be a consequence?

    A. The bank will increase lending and spending in order to rebuild its reserves.

    B. If everyone tried to withdraw money from the bank at the same time, there would not be enough funds.

    C. The Federal Reserve will relinquish control.

    D. The bank will increase credit availability, which will lower interest rates, increase the money supply, and lead to an increase in total spending.

69. Mr. Lyle's class is reviewing for an economics test. Mr. Lyle said, "The following words are related to this concept: *par value, date to maturity, coupon,* and *promise*." What is the concept?

    A. credit

    B. bond

    C. investment

    D. dividend

70. Ms. Jacobson is a geographer who studies *fauna*. What would be of most interest to her?

    A. different kinds of soil

    B. interactions between weather and the environment

    C. crops and plants found within a specific region

    D. the animals found in a location

71. Air conditioning is an example of how humans

    A. modify their environment.

    B. adapt to their environment.

    C. depend on their environment.

    D. destroy their environment.

72. Who wrote the Bill of Rights?

    A. Alexander Hamilton

    B. Thomas Jefferson

    C. George Washington

    D. James Madison

73. How does the Constitution provide for political parties?

    A. Political parties are considered viable if they are on ballots in two-thirds of the states.

    B. The United States' bicameral legislature system is set up for two parties.

    C. Political parties are not mentioned in the Constitution.

    D. Political parties are mentioned as an area of state authority.

74. Which of the following actions are primarily the responsibilities of the states?

    A. Ensuring public safety, administering and certifying elections, and recording birth and death certificates
    B. Regulating interstate commerce as well as television and radio
    C. Regulating immigration and naturalization
    D. Providing for national defense and creating money

75. The modern democratic state in which the people do NOT take a direct role in legislating or governing, but elect representatives to express their views and wants is called a

    A. republic.
    B. dictatorship.
    C. constitutional monarchy.
    D. totalitarian state.

76. Which amendment to the Bill of Rights states in part that "Congress shall make no law respecting an establishment of religion?"

    A. Amendment 14
    B. Amendment 5
    C. Amendment 1
    D. Amendment 10

77. What President called the Soviet Union an "evil empire"?

    A. Ronald Reagan
    B. Jimmy Carter
    C. Richard Nixon
    D. John F. Kennedy

78. Kevin is watching the news. Two members of the president's cabinet are discussing the *unitary/rational actor model*. What is the focus of the discussion?

    A. foreign policy
    B. economic policy
    C. military policy
    D. domestic policy

79. Which political entity is correctly matched with its example?

    A. nation state: ISIS/ISIL

    B. non-state actor: Mexico

    C. non-territorial transnational organization: McDonald's

    D. intergovernmental organization: United States

80. Which Mesoamerican civilization was the earliest?

    A. Incan

    B. Mayan

    C. Olmecs

    D. Aztec

81. Which nation was the first to declare war in World War I?

    A. Germany

    B. Russia

    C. Austria-Hungary

    D. France

82. The major contribution of the Phoenicians was

    A. cuneiform

    B. hieroglyphics

    C. common language

    D. alphabetic system

83. Which of the following identifies Adam Smith's concept that stated that if everyone followed their own self-interests, it would be for the economic good of everyone, since everyone will do what they do best.

    A. laissez faire

    B. utopian societies

    C. the invisible hand

    D. communism

Practice Test 2

84. In what time period did the Holocaust occur?

    A. World War II

    B. Russian Revolution

    C. Age of Discovery

    D. French Revolution

85. Which of the following was an outcome of the Industrial Revolution?

    A. the Commercial Revolution

    B. an increase in population in Europe

    C. the Age of Exploration

    D. the rise of big business

86. Which country is most identified with the Renaissance?

    A. Egypt

    B. United States

    C. England

    D. Italy

87. What is the opposite of a federal form of government?

    A. Anarchy

    B. Confederation

    C. Plutocracy

    D. Parliamentary

88. Which of the following do historians generally consider the earliest cause of World War II?

    A. The Treaty of Versailles

    B. The rise of Adolf Hitler to power

    C. The alliance of Adolf Hitler and Benito Mussolini

    D. Japan's success in China

89. In what year was Florida admitted to the United States?

    A. 1843

    B. 1845

    C. 1846

    D. 1844

90. The Twenty-Fifth Amendment established the line of succession for the president of the United States. Who succeeds the president if the president and vice president are killed at the same time?

    A. Speaker of the House

    B. President pro tempore of the Senate

    C. Secretary of State

    D. Secretary of the Treasury

91. Which of the following is considered a river valley civilization?

    A. Sumer

    B. Ming Dynasty

    C. Aztec Civilization

    D. Ottoman Empire

92. The Vedic religions evolved into which one of the following religions?

    A. Buddhism

    B. Hinduism

    C. Calvinism

    D. Islam

93. Where would you most likely see the impact of the *Carolingian Miniscule* of the Lower Middle Ages today?

    A. government organization

    B. publishing

    C. military campaigns

    D. crop production

94. What was a goal of the Crusades?

    A. to explore different religions

    B. to expand the Roman Empire

    C. to capture Jerusalem for the papacy

    D. to develop trade routes to the East

Practice Test 2

95. Which religion had its greatest impact on China?

    A. Hinduism

    B. Buddhism

    C. Christianity

    D. Islam

96. If the federal government wants to influence state governments in an area that the Constitution establishes as a responsibility of the states, what action can it legally take?

    A. The federal government can use executive privilege.

    B. The federal political leaders can pressure state leaders.

    C. The federal government can threaten to withhold money for projects administered by the states unless states comply.

    D. The states can ignore the federal government.

97. When colonial Massachusetts Governor Thomas Hutchinson attempted to force the sale of taxed tea in Boston in 1773, Bostonians reacted with the

    A. Boston Massacre.

    B. Boston Tea Party.

    C. Declaration of Independence.

    D. Articles of Confederation.

98. When did the young United States decide to form a militia?

    A. After the Second Continental Congress

    B. After the First Continental Congress

    C. After Great Britain's retaliation for the Boston Tea Party

    D. After passage of the Stamp Act

99. The Twenty-sixth Amendment was passed in 1971 during the Vietnam era. What did it accomplish?

    A. The amendment established age 18 as the legal drinking age throughout the United States.

    B. The amendment ended the draft.

    C. The amendment established age 18 as the legal voting age throughout the United States.

    D. The amendment repealed the 18th amendment.

100. What is true of *samurai* during the feudal Japanese period?

   A. They were similar to the feudal barons in medieval Europe.

   B. They were mercenary warriors who fought against the emperor.

   C. They were religious leaders who were at the pinnacle of Japanese society.

   D. A samurai was the same as a shogun.

101. Susan B. Anthony would most likely have supported which Constitutional amendment?

   A. Fourteenth

   B. Seventeenth

   C. Nineteenth

   D. Twenty-second

102. Which of the following statements best represents the Humanist movement of the Renaissance?

   A. *I am inspired by the Aztec and Mayan civilizations.*

   B. *Humans are nothing compared to God.*

   C. *Eat, drink, and be merry: Let's celebrate!*

   D. *A life of sacrifice and prayer paves the way to eternity.*

103. What characterized *manorialism* in the Middle Ages?

   A. a highly centralized political, economic, military, and social system

   B. contracted labor between the lord of an estate and serfs

   C. less availability of agricultural goods

   D. an increasing use of slave labor to support the work of the manor

104. The Watergate scandal led to Richard Nixon's downfall primarily because of his

   A. failed trip to China.

   B. Vietnam War policies.

   C. role in directing the cover-up of the break-in of the Democratic National Committee offices.

   D. involvement with organized crime.

Practice Test 2

105. The "War on Poverty" was an attempt by
    A. President Johnson to end hunger and economic despair in America.
    B. President Kennedy to organize the Peace Corps.
    C. George Marshall to feed the people of Europe after World War II.
    D. President Eisenhower to reduce the number of people on public assistance.

106. When did the social science disciplines emerge?
    A. mid-1800s
    B. early 1900s
    C. late twentieth century
    D. mid-twentieth century

107. The four major subfields of which subject are archaeological, biological, linguistic, and socio-cultural?
    A. sociology
    B. psychology
    C. anthropology
    D. history

108. Mrs. Carson has the following terms written on the board: *norms, values, culture, customs, traditions*. What is most likely to be the course that Mrs. Carson teaches?
    A. Political Science
    B. Civics
    C. Sociology
    D. Geography

109. Which of the following is the study of how people choose to use limited or scarce resources to obtain maximum satisfaction of unlimited wants?
    A. Economics
    B. Education
    C. Political Science
    D. Anthropology

110. Mr. Smith is majoring in a field focused on *pedagogy*. What is he studying?

    A. History

    B. Civics

    C. Geography

    D. Education

111. *Environment and Society* is one of the essential elements of the field of

    A. geography.

    B. education.

    C. political science.

    D. history.

112. Ms. Hill teaches Anthropology. She is referring to CPALMS in order to

    A. find valid instructional tools for teaching.

    B. identify the appropriate subfields of anthropology.

    C. determine which Florida Educator Accomplished Practice (FEAP) is relevant.

    D. review which students require instructional accommodations.

113. Mr. Stolte is helping his students prepare for a civics test. He demonstrates how he eliminates incorrect options by verbalizing his thought process. He then puts students into groups and assigns each group a question. The students work together and then explain to the class how they determined which option was correct, and why the other options were incorrect. This instructional strategy focuses on

    A. metacognition.

    B. using mnemonics to recall information.

    C. the lower levels of Bloom's Taxonomy.

    D. the scientific method.

Practice Test 2

Use the table below to answer questions 114-116.

Population of the United States by Sex, Age, Hispanic Origin, and Race: 2008 (Numbers in thousands. Civilian non-institutionalized population[1])

Sex and age	Hispanic		White alone		All other races	
	Number	Percent	Number	Percent	Number	Percent
Male	**23,652**	**100.0**	**96,613**	**100.0**	**26,591**	**100.0**
Under 5 years	2,563	10.8	5,742	5.9	2,390	9.0
5 to 9 years	2,216	9.4	5,774	6.0	2,243	8.4
10 to 14 years	2,036	8.6	5,997	6.2	2,217	8.3
15 to 19 years	1,943	8.2	6,538	6.8	2,343	8.8
20 to 24 years	1,899	8.0	6,480	6.7	2,005	7.5
25 to 29 years	2,413	10.2	6,286	6.5	2,022	7.6
30 to 34 years	2,030	8.6	5,657	5.9	1,802	6.8
35 to 44 years	3,638	15.4	13,469	13.9	3,773	14.2
45 to 54 years	2,478	10.5	15,505	16.0	3,556	13.4
55 to 64 years	1,342	5.7	12,452	12.9	2,285	8.6
65 to 74 years	665	2.8	7,062	7.3	1,250	4.7
75 to 84 years	344	1.5	4,431	4.6	530	2.0
85 years and over	85	0.4	1,220	1.3	174	0.7
Female	**22,374**	**100.0**	**100,155**	**100.0**	**29,721**	**100.0**
Under 5 years	2,451	11.0	5,468	5.5	2,288	7.7
5 to 9 years	2,120	9.5	5,508	5.5	2,156	7.3
10 to 14 years	1,950	8.7	5,645	5.6	2,193	7.4
15 to 19 years	1,856	8.3	6,276	6.3	2,359	7.9
20 to 24 years	1,717	7.7	6,262	6.3	2,166	7.3
25 to 29 years	1,863	8.3	6,258	6.2	2,217	7.5
30 to 34 years	1,831	8.2	5,651	5.6	2,118	7.1
35 to 44 years	3,266	14.6	13,577	13.6	4,409	14.8
45 to 54 years	2,410	10.8	15,826	15.8	4,160	14.0
55 to 64 years	1,450	6.5	12,957	12.9	2,816	9.5
65 to 74 years	865	3.9	8,164	8.2	1,582	5.3
75 to 84 years	447	2.0	6,185	6.2	975	3.3
85 years and over	149	0.7	2,380	2.4	281	0.9

1. Plus armed forces living off-post or with their families on-post.

2. Hispanic refers to people whose origin is Mexican, Puerto Rican, Cuban, Spanish-speaking Central or South American countries, or other Hispanic/Latino, regardless of race.

SOURCE: U.S. Census Bureau, Current Population Survey, Annual Social and Economic Supplement, 2008. Internet release date: September 2009

114. How many Hispanic women are between the ages of 20 and 29 years old?

　　A.　3,580

　　B.　1,717,000

　　C.　3,580,000

　　D.　Data not available in this table.

115. What percentage of the population are African-American males between the ages of 5 and 19?

　　A.　25.5%

　　B.　8.8%

　　C.　Data not available in this table.

　　D.　17.1%

116. If the population trends of 2008 continue, what would be a logical conclusion about the population in the year 2078?

　　A.　Data not available in this table.

　　B.　There will be more white females than white males.

　　C.　There will be more members of the category *all other races* than in *whites only* and *Hispanics* combined.

　　D.　Hispanics will be the race with the highest percentage of the population.

117. Which of the following is an example of a *primary source*?

　　A.　a documentary on George Washington

　　B.　a teacher's lecture on the three branches of the government

　　C.　a diary entry about Martin Luther King's "I Have a Dream" speech from an individual whose grandmother heard the speech on the radio

　　D.　an audio recording of Martin Luther King delivering his "I Have a Dream" speech

118. What was the significance of the Peace of Westphalia?

　　A.　It created the concept of nation-states.

　　B.　It introduced the idea of the treaty as the basis of international law.

　　C.　It ended World War I.

　　D.　It redefined the boundaries of Europe following the French Revolution to preserve the peace in Europe.

119. President Franklin D. Roosevelt's programs of relief designed to end the Great Depression were called

    A. the Great Society

    B. Fireside Chats

    C. the New Deal

    D. the Fourteen Points

120. In the American system of government, checks and balances

    A. regulate the amount of control each branch of government wields.

    B. make each branch of government independent.

    C. give the president control.

    D. give the Supreme Court control.

PRACTICE TEST 2 ANSWER KEY

Question	Answer	Field	Competency
1	D	Economics	Competency 2.2
2	A	Geography	Competency 1.2
3	C	Political Science	Competency 3.1
4	B	U.S. History	Competency 5.6
5	B	U.S. History	Competency 5.13
6	A	U.S. History	Competency 5.5
7	B	Social Science	Competency 6.5
8	B	Social Science	Competency 6.2
9	D	Geography	Competency 1.4
10	D	World History	Competency 4.3
11	A	Economics	Competency 2.6
12	A	Economics	Competency 2.4
13	A	World History	Competency 4.13
14	A	World History	Competency 4.3
15	A	Economics	Competency 2.7
16	B	Economics	Competency 2.5
17	B	U.S. History	Competency 5.4
18	C	World History	Competency 4.11
19	C	Political Science	Competency 3.3
20	B	World History	Competency 4.2
21	A	Political Science	Competency 3.7
22	A	Social Science	Competency 6.5
23	A	Political Science	Competency 3.1
24	D	Political Science	Competency 3.2
25	D	Political Science	Competency 3.2

Practice Test 2 Answer Key

Question	Answer	Field	Competency
26	C	Political Science	Competency 3.2
27	A	Economics	Competency 2.1
28	C	Economics	Competency 2.1
29	A	Economics	Competency 2.4
30	A	Economics	Competency 2.3
31	B	U.S. History	Competency 3.1
32	B	Social Science	Competency 6.1
33	D	Social Science	Competency 6.4
34	C	U.S. History	Competency 5.14
35	C	Political Science	Competency 3.1
36	B	U.S. History	Competency 5.11
37	B	Political Science	Competency 5.10
38	A	Economics	Competency 2.3
39	A	U.S. History	Competency 5.13
40	A	U.S. History	Competency 5.11
41	D	Geography	Competency 1.1
42	D	U.S. History	Competency 5.11
43	D	World History	Competency 4.10
44	C	World History	Competency 4.12
45	B	Political Science	Competency 3.1
46	A	Political Science	Competency 3.6
47	D	Geography	Competency 1.1
48	A	Economics	Competency 2.4
49	B	Economics	Competency 2.4
50	C	Economics	Competency 2.5
51	A	World History	Competency 4.6

Question	Answer	Field	Competency
52	B	World History	Competency 4.1
53	D	World History	Competency 4.6
54	B	U.S. History	Competency 5.7
55	A	U.S. History	Competency 5.8
56	B	World History	Competency 4.7
57	D	U.S. History	Competency 3.1
58	D	U.S. History	Competency 3.5
59	A	Geography	Competency 1.2
60	A	World History	Competency 4.1
61	D	World History	Competency 4.4
62	D	Economics	Competency 2.3
63	C	Economics	Competency 2.4
64	D	World History	Competency 4.2
65	C	Social Science	Competency 6.5
66	A	Geography	Competency 1.2
67	D	Economics	Competency 2.1
68	B	Economics	Competency 2.4
69	B	Economics	Competency 2.4
70	D	Geography	Competency 2.1
71	B	Geography	Competency 1.3
72	D	U.S. History	Competency 5.4
73	C	Political Science	Competency 3.3
74	A	Political Science	Competency 3.4
75	A	Political Science	Competency 3.1
76	C	Political Science	Competency 3.1
77	A	U.S. History	Competency 5.13

Practice Test 2 Answer Key

Question	Answer	Field	Competency
78	A	Political Science	Competency 3.5
79	C	Political Science	Competency 3.5
80	C	World History	Competency 4.3
81	C	World History	Competency 4.11
82	D	World History	Competency 4.1
83	C	World History	Competency 4.8
84	A	World History	Competency 4.11
85	D	World History	Competency 4.8
86	D	World History	Competency 4.4
87	B	Political Science	Competency 3.6
88	A	World History	Competency 4.11
89	B	U.S. History	Competency 5.16
90	A	Political Science	Competency 3.1
91	A	World History	Competency 4.1
92	B	World History	Competency 4.13
93	B	World History	Competency 4.4
94	C	World History	Competency 4.4
95	B	World History	Competency 4.13
96	C	Political Science	Competency 3.4
97	B	U.S. History	Competency 5.3
98	B	U.S. History	Competency 5.3
99	C	Political Science	Competency 3.1
100	A	U.S. History	Competency 4.3
101	C	U.S. History	Competency 5.14
102	C	World History	Competency 4.4
103	B	World History	Competency 4.4

Question	Answer	Field	Competency
104	C	U.S. History	Competency 5.13
105	A	U.S. History	Competency 5.14
106	A	Social Science	Competency 6.1
107	C	Social Science	Competency 6.1
108	C	Social Science	Competency 6.1
109	A	Social Science	Competency 6.1
110	D	Social Science	Competency 6.1
111	A	Social Science	Competency 6.2
112	A	Social Science	Competency 6.5
113	A	Social Science	Competency 6.5
114	C	Social Science	Competency 6.4
115	C	Social Science	Competency 6.4
116	D	Social Science	Competency 6.4
117	D	Social Science	Competency 6.6
118	B	Political Science	Competency 3.5
119	C	U.S. History	Competency 5.11
120	A	Political Science	Competency 3.6

PRACTICE TEST 2 SELF-ASSESSMENT GUIDE

Knowledge of Economics —/18

1	11	12	15	16	27	28	29	30	38	48

49	50	62	63	67	68	69

Knowledge of Geography —/8

2	9	41	47	59	66	70	71

Knowledge of Political Science —/23

3	19	21	23	24	25	26	35	37	45	46

73	74	75	76	78	79	87	90	96	99	118	120

Knowledge of Social Science —/18

7	8	22	32	33	65	106	107	108	109	110

111	112	113	114	115	116	117

Knowledge of U.S. History —/24

4	5	6	17	31	34	36	39	40	42	54

55	57	58	72	77	89	97	98	100	101	104	105	119

Knowledge of World History —/29

10	13	14	18	20	43	44	51	52	53	56

60	61	64	80	81	82	83	84	85	86	88

91	92	93	94	95	102	103

DETAILED EXPLANATIONS FOR PRACTICE TEST 2

1. **D**

    "Custom plays a very large role in this rather competitive market" is the incorrect sentence. The other statements (A, B, and C) are true.

2. **A**

    Earthquakes occur along the boundaries between colliding tectonic plates. Earth's lithosphere is broken down into a dozen plates that float, and plate movement occurs under land as well as under the ocean (B). Plate tectonics has nothing to do with hurricanes (C). Plates do not seem to be affected by gravity or ocean tides (D).

3. **C**

    Only states can approve a proposed Constitutional amendment. An amendment requires approval of a three-fourths majority of the states to be ratified. The federal government is responsible for raising and maintaining an army and navy (A), granting copyrights and patents (B), and regulating naturalization and immigration (D).

4. **B**

    The principle of popular sovereignty was a central feature of the Kansas-Nebraska Act. A favorite policy of Democrats during the late 1840s and early 1850s, it proved a failure in solving the impasse over the status of slavery in the territories. The Kansas-Nebraska Act repealed the Missouri Compromise (A). Popular sovereignty was not a factor for the United States to enter World War I (C). The Albany Plan of Union provided for an intercolonial government that would regulate dealings with the Native Americans, organize and run a colonial army, manage the public lands, legislate, and supervise the collection of taxes for a common defense fund. It did not relate to the principle of popular sovereignty (D).

5. **B**

    Kennedy came off looking better in the televised debates. Americans were perhaps somewhat bored with Eisenhower, though not deeply dissatisfied (A). From the standpoint of gaining a valuable edge in an extremely tight race, Kennedy's political record did not matter as much as how he performed on his feet (C). Nixon, like Kennedy, had served in the Navy during World War II (D).

6. **A**

    The French and Indian War, or the Seven Years' War, occurred prior to the Revolutionary War. The War of 1812 occurred several decades after the Revolution that created the United States.

Detailed Explanations for Practice Test 2

7. **B**

    Choice is an important element in motivating students to learn. Answer choice (A) does not provide opportunities for research. The students proposed the questions, so covering all the questions should not be a problem. Answer choice (C) is incorrect because the students have chosen what they consider to be key questions. Answer choice (D) is a possibility, but only if there is a specific reason why all the students should not research all the questions.

8. **B**

    The terms *environment, human systems, physical systems,* and *environment and society* relate to the subject of geography, more than to civics, history, or economics.

9. **D**

    A pie chart is the best choice because each set of classrooms is part of the total of 40 classrooms. A scatterplot (A) is not appropriate because it shows one variable on the horizontal axis and another value on the vertical axis. A line graph (B) plots the value of data in a data point and then "connects the dots" in order to illustrate the relationship of consecutive points. It is usually used to show how something changes over time. An area chart (C) is used to show how something changes with respect to time. It shows the contribution, over time, of each type of data in a series, in the form of a whole picture.

10. **D**

    Kush was involved in trade and also collected taxes from trade items that were transported through it. Axum traded in ivory and gold. The Swahili coast traded in gold, ivory, and slaves. Many of the individuals in these kingdoms and countries were of the Islam or Christian faiths (A). They had not been British colonies (B) and were not ruled by brothers (C).

11. **A**

    Adam Smith was a Scottish economist who wrote *The Wealth of Nations* in 1776. James Madison (B), Benjamin Franklin (C), and Thomas Jefferson (D) were American revolutionary leaders and statesmen.

12. **A**

    Functional unemployment, by definition, is the result of a mismatch of skills or location. This question presents a mismatch of job skills, as the robot has replaced the worker. Educational unemployment (B) is not an unemployment type. Cyclical unemployment (C) takes place when the economy falls as the result of a recession. Frictional unemployment (D) occurs when workers voluntarily move from one job to another with time in-between.

13. **A**

    The writers of most Hindu sacred texts are unknown. Although the authority of the *Vedas* (a collection of ancient sacred texts from the Vedic religion) and the Brahmans (the priestly class) is accepted and respected, some Hindus reject one or both. The *Qur'an* is the book of sacred writings for Islam (B). The *Torah* and books of the *Old Testament* are sacred writings of Judaism (C). There is no single religious text for Buddhism (D), although several dozen texts have religious significance.

14. **A**

    The cities the Mayas built were ceremonial centers for religion. A priestly class lived in the cities, but for the most part the Maya population lived in small farming villages. The priestly class would carry out daily religious duties, particularly sacrifices, and the peasants would periodically gather for religious ceremonies and festivals. While functions such as government (B), trading marketplaces (C), and festivals and celebrations (D) would have been held in cities, the development of cities was primarily based on serving religious purposes.

15. **A**

    The definition of credit is "a promise to pay for goods or services that have already been provided." Bonds (B) are financial instruments frequently used by government and business as a way to borrow money. Interest (C) is a small amount of money owed to the lender for the privilege of borrowing money. A liability (D) is a debt.

16. **B**

    In a monopoly, one firm controls an entire industry, so the firm is the industry. Since only one firm controls the industry, the result is generally not fair pricing (A) because there is no competition. By definition, there is only one, not multiple, sellers (C). There is no competition to drive down prices (D).

17. **B**

    Hamilton is arguing for a mechanism to create revenue (a source of funds) for military and other expenses of the country. Taxation is the only response option that involves money. Public defense (A), governance (C), and civilians (D) would not be that mechanism.

18. **C**

    Japan's attack on Pearl Harbor drew the U.S. into declaring war. Japanese aid to Germany (A) was not a factor. The U.S. did not want to annex Pacific islands held by Japan (B). The Americans did not resent Japanese trading policies (D).

Detailed Explanations for Practice Test 2

19. **C**

    The antiparty feeling was rooted in three basic beliefs: First, the Founders thought parties created and exploited conflicts that undermined consensus; second, they thought parties were instruments by which a small and narrow interest could impose its will on society; and third, they believed parties stifled independent thought and behavior. It is not surprising that the Constitution doesn't mention political parties, but it created a system in which parties, or something like them, was inevitable. When the Founders established popular elections, they needed some kind of agency to organize and mobilize supporters of the candidates. Therefore, options (A), (B), and (D) were basic beliefs regarding political parties. The correct answer—that parties only provide a general understanding of where the candidate stands—was not one of the beliefs.

20. **B**

    The Silk Road crossed Central Asia and branched out in several directions to form a network of land-based routes, not following just a single route. The Silk Road developed during the Han Dynasty (A). It was not a system of waterways (C) and was not developed for military use (D).

21. **A**

    The critical word in this question is *civil*, which refers to the law. Freedom of worship is guaranteed in the Bill of Rights. Bonuses (B) and subsidies (D) are not guaranteed by law. Yelling "fire" in a building when there is no fire is not a legal expression of free speech (C).

22. **A**

    Social studies instruction requires the teaching of facts, concepts, and generalizations. Because each category depends upon the other, they cannot be taught in isolation. Concepts rely on facts, but facts are meaningless unless they relate to concepts and generalizations. Generalizations organize and summarize information obtained from an analysis of facts. While a generalization contains a broad assertion, a fact is a truth about a particular incident. Inquiry is not useful for learning specific facts such as the order of the Bill of Rights (B) or specific historical events (C). Since metacognition focuses on self-knowledge rather than content knowledge, inquiry does not develop metacognitive thinking (D).

23. **A**

    The three-branch system of government created a system of checks and balances that would prevent any one branch from becoming too powerful, thus protecting the people from an oppressive government. Checks and balances is not related to foreign intervention (B), financial stability (C) or a national bank (D).

24. **D**

    Two Senators serve from each state for a total of 100. The number is determined by the number of states, not the population of the state (A). Washington, D.C., is not represented in Congress by a Senator or a Representative (B). There are 435 members in the House of Representatives (C).

25. **D**

The Constitutional requirements for the office of president and vice-president are as follows: candidates must be at least 35 years of age, must be natural-born citizens, and must have resided in the United States for a minimum of 14 years. Marcia N. is over 35. Since she was born in Orlando, she is a natural-born citizen. She has lived in the United States her entire life. James S. (A) is not a natural-born citizen. Faith J. (B) is not old enough to run for president. Carl K. (C) has lived outside the United States for 26 years. Since he is 37 years old, he has not resided in the U.S. for the required 14 years.

26. **C**

Supreme Court justices are appointed for life by the president. They are not appointed for a limited time such as 6 years (A), 1 year (B), or 10 years (D).

27. **A**

The "4Es" are universal economic goals that enable a society to use its existing resources to reduce scarcity and obtain the maximum satisfaction possible. They are not strategies used by the Federal Reserve to avoid a stock market crash (B); techniques used by capitalists in a traditional market to stabilize prices (C); or principles used in a command economy to maximize control (D).

28. **C**

Since the curve represents technical efficiency, any point on the curve is valid. 9 cars and 4 motorcycles is at point C on the curve. 9 cars and 9 motorcycles is above the curve. 7 cars and 4 motorcycles is below the curve. 4 cars and 10 motorcycles is above the curve.

29. **A**

The primary function of the Federal Reserve Board is to implement monetary policy. The Federal Reserve does not control government spending (B), regulate commodity prices (C), or help the president run the executive branch (D).

30. **A**

GDP (Gross Domestic Product) is the total dollar value of all finished goods and services sold in the product market in a given year. The GDP does not involve the federal budget (B), national income (C), or national debt (D).

31. **B**

James Madison was one of the authors of *The Federalist Papers* and wrote the initial draft of the Bill of Rights in 1789. Although Alexander Hamilton (A) and John Jay (C) were authors of the *The Federalist Papers*, neither authored the initial draft of the Bill of Rights. Thomas Jefferson (D) did not contribute to the writing of *The Federalist Papers* or the Bill of Rights.

Detailed Explanations for Practice Test 2

32. **B**

    Ethnography is the systematic description of a human society, usually based on firsthand fieldwork. All generalizations about human behavior are based on the descriptive evidence of ethnography. Since it involves firsthand fieldwork, it would not apply to the study of prehistoric peoples (A). It is not an interpretative explanation of human behavior (C). It is not a form of experimental research (D).

33. **D**

    The assignment is at the extended level in terms of Webb's DOK because it asks students to evaluate and create. It is beyond the skill/concept level (A). Evaluation (C) and synthesis (B) are part of Bloom's Taxonomy, not Webb's DOK.

34. **C**

    Title IX of the Education Amendments banned sex discrimination in schools. As a result of Title IX, the enrollment of women in athletics programs and professional schools increased dramatically. Title IX did not impact organizations for peace and justice (A), co-ed residential halls (B), or LGBT organizations (D).

35. **C**

    The Bill of Rights was written to overcome concerns about federal overreach and guarantee powers of the states and people. There is no amendment that delegates the federal government rights not given to the states (A). There is no amendment that establishes political parties (B). The amendments are not the same as the Articles of the Constitution (D).

36. **B**

    The Harlem Renaissance is considered the first important movement of Black artists and writers in the United States. Centered in the Harlem neighborhood of New York City, the movement dispersed to other urban areas during the 1920s and promoted the publication of more Black writers than ever before. While it occurred during the Roaring Twenties, the Harlem Renaissance involved Black artists and writers (A). The Lost Generation describes the generation—of all races—that came of age during World War I (C). The Jazz Age occurred during the same time period, but included European countries as well as the United States. It also involved a variety of races (D).

37. **B**

    The Eighteenth Amendment made the sale of alcohol illegal. The amendment was repealed by the Twenty-first Amendment in 1933. Both the Fifteenth and the Nineteenth amendments involved voting rights (A). No amendment addressed the Great Depression (C). The Twenty-Second Amendment limited presidential terms (D).

38. **A**

The intersection of the supply and demand curves is referred to as the equilibrium. In terms of standard of equity (B), a society wants the distribution of goods and services to conform to its notions of "fairness." There is no objective standard of equity because different societies have different notions of what constitutes equity; however, there are three widely held Standards of Equity: (1) Under a contributory standard, people are entitled to a share of goods and services based on what they contribute to society; (2) Under a needs standard, a person's contribution to society is irrelevant, and goods and services are distributed based on the needs of different households; (3) Under an equality standard, every person is entitled to an equal share of goods and services, simply because he or she is a human being. A mixed economy (C) contains elements from traditional, command, and market economies. Technical efficiency (D) occurs when a country produces the greatest quantity of goods and services possible from its resources at a minimum cost, thus using fewer resources and increasing production quantities.

39. **A**

In February 1950, Republican Senator Joseph R. McCarthy of Wisconsin claimed that he had a list of Communists and Communist sympathizers in the U.S. Department of State. The Franklin Roosevelt administration (B) ended in 1945, and McCarthy did not explore corruption in his administration, if any occurred. McCarthy was not interested in misuse of corporate funds for political purposes (C) or the dangers of nuclear energy (D).

40. **A**

Franklin D. Roosevelt was the architect of the New Deal, a plan to bring the United States out of the Great Depression, so answer choice (A) is most accurate. Adolf Hitler rose to power largely due to the economic misery that enveloped post–World War I Germany (B). Black codes were laws passed by Southern states to tie slaves to the land. With regard to choice (D), Charles de Gaulle, president of France during the late 1950s and most of the 1960s, was not at the Tehran Conference attended by Roosevelt, Winston Churchill, and Josef Stalin.

41. **D**

Space-time compression is defined as the decreasing effect of distance on the speed of human travel across space. Choice (A) is the decreasing impact a phenomenon has on something as the distance from its origin increases. Choice (B) refers to the negative impact of globalization in causing a growing divide between countries in the periphery and those in the core. Choice (C) is diffusion of an innovation that takes a new and unique form as it's spread from one place to another, and seeks to match cultural customs where it's transplanted.

Detailed Explanations for Practice Test 2

42. **D**

    The Civilian Conservation Corps (CCC) was a New Deal program during the Great Depression which created work camps around the country where young men performed reforestation and conservation tasks. The Agricultural Adjustment Act (A) protected farmers from price drops by providing crop subsidies in exchange for an agreement to reduce production by up to one-half. The National Industrial Recovery Act (B) sought to stabilize the economy by preventing extreme competition, labor-management conflicts, and overproduction. The Glass-Steagall Act (C) created federally insured bank deposits to prevent bank failures.

43. **D**

    Nationalism is a unifying force because it creates a sense of identity; however, it can also result in an unhealthy "us vs. them" mentality. Nationalism does not create smaller economic units (A), inspire revolutionary change (B), or encourage multiculturalism (C).

44. **C**

    Technologies such as the Internet, media, and satellite communications as economic changes (e.g., multinational corporations; trade agreements) have increased globalization. Globalization is not defined by the United Nations (A). Buying local (B) is a movement that offers a counterweight to globalization. Globalization blurs a country's borders and boundaries (D).

45. **B**

    Article I of the Constitution describes the Legislative Branch. Article III (A) describes the Judicial Branch. Article V (C) involves amending the constitution. Article VII (D) focuses on ratification of the Constitution.

46. **A**

    Government by the many is what we have in the United States: a constitutional democracy. An oligarchy (B) is rule by a small, elite group that makes all of the decisions in government. A monarchy (C) is rule by a single person (e.g., king, queen, emperor) who rules until death or abdication. Anarchy (D) occurs when there is no rule or authority.

47. **D**

    Relative location implies a relationship in which the identification of one location depends on another location. Thus, if either the house or the shops are torn down, the description is no longer accurate. Regional geography (A) organizes areas of the Earth that have some degree of similarity and divides the world into different realms. Both (B) and (C) are examples of absolute location because they specify exact and unchanging locations.

48. **A**

    When the Fed purchases bonds, it pays for them with money, which increases money supply. Choices (B), (C), and (D) are contractionary moves by the Fed.

49. **B**

Decreasing spending and increasing taxes will result in less money in consumers' pockets and, thus, less money to spend. This will contract the economy and slow it. Buying bonds on the open market (A), reducing the reserve requirement (C), and lowering the discount rate (D) all will expand the economy.

50. **C**

In a command economy, the government controls all aspects of the economy. Authoritarian (A) is not a type of economy. It is a form of government in which a strong central power rules, and political freedoms are limited. A traditional economy (B) operates by custom. A mixed economy (D) combines features of traditional, mixed, and market economies.

51. **A**

An empiricist is someone who believes knowledge from sensory experience and who would use evidence and reason as the basis of understanding. Classification of human knowledge would exemplify that sort of thinking. The other examples—Genghis Khan (B), Samuel Richardson (C), and Pope Alexander VI (D)—do not provide information about how the individual used reason and evidence for decision-making or organization of information.

52. **B**

The Stone Age is the time early in the development of human cultures, before the use of metals, when tools and weapons were made of stone. The dates of the Stone Age vary considerably for different parts of the world. In Europe, Asia, and Africa the Stone Age began about 2 million years ago. "Ancient times" (A) is more of a colloquial than a historical term. There was not a Horse Age (C) in history. The Bronze Age (D) involved the use of metalwork.

53. **D**

The philosophes were the intellectuals of the Enlightenment who questioned the traditions of society and began to look at the universe in a scientific, critical light. Priests (A) were more likely to think from a traditional perspective. Merchants (B) and warriors (C) were not considered to be intellectuals of the time period.

54. **B**

Southern states were required to ratify the Fourteenth Amendment in order to regain admission to the Union. Black people had not always been granted full civil rights even in Northern states before the Civil War (A). The Sixteenth Amendment (C) authorized income taxes. There was never a law mandating that recently freed slaves would get free land and farming tools (D).

Detailed Explanations for Practice Test 2

55. **A**

    The Old Immigration, made up of those from Northern and Western Europe, still predominated after the Civil War until about 1890. Thereafter, the New Immigration composed primarily of those from Southern and Eastern Europe, prevailed, rather than immigration from South America (B), Asia (C), or Africa (D).

56. **B**

    Prince Henry of Portugal was a key contributor to the Age of Exploration in terms of expansion of shipping and the development of a school for navigation connected to a shipyard that provided opportunities for experimentation and innovation. This created a maritime revolution that sparked advances in technology like the astrolabe and the magnetic compass. Better maps and improvements in shipbuilding opened the possibilities of long-distance sea travel that had seemed rather risky and impossible earlier. Christopher Columbus sailed for Spain, not Great Britain (A). John Cabot sailed for England, not for Norway (C). Cartier sailed for France, not for Spain (D).

57. **D**

    Under the Articles of Confederation, the United States government was weak and ineffective. It was more like a confederation of sovereign states, rather than a united country. One of the key weaknesses was lack of a national court system. In the government under the Articles of Confederation, the chief executive was weak, not powerful (A). Another weakness was that it required unanimous approval of amendments, not approval of half of the states (B). The legislature was unicameral, not bicameral (C).

58. **D**

    Americans' primary objection to the Stamp Act was its purpose of raising revenue from the Americans without the consent of their representatives. Colonists did not accept external taxes, such as those imposed by the Townshend Acts (A). The Stamp Act was not the first tax imposed on the colonists. For example, taxes from the Sugar Act in 1764 preceded those of the Stamp Act in 1765 (B). The taxes were not so high that they would cripple the economy (C).

59. **A**

    The hydrologic cycle is the water cycle; therefore, rain is part of the hydrologic cycle. Animals (B), plants (C), and earthquakes (D) are not part of the hydrologic cycle.

60. **A**

    It is critical to understand the importance of the Hammurabi Code. This code of laws is the earliest-known example of a ruler proclaiming publicly to his people an entire body of laws, arranged in orderly groups, so that all men might read and know what was required of them. The code was carved upon a black stone monument, eight feet high, clearly intended to be in public view. The code was written on stone and clay tablets (B). It did not establish a legislature (C). It was not based on human rights (D).

61. **D**

John Calvin, a French reformer, arrived in Geneva, a Swiss city-state that had adopted an anti-Catholic position. Although he left after his first efforts at reform failed, when he returned to Geneva, his doctrine became the center of the Reformation. Calvin's analysis of Christianity was called Calvinism, which spread to Scotland, the Netherlands, England, and New England. René Descartes (A) was more of a mathematician and philosopher than a religious reformer. Mary, Queen of Scots (B) was not a religious reformer. Machiavelli (C) was an Italian historian, politician, philosopher, and writer; however, he was not a religious reformer.

62. **D**

A demand relation shows the quantity demanded at a particular price. The supply and demand diagrams are done sideways, with the price put on the *y-axis* and the quantity on the *x-axis*. Demand graphs usually slope downward because people buy less when the price is high and more when the price is low. Supply graphs, on the other hand, usually slope up from left to right, as the higher a price is, the easier it is to make a profit selling a good on the market. Command and market (A), microeconomics and macroeconomics (B), and frictional and functional (employment) (C) are not depicted on graphs.

63. **C**

Macroeconomics is the study of the economy as a whole. Macroeconomists ascertain the health of an economy by examining national output, the role of inflation, and unemployment. Generally, all economies include components of traditional, command, and market components and that is not one of the factors that macroeconomists examine (A). Similarly, macroeconomists do not focus on consumption and investment (B), or equity and equilibrium (D).

64. **D**

The Romans adopted a Republican-style government that included a system of checks and balances in which each government constrained the actions of others, so that no one person would gain too much power. The Roman Empire was not isolationist; rather, it was always conquering other countries and adding them to the empire (A). The Romans shared their citizenship with those elites that they conquered in order to guarantee loyalty and to strengthen Rome's grip on their territories; however, in consolidating their power over huge territories, the Romans committed atrocities, enslaved whole peoples, and destroyed cities with little provocation (B). The main language of the Romans was Latin, not Italian (C). Rome was composed of three tribes that were further divided into clans, which were composed of groups of families. In each of these divisions was a class of nobles and a class of commoners.

65. **C**

Since Ms. Alvarez wants to focus the development of critical thinking and collaboration, the best choice is for the questions to emphasize higher order thinking skills, rather than content of only the print materials (A), student perceptions (B), or research skills (D).

Detailed Explanations for Practice Test 2

66. **A**

    Soil samples are part of the lithosphere, the study of the land masses of the Earth. Atmosphere (B) is the study of air including climate and meteorology. The biosphere focuses on life: plants, animals, and other living things (C). The hydrosphere involves water and water processes (D).

67. **D**

    Answer choices (A), (B), and (C) are all assumptions that the model takes as given, to illustrate the axiom that economic choices we make result in trade-offs that can be measured. The Production Possibilities Frontier Curve is just one of the models that inform the realities governing behavior in a free market system. As trade-offs are measured, we realize that various combinations of goods and services can be produced, but at a cost to production of an alternative good or service. Option (D) is not part of the model.

68. **B**

    When a bank is deficient in its reserves, it doesn't have enough resources to meet the demands of depositors. Thus, if all of the depositors tried to withdraw money, the bank would not have enough. Both (A) and (D) are the opposite of what a bank can do to increase reserves. The Federal Reserve does not relinquish control; rather, it implements monetary policies to change the level of money in the banking system (C).

69. **B**

    Every bond comes with a *par value* (face value), a *date to maturity* (ranging from 90 days to 30 years), a *coupon* (a promise to pay a certain amount of money each year to the bondholder until maturity), and a *promise* to repay the par value on the maturity date. That combination of terms does not apply to credit (A), investment (C), or dividend (D).

70. **D**

    Fauna refers to animals. Kinds of soil are part of the study of the lithosphere (A). Interactions between weather and the environment is part of physical geography (B). Crops and plants are living organisms and part of the biosphere (C).

71. **B**

    Humans have learned to use technology like air conditioning to adapt to their environment. Modifying their environment would change the environment itself (A). Depending on the environment would involve reliance on the environment, e.g., reliance on plants or animals as food (C). Though some may view air conditioning as a contributor to the destruction of the environment (D), choice (B) is still the *best* answer.

72. **D**

Initially drafted by James Madison in 1789, the Bill of Rights was written at a time when ideological conflict between Federalists and anti-Federalists, dating from the Philadelphia Convention in 1787, threatened the Constitution's ratification. The Bill of Rights was largely a response to the Constitution's influential opponents, including prominent Founders, who argued that it failed to protect the basic principles of human liberty. Alexander Hamilton contributed to *The Federalist Papers* (A). Thomas Jefferson (B) wrote the *Declaration of Independence*. George Washington (C) did not contribute to the Bill of Rights.

73. **C**

The Constitution does not mention political parties. In fact, "factions" with "jealousies and false alarms" were feared as possible causes of damage to the country. Political parties were thought of as searching for profit, not providing for the common good. The Constitution does not address political parties in terms of appearance on ballots (A), relationship to the bicameral nature of the legislature (B), or area of state authority (D).

74. **A**

Option choices (B), (C), and (D) list activities that happen across state borders, so they are federal responsibilities. The actions in option choice (A) are local responsibilities.

75. **A**

The United States is a republic. The modern democratic state is usually a republic, in which the people do not take a direct role in legislating or governing, but elect representatives to express their views and wants. A democratic government exists when these representatives are freely chosen by the people, and the people's demands are then recognized by the duly elected government. Both a dictatorship (B) and totalitarian state (D) rule from a strong central power with limited freedoms for individuals. In a constitutional monarchy (C), the monarch's (ruler's) authority is restricted by a constitution.

76. **C**

Most people remember Article 1 of the Bill of Rights as the "free speech" article. It states: "Congress shall make no law respecting an establishment of religion, or prohibiting the free exercise thereof; or abridging the freedom of speech or of the press; or the right of the people peaceably to assemble, and to petition the government for a redress of grievances." Amendment 14 defines citizenship (A). Amendment 5 states that you cannot be a witness against yourself or face double jeopardy (B). Amendment 10 states that any rights not given to the federal government are given to the states and the people (D).

Detailed Explanations for Practice Test 2

77. **A**

    President Ronald Reagan was elected on a platform that strongly opposed Communism, and Reagan spoke of waging war with the Communists wherever they may be. In expressing his views, Reagan described the Soviet Union as "an evil empire." This perspective was, in part, a backlash against his predecessor President Carter's (B) administration, which was viewed as militarily weaker than it should be. While Richard Nixon (C) and John F. Kennedy (D) were presidents during the Cold War, neither described the Soviet Union as "an evil Empire."

78. **A**

    The *unitary/rational actor model* is a foreign policy model that assumes that all nations or primary players share similar goals and approach foreign policy issues in like fashion. The actions players take, according to this theory, are influenced by the actions of other players, rather than by what may be taking place internally. The model does not relate to economic policy (B), military policy (C), or domestic policy (D).

79. **C**

    Non-territorial transnational organizations are institutions, such as the Catholic Church, that conduct activities throughout the world, but whose aims are largely nonpolitical. A relatively new non-territorial transnational organization is the multi-national corporation (MNC). McDonald's is an example of an MNC. A nation-state (A) is a legal entity occupying well-defined geographic areas and organized under a common set of governmental institutions. Countries are examples of nation-states. A non-state actor (B) is a movement or group that functions as an independent state. ISIS/ISIL is an example of a non-state actor. An intergovernmental organization (D) is made up of nation-states. NATO and the United Nations are examples.

80. **C**

    The Olmec Civilization was the first Mesoamerican culture, which existed from about 1200 BCE to 400 BCE. The Mayan (B) civilization occurred from about 300 BCE to 900 CE. The Aztec (D) and Incan (A) civilizations began and ended in much the same time periods: from the 1200s CE until the 1500s CE.

81. **C**

    Austria-Hungary declared war on Serbia, thus beginning World War I. Once Austria-Hungary declared war, Russia (B) began mobilizing its forces. Germany (A) advised Russia to stop, and it then declared war on Russia. France (D) joined the war after that.

82. **D**

    The Phoenicians developed the first alphabet. The Sumerians created a form of writing called cuneiform, which used wedge-shaped figures (A). The Egyptians created a system of writing using symbols and simple syllabic and alphabetic elements called hieroglyphics (B). There is not a world common language (C).

83. **C**

In his book *The Wealth of Nations*, Adam Smith wrote, "Every individual necessarily labors to render the annual revenue of the society as great as he can ... . He intends only his own gain, and he is in this, as in many other cases, led by an invisible hand to promote an end which was no part of his intention ... . By pursuing his own interests, he frequently promotes that of the society more effectually than when he really intends to promote it. I have never known much good done by those who affected to trade for the public good." Laissez-faire (A) is a type of economics that occurs when the government removes itself from control, and the people do what they choose. A variety of economists developed the idea of socialist utopian societies (B), which would be a kind of perfect world in which people would look out for the economic benefit of each other, rather than profiting from each other. Communism (D) is a political theory developed by Karl Marx which advocates a society in which all property is publicly owned, and each person works and is paid according to their abilities and needs.

84. **A**

The Holocaust was a genocide in which about six million Jews were killed in the World War II Nazi Germany regime of Adolf Hitler. The Russian Revolution (B), Age of Discovery (C), and French Revolution (D) all preceded World War II and the Holocaust.

85. **D**

The Industrial Revolution introduced mass production into the production of goods. As a result, businesses could grow and expand by producing more and selling more. The Commercial Revolution (A) spurred the great economic growth of Europe and brought about the Age of Exploration (C). These both preceded and contributed to the Industrial Revolution. The increase in population in Europe (B) also preceded the Industrial Revolution and contributed to it.

86. **D**

The Renaissance, which means "rebirth," emphasized new learning, including the rediscovery of much classical material and new art styles. Italian city-states, such as Venice, Milan, Padua, Pisa, and especially Florence, were the home to many Renaissance developments, which were limited to the rich elite rather than to Egypt (A) and England (C). The United States (B) was not yet a country at the time of the Renaissance.

87. **B**

A federal government is the opposite of a confederation, a form of government in which most of the power is allocated to regional governments that can defy the national government to which they grant only a limited amount of power. Anarchy (A) is not a form of government. A plutocracy (C) is a type of oligarchy that has rule by only a few, super-wealthy individuals. A parliamentary (D) system of government is a fusion of the executive and legislative branches.

Detailed Explanations for Practice Test 2

88. **A**

    The Treaty of Versailles, signed in 1919, is cited as the earliest cause of World War II. The atmosphere in Europe and the attitude toward Germany in the period just after World War I was very anti-German. President Woodrow Wilson wanted a secure peace based on his Fourteen Points, because he wanted a peace that would be based on justice, that would have liberal principles at its core, and that would be maintained by a new international organization (The League of Nations). While Wilson agreed that Germany needed to be punished for their involvement in the war, he wanted the punishment to be fair. However, Europe took the punishment to the extreme, setting the stage for the next conflict, World War II. As a result of the treatment of Germany by Europe, Adolf Hitler rose to power (B) and formed an alliance with Benito Mussolini (C). Japan's success in China was not the earliest cause of World War II (D).

89. **B**

    Florida became the twenty-seventh state on March 3, 1845.

90. **A**

    The succession after the vice president is Speaker of the House, President pro tempore of the Senate (B), Secretary of State (C), and then Secretary of the Treasury (D).

91. **A**

    The Sumerians were part of the Mesopotamian Civilization that developed on the Tigris and Euphrates rivers. While all civilizations and peoples depend on freshwater supplies, rivers do not always form the nucleus of their civilization. The Ming Dynasty (B), Aztec Civilization (C), and Ottoman Empire (D) are not considered to be river valley civilizations.

92. **B**

    Hinduism, the name given to the Sanatana Dharma by Muslim invaders, is the result of the evolution of Vedic religions. Buddhism (A) is named for the historical Buddha, who was born Prince Siddhartha Gautama to a wealthy Kshatriya family in the Himalayan foothills of a border region between India and Nepal in the 500s BCE. Calvinism (C) is a religion that developed as part of the Protestant Reformation. Islam (D) is a religion that traces its roots to Abraham in the Old Testament.

93. **B**

    The Carolingian miniscule was the creation of a uniform writing style with capital and small letters, as well as spacing, so that the Roman alphabet could be read more easily. This advancement became a standard in all of the languages of Western civilization and would contribute to today's publishing industry. It does not have a significant impact on the organization of government (A), military campaigns (C), or crop production (D).

94. **C**

The increased authority of the papacy and the relative decline in the power of the emperor became clear in the emergence of the Crusades as a major preoccupation of Europe. Although the capture of Jerusalem (1099) and the establishment of a Latin kingdom in Palestine were offset by disasters and quarrels, the papacy gained greatly in prestige and strengthened its position in relation to the emperor and Germany, which had avoided participation in this first of many Crusades. Since the Crusades emphasized development of the Catholic Church, exploration of other religions was not a focus (A). The Crusades of the Middle Ages occurred far later than the fall of the Roman Empire in the 400s CE (B). Although one benefit of the crusades was the expansion of trade routes across the Mediterranean (D), development of trade routes was not a purpose.

95. **B**

Buddhism first came to China during the Han era, but few Chinese adopted the religion at that time. By the Tang Dynasty, Buddhism was well established, as many of the Tang rulers were Buddhists and supported the religion. Hinduism was practiced most widely in India (A). Christianity (C) was a dominant religion in Europe. Islam (D) dominated the Middle East and Africa.

96. **C**

The federal government has what is called "the power of the purse," which is the Constitutional power given to Congress to raise and spend money. With that power, Congress can compel states to act or not to act in a given area. Recent examples include money allocated for maintenance of the federal highway system, which was tied to states changing the speed limit within their jurisdiction and the requirement of states to meet minimum education standards to receive federal education allocations. Executive privilege (A) allows members of the executive branch, including the president, to resist certain interventions of the legislative and judicial branches to access information and personnel related to the executive branch. While the federal government can pressure state leaders (B), this is an informal method of influence. Although the states can ignore the federal government, they do so at the loss of funding (D).

97. **B**

The Bostonians reacted by throwing the tea into the harbor rather than allow the tax to be paid on it. The Boston Massacre (A) occurred in 1770 when British soldiers killed and injured civilians. This incident was used to build animosity toward the authorities. The Declaration of Independence (C) was fueled by many incidents, including the tea tax, but was not signed until 1776. The Articles of Confederation (D) ratified in 1781 were the first U.S. Constitution.

98. **B**

The members of the First Continental Congress (A) met in 1774 and had no desire to break away from Great Britain. However, by the time the Second Continental Congress met in 1775, military conflict seemed imminent. The Boston Tea Party (C) occurred in 1773. The Stamp Act (D) was passed in 1765.

Detailed Explanations for Practice Test 2

99. **C**

    Congress proposed the Twenty-sixth Amendment on March 23, 1971, after the House of Representatives passed it, following the Senate's passage of an identical resolution on March 10, 1971. It was quickly ratified by the states. The amendment states that the right of citizens of the United States eighteen years of age or older to vote shall not be denied or abridged by the United States or by any state on account of age. Alcohol consumption laws are under state authority (A). The end of the military draft was not the result of an amendment (B). The Twenty-first Amendment repealed the Eighteenth Amendment. (D).

100. **A**

    Samurai during the feudal Japanese period were similar to the feudal barons in medieval Europe. They were not mercenary warriors (B) or religious leaders (C). A shogun (D) was a general.

101. **C**

    Susan B. Anthony was a 19th century reformer and suffragette who fought for voting rights for women. Therefore, she would have been in favor of the 19th Amendment, which gave women the right to vote. The 14th amendment (A) defined U.S. citizenship. The 17th Amendment (B) provided for direct election of senators. The 22nd amendment (D) limited the president to a maximum of two terms or 10 years.

102. **C**

    Humanists believed that this life was important and should be enjoyed, and that human accomplishments in the scholarly, artistic, and political realms should be celebrated. Humanists were inspired by the classical Greek and Roman civilizations, not the Mesoamerican civilizations (A). They believed that humans were capable of anything, and would not characterize them as being "nothing compared to God" (B), and that humans should enjoy life instead of waiting for the next one (D).

103. **B**

    Manorialism was an economic system in which large estates, granted by the king to nobles, encompassed one or more self-sufficient villages, which were populated largely by serfs. By 800 CE, about 60% of Western Europe was *enserfed,* meaning that there was a contractual agreement between lords, who provided justice and protection, and serfs, who provided their labor for a fixed amount of time each year. It did not feature a centralized political, economic, military, and social system (A), less availability of agricultural goods (C), or an increased use of slave labor (D).

104. **C**

The *Watergate Scandal* is a general term that describes a web of political scandals from June 1972 to April 1974. All of the scandals relate to the burglary of the national headquarters of the Democratic Committee, which was housed in the Watergate office complex in Washington, D.C. President Nixon, facing impeachment for his involvement in covering up White House involvement with the entire Watergate Affair, was forced to resign. Nixon's trip to China (A) was successful and opened relations between the U.S. and China. Nixon ended the Vietnam War (B). He was not involved with organized crime (D).

105. **A**

In his 1964 State of the Union message, President Lyndon Johnson called for a "War on Poverty." The Economic Opportunity Act of 1964 established the Office of Economic Opportunity to carry out antipoverty programs. While Kennedy did organize the Peace Corps (B), he did so prior to 1964. George Marshall's plan was to provide funds for military and rebuilding in Europe, not for food (C). Public assistance would not have been an issue under President Eisenhower (D).

106. **A**

The field of social science emerged as a distinct field in the middle of the nineteenth century (1800s). It emerged prior to the 1900s (B), or the mid- or late twentieth century (C, D), so (A) is the only possible answer.

107. **C**

The four major subfields of anthropology are archaeological, biological, linguistic, and sociocultural. Sociology (A) is the study of human interaction, specifically how groups influence individual values, norms, and sanctions. Psychology (B) is the scientific and systematic study of mental processes and/or behavior. History (D) is the study of political, economic, social, and cultural aspects of the past through the use of material, oral, and written sources.

108. **C**

Norms, values, culture, customs, and traditions are concepts related to sociology.

109. **A**

Economics is the study of how people choose to use limited or scarce resources to obtain maximum satisfaction of unlimited wants. Education (B) is the social science field that is concerned with the pedagogy of teaching and learning. Political science (C) is the study of the principles of government, the manner in which government conducts itself, how we identify ourselves as citizens of a particular nation, how we participate in our political structure and how it affects us, and what motivates us to affiliate ourselves with certain points of view or parties. Anthropology (D) is a science of the entire panorama of humankind, from human origins to contemporary life.

Detailed Explanations for Practice Test 2

110. **D**

Pedagogy is defined as the method and practice of teaching, especially as an academic subject or theoretical concept; therefore, education is the correct choice. History (A) is the study of political, economic, social, and cultural aspects of the past through the use of material, oral, and written sources. Civics (B) is the branch of political science that examines civic affairs and the rights and duties of citizenship. It focuses on the role of citizens in a government. Geography (C) is the study of the Earth's surface, including such aspects as its climate, topography, vegetation, and population.

111. **A**

Environment and Society is one of the six elements of the field of geography.

112. **A**

The Florida Department of Education defines Florida's CPALMS (Curriculum Planning and Learning Management System; *http://www.cpalms.org/Public/*) as "an online toolbox of information, vetted resources, and interactive tools that helps educators effectively implement teaching standards." It provides excellent content and ideas for teaching and learning by subject area. It also provides resources for students and parents to use. Anthropology is not a specific standard in CPALMS (B). FEAPS (C) are standards for teachers. While CPALMS does provide information about instructional accommodations (D), choice (A) is the best response.

113. **A**

Metacognition is thinking about thinking and involves awareness and control of cognitive processes. Mnemonics (B) are strategies for remembering information. The lower levels of Bloom's Taxonomy are recall and comprehension (C). The scientific method (D) is an inquiry strategy consisting of the following steps: identify and clarify an issue; propose a hypothesis; locate, collect, and organize the data or evidence information they receive; evaluate, interpret, and analyze the data; then, finally, draw inferences and conclusions about it and use this information to make generalizations.

114. **C**

The question requires you to add the numbers of Hispanic women in each of the age brackets (20 to 24 and 25 to 29) together to get the answer: $1,717 + 1,863 = 3,580$. And, since all the amounts in the table are shown as thousands, your answer must be 3,580,000. All of the other options are incorrect.

115. **C**

The tabular information in the "All other races" column does not break out the data by African-American, Asian, or any other races; therefore, the data is not available. This table's main purpose is to display the population by sex, age, and hispanic origin, white alone, and race. However, race is constructed as white and other. Any analysis would need to account for the limits of any discussion of race other than white, since Hispanic is not a race; rather it is an ethnic identification. Many people who self-identify as Hispanic also identify as white. This table does account for that phenomenon since it has the category "White alone."

116. **D**

The number of individuals who are currently in the age group 30–34 would be 100–104 in the year 2078; therefore, for the purpose of this question, the age groups for comparison would be those under 30. With the exception of the 15–19 age group for *all other races*, all other age groups for *Hispanic* are higher than either the *whites only* or the *all other races* groups; therefore, the Hispanic group will have the highest percentage of the population. The table provides information that can be used to answer the question (A). Comparing the *whites only males* column at the top of the chart with the *whites only females* at the bottom of the chart, the number of males in each age group under 30 is higher than that of the females. Thus, there will be more white males than white females (B). Since the number of Hispanics has the highest percentage, the category *all other races* cannot be greater than the combination of *whites only* and *Hispanics* (C).

117. **D**

A primary source is an account of an event created by someone who witnessed the event or that wrote about it during the period being studied or immediately after it; therefore, an audio recording of the event as it occurred would be a first-person source. A documentary on George Washington (A), a teacher's lecture on the government (B), and a diary entry from an individual who was not the individual who witnessed the event (C) are secondary sources.

118. **B**

The Peace of Westphalia introduced the idea of the treaty as the basis of international law. There was no document that created the concept of nation-states (A). The Treaty of Versailles ended World War I (C). The Congress of Vienna met in 1814 and 1815 to redraw the map of Europe after the Napoleonic era and to endeavor to preserve the future peace of Europe (D).

Detailed Explanations for Practice Test 2

119. **C**

While Roosevelt did have "Fireside Chats" (B), that was not the name given to his legislative priorities. The New Deal (C) was a collection of programs and legislation designed by Roosevelt's "brain trust" to bring the country out of economic crisis. The way to end the depression was that government had to regulate business and restore purchasing power to the masses by cutting production. Roosevelt and his "brain trust" believed this would lead to rising prices and rising wages, which made sense according to the economics of scarcity. Roosevelt also believed in direct unemployment relief and repealing prohibition. Answer option (A) refers to President Lyndon Johnson's legislative War on Poverty, which was patterned after Roosevelt's New Deal, but Johnson's legislation was enacted in the 1960s. Answer option (D) is the document created by President Wilson to put an end to World War I.

120. **A**

Answer choice (A) is correct: checks and balances provide each branch of government with the ability to limit the actions of the other branches. Choice (B) is not correct because the Founders wanted each branch to be interdependent. Choices (C) and (D) are also incorrect because they deal with only one branch of the government.

INDEX

A

Abolitionist movement, 53, 227, 288
Abortion, 68, 96, 293, 294
Absentee ballots, 71
Adams, Henry, 53
Adams, John, 76, 77, 209, 211, 213, 215, 288
Adams, John Quincy, 67, 218
Adams, Sam, 53
Adams-Onis Treaty, 217, 301
Advertising industry, 171
Affirmative action, 65, 96
Afghanistan 82, 83, 276, 277
   Soviet invasion of, 96, 277
   war on terrorism and, 83–84
Africa 87, 101–103, 117, 121–122, 125–129, 148–151, 164, 167–168, 172, 177–179, 192, 200, 225–226, 250, 279, 286
   before 1500, 125, 148
      Axum, 126–127
      Ghana, 127–129, 151
      Islam and, 129, 150, 184
      Kingdom of Kush, 126
      Mali, 127–129, 151
      Songhai, 127–129, 151
      Swahili Coast, 126–127
      Western Africa, 127
   from 1500 to 1850
      African traditional religion, 150
      cultural developments, 250
      economic developments, 247, 252
      political developments, 248
      slave trade, 148–151, 166, 177, 221, 232
      social impacts, 201–203
   impact of imperialism on, 177
African Americans, 95, 176, 221, 230, 232–233, 238, 244–245, 248, 250–251, 261, 266–267, 278, 282, 286–287, 302
   civil rights, 55, 57, 64, 94–95, 230, 233, 261, 267, 277–278, 280–287, 289, 293
   Great Depression and, 252, 303
   World War I and, 242–243
   World War II and, 79
Age of Exploration, 163–166, 191
Age of Reason, 159
Agrarianism, 233
Akhenaten, 112–113
Akkadians, 106, 108
Albany Plan of Union, 204
Albuquerque, 167
Alexander II of Russia, 269
Allocative efficiency, 27–28, 31
al-Qaeda, 83–84
Amendments to U.S. Constitution, 54–58. *See also* specific amendments
   civil rights and liberties, 94–95
American Federation of Labor, 238, 262
American history 166, 240, 253, 284
   agrarianism, industrialization, urbanization and reform movements, 233
   antebellum period, 221, 225
   Civil War and Reconstruction era, 226
   Cold War era, 268
   colonial period, 194
   Constitutional era and early republic, 214–215
   contemporary domestic and foreign affairs, 294
   Florida history, 296
   immigration in late nineteenth and twentieth centuries, 240–245
   Revolutionary era, 204
   westward expansion, 216, 220, 225
   World War I era, 242
   World War II era, 262
American revolution 198, 205, 300–301
   Albany Plan of Union, 204
   Battles of Lexington and Concord, 212
   Boston Massacre, 209
   Boston Tea Party, 210–211
   Declaration of Independence, 52, 94, 213, 288
   First Continental Congress, 211–212
   Grenville Acts, 207
   Intolerable Acts, 211–212
   Second Continental Congress, 212

Seven Years' War and Treaty of Paris, 205–207
Tea Act, 210
Townshend Acts, 209
Treaty of Paris (1783), 205–207
American Samoa, 78
Americas 77, 79, 103, 122,135, 142, 152, 165–166, 168, 177, 191–194
   Age of Exploration impact on, 191–193
   Aztecs, 137, 168, 177, 192
   Mayan civilization, 136
Analects, 116, 188
Anarchy, 91
Andean Society, 137–138
Anglican Church, 145, 201
Antebellum period, 221, 225
Anthony, Susan B., 240, 288–290, 292
Anti-Federalists, 53, 215
Aquinas, Thomas, 140, 142
Articles of Confederation, 51–52, 54, 214
Aryabhata, 123
Aryans, 114
Ashoka Maurya, 123
Atlantic Slave Trade, 148,166
Atomic bomb, 79, 183, 268–270, 272
Authoritarian government, 93
Autocracy, 92, 180
Avignon Exile, 144
Axum, 126–127
Aztecs, 137, 168, 177, 192

B

Babylonian Empire, 108
Babylonian Period, 102
Bakke v. Regents of the University of California, 96
Balance of payments, 45
Balance of power, 75,76, 86,172
Balboa, Vasco Núñez de, 168
Bay of Pigs, 275
Beauregard, P.G.T., 227
Bentham, Jeremy, 172
Berlin Wall, 82, 275, 277
Bill of Rights, 52, 53, 55, 94, 96, 215
Birth control, 250, 292
Black Codes, 278
Black Death, 142

Black Panthers, 286
Bonaparte, Napoleon, 174,
Bonds, 38, 39, 45, 64, 69, 248, 300
Boston Massacre, 209
Boston Tea Party, 211
Boxer Rebellion, 157
Bronze Age, 102, 104
Brown v. Board of Education, 95, 281, 282
Bruni, Leonardo, 195
Bryan, William Jennings, 235
Buddhism, 123, 130, 134, 187
   basic beliefs of, 187
   historical overview, 187
   spread of, in China, 130
   types of, 187
Bull Moose Party, 67
Bureaucracy
   Chinese civil service and, 188
   federal, 63–65
Bush, George H. W., 83, 85, 88
Bush, George W., 83
Bush Doctrine, 83, 84

C

Cabal, Pedro, 167
Cabot, John, 168, 192
Calvin, John, 145
Capitalism, 33, 172, 180, 193, 195, 224, 237, 238, 247, 270, 280, 313
Carolingian Renaissance, 138, 139
Carter, Jimmy, 82
Carter Doctrine, 82
Cartier, Jacques, 168, 192
Castro, Fidel, 274, 275
Catherine de' Medici, 147
Catherine II "the Great," 158
Catholic Church
   Counter Reformation, 146
   Crusades, 138, 141
   Inquisition, 142
   integrated into feudal system, 139
   Lower Middle Ages and, 138
   monasticism and monasteries, 138
   Reformation and, 139, 164
Chaldeans, 108
Champlain, Samuel de, 168, 194
Charts, 22, 23

Index

Checks and balances, 52, 54, 91, 120, 162, 214
Chesapeake colonies, 196, 197
China, 114, 123, 154, 295
   earliest civilizations, 114–124
   Han Dynasty, 123
   Ming Dynasty, 133, 154
   Mongols and, 132
   Opium War, 223
   Qing (Manchu) Dynasty, 155
   Song Dynasty, 131
   spread of Buddhism, 130
   Sui Dynasty, 130
   Tang Dynasty, 131
   Yuan Dynasty, 133
Chinampas, 137
Chinese Exclusion Act, 241
Christianity, 186
   basic beliefs of, 186
   historical overview, 186
Cities, Industrial Revolution and, 169
Citizens
   political beliefs and characteristics of, 68
   rights, privileges and responsibilities of U.S., 94
Civics, social study concepts of, 308, 313
Civil liberties, 94, 277
Civil rights, 94, 277, 278
   civil rights era, 280, 281
   defined, 94
   early twentieth century roots of civil rights era, 95
   reconstruction and failures of, 94
   significant individuals, 279
Civil Rights Act of 1964, 285
Civil War
   advantages of Confederacy and Union, 228
   antebellum period, 221
   causes of, 226
   Florida during, 302
   hostilities begin, 227
   progress of war, 228–229
   reconstruction, 227, 229, 230, 232, 278
Cold War, 80, 82, 272, 275, 276
   during 1960s, 275–276
   containment, 80, 26, 268
   détente, 80, 82, 275, 276
   domino theory, 80, 272
   under Eisenhower, 275
   emergence of, and containment, 80–81
   Marshall Plan, 80, 85, 270
   Truman Doctrine, 80, 270
   unrestricted competition, 80
   Vietnam War, 96, 274
Colonial America, 194–195
   economic changes and, 194
   government in, 185
   Middle Atlantic colonies, 197
   New England colonies, 196, 204
   reasons Europeans came to America, 197–198
   social changes during, 203
   societies in, 196
   Southern and Chesapeake colonies, 197
Colonialism
   Age of Exploration and Americas, 191
   compared to imperialism, 177
   extent of, 178
   impact of, 178
Columbian Exchange, 166
Columbus, 142, 167, 168
Command economy, 43, 44
Commercial Revolution, 164, 169
Communism, 80, 81, 83, 87, 173, 271, 272, 276
   Cold War and, 83, 268, 276
   Red Scare and McCarthyism, 271
   as type of government, 173
Comparative advantage, 44
Concord, Battle of, 212
Concurrent powers, 58
Confederate States of America, 223, 227, 302
Confederation government, 214
Confucianism
   basic beliefs of, 188
   historical overview of, 188
Confucius, 116, 124, 188
Congress
   committee system of, 60
   constitutional qualifications for, 61
   legislative process, 60, 61
   powers of, 59
Congress of Vienna, 174
Conservatives, 68
Constitution, United States, 50–65
   Amendments to, 55, 278, 303
   Articles of, 51
   Articles of Confederation, 51, 52, 54, 214

basic principles of, 53
Bill of Rights, 52, 53, 55, 94, 215
checks and balances, 50, 52, 53, 54, 91, 120, 162, 214
concurrent powers, 58,
Constitutional Convention, 51, 232
development and ratification of, 51–52
Electoral College, 53, 60, 62, 215
federal government powers, 65
federalism, 50, 53
framework for foreign policy, 75
Great Compromise, 52
historical background for, 51
legislative powers and, 59–68
New Jersey Plan, 52,
Preamble, 51, 54, 140
state government powers, 65–61
Three-Fifths Compromise, 53, 215
Constitutional Convention, 51, 232
Constitutional form of government, 93
Consumption, 33, 35, 171, 172, 236
Containment policy, 80
Coolidge, Calvin, 248, 249
Congress of Racial Equality (CORE), 280, 283
Cortés, Hernando, 168
Cossacks, 159
Costs, law of increasing costs, 29
Cotton is King, 225
Counter-Enlightenment, 162
Counter Reformation, 146
Covenant of the League of Nations, 89
Cow Cavalry, 303
Credit, 47, 248
Crusades, 138, 140, 141
Cuba, 78, 274
Cuban Missile Crisis, 80, 275
Cuban Revolution, 274
Cuneiform, 106
Currency Act, 207

D

da Gama, Vasco, 142, 164, 167
Daoism, 116
Daughters of Liberty, 209
da Vinci, Leonardo, 143
Davis, Jefferson, 223, 228
Dayton Accords, 83

Declaration of Independence, 52, 94, 213
De facto segregation, 95
De jure segregation, 95
Demand, 33, 34
Democracy
   ancient Greece, 116, 117, 118, 119
   as government system, 117
Democratic Party, historical perspective, 67, 227, 261, 285
Democratic Republicans, 66, 67
Descartes, René, 161
de Soto, Hernando, 297, 298
Détente, 80, 82, 275, 276
Dias, Bartolomeu, 164, 167
Dictatorship, 92, 93
Diderot, 162
Discount rate, 40
Domino theory, 80, 81, 272
Double jeopardy, 94
Dred Scott v. Sandford, 95
DuBois, W.E.B., 245, 279
Due process, 94, 277

E

Economics, 25
   allocative efficiency, 27, 28, 31
   balance of payments, 45
   bonds, 38, 39, 45
   command economy, 43–44
   comparative advantage, 44
   consumer economy, 47
   credit, 9, 37–40, 47
   defined, 14, 35
   in developing nations, 46
   discount rate, 38, 40
   economic growth, 26, 27, 31, 37, 42, 46
   equity, 27–28
   exchange rate, 44–45
   Federal Reserve System, 37, 42
   fiscal policy, 37
   full employment, 27, 29
   GDP, 35, 36, 42
   inflation, 26, 35–37, 42–43
   law of increasing costs, 30
   macroeconomics, 26, 35
   market economy, 25, 41–43
   microeconomics, 26

Index

national output, 35–36
open-market operations, 38
phases of economic cycle, 36
price, 32–39, 41
production possibilities frontier curve, 29
productive efficiency, 28
reserve ratio, 39
scarcity and resource allocation, 44
supply and demand relationships, 34
technical efficiency, 28, 30
trade-offs and opportunity cost, 29
unemployment, 35–37
universal economic goals, 27–28
Egypt, ancient, 110–113
1848 Revolutions, 174–176
   in Austria, 175
   causes of, 174–176
   effects of, 176–178
   in France, 174–175
   in Italy, 174–175
   in Prussia, 175
Eighteenth Amendment, 57, 67, 246
Eisenhower, Dwight, 272–274
Eisenhower Doctrine, 272–273
Elastic clause, 59
Electoral College, 53, 56, 60, 62, 215, 235
Elizabeth I, English queen, 147
El Salvador, 82
Emancipation Proclamation, 228, 278
Empiricists, 161
England
   Age of Exploration, 163–165
   individuals in Age of Exploration, 163–166, 191
   Reformation in, 145
Enlightenment, 52, 94, 159–163, 173, 187
   elite culture of, 162
   empiricists, 161
   overview of, 54, 84
   rationalists, 161
   Rococo and Neoclassicism, 162, 163
Equal Opportunity Commission, 285, 293
Equal Rights Amendment, 292–293
Escobedo v. Illinois, 96
Euphrates River, 106
Europe
   Counter Reformation, 146
   Middle Ages, 138, 140, 142
   Reformation, 118, 138–139, 144–146, 164
   Renaissance, 118, 138–139, 142–144, 146, 153, 164, 251
European Community (EC), 85
Exchange rate, 44–45
Executive branch, 55, 61, 91, 229
   budget, 42, 60, 62, 153, 261
   Cabinet, 55, 60–64, 83, 231, 265
   constitutional requirements for, 62
   powers of, 53, 59, 145, 160, 162
   veto power, 62
Expansionism, 78
Exploration, Age of, 163
   Atlantic Slave Trade, 148, 166
   causes of, 163–165
   Columbian Exchange, 166
   effects of, 165–167
   impact on Americas, 165–167
   main events early in, 167
   mercantilism, 166
   part of, 169, 176, 180
   Prince Henry the Navigator, 164, 167
   significant individuals in, 163
   Treaty of Tordesillas, 167, 191
Ex post facto laws, 60
Expressed powers, 59

F

Factory system, 169, 171
Fair Employment Practices Committee, 262, 267
Federal budget, 62
Federal bureaucracy, 62–63, 65
Federal Deposit Insurance Corporation, 64, 258
Federal government
   powers of, 53, 59
   size of, 42, 61, 68, 90
   as type of government, 91
Federalism, 50, 53, 390
Federalist Party, 66–67
Federalists, 53, 66–67, 215
Federal Reserve Board, 64
Federal Reserve System, 37, 42
   discount rate, 40
   open-market operations, 38
   reserve ratio, 39
Federal Trade Commission, 64, 248

Ferdinand, Archduke Franz, 178
Fertile Crescent, 105, 108, 115
Feudalism
    Catholic Church integrated into, 139–140
    Japanese, 134–135
    during Lower Middle Ages, 138
Fifteenth Amendment, 73, 231, 278, 285, 288, 290
First Continental Congress, 211–212
First New Deal, 255–256
Florida history, 296
    during booming years, 303
    British period, 300
    in Civil War, 303–303
    conquistadors, 137, 165, 168
    Disney World and tourism, 305
    French colonists, 299
    Great Depression and New Deal, 247, 252–253, 262, 303
    Indian tribes and, 297–298
    Kennedy Space Center and NASA, 304
    under Reconstruction, 303
    Seminole Wars, 301
    Spanish colonists, 299–300
    during World War I, 304
Foreign policy
    Bush Doctrine, 83–84
    Cold War, 79–80, 82–85, 88, 182, 268–270, 272–277
    constitutional framework for, 75
    current issues in, 294–296
    global system, 85–88
    international relations and, 88
    isolationism, 76, 78–79
    models of, 84–85
    Obama Doctrine, 84
    theoretical framework for international relations, 75–76
    war on terrorism, 83
    World War I, 78–79, 85
    World War II, 76, 79, 85
Fourier, Charles, 172
Fourteen Points, 78, 245
Fourteenth Amendment, 73, 94–95, 230, 233, 278, 281, 289–290
France
    Age of Exploration, 163–166
    colonialism of, 176–178
    1848 revolution, 174

    Florida history and, 299
    French and Indian War, 205–206, 300
    French Revolution, 86–87, 139, 173–174
    individuals in Age of Exploration, 163
    World War I and, 244
Franklin, Benjamin, 204–205, 213–214
Freedmen's Bureau, 279
Freedom Ride, 283–283
French and Indian War, 205–206
French Revolution, 86–87, 139, 173–174
    causes of, 173–174
    Congress of Vienna, 174
    era of Napoleon, 173–174
    phases of, 174–176
Frobisher, Sir Martin, 168
Fugitive Slave Law, 221–222

G

Gadsden Purchase, 217–218
Galen, 121
Garvey, Marcus, 250, 286
GDP, 35–36, 42
General Agreement on Tariffs and Trade, 80
Genghis Khan, 132–133
Geography, 11–13, 15, 17, 19, 21, 114, 118, 134, 186, 194, 196, 308, 312, 321
    branches of, 11, 90, 186, 308
    defined, 9, 14, 35, 53, 66, 69, 75, 92, 96, 109, 143, 176, 186, 224, 230, 278, 311
    environment and society, 16, 312
    graphs and charts, 22
    human systems, 15–17, 312
    location, 11, 13–15, 21–22
    maps, 12–13, 20–22
    new standards in geographic education, 12
    physical systems, 15–17, 19, 312
    place, 11–17, 20, 23
    regions, 13–14
    social study concepts of, 310–312
    themes of, 309
    uses of, 17
    world in spatial terms, 12
George III, English king, 206–208, 212
Germany
    colonialism of, 92, 141, 146–148
    World War I, 181–182
    World War II, 181–182, 270–273
Gettysburg Address, 229

Index

Ghana, 127–129, 151
Gideon v. Wainwright, 96
Gitlow Case, 94
Glasnost, 82, 277
Globalization, as current trend, 183–184
Global system
    contemporary, 87–88
    historical context of modern, 86
Golden age of diplomacy, 86
Gorbachev, Mikhail, 82, 277
Government
    in command economy, 43
    comparison of types of, 90–99
    in market economy, 41–44
    municipal, 71, 74
Government corporations, 64–65
Granges, 234
Grant, Ulysses S., 229, 231, 288, 290
Graphs, 20, 22–23, 33
Great Awakening, 203, 219, 223
Great Britain
    American revolution and, 198, 205, 300–301
    colonialism of, 206–211
    Florida and, 227, 296–297, 300–301, 304
    Opium War, 157, 178
    World War I, 263–268
    World War II, 183, 209
Great Depression, 79, 181, 247, 252–253, 262, 303
    election of 1932, 254
    First New Deal, 255–256
    Florida during, 303–304
    Hoover's policies during, 254
    reasons for, 252, 273
    Second New Deal, 259
Great Schism, 144
Greece, ancient, 116–118
Grenville, George, 206, 208
Grotius, Hugo, 89
Guadalupe-Hidalgo, Treaty of, 218–219
Guam, 78
Guatemala, 88, 136, 274
Guilds, 152, 154
Gulf of Tonkin Resolution, 81
Gunpowder Empires, 151
Gupta Empire, 123

H

Habeas corpus, 60, 94
Hamilton, Alexander, 52–53, 64, 66–67
Hammurabi, 108
Han Dynasty, 123–124
Hanging Gardens of Babylon, 108
Harappa, 113
Harding, Warren G., 248–249
Harlem Renaissance, 247, 251, 280
Hatshepsut, Queen, 112, 126
Hazelwood School District v. Kuhlmeier, 96
Hebrews, earliest, 109
Heinan period, 178
Helsinki Accords, 82
Henry, Patrick, 211
Henry II, English King, 140
Henry VIII, English king, 145
Hieroglyphics, 111, 135
High Middle Ages, 138, 140
Hinduism, 190
Hindus, Mughal Empire, 133
Hiroshima, 268
History. *See also* American history; World history
    defined, 143, 176, 186
    periodization of, 101
    study of, 99, 118
    time and, 100, 117, 165
Hitler, Adolf, 92, 181
Hittites, 107–108, 112–113
Ho Chi Minh, 81, 274
Holding companies, 237
Holocaust, 182, 320
Holy Roman Emperor, 86, 146–147
Holy Roman Empire, 88, 122
Homeland Security, Office of, 83
Homo sapiens, 101–102
Hongwu, 133
Hoover, Herbert, 244, 248–249
Hoover, J. Edgar, 246
Humanism, 143
Hume, David, 161
Hundred Schools of Thought, 116
Hus, Jan, 144
Hussein, Saddam, 84–85
Hyksos, 112–113

I

Ignatius of Loyola, 146
Immigration, in late 19th and early 20th century America, 240–242
Impeachment, 59, 61, 276, 434
Imperialism
  compared to colonialism, 177–178
  motivations for, 200–201
  political, social, geographic and economic impact of, 87–88
Incas, 137–138, 168, 192
Independent executive agencies, 64
India
  earliest civilizations, 104–106
  impact of imperialism on, 177
  Mauryan and Gupta Empire, 123
  Mughal Empire, 133
Indian Removal Act, 301
Industrialization, in U.S. from 1860 to 1900, 236–240
Industrial Revolution, 87, 157, 164, 169–173
  causes of, 169
  economic effects of, 169
  political effects of, 172–173
  social effects of, 170
Inflation, 26, 35–37, 42–43, 51, 155, 180, 193, 198, 231, 234, 246, 266, 308
Inflation rate, 37
Inquisition, 142
Interest groups, 65, 69–70, 85, 248
International Court of Justice, 89
International law, 75, 82, 89–90, 182, 242–243
International Monetary Fund, 45, 80, 185
International relations
  contemporary global system, 87–88
  international law, 75, 82, 89–90, 182, 242–243
  modern global system, 85–86
  overview of, 84
  theoretical framework for, 75–76
Interstate Commerce Act, 234, 236
Interstate Commerce Commission, 64, 248, 284
Interwar period, 78
Intolerable Acts, 211–212
Invisible hand, 25, 172
Iran, Safavid Empire, 151
Iraq, invasion of Kuwait, 83, 85
Iraq war, 83
Irish Republican Army (IRA), 87
Iron Age, 102, 104
Islam, 125–129, 150, 153, 184, 188–190, 286–287
  ancient Africa and, 125–127
  five pillars of, 189
  life of Muhammad, 188–190
  Qur'an, 127, 189
  spread of, 125
Isolationism, 76, 78–79
Italy, 1848 revolution, 174
Ivan III, Russian tsar, 159
Ivan the Terrible, 157, 159

J

Jackson, Andrew, 65–67, 217–218
Janissaries, 152–153
Janissary Corps, 153
Japan, 88, 134, 151, 181–182, 241–243, 247, 264–268
  feudal, 134–135
  Heinan period, 134
  Takia Reforms, 134
  Yamato Clan, 134
Jay, John, 52, 211, 213
Jefferson, Thomas, 52, 66–67, 121, 213, 217, 288, 315
Jeffersonian Republicans, 66
Jim Crow Laws, 233, 278
Johnson, Andrew, 59, 230
Johnson, Lyndon, 81, 276
Judaism
  basic beliefs of, 186
  branches of, 186
  historical overview, 186
Judicial branch, 55, 63
  other courts, 55
  Supreme Court, 63
Just war, 89

K

Kansas-Nebraska Act, 222
Karlowitz, Treaty of, 154
Kellogg-Briand Pact, 79, 89
Kennedy, John F., 275, 287
Kennedy Space Center, 304
Khan, 132

Index

Khrushchev, Nikita, 273
King, Martin Luther, Jr., 282–284, 286–287
King George's War, 206
Knights of Labor, 237–238
Korean War, 272
Korematsu v. United States, 95, 267
Kshatriyas, 187
Kublai Khan, 133
Ku Klux Klan, 233, 251, 278
Kush, Kingdom of, 126–127
Kuwait, 83, 85

L

Labor unions, 41, 69, 237, 262
Laissez-faire economics, 67, 172, 237
League of Nations, 78, 89, 179, 245, 247
League of Women Voters, 292
Lee, Robert E., 228
Legislative branch, 54–55, 59, 66, 91
    committee system of, 60–61
    constitutional qualifications for, 61
    powers of, 53, 59
Leibniz, Gottfried Wilhelm, 161
Lend-Lease Act, 79, 264
Leo X, Pope, 145
Lexington, Battle of, 212
Liberals, 68, 70, 1175, 279
Lincoln, Abraham, 218, 222, 227, 302
Livy, 122
Lobbying, 248
Local government, 53, 58, 71–74, 241
Location, 11, 13–15, 21, 36, 74, 91, 100, 103–104, 126, 129, 264, 301, 321
Locke, John, 52, 161
Louisiana Purchase, 217, 221
Lower Middle Ages, 138
Luther, Martin, 145

M

Machiavelli, 144
Macroeconomics, 26, 35, 308
Madison, James, 52–53, 56, 67, 215
Magellan, Ferdinand, 168
Magna Carta, 52, 140
Malcolm X, 286–288
Mali, 127–129, 151

Malthus, 172
Manchu Dynasty, 154–155
Mandate of Heaven, 115
Manifest Destiny, 77, 216, 218–219
Manorialism, 140
Manu's Laws, 123
Mao Zedong, 271
Mapp v. Ohio, 95
Maps, 21–22
March on Selma, 285
March on Washington, 261, 267, 284, 286
Market economy, 25, 41–43, 151
Marshall Plan, 80, 85, 270
Marx, Karl, 172, 181
Mary, Queen of Scots, 147
Mary I, English queen, 147
Mauryan Empire, 123
McKinley, William, 235, 275
Mehmed the Conqueror, 152
Mercantilism, 166, 169, 194, 197
Meritocracy, 154, 188, 239
Mesoamerica
    Andean Society, 137
    Aztecs, 137, 168, 177, 192
    Mayan civilization, 136
    Olmecs, 135
Mesolithic period, 103
Mesopotamia, 101, 104, 106–111, 113–115
Mexican-American War, 218, 243
Microeconomics, 26, 308
Middle Ages, 138, 140, 142
    Black Death, 142
    Carolingian Renaissance, 138–139
    creation of schools, 139
    Crusades, 138, 140–142
    defined, 143
    feudalism during, 138
    Gothic architecture during, 140–141
    High, 138, 140–141
    integrated Church into feudal system, 138–139, 142
    Late, 138, 142
    Lower, 138
    Magna Carta, 52, 140
    manorialism, 140
    monasticism and monasteries, 139
    rise of European monarchies, 138
    scholasticism, 141
    social classes during, 139

Middle Atlantic colonies, 197
Middle Kingdom, 110, 112–113
Ming Dynasty, 130, 133, 154–156
Miranda v. Arizona, 96
Mississippi Freedom Summer, 285
Mixed economy, 33
Monarchy, 52, 87, 93, 109, 120, 140, 160, 173
    rise of European, during Low Middle Ages, 138
Monasteries, 130, 139
Monasticism, 139
Mongols, 130, 132–133, 151, 155, 157, 164
    Gunpowder Empires and, 151
Monotheism, 109, 112–113
Monroe, James, 77
Monroe Doctrine, 78, 242, 245
Montesquieu, Baron de, 162
Morgenthau, Hans J., 75
Mughal Empire, 133
    cultural development, 105, 250
    political developments, 248
    social development, 155, 197, 249
Multiculturalism, 90
Multi-national corporation (MNC), 88
Municipal government, 74
Muslims
    five pillars of Islam, 189
    life of Muhammad, 188–190
    Mughal Empire, 133
    Ottoman Empire, 120, 152–154, 178–179
    Safavid Empire, 151
    spread of Islam, 125
    tenants of Islam, 189

N

Nagasaki, 268
Napoleon, 86–87, 174, 217
Napoleonic Wars, 86
NASA, 273, 304–305
National Advancement for the Advancement of Colored People (NAACP), 279
National government, 51–52, 54, 59, 62–63, 66, 90, 91, 214
    executive branch, 42, 55, 61, 63, 91, 215, 229
    federal bureaucracy, 62–63, 65
    judicial branch, 55, 63
    legislative branch, 54, 55, 59, 66, 91
Nationalism, 81, 85, 87, 152, 154, 174–179, 181, 184, 216, 221, 242, 270

Nationality, 86, 176, 285
National Republicans, 67
Nation-state, 50, 86–87, 89, 176
Native Americans
    Columbian Exchange, 166
    in Florida, 1, 3, 16, 69, 296, 299–304
    horses and, 132, 159, 194
    Pontiac's Uprising, 206
    Proclamation of 1763, 206, 242
Natural Bridge, Battle of, 302
Nazi Germany, 79, 92
Near v. Minnesota, 95
Nehru, Jawaharlal, 80
Neoclassicism, 162
Neolithic Period, 104
Neolithic Revolution, 103–104
Neutrality, 79, 89, 242, 263–264
Neutrality Acts, 79, 263
New Deal, 64, 247, 252, 255, 256, 259, 261, 303
New England colonies, 196, 204
New Kingdom, 110, 112–113, 126
New World Order, 83, 88
New York Times v. United States, 96
Ngo Dinh Diem, 81
Nicaragua, 78, 82
Nicholas, Russian tsar, 180
Nile Delta, 104
Nineteenth Amendment, 73, 240, 246, 288, 292
Nineveh, 108
Nixon, Richard, 82, 275–276
Nixon Doctrine, 276
Non-Aligned Movement, 80
Non-interventionism, 67, 76–77
Non-state actors, 87
North Atlantic Treaty Organization (NATO), 80, 270
Northwest Ordinance, 216
Nubia, 126

O

Obama, Barack, 84
Obama Doctrine, 84
Old Kingdom, 110–113
Oligarchy, 92
Olmecs, 135
Olustee, Battle of, 302
Open Door Policy, 78

Index

Open-market operations, 38
Opium War, 157, 178
Opportunity cost, 26, 29–31, 44
Organization of Petroleum Exporting Countries (OPEC), 85
Osman, 152
Ottoman Empire
    cultural developments, 153
    economic developments, 154
    highlights of, 152–154
    political developments, 153
    Safavid empire and, 151
    social structure of, 152
Owen, Robert, 172

P

Paleolithic period, 102–103
Palestine Liberation Organization (PLO), 84, 87
Panic of 1873, 350
Paper, 231
Paris, Treaty of (1763), 205–207
Paris, Treaty of (1783), 213–214
Parks, Rosa, 281–282
Parliamentary system of government, 91
Patricians, 119, 122
Pax Mongolica, 133
Peace of Augsburg, 147
Peace of Westphalia, 86, 89
Pearl Harbor, 79, 182, 265, 267
Perestroika, 82, 277
Perot, H. Ross, 67
Persian Gulf War, 83, 88
Peter the Great, 158
Pharaohs, 110, 112, 126
Philip II, Spanish king, 147
Philippe, King Louis, 174
Philippines, 77–78, 265
Philosophes, 160, 163
Phoenicians, 108
Pickens, Fort, 227, 302
Place, 5–6, 9, 11–17, 20, 36, 41, 43, 69
Planned Parenthood Federation of America, 292
Plate tectonics, 17–19
Plebeians, 122
Plessy v. Ferguson, 95, 233, 279, 282
Plutarch, 122

Plutocracy, 92
Political Action Committee (PACs), 70
Political parties, 49, 65–68, 85, 184
    defined, 14, 35, 54, 66, 69, 75
    elements of, 43
    functions of, 71
    historical perspective on, 65–66
    primary elections, 67
Political science, 49–97
    citizenship rights, privileges, responsibilities, 57–58, 62
    civil rights and individual liberties, 94–95
    Cold War, 79–85, 88, 182, 268–277
    Constitution of United States, 50–77
    development of discipline of, 50
    executive branch, 61, 63
    expansionism and unilateralism, 77
    federal bureaucracy, 62–63, 65
    federal government, 53–59, 63, 66, 71–75, 91, 94
    foreign policy, 51–52, 60, 62, 66, 75–82, 84–85, 87–88
    global system, 85–88
    interest groups, 65, 69–70, 85
    international law, 75, 82, 89–90
    international relations, 50, 75, 84, 86–88
    isolationism and non-interventionism, 76
    judicial branch, 49, 55, 59, 63
    landmark Supreme Court cases, 95
    legislative branch, 54–55, 59, 66, 91
    media and public opinion, 71
    municipal government, 74
    national government structure and functions, 59–65
    philosophy and ideology of founders, 52
    political beliefs and characteristics of citizens, 68
    political parties, 49, 65–68, 85
    political systems compared, 90–93
    state government, 58, 66, 71–74, 91
    subfields of, 49
    voter apathy, 71
    war on terrorism, 83
Political socialization, 68
Polyarchy, 92
Ponce de Leon, 296, 298
Pontiac's Uprising, 206
Populist Party, 67, 234

Portugal
  Age of Exploration, 167, 169
  individuals in Age of Exploration, 167
Postal Service, United States, 65, 72
Prehistory, 101
Presidential system of government, 91–93
President of United States
  budget, 62
  Cabinet, 63
  constitutional requirements for, 62
  powers of, 54, 59
  veto power, 62
Price, 33–35, 39, 41, 43, 127–128, 132, 164, 170, 206, 217, 225, 252, 256–257, 266
Primary elections, 67
Primary sources, 99–100, 144, 321–322
Prime minister, 80–81, 91, 182, 206–209, 264
Prince Henry the Navigator, 164, 167
Printing press, 143–144
Proclamation of 1763, 206
Production possibilities frontier curve, 29
Progressive Party, 292
Prussia, 1848 revolution, 86, 174–175
Ptolemy, 122, 141
Public opinion, 65, 70, 85, 184, 211, 232
Puerto Rico, 77
Pyramids, 111–112, 135

Q

Qing (Manchu) Dynasty, 155
Quartering Act, 207, 211
Quipu, 138
Quota Act, 242
Qur'an, 127, 189

R

Radical Republicans, 229, 231, 279, 285
Raleigh, Sir Walter, 168
Ramses, 112
Randolph, A. Philip, 286
Raphael, 143
Rationalists, 161
Reagan, Ronald, 82, 277
Reason, Age of, 159
Reconstruction period, 226–233
  civil rights failures of, 226–228
  Florida under, 303
Red Scare, 271
Reformation, 118, 138–139, 144–145, 164
  causes of, 144
  in England, 145
  Martin Luther and, 145
  other reformers, 145
Reform movements, 223–224, 233, 239, 241
Regions, 13–14, 122, 125, 137–138, 166, 177, 193, 196, 220, 312
Regulatory commissions, 64
Religion
  Buddhism, 123, 130, 134, 187
  Christianity, 122, 126–127, 145, 150, 164–165, 184, 186–188, 192–194
  Confucianism, 116, 131, 133–134, 156, 188
  Islam, 125–129, 150, 153, 184, 188–190, 286–287
  Judaism, 109, 122, 150, 186–188
Renaissance, 118, 138–139, 142–143-144, 146, 153, 164–165, 247, 251, 280
  Carolingian, 138–139
  humanism, 143
Representatives, House of
  committee system of, 60–61
  constitutional qualifications for, 61
  powers of, 59
Republican Party, historical perspective, 67
Republic of letters, 162
Reserve ratio, 39
Revere, Paul, 212
Revolutionary era. See American revolution
Revolutions, Age of, 173
  1848 Revolutions, 174
  French Revolution, 86–87, 139, 173–174
Ribault, Jean, 299
Rigveda, 114
River Valley Civilizations, 104–105, 113–114, 116
Roaring Twenties, 247–248, 251
Roberts, Justice Owen, 261
Rococo art, 162–163
Roe v. Wade, 96, 293
Roman Catholic Church. *See* Catholic Church
Romanov, Mikhail, 158
Romanov Dynasty, 158
Roman Period, 102
Romans
  compared to ancient China, 124

Index

legacy of, 121
Roman Empire, 119–122
Romantic poetry, 163
Roosevelt, Franklin, 64, 79
    election of 1932, 254
    First New Deal, 64–65
Roosevelt, Theodore, 67, 242, 275
Roosevelt Corollary, 78
Russia
    Ivan III, 157–159
    Ivan the Terrible, 157, 159
    Peter the Great, 158
    revolution of 1917, 180
    Romanov Dynasty, 158
    Time of Troubles, 157, 159

S

Safavid Empire, 151
    cultural developments, 151
    economic developments, 151
    political developments, 151
    social developments, 151
Samurai, 135
Sanger, Margaret, 250, 291–292
Satire, 122, 163
Scarcity, 25–29, 31, 255, 313
Scholasticism, 141
Scientific Revolution, 169
Secondary sources, 99–100, 321–322
Second Continental Congress, 212
Second Great Awakening, 219, 223
Second New Deal, 256, 259
Sedition Act, 244
Segregation, 95, 233, 242, 261, 279, 280, 281–284, 287
Seljuk Turks tribes, 152
Seminole Wars, 301
Senate
   committee system of, 60
   constitutional qualifications for, 61
   powers of, 54, 59
Separation of church and state, 94
Seven Years War, 205
Shakers, 225
Shang dynasty, 115
Sharecropping, 232–233
Shays' Rebellion, 51
Shi'ite muslims, 190
Shogun, 135
Silk Road, 124
Sinan, 153
Slaves/slavery
    Atlantic Slave Trade, 148, 166
    Compromise of 1820, 221
    Compromise of 1850, 221
    effect on Africa, 148–151
    Fugitive Slave Law, 221–222
    imperialism and, 85, 176
    Kansas-Nebraska Act, 222
    in Ottoman Empire, 152–154
    Southern slave owners during antebellum period, 221–226
    Triangular Trade System, 166
Smith, Adam, 25, 44, 172
Social-Darwinism, 237
Socialism, 33, 87, 173, 175, 179
Social science, 1–10, 20, 25, 307–310, 314, 317, 320
    concepts of, 309–310
    disciplines of, 309
    primary and secondary sources, 321–322
    strategies and methods to teach, 317
    tabular and graphic representations of information, 314
    tools and technologies to teach, 320
Song Dynasty, 131
Songhai, 127–129, 151
Sons of Liberty, 208
Southern colonies, 201–202
Soviet Union
    Cold War and, 83, 268, 276
    détente and, 80–81
    glasnost and perestroika, 82, 277
    invasion of Afghanistan, 82, 276–277
Spain
    Age of Exploration, 191
    Florida history and, 296
    individuals in Age of Exploration, 191
Spanish-American War, 77
Spheres of influence, 78, 117
Spinoza, Benedict de, 161
Stalin, Joseph, 80, 267–268, 273
Stamp Act, 207–208
State government
   powers of, 59
   responsibilities of, 49

Stock market, 41, 43, 181, 235, 253, 257, 259
   crash of 1929, 253
Stone Age, 101–103
Strategic Arms Limitation Treaty (SALT I), 82
Student Nonviolent Coordination Committee
   (SNCC), 281
Suez Crisis, 274
Sugar Act, 207
Sui Dynasty, 130, 132
Suleiman the Magnificent, 153
Sultan, 133, 152–153
Sumerians, 106–107, 109, 114
Sunni muslims, 191,
Superpower, 80, 82, 87–88, 182
Supply, 25, 27, 33–43, 45, 64, 105, 127, 129,
       131, 135, 166, 170, 172, 228, 234–235,
       251, 259, 267, 298, 302
Supreme Court, U.S.
   justices of, 63
   landmark cases of, 95
   role of, 63
Swahili Coast, 126–127

T

Tacitus, 122
Takia Reforms, 134
Tamerlane, 133
Tang Dynasty, 130–131, 134
Tea Act, 210
Technical efficiency, 28, 30
Temperance Societies, 224
Tenochtitlan, 137
Ten Percent Plan, 229–230
Terrorism, war on, 83–84, 137, 177, 184,
    278, 294
Theocracy, 111
Third parties, 67
Thirteenth Amendment, 73, 230, 278
Thirty Years War, 86
Thirty Years' War, 147
Thutmose III, 112
Tigris River, 106
Time, 16, 23, 35, 94, 122–123, 144, 309
Time of Troubles, 157, 159
Timur the Lame, 133
Tinker v. Des Moines School District, 96
Tithe, 139
Titian, 144

Tordesillas, Treaty of, 167, 191
Townshend Acts, 209
Trade reciprocity, 77
Transcendentalists, 225
Triangular Trade System, 166
True womanhood, 224
Truman, Harry S., 268
Truman Doctrine, 80
Trusts, 236
Tsar, 157–159, 180
Twenty-fourth Amendment, 285

U

U-2 incident, 273
Underground Railroad, 225, 289
Unemployment, 26, 35–37, 42–46, 74, 175,
    183, 235, 255–256, 259–261, 278, 308
Unilateralism, 77, 79, 84
Unions, 142, 237–238, 285
United Fruit Company, 88
United Nations, 50, 79, 88, 89, 182, 184,
    265, 272
Universal Negro Improvement Association,
    250, 286
Untouchables, 114
Urbanization, 170, 224, 233, 238–239, 311
Utopian societies, 172

V

Valide-sultan, 153
Vedas, 114, 190
Verrazzano, Giovanni da, 168
Versailles, Treaty of, 78, 180–182, 213, 247
Vespucci, Amerigo, 167
Veto power, 62
Vienna, Congress of, 174
Vietnam War, 96, 272, 274
Virgil, 122
Voltaire, 161–163
Voter apathy, 71
Voter Education Project, 283
Voting
   incidence of, 74
   voter apathy, 71
   women's right to, 288
Voting Rights Act of 1965, 285

Index

W

Wade-Davis Bill, 230
War on terrorism, 83
Warring States, 116
Warsaw Treaty Organization, 270
Washington, Booker T., 279–280
Washington, George, 51–52, 58, 62, 66, 76, 205, 211, 214–215, 264
Watts Riots, 286
Wealth of Nations (Smith), 25, 44, 172
Weathering, 17–18
Westmoreland, William, 81
West Virginia Board of Education v. Barnette, 95
Westward expansion, 216, 220, 225
Whigs, 67
Wilson, Woodrow, 78, 179, 242, 247
Woman's Christian Temperance Union, 291
Women
   in roaring twenties, 374
   suffrage, 71, 238, 240, 246, 285, 228–292
   true womanhood, 224
   voting, 288–291
   women's rights movement, 224, 288, 290
   World War I and, 247
   World War II and, 247
World Bank, 45, 79, 185
World history
   African, Asian and Eastern European societies from 1500 to 1900, 148
   African, Asian and Mesoamerican societies before 1500, 125
   Age of Exploration, 163–166
   Age of Reason through Age of Enlightenment, 159–160
   Age of Revolution, 173
   ancient civilizations, 106, 113, 116–117, 120
   contemporary global trends, 183–184
   imperialism and nationalism, 176
   Industrial Revolution, 87, 164, 169–173
   Middle Ages, Renaissance and Reformation, 138
   military conflicts in twentieth century, 178–183
   prehistory and early civilizations, 101–143
   world religions, 186, 190
World War I
   American involvement in, 178–179
   causes of, 178–179
   creation of new states after, 178–180
   economic effects of, 179
   Florida during, 304
   main rivalries between power before, 179
   political effects of, 172–173
   return to isolationism after, 78
   social effects of, 149, 170
World War II
   American involvement in, 182
   American response to war in Europe, 263
   causes of, 181
   effects of, 182–185
   end of isolationism, 76
   home front, 265–266
   Neutrality Acts, 79, 263
   social changes at home, 266
Writing system, 106, 108, 135, 137
Writs of certiorari, 63
Wudi, 123–124
Wycliffe, John, 144

X

Xia dynasty, 115

Y

Yalta Conference, 267
Yamato Clan, 134
Yuan Dynasty, 133

Z

Zhou dynasty, 188
Ziggurat, 107, 109

Notes

Notes

Notes

Notes

Notes

Notes